The Promotable Woman

Becoming a Successful Manager

Revised Edition

The Promotable Woman

Becoming a Successful Manager

Revised Edition

Norma Carr-Ruffino

San Francisco State University

Wadsworth Publishing Company

Belmont, California

A Division of Wadsworth, Inc.

To Fredo
And to Brian, Carrie, and Randy

Editor: *Carol Butterfield*

Production: *Mary Forkner and Martha Simmons,
    Publication Alternatives*

Designer: *Michael Rogondino*

Copy Editor: *Kathleen Engelberg*

Cover: *Design Office, Bruce Kortebein*

Cover Photograph: *Steve Frisch*

Back Cover Photograph: *Gage White*

Printed in the United States of America

15 — 93 92 91

ISBN 0-534-05052-2

Library of Congress Cataloging in Publication Data

Carr-Ruffino, Norma.
  The promotable woman.

  Includes bibliographies and index.
  1. Women executives.   2. Executive ability.
3. Management.   I. Title.
HD6054.3.C37   1985   658.4'09'024042   84-25683
ISBN 0-534-05052-2

Contents

How This Book Can Change Your Life

You are on your way to becoming a promotable woman, and this book can increase your level of promotability by making you a more confident, competent leader. The fact that you're reading this book indicates that you have either moved into the managerial level or that you are thinking very seriously about making a commitment to a management career. That means you're able to picture yourself in an assertive, decision-making position of responsibility.

But can you picture yourself solving the problems unique to women in management? And, how do you plan to overcome cultural barriers to acquiring the skills necessary to any successful manager? For example, you may have to overcome cultural conditioning that can create internal conflict between your personal-life roles (woman, wife, mother, other) and your role as an upwardly-mobile manager. And you will probably have to deal with the stereotypes others have of women, their acceptable roles, their place in business, their traits as a boss.

Most of the specific problems unique to women managers are rooted in two general elements: (1) the woman's own image of what her role and behavior should be and (2) the stereotypes others have about women. Finding the appropriate level of femininity, firmness, friendliness, and assertiveness is

directly related to understanding these two elements and how they affect the woman manager.

This book can change your life dramatically if you take advantage of the opportunities it offers you (1) to understand how your self-concept affects your management style, (2) to make constructive behavioral changes that help you to function more effectively as a person, (3) to understand how the stereotypes of others affect your management style, and (4) to develop specific management skills that establish your competence and deal effectively with stereotypes. In this way, the book can help you to take advantage of the **opportunities** unique to women managers and at the same time deal effectively with their unique **problems.**

What's Different About Women Managers?

In 1983 nearly 44 percent of all paid workers in the United States were women, and most were in low-paying jobs. In fact, on the average, women were making only about 62 percent of what men were making. Only 4 percent of women workers were in jobs paying more than $25,000, while 25 percent of men workers held such jobs.* About 53 percent of all women over 16 were in the paid labor force in 1982. Although most of them were working because they wanted to, a large percentage worked because they were the sole source of support for themselves or their families or because their salaries were needed to raise the family out of the low-income level.**

While 32 percent of all managers and administrators are women, 80 percent of the clerical workers are women. Many women managers and administrators are stuck at the lowest managerial level with little hope for advancement—for example, first-line supervisors of clerical workers or personnel administrators. While more and more women are learning to break the barriers into middle management, very few are making it into top management. Only 5 percent of top-level managers are women.**

Women who move up from worker or trainee to supervision and management often find themselves in a rather lonely position. They are frequently the only women in either small or large meetings of managers. They may have difficulty "fitting in" with the groups. At the same time, they can no longer be "one of the girls" among the female workers.

Women managers must deal with preconceived attitudes about the "woman boss." Because they are frequently the first women in their position, they must also deal with their own uncertainties about the most desirable approach to various situations. Therefore, women can profit from a specialized approach to developing management

skills. Although women's *goals*—the managerial functions they must master—are the same as the *goals* of male managers, the *process* of reaching those goals, of mastering those functions, is somewhat different for most women.

The Women Who Will Profit from This Book

This book is for women who are moving into relatively lonely, but very exciting, supervisory or management positions. Such women come from a variety of backgrounds:

Women who are currently in the business world as workers and who have been (or are anticipating being) promoted

College students enrolled in courses to prepare them for management positions

Women returning to the work force who want to prepare for management positions

This book is designed to be used

In college courses

In seminar groups

In training sessions within companies

By women studying on their own

If you are in one of these categories, this book should help you to prepare for the move into management, to make a smooth transition, and to become an increasingly effective manager. If you keep the book at your desk after you have completed it, it should serve as a handy reference guide for

Handling difficult situations

Regaining perspective after crises

Reviewing certain principles and techniques

---

*U.S. Department of Labor, Bureau of Labor Statistics, *Employment and Earnings*, January, 1984.
**U.S. Department of Commerce, Bureau of the Census, *Money Income of Households, Families, and Persons in the U.S.*, Series P-60, No. 142, 1984.

Reinforcing new awarenesses, attitudes, or perspectives you have gained in the process of completing the book

How Your Learning Will be Enhanced

Every effort has been made in this book to provide opportunities for you to actually experience situations, actions, and viewpoints—either vicariously through reading and analyzing cases or directly through participating in simulations or role-plays of situations. Each chapter includes a statement of learning objectives so that you can know what you should achieve by completing it. You can also evaluate how well you have actually achieved those objectives after completing a chapter by going back and reviewing them and making a self-analysis.

You can vicariously experience situations typically encountered by the woman manager through following Carrie Dickeson and her colleagues as they successfully and unsuccessfully cope. You will get to know Carrie as she is promoted through the ranks of the Sales Department of a large clothing manufacturer. These case incidents provide role models of successful actions and approaches to guide you. They can also help you to become aware of some of the pitfalls to avoid. These problems and opportunities are analyzed and discussed within the chapter. The principles and techniques involved in these cases are pinpointed and listed.

Each chapter has a number of experiential learning devices to help you apply the principles and techniques so that they are reinforced. These experiences can help you to have strategies readily available in your memory and to feel confident in applying them to actual business situations in the future. These learning devices include self-analysis through completing checklists, answering questions, and making evaluations;

analysis of cases; role-playing; games; and other exercises. Many of the exercises and games are ideal for working with a partner or a small group. Most of them can also be done by one person alone.

What You Will Work On in This Book

In Part 1, "Developing Personal Skills," you will focus on self-development—increasing the kind of awareness, attitudes, skills, and approaches that will make you the *kind* of manager most likely to succeed. The particular problems of women in developing or maintaining an appropriate self-concept and healthy self-esteem are addressed. The image you convey to others is stressed. In the opening part of the book, then, your goal is success as a person first and as a manager second.

In Part 2, "Developing Management Skills," you will focus on developing the skills that are most essential to the management functions of planning, organizing, staffing, directing, and controlling. In this section of the book, as in the first part, problems unique to woman managers are stressed along with the basic management information.

What You Will Achieve by Completing This Book

If you apply yourself well to reading this book and completing all the exercises that are appropriate to you, you should

Be aware of the major problems you are likely to face as a woman manager

Be aware of most of the common pitfalls to avoid

Have experience in applying specific principles and techniques for handling common management situations

Be able to cope with the stress inherent in the manager's role

Project the image of a competent, assertive, fair manager

Be skilled at setting goals and priorities and at achieving measurable results—both for your company and for yourself

Know how to get promotions and raises

Know how to effectively delegate tasks as well as motivate and supervise others

Communicate more effectively

Have a better understanding of the financial operations of businesses

This book is intended to help you grow personally and professionally. As you build your reputation as a successful person and effective manager, you also build the reputation of women managers in general. I urge you to share with other women the knowledge and awareness you gain through this exciting process of growth and development. As we support one another, we not only help ourselves, we also increase the level of acceptance for women in leadership roles. We help open up new career paths for women everywhere.

Such mutual support and self-effort can also help us to build a stronger democratic society, to create a better world for both sexes. Shirley MacLaine recently shared a message from a very special being called Mayan: "All women need to believe in themselves as women; they need to be secure in that belief. . . . Women have the right—even with the independence already achieved in the United States—to be even more independent and free. No society can function democratically until women are considered equal on every basis—particularly to themselves. And women will never attain such a thing other than through their own self-effort. In fact, nothing is worth having,

except that which is won through self-effort."*

The People Who Contributed to This Book

Carol Butterfield, Editor and Marketing Director for Wadsworth, picked up where former editor Nancy Taylor left off on the further development and refinement of *The Promotable Woman* for this revision. Both women have made invaluable contributions to the final product. Publications Editor Mary Forkner has once again done an excellent job.

Suggestions from the following reviewers have been most helpful: Margaret C. Hopfl, Pennsylvania State University, Altoona, Pennsylvania; H. Ervin Lewis, Wellman Industries, Inc., Johnsonville, South Carolina; Dr. Joanne Rettke, Mohawk Valley Community College, Utica, New York; Connie Sitterly, Amarillo College, Amarillo, Texas; June Webb-Vignery, University of Arizona, Tucson; and Dr. Elizabeth Woolfe, Palm Beach Junior College, Palm Beach, Florida.

A special thanks goes to the many women who have attended my seminars throughout the United States and my *Women in Management* courses at San Francisco State University. Their help was essential in refining these materials, especially the exercises. These women also shared helpful research information and references. Frances Gusman deserves special mention for her work on the key terms and Sonia Medina for her work on the model of the job-getting process.

Many of the women mentioned here have shared with me the ways in which the materials in this book have changed their lives. Our goal is to create a book that will also change your life.

Norma Carr-Ruffino, Ph.D.

Out on a Limb by Shirley MacLaine. New York: Bantam Books, 1983.

The Promotable Woman

Becoming a Successful Manager

Revised Edition

Developing Personal Skills

That Promote Managerial Effectiveness

All the skills that help you manage effectively are important. Some of those skills are fairly technical and directly related to the traditional management functions. Others are more general, stemming from your personal effectiveness as a human being; however, they also greatly enhance your effectiveness as a manager. Indeed, such skills are frequently more important to managerial success than are the technical skills.

In Part 1, we'll discuss the personal skills, attitudes, habits, and traits that will lead to personal growth and will help you to become a stronger person and to overcome barriers to acceptance by others in your organization. Research by Dr. Alma Baron and other management experts turned up seven interesting reasons men gave for not wanting a female boss: she's not confident, she doesn't have clout, she doesn't know how to play the game, she comes on too strong, I don't know how to treat her, working for a woman makes me look bad, and I'm paying the consequences because she's only a token. The major goal of Part 1 is to help you overcome such preconceived notions by becoming a stronger, more vital, more aware woman with increased business savvy. As such, you are bound to become a better manager.

To help you overcome these seven barriers (and others), we'll focus on eight keys to leadership success: review your strengths and achievements daily, choose a career doing something you care deeply about, set clear goals and priorities, relax and visualize yourself achieving your goals, take calculated risks every day, get rid of any "victim mentality" you may have, learn the political ropes in your organization, and become a team player. To put your personal and managerial development into perspective, we'll start with an overview of the business world—its evolution, culture, key values, and power structure.

Chapter One

Surveying the Management Scene

"If you're going to play the game properly,
you'd better know every rule."

Barbara Jordan

It's important that you know how your viewpoints, attitudes, and habits compare with those of men (and other women) who are functioning successfully in management positions. It's also helpful to know something about others' expectations of you as a woman and as a manager. Being able to identify the **fast track*** to advancement and being able to distinguish between **dead-end jobs** and those that lead to further advancement is crucial to your career. Just as crucial is understanding something about how power is gained and used within the typical organization and the resulting "politics" that inevitably accompany power bids and power struggles. And, when you start recognizing how upward mobility, visibility, and power interact and go hand in hand in achieving career success, you'll know you're developing the kind of savvy necessary for the promotable woman.

In this chapter you will have the opportunity to

1. Understand how women's roles evolved and how they are changing

2. Become aware of male/female attitudinal differences toward their jobs, their careers, and the business world in general

3. Verify that you really want to be a manager

4. Become aware of some essential steps to moving up in a management career

5. Become aware of some types of dead-end jobs women are frequently assigned to

6. Understand why women are frequently excluded from true management positions

7. Understand some differences between supervisory and middle-management jobs and between line and staff jobs

8. Understand how the secretarial role affects women's **self-concepts** and career plans

9. Understand how opportunities for advancement affect attitudes and behavior and how organizational power and politics affect morale, leadership, and supervision

---

*Terms in bold type are defined in Appendix 4, Key Terms.

3

10. Understand some ways organizational power is gained, withheld, and used

Before we go too deeply into the specifics of developing personal skills and management skills, we will step back and survey the evolution of women's roles and their impact on the management scene in the United States today. Because that scene has historically been a male scene, most women are woefully unaware of the rules of the business game.

The term "business game" does not necessarily imply game-playing in the sense of ulterior motives, dirty tactics, and negative results for the losers. Like the game of life, the business game can be played in many ways and doesn't necessarily require losers or negative results. Some rules vary from one organization to another, while others tend to be common to most organizations. If you don't like the way the game is played in one firm, perhaps you can find another organization more to your liking. In this chapter you'll get an overview of the business game, which should help you put specific situations and problems you encounter into perspective.

 Career Decisions

To help you achieve these objectives, we'll follow the career path and the skill development of Carrie Dickeson throughout this book. Carrie, a business administration major at San Francisco State University, will be graduating in three months. For the past three years she has been working for Lighthouse Designs, Inc. Her first year she worked full-time as a sales representative, and for the past two years she's worked part-time as an administrative assistant to

Jan Arguello, Vice-President of Sales. Lighthouse Designs is a large company that manufactures women's clothing. Its headquarters are in San Francisco, and it has a number of regional branch offices throughout the United States.

Today Carrie has career plans on her mind. Sipping a cup of coffee in the employees' lounge, she confides to her co-worker Gail Blocker, "Gail, some of the big corporations will be interviewing on campus in a couple of weeks. I started working on my résumé last night, and I just realized that I'm not sure exactly what type of job I'm looking for, much less what kind of company."

"I thought you wanted to be a manager, Carrie. Isn't that all you need to know right now?"

"Evidently not. The Placement Center sent out a list of questions interviewers often ask about your career plans, job objectives, and so forth—and I'm not really prepared to answer any of them!"

"I thought you were going to stay with Lighthouse, Carrie, and try to work into a management position here."

"I think I would like that, Gail. But why should I put all my eggs in one basket? I mean, it seems to me that I'll be in a much stronger position to negotiate for a promotion if I can generate some other good job offers."

"Well, I don't envy you having to go through the ordeal of being interviewed. I *hate* looking for a job. It just makes me a nervous wreck. And I feel so rejected when I don't get the job I applied for."

"I guess that's one way of looking at it, Gail. On the other hand, I think it may be an exciting experience. The seminar instructor from the Placement Center suggested that we view any jobs we *don't* get as lessons in job campaigning. She smiled at Gail's puzzled look. "You know—we ask ourselves what lessons we can learn from that experience and use it to increase our effectiveness in the next interview."

"Well, I'm still more comfortable just staying here with a company I'm familiar with, even if it doesn't carry much status or pay. I know Mr. Barker appreciates my work as his secretary, and one of these days he's bound to recommend me for promotion to a management job."

"Hey, Gail, I can understand that. I may end up here myself. In the meantime, I'm planning to wage as effective a job campaign as I can. To me it's like a game—it will be a kick if I can play it really well, but it's not the end of the world if I blow it. Say, haven't you been waiting around for a promotion for three or four years now?"

"Yes, I have. In fact, I've watched several men come through this department who learned most of what they know from me. They've moved on to better-paying positions, and here I sit."

"Gail, have you ever talked to Mr. Barker about this?"

Looking upset, Gail pushes back her chair and begins gathering up her things. "Well, I don't want to complain. Mr. Barker knows all this, and he knows the kind of work I do. I've always felt that when the time was ripe, he would see that I got a good promotion."

As Gail walks away, Carrie smiles and shakes her head.

These two situations, Gail's and Carrie's, provide food for thought. Both women are in the process of making and implementing career decisions, but in different ways. Can you identify some of the differences?

1. List specific actions and attitudes mentioned in this case that tend to enhance a person's promotability. _____

_____

2. List specific actions and attitudes mentioned in the case that tend to sabotage career goals. _____

_____

3. What words do you associate with the word "risk"? (Be spontaneous.) _____

_____

4. How do you think most successful business people view risk? _____

_____

Throughout the next few chapters, we'll be generalizing, indirectly, from both Gail's and Carrie's experiences as we look at approaches women can take to management careers.

EXERCISE 1-1: ASSESSING VIEWPOINTS THAT AFFECT PROMOTABILITY

Place a checkmark beside the response that best reflects your viewpoint at first glance. Don't try to analyze your answer or figure out which response is "right." For some specific comments and interpretations of answers, see the answer key at the back of the book.

1. Several important people in your life seem to believe that highly successful career women are not good wives or mothers, are not "truly

feminine," and by implication are not successful as women. Your response is:

(a) Maybe you're right.

(b) I'll live my life the way I see fit!

(c) Women, as well as men, can be successful in both their personal and their professional lives, if they learn how to set priorities that reflect balanced life goals.

2. How long do you expect to be working?

(a) Until I have children

(b) Most of my life

(c) Until I get married

(d) Other _____

3. What do you expect in return for these years of work?

(a) Money for the "extras" in life

(b) A high income plus a chance to make a contribution and develop my talents

(c) Money for the essentials of life

(d) Other _____

4. What position do you expect to hold within the next ten years?

(a) Vice-President

(b) Department head

(c) Chief Executive Officer

(d) I don't know

(e) Other _____

5. Which type of job is most likely to lead to advancement?

(a) Personnel specialist

(b) Salesperson

(c) Administrative Assistant to the President

6. A "fast track" is

(a) An express method for getting services or products to customers

(b) The most direct career path to middle or top management

(c) A computer-aided procedure for executive decision-making

7. You're most likely to gain favorable visibility in an organization by

(a) Taking calculated risks and succeeding

(b) Dressing for success

(c) Attending all social functions and talking to the top decision-makers

8. A calculated risk is mainly

   (a) A chance to make a gain

   (b) Dangerous but can pay off

   (c) To be taken only if necessary

9. Teamwork in organizations mainly involves

   (a) Joining forces with people you work well with

   (b) Working toward specific goals with people you like, despise, or feel neutral about

   (c) Helping those who need your help

10. Your boss tells you he's thinking about expanding your unit or department to include a new area of responsibility. Your group is already overloaded with work. What would you do?

    (a) Wait for him to come up with the detailed plans and instruction for implementing them

    (b) Work out your own ideas for the best way to plan and implement the expanded areas of authority and responsibility, then discuss them with him

    (c) Tell him your group simply can't take on more work

A WOMAN'S PLACE—GAINING PERSPECTIVE

About 95 percent of the top decision-makers in American organizations are men. This means that—for better or worse—you're going to be operating in a male culture where the rules are made by men. To be successful, you must learn the rules of the game, which are quite different from the rules governing woman's traditional place in the home. To further complicate matters, some of the rules are beginning to change.

The changing ideas about what constitutes "a woman's place" are having far-reaching effects on nearly every person and every aspect of our society. Male/female relationships, family life, work life, educational programs—all are in the process of change as women move into new roles. But the rate of change is not consistent; it varies from community to community and from organization to organization.

In some communities and organizations, general agreement about woman's place has changed very little in the past fifty years. In others it may depart drastically from the traditional ideal, even to the extent that woman's place is little different from man's place. It depends on the woman, what she wants to do, and what she's able to do. The general viewpoint of most communities and organizations lies somewhere between these two extremes.

Women like you who are moving into management roles will therefore encounter a variety of changing attitudes and practices, depending upon where you live and the company you work for. These attitudes and practices, and your responses to them, will have a large impact on the opportunities and the barriers you will meet throughout your career.

To put all this in perspective, we'll look backward briefly to see how this state of affairs came about. Then we'll survey the most important ways in which it is changing and how these trends may affect your future. This perspective can help you to identify and overcome traditional barriers that you may face as a woman manager. It can also help you to recognize new opportunities, which we will explore as well.

How It All Began

"Woman's place is in the home." This predominant idea about a woman's role is the foundation of division of labor by sex. Some people say it's always been that way because it's natural and is essential to the survival of the species—this is the nature theory. Others say that we can never know for sure how it all began. What we do know is that throughout history both sexes, and the community as a whole, have trained children to conform to the roles implied by the division of labor by sex—this is the nurture theory.

The Nature Theory   Based on the premise that the average male apparently has always been larger and stronger than the average female, this theory holds that the male was the logical one to hunt for the family food and to defend the mother and babies. The female was the bearer and nurser of children and therefore stayed near the home to carry out her nurturing and caretaking functions.

The Nurture Theory   Advocates of this theory say that regardless of how division of labor by sex originally came about, its existence is reinforced when a community believes that that is what works best. Here is how the nurturing, or socialization, process

works: When women act in nurturing, dependent, serving ways, they are rewarded through such payoffs as approval, support, recognition, help, and protection. These rewards are given in the interest of keeping women in the home, caring for their men and children. Men receive the same types of rewards when they show the strength, aggression, and independence considered desirable for defending and providing for their women and children.

At the same time, both women and men are punished for acting in ways that conflict with these basic roles. Community members may show disapproval, shun or ostracize violators, withdraw support, or carry out similar reprisals. For example, people might openly criticize a woman who acts in ways normally associated with the male role, such as venturing alone into the forest or going hunting. The criticism intensifies if she also neglects some of the housework. Likewise, the man who prefers household activities to hunting will be criticized.

The general belief that women are not good at performing masculine activities, and vice versa, serves to reinforce this socialization process. For example, people in the community might expect women to fail or do poorly if they attempt to hunt or tame a wild horse and men to be ineffective at cooking, child care, and sewing.

This type of socialization is still practiced in some communities today and its vestiges are felt in virtually every community and organization in our society. But it's been changing, especially in the last twenty years.

Before the Industrial Revolution

Before the 1800s most pioneer women in the United States were married to farmers or small business owners. It was a family economy jointly occupied by men and women.

The men tended to be responsible for producing commodities or providing services for the community, while the women's major responsibilities revolved around providing for family needs. Some of a wife's specific duties depended on her husband's occupation; she was expected to help him and respond to his specific needs. If he was a farmer, she might help with the milking and gardening. If he was a store keeper, she might help out as a store clerk or record keeper. However, the average wife was not expected to work outside the home or family business. Black slave women were the only major exception to this arrangement; they were expected to care for their own family's needs while also working outside their homes for their master. Black or white, rich or poor, women generally were thought to be inferior to men; their roles, therefore, were "properly" subservient to male roles.

The Development of Industrialism

During the 1800s family activities and economic activities began to emerge as distinct spheres. More and more husbands provided for their families by working in corporate factories and offices. The successful man won the struggle for wealth through competition with others and ultimately through power over others. His wife won approval through supporting his advancement and that of the children and ultimately through subordinating her personal desires and needs to theirs.

The ideal wife's sphere of "social homemaking" gained value. In fact the privileged woman probably went to school or college to train for this role. She was held responsible for establishing the emotional bond of love within the family and for molding the personalities of the children. In her social homemaking sphere, individual personalities

and the willingness to cooperate and to share were appreciated. This realm contrasted with her husband's economic sphere of impersonal, competitive, "you scratch my back, I'll scratch yours" relationships.

The contrasting sets of life principles that emerged were distinct and complementary: for men, an impersonal, public, competitive set; for women, a personal, private, charitable one. This difference in life principles and spheres was asserted to be natural and God-given by many nineteenth-century writers.

If a married woman worked outside the home, it was almost always assumed that her husband was unsuccessful in the struggle to provide for his family. In 1890 only 19 percent of all women worked outside the home, with less than 5 percent of all married women in this labor force. The female labor force was made up predominantly of young, not-yet-married women.

Most of these women worked in jobs considered compatible with "woman's function" and some in menial factory, office, or sales jobs. Over 95 percent of the servants in private homes were women [10].* Even when women found a position of authority and power outside the home, it was within a primarily female space, such as the public schools, hospitals, libraries, and welfare agencies. To this day the only professional roles dominated by women are public school teacher, nurse, librarian, and social worker.

Developments During the Twentieth Century

Several recent developments that have further undermined the sexual division of labor are (1) the streamlining of housework, (2)

---

*See item 10 in "References" at the end of the chapter; books and articles cited within each chapter and other books of general interest are listed there. The number in brackets corresponds to the item numbers in the listing.

the temporary need for women to fill men's jobs during World War II, (3) more reliable birth control methods, (4) the Civil Rights movement, and (5) increased life expectancy rates.

The Streamlining of Housework   Housework has come a long way since 1910, when it was tedious, often backbreaking drudgery, all done by hand. Today virtually every American home is equipped with an array of labor-saving devices, and supermarkets offer numerous prepared foods at reasonable prices. Such developments have allowed women to reduce drastically the hours they must spend doing essential household chores.

World War II   As this streamlining process was occurring, World War II created a dire shortage of workers in the United States. Women—even married ones—were urged to take over jobs vacated by men who were now serving in the military. Not only did women prove to be quite capable in filling these jobs, but they enjoyed doing needed work and bringing home an extra paycheck. Their families found they could function quite satisfactorily with a working mom; in fact many families were happier because Mom was happier. But when Johnny came marching home again, he wanted his job back. And women were urged to have babies and devote themselves full-time to the homemaking role. Family togetherness was the order of the day. It translated into husbands in the work place and wives at home. Many women reluctantly complied, but the entire experience was not lost upon their daughters. Some noticed, for example, that home life was more pleasant when Mom was purposefully occupied with her paid job. Most sensed the general acceptance (even approval) of working moms. And they noted that some of the moms continued working.

The Development of the Birth Control Pill
Along with a greater acceptance of tubal ligations and vasectomies to limit the child-bearing years, the development of the pill during the 1960s meant that for the first time women could control the timing and number of their pregnancies. This made them less dependent on a husband's ability to provide and more in control of the pattern of their work lives.

The Civil Rights Movement   Occurring at about the same time, the Civil Rights movement was mainly a bid for equal opportunity by blacks, but it led to legislation that was to affect dramatically the sexual division of labor. Some Southern legislators who opposed pending civil rights legislation added a sexual discrimination clause to it, thinking that would lead to sure defeat. Much to their dismay, it passed.

As a result of this and other legislation, the **Affirmative Action** programs that were eventually imposed upon virtually all large corporations included guidelines for ensuring equal opportunity for women as well as racial minorities. These programs required corporations to move women into higher-level, better-paying positions (for example, managerial and professional positions) in proportion to the total number of female workers in the organization.

Life Expectancy Rates   Throughout this century life expectancy rates have been increasing. At about the time that the career doors were opening legally for them, women began to realize that they had many productive years to fill, even after their childbearing years were over. Many women who had thought of themselves as part-time or temporary workers now had all their children in school and could confidently choose to have no more children; yet they were only in their 30s. Now what? Suddenly they realized they would probably be working another thirty years, and many decided they might as well make the most of it. They wanted careers that were satisfying, challenging, exciting, and well-paying.

Many of today's women managers, therefore, were late bloomers. During their 20s and early 30s—when their male counterparts were busy "paying their dues" in the organization by putting in long hours, learning the ropes, getting promotions, and gaining invaluable expertise—these women were mainly concerned with raising children. Perhaps you're one of these women.

Or perhaps you're one of their children, one of the new breed of women who are moving into their own careers. A major concern for many of these women is how they will integrate the wife and mother role with the career role. These new career women are *not* late bloomers; they know they want managerial or professional careers, and many of them plan to make it to the top.

Where We're Headed

Most of the important trends today—trends that give clues to what our lives will be like in the future—offer exciting opportunities for career-oriented women. These trends include (1) the movement of women into new, more powerful roles outside the home; (2) the transition from an industrial to an information society; (3) the resulting increased need for the human touch; (4) the decentralization of many centralized institutions, which eliminates much red tape and allows more autonomy at local levels; (5) the related focus on improving sagging productivity in American businesses through encouraging more cooperation, participation, and individual decision-making at all levels; (6) a tendency to depend more on self-help and less on institutional help; (7) more reliance on informal networks and less on formal

communication through the organizational hierarchy; and (8) multiple lifestyle options as opposed to either/or choices [9]. These trends all tend to be favorable for women who want careers in management.

The new roles of women and the transition from an industrial society to an information society are by far the most profound changes of this century. In an organization that relies on securing, processing, and disseminating information, physical size and strength are obviously not bona fide job requirements. In addition, the increased use of the computer and other high technology applications tends to create a greater need for personal involvement, the human touch—empathy, warmth, understanding, supportive conversation, cooperation—skills most women have been encouraged to develop from childhood. To prepare themselves for management positions, therefore, women should expand on these skills. At the same time they must become knowledgeable and comfortable with computer functions. Since the computer is an essential tool that affects virtually all important jobs in the information society, women must overcome any reticence they may have about gaining computer skills.

Other important trends toward decentralization of organizations, participation in decision-making, networking within organizations and among business and professional people, self-help, and multiple lifestyle options all represent a movement away from traditional, hierarchical, authoritarian organizations. This translates into less elitism, fewer directives from on high, and more participation and cooperation from all levels of the organization. Such a movement should remove many of the traditional barriers to full participation in organizations that women have typically encountered, provided we are ready to accept the challenges and demands of the new responsibilities.

Two of the major barriers to full participation that still remain are (1) comparable pay for jobs typically held by women and (2) high-quality, affordable child care. The resolution of these two problems are major issues for women of the 1980s and will dramatically affect the status of women in the 1990s. A third barrier may be the reluctance of top managers and administrators to admit significant numbers of women to their ranks.

Comparable Pay for Comparable Worth
This concept (also called "Comparable Worth" or "Pay Equity") carries the equal pay for equal work idea a step further. Equal pay laws require, for example, that a female senior accounting clerk receive the same base pay as a male senior accounting clerk within the same company. Comparable pay rulings, where enforced, might require that a junior secretary receive the same base pay as a journeyman electrician working in the same community. Pay scales would be based on a system of analyzing and evaluating jobs based on such factors as level of education and experience required, level of responsibility and difficulty, and hardships involved.

Advocates of comparable pay laws believe their passage may be the only way to eliminate the "female ghetto" of low-paying jobs found in most organizations. They point to statistics showing that when an occupation formerly dominated by male incumbents—such as high school instructor or sales clerk—becomes dominated by women incumbents, the pay and status decline. At the same time, jobs held mainly by men—such as the building trades or maintenance jobs—may increase in pay, if not in status. As a result, female high school instructors with college degrees may receive less than half the pay of plumbers or city street sweepers without high school diplomas. A system of

comparable pay would be designed to eliminate such inequities. A major barrier is the cost to organizations. Since lowering the pay of male workers would be impractical, they must raise the pay of female workers. One solution involves gradual increases for underpaid female workers and decreases in the starting pay of **new hires** in overpaid male positions.

While the courts have ruled in favor of comparable pay in some cases, the outlook for general application of the concept is uncertain.

High-Quality, Affordable Child Care   This is essential for women who want a relatively uninterrupted career. The greatest problems center around care for infants during the extremely impressionable, formative years from birth to age 3. Care problems become less intense as toddlers move into the nursery school-kindergarten phase, socializing more with their peers and needing less one-on-one adult supervision.

Women caught in the crunch of low pay for typically female jobs and high expenses for top-notch child care often give up their careers in frustration. Even those women who make it into management may experience this financial crunch if they start their families while they are in a relatively low-paying supervisory or lower-management job.

Most of the practical solutions to this dilemma center around employer support of high-quality child care. The most satisfactory solution to date appears to be the on-site day-care center that also includes after-school programs for school-age children. This arrangement even allows mothers to continue breast-feeding after they return to work. It provides for regular mother-child contact throughout the work day.

The 1982 Dependent Care Assistant Plan allows employers to provide such services on a tax-free basis. Costs to employers are further offset if they use the **"cafeteria approach"** to employee benefits. In this setup, employees can select from a variety of benefits, tailoring a "benefit package" to their particular needs. Young parents, for example, might choose $100 per month worth of child-care benefits and forgo the same amount in retirement benefits or stock options.

Other solutions offered by employers include operation or support of off-site day-care centers, reimbursement of child-care expenses directly to the employee, and information and referral services to help parents find good child-care facilities. During the past ten years, over 100 child-care resource and referral agencies (R & Rs) have sprung up around the country. For example, Patty Siegel of San Francisco, Executive Director of California Child Care Resource and Referral Network, has set up 55 R & Rs in California. Similar agencies in other cities might be found in the yellow pages under "child care services" or a similar heading. For women who can afford it, a new version of the English "nanny system" may be the answer. Several training schools for modern-day governesses who come to the child's home are now operating around the country.

Admittance to Top Management This is still a major problem for women. While more than 42 percent of all workers are women, only 5 percent of top-level managers are women. In the past there was a very small pool of qualified women who sought such positions. That pool has grown rapidly; yet corresponding numbers of women are not being promoted to the really powerful positions. How can we remove this barrier to equal opportunity for women in the work place? Many women are no longer willing to wait and see when (if ever) **top managers*** may be ready to admit significant numbers of women to their ranks. The

most realistic solution may be national legislation that would set Affirmative Action requirements for moving women into top slots. (See Exhibit 1–1 on page 18.)

How Key Women's Issues Will Be Resolved Much depends on the willingness of women to work together to bring about needed change. The ways in which women use—or don't use—their individual and collective economic and political power will determine the outcome. In the economic arena, for example, women who have qualified themselves to fill needed jobs—such as those calling for computer skills combined with human relations skills—will be in demand. They can let employers know that high-quality, on-site day-care facilities will be a key factor in their job choice decisions. They can also let employers know that they prefer organizations with established systems of comparable pay. Women who reach positions that carry influence or decision-making clout can use it to bring about such organizational change.

Governmental and legal support of these key issues also depends on women's involvement. Women can wield political power, both as individuals and within groups, by letting politicians know that comparable pay and issues related to child care will be key factors in their voting decisions.

Old Barriers and New Opportunities

We've come a long way—further than any other group of women in the world—toward enjoying opportunities to choose those roles that fit each of us best and toward breaking out of rigid, stereotyped roles based on the expectations of others. And we still have a

---

*Top managers are executives who make those decisions that affect the entire organization.

long way to go. How far? It depends on the community and the organization. Some companies offer more opportunity for advancement than others, just as some communities tend to cling to the past while others are more future oriented.

Overcoming Old Barriers Traditions from the past affect today's career woman in two basic ways: (1) how she pictures herself and therefore the roles and behaviors with which she is comfortable, and (2) what others expect of her—their preconceived notions of her abilities, traits, strengths, and weaknesses, and their resulting beliefs about proper roles and behaviors.

The self-limiting beliefs of many women tend to create gaps in their preparation for a managerial role. Such beliefs lead to typical behavior, or traits, that may be quite appropriate in some situations but are frequently self-defeating in business situations. Which of these typical traits might create a career barrier for you?

- A tendency to suppress or hide ambitions and goals, to wait to be asked, to expect those in command to notice and acknowledge your potential and achievements and to direct your career progress

- A reticence to talk about your abilities and achievements, even in a business setting with people who need to know about them

- Avoidance of being the focus of attention, of taking action that will result in increased visibility within the organization

- Lack of confidence in ability to handle financial matters, projects requiring math or technical skill, situations requiring astute problem-solving and decision-making abilities

- Avoidance of office politics, the gaining and effective use of power

- A lack of curiosity about the inner workings of organizations: the hierarchy, the chain of command, sources of power, career paths

- A tendency to capitulate quickly to the wishes of others, especially men, when they attempt to dominate

- A tendency to personalize events, criticism, and messages of others, to react emotionally, and to act out such reactions

- A tendency to react to risky situations by focusing on the possible loss or danger involved rather than by balancing the probabilities and magnitude of possible gain versus loss

- More focus on self-development than on working as part of a team to meet organizational goals (and in the process some personal goals) and on developing an organizational power base

- A tendency (conscious or subconscious) to fear success in the business world

Role conflict is a common problem for career women. Both men and women are sometimes afflicted with fear of failure—fear that if they let people know they're trying to achieve a particular goal and actually go for it, they will experience humiliation and perhaps rejection if they don't succeed. The fear of success is generally a woman's problem and is based mainly on the belief that if she becomes a successful career woman, she will not be viewed as a desirable mate. Dr. Matina Horner found that 65 percent of the women she studied indicated a fear of success, compared with only 10 percent of the men.

The fearful reactions range in intensity from disturbing to terrifying. Horner concluded that women's desire for a close relationship is more primary than men's and takes precedence over everything else. The results, mostly unconscious, take several forms, including (1) mild to severe paralysis—the woman allows her career to lie stagnant between the two conflicting needs; (2) self-sabotage—she manages somehow to take actions and make moves or decisions that undermine her career goals; (3) energy drain—she uses so much emotional energy trying to repress those parts of her personality she subconsciously believes are unacceptable, threatening, or otherwise frightening that she has little energy left to devote to achieving goals.

Author Colette Dowling [3] labeled one version of this fear of success the "Cinderella complex." She described the tendency of some women to sabotage their careers because they fear they'll become so independent, and perhaps aggressive, that they won't appeal to a potential "Prince Charming." The major problem is that their expectations, fears, and resulting self-sabotage are all going on at a subconscious level and therefore are difficult to pinpoint. Deep down, such a woman fervently hopes that someone will come along to make her happy, which implies that she lacks confidence in her ability to assume control and responsibility for her own life.

Do you have just a touch of the Cinderella syndrome lurking in the back of your mind? Deep down, are you really waiting for Prince Charming to come along and make you happy ever after? There are other versions of Prince Charming, such as Santa Claus or Sugar Daddy. It's important to identify such fantasies and decide if you need to replace them with more realistic goals that allow you more autonomy. After all, Cinderella was a victim who needed rescuing—hardly a role compatible with that of manager. The fantasy usually implies that the male rescuer would be resentful and probably threatened by an independent, competent woman. Do you really need such a man?

Doesn't it make more sense to build a satisfying life of your own and hold out for a partner who has a deep inner confidence in his own competence and manhood, one who prefers to relate to a woman on an equal basis? Such a man is unlikely to resent your accomplishments or to try to dominate you. This approach to close relationships can free you to grow and develop and to advance unfettered toward all your goals. It allows you to be open and direct about your abilities and achievements in your dealings with men. In turn, you can gladly let those men who are threatened by your competence move on, rather than cluttering up your life with problem relationships.

Many women reach adulthood with a number of these self-limiting beliefs and resulting fears that they picked up from their families and the people in their communities. These beliefs are also absorbed from the culture at large via books, newspapers, and television. Such beliefs are usually based on what we perceive as the expectations of others about how we probably are and how we should behave. Later we'll explore some alternate behaviors you may want to consider adopting—approaches that will enhance your managerial image. The fact that other's expectations of appropriate behavior for managers often conflicts with their ideas of appropriate feminine behavior creates problems for many women managers.

The expectations of others about appropriate roles and behaviors for women (or any other category of persons), as well as the rewards and punishments women experience as a result of these expectations, help mold women's behavior. When nearly all women conform to the expected behavior patterns generation after generation, it becomes impossible to determine whether such behavior is innate or learned. Many people have acted as if such behavior is innate, however, and treated women in a stereotyped manner.

A **stereotype** is a belief about a certain group of people and their predictable characteristics. We use stereotypes as shortcuts—to categorize people and free us from having to judge each person independently. In the process, however, we usually ignore important information about individuals within that group. Most importantly, stereotyped expectations frequently lead individuals to behave in the expected ways and therefore fail to act naturally or to develop alternate behaviors and skills. We see a cycle in operation here: Community expectations of desired behavior from a subgroup within the community can lead to fairly rigid behavior patterns, which in turn lead to stereotyped expectations about the subgroup, which further reinforces the limited behavior patterns.

These stereotyped expectations of others exert a powerful influence in our lives, especially when we are young. This socialization process, discussed earlier, molded much of our behavior as children because we got payoffs—admiration, approval, and other good things—for acting in expected ways. By the time we're adults, we've forgotten how the process occurred, and we've internalized many of the expectations as our own beliefs about proper behavior.

Even if your community, family, or personal beliefs about appropriate behavior for women differs from that of the culture at large, operating on your own terms can be most difficult in the face of cultural expectations. As recently as 1972, research showed a wide disparity between traits that people valued in women as compared to men.

Loring and Wells [8, p. 103] of Stanford University, for example, found that the most valued traits in men were the following: "aggressive, independent, unemotional, objective, team player, dominant, likes math and science, not excitable in a minor crisis, active, competitive, logical, worldly, skilled in business." Notice that these traits are those typically expected of successful business and professional persons.

On the other hand, the traits most valued in women were the following: "does not use harsh language, talkative in appropriate situations, tactful, gentle, aware of feelings of others, religious, interested in her appearance, neat, quiet, strong need for security, appreciates art and literature, expresses tender feelings."

Women managers who find themselves in communities and organizations still adhering to these expectations of feminine behavior must convey a professional image that is usually identified with masculine traits and still retain the best aspects of their femininity. It takes skill, but a number of women have managed it and have won over the people they need as a support base in order to succeed. They've done it by building on their present strengths, adapting them to business settings, and developing other traits typical of effective male managers.

Do you need to develop strengths you've neglected because they weren't typically expected of women in your community? Alice Sargent suggests *some typical male strengths* that most women can develop further [12].

- Learn how to be powerful and forthright.

- Become **entrepreneurial.**

- Have a direct, visible impact on others, rather than just functioning behind the scenes.

- State your own needs and refuse to back down, even if the immediate response is not acceptance.

- Focus on a task and regard it as at least as important as the relationships with the people doing the task.

- Build support systems with other women and share competence with them, rather than competing with them.

- Build a sense of community among women instead of saying, "I pulled myself up by my bootstraps, so why can't you?"

- Intellectualize and generalize from experience.

- Behave "impersonally," rather than personalizing experience and denying another's reality because it is different.

- Stop turning anger, blame, and pain inward.

- Stop accepting feelings of suffering and victimization.

- Take the option of being invulnerable to destructive feedback.

- Stop being irritable, a "nag," and/or passive-resistant about resentments and anger.

- Respond directly with "I" statements, rather than with blaming "you" ones ("*I'm* not comfortable with that" rather than "*you* shouldn't do that.").

- Become an effective problem-solver by being analytical, systematic, and directive.

- Change self-limiting behaviors, such as allowing interruptions or laughing after making a serious statement.

- Become a risk-taker (calculating probabilities and making appropriate trade-offs).

Recognizing New Opportunities The traditions of the past hold the seeds of new opportunities for women in the future; for example, the way you were raised (that socialization process again) no doubt provided you with many special skills and advantages. Not only that, prevailing views of "woman's place" are changing in many organizations and cultures.

First, let's explore some of your special strengths so you can become more aware of them, build on them, and adapt them to business situations. In addition to typical male strengths, Sargent has identified *some typical female strengths* that you may want to enhance.

- Ability to recognize, accept, and express feelings

- Respect for feelings as a basic and essential part of life, as guides to authenticity and effectiveness rather than as barriers to achievement

- Acceptance of the vulnerability and imperfections of others

- Belief in the right to work for self-fulfillment as well as for money

- Belief in the value of nonwork roles as well as work identity

- Ability to fail at a task without feeling failure as a person

- Ability to accept and express the need to be nurtured at times

- Ability to touch and be close to both men and women without necessarily experiencing or suggesting sexual connotations

- Skill at listening empathetically and actively without feeling responsible for solving others' problems

- Ability to share feelings as the most meaningful part of one's contact with others, accepting the risk and vulnerability such sharing implies

- Skill at building support systems with other women, sharing competencies without competition, and feelings and needs with sincerity

- Ability to relate to experiences and people on a personal level rather than assuming that the only valid approach to life and interpersonal contact is an abstract, rational, or strictly objective one

- Acceptance of the emotional, spontaneous, and irrational parts of the self

Which of these traits and skills are a part of your repertoire? Like most traits and skills, these can be either a strength or a liability, depending on the situation and how you use them. How can you build on these special skills in your managerial role? How can you adapt them to the rules of the business game so that they create opportunities rather than barriers? We'll discuss various aspects of this issue in other chapters.

Opportunities for women in management have expanded rapidly in recent years, as shown in Exhibit 1-1. As you can see, women's opportunity to enter the lower management ranks has increased significantly during this century. However, the number of women making it to the highest levels of corporate management is still relatively small. One reason is that women have not planned and prepared for such careers in the past.

Another reason is that while many companies have been complying with Affirma-

tive Action guidelines by placing women in the positions of working supervisor, first-line supervisor, staff specialist, or even middle manager, they've been excluding them from positions on the career paths that lead to top management.

One way for women to capitalize on the opportunities that have been opening up for women is to focus on what the decision-makers are looking for in promotable people. Loring and Wells [8, p. 61] found that the promotable manager is

1. Able to develop goals and objectives

2. Able to build a plan to implement these goals, interrelating them with others

3. Capable of effective communication, especially face to face, but also written and formal presentation

4. Able to resolve or balance conflicts between work, interests, and people

5. Good at problem-solving and all its phases, with work processes and people problems

6. Capable of balanced decision-making, carefully weighing the important elements, and generally using good judgment

7. Able to determine priorities, with flexibility to change as needed, and stick with them when necessary

In summary, top management looks for people with the will to succeed, the asser-

EXHIBIT 1-1: Women's Participation in Management Positions, 1900–1983

	1900	1950	1980	1983
Management positions—supervisor through top manager	3.0%	12.0%	26.0%	33.0%
Top-management positions	0 %	0.4%	5.0%	5.0%

From U.S. Department of Labor, Bureau of Labor Statistics, *Employment and Earnings*, January 1984.

tiveness to get what they want, and the judgment to know when to compromise for the good of the organization. These are key abilities of *all* managers. Loring and Wells also attempted to determine how managers spot a *woman* with a primary, long-range interest in her career [8, p. 54]. They found this profile of *The Promotable Woman:*

1. An achieving person

2. A high level of motivation and achievement need

3. An identification with a field or profession

4. A high degree of individuality

5. A strong sense of self-esteem

If you are (or become) a person who *acts* out of her own convictions rather than one who merely *reacts* to people and situations, you'll stand the best chance of seizing new opportunities—and you'll probably handle a leadership role successfully. Women who function as mere *reactors* either live up to other people's expectations of them, acquiescing passively to others' demands, or, by doing the opposite of what's expected, operate at some level of rebellion. Either way, they are operating on *others'* terms rather than on their own. When a woman becomes her own person, she is ready to move up in the organizational hierarchy and to gain and use power.

THE ORGANIZATIONAL HIERARCHY

In planning your career, you need to be aware of the various levels of management positions, as well as the differences between **line** and **staff jobs.** You need to be able to identify the career path most likely to lead directly to the ultimate position you set your sights on. You'll want to avoid getting sidetracked into what the organization views as a dead-end position going nowhere. And you'll want to know which job moves represent the fast track to the top, why women have traditionally been excluded, how barriers to advancement usually affect people's behavior, and some ways of identifying companies that actively seek to promote women. In this section we'll discuss the organizational hierarchy as it applies to your career decisions. In Chapter 10 we'll examine in detail various types of organizational structure and their implications.

Levels of Management

At least three levels of management are found in all but the smallest organizations: supervisor, middle manager, and top manager. Very large organizations may have a dozen or more levels, but they can usually be further categorized into one of the three basic levels. Figure 1–1 shows the corporate hierarchy in a large organization.

The First-Line Supervisor The person in this position directly supervises a group of workers who are usually doing similar kinds of work. They therefore perform a single function within a department, such as the Pattern Makers Unit in a **Production Department.** Sometimes the first-line supervisor is called a foreman, sometimes an office manager. The key to identifying her level is determining the function she fulfills. She is usually technically competent at the work itself and spends most of her time directly involved with the workers and the work; that is, she is usually considered a specialist in the work being done.

The Managerial Supervisor The person in this position has a broader scope of authority within the department and usually has two or more first-line supervisors in sepa-

FIGURE 1-1: The Corporate Hierarchy

Note that line jobs lead to movement up the chain of command into the ranks of top management. Staff positions lack authority outside the immediate staff departments and may be career dead ends.

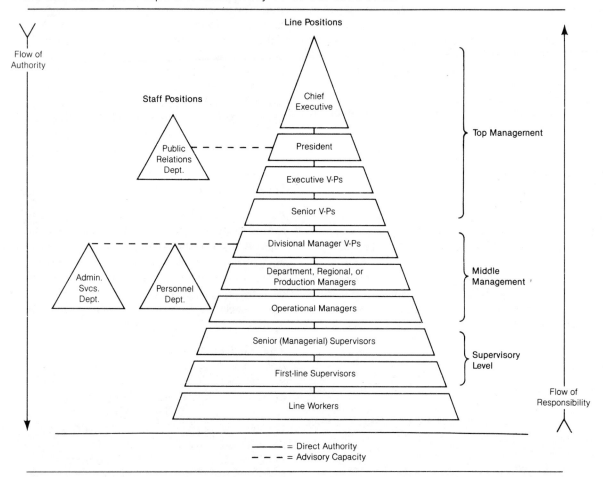

rate functions reporting to her. For example, the supervisors of the Pattern Makers Unit and the Fabric Cutters Unit might report to her. She may be responsible for scheduling and coordinating the tasks of different work sections, or she may simply be responsible for a larger variety of functions or work than the first-line supervisor.

At the managerial level a supervisor is no longer a specialist. She does not *do* the work her subordinates do, and she needn't know *how* to do it. Her job involves getting work done through other people. She judges results and ensures the performance of others. She spends more time planning, coordinating, motivating workers, handling personnel problems, and dealing with aspects of company finances, such as budgets or profit figures.

Middle Managers These people are responsible for all aspects of an entire division, department, region, plant, branch office, product line, or service area. They not only coordinate the activities of the supervisors who report to them, they spend a great deal of time with other middle managers and top managers to see that companywide objectives and policies are integrated and coordinated. They are normally much more involved than supervisors in making decisions about long-term company objectives and in setting policies.

Top Managers The top managers are responsible for determining the long-term direction the company will take, its major purpose for being, and its broad, overall strategies for dealing with competition, change, and the external environment. Top managers are also responsible for establishing companywide objectives and policies and for providing leadership and guidance to the firm as a whole. They coordinate the activities of the middle managers who report to them, and they work with other top managers to integrate activities to achieve companywide objectives. They also interact with managers of staff departments, who provide them with information, expertise, and advice. They often spend much of their time interacting with other business, government, and community leaders, as well as the company's owners (board of directors) or other governing body.

Line Versus Staff Positions

Staff departments are made up of people who specialize in various fields. Their function is to assist the line executives. They *may* include such departments as personnel, accounting, data processing, advertising, public relations, research, traffic, billing, industrial relations, medical, home economics, legal, and such technical specialties as engineering, sciences, and architecture, *if*

they are not the main service provided by the organization.

Staff jobs are *not* in the direct chain of command. Staff specialists and managers make recommendations and give advice to the line manager to whom they report. Although staff departments may have internal authority levels and chains of command, the top job is head of the department. Staff department heads make decisions that affect their own departments, but they do not normally make decisions that affect other departments, simply because they have no other departments under them. In contrast, the top job in the line structure is Chief Executive, as shown in Figure 1–1. Line managers make decisions that can affect everyone below them in the organization. More importantly, when top managers are looking within the company for promotable candidates, they usually select line managers. We'll discuss some exceptions to this practice later in this section.

Line jobs in private enterprise may be viewed as **profit centers.** Managers in these jobs find it relatively easy to pinpoint their contributions to company profits. In any firm that handles a product, sales jobs are line jobs. If the company makes products, jobs in the production department are line jobs. If it's a wholesale or retail firm, buyers as well as salespersons are in line jobs. If the company provides a service, jobs directly connected to providing that service are line jobs. In banks, it's getting and investing money; in insurance companies, it's getting and investing the money from premiums and handling claims; in a repair company, it's making the repairs; in a computer services firm, it's providing the actual service. Top management views these departments as absolutely essential to the survival of the organization; therefore, the budgets required to operate these departments are accepted as a necessary cost of doing business.

Staff departments, on the other hand, are sometimes considered by top managers to consist largely of "extras, frills, or nice-to-haves." It follows that their budgets may be viewed largely as expenses—that is, as profit drains. While staff services may be valuable, even vital, to optimal company operation, staff budgets and jobs are usually the first to be cut when business falls off.

You'll find many variations on the hierarchy depicted in Figure 1-1 when you check out companies you're interested in. The **matrix organization** is a recent innovation that can provide opportunities for women to gain valuable experience and to become visible. In this setup a parallel organization operates alongside and concurrently with the main, ongoing organization. The parallel organization is made up of project teams that disband after each project is complete. The structure of the main organization is usually similar to the one shown in Figure 1-1. In such a setup new people (like you) have a greater chance to learn about other phases of company operations and to expand their support networks. They can also become more visible to peers, through interaction on teams, and to top management, through progress reports and achievement on the team. Structures of organizations will be discussed further in Chapter 10.

The rewards for moving up in the hierarchy can be great, as indicated in Exhibit 1-2. Degrees in business are serving as entry papers for many women, especially young women and those with limited business experience.

Although comparisons of male/female salaries at various managerial levels are not included in Wright's almanac, it is noted that only 5 percent of the managers who earn over $40,000 in the fifty top U.S. industrial firms are women.

Potentially Dead-End Jobs

Companies vary widely in their commitment to opening up management opportunities for women. Therefore, you should be aware of the types of dead-end "management" positions you may get stuck in. (We'll discuss breaking out of dead-end positions later in this chapter.) Here are some examples.

The Working Supervisor This job may be labeled a management position for Affirmative Action purposes. But the label is misleading. Actually the woman still has responsibility for producing her own work while assuming a relatively small increase in pay and in authority in return for a large in-

EXHIBIT 1-2: Average Salaries by Managerial Level

Top managers—highest ten CEOs (includes stock gains and deferred compensation plans)	$5,000,000
Basic salary/bonus pay range: $250,000 to $2,300,000	
Top five officers in 10,000 corporations	120,000
Small company—CEO	75,000
Small company—other top managers	50,000
Middle managers, large company or department	60,000
Middle managers, small company or department	30,000
Supervisor	25,000
Trainee starting salary, MBA	24,000
Trainee starting salary, business degree	17,000

From *The American Almanac of Jobs and Salaries* by John W. Wright (New York: Avon, 1984).

crease in responsibility and time demands. She probably lacks adequate time for proper planning, organizing, directing, and controlling because she is too busy doing her own work.

First-Line Supervisors in Highly Routinized Functions   Women in these positions are often functionally powerless. They are frequently caught between conflicting demands of a management hierarchy they are not likely to have an opportunity to enter and the resistance of workers who resent their own highly routine and repetitive work. Women are especially likely to be given such jobs overseeing other women clerical or secretarial workers. Even when they are relieved of their own work duties and are given adequate time to supervise or manage, these women are likely to be powerless and stuck in dead-end positions.

Certain Staff Jobs   Women in some staff positions, such as personnel or public relations, may be organizationally powerless because they have no line authority and are dependent on line managers to carry out their recommendations and to implement their decisions. Staff managers usually lack the authority given line managers to make operational decisions and see that they're carried out. The staff person must be an expert in a particular area, such as public relations, research, or personnel relations. Association with operational employees is indirect. In staff positions the most important requirement is *expertise* in a specialized area of an operation. Women are especially likely to find themselves in a "stuck" position in the personnel department, which is thought of as a "woman's area" in some companies.

Recently, however, some innovative companies have renamed and reorganized this area to function as the **human resources department**. The head of the department is involved in virtually every company function

that requires people, often reports directly to the president, and may wield a great deal of power. The central function of personnel should be helping people gain the tools, knowledge, attitudes, viewpoints, and information they need in order to be productive and to succeed in their jobs. Unfortunately, this role gets lost in mounds of paperwork in many companies.

Jobs Likely to Lead to Advancement

Line jobs are more likely to lead to advancement than staff jobs, especially line jobs that directly affect company profits. However, staff jobs that are directly connected to solving a major company problem can also be a steppingstone to promotion.

Line Jobs That Contribute Directly to Profit   These are potentially the most powerful positions in most companies. If you can, find out how the people in top management in your company made it to the top. Chances are they came up through the ranks of the production and/or sales departments. Recently some top executives have been emerging from financial operations, since managing money once it has been made has become a high priority for many companies.

In simple terms, the jobs connected with the dual functions of producing and selling are potentially the most powerful. The dual functions involve (1) buying something, making something, or bringing in something and (2) selling something or servicing something for a profit.

Key Line Jobs in Nonprofit Organizations   The jobs most likely to lead to the top in government and other nonprofit agencies are those most directly connected with providing the major service of the organization. In health care organizations, the key jobs are the administrative positions involving direct patient services; in educational institutions, providing programs of study; in the postal service, collecting, processing, and delivering mail; in the Salvation Army, collecting contributions and distributing meals and other help to the needy.

In these examples the positions that include responsibility for attracting users of the services or for securing the necessary funds to provide the services vary in importance, depending on the purpose and nature of the organization. For example, attracting students to a private university has become a key responsibility in recent years. Securing funds has always been a key responsibility in charitable organizations like the Salvation Army.

Jobs on the Fast Track Top management in many organizations tags the most promising management trainees for promotion along an accelerated career path often called the "fast track." These candidates usually spend shorter periods of time in fewer jobs before being promoted to key middle management positions. They may then become the prime candidates for top management positions.

Jobs in Areas Crucial to Solving Current Company Problems When a company needs to computerize its operations, the staff position of systems analyst can become quite visible and important. When a company is threatened with a ruinous lawsuit, the legal staff gains status. Although such jobs may have relatively temporary value for advancement purposes, you may be able to gain visibility and be "in the right place at the right time" by accepting such a position. If the job is a staff function, however, think twice.

Why Women Have Been Excluded

Women have traditionally been excluded from management, especially middle and top management. Their opportunities for ad-

vancement have been practically nonexistent for three major reasons: the conformity pressures on managers to look and act alike, management's need for certainty about the attitudes and actions they can expect from people they bring into their inner circle, and the fact that the secretarial positions in which many women begin are completely outside the corporate hierarchy.

Conformity Pressures Rosabeth Kanter has noted that managers of the typical large corporation must look the part [7, pp. 47–68]. The similarities in their appearance are striking and reveal the extent of **conformity pressures** on managers. The managers in the typical corporation she investigated were usually white and male, with a "certain shiny, clean-cut look." Not only is social conformity important in managerial careers, but studies show that leaders in many types of situations are likely to show preference for socially similar subordinates and help them get ahead. Clark Kerr and his associates found that "incumbents in the managerial hierarchy seek as new recruits those they can rely upon and trust. They demand that the newcomers be loyal, that they accept authority, and that they conform to a prescribed pattern of behavior" [7, p. 63].

Uncertainty Conformity pressures and the development of exclusive management circles closed to "outsiders" are closely related to the degree of uncertainty found in all organizations. Managers are searching for all the security they can find. They are reluctant to give up some control and turn over some of the discretionary powers they have held within the organization to persons they're uncertain about. Therefore, they tend to reproduce themselves in kind. Women are occasionally included in the inner circle when they are part of an organization's ruling family. In most cases, however, this system leaves women out, along with other people who are socially different.

Some common perceptions of women also lead to exclusion. For many managers, "trust" means total dedication and complete loyalty. This viewpoint tends to omit female workers, who are seen as incapable of such a single-minded attachment. Many managers believe women generally don't have strong beliefs about their ability to become a manager and don't have driving aspirations to achieve that position. Kanter did in fact find that many women in the company she studied did not picture themselves as potential managers. However, she concluded that the limited self-concept held by these women was not based on any actual lack of the innate traits considered necessary for managerial success. Rather, it had developed as a result of the traditional, limited female roles these women held within the organization, especially the clerical and secretarial roles.

The Secretarial Ghetto In this century, women's roles have centered around the secretarial and clerical functions, and this has powerfully affected women's self-concepts and aspirations. In nearly all companies, the secretarial ladder is short, and rank is usually determined by the boss' status. In other words, secretaries derive their formal rank and level of reward not from the skills they use and the tasks they perform but from the formal rank of their bosses.

Nearly half the women in top management who are over 50 started in clerical positions, compared with only 23 percent of those under 50 [15]. However, you may find it necessary to take a clerical or secretarial position in order to get your foot in the door and to gain some work experience. Assisting an executive is a great way to learn about managing if you look and listen intelligently. However, you should keep in mind that decision-makers in a traditional company may be unwilling to promote anyone categorized as secretarial. You may have to find a way

to break out of this dead-end position, a topic we'll discuss later in this section. Kanter discovered other potential traps for women following the secretarial route; some of them could be traps for any woman worker.*

Narrow specialization and orientation to one boss and one job. Ambitious secretaries who try to get ahead through the initiative/efficiency route run the risk of becoming a threat to their bosses. Most secretaries find it safer to learn the *boss* rather than the company. In this way he comes to depend on her ability to anticipate his needs and to respond to requests without detailed orders.

Timidity and self-effacement. Because of their lack of independence and autonomy in the job and because of their dependence on one man, older women especially tend to display timid, self-effacing, nonassertive behavior.

Praise-addiction. Many secretaries tend to become addicted to praise because the boss gives them regular doses of thanks and praise in return for compliance with a continual flow of orders. Most secretaries are protected from responsibility or criticism because their boss serves as a buffer between them and other employees. This condition tends to intensify their dependence on the boss.

Emotionality and gossip. Many secretaries resort to assumed helplessness and emotional manipulation to get what they want. They take advantage of the discomfort of many men with displays of

---

*Since Kanter found that nearly all bosses in the corporation she studied were male and nearly all secretaries were female, this discussion refers to the boss as "he" and the secretary as "she."

emotion, such as anxiety or tears. These secretaries, of course, pay the price of becoming more and more accustomed to emotional displays that are considered inappropriate for managers.

Some secretaries also use their privileged access to information to gain status with others through gossip. Men in most status and power positions also earn status with others through gossip. However, it is usually referred to as "rumor" or "the grapevine." When secretaries use these powers and control tactics, they tend to reinforce stereotypes of women as gossipy and emotional.

How Opportunities for Advancement Affect Attitudes and Behavior

In most companies, the incentives are all for upward mobility. Therefore, the people who believe they're in line for advancement are "turned on" by the prospects of reaping rich rewards. On the other hand, those who believe they're stuck in dead-end positions must adjust to the prospect of limited rewards. The resulting attitudes and behavior of the two groups are quite different.

The Movers A typical career path to the best managerial positions is a track providing opportunities for a person to hold a variety of jobs across functions for two or three years each, including a period of time in the central headquarters of the company. The promotability that results from such diverse experience is essential not only to success but to other human values as well—to autonomy, independence, growth, a sense of challenge, and a chance to learn. In most companies the message is clear: Be promoted or be stuck. Upward mobility not only enhances a person's self-esteem dramatically, it

also affects the way people involve themselves in their work.

For those who have it, opportunity is seductive. Those on the fast track to middle or top management invest themselves heavily in work and concern themselves with learning the things that will be useful to them on their journey upward. They learn how to be political and how to watch what they say and to whom. As they move, they are usually willing to take on any extra tasks that will advance their careers. Once the excitement of opportunity takes hold, people's aspirations tend to soar. People can be turned around and turned on by realizing they have a wide-open opportunity to move up.

The Stuck It's a different story with the "stuck." These are people with low ceilings in their jobs, people at dead ends. Blocked from movement, lacking opportunity in a system where mobility above all means success, they make a variety of adjustments to their situation. They relate to work, to the organization, and to its people in a very different way from high-opportunity movers.

The largest category of stuck people are those who never had much opportunity to begin with. Low promotion rates, or short ladders and low ceilings in their job category, mean that they developed little or no expectations of upward mobility. Rosabeth Kanter found that most women clerical workers, supervisors of office workers, and some staff managers, especially in personnel, were in this situation [2, pp. 30–163]. Since their expectations were low from the start, these people were not necessarily alienated from the organization. Instead, they became more involved with their peers. Staff people might invest more time in their "professional" organization.

Another group of the stuck are the ones who either (1) competed for promotions and were turned down or (2) were promoted along dead-end career paths. These people are more likely to be frustrated because their expectations of opportunities have been encouraged and then blocked.

Male and Female Responses to Being Stuck
Women and men tend to respond in similar ways to the realization that their jobs offer them little hope of advancement.

1. *Low commitment to the company and to their work.* They become marginal employees, doing just enough to hold onto their jobs.

2. *Lack of initiative and withdrawal from responsibility.* Even if they continue doing an excellent job, they make no effort to expand it or to look for opportunities for the company to excel or prosper. They play it safe, shying away from new assignments outside their job description.

3. *Loyalty to their stuck peer group.* Cliques of the stuck may find their solidarity in open rejection and criticism of managers further up the ladder. Such criticism tends to take the form of passive resistance such as gossiping, joking, and ridiculing.
   Members of any such closed peer groups are under pressure to remain loyal to the group. Leaving the group, even for a promotion, may be seen as disloyalty. This tends to be especially true for women in clerical and secretarial jobs. To compound the problem, as a woman moves up, social contacts usually become fewer and more difficult, while men usually find a male peer group at every level. Concern about "leaving friends" and the social discomforts that go along with a promotion is therefore often expressed by women in the secretarial or clerical ranks.

4. *Preoccupation with social recognition.* The stuck seek status through social, rather than technical or professional, skills—perhaps by having the juiciest gossip, the latest inside information, or the best jokes. Some gain status by being the most compatible on the golf course, at the convention, and at other semisocial functions, especially where they're in frequent contact with outsiders who don't know their true position within the company. Others focus on getting recognition from younger or newer employees within the company.

5. *Resistance to innovation.* The stuck may get their kicks by resisting the ideas and projects of those people who did make it to higher positions. These chronic complainers and criticizers tend to offer no new ideas of their own, only barriers to the implementation of others' ideas. Barriers often take the form of foot-dragging or delaying projects through bureaucratic red tape.

Several studies have shown that men in low-opportunity situations take on the characteristics usually attributed to women in their orientation to work. Kanter found that such men "limit their aspirations, seek satisfaction in activities outside of work, dream of escape, interrupt their careers, emphasize leisure and consumption, and create sociable peer groups in which interpersonal relationships take precedence over other aspects of work" [7, p. 161].

If most women seem to be less motivated or committed to business careers, then, it is probably because their jobs carry less opportunity. When they perceive they have the same opportunities as men, women tend to behave in ways usually attributed to men on the job: They become more ambitious, task oriented, and involved with work.

Breaking Out of a Dead-End Position

Your best strategy, of course, is to avoid getting stuck in a dead-end position by exchanging the right information with your potential boss when you interview for a job or a transfer. Make your career goals known, and find out about alternate career paths and the likelihood of their leading to your goal. Understand the difference between low-mobility and high-mobility positions, and ask questions that will help you determine which type you're being offered. (See Exhibit 1-3.) Also refer to Exhibit 1-4 for clues on evaluating the power potential of a job, which is related to job mobility and promotability. Suggestions for specific interview questions are provided in Chapter 2.

After you accept a position, keep your eyes and ears open and keep evaluating whether you are still in line for a promotion that will be a good step toward your goal. After you've been in a position for two years, start making inquiries about when you're scheduled to move up. If you're still in the same job after three years, it's likely that you're stuck.

Here are a few strategies for breaking out of a dead-end job; they should give you some ideas for developing your own strategy.

EXHIBIT 1-3: The Promotability Factor of Jobs

High-Mobility Positions	Low-Mobility Positions
A high probability of advancement	Low promotion rates
A short time-span between advances	Long time-span between moves
The chance for increasing challenges	Unchanging tasks
	Static level of skill and mastery
Eventual access to the most rewarding jobs	No pathway into rewarded positions

- Make your goals known to appropriate decision-makers; gain their support. (See the section on mentors in Chapter 3.)

- If a better position is unavailable, try to expand your job responsibilities and get the title changed; later ask for a pay raise commensurate with your increased responsibilities.

- Ask for a lateral transfer if it would provide necessary experience and put you in a better position for promotion later.

- Look for ways to become more visible to decision-makers and to impress them favorably with your abilities and potential. See the discussion of gaining power later in this chapter, as well as relevant discussions in Chapter 14.

- Ask if there are some seminars, courses, or training programs that will prepare you for promotion; see if the company will provide funds.

- If you cannot get a commitment from your boss to promote you by a certain date, start planning your move to a company that offers better opportunities for advancement.

ORGANIZATIONAL POWER

How do you feel about gaining and using power? Exercise 1-2 at the end of this chapter is designed to help you identify your attitude toward power. Many women associate negative feelings and thoughts with the word "power" and are somewhat uncomfortable with the idea of assuming and using power. This attitude contrasts vividly to the typical male attitude. Most men assume that they will be expected to wield power in many capacities throughout their lives and tend to be comfortable with the idea. The first definition of power in the *American*

Heritage Dictionary is "the ability or capacity to act or perform effectively." In other words,

> *Power is the ability to make things happen, to influence people and events.*

Implied in this definition is the ability to influence yourself—that is, to direct your own life and to command your inner resources.

Because the ability to gain and use power effectively and to be comfortable with a powerful role is essential to managerial success, we'll discuss power from several angles throughout this book. In this chapter we'll take a broad view of power as used in an organizational setting. In Chapter 3 we'll discuss interpersonal power, your power as perceived by others; in Chapter 4, personal power, the ability to command your inner resources; and in Chapter 7, the need for power, a drive that motivates some people.

All these discussions are based on the premise that power itself is neither good nor bad; it's the ways in which power is used—and the effect of those methods on others—that may be judged either positive or negative. If you are uncomfortable with the idea of wielding power, this thought may help: Wherever you find groups of people, you find leaders—people who exercise power. Someone therefore is going to exercise power in any group; if you have leadership qualities, the leader might as well be you. In fact, the way you exercise power might have a more positive effect on the group than the way your competitors might go about it.

Organizational power represents different things to different people. For some, organizational power meets a real need. Most people, however, are interested primarily in gaining enough organizational power to survive within the system. They merely want enough power to carry out their responsibilities—to conduct their business with relative autonomy and to get the resources they need to meet their objectives. The formal, hierarchic power that comes automatically with a manager's job is rarely adequate. To function effectively, managers must also gain informal power through organizational politics. In any organization the powerful are the ones who have access to tools for action; so as a manager you must figure out what tools you need and how to go about getting them.

Types and Sources of Informal Organizational Power

Kanter found general agreement among managers about what constitutes credibility—competence plus power, the known ability to get results [7, p. 169]. People will do almost anything for a boss when they believe he or she has their interests at heart and will fight for them. However, they must see that the boss has the power to produce for them; they must believe the fight will pay off for them. This means that the boss must have some power within the system.

In order to be an effective manager, therefore, you must tap into informal organizational power and project the image of a powerful boss. And to maximize your power and promotability, you must seek a powerful boss any time you interview for a new job. Some sources of organizational power are (1) upward influence in the decision-making process, (2) the ability to get needed resources and information, (3) the ability to reduce people's sense of dependency and uncertainty, and (4) upward mobility. While these categories are closely related and sometimes overlap, they are helpful in identifying power sources.

Upward Influence Work groups with high morale invariably believe that their leaders have upward influence—that is, they are able to influence their own bosses and have a say in decisions affecting the department as a whole. When a boss has both good human relations skills *and* power, the workers tend to have high morale. Both men and women attach more importance to having a boss who can get things done than to working for someone who is "nice." Praises and promises mean little if the leader can't deliver.

Resources/Information People invariably sense who is powerful and are most likely to accept direct attempts to influence them from people they perceive as powerful. The most effective and best-liked leaders are those who can command more of the organization's resources, who can bring something that is valued from outside into the group, and who have access to the information that directly affects those in the work group.

Dependency/Uncertainty The larger and the more complex an organization is and the more rigid the hierarchy within the organization, the more people are dependent on others in the organization to get the things they need to carry out their tasks. People are generally willing to work quite hard to reduce this sense of dependency. One way to reduce it is to become allies with powerful people who can make them more independent by bringing more certainty to their lives.

People who want to gain power, then, must be able to solve the dependency problems of others and have some control over the major sources of uncertainty. People who have some control over situations currently creating problems for the company tend to have access to this type of power. Finance and accounting people have more power when business is bad or when money is tight. Production experts are a source of power when materials are scarce and demand is high. And so forth.

Upward Mobility Workers want to ally themselves with managers they perceive to have power for several reasons. (1) Powerful managers can get more for their workers. (2) They can back up both their promises and their threats. (3) They can more easily make changes in the situation of workers. (4) They can take the workers along with them when they move so that a worker's upward mobility is affected. (5) They are more likely to adopt a participatory management style in which they share information, delegate authority, train the worker for more responsibility, and give the worker more responsibility and autonomy.

Powerful bosses are promotable bosses, and they want to show that they are not indispensable in their current jobs. They train people to take their place when they advance. They delegate authority as a means of training replacements. This is in vivid contrast to powerless and unpromotable bosses. They tend to try to retain control and to restrict opportunities for workers to learn new skills and attain a higher level of responsibility. They're insecure and want to make it clear that no one else can take their place. A capable subordinate represents a serious replacement threat to the unpromotable boss, and the subordinate's growth and advancement are seriously blocked.

Being upwardly mobile in an organization confers a degree of power upon a person. Conversely, individuals who know how to gain power are likely to *become* upwardly mobile within the organization.

Ways of Gaining Organizational Power

Most of the ways people within large organizations gain power involve growth activities and alliances. Activities that result in an increase in power must be (1) out of the ordinary, (2) visible to key people within the organization, and (3) seen as part of a solution to a crucial organizational problem. Ways of doing something people consider extraordinary are by

1. Making organizational changes

2. Taking major risks and succeeding

3. Being the first in a new position

Reorganizing New managers must handle changes or crises to demonstrate their abilities. If their department has been running smoothly and continues to run smoothly, no visibility is gained. By reorganizing, a manager can ensure that his or her own team is well placed and that opposition is eliminated. Reorganizing provides the manager with rewards to bestow on followers in the form of new opportunities and job changes. Such managers create new uncertainties that make people more dependent on them; in this way they increase their power. In addition, the reorganization can be presented as a problem-solving innovation, which by design is highly visible.

Risk-Taking This approach requires a willingness to take calculated risks. Since many women have a negative view of risk—focusing on what may be lost in case of failure instead of what may be gained in case of success—it's a good idea to analyze your approach to risk-taking. Most men view calculated risk-taking (awareness of the probabilities and the implications of both failure and success) as a welcome challenge. (See Chapter 10 for a discussion of risk-taking in connection with problem-solving and decision-making.) Fewer managers are able to pull off extraordinary risks. When they do, the payoffs can be very high. Successful risk-takers show the company they can perform in the most difficult of circumstances, and they develop charisma in the eyes of others.

Visibility Jobs in which people are heavily involved in more than one department or with other organizations tend to have the most visible activities. Serving on task forces and committees can also gain visibility for the participants. Some managers gain visibility for their activities by making sure they appear relevant to solving company needs. This strategy may involve finding an acceptable label for an activity, then finding an organizational need to hang the label on, and finally selling the project to the appropriate persons.

Power Base In a large company it's also necessary to make social connections with people outside the immediate work group; these relationships need to be long term and stable. Gaining power, in fact, requires developing a support network, or **power base,** throughout the company that includes (1) subordinates, (2) colleagues, (3) mentors, and (4) other decision-makers. The value of a **mentor** (a decision-maker who befriends a younger manager and serves as teacher and supporter) will be discussed in Chapter 3, along with a general discussion of support networks.

How can you size up a potential job in terms of the power you may be able to generate within that position? One way is to get as much information as possible about the job factors, as listed in Exhibit 1–4. You can add other relevant factors for the position you're considering. Then analyze the factors for their power potential; for example, if the job functions are governed by few rules, that's a plus. If you're following a long line of predecessors in the job, that's a minus. Compare and evaluate the pluses and minuses for all the relevant factors to determine the job's potential for power.

The Powerless

Although it is no longer unusual for women to be given jobs of heavy responsibility where they are accountable for the results of subordinates, it's still relatively unusual for

EXHIBIT 1-4: Evaluating the Power Potential of a Job

Job Factors	Potential for Power (+) When Factor Is:	Potential for Powerlessness (−) When Factor Is:
Number of rules that must be followed	Few	Many
Number of predecessors in the job	Few	Many
Number of routines already established	Few	Many
Variety of tasks involved	Many	Few
Quantity and quality of rewards for unusual performance	High	Low
Degree of flexibility about how to use people	High	Low
Amount of approval needed for nonroutine decisions	Little	Much
Proximity of physical location to company headquarters	Central	Distant
Extent of publicity about job activities	Great	Small
Relevance of tasks to current organizational problem areas	Central	Peripheral
Focus of tasks	Outside dept.	Inside dept.
Extent of contact with top management	Great	Small
Number of opportunities to participate in programs, conferences, meetings, problem-solving task forces, committees	Many	Few
Advancement prospects of subordinates	Great	Small

Adapted from ''Power Dimensions in Your Job: Analysis for Action,'' by Goodmeasure, Inc., 1979.

women to have much power within the organization. This lack of power affects management style.

Sources of Powerlessness Frequently women supervisors or managers find themselves without the informal power that their formal roles demand—for some or all of these reasons:

They lack informal political influence as well as powerful mentors or sponsors; they are not on an upwardly mobile career path.

They are unable to get adequate **resources**, such as budget money, staff services, supplies, and additional workers.

They have little input to or influence in the planning and decision-making that directly affect them and their subordinates, and their area of independent decision-making is too limited.

Their situations don't permit them to take risks. Their bosses solve their problems for them rather than serving as **resource persons**.

Their authority is sometimes undercut by their bosses.

They convey a sense of insecurity as a leader and appear to anticipate resistance from their subordinates rather than cooperation.

Being aware of the sources and symptoms of powerlessness can help you avoid job "traps" that appear to be desirable promotions but are actually dead ends. Look carefully at the positions of working supervisor, supervisor of clerks or secretaries, and staff jobs. They may be steppingstones to powerful jobs, but they can also be dead ends.

How Powerless Managers React Powerless managers—whether male or female—tend to concentrate their power needs on their subordinates, over whom they have at least some degree of authority. The following behavior patterns are typical:

1. *Controlling Behavior and Close Supervision*

   Powerless managers tend to "lord it over" their subordinates. They tend to find talented subordinates threatening and rarely help such people get ahead. They usually select their immediate assistants from the mediocre rather than from the outstanding members of the group. They tend to resort to discipline or threats to gain cooperation from workers more frequently than their powerful counterparts do.

   They tend to make most or all of the decisions.

   They frequently do an excessive amount of the routine work.

   They rarely or never let a subordinate represent them at meetings.

   They attempt to control communications coming in and out of their department, so that all communications pass through them.

   They may attempt to take all the credit themselves for what is accomplished in the department. Because technical mastery of job content is one of the few areas where they do feel powerful, they are likely to take over tasks of subordinates or supervise them too closely.

   They may exert excessive control over their subordinates.

   They tend to jump in too quickly to solve problems for subordinates.

   They nitpick over small things subordinates do differently.

   They may overdo demands of strict conformity to their procedures, thus blocking subordinates from learning or developing their own styles.

   They spend too much time taking over the work of the next level down instead of devoting themselves to more general leadership activities.

2. *Overconcern with Rules and Procedures*

   Powerless managers give subordinates no room for freedom or experimentation with procedures.

   Since their superiors may not back them up, they depend on the rules as their only safe and sure legitimate authority.

   Getting everything "right" according to the rules is one of the few ways they have to impress superiors or to secure their positions.

   Control of the rules gives them some added power. They bend the rules for subordinates who are compliant and reward favored subordinates with a lighter application of the rules.

3. *Excessive Focus on Territorial Rights*

   Powerless managers tend to narrow their interests to their particular small territory or piece of the system.

   They try to insulate and protect it.

   They attempt to prevent anyone else from engaging in similar activities without their approval or participation as "the expert."

They focus on meeting their own goals. They show little interest in company goals.

Staff managers indulge in territoriality more frequently than line managers. Staff managers usually have fewer subordinates to supervise closely and fewer rules and procedures to resort to.

These findings have three important implications for women. First, powerless managers tend to display the types of behavior often attributed exclusively to women managers. Such behavior results from organizational powerlessness, *not* from any sex-related characteristics. Second, women who are upwardly mobile should seek to work for powerful bosses. They are more likely to encourage growth and development and to help talented women move on up the ladder. Third, women can avoid behaving as if they are powerless by avoiding the behaviors listed here and by adopting behaviors typical of the powerful. (See Chapters 3, 4, and 5.) Acting as if you have power is frequently half the battle! Many of the powerful got that way by surrounding themselves with the "aura" of power.

Now you know some basic rules of the business game, including how it came to be a male domain and how it's changing. If you don't like the business game or its rules, you have two choices: (1) Find something else to devote your energies to. (2) Play the game until you have enough power to change some of the goals or rules (keeping in mind that many who start out as radical reformers end up as conservative supporters). If you do like the game, you've probably found your niche.

If you're wavering, read on and find out more about the game. Start asking successful business executives how they view the game. Most say it helps them to think of the business world as a game. They're not likely to tie their sense of self-esteem and value as a person to winning a mere game. They can put skirmishes—and even major battles—into perspective. The setbacks and defeats that inevitably occur in even the most successful careers can then be viewed philosophically. The executive can ask, "What lesson can I learn from that one?"—"What new opportunity does this open up?"—and move on to the next round. This approach can be especially helpful for women who tend to take things too personally, overreact to criticism, let their emotions get the best of them, or carry a chip on their shoulder. It is conducive to "rolling with the punches." We'll discuss these particular problems in further detail in Chapter 4.

Keep in mind too that any organization—including government agencies, schools, churches, and other charitable or volunteer organizations—has its hierarchy, politics, and questionable practices. Whatever career path you choose, it's important to learn the rules of the game. Then you're in a position to decide how they fit in with your values, which of your viewpoints you'd be willing to change, and just how far you're willing to go toward compromise. Above all, it's important to deal with reality. This book is designed to help you do that. The next step is to identify the specific niche you want to aim for—to set your goals and priorities and to develop an action plan for reaching them.

SUMMARY

Although openings for women in management positions have more than doubled in the past thirty years, only 5 percent of top-management jobs are held by women. Those who succeed understand that they are operating in a male culture where the rules are made and enforced by men. They learn the rules of the game.

Traditionally woman's place was thought to be in the home. The industrial revolution separated male and female spheres even more; men ran the businesses and their wives ran the homes. During World War II women were called on to do "men's work" and discovered they were good at it. Several developments since that time have caused a large increase in the percentage of career-oriented women. These developments include the birth control pill, the Civil Rights movement, the women's movement, and higher life expectancy rates. Now we are in the midst of the computer revolution, and we're changing from an industrial society to an information society. This trend, along with other trends, offers even greater opportunities for women to move into new, challenging, and exciting careers.

The major barriers to success for most women involve their own self-limiting beliefs and attempts to live up to the stereotyped expectations of others about their place. Many women have overcome these barriers through awareness of unproductive behaviors and attitudes, such as fear of success, and the adoption of new behaviors and viewpoints.

Decision-makers in organizations are looking for promotable people with key managerial skills such as the ability to (1) develop goals, objectives, and plans; (2) communicate, solve problems, and make decisions; (3) handle conflicts between work, interests, and people; and (4) determine priorities. Companies are looking for *women* to promote into management who are highly motivated to achieve, feel a strong sense of identification with a particular field or profession, and have a high degree of individuality and self-esteem.

Upward mobility, visibility, and power go hand in hand for career success. The following jobs *may* be upwardly mobile but are frequently dead ends: working supervisor, first-line supervisors in highly routinized functions, and certain staff jobs, such as personnel. Jobs most likely to lead to advancement are (1) line jobs that directly contribute to profit and (2) jobs in areas considered crucial to solving current company problems.

Most women classified as "managers" are actually supervisors. It's important to recognize the difference between supervision and middle management. Middle managers are more closely involved in making decisions about objectives and developing policies for entire functional areas in order to integrate and coordinate companywide operations. Supervisors make fewer decisions, and their influence is usually limited to matters that directly affect their unit.

People who believe they have a high opportunity for advancement tend to become highly motivated. Conversely, people who believe they have little opportunity to advance tend to show (1) low commitment to the company and to their work, (2) lack of initiative and withdrawal from responsibility, (3) loyalty to their "stuck" peer group, (4) preoccupation with social recognition, and (5) resistance to innovation. Both men and women respond the same way to high-opportunity and low-opportunity situations.

Access to power is important for success as a manager. Work groups with high morale invariably perceive that their leaders have upward influence. Ways to gain power include (1) doing something out of the ordinary, (2) being visible to key people within the organization, and (3) being seen as part of a solution to a crucial organizational problem. Some actions that people might consider extraordinary are making organizational changes, taking major risks and succeeding, and being the first in a new position.

Male and female managers tend to react in similar ways to powerlessness: (1) controlling behavior and close supervision of workers, (2) being overly concerned with rules and procedures, and (3) focusing excessively on territorial rights.

Additional Exercises

EXERCISE 1-2: YOUR POWER PROFILE

Write the first things you think of in response to the following five statements. Don't try to analyze what you "should" respond. The first things that pop into your mind will be the most valuable for this exercise.

Statement 1. *Power.* When I think of power, I think of _____

_____

Statement 2. *Powerless.* Some situations in which I have felt powerless are _____

_____

Statement 3. *Powerful.* Some situations in which I have felt powerful are _____

_____

Statement 4. *Power Drains.* Some typical behaviors that drain away a woman's professional power image (that make her appear less powerful) are _____

_____

Statement 5. *Power Boosts.* Some typical behaviors that boost a woman's professional power image (that make her appear more powerful) are _____

_____

Recap. Now, go back and categorize your responses to Statement 1 by identifying each response as (a) a positive aspect of power, (b) a negative aspect of power, or (c) a neutral aspect of power. Which category is predominant in your responses? What do you think this reveals about your attitude toward power? _____

_____

Compare your responses to Statements 2 and 3. How can you eliminate or minimize situations in which you feel powerless? How can you expand or increase the situations in which you feel powerful? _____

_____

Compare your responses to Statements 4 and 5. How can you eliminate or minimize your own actions that are power drains? How can you expand or increase your actions that represent power boosts? _____

_____

EXERCISE 1-3: PINPOINTING YOUR ATTITUDE

Step 1. Finish the following story. Be as spontaneous as possible; don't try to analyze what you should write or figure out the best response. This exercise will have the most value to you if it reflects your first reactions. Write anything that occurs to you, whether it makes sense or not.

Step 2. If you are meeting with a group, your instructor may want you to print your initials on the back of your story and turn it in to be analyzed by the instructor or redistributed to another group member.

Step 3. See the answer key for instructions on analyzing your paper and, if appropriate, another group member's paper.

The Story: Carrie Dickeson decides to enter graduate school to work on her Master of Business Administration degree. She finds that about one-fourth of the graduate students are women. Only one of her instructors is female. When grades come out at the end of the first semester, Carrie learns she has the highest grade point average in the Business Department. (Continue the story to its conclusion.)

EXERCISE 1-4: OVERCOMING FEAR OF SUCCESS

Is it possible that you have hidden reservations about achieving a successful career? Could it be that you actually fear some aspects of success? Such fears can result in self-sabotage of career goals. The analysis of your response to Exercise 1–3 may indicate that you do in fact harbor some of these fears. The best way to overcome them is to uncover them and then to establish new beliefs about success. Steps 1 and 2 of this exercise are designed to help you further identify success fears and their sources. Steps 3 and 4 are designed to help you establish new beliefs about success. (More about this in Chapter 2.)

Instructions for Steps 1 through 3: Read the statement; then close your eyes, breathe deeply, and relax. Focus on the statement; don't analyze it or try to figure out what the "best response" should be. Notice what comes up, what spontaneously occurs to you. Then open your eyes and finish the statement by writing your responses in approximately the sequence in which they occurred to you.

Step 1: (a) I want to reach my career goals, but . . .

   (b) To achieve my career goals, I might have to give up . . .

   (c) Maybe I don't really deserve to succeed because . . .

Step 2: Some "don't deserve" or warning messages my parents or others gave me are . . .

Step 3: (a) I can handle abundant success because . . .

   (b) My top three priorities are . . .

   (c) I deserve abundant success because . . .

Step 4: Put each item you wrote in Step 3 on a separate card. Each week select a different card and place it where you'll see it several times a day. Become your own best supporter. Repeat one of these affirmations at least once a day.

EXERCISE 1-5: YOUR SELF-CONCEPT

Draw a picture of yourself:

1. When you feel down

2. When you feel your very best

3. Who you are in your wildest fantasies

4. The way people see you who think you're "just great"

5. The way people see you who think you're "for the birds"

6. Your ideal self—who you would really like to be and think maybe you could be

REFERENCES

1. Berch, Bettina. *The Endless Day: The Political Economy of Women and Work.* New York: Harcourt Brace Jovanovich, 1982. This book provides an explanation of how our economic system operates and how it structures the economic life of women in the marketplace, in housework, and in childrearing, along with some alternatives for change.

2. Colwill, Nina L. *The New Partnership: Women and Men in Organizations.* Palo Alto, Calif.: Mayfield, 1982. An examination of the interaction between women and men as it affects today's organizations, this book explores sex roles and sex-role myths, as well as their impact in the work place.

3. Dowling, Colette. *The Cinderella Complex.* New York: Simon and Schuster, 1981. The author examines the tendency of many women unconsciously to sabotage real career success for fear it will prevent their rescue by "Prince Charming" from the workaday world. The tendency to back away from career success once marriage takes place is also examined.

4. Fenn, Margaret. *Making It in Management: A Behavioral Approach for Women Executives.* Englewood Cliffs, N.J.: Prentice-Hall, 1978. This book gives an explanation of the management process and the relationships most

important to successful leadership, with a focus on opportunities and barriers women may encounter.

5. Higginson, Margaret V., and Thomas L. Quick. *The Ambitious Woman's Guide to a Successful Career.* New York: AMACOM, 1975. The authors explore the important factors in planning a career, developing organizational savvy, and understanding key relationships.

6. Hull, J. B. "Female Bosses Say Biggest Barriers Are Insecurity and 'Being a Woman.' " *Savvy* (November 2, 1982).

7. Kanter, Rosabeth Moss. *Men and Women of the Corporation.* New York: Basic Books, 1977. A classic in the field of women in management, this book is especially valuable for its insights into the ways organizational power and mobility affect women in the corporate world, the status of women, and some barriers women must overcome to succeed as managers.

8. Loring, Rosalind, and Theodora Wells. *Breakthrough: Women into Management.* New York: Van Nostrand Reinhold, 1972. This is a landmark study of attitudes and cultural factors that facilitate or hinder the movement of women into management positions.

9. Naisbitt, John. Megatrends: *Ten New Directions Transforming Our Lives.* New York: Warner Books, 1982. The author explores the major trends occurring today that will affect our lives in the future.

10. Matthaei, Julie A. *An Economic History of Women in America.* New York: Schocken Books, 1982. A history of women's work in America since colonial times, this book focuses on how the sexual division of labor developed and changed with the advent of industrialism.

11. Ryan, Mary. *Womanhood in America: From Colonial Times to the Present.* New York: Franklin Watts, 1983. This work explores the history of woman's role in American society, including the sexual division of labor and the current trend toward gender symmetry.

12. Sargent, Alice G. "The Androgynous Blend: Best of Both Worlds?" *Management Review* (October 1978), pp. 60–65.

13. Sheehy, Gail. *Passages.* New York: Dutton, 1974. This is an excellent book for helping you understand the predictable crises of adult life. It helps to know you are not alone!

14. U.S. Department of Labor. Bureau of Labor Statistics. *Employment and Earnings,* January 1984.

15. *Wall Street Journal,* November 2, 1981.

16. Wright, John W. *The American Almanac of Jobs and Salaries.* New York: Avon, 1984. See listing in Chapter 2 References.

Chapter Two

Clarifying Your Goals and Setting Priorities:
Life Plans and Career Plans

"There are no doors we cannot unlock. We will place no limits on achievement."

Geraldine Ferraro

The people in power in business organizations are looking for promotable men and women. They want people who know what they want and where they're going, people who can develop goals as well as action plans to implement their goals. They also want people who are able to balance conflicts between work, interests, and people. In this chapter, you will focus first on identifying your key skills and interests. Then you can use that self-awareness to develop personal goals and action plans for your career, your family or private life, and your personal growth and development, so you will be able to balance or resolve conflicts that occur. Later, in Chapter 9, you'll apply goal-setting skills to developing organizational, departmental, and other job-related goals.

In this chapter you will have the opportunity to

1. Analyze and package your unique set of skills and interests

2. Distinguish between goals and activities

3. Formulate effective goals that lead to achievement

4. Develop skills in balancing your career, your family life, and your personal development

5. Develop action plans that lead to the attainment of your most important goals, and use your plan to improve your career and your life

6. Develop a plan for getting the job you want

7. Design a résumé that helps you sell yourself

8. Write an application letter that captures favorable attention

9. Learn how to handle job interviews so that you get the job that's best for you

---

 Life Directions

"Come in, Carrie, have a seat." Jean Simon, Placement Counselor at San Francisco State University, points toward the chair beside her desk. "I looked over the résumé you left with the secretary yesterday, but I'm afraid I wasn't able to do much with it."

"Is it that bad?"

"No, no. It's just that your job objective is so broad—'a management trainee position.' You see, your résumé should focus on those aspects of your background that qualify you for the particular job you're after. And when you don't identify a particular kind of job with a specific type of company, then it's impossible for me to evaluate effectively how well your résumé highlights your qualifications."

"I knew I should have been more specific. Believe me, I've wrestled around with this problem for over a week. But I hate to just pick a type of job and a kind of company out of the air. The truth is, I can't decide exactly what I want to do. I feel that I don't know enough about what's out there."

"Okay, Carrie. I can see you have lots of work to do before you begin any serious interviewing. Job objectives are based on career goals and on life goals—and a week is hardly an undue length of time to consider these matters. You need to hammer out your goals, decide which ones have top priority, and set up some action plans for the major ones. And all this should be done in writing, so you'll have something concrete to refer to when you're conducting your job campaign and later when you're making on-the-job decisions about how to manage your time."

Carrie sighs. "I suppose so, but it's such a drag. I mean I'm so busy already—with school, and my job, and now these interviews. Besides, I'm not really comfortable with the idea of planning every aspect of my life for the next ten or twenty years."

"Whoa! I can see you've thrown up some real barriers to the whole planning process. First of all, goals should be stated in concrete terms, but they should never be set in concrete. The best plans are always flexible, and the best planners are alert to times when their goals should be changed." She smiles at the spark of interest in Carrie's eyes. "You see, goals should serve you—you should never become a slave to your goals."

"I like that idea."

"Sure. Your goals and plans simply provide you with a mental map to help you direct your energy. They help you create the life you want for yourself. Instead of wasting a lot of energy in hoping and wishing, you use it to achieve what you want in life. Even if you make some false starts, you'll probably be moving in the general direction of your heart's desires. It's fine to dream, but people with just dreams—no specific goals—tend to drift along through life, never really getting anywhere."

Carrie nods. "Waiting for their ship to come in."

"Yes, and later wondering why it floundered. That's why I'm convinced that your chances of creating the life you want in minimal time are far greater when you're armed with some goals that are based on honest soul-searching."

"You're beginning to convince me," Carrie replies.

"Let me share with you a story I came across the other day. It says it so much better than I can." Jean pulls a little booklet from her desk drawer and begins reading:

The California Coast was shrouded in fog that fourth of July morning in 1952. Twenty-one miles to the west on Catalina Island, a 34-year-old woman waded into the water and began swimming toward California, determined to be the first woman to do so. Her name was Florence Chadwick, and she had already been the first woman to swim the English Channel in both directions.

The water was numbing cold that July morning, and the fog was so thick she could hardly see the boats in her own party. Several times sharks had to be driven away with rifles. As the hours ticked off, she swam on. Fatigue had never been her big problem—it was the bone-chilling cold of the water.

Fifteen and one-half hours later, numbed with the cold, she asked to be taken out. She couldn't go on. Her mother and her trainer alongside in a boat told her they were near land. They urged her not to quit. But when she looked toward the California Coast, all she could see was the dense fog. After another twenty-five minutes—when she had been in the water almost sixteen hours—she quit and was lifted into the boat.

It was not until hours later, when her body began to thaw, that she felt the shock of failure. To a reporter she explained, "Look, I'm not excusing myself. But if I could have *seen* land, I might have made it."

After swimming over twenty miles of the twenty-one-mile channel, she had been pulled out only a half-mile from the California Coast! Later she was to reflect that she had been licked not by fatigue or even by the cold—the fog alone had defeated her because it obscured her goal. It had blinded her reason, her eyes, and her heart.

It was the only time Florence Chadwick ever quit. Two months later she swam the same channel, and again the fog obscured her view, but this time she swam with a clear vision of her goal in her head—a mental map of where she was going. Not only was she the first woman to swim the Catalina Channel, but she beat the men's record by some two hours!"*

Carrie blinks. "Sold! When is your next goal-setting seminar?"

---

1. Do you think Carrie's initial attitude toward goal-setting is a typical one? How would you describe that attitude? What new insights do you think Carrie gained from Jean Simon's suggestions and the story she told about Florence Chadwick's experience? _____

2. Have you made a practice of setting specific goals for yourself and developing plans to achieve them? _____

3. How would you describe your attitude toward goal-setting up to this point in your life? _____

4. Did the Florence Chadwick incident bring to mind any related experiences from your own life? If so, explain. _____

5. How can you use insights similar to the ones Florence Chadwick experienced to achieve what you want in your life? _____

---

*Adapted from *Bits & Pieces*, ed. by Marvin G. Gregory (Fairfield, N.J.: The Economics Press, 1979).

IDENTIFYING PLANNING BARRIERS AND PAYOFFS

If your answers to the questions above reveal some internal resistance to setting goals and developing a career plan, you are not unusual. The first step toward success for many people is getting over the planning barriers they erect for themselves. Exercise 2-1, Identifying Planning Barriers and Payoffs, is designed to help you identify your own barriers and to move on to a greater awareness of the payoffs for planning.

Perhaps you can identify other barriers to success from your responses to the exercises at the end of Chapter 1. Do you feel uncomfortable about exercising power? Are you afraid to set goals because you may fail? Do you fear success even more than failure? How about your self-concept? Who are you? Can you picture yourself in a role that symbolizes success to you? What is success to you? Three troublesome types of fears that form barriers to success are (1) fear of success itself, (2) fear of failure, and (3) fear of risk-taking.

Success means different things to different people. Here's a definition that could apply to everyone:

Success is the ability to visualize the life you want to live and to enjoy the process of moving toward that vision and achieving it.

EXERCISE 2-1: IDENTIFYING PLANNING BARRIERS AND PAYOFFS

1. "Set your goals and plan your life." Do you have any resistance to that suggestion? If so, list your negative or doubting responses. _____

   _____

2. "If only I had . . . " Does that phrase bring to mind any regrets you've experienced? If so, list the first few that come to mind. _____

   _____

3. Look over the situations you listed in No. 2. Note how the results might have differed if you had clearly identified your top goals and thought about some key activities for reaching them. _____

   _____

4. "I did it!" "I made it!" "I got it!" Do these words bring to mind some high points in your life? List the first few that come to mind. _____

   _____

5. Look at the situations you listed in No. 4. Compare them to the situations listed in No. 2. Were you more committed to achieving the re-

sults you got in the latter situations? Did you put more thought and planning into them? How many of them were "lucky breaks"? How much of your desire or commitment was subconscious? Conscious? Do you think your subconscious desires and intentions may have helped create any of the "lucky breaks"? Explain. _____

_____

6. Are you willing to depend on lucky breaks or subconscious desires to determine the kind of life you have? Or do you want to exercise a higher degree of conscious control in creating the life you want? Comment.

_____

_____

7. What payoffs can you identify for setting goals and planning your life direction? Refer to the resistant responses you listed in No. 1; list any rebuttals that come to mind. _____

_____

_____

To visualize the life you want, you must be able to see yourself functioning comfortably in it. You must have a sense of who you are. Did the drawings you made of yourself in Exercise 1-5 help you to identify who you are in your own mind? How would you answer the question, Who are you? _____

_____

Many people respond to that question in terms of the roles they play or what they do. But you are something more all-encompassing than that. Ruth Ross, author of *The Prospering Woman* [19], goes even further and says you are not your feelings, your body, or your mind. She says:

You are a center of consciousness—designed to be self-aware.

Many of the exercises in this book are designed to help you reach new levels of self-awareness. For example, becoming aware of your fears is often a first step to overcoming the three barriers to success discussed next.

Fear of Success

Did Exercise 1-4 uncover some fear of success you may have been subconsciously harboring? If so, you'll need to work out any role conflict that underlies the fear. The best way to root out fear is to get down to specifics and examine it in detail by asking yourself questions similar to the following ones:

Do you fear that success will have some scary consequences? Dig them out and face them. Here are some common ones: I won't be as attractive to men. I won't be able to catch (or hold) a husband. It will involve too much responsibility. I'll be in the spotlight too much. I'll be blamed when things go wrong. I won't have enough free time for a personal life. People won't like me if I'm the boss . . . a strong, aggressive woman . . . more successful than they are.

Do you fear that success doesn't fit your self-image? Maybe you need to work on changing it. Deep down, do you picture yourself as an underprivileged type? Slightly inferior in some way? A follower, not a leader? A victim? A sweet young thing?

Are you afraid of your parents' reaction to your success? Are you afraid your mom won't like you if you're more successful than she was? Do your parents generally resent successful people?

Conversely, are you afraid you *will* fulfill your parents' wishes? Perhaps you still resent their pushing you. Or maybe there's another reason you decided as a child that you would "show them" by not giving them what their hearts desired.

Do you merely fear the unknown aspects of success? Moving into new roles, especially leadership roles, is risky. So much of the territory is uncharted.

Or, maybe you fear that you don't really deserve success. This ties in with self-image again. If as a child you received messages from important people in your life that you interpreted as, "You don't deserve success," then you may have decided you aren't deserving. Or perhaps your behavior didn't meet the standards you had internalized, so you decided you were undeserving. Chances are you don't remember making that decision, but it can exert a strong subconscious influence on your actions. In fact, psychological research indicates that we'll do almost anything to prove we are right in these basic life decisions. We'll focus on proving we don't really deserve success instead of focusing on opportunities for achieving it. After all, achieving it would make us wrong, a situation our subconscious selves will fight valiantly to avoid!

You can reverse such negative cycles through self-awareness and through changing your subconscious beliefs and goals. We'll focus on the latter in Chapter 4. It also helps to take a realistic look at the alternatives to success—in the long run you are much more vulnerable and have far fewer options in life without success!

Fear of Failure

The other side of the coin is fear of failure, which involves the fear of revealing yourself as inadequate or wrong. It involves focusing on wrong versus right instead of moving toward the life you want. When you experience fear of failure, focus on this thought:

All is to my benefit.

This idea is based on the concept of life as a game in which we are constantly learning, growing, and improving. Situations in which we don't get what we aim for can serve as valuable lessons and signals for future guidance if we choose to use them that way.

Fear of Risk-Taking

Both the fear of failure and the fear of success are often based on a fear of taking risks. Throughout this book we'll be discussing various aspects of risk-taking, including calculating the probabilities of success. It's easy to forget, also, that avoiding a risk can be a risk itself—a risk that we won't grow or be all that we can be.

Any of our fears can exert power over us only so long as they are vague or nebulous.

When we keep them in a mental closet and refuse to bring them into the bright light of awareness to examine them and their possible consequences, they retain the scary power of ghosts or goblins. Exercise 2-2, Handling Fear, is designed to help you face your fears. If you can become comfortable with handling the worst that can happen, the consequences cease to have the power to bring fear and tension into your life. Only then can you truly let go of your fears and focus on setting and achieving your goals. Letting go of the desperate need to avoid fearful consequences is one of the keys to self-mastery. In Chapter 4 we'll discuss letting go of the intense need—versus the relaxed intention—to achieve your goals, which is another self-mastery key.

EXERCISE 2-2: HANDLING FEAR

Step 1. List all the fears that come to your mind. _____

_____

_____

Step 2. Rank the fears you listed according to the power you think they have over your willingness to set goals and achieve them.

Step 3. For your most crippling fear ask, "Why do I experience fear in this type of situation? What am I really afraid will happen?" Write your answer next to the fear statement. Then ask why again and write your answer. Keep asking why until you feel you've discovered the root of the fear, the ultimate consequence you're really afraid of.

Step 4. Visualize the ultimate consequences you uncovered in Step 3. (See Exercises 4-4, 4-5, and 4-6 if you need help with this step.) Ask yourself, "What are the worst things that can happen in this situation?" Imagine all the consequences. List them here. Next, relax and let go of the desperate need to avoid those consequences. See yourself handling them comfortably. (You may have to spend days or even weeks getting to the point where you can honestly say, "I can handle those consequences; it wouldn't be the end of the world; I could move up and out from there.") _____

_____

Step 5. Ask yourself, "What goal(s) was this fear blocking my whole-hearted commitment to?" List them here. Next, picture yourself moving toward each goal with the relaxed intention of achieving it. Whenever you think about this goal, relax and focus on achieving it, free of fear.

(See the exercises in Chapter 4 for tips on achieving a deeply relaxed state of concentration.) _____

_____

Step 6. Repeat Steps 3 through 5 for your other major fears, one at a time.

Handling your fears can help you to deal effectively with risk and to estimate more objectively the actual probabilities of various outcomes. Taking calculated risks is essential for success in life and is certainly a key to success in business. Nothing ventured, nothing gained is one of the rules. What types of risks have you been unwilling to take? How does this unwillingness affect the goals you set for yourself? Often people miss opportunities because they won't risk rejection. As one wit has said, "If you haven't experienced rejection at least once this week, you're simply not out there trying." In other words, playing it safe may make you feel better temporarily, but to experience that heady excitement that comes from a high level of achievement, you must go after challenging goals, goals that involve the risk of rejection or failure.

Identifying with Successful People

How do you relate to other people's successes? With envy? Resentment? Awe? Appreciation? Enjoyment? Sincere applause? Your responses are clues to your self-concept and to your fears. If your feelings are negative or involve a sense of awe, you are separating yourself from success. Chances are you don't want to be reminded that you are not risking and achieving. On the other hand, when you identify with success and see yourself moving toward your vision of success, your feelings about others' success tend to be positive.

It's important to identify your own barriers to successful goal-setting and planning and to overcome them so they don't dominate your thoughts. Your dominant thoughts are what you will get next in your life. Learn to focus on what you want, not on your supposed inadequacies. Then you'll be open to the opportunities that come along—you're more likely to see them and grab them. You'll focus on what you *can do*, not on what you can't.

IDENTIFYING AND PACKAGING YOUR SKILLS AND INTERESTS

One of the keys to success is to choose a career doing something you really care about. What you care about, what you enjoy, is closely related to what you're good at doing. But many people are not clear about the kinds of things they're good at and really enjoy. They feel there may be many things they could do or would like if they only knew more about them or had a chance to try them—especially in the career area.

The only way to identify your skills and interests is to start with what you know now. Then as you learn more about various jobs and careers, you have a basis for evaluating how well they fit your set. Exercise 2-3, Analyzing Your Key Interest/Skill Areas, is designed to help you identify your skills and interests and to go a few steps further. By analyzing what it is you enjoy most about various activities, you may be able to iden-

EXERCISE 2-3: ANALYZING YOUR KEY INTEREST/SKILL AREAS

Step 1. List randomly, as they come to mind, all the things, past and present, that you have done well, that you enjoyed doing, or that you are interested in doing. _____

_____

Step 2. Now analyze each item you listed in Step 1 by identifying the particular portion or aspect of the activity you enjoyed the most. (Example: "Giving parties" can be broken down into planning, organizing/coordinating, and social interaction. Planning involves making decisions about the type of party, when and where to have it, whom to invite, and the type of dress, food, and activities that will be appropriate. Organizing includes rounding up invitations, food, supplies, and helpers, and coordinating all these elements so the party runs smoothly according to plans. Social interaction includes seeing that people feel welcome, get to know each other, and have a good time. Another type of analysis is to identify the specific needs you met by engaging in the activity. What was most fulfilling—the sense of power you felt from engineering the party? The sense of achievement you experienced from bringing it off well? Or the sense of cameraderie you felt from getting together with people and promoting a good time?) _____

_____

_____

_____

Step 3. Now look over the items you listed from your analysis in Step 2. Can you identify some common building blocks of skills and interests? List them. Finally, rank them in order of their importance to you. _____

_____

_____

tify some commonalities. Then you can package your skills and interests into some building blocks that could be rearranged in any number of ways to suit various career paths. Exhibit 2-1, Repackaging Your Skills, may give you some ideas.

EXHIBIT 2-1: Repackaging Your Skills

Key Skills	Related Business Needs/Applications	Employment Areas
Creative/Artistic Writing, editing, graphic arts, announcing, performing arts, modeling	Communication skills, public relations/media skills, establishing/building client relationships, technical supervision	Managers/administrators, marketing/sales, communications, clerical/administrative support, services
Business Detail Clerical, bookkeeping, accounting, administrative, computer operations, interviewing, claims handling, statistical analysis, records processing	Organizing, coordinating, processing, follow-up and control, evaluation, information management, administrative procedures	Managers/administrators, marketing/sales, computer-related jobs, finance/real estate/ insurance, professionals, communications
Humanitarian Child care, counseling, religious or social work, nursing, therapy, rehabilitation services	Consensus-style management, service orientation, direct client/customer contact, skills in communicating, motivating, training, supervising	Managers/administrators, marketing/sales, finance/real estate/ insurance, professionals, communications
Accommodating Services Social/recreational services, food services, beauty/barber services, customer services, attendant services, passenger services	Customer/client orientation, building and maintaining business relationships, skills in communications/ public relations	Managers/administrators, marketing/sales, finance/real estate/ insurance, services
Selling Retail, real estate, and technical sales, advertising and promotion, clerical work related to sales	Persuasive communication, human relations skills, establishing business relationships, customer/client orientation, results/profit focus	Managers/administrators, marketing/sales, finance/real estate/ insurance, services, communications
Physical Performing Coaching and instruction of sports, officiating	Decision-making, problem-solving, training, coaching, directing workers, setting motivational work climate, setting goals, managing achievement, productivity	Managers/administrators, marketing/sales, services, communications
Plants/Animals Farming, forestry, animal services, nursery/groundskeeping, specialty breeding	Planning, organizing, coordinating, technical applications/supervision, achievement/productivity orientation, problem-solving, decision-making, follow-up and control	Managers/administrators, professionals, services, technicians

EXHIBIT 2-1: Continued

Key Skills	Related Business Needs/Applications	Employment Areas
Leading/Influencing Educational/library services, social research, law, politics, public relations, health and safety services, finance communications	Managing information, handling authority/accountability, being responsible for results and productivity, dealing with the public/media	Managers/administrators, marketing/sales, computer-related jobs, finance/real estate/ insurance, communications
Industrial All production work, manual work, equipment operation, quality control supervision	Technical applications/ supervision, union relationships, productivity orientation	Technicians, services, computer maintenance, contract construction
Scientific/Technical Physical/life sciences, laboratory technicians, medical practitioners	Math skills, technical applications/supervision, design and use of rational procedures, problem-solving, decision-making	Managers/administrators, professionals, technicians, computer-related jobs, marketing/sales, services, mining, finance/real estate/insurance

DEVELOPING CLEARLY STATED GOALS

Now that you have dealt with potential barriers to effective goal-setting and have analyzed your unique package of skills and interests, you should be ready to move into the goal-setting process. The process of developing clearly stated goals involves understanding the difference between goals and activities, learning to state goals in specific terms, brainstorming a comprehensive set of goals, refining and ranking them, categorizing them according to career, personal development or family orientation, and recognizing the relative importance of these categories for you.

Defining a Goal

The term "goal" as used here is synonymous with "objective." Let's define it further: (1) A goal is a specific end result you want by some stated point in time. (2) Activities are things you *do* in order to achieve your goal. (3) You may *enjoy* an activity, but that doesn't make it a goal. (4) There may be a variety of feasible and acceptable activities that can help you reach your goal.

The activities are a means to an end. The end is your goal. That's why it's important to separate goals from activities—so you'll be clear about what you're really after and feel free to consider alternative activities for getting there.

It's also important to have a clear picture of your goals. Write them down. Exercise 2-4 provides space for you to list your five most important goals. You're much more likely to achieve written goals than mental ones. They're more specific, as you will see in the pages that follow. You'll also see that written goals are easier to remember, to update, to revise, and to mark off once they're achieved. And the marking-off increases

EXERCISE 2-4: INITIAL STATEMENT OF GOALS

Keeping in mind that a goal is a specific end result, try to list your five most important goals. Include goals related to family, career, and personal development.

1 _____

2 _____

3 _____

4 _____

5 _____

your sense of satisfaction and your motivation to keep achieving.

Distinguishing Between Specific and Vague Goals

Most of us tend to carry around a mixed bag of "wants." Many of them are vague; some we picture as activities instead of what we hope to gain *from* those activities. We usually wish we had these wants now, and we dreamily hope to have them some day. We must transform such dreamy wants into clear, specific goals in order to achieve them.

Most of us need to clarify what we really want to *be,* what we want to *have* in our lives, and what we can *do* in order to achieve our goals. We need to be specific about exactly what we plan to achieve. How specific? Preferably specific enough so that on the target date we've set for attainment of the goal, we *know* for sure whether we've achieved it or how close we've come to it, and anyone knowledgeable on the subject could also tell. To illustrate, let's compare the stories Carrie

recently heard from two friends, Pat and Ann.

Pat's story: Last summer my sister came to visit for a couple of weeks. We've always been able to wear the same clothes. One day I tried on one of her skirts and couldn't close the zipper. Sis teased me about "putting away a few too many groceries." After she left, I looked in the mirror and said to myself, "Pat, ole girl, you've got to do something about this flab." I'm going to join an exercise class and cut down on desserts. I'm determined to lose this excess weight. The next time Sis visits me, I want her to see that I'm my old, trim self.

Ann's story: The other day I got out my fall and winter clothes. When I tried on my after-five things, I couldn't get the zipper closed on some of them. Later, I weighed myself. That's when I realized for the first time I had gained fifteen pounds since last Christmas. I have a clear picture of how I want to be physically and that includes *being* slender. My goal is to lose fifteen pounds— about two pounds a week over the next eight weeks. By December 1, when the holiday parties begin, I will be down to my previous weight and able to look great in all those party clothes hanging in my closet. I figure that in order to achieve this, I'll have to cut my food intake to twelve hundred calories a day. I'll use the balanced diet my health club recommends. I'll also exercise an extra thirty minutes each day in order to use up a few more calories and improve my muscle tone.

Which person do you think is most likely to achieve her goal? Pat or Ann? Why? We can see several factors operating in these two cases.

1. *Ann* is clear about what she wants to *be*: slender, slender enough to fit into her party clothes. *Pat* is focusing on what she is going to *do*: get rid of the flab.

2. *Ann* is clear about the end result she wants. Her goal is specific, and she has a time target: lose fifteen pounds, about two pounds a week, by December 1. She will know for sure how well she has achieved her goal by December 1, or just how close she came to achieving it. And anyone else could tell if they watched her as she stepped on the scales on the beginning date of her project, October 1, and again on the target date, December 1.

   Pat will have no way of knowing for sure how well she has met her goal. It is too vague. She has specified neither how much weight she plans to lose nor a specific target date for losing it. Since her goal is vague in her own mind, it will be easy for her to mentally change her ideas about how much she needs to exercise, what and how much she should eat, and so forth.

3. *Ann* is separating her goal from what she will *do* to achieve it. Her activities include cutting her food intake to twelve hundred calories a day and exercising thirty minutes more each day. She could choose many alternative activities in order to achieve her goal. Notice that her activities, like her goal, include specific and measurable standards. She has also included a standard of quality for her activities—a balanced diet and exercises that are designed to improve muscle tone.

   Pat is focusing on activities and not separating them from her goals: "to do something about this flab," "to join an exercise class and cut down on desserts," "to lose this excess weight." Her activities are as vague as her goal, and she hasn't thought about what standards she wants to maintain in the course of this project.

Additional examples of vague and specific goals are listed in Exhibit 2-2.

EXHIBIT 2-2: Vague Versus Specific Goals

Vague Goals	Specific Goals
To make more money	To earn $30,000 next year
To move up in the company	To be General Manager of a regional branch by 19xx
To get ahead in life	To have a net worth of $500,000 by 19xx
To go back to school	To have an MBA degree by 19xx
To have more free time	To have at least one month of free time per year by 19xx
To travel more	To travel to the Far East in 19xx for three weeks

Distinguishing between Goals and Activities

In many cases, only you can decide whether a "want" is a goal or just an activity. Ask yourself, "*Why* do I want to do this?" If the act or process of doing something is what you desire, then it's probably a goal for you. If the activity is mainly a *means* to having something you desire, then it's not a goal for you. For example: *Why* do you want more free time? Is it to have more time to pursue a hobby, develop a skill, travel? If so, then those activities are your goals and having more free time is a *means* to that end. On the other hand, you may want freedom to do things on the spur of the moment, to pursue whatever tickles your fancy from time to time. If so, then having more free time is indeed your goal.

Here is another example: *Why* do you want to have a college degree? Is it to get a better job, make more money, or feel the personal satisfaction of having the degree, regardless of its other advantages?

Analyzing your "wants" in this way will help you to determine what you really desire. If an item is more an activity than a goal, you may be able to find an alternate activity that is much easier for you to engage in and will lead to comparable or even superior results. For example, suppose you find that the major reason you want a degree is to increase your earnings. You might find a number of alternate career paths or ways of becoming qualified for a particular career path that would take less money, time, and energy than getting a degree.

When you find it difficult to make that kind of decision, try this: Get comfortable; relax as fully as possible. Close your eyes and try to visualize yourself once you have achieved your goal. How do you feel? Are you satisfied with that particular end result? Are you satisfied with the *way* you got it? Is anything missing? What would you have done differently if you could?

Sometimes visualizing the end results and how you feel about them can help you decide what you really want. For example, if you visualize yourself holding a particularly desirable job *without* having gotten the degree, you may determine whether having a degree is your true goal. (See also Richard Bolles' paperback *What Color Is Your Parachute?* [7], or order his brochure *The Quick Job-Hunting Map* [6].)

Refining and Ranking Your Goals

Exercise 2-5, Refined List of Goals, is designed to help you state your goals specifically and reflect on their relative importance. Some of the items are probably variations of the goals you listed in Exercise 2-4. If you have trouble deciding what your goals really are, complete Exercise 2-6, Self-Starters to Help Clarify Goals.

EXERCISE 2-5: REFINED LIST OF GOALS

1. *Distinguish between goals and activities.* Look at the list of goals you made in Exercise 2-4. How many are actually activities? Eliminate them.

2. *Redefine your goals to make them more specific.* Select the following items that reflect your goals and fill in the blanks in order to make them

specific. At this point, don't rank or evaluate their practicality or relative importance.

Rank

———————   To have $———— in assets by ————
                                                 (date)

———————   To be ———————— by ————
                  (job position)   (date)

———————   To earn $———— next year

———————   To have a relationship with ———————————— in which we ————————
                                          (description of person)   (feel, believe,

            ———— by ————
             do . . .)   (date)

———————   To weigh ———— by ————
                      (pounds)   (date)

———————   To have a ———————————— by ————
                       (degree or certificate)   (date)

———————   To retire with $———— a month income (or equivalent) by ————
                                                                     (date)

———————   To have ———— days of free time per year by ————
                                                        (date)

———————   To learn ———————————— by ————
                     (specific skills or knowledge)   (date)

———————   To travel to ———————————— in ———— for ————————————
                                          (date)   (no. of days, weeks, or months)

———————   To spend ———— hours a ———————————— in mutually satisfying activities
                                  (day, week, month)

            with ————————
                  (name)

3. *Brainstorm.* List other goals that don't fit into the preceding categories. Be as outrageous as you like. Use the enthusiastic, creative-child part of your personality to brainstorm. Send that critical, practical part of you "down the hall" till later. Make your goals as fantastic or as simple as you like. Anything goes! (Remember to try Exercise 2-6 if you're blocked.)

———————   To ————————————————————————————————

———————   To ————————————————————————————————

———————   To ————————————————————————————————

———————   To ————————————————————————————————

———————   To ————————————————————————————————

4. *Evaluate and rank.* After you've freely and wildly listed any goals you can think of, start asking which one of all your goals is the most important (include all goals in items 2 and 3). Put the number "1" in the space to the left of that goal. Continue the process for the second most important goal, the third, and so forth until all are ranked. Do you want to delete any goals? Can any outlandish ones be modified or combined to make them more realistic? Are they all specific?

EXERCISE 2-6: SELF-STARTERS TO HELP CLARIFY GOALS

PROGNOSIS: SIX MONTHS: Pretend that you have been given six months to live. Close your eyes and visualize the situation in as much vivid detail as possible. Assume that you'll be in perfect health up to the day you die and that all the necessary arrangements for your death have been taken care of. List the first five things you think of that you would want to achieve in your last six months.

1 _____

2 _____

3 _____

4 _____

5 _____

SUDDEN WEALTH: Pretend someone just gave you $5 million tax-free. Close your eyes and visualize the situation in vivid detail. List the first five things you think of that you would want to achieve in the next six months—your last.

1 _____

2 _____

3 _____

4 _____

5 _____

Analysis: Which items on these lists are not connected with pressures of time or money? Which can you achieve now, even without a gift of money? Which can you have in the next six months, even without the pressure of time? Can those items be phrased as goals? How many of them can become obtainable goals with some simple modification to your current situation?

Now go back to Exercise 2-5 and continue refining your goals.

Prioritizing Three Areas of Your Life

Your goals probably include several kinds of "wants," for few people lead a one-track life where *only* their careers or *only* their personal growth or *only* their family is important. Women frequently have more difficult choices to make than men when it comes to conflicts between career and private life. In the past, highly trained women have usually given up their career aspirations when they married. Today, some women attempt to be Superwoman. They set unrealistically high goals and standards for all areas of their lives, which may lead to frustration, exhaustion, and even depression (currently referred to as "burn-out"). Other women are unaware of the implications of the choices they're making until problems begin cropping up.

To have a clear picture of your career goals, you'll need to analyze their importance in relation to the other goals in your life. Exercise 2-7, Deciding Your Most Important Life Areas, presents an opportunity to do this. It asks questions concerning the choices you will make among three areas of your life—career, private life, and personal development. Base your responses on your *current* life circumstances, not on possible later phases. In attempting to answer the first question, about private life versus career goals, picture yourself in a situation where you must make a choice. For example, you might have the opportunity to ob-tain a high-level position in a foreign country in which you've always wanted to live for a while, but your husband can't go with you. Even if you live alone, you probably have some family or private life considerations and goals. If not, you can concentrate on the other two categories.

In answering the second question, concerning conflicts between your career and personal development, you might visualize a situation in which you must regularly give up your personal reading time or your favorite sport in order to attend job-related meetings or seminars. In resolving conflicts between personal development and family goals (question 3), a sample scene might be giving up Saturdays with your family for four months to attend a creative-writing class.

Don't worry about the complexity or inter-relatedness of the questions. It's obvious that you may be a better daughter, wife, or mother when you're a better person generally. For now, just try to choose among the categories so that you can set priorities and determine the most important area of your life.

After you have analyzed your life areas in Exercise 2-7, go back to the goals you refined in Exercise 2-5 and decide whether each is a career, private life, or personal goal (or some combination of the three). Which are so important that you would like to work on them in more than one area of

EXERCISE 2-7: DECIDING YOUR MOST IMPORTANT LIFE AREAS

1. If you had to choose between career goals and private life goals during this phase of your life, what would you choose? (If you have no private life goals, skip this question.)

   _____ Private Life Goals

   _____ Career Goals

2. If you had to choose between pursuing career goals and personal development goals, which would you choose? (It may be helpful to refer to your list of goals in Exercise 2-5.)

   _____ Career Goals

   _____ Personal Development Goals

3. If you had to choose between private life goals and personal development goals, which would you choose?

   _____ Personal Development Goals

   _____ Private Life Goals

4. If you had to choose one life area to work on this month, what would it be?

   _____ Career

   _____ Private Life

   _____ Personal Development

5. List the three life areas in order of importance to you.

   Most important _____

   Less important _____

   Least important _____

your life—by taking a course with your husband, for instance? Which aren't leading to achievement or satisfaction for you in one area but might fit well in another area? For example, getting training in making presentations through company-sponsored seminars versus joining a toastmasters group on your own time.

You'll probably find that one broad goal applies more to a specific area rather than to all three areas of your life. For example, you may want increased freedom in your job but feel no need for it in the private life or personal development area.

Balancing Your Life Areas

People who make it to middle and top management almost invariably must pay their dues by putting their career first during some phase of their lives. This emphasis can have real payoffs: A 1980 study revealed that most millionaires gain their fortunes through their work or profession, not through inheritance [3]. However, if you keep putting your career first throughout your adult life, you may miss out on some of your most cherished goals. For example, most happy couples report that they both put each other first in the scheme of things. So there may be times when you'll place your career second, though let's hope not because of any Cinderella complex.

A 1978–1980 study to determine what contributes most to women's self-esteem and enjoyment of life led to the conclusion that married women with children and careers are the happiest [2]. So the good news is that many women are managing to "have it all," and they seem to be the happiest women in our society.

The bad news is that no matter how hard they work, women still remain almost entirely responsible for the child care and housework. So said the majority of 6,000 couples, mostly in their 20s and paired in various types of relationships, who responded to a survey in 1977 [4]. Despite new views about work, money, and sex—and the ease of ending relationships—this generation is pairing up and seeking long-term relationships. They are reaffirming the institution of marriage, even though they don't necessarily buy the whole package of traditions that go with it. While the couples were struggling toward equality, many of the traditions that make careers difficult for married women still prevailed.

These researchers also report that husbands with successful wives are happier in their marriages, but most of them don't want the wives to take over the provider role. And there seems to be a point at which most males feel threatened. The more successful wives had a higher breakup rate unless their husbands achieved a similar level of success.

All this is a further indication of the need for selectivity in close relationships. In addition, some frank discussions about areas of responsibility in the home may prevent later stress and undue burdens on you. Here are a few questions you might want to consider: Who should manage the money? Do the cooking? Clean the house? Take out the garbage? Mow the lawn? Be responsible for the children? Stay home when a child is sick? How are you going to handle career opportunities that require travel? Relocating? Will it depend on which career phase either of you is in, or will the decision be automatically in favor of his career? It's important to discuss priorities and joint decision-making techniques *before* becoming too committed to a relationship, rather than after.

Balancing your life areas requires skills in assertiveness, delegation, and time management, topics that are discussed in later chapters. If you are to avoid the burn-out caused by playing a wonder-woman role for too long, you must identify your rights within your close relationships, especially where children are involved. Assertiveness on your part will probably be required in order to reach constructive agreements on how everyone in the household will contribute toward its maintenance. You will need delegation skills to assign tasks to your children or paid household helpers. And you'll need time management skills to be sure you're taking care of your own top priority items rather than unwittingly spending too much of your precious time on other people's priorities.

REACHING YOUR GOALS: PLANNING ACTIVITIES AND SETTING PRIORITIES

You probably have a sense now of what goals are most important in each area of your life. The next step is to consider what activities will provide the best avenues for reaching these goals.

Exercise 2-8 lays out an activities list for all three areas of your life. (You'll probably wish to elaborate on it on your own worksheet.) To use it, you'll need to check back to Exercise 2-5; then list your three most important goals in each category in Exercise 2-8. Fill in the life area priorities you developed in Exercise 2-7, item 5. You'll then have a summary of what you want in life, right now.

Next, start writing down any and all activities you can think of that might help you achieve your goals, taking one goal at a time. At this point, do not rank the activities. Again, fantasize, brainstorm, let the creative-child part of you take over. Send your judgmental counterpart out of the room; she can come back later and help you evaluate the activities. Be daring. Be outrageous. If you're stymied in the career category, see Exhibit 2-3, Finding the Best Field,

turn to Exercise 2-9 as a self-starter, and then return to Exercise 2-8.

When you have listed activities for all life areas, summon your critical, practical, reasonable side to help you select the activity that is the most feasible and the most likely to contribute to your first goal. Rank that activity number 1 on the list in Exercise 2-8. Rank the second most likely activity number 2, and so forth down to the least likely activity. Repeat for each goal.

Does your list of activities boggle your mind? If so, start picking out the activities *you are willing to spend at least five minutes on during the next week*. Now remove from your list all activities you are *not* willing to spend five minutes on. Such activities may be important, but obviously they're not important enough to occupy your time right now. Since *now* is all any of us has, remove them from your list.

Do some of your goals now have no activities listed for them? Then go back and list other activities, ranking them and deleting them. Keep going until you have for each goal a list of activities that are important to you and are things you are willing to begin acting on right away.

If you've completed all the exercises to this point, you should be closer to knowing (1) what you want, (2) what you can do to get it, and (3) what you will do about it in the next week.

Developing Short-Term and Long-Term Action Plans

Here's the total process you'll be following to get what you want in life: (1) setting goals and priorities, (2) developing specific action plans with prioritized activities to help you reach those goals, and (3) periodically reevaluating your goals, action plans, and priorities.

Exercise 2-10 provides a format for a one-month action plan. Exercises 2-11 and 2-12 provide for a one-year plan and a five-year plan. Think broadly as you complete the longer-range plans, focusing on goals rather than on activities. Do you need to plan even further ahead? For ten years? If so, use a similar format.

To accomplish the most, make a one-month plan *every* month. Use it as the basis for your weekly and daily **"To Do" lists** (see Chapter 13). Compare months to see how you're progressing toward long-term goals. Finally, remember to reevaluate your decisions regularly to be sure that your goals reflect what you really want in life and that your activities are the best ones for getting you there.

EXERCISE 2-8: ACTIVITIES FOR ACHIEVING CAREER, PERSONAL DEVELOPMENT, AND PRIVATE LIFE GOALS

Career (Life Area Priority No. _____)

Goal 1 _____

Activities	Rank*
1 _____	_____
2 _____	_____
3 _____	_____
4 _____	_____

Goal 2 _____

Activities	Rank*
1 _____	_____
2 _____	_____
3 _____	_____
4 _____	_____

Goal 3 _____

Activities	Rank*
1 _____	_____
2 _____	_____

*Only *after* you have listed activities for *all* goals should you rank the importance of the activities listed for each goal.

3 _____ ____

4 _____ ____

Personal Development (Life Area Priority No. _____)
Goal 1 _____

Activities   Rank*

1 _____ ____

2 _____ ____

3 _____ ____

4 _____ ____

Goal 2 _____

Activities   Rank*

1 _____ ____

2 _____ ____

3 _____ ____

4 _____ ____

Goal 3 _____

Activities   Rank*

1 _____ ____

2 _____ ____

3 _____ ____

4 _____ ____

*Only *after* you have listed activities for *all* goals should you rank the importance of the activities listed for each goal.

Private Life (Life Area Priority No. _____)

Goal 1 _____

Activities   Rank*

1 _____ ____

2 _____ ____

3 _____ ____

4 _____ ____

Goal 2 _____

Activities   Rank*

1 _____ ____

2 _____ ____

3 _____ ____

4 _____ ____

Goal 3 _____

Activities   Rank*

1 _____ ____

2 _____ ____

3 _____ ____

4 _____ ____

*Only *after* you have listed activities for *all* goals should you rank the importance of the activities listed for each goal.

EXHIBIT 2-3: Finding the Best Field

	Keys to Power	Need for Mentor	Tolerance for Individuality	Style	Future
Accounting	Personal influence; building relationships with clients, partners	Great	Very low	All-American	Clients may start shopping for brilliance and originality, which will change internal power game
High technology	Original ideas in product development, marketing, productivity	The larger the org., the greater the need	Much greater than in past; innovators who can work within system in great demand	Consensus-style mgmt pushing out former autocratic styles	Risk-taker's paradise; high stakes, huge payoffs
Banking/ finance	Profitable ideas; technical analysis; building relationships	Helpful, not essential if self-motivated with money-making ideas	Growing	Low-key; facts/ numbers focus; serious, fairly trendy, not overly ambitious	Much change, rethinking about mission, services, methods
Health care	Influence with M.D.'s, adminis-trators	Not great if skilled politician; hard to find	Medium to high	Analytical; firm, sticking to point; respectful attitude toward doctors	Booming, but government and insurance companies are setting limits
Nonprofit	Often on edge of org., managing special projects; fund-raising skills, consensus mgmt skills, public relations skills	May be only way to learn ropes	Fairly high	Project image of idealism; practice rules of political survival	Change; erratic spurts of growth and decline
Glamour/ media	Ideas supreme; profitability all; risk-taking essential; boldness a must	Self-promotion more important in many cases; access to powerful people important	Highest	Outgoing; negotiating skills, political savvy	Always important; perhaps some altered forms

Adapted from "The Keys to the Kingdom" by Marilyn Moats Kennedy, *Savvy* (February 1984), pp. 48–55.

EXERCISE 2-9: SELF-STARTER TO HELP IDENTIFY THE MOST PRODUCTIVE CAREER ACTIVITIES

By now you should have a specific type of job in mind as your key career goal. You should also be able to describe your ultimate career goal—the top position you're aiming for. To help you identify the activities most likely to help you reach that goal, look at these questions:

1. What type of company do you have in mind? Can you pinpoint a specific company?

2. What type of degree, courses, or other training will you need?

3. What specific skills and knowledge will be required? At what level of ability?

4. What kinds of people could tell you more about the job, help teach you what you need to know, help you get your foot in the door, help you gain favorable visibility within the company, introduce you to people who can help?

5. What jobs will you need to hold in order to prepare yourself for your *ultimate* career goal? What functions do you need to have experience with? How do these functions link up with each other? (For example, what are the links between production and sales, sales and marketing?) Can you get some actual job descriptions your target company has prepared for these jobs? Which staff positions would give you the best chance of moving into a line job? Which line jobs provide the basic experience you'll need? (See also *The American Almanac of Jobs and Salaries* [25].)

6. Once you have a career plan, who can give you the most helpful evaluation of its effectiveness? Is the plan workable in view of the other top priorities in your life?

Use your answers to help complete Exercise 2-7.

EXERCISE 2-10: ONE-MONTH ACTION PLAN FOR _____ 19__
(MONTH)

Career

Goal 1 _____

Activities   Target Date

*1 _____   _____

2 _____   _____

3 _____   _____

Goal 2 _____

Activities   Target Date

*1 _____   _____

2 _____   _____

3 _____   _____

Goal 3 _____

Activities   Target Date

*1 _____   _____

2 _____   _____

3 _____   _____

Personal Development

Goal 1 _____

Activities   Target Date

*1 _____   _____

2 _____   _____

3 _____   _____

*Put this activity on your "To Do" list for *today* and keep it on the list until you have accomplished it. If you haven't acted on the starred activities within seven days, go back and reevaluate your goals and activities.

Goal 2 _____

Activities   Target Date

*1 _____   _____

 2 _____   _____

 3 _____   _____

Goal 3 _____

Activities   Target Date

*1 _____   _____

 2 _____   _____

 3 _____   _____

Private Life

Goal 1 _____

Activities   Target Date

*1 _____   _____

 2 _____   _____

 3 _____   _____

Goal 2 _____

Activities   Target Date

*1 _____   _____

 2 _____   _____

 3 _____   _____

*Put this activity on your "To Do" list for *today* and keep it on the list until you have accomplished it. If you haven't acted on the starred activities within seven days, go back and reevaluate your goals and activities.

Goal 3 _____

Activities   Target Date

*1 _____   _____

2 _____   _____

3 _____   _____

*Put this activity on your "To Do" list for *today* and keep it on the list until you have accomplished it. If you haven't acted on the starred activities within seven days, go back and reevaluate your goals and activities.

EXERCISE 2-11: ONE-YEAR ACTION PLAN FOR 19__

Last updated _____

	Career Goals	Target Date
1	_____	_____
2	_____	_____
3	_____	_____
	Personal Development Goals	Target Date
1	_____	_____
2	_____	_____
3	_____	_____
	Private Life Goals	Target Date
1	_____	_____

2 _____   _____

3 _____   _____

EXERCISE 2-12: FIVE-YEAR ACTION PLAN FOR 19__ TO 19__

Last updated _____

	Career Goals	Target Date
1	_____	_____
2	_____	_____
3	_____	_____

	Personal Development Goals	Target Date
1	_____	_____
2	_____	_____
3	_____	_____

	Private Life Goals	Target Date
1	_____	_____
2	_____	_____
3	_____	_____

Tips for Implementing Your Plan

Here are some general suggestions for using your plan:

1. *Visualize.* Use relaxed concentration and visualization as a technique to command your inner resources so that all your actions tend to move you toward your goals. (See Exercise 4-7, Self-Mastery Visualization.)

2. *Act.* Begin this week, even if you undertake only a five-minute activity for each goal.

3. *Communicate.* Let the important people in your life *know* about the goals they may be able to help you with. For example, let your boss or mentor know about appropriate career goals.

4. *Get support.* Make a list of the people who can help you and give you support as you work toward your goals. Decide the best way to enlist their aid. Include support systems in your plan.

5. *Enjoy.* Make the *process* of achieving your goal as enjoyable as possible. It's important to keep your eye on the end result you want, but it's also important to relax and enjoy yourself along the way. In fact, your enjoyment of an activity should be one of the criteria for selecting it.

6. *Negotiate.* Use your goals to help you achieve specific results on the job that will serve as the basis for negotiating promotions and raises later.

7. *Stay focused on your goals.* Don't get so carried away with the *activities* that you lose sight of the *goal.* Use your action plan to chart activities; mark them off as they are completed and as the goal is achieved. It helps if you keep a list of your top three or four goals handy and refer to it regularly. Some successful women keep their list (or symbolic pictures of their goals) posted where they'll see it daily in their home or office.

8. *Overcome barriers to achieving goals.* Don't let procrastination, interruptions, and distractions keep you from achieving your goals. See the discussion of time management in Chapter 12 for suggestions on overcoming these barriers.

9. *Reevaluate.* If you are having unusual difficulty in achieving a goal, ask yourself whether the goal is right for you. If it is, then reevaluate the activities you have selected and look for new ones. If it's not, spend some time formulating another goal that's more appropriate and focus on it.

10. *Keep goals flexible.* Your goals are not set in concrete. They're just part of a plan that can be changed as *situations* change.

11. *Congratulate yourself.* When you achieve a goal, remember to give yourself credit and lots of positive reinforcement for your achievement.

12. *Keep setting goals.* Once you have achieved a major goal, set another one to take its place. You say you've earned a rest? You don't want another major project for a while? Then your new goal might be to have a specific number of additional unstructured hours each week, month, or year to do as you please. The object is to be clear about what you want and what you are doing with your time and your life—so that you are making clear choices rather than drifting and dreaming.

USING YOUR PLAN TO GET THE JOB YOU WANT

Once you have a clear picture of your interests, likes, dislikes, skills, abilities, and resulting career goals, you're in a better position to develop an effective action plan for getting the specific job you want next. In this section we'll discuss the other steps to landing that position, as illustrated in Figure 2-1.

If you are a college student, you'll need a job-getting action plan before you graduate. If you're in a secretarial, clerical, or staff position, you may have to wage a job campaign and change companies in order to have the best chance of moving into management.

Even if you plan to move up within your present company, many of the suggestions that follow can be helpful to you. If you're not sure exactly what you want to do next, you're not alone. That's why the "reevaluate" step is shown in Figure 2-1. Once you've done your best to analyze your situation, make a wholehearted commitment to the resulting action plan and give it your best shot. At least you'll be gaining valuable experience and learning more about yourself.

Designing a Winning Résumé

The right kind of résumé can open doors for you. Even if you already have the job you want, it's a good idea to periodically update

FIGURE 2-1: The Job-Getting Process

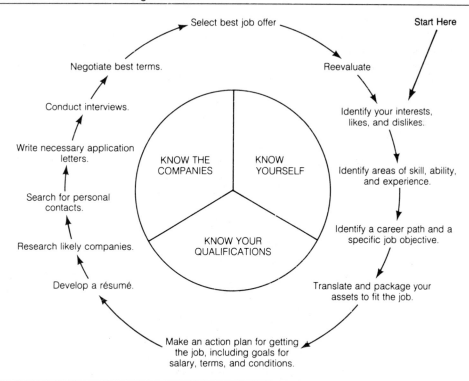

your résumé. The process can sharpen your awareness of your strengths and achievements.

Keep your résumé in a file folder. From time to time add to the file any letters, reports, memos, honors, or awards that reflect your achievements, career growth, and personal development. At least once a year pull the file and update your résumé. Review it before you ask for a promotion or raise. If someone asks you for your biography or for background information for a news release or a group introduction, use your résumé as a basis for preparing it quickly. Your résumé is a handy reference document, and you will probably find other uses for it.

The most important use of résumés is in applying for a job. Interviewers review them to determine which applicants probably have the right "product" to sell.

Selling Yourself Your résumé is a selling document. Its major purpose is to persuade the reader to grant you an interview. To do that, it must hook your reader's attention immediately. Interviewers frequently screen large numbers of résumés in order to select three or four candidates to interview. Therefore your résumé may have only about thirty seconds to make an impression, good or bad, on the reader.

Put only your name and phone number at the top of the page. Don't clutter it with personal data because this is the place to state your job objective and a summary of your most attractive qualifications. Should you include a picture at the top? Normally, no. If you use a high-quality reproduction process in which the picture becomes an integral part of the résumé, interviewers might back away from the slickness of the presentation. On the other hand, if you merely glue a small photograph to your résumé, the effect tends to be a little corny and unprofessional. A major exception is when you're applying for a job in a distant city and you feel your appearance is a definite asset for the job. The

interviewer naturally prefers maximum input before incurring the expenses involved in a personal interview in such cases.

You'll have a better chance of selling yourself to the right company if you aim for a specific type of position. It's standard practice to reproduce the résumé and send it to several companies. However, the most successful applicants avoid the "shotgun approach"—that is, hoping to get interviews for a wide range of jobs by stating a general job objective, such as the one shown in Exhibit 2-6, and mailing the résumé to numerous companies. Remember, résumés that get results usually include (1) a specific job objective and usually a clue to the type of career path desired, (2) a "bait" paragraph showing major qualifications for the job, and (3) a detailed but concise description of experience and education, all tailored to fit the job objective. (See the example in Exhibit 2-7.) If you wage a job campaign that zeroes in on your first-choice job objective, you're likely to get that type of job. At the same time, you avoid giving the impression you'll take almost anything or that you don't know your own mind.

Your résumé must answer some basic questions, such as what sort of position you want and perhaps your ultimate target position or career path. At the beginning, therefore, state clearly your own specialty and the area you're aiming for—for example, a systems analyst with a large bank, a management position in the production department of a textile manufacturing firm, a financial manager for an investment counseling firm.

Follow the statement of job objective with a brief summary of your *major* qualifications for the position. This is your selling pitch, your bait to hook the reader into reading further. The way you phrase your job objective and your summary of qualifications can mean the difference between success and failure in getting a chance to in-

EXHIBIT 2-4: Action Verbs That Describe Management Functions

Administered	Developed	Managed
Advised	Directed	Negotiated
Analyzed	Edited	Organized
Applied	Evaluated	Participated in
Approved	Executed	Performed
Arranged	Expedited	Planned
Clarified	Facilitated	Prepared
Communicated	Forecast	Promoted
Compared	Generated	Recommended
Compiled	Handled	Recruited
Computed	Have knowledge of	Reduced
Controlled	Implemented	Reported to
Cooperated with	Initiated	Researched
Coordinated	Improved	Reviewed
Counseled	Integrated	Solved
Created	Interviewed	Supervised
Decided	Investigated	Surveyed
Delegated	Made decisions	Trained
Demonstrated	Maintained contact	

terview, so spend time perfecting this section of your résumé. See the bait lines following the statement of job objectives in Exhibit 2-7; see also the Summary of Qualifications section in Exhibit 2-8. Put yourself in the interviewer's place and ask which of your qualifications he or she will view as most important for success in the position you're seeking. Then select those items from the experience and education sections of your draft résumé and rephrase them concisely into three or four bait lines. Use the kinds of management terms we'll discuss next.

Describing Past Experience in Management Terms In the experience section of your résumé, back up what you claimed in your bait. Stress experience that relates to the job you want (no matter how insignificant or limited it was, if you're relatively inexperienced). List it first. You must learn to view these past experiences in terms of the management functions you performed. Think back over the functions you have fulfilled in previous jobs, at home, and in social, chari-

table, religious, or professional organizations. Then picture yourself doing something similar in a management position. Did you plan and organize a rummage sale? Then you can plan and organize business projects. Did you call club members and persuade them to take on responsibilities and work toward club goals? You can do the same with employees in meeting company goals.

Exhibit 2-4 lists some verbs that might be appropriate for describing what you actually did in the jobs you held. Choose the ones that express the highest level at which you performed ("implemented" instead of "assisted," "supervised" instead of "performed").

Even if the highest-level position you've held is sales clerk, secretary, or office clerk, you have performed many of the functions listed in Exhibit 2-4. For example, if you've been responsible for showing a new worker how to handle certain jobs, you've been involved in training and perhaps in delegating and supervising. If you've ever been responsible for even a part of a major project, you no doubt organized, handled, decided, and executed items in completing your assignment,

EXHIBIT 2-5: Functional Areas of Business

Accounting	Merchandising
Administration	Operations Research
Administrative Services	Personnel/Human Resources
Advertising	Production
Budget and Control	Purchasing
Communications	Real Estate
Data Processing	Research and Development
Finance	Retailing
Industrial Relations	Systems
International Trade	Traffic
Inventory Control	Training
Legal	Transportation
Marketing	Wage and Salary Administration

and you were probably involved in other functions as well. Even if none of the action verbs apply to your involvement in a task, you can always use "was responsible for," "was accountable for," "am familiar with," or "reported to." By expressing your experience in this manner instead of merely listing job titles and duties, you show an executive orientation. Your résumé becomes more businesslike and impressive in tone.

If you have participated in charitable, academic, religious, or other nonprofit organizations, analyze your activities and responsibilities for their administrative or managerial components. If such experience helps fill in gaps in your qualifications for your target position, by all means include it in the experience section of your résumé. (Exercise 2-13 can help you translate your experiences into management terms. If you will first read the discussion and examples that follow, however, the whole process will make more sense to you.)

Look over all your activities and recall specific achievements related to each. Were there instances in which you produced more than was expected? By how much? Estimate, if necessary. Use percentages, where appropriate. "I exceeded the target number of claims

to be processed by 10 percent." Did you accomplish something with less money, time, or supplies than expected? Again, be as specific as possible and use numbers, dollars, or percentages. "I figured out a way to save $1,500 a year on office supplies." Are you in the habit of meeting deadlines and target dates, even when the going gets tough? Say so. "My reports were regularly submitted on or before the deadline dates."

Now describe specific activities and achievements for each job you held. If one job is obviously more relevant to the position you're seeking than the others, consider listing it before other more recent jobs so it will attract more attention. Otherwise, list your most recent job first. While you're at it, relate each accomplishment to a given job unless you performed virtually the same functions in more than one job. Many résumés are so full of accomplishments—whole pages of them—that they neglect to tell what actual jobs the person has held and at what companies. In order to get an accurate picture of you, the interviewer needs a framework to hang your accomplishments on.

Once you have completed the experience section, analyze it to identify the broad functional business areas you've been involved in. Exhibit 2-5 lists a few of the functional areas of business to give you some ideas for categorizing your experience. Use these as headings in the left margin of your résumé to emphasize general areas of valuable experience.

Highlighting Appropriate Aspects of Your Education If you have any work experience that can possibly relate to the job you want, present the experience section before the education section. This approach may set you apart from the numerous graduates who will probably be applying for similar positions. If not, then highlight your academic achievements. Mention your grade point average only if it's good (3.0 or better). Call attention to any academic honors and special achievements. If you have a college degree, don't bother to list community college or high school information unless you received special honors or your training there is more relevant to the job requirements than your university courses. Mention only those courses that are beyond the required courses in your field and that apply to your job objective. If your education was completed years ago, merely list the degrees or diploma and schools. If you've done any significant postgraduate work, including professional seminars, that fill in gaps in your qualifications, list it.

Selecting the Right Personal Data and Interests Normally the interviewer will be calling you for an interview, so your address is not important and can go near the end of the résumé under personal data. In the past many applicants also listed here such items as sex, marital status, number of children, height, weight, and health condition. With the advent of Equal Employment Opportunity laws, this practice is changing. The pur-

pose of these laws is to help you have a fair chance to be considered for jobs you want. Therefore, you need only include such information if you think it will favorably impress the interviewer. If you believe the interviewer is looking for women to fill an Affirmative Action quota, by all means mention that you're female. (It's perfectly legitimate to put only your initials and last name at the top of the page if you don't want your sex revealed.) If you think the interviewer might prefer a single woman with no children, and you're married with two children, don't mention marital status or children. (Various aspects of EEO laws are discussed in the interview sections of this chapter and Chapter 12.)

The personal data section is the place to put *brief* relevant information about yourself that doesn't fit in any of the other categories. For example, you can mention your willingness or unwillingness to move to another locale, to travel, or to use your own car for company business. A graduate might mention that she worked to provide partial or full self-support while in college. Information given here should overcome possible obstacles or further enhance your chances of getting an interview.

In the interests section mention any activities, skills, or special interests that might enhance your success on the job or give you something in common with the interviewer or your future coworkers. If you have been recognized for special achievement in these areas, refer to it but keep this section very brief. Avoid a childlike show-and-tell tone. Analyze this information to see whether any of it can be moved into your experience section to round out your qualifications for the job.

Using Personal References Discreetly Interviewers do not normally check out references until after they have selected, interviewed, and screened the applicants for a particular job. Only when they are seriously considering the top two or three candidates do they bother with this step, which is somewhat of an imposition on the people listed as references. If you include their names, addresses, and telephone numbers on your résumé, which everyone knows you had reproduced and probably sent to a number of companies, you are in effect "advertising" your connections. You certainly want to avoid the possibility that inexperienced or thoughtless interviewers may contact your references unnecessarily. Protect their privacy and exhibit your savvy and thoughtfulness by merely mentioning that references are available upon request.

Do spend some time deciding whom you should give as references when the time comes. The interviewer may want the names of the people you reported to in your former jobs as well as other people who can give a fairly objective evaluation of your personal habits and characteristics.

If you didn't get along with a former boss and were fired or quit in a huff, are you going to list him or her? If those job experiences are an important part of your qualifications, see whether you can get another of your bosses there to give you a good recommendation. List him or her instead; you may even want to go ahead and put that name in the experience section in case the interviewer checks job references before calling you. If you think you won't get a good recommendation, be vague on your résumé about the exact department or unit you worked in and handle the reference problem at the interview. (More about that in the interview section.)

If you have little or no work experience, you can ask teachers and others familiar with your academic performance to serve as references. In addition you may want to ask a business or professional person—one who is respected in the community and who has known you for several years—to vouch for your personal integrity and dependability.

Regardless of the types of references you give, be sure they will be fully supportive of you. Always contact them first and ask whether you may give their names. Let them know the type of job you're seeking and remind them of your qualifications. You may want to send them a copy of your résumé. After you get a job, acknowledge their help by writing them a note of thanks and telling them about your new position.

Learning from Sample Résumés Although you may benefit from the advice of a professional résumé-writer, you should write your own résumé. The process of writing it is as important as the finished product in helping you get your job. The process of translating past experiences into management terms and organizing your qualifications into a selling package is invaluable to you in preparing for the interview. Since the résumé is totally and uniquely yours when you write it yourself, you'll be able to back it up and expand on it with confidence. This approach also implies that copying a sample résumé almost verbatim, merely plugging in your data, is self-defeating. On the other hand, you can learn something about applying the suggestions given here to your situation if you analyze how they're carried out in sample situations.

Suppose, for example, your job-to-be called for selling fashion merchandise, and helping retail clients with sales promotion, merchandising, and sales forecasting. The career path might include advancement into higher-level management positions. This was the case with Joan Kerr, a senior at State University. She had been a part-time sales clerk, an officer of the honorary marketing fraternity, and a Girl Scout leader. How could that qualify her for this top-level sales job? Joan's first-draft résumé, the draft shown in Exhibit 2-6, doesn't make the most of her experience.

Joan discussed her first draft with her communications instructor. They agreed it needed revising. Working together, they first broke down Joan's job and organizational responsibilities into separate activities or functions. They found that she had valuable experience in sales promotion, merchandising, planning, and forecasting. After all, Joan had been selling women's clothing for years, arranging and displaying some of the merchandise. She had talked with her supervisor about sales expectations for upcoming seasons (part of sales forecasting). She looked at these ordinary duties to see which parts of them were transferable to a manager's duties; then she rephrased the description of her experience to reflect those skills. It's important for managers to produce measurable results, so Joan did some figuring and noted that she had regularly exceeded her sales quotas by an average of 15 percent.

Joan's teacher pointed out to her that she has performed a number of administrative functions as an officer of a school organization. As a professional fraternity officer, she has also gained marketing experience and understanding, which could be used as part of her bait. In the final version of Joan's résumé, shown in Exhibit 2-7, the words "part-time sales clerk," "student-organization officer," and "Girl Scout leader" are buried or omitted. However, her transferable skills *do* relate to the seemingly different job she's aiming for now.

How about the woman who has been out of school for several years and has a great deal of valuable experience, but not in the area of business management? This was the case with Helen Jay, who taught high school math for ten years. Helen wanted to move into a career path leading to top management, but she realized she knew very little

about profit-making organizations. She does know about helping people gain new skills. She decided the best way to get her foot in the door was through personnel training. She figured she would learn about all aspects of a personnel department while in a training position and eventually move into a head slot. As head of personnel she planned to learn about the functions and interactions of other departments and move into a line-manager slot. Helen is willing to change companies each time she makes a major job move, if necessary, and she will tailor her experience to fit her new job objective at each step. The résumé Helen sent to the Personnel Director at Lighthouse Designs, Inc., is shown in Exhibit 2-8.

Pulling It All Together Before you write the final draft of your résumé, be sure you're making the most of what you have. Exaggerating your accomplishments is expected and tolerated by most experienced interviewers. In fact, most instinctively discount claims by a certain percentage; therefore, you're at a disadvantage if you *don't* embellish your record. Take full credit for every project you've shared in and every management function you've performed. You can explain your claims when you come in for an interview. What you clearly should *not* do is take credit for projects or functions you were scarcely involved in at all. If you're still unsure about how to apply all this to your situation, complete Exercise 2-13.

Edit your final draft for conciseness. Most recent graduates should be able to include their essential information on one page. The absolute maximum for older, more experienced applicants is two pages. Never crowd the information on the page.

Be sure your finished résumé is neat and simple. A sloppy, smudged document that's hard to read won't impress anyone

EXHIBIT 2-6: Joan's Résumé: First Draft

Joan Kerr
831 Foothill Drive
Colma, California 94015
(415) 555-3809

JOB OBJECTIVE:	A management position with a clothing manufacturer

EDUCATION:

B.A. in Marketing
State University
January 19xx

G.P.A. State University 3.67
G.P.A. Marketing. 3.77

Marketing Courses:	Units
Intro to Marketing	3
Intermediate Marketing	3
Advanced Marketing	3
Sales Techniques	3
Advertising	3
Merchandising	3

A.A. in Retailing
West Community College
January 19xx

Salutatorian, Westmoor High School, 19xx

SCHOOL ACTIVITIES: President of student organization, Beta Gamma Psi. Arranged luncheons, dinners, and banquets with guests from business firms, the AMA, and government agencies.

WORK EXPERIENCE: Part-time salesclerk for Gemex Department Stores for seven years.

PERSONAL DATA:
Date of Birth: January 27, 19xx
Marital Status: Single
Height: 5'7"
Weight: 135 lbs.

INTERESTS: Helping girls in the Girl Scouts. Physical Fitness. Sports (tennis, swimming, surfing, etc.). Sewing.

REFERENCES:

Mr. Bill Jensen, Vice-President
Acme Company
4509 Green Road
San Francisco, CA 92703
(415) 289-3605

Ms. Violet James
Violet's Boutique
98 Beach Road
San Francisco, CA 93251
(415) 382-4621

EXHIBIT 2-7: Joan's Résumé: Final Version

Joan Kerr
(415) 555-3809

JOB OBJECTIVE: Marketing graduate with top grades seeking position as sales representative with women's ready-to-wear manufacturer.

Seven years' experience in sales and merchandising.

Knowledge of and experience with activities of marketing department; clothing manufacturers, wholesalers, and retailers; and American Marketing Association.

EXPERIENCE: Gemex Dept. Store—19xx to present

Sales and Merchandising Promoted sales of women's ready-to-wear. Participated in planning of merchandising strategies. Was responsible for implementing merchandising plans. Regularly exceeded sales quotas by an average of 15 percent. Exposure to sales forecasting.

Training Trained new workers in the department.

Administration President, Beta Gamma Psi, 19xx. Planned and supervised correspondence with members, national offices, firms, and agencies. Planned and directed meetings and banquets with guests from the marketing division of business firms and the AMA. Organized and administered a tutorial program for marketing students.

EDUCATION: B.A. in Business Administration, State University
Degree to be granted in 19xx
Overall G.P.A. 3.67, Marketing G.P.A. 3.77
Concentration in Marketing, including advanced elective courses in Sales Techniques, Advertising, Merchandising.

A.A. in Retailing, West Community College, January, 19xx
Westmoor High School, 19xx, Salutatorian

PERSONAL DATA: Address: 831 Foothill Drive, Colma, California, 94015
Willing to travel and to transfer, although prefer Bay Area.

INTERESTS: Civic activities, sports (tennis, swimming)

REFERENCES: Available upon request.

EXHIBIT 2-8: Helen's Résumé: Career Change

Helen Jay
(415) 362-8519

JOB OBJECTIVE: Assistant Director/Manager, Personnel—Training

SUMMARY OF   A results-oriented organizer, able to establish and lead pro-
QUALIFICATIONS: ductive, creative group-learning processes. A background in
education and administration that illustrates competency in
managing, training, evaluating, coordinating, communicating,
researching, and reporting complex situations.

PROFESSIONAL   Planned, organized, and administered the High Intensity Learn-
EXPERIENCE: ing Center for basic math skills, which provided an innovative
tool for creative teacher-student interaction.
Bennington High School, 19xx-19xx.

Management   Responsible for the planning and organizing of the Demonstration
Summer School. University of California, Bennington.
Supervised the summer school office staff. Publicized the
summer school by editing and distributing brochures. Completed
summer school annual report.

Responsible for adding new equipment in the Science-Math Lab
due to the funding of a proposal I prepared.

Training   Conducted workshops to train teachers to use the High Intensity
Learning Center at Bennington High School.

Managed a full-time teaching load while involved in numerous
professional activities, 19xx-19xx.

Responsible for the Teaching Assistant Program.

Coordination   Coordinated new curriculum for a Biology-Math course and a
Consumer Math course.

EDUCATION: B.A. Mathematics, University of California, Bennington

PERSONAL DATA: Address—4021 Maple Avenue, Bennington, CA 94705
Willing to travel and to relocate.

INTERESTS: Toastmasters Club, honored as Outstanding Speaker in Region V.
Skiing, tennis.

REFERENCES: Available upon request.

EXERCISE 2-13: SELF-STARTER TO TRANSLATE EXPERIENCE INTO MANAGERIAL LANGUAGE

Objective: To help you identify and organize your past experience in ways that focus on your managerial skills, even if you've never held any sort of "management position."

1. List every job you've ever held, including officer and committee positions in any type of organization and any volunteer work.

2. Break down each job in terms of what you learned—new skills, upgraded skills, new knowledge. Include the level of ability you achieved.

3. List specific projects, achievements, deadlines met, as well as any incidents, crises, or tests you handled successfully.

4. How did you do it? What technical and behavioral skills were necessary?

5. Now describe in managerial terms the skills, knowledge, and achievements mentioned in items 2, 3, and 4 (see the list in Exhibit 2-4).

6. Now regroup. What broad functional areas have you had experience with (see the list in Exhibit 2-5). Which jobs, along with your skills and achievements in each, fall under this function? These functional areas become your marginal headings under "experience" in your résumé.

7. Keep rewriting and editing until you've refined your experiences into those that best represent your ability to succeed in the job you're seeking.

favorably. To be effective at all, the résumé has to look good. At the other extreme, one that's too glossy or professional worries experienced interviewers. They wonder if the applicant is all glitter and razzle-dazzle. They much prefer a résumé that is neatly typed (rather than printed) on high-quality paper and then duplicated on a good copier. Your next step is to decide who gets copies.

Finding the Right Organizations

You need as much information as possible about the types of companies that might use your services. You're looking for the best fit between your package and the company's needs and objectives. What are the advantages and disadvantages of large, medium, and small organizations, for example? In a large firm you might have the most opportunities for advancement and access to the most sophisticated operations, but you might also find yourself stuck in a highly specialized job. Talk to anyone and everyone who has knowledge or experience with the types of organizations you're considering. Ask your librarian for reading sources. Narrow the field to your first-choice geographical area and company size.

Geography and Opportunity In selecting a geographic area, it's wise to investigate prevailing attitudes toward new roles for women. When attitudes are generally supportive of career women, doors tend to open more readily, and support is more abundant and easier to find. According to Dun's Marketing Services, the best regional area is the West, based on percentage of women who are managers. By state, California has the most women executives, followed by New York, Texas, Florida, Illinois, and Pennsylvania.

But opportunities can vary greatly by city within a state. Furthermore, in any large city, you're likely to find some companies that open doors for women managers and others that resist such new trends. However, some cities do have more of one type of company than the other, according to a 1983 survey reported by *Savvy* [20]. Based on percentages of women who are managers and are active in management and professional clubs, local chambers of commerce, city government, and women's support groups, *Savvy* designated the following cities the best: New York, Chicago, San Jose, Minneapolis-St. Paul, San Diego, and Atlanta. Cities judged too small or undiversified to qualify for the best category but tempting enough to rate honorable mention are Miami, Hartford, San Antonio, and Wilmington. Sleepers that should come alive for women in the near future are Austin, Santa Rosa, Portland (Maine and Oregon), and Salt Lake City.

The worst, those steeped in tradition, male oriented, and full of stereotypes, are Tulsa, Cleveland, Baltimore, Birmingham, Detroit, Pittsburgh, and Boston.

Clues to an Organization's Openness Even though it's a real asset to live in a city where women tend to be welcome in management circles, it's even more important to find or-

ganizations with good track records in supporting women. Listed below are some policies, programs, and structures to look for in organizations you're investigating. When you're preparing for your job interviews, use this list to help you formulate questions you'll want to ask. Add them to your total list of questions. (See section on preparing your questions, later in this chapter.)

1. *Antidiscrimination guidelines.* Progressive organizations publish a statement of organizational policy regarding equal opportunity and sexual harrassment. They provide specific guidelines for behavior in situations involving women so that discrimination and harrassment can be avoided.

2. *Decentralization.* More and smaller units are created within the organizational structure to increase the number of managerial positions available. Increased autonomy in work units gives supervisors and managers more opportunity for making decisions and taking risks. "Flattened" managerial hierarchies with short chains of command bring workers in closer contact with top management, increasing the influence of leaders and building worker morale.

3. *Project management.* Temporary teams are created to carry out particular tasks. Workers from different departments and hierarchical levels work on new tasks and share learning experiences, even though their routine jobs remain the same.

4. *Open communication channels.* System knowledge (information about budgets, salaries, minutes of some meetings, and so forth) is routinely available to all employees, eliminating a "closed club" effect.

5. *Management by objectives.* This formal system of objective-setting, problem-solving, positive reinforcement, and upward mobility can pinpoint performance requirements for promotions.

6. *Job opportunities within the organization.* Openings are posted and employees are free to apply for any job. Position descriptions list actual tasks to be performed, identify abilities needed, and identify special opportunities to move beyond the limits of the formal job title.

7. *Personnel assessment centers.* Such centers provide objective evaluative data about employees' performance. A male executive takes less risk in promoting a woman if he can back up his decision with impartial data from the center. (More information about assessment centers can be found by looking in the classified telephone directory under "Career Services" or "Vocational Consultants.")

8. *Opening up dead-end jobs.* Achievement at all levels—including secretarial and clerical—is rewarded by promotion. Job enrichment rewards skill development with new challenges and increased pay. Apprenticeship systems are developed. Managers are rewarded for helping low-mobility employees, like secretaries, develop skills, further their education, and move up the career ladder. New jobs are developed in a sequence of skill levels to bridge the gap between high- and low-status work. Project teams and committees include secretaries and clerical workers.

9. *Formal mentor-type programs.* A formalized mentor/protégé system can reward mentors for producing successful protégés, especially women. Similar pro-grams can help ensure that someone will help women manage their career paths, including access to a progression of sympathetic and supportive superiors. (See discussion in Chapter 3.)

10. *Formal career review procedures.* Workers discuss their career goals and the means of achieving them with the appropriate person in the company on a regular basis. Workers receive both positive and negative feedback about their performance.

11. *Management development programs.* Formal management training helps new managers to eliminate inappropriate behaviors and develop skills and understanding necessary for working with groups. Formal training programs for new managers have an added bonus of bringing people together within the organization. They help lay the groundwork for powerful peer alliances.

12. *Aids for dual-career women/families.* Some company practices that may be especially helpful for career women with families are provision of maternity/paternity leaves, on-site day-care centers, **job sharing, flexitime,** and flexible job transfer and travel policies. For example, a few organizations provide for a choice or combination of paternity and maternity leaves, which signals that management considers child care a family issue, not a woman's issue. Job-sharing (two professionals or managers each working half-time to cover one job position) and flexitime (choice of beginning and ending work hours) are company practices that help career women through the child-raising years.

After you collect information about specific companies that might fit with your package, select a few to focus on and learn all you can about them. Many reference sources at university and public libraries contain such information. Such directories as Moody's and Standard & Poor's can help you learn about company operations, financial performance, and key personnel.

Each June *Savvy* publishes a report on the sixteen large corporations they believe offer the best opportunities for women. They report that all have a rich tradition of change, aggressive recruitment, objective systems of promotion, management training programs, companywide job postings, Affirmative Action programs, and an open management style. All show good prospects for growth and have a growing percentage of women in management [20]. See also *The 100 Best Companies to Work for in America* [15].

Try to determine the salary range for the type of job you want. Also, find out about usual benefits and perquisites (these "perks" include such things as a company car, an expense account, and so on). The *American Almanac of Jobs and Salaries* [25] is a good place to start. Once you have some general salary information, see if you can identify what your target companies offer. This may be hard to come by; personal contacts can be invaluable sources of such information.

Once you have a few likely companies firmly in mind, begin an all-out campaign to find personal contacts within them. Find out whether any of your friends, relatives, or acquaintances knows anyone connected with the companies. Don't forget people from your past: teachers, fellow students, business acquaintances. Personal contacts can not only provide valuable information, they can do wonders in helping you get your foot in the door, so effort spent developing them can really pay off. If you're a student, doing a research project that requires interviewing someone in a business organization can help you get your foot in

the door. Of course you won't mention at this point that you're interested in a job. Simply establish one or more contacts in the company and get as much information as you can about company operations. If you simply can't establish any kind of personal contact, you may have to send your résumé in "cold" and depend on an attention-getting, persuasive cover letter as the contact point.

Writing an Application Letter That Gets Attention

Each résumé that you send out should be accompanied by an original covering letter or application letter. *Never* send a photocopy of your covering letter. Even the best résumés tend to have a mass-produced look. You can make your own individual mark most effectively in your covering letter.

Get the name and title of the particular person within each company who is most concerned with the skills and services you have to offer and address your letter to that person. Show how your particular experience, skills, interests, and traits fit the specific job you want in this particular company. Refer only to the high points of your résumé. Don't repeat large segments of it in your letter. Stress what you can contribute to the operations and goals of the company. Where appropriate, show that you know something about what's going on in the field that affects this company as well as company achievements, objectives, and problems. The person who receives your letter should always feel that your pitch is directed solely to this one company.

Start off with a statement that's likely to grab the reader's attention; include your bait early. Remember, the recipient of the letter is mainly interested in the needs and problems of the company. She or he is interested in you only to the extent that you can help solve a problem or meet a need. So state briefly how you can do that.

You might need another paragraph or two to describe how your knowledge, skills, interests, and personal traits fit the needs of the company. Try to show how and why you are just the person the company is looking for. Remember to keep your letter brief, however; from three to five short paragraphs are plenty.

In the last paragraph ask for an interview. Make it as easy as possible for the reader to set up an interview with you. Give some specific dates for follow-up purposes so you'll have a good reason to call later and won't be left wondering and waiting. Before you sign the letter, proofread it carefully. Make it as letter-perfect as your résumé. Be sure to keep a copy so you'll know exactly what you said.

Exhibit 2-9 shows the letter Joan Kerr wrote to Jan Arguello to apply for a job on the sales staff. See how it illustrates the points we've just covered. Such a letter is very likely to land you an interview. But how should you handle this important meeting?

Handling the Job Interview

The purpose of the interview is to give the company an opportunity to see whether you have the right "product" to sell them and to give you a chance to see whether the company has the right "product" to sell you. *Your* basic approach should be: I have a product that is good and that I want to sell to the right buyer. You will be in a better bargaining position if you can set up several interviews within two or three weeks of each other and generate at least two job offers.

Most interviewers are looking first for confidence and second for competence—not overconfidence or underconfidence, simply confidence. If necessary, they'll trade competence for confidence because they can't teach confidence or unteach overconfidence. The key to a successful interview is a combination of reasonable humility (not expecting to be President right away), enthusiasm, and strong self-respect.

The main part of the interview consists of explanations as well as questions and answers about job requirements and your qualifications. After the routine matters have been handled, it's your turn to show whether you have the mentality of an executive or a worker (see Exhibit 2-10).

Bring a folder with relevant information to the interview. As the interviewer talks, take a few brief notes about important information on the company and the job. Have a list of reminders on questions you want answered and points you want to cover.

Use the executive approach in your job application letter and résumé as well as in the interview. Every contact you have with a prospective employer is an opportunity to show you are executive material. Here are some pointers.

Dress the Part The way you dress communicates a great deal about your self-concept and about the type of person you are. Your image is especially crucial during job interviews and the first few weeks or months on the job. The people selected for higher-level positions tend to look and act as if they fit the new role even *before* they're given the nod. Test your savvy by completing Exercise 2-14, Identifying the Executive Image, and comparing your ideas with those of other career women [22].

Many articles and books have been written on the subject of appropriate dress for

EXHIBIT 2-9: Job Application Letter

April 22, 19xx

Ms. Jan Arguello
Lighthouse Designs, Inc.
206 Market St.
San Francisco, CA 94102

Dear Ms. Arguello:

The enthusiastic response to your new lines reported recently in the San Francisco Star indicates your company will continue to grow and expand. You will
no doubt be looking for additional top-notch sales representatives to handle your
lines. I have over seven years of sales experience in fashion merchandising that
includes sales promotion, merchandising strategies, and sales forecasting. It
also includes the successful handling of various responsibilities that called for
executive planning, organizing, administering, training, and supervising.

I think this experience, along with my college degree in marketing and my lifelong interest in the fashion industry, can help me contribute to your goals of
meeting the increased demands of your market.

I am sure you are looking for someone who also has the intelligence and ambition
to advance to more responsible positions within the firm. The enclosed résumé
shows that I have maintained a high grade point average in my college work while
taking a leadership role in professional and civic organizations. At the same
time I was also successful in assuming increased responsibility on the job.

I am graduating with a BBA in marketing from State University and will be ready
to move into a full-time position by June 1. My résumé lists some of my past
achievements which show that I am accustomed to getting results. I am eager to
bring the same high level of drive, intelligence, know-how, and willingness to
learn to my future position on the sales staff of a firm such as Lighthouse
Designs.

May I meet with you between now and Wednesday, May 15, to discuss the possibility
of joining your firm? I will call your office on Wednesday, May 1, to discuss a
meeting date that is convenient for you. If you wish to reach me in the meantime,
my home phone number is 555-3809.

Very truly yours,

Joan Kerr

Enclosure: Résumé

EXHIBIT 2-10: Executive and Worker Mentalities

Executive Mentality	Worker Mentality
You are a self-confident salesperson. You approach job-getting as a courting-for-marriage relationship. Each party must have something of value to bring.	You have a "beggar" attitude. You approach job-getting as a master/slave relationship.
A Focus on Primary Concerns	*A Focus on Secondary Concerns*
The firm and its future	Fringe benefits
The salary	Holidays
Opportunities for continued advancement *after* you prove yourself	Working conditions
Second Part of the Interview	*Second Part of the Interview*
You know about the company and the job.	You reveal that you know little or nothing about the company.
You are able to provide relevant information.	
You smoothly point out how your experience fits the job—what you have to sell.	You seem to want a job, any job.
You ask for information about what the company has to offer you. Show no fear about doing this.*	You imply that your main concern is "What's in it for me?"
You do not ask about secondary concerns.	You focus too intently on secondary concerns— work hours, holidays, coffee breaks, fringe benefits, carpets, windows, desks.
You discuss salary in terms of an *annual* amount and negotiate assertively.	You show little or no interest in primary concerns.

*Put the responsibility on the interviewer to volunteer information about primary concerns. If the interviewer doesn't and starts to discuss secondary concerns, you should politely put aside the secondaries and zero in on the primaries. In this way you will show the interviewer that you're aware of the difference between the two and are interested in the primaries.

the business woman. Here is a very simple formula: When in doubt, select

A conservative approach

Simple lines, classic styles

Neutral colors (gray, navy, black, brown, beige, tan)

Clothes and accessories that are as expensive as you can afford (It's better to have a few expensive items than several cheaper ones.)

Natural fibers (wool, silk, cotton) or at least fibers that look natural

Real leather pumps, bag, briefcase

Minimal, simple, "real" jewelry (gold, pearls, classic styles, appropriate heirlooms)

Simple, neat, natural hairstyles

When dressing for a job interview, you frequently know very little about the people you'll be meeting, their viewpoints and values. However, as a potential manager for a company, it's better to be considered slightly plain or dowdy than to be considered the least bit far-out, cheap, or flashy. Once you are on the job and get to know the organization and the people in it, you will find out how much leeway you have. But for the interview, be conservative.

For more specific details and information, read John Malloy's *Woman's Dress for Success* [16]. Malloy recommends a business woman's "uniform" of conservative, skirted suits, and he illustrates in great detail what is meant by the simple formula described here. Although the "uniform" might bore

EXERCISE 2-14: IDENTIFYING THE EXECUTIVE IMAGE

Step 1. Rank the twelve different outfits shown below according to how well each reflects your idea of the executive image.

Step 2. Compare your decisions with those of other career-oriented women (*Savvy* readers who participated in a 1983 survey). See their responses at the end of the chapter on page 97.

© 1984 SAVVY Magazine, SAVVY Co., New York, NY. Reprinted with permission.

you, you won't go far astray by following his advice. See References section for other sources.

Stress Specific Achievements The job interview is *not* the time to be shy or modest, regardless of your childhood training. Toot your own horn, just as you did in the résumé, when you discuss your qualifications. You might say, for example, "I'm good at problem-solving." Then be ready to back it up by giving some examples—how you solved a problem, how you would do it again. Look for interdisciplinary experience and skills that make your product unique or at least special: "I've been especially successful in solving problems involving research design, product quality, and sales promotion. I think this experience will be especially helpful in promoting your new product line."

When you discuss your experience and educational background, describe projects you successfully initiated, participated in, or completed; company savings you effected; contributions to company profits and goals; activities that show you're in the habit of producing results. If you developed your own résumé, following the suggestions given earlier, you will probably be comfortable and confident in discussing your achievements and skills in a businesslike way.

Be Prepared to Handle Difficult Questions and Situations Some interviewers may, through ignorance or by design, set up uncomfortable situations. For example, you may be kept waiting in the reception room. If so, take the time to review your résumé and notes for the job. Breathe deeply and relax. Or when you are ushered into the interviewer's office and introduced, the interviewer may glance up briefly and keep on working. If that happens, ask whether you should come back another time when she or he is not so busy. Standing around nervously or fading into the woodwork does *not* signal self-confidence.

Here are some difficult questions you should be prepared to answer. You might want to role-play them with a friend. In general, avoid one-line answers. The interviewer's purpose is to find out as much as possible about your qualifications and your personality. Expand on appropriate questions in order to give the information *you* want the interviewer to have.

"Tell me about yourself." Be ready to focus on the aspects of your background that qualify you for the job.

"Where do you want to be in five years?" Your career goals are well planned. Review them just before the interview. Relate them to a specific career path within the company, if possible.

"What is your major strength?" Talk about strengths that are especially important for success on this particular job.

"What is your major weakness?" Don't fall for this one (and of course don't be the one to bring up weaknesses). It's up to you to present your *best* self at the interview. Turn this negatively phrased question into a positive by saying something like, "I tend to take my career too seriously," "I'm a perfectionist in my work." "I sometimes get carried away with exciting projects on the job and push myself too hard." "I sometimes put too much pressure on myself to achieve."

"What did you like best about your last job (or in school)?" Your answer should reflect your ability to succeed in this job. For example, if human relations is an important part of the job, you can say "the people" and then tell why.

"What did you like least about your last job (or in school)?" Again, turn a negative question into a positive one. A good answer might be, "the limits on my ability to use all my skills to the fullest," or "the limited opportunities for advancement." Studiously avoid saying anything negative about any person or organization you've been involved with. You want to come across as a person who has a positive outlook, who foresees and prevents problems, who handles any problems that do occur effectively, and who doesn't harbor resentments or grudges. Also, the interviewer may figure that if you bad-mouth your previous boss or company, you'll eventually bad-mouth your new boss or firm.

There is one exception to the advice about avoiding negative comments. When you are reasonably sure that the person the interviewer will contact will not give you a favorable recommendation but you must list that company on your résumé because your experience there represents an essential part of your job qualifications. In this unfortunate situation, it's best to inform the interviewer of the circumstances from your viewpoint. If you are reasonably sure that the interviewer will check out this job reference and will therefore probably get some negative feedback about you, give your side of the story at the initial interview. Be as objective and matter-of-fact as possible. Describe the un-fair *situation* and avoid condemning the *people* involved. If personalities played a part, your attitude can convey "how unfortunate" it is that certain personality traits were involved. You can stress that you learned a great deal from the experience and know how to avoid such problems now.

"What salary are you earning now?" If you're after a job that pays more than you are now earning, you may weaken your bargaining position if you reveal your current salary. The interviewer probably has an idea of your general salary range but will be unable to verify it. You can answer, "Actually, quite a bit less than I think I am worth and will be able to get. That is one reason I'm looking for an opportunity elsewhere."

"Can you type?" If you have the experience or education to qualify for a managerial or management trainee position, don't let anyone steer you into a clerical or secretarial position except as a last resort. You can re-

spond either "No," or "I'm not interested in a position in the clerical or secretarial area." The latter response implies, " . . . even if it has a glorified title."

If you do your homework in identifying and packaging your skills and interests, developing a career action plan, translating past experience into results-oriented management action terms, and investigating potential employers, you'll be ready for many of the questions that are difficult for less-prepared candidates. Questions such as, "Why do you want to work here?" "Why should I hire you?" "How have you helped sales/profits/cost reductions?" and "How many people have you supervised?" will merely serve as opportunities for you to highlight your key qualifications and your preparation for the interview.

You need to think about responses to such questions as, "Why do you want to change jobs?" if you're currently employed full-time. "How long will you stay with the company?" and "Are you willing to go where the company sends you?" are other questions that should not catch you by surprise. If your potential boss asks, "Would you like to have my job?" a good answer might be, "I would certainly like to follow in your footsteps when you move up—of course, a job at a similar level to yours might be quite appropriate, too."

Anticipate Sexist Questions What will you do if an interviewer asks you a question that you believe is discriminatory? That depends on how sexist the interviewer seems to be, how much you want the job, and how you feel about the particular situation in which the question occurs. Here are some possibilities:

1. *Sidestep the question* by not responding directly to it. Instead, mention a related bona fide job qualification you meet, or

make a reference to your professionalism, commitment, or relevant trait. For example, a response to, "What arrangement have you made for the care of your children?" might be, "My personal responsibilities won't interfere with my job."

2. *Downplay the question* by answering as briefly as possible, and then move on to a related topic. For example, in response to, "Will your husband object to your traveling?" your answer might be, "We support each other's career objectives. What sort of travel does the job entail?"

3. *Challenge the relevance* of the question by asking if it refers to a requirement for the job and just how it is connected with your qualifications. For example, a response to whether you plan to have children might be, "Is motherhood a requirement for this job?"

4. *Return the question* to the interviewer by saying, "Yes, are you?" or some similar question that fits. This can make a pointed statement, especially with male interviewers.

5. *Tactfully confront the legality* of the question by asking, "Isn't that type of question now considered sexually discriminatory?" or a similar question.

Federal legislation and court decisions now make it unlawful to ask certain questions *before* hiring that might be used to discriminate against an applicant because of sex, race, age, physical handicap, or arrest record. Some questions are essential to establish whether you can meet a bona fide occupational qualification. Other inquiries—about your previous name(s), family status, age, health, race, birthplace, people you live with, home ownership, arrests, club memberships, credit rating, religion—

may be unlawful, if the answers might eliminate you from consideration for a job you're actually qualified for.

Decide in advance which kinds of attitudes you're willing to tolerate and which you will not (as well as which attitudes will probably limit your advancement, if held by one of your bosses). If the interviewer's questions reflect an attitude that you find intolerable, you probably should think twice before accepting a position with the firm. In this case, do you want to confront the interviewer with the illegality of the question (or later report it to the EEOC, after you find a job with another firm)?

As a practical matter, let the interviewer know the facts that you think will put you in a favorable light. Sidestep or downplay possibly unlawful questions that might be unfavorable to you. If the interviewer persists, return the question or challenge its relevance and/or legality. You may have to make the choice of cooperating if you want the job or calling the interviewer's hand if you don't.

Prepare the Questions You'll Ask Remember, you're interviewing the company too, so prepare a list of questions. You certainly won't read from it during the interview, but you'll probably want to glance at it before the interview is over to be sure you've covered the important items. The items listed as clues to an organization's openness in this chapter should trigger some questions you'll want to ask. See Exhibit 1-4, Evaluating the Power Potential of a Job, for more ideas. Here are a few other questions to get you started:

- What percentage of your employees are women? What percentage of supervisors, middle managers, and top managers are women? Are there any women on the board of directors? Have percentages increased in recent years?

- Do you have an Affirmative Action program? What does it include?

- What sort of career paths were followed by your top managers?

- What job moves are actually possible from this position?

- Which moves would be vertical and which are lateral?

- What capabilities and experience are needed to move from one job to another?

- Are jobs with similar requirements grouped as job families? If so, what moves within job families are available in order to broaden experience and gain exposure to different working situations?

- Is there any systematic way that career paths are managed in this company? Do you have a formal career development program?

- Do you have a special career track for top performers?

- Is it company policy to promote from within (as opposed to looking outside the company for top managers and staff people)?

- What percentage of trainees make it to middle management? Top management? (Or perhaps a specific staff position you have in mind)

- What departments or areas are expanding most rapidly?

- Do you have a career development program? If so, how does it work? What services does it offer employees? Do you have a career resource center or something similar?

- Does management support individual career planning? If so, in what ways? (For example, counseling, workshops, self-development assessment centers)

- Is information about career opportunities and career development resources made available to employees? How? (For example, by posting available job positions, through workshops, or through counselors)

Negotiate the Best Terms   If your research has been successful, you will know the salary range the company pays for the type of position you want. You should at least know the salary range most companies generally pay for that type of position. Your goal is to get the top of that range. If your information about what the company pays is sketchy or nonexistent, try to ask about the salary *range* before the interviewer asks what salary you expect. Then you can set your asking price at the top of the range or a little above the annual salary the interviewer mentions.

Delay talking about money as long as possible. Wait until you feel the interviewer wants you for the job, if possible. You're more likely to get your price once the interviewer is convinced of your worth and is psychologically committed to trying to hire you.

If the interviewer tries to pin you down to a salary figure too soon, a tactful delaying maneuver might be: "I'm really intrigued with the areas of responsibility in this job. Tell me more about those first. I'm sure we can arrive at an agreeable salary figure if everything else fits."

Once you get an offer that seems acceptable, thank the interviewer, say you're very interested, and ask when he or she wants your decision. If you avoid accepting right away, you can review your job offers at your leisure and try to find out what perks and benefits you may be able to negotiate (such as an expense account, stock options, or company car) as well as a higher salary. Your chances of getting these extras are small just after a salary discussion. You have a better chance to negotiate for them during the next meeting. If the interviewer balks, perhaps you can tie them to additional job responsibilities you're willing to accept. If you have a slightly better offer, you can say you really prefer the interviewer's company but Company X has made you an offer that's hard to refuse.

Logical and patient insistence on an annual salary that is within reason will win you respect that will probably be remembered in the future. It sets the stage for assertiveness in future negotiations for promotions and raises. Since raises are usually figured on a percentage of what you're already earning, negotiating the best starting salary provides a basis for larger raises as long as you're with the firm.

As part of your preparation for interviewing, prepare one or two possible parting comments that may enhance your prospects: "I've enjoyed learning more about Lighthouse Designs. You're doing some exciting things." Or: "I think this job is my cup of tea."

Within a few days after the interview, send a follow-up letter referring to key points that were covered and thanking the interviewer for the opportunity to discuss the position. Such a followup (1) shows you are thoughtful and considerate, (2) keeps your name on the interviewer's mind, and (3) provides you with a record of the transaction via the carbon copy.

When you select the best job offer, keep in mind the intangibles as well as salary and extras. Weigh your feelings about chances for advancement, attitudes toward women managers, lifestyles and attitudes of management, and your emotional reaction and enthusiasm toward the job. If there's no significant difference among the tangible factors, go with your emotions. Remember, your commitment and enthusiasm will be major factors in your success on the job.

SUMMARY

Before you begin setting goals, you may need to identify barriers in your own mind to planning your life direction. Typical barriers are fears concerning regimentation, failure, success, and risk-taking. If you handle such fears, define your ideas of success and who you are, and focus on the payoffs for planning, you will be able to set your goals with more energy and direction. The next phase is identifying and packaging your skills and interests so you have a better idea of the type of career that will spell success for you.

A goal is a specific end result you want by some stated point in time. Activities are things you *do* in order to achieve your goal. You may enjoy an activity, but enjoyment doesn't make it a goal. There may be a variety of feasible and acceptable activities that can help you reach your goal.

Specific goals include amounts, places, exact items, and time targets. *Vague goals* reflect wishes and dreams. The more specifically you state your "wants" as goals, the more likely you are to get them. If you have difficulty determining if a "want" is a goal or an activity, ask yourself *why* you desire it.

To identify your major goals, follow these steps: (1) Brainstorm all the "wants" you can think of. (2) Separate goals from activities. (3) Rank your goals in order of importance. (4) Restate goals, if necessary, so they are specific and clear. (5) Decide the relative importance to you of the major areas of your life: career, private life, and personal development. (6) Categorize your list of goals according to the major areas of your life.

After you have identified your major goals, your next step is to find activities that will help you achieve them: (1) Start with the top-priority goal in your most important life area. Brainstorm activities that can help you reach this goal. (2) Rank the activities according to their likelihood of helping you achieve the goal. (3) Select the activities you're willing to spend at least five minutes on during the coming week. (4) Repeat this process for your other goals.

Next develop action plans, beginning with a one-month plan: (1) List the top three goals in each life area. (2) Under each goal (a total of nine goals) list the three top-ranking activities for achieving those goals, along with target dates (a total of twenty-seven activities). Adapt the number of goals and activities to reflect your situation and preferences. Use the most important activities as the basis for your daily "To Do" list. Make long-range action plans—one-year, five-year, ten-year—to suit your needs.

Use your action plan to move ahead by designing a résumé that reflects your goals. The process of preparing your résumé should sharpen your awareness of your strengths and achievements and help you sell yourself. The main purpose of the résumé is to persuade the reader to grant you a job interview. It should begin with a clear statement of your specific job objective, followed by a brief statement of your major qualifications for that position. This selling pitch or "bait" is designed to capture the reader's attention and interest immediately. Describe your past experiences in terms of the management functions you've performed even if you haven't actually held a management position. List specific activities and achievements, using administrative action verbs and quantifying where possible. Get all the information you can about the companies you may want to interview. Make every effort to establish personal contacts.

A covering letter is necessary any time you mail your résumé. Write it especially for the person who can grant you an interview. Show how your particular experience, skills, interests, and traits fit the job you're applying for and meet the needs of this firm. Stress what you can contribute.

The job interview is your opportunity to show that you are executive material. Focus on the primary concerns: the firm and its future, the salary, and the opportunities for advancement after you prove yourself. The way you dress for the interview also communicates a great deal about your self-concept and the type of person you are. When in doubt, select a conservative, simple, classic, well-tailored suit and accessories.

During the interview, stress your most relevant skills, specific achievements in past situations, and unique combinations of skills and experience. Be prepared to handle difficult questions and situations so that you (1) project self-confidence, (2) take advantage of every opportunity to communicate your strengths and achievements, (3) avoid bringing any shortcomings into the conversation, and (4) tactfully sidestep or confront unlawful, discriminatory questions. Know the going salary range for the position, and try to get the top of the range by postponing the salary discussion until you feel the interviewer is ready to offer you the job.

Try to set up several interviews and generate more than one job offer so you'll be in a better bargaining position. Respond to offers with a show of interest and an agreement to give a decision within a reasonable time. Then see which company will up its ante in salary or other benefits before accepting the best offer.

REFERENCES

1. August, Bonnie. *The Complete Bonnie August Dress Thin System*. New York: Rawson, Wade Publishers, 1981. The author shows numerous ways to look up to thirty pounds thinner, to conceal figure problems, and to make the most of figure assets. She includes how to dress for a power image.

2. Baruch, Grace; Rosalind Barnett; and Caryl Rivers. *Lifeprints: New Patterns of Love and Work for Today's Woman*. New York: McGraw-Hill, 1983. In a two-year study financed by the National Science Foundation, the authors concluded that married women with children are the happiest of all women.

3. Blotnick, Srully. *Getting Rich Your Own Way*. New York: Doubleday, 1980. This study uncovers facts about the wealthy and how they got that way (mainly by working hard in careers they loved.)

4. Blumstein, Philip, and Pepper Schwartz. "American Couples: Money, Work, Sex." University of Washington, 1983. The authors surveyed 12,000 people to determine new trends in couple relationships.

5. Bolles, Richard N. *The Three Boxes of Life*. Berkeley, Calif.: Ten Speed Press, 1984. This text contains excellent exercises for life planning.

6. Bolles, Richard N. *The Quick Job-Hunting Map*. Berkeley, Calif.: Ten Speed Press, 1984. This handy packet of key exercises from *What Color Is Your Parachute* can be ordered from the publisher (Box 7123).

7. Bolles, Richard N. *What Color Is Your Parachute?* Berkeley, Calif.: Ten Speed Press, 1984. This classic in career planning includes excellent exercises for determining what you really want to do and how to create an ideal job for yourself.

8. Butler, Diane. *Future Work: Where to Find Tomorrow's High-Tech Jobs Today*. New York: Holt, Rinehart and Winston, 1984. The author explains the various technologies and presents a method for finding openings.

9. Dietch, Joan K. *The Success Look: For Women Only*. New York: Grosset & Dunlap, 1979. The author defines six personality/body types and presents a summary of looks for each. Less-experienced women should be wary of adopting such types as the "Seductive." Read Malloy first.

10. Fraser, Jill Andresky. "You Are Where You Live." *Savvy* (October 1983), pp. 38–48.

11. Hollands, Jean. *The Silicon Syndrome: A Survival Handbook for Couples*. Palo Alto, Calif.: Coastlight Press, 1983. The author discusses how to balance your life when it includes a relationship with a technical professional.

12. Jackson, Carole. *Color Me Beautiful*. New York: Ballantine Books, 1980. All items in your wardrobe will work better together once you identify your best colors. The secret is discovering your underlying skin tone. Carry the removable color chart with you when you shop.

13. Kennedy, Marilyn Moats. "The Keys to the Kingdom." *Savvy* (February 1984), pp. 48–55.

14. Lakein, Allen. *How to Get Control of Your Time and Your Life*. New York: P.H. Wyden, 1983. This is a basic text on using goals to manage time.

15. Levering, Robert, and Milton Moskowitz. *The 100 Best Companies to Work for in America*. Reading, Mass.: Addison-Wesley, 1984. This book includes not only the best places for women but the best companies for ambience, pay, job security, and benefits.

16. Malloy, John. *Woman's Dress for Success*. New York: Follett, 1977. This is a basic resource for proper business dress. All suggestions are based on extensive research into actual reactions of business decision-makers.

17. Medley, Anthony H. *Sweaty Palms: The Neglected Art of Being Interviewed*. Belmont, Calif.: Wadsworth, 1978. This book includes all aspects of going through a job interview.

18. *National Job Market*. This newspaper reprints help-wanted ads gleaned from nearly 3,000 newspapers each week. Buy at some newsstands or order the full edition that includes helpful articles and other data (P.O. Box 286, Kensington, Md. 20895; $29 for 6 weeks).

19. Ross, Ruth. *The Prospering Woman*. Mill Valley, Calif.: Whatever Publishing, Inc., 1982. This book can change your life by helping you to know yourself and what you truly want, to come from a stance of abundance versus scarcity, and to make room in your life for success.

20. Scholl, Jaye. "The Corporations of the Year." *Savvy* (June 1983), pp. 30–31.

21. Sher, Barbara. *Wishcraft: How to Get What You Really Want*. New York: Ballantine Books, 1979. This book presents a detailed, step-by-step plan to pinpoint your goals and make your dreams come true.

22. Solomon, Michael, and Susan Douglas. "The Power of Pinstripes." *Savvy* (March 1983), pp. 60–62.

23. Stein, Frances Patiky. *Hot Tips: 1000 Fashion and Beauty Tricks*. New York: Putnam, 1981. This is a good supplement to Malloy's book.

24. Thompson, Jacqueline, ed. *Image Impact: The Aspiring Woman's Personal Packaging Program*. New York: A & W Publishers, 1981. A valuable addition to Malloy's work, this book also covers personality and public speaking.

25. Wright, John W. *The American Almanac of Jobs and Salaries*. New York: Avon, 1984. Here's a wealth of previously unobtainable information about salaries for all types of positions. Covering both profit and nonprofit organizations, it includes job descriptions and salaries by region and metropolitan area. You must buy or borrow this reference before launching your job campaign. First published in 1982, it will be revised regularly.

Survey Responses for Exercises 2-14 (p. 88)
Best: number 1 choice was outfit 12; number 2 choice was outfit 5.
Worst: number 9 choice was outfit 4; number 10 choice was outfit 2; number 11 choice was outfit 6; number 12 choice was outfit 11.

Chapter Three

Surviving the Transition to Manager

"I don't ride to beat the boys, just to win."

Denise M. Boudrot (jockey)

You've already made your most important career decision: to move into management. Once that is done, the next step is actually landing a management position. At that point you face perhaps the biggest test—and hurdle—of them all: surviving the transition from worker or trainee to manager. This chapter is about coming through that crucial period with flying colors.

In this chapter you will have the opportunity to learn how to

1. Identify the common pitfalls in making the transition from worker to manager and apply some techniques for avoiding them

2. Identify the top priorities of the manager's job and change your focus to getting the work done through subordinates

3. Take steps toward developing interpersonal power and a support network

4. Handle office politics

5. Avoid becoming identified by others with stereotyped female roles

6. Prevent or deal effectively with sexual overtures and harassment on the job

In this chapter we'll focus on some of the common pitfalls to be avoided as you make the transition from worker to manager. Most of them result from the lack of awareness of the politics and power structure within an organization that we discussed in Chapter 1. We'll expand on that topic in this chapter and discuss establishing your own power base of supporters. You will learn about the importance of including a mentor in that power base, along with suggestions for establishing, maintaining, and eventually outgrowing that important relationship.

We'll also discuss changes you may need to make in your approach, attitude, and goals in performing your job functions. You'll have a chance to review stereotypes, myths, and sexual games that you'll undoubtedly encounter as a woman manager, along with ways of sidestepping or coping with them.

First, though, examine your current attitude toward handling some of the situations new women managers often face by completing Exercise 3-1. When you have finished reading Chapter 3, take another look at your responses to this self-assessment to see whether you would change any of them.

EXERCISE 3-1: SELF-ASSESSMENT: MAKING THE TRANSITION TO MANAGER

Select the response (a, b, or c) that best describes your opinion or the way you would handle the situation. Then determine how strongly you feel about that response and place the appropriate number in the appropriate space. For example, if your response is "a" and you feel strongly about it, place the number 3 under "Strongly Agree." See the answer key for scoring and interpretation.

	3 Strongly Agree	2 Agree	1 It Depends
1. The most important task of the new woman manager is to			
(a) Do her job the way her boss wants it done.	___	___	___
(b) Get the work done by her subordinates.	___	___	___
(c) Perform her job duties efficiently.	___	___	___
2. The first few weeks of the job, it is best to			
(a) Pay attention to office cliques, gossip, and personalities.	___	___	___
(b) Ignore office gossip.	___	___	___
(c) Concentrate on learning the paperwork necessary to the job.	___	___	___
3. Your boss has been your sponsor or mentor within the organization. He constantly gives you advice and warns you about mistakes. Your best response is to			
(a) Confront him with his overprotective attitude and tell him he must stop undermining your confidence.	___	___	___
(b) Encourage his nurturing tendencies in order to get all the information and help you can.	___	___	___
(c) Start changing the relationship from one of mentor/pupil toward one of two colleagues.	___	___	___
4. The best approach to molding your department into a more productive unit is to			
(a) Make minor changes and improvements first.	___	___	___
(b) Ignore minor inefficiencies in the beginning and concentrate on developing support for a major reorganization later.	___	___	___
(c) Launch a comprehensive reorganization as soon as possible.	___	___	___

	3 Strongly Agree	2 Agree	1 It Depends
5. When you report for your new job as a manager, you find a typewriter by your desk. None of the other managers (all male) has a typewriter in his office. Your best response is to			
(a) Say nothing. This is your chance to show how much more efficient you are than managers who can't (or won't) type. You can compose some of your own rough drafts of reports at the typewriter, type short business messages yourself, and so forth.	____	____	____
(b) Tell your boss that you are shocked at the blatant display of male chauvinism and that you will report the company to the EEOC if the typewriter isn't removed immediately.	____	____	____
(c) Arrange to have the typewriter removed to an area where clerical personnel can use it.	____	____	____
6. In your previous jobs, you developed a fairly high degree of skill in typing, taking shorthand notes, and filing. Your most effective use of these skills now is to			
(a) Capitalize on your experience to supervise the clerical tasks of subordinates but don't use these skills yourself.	____	____	____
(b) Capitalize on them to improve your efficiency as a manager.	____	____	____
(c) Forget you ever knew them.	____	____	____
7. At the first weekly staff meeting you attend on your new job, your boss insists that you take notes and have them typed and distributed to the other managers present. Your best response is to			
(a) Do the job as quietly, efficiently, and professionally as possible.	____	____	____
(b) Tell him you'll be glad to take turns with the other managers in performing this task and let him know you prefer to take your turn at a later meeting.	____	____	____
(c) Tell him it's too bad he has put you in such a spot but you'll have to refuse since this task is not appropriate to your new job assignments.	____	____	____

	3 Strongly Agree	2 Agree	1 It Depends

8. You are required to attend many company meetings as a part of your new job. A good way to alleviate your restlessness during these meetings is to

(a) Take copious notes: This keeps you occupied and the notes may serve as a valuable source of information later. ___ ___ ___

(b) Keep some therapeutic project handy in your desk—such as knitting, crocheting, or needlework—that can help occupy your hands and mind during these meetings. ___ ___ ___

(c) Concentrate on observing the people in these meetings by noticing their nonverbal behavior as well as what they say. ___ ___ ___

9. You have been active in a charitable organization for the past several years. The people in your office have been supportive of the various projects of this charity by buying raffle tickets, Christmas cards, and so forth. Now that you are a manager, it is best to

(a) Dissociate yourself from volunteer projects completely. ___ ___ ___

(b) As far as the company is concerned, no longer associate yourself with volunteer projects unless they are also the pet project of a top corporate officer. ___ ___ ___

(c) Capitalize on the fact that you are involved in the community and continue to ask for support for your volunteer activities. ___ ___ ___

10. Your new boss starts confiding in you about his marital problems and asks you about your personal life. Your best response is to

(a) Keep steering the conversation back to professional and business interests. ___ ___ ___

(b) Tell him he is getting too personal and you won't put up with sexual overtures on the job. ___ ___ ___

(c) Capitalize on the opportunity to develop a close relationship. ___ ___ ___

Preparing for the Big Move

One day a few weeks after Carrie has discussed her career goals and job offers with her boss, Jan Arguello, Jan walks in from an Executive Committee meeting with good news.

"Carrie, how do you feel about moving to San Diego?"

Carrie's eyes widen. "What's happening, Jan?"

"Well, I've just been authorized to offer you the Assistant Sales Manager's position at our San Diego branch office."

"All right! When do I start packing?"

Jan smiles. "Come into my office and let's talk about it."

When Carrie learns that she will move to the San Diego office in less than a month, she realizes she's not really sure about how to make the transition from worker to manager. As Jan's administrative assistant, she's been viewed as a glorified clerical/secretarial worker. Her major responsibility has been to keep Jan happy, and Jan has protected her from the criticism of others. As Assistant Sales Manager, she'll be viewed as a manager with responsibilities for directing the work of many others throughout the region.

Carrie begins formulating questions to ask Jan and other women who have made the transition to manager successfully. With Jan's blessing, she meets with the company President and talks with him about company goals and policies. She shares her goals and plans with him, and he gives her further ideas for carrying out company plans.

In her last session with Jan before leaving for San Diego, Carrie says, "Jan, we've talked a lot about this new job. But what do you think are the key aspects I must keep in mind?"

Jan, looking thoughtful, stares out the window for a while. Turning back to Carrie finally, she says, "First, I'd say focusing on the people you'll be dealing with. You already know a great deal about the actual work to be done—and you'll easily learn what you need to know about that. But your main job from now on is to get the work done through the people you'll be directing—instead of doing it yourself as you've been doing."

"Okay, but I'm not clear just how I go about focusing on the people."

"A good start is to become a listener, an observer, a sponge. Take in every detail about the people—their habits, likes, dislikes, working patterns, cliques, enemies, histories. Find out who the game players are and what their games are. Office politics will make or break you, Carrie. You can play it as honorably as possible, but you can't avoid it or ignore it if you expect to survive in a large organization."

Carrie smiles. "I think I have a lot to learn in that department."

"Yes, and you won't learn it overnight, but I'm as near as the telephone, and I'll support you any way I can. Which reminds me, another aspect of focusing on the people is to begin right away to build a support network."

"Well, I already have one supporter."

"That's for sure," laughs Jan. "And you'll need all you can get—among your people, the other managers like you, the higher-level managers, the customers—and don't forget to cultivate some support people outside the company circle."

"I guess I'd always thought of supporters as being my bosses."

"Many people make that mistake and pass up some important sources of power. Before you leave, you've got to hear one more of my little stories. I'm not sure where this one originated, but it's been making the rounds, and it also makes a point about peers supporting each other.

Not long ago, there were two junior officers in the Dutch Navy who made a pact. They decided that when they were at various Navy social functions, they would always go out of their way to tell people what a great guy the other was. They would appear at cocktail parties or dances and say, "What an unbelievable person Charlie is. He's the best man in the Navy." Or, "Did you hear about the brilliant idea Dave had?"

They revealed that pact to the public the day they were both made admirals—the two youngest admirals ever appointed in the Dutch Navy. Their pact had influenced the perceptions of their superiors and their peers in the organization. The point: Believing is seeing. It's much more effective than the old idea that seeing is believing [8].

"That's a powerful idea." Carrie smiles. "When people believe you are exceptional, they're more likely to notice the good things you do—and to perceive your performance as exceptional. Can you imagine what would have happened if those guys had developed a whole support network?"

"I don't think the Dutch Navy could have handled that!" laughs Jan. "But getting back to our key points for making a smooth transition, let's talk about a couple of special points the woman manager must consider. First, you have to learn to sidestep stereotyped roles. There are still many people who try to treat women employees as if they are really clerks, secretaries, waitresses, house mothers, kid sisters, sex symbols—you get the idea. And it's easy for you to fall into one of those roles if you unconsciously think of yourself that way."

Carrie frowns. "But how can I avoid it if it's unconscious?"

"By becoming aware. And by regularly and continuously picturing yourself as a competent professional person when you're at work. When you focus on this self-concept, it helps you project your chosen self-image to others, including guys at all levels who make sexual overtures."

"You mean I still have to cope with that—even when I'm a manager?"

Jan laughs. "The rarer and the bigger the catch, the more status it gives the man who does the catching. No, you'll probably find that the sexual game-playing just becomes more subtle and sophisticated. And you have much more to lose. Not only that, you'll almost certainly stand to lose more than he will—unfortunately, the double standard is still alive and well in most organizations." Jan glances at her watch. "Hey, it's almost time for that staff meeting."

Carrie stands up. "Well, to be forewarned is to be forearmed. I can see there are many traps I could fall into, but you've shown me there are also ways to avoid them."

"Or cope with them—or redeem yourself. It would be nice if you could set some kind of record and avoid all the problems, but don't count on it."

---

1. What do you think is the most important aspect of making a successful transition to a management position? _____

2. Of the potential problems or traps mentioned, which is most likely to trip you up as a manager? _____ Why? _____

3. What can you do to prevent or cope with this potential problem? _____

_____

4. What special strengths do you already possess that will help you make an effective transition? _____

REDEFINING YOUR TOP PRIORITIES

If you move from a trainee position to manager, your top priorities will shift from learning to leading. Of course, you were demonstrating your leadership potential before—and you'll continue to learn in your new role. But now your top priority is functioning effectively as a leader, and you'll spend most of your time in that capacity. If you are promoted from a worker position to manager, your top priorities will shift from technical effectiveness in doing the actual work to leading and directing others in the performance of such work. You'll shift from a focus on pleasing your boss in every detail to leading your team in achieving objectives you and your boss have agreed upon.

To be an effective leader, you must be adept at organizational politics, for there will be times when you must outwit the politicians before they outwit you (and do you in). You must establish your credibility as a competent leader. If your working style has had a strong element of dependence and deference, you must replace it with autonomy and assertiveness. You must replace any out-of-balance need to please or to win popularity contests with the ability to establish appropriate distances in your work relationships. The effective woman manager has the self-confidence to "be her own person."

First, let's review some key elements you'll want to consider in redefining your priorities to suit your new managerial role. Later in this chapter we'll expand on some of these elements in discussions of how to establish a support network and how to handle game players.

Fine-Tuning Your Focus

Your new priorities call for fine-tuning your focus in two major ways. First, you'll need to shift from a focus on doing all the work necessary for meeting your personal job goals to a focus on leading and directing others in doing the work necessary to meet department goals. Second, if you've relied on a dependency relationship in which your boss dealt with the unwritten mysteries of organizational power, rules, customs and habits, you must now concentrate on gaining that kind of political savvy yourself.

Focusing on Getting the Work Done Through Others   As a manager you're now responsible for planning, organizing, implementing, and evaluating the work of your group, since your boss has delegated some of his or her authority to you. Instead of implementing the work yourself, you delegate it to the people on your work team, then coach them on how to complete it successfully. Therefore, you must learn what you can expect from your people as individuals, as groups, and as a total team.

Identifying the True Power   You'll check out the organization chart, of course, to identify formal power sources and relationships in your company. But keep in mind that informal power sources and relationships may be even more important to your success. Of course, you won't be so naïve as to ask directly about who the most powerful people are, but get all the information you can from old-timers, your boss, and others. Questions about how decisions are made, whether committee recommendations are acted upon, and what jobs the top people previously held can be fruitful.

Do your career goals include reaching a top-management position? If you haven't been able to learn a great deal about the power elite in your company before joining it, now's the time to learn so you can weigh your chances of moving up. The most important step may be to determine if you have a disqualifying characteristic. For example, in some technically oriented companies, lack of a technical degree and background is a disqualifier. Your inquiries should also turn up clues about other organizational values—or dos and don'ts.

Learning the Unwritten Rules Every organization has its own variation of the typical dos and don'ts we discuss throughout this book. Your indirect questions—and your careful listening and observation—will help you learn these. Here are some typical taboos you should investigate:

Talking too much about favors you've received from higher-ups, matters told you in confidence, others' shortcomings, and so forth

Being brutally frank about what's wrong with the company, someone in it, a client, and so forth

Being a pest by making an issue of trivia or by constantly complaining

Throwing temper tantrums or displaying lack of emotional control

Cheating on the expense account—is it worth jeopardizing your career?

Complaining about a former boss needlessly

Deviating too far from custom in such matters as dress, speech, courtesy, habits

Violating the chain of command by going over your boss' head to complain about her or him or to get a decision revoked

Making a big issue of new male/female roles so that others feel put down or awkward in your presence or consider you touchy or difficult

Failing to cooperate with top management. For example, suppose you receive a request that would create an unreasonable burden. Instead of automatically refusing, consider some alternatives. If you can get the okay for additional staff to help you, you can cooperate *and* expand your area of authority.

Knowing the unwritten rules in your company will ease your transition to manager. Of even more immediate importance is learning about the department you inherit.

Learning About Customs and Habits in Your Department These are the sorts of things you need to know: Who's called by his or her first name, last name, nickname? Is the order of names on distribution lists of great importance to people? Are memos sent to everyone or just to people who need the information? Does everyone get to work on time? How flexible are lunch hours and coffee breaks? What other habits and quirks may be important?

Learn the informal system but don't disrupt it at first; introduce small changes gradually. Every department has its own little idiosyncrasies. They may seem unimportant or silly to you, but they can have tremendous influence on your effectiveness in managing your group. If you get people upset over the little things, you'll have a difficult time winning their cooperation on major changes. You'll also reinforce one of the many stereotypes of women managers—that they nitpick about trivial details and are overly concerned with efficiency.

Establishing Your Credibility

Convincing others that you are indeed an effective leader can be easy if you avoid the common pitfalls awaiting the woman manager. One pitfall is remaining dependent on an overprotective boss or mentor and not projecting the image that you are your own person. Other pitfalls revolve around the tendency of some women to reveal their thoughts and feelings too freely and indiscriminately in work relationships.

Being "Your Own Person" Beware of the overprotective boss who is constantly giving you advice and warning you about mistakes. This is a subtle way of undermining your authority and confidence. Before taking a management position, get clear with your boss what your areas of responsibility and authority are. Make it clear that you're ready to use your authority and to accept responsibility for the consequences of your decisions and actions.

This can be especially difficult for you if your boss has been your mentor—the person who has promoted your interests, put in a good word for you with superiors, coached you in assuming more responsibility, and so forth. Once you become a manager, you must wean yourself from dependence on this person, while still retaining his or her support. One way to do this is to communicate your concern about dependence.

If your mentor or boss sometimes fights your battles for you, you can request that he or she not go to bat for you in problem situations unless you request it. You can say you prefer asking for his or her opinions and information and then making your own decisions. You can stress that you think you're at a point in your professional growth and development where you need to try your wings more, even if this means making some mistakes. Of course, it's wise to also stress how much you appreciate the advice and support—that you still welcome it at the same time that you're developing more autonomy. The idea is to maintain your boss' support, your subordinates' respect for your autonomy, and your growing self-confidence.

Distancing in Work Relationships While you want to be known as a human, people-oriented manager, your leadership role requires that you earn and maintain respect. You are responsible for the productivity of your unit, and you must sometimes make decisions that will not please everyone. Developing intimate friendships and striving for popularity are therefore incompatible with your leadership role.

The tendency to become too personal in work relationships is a success barrier that affects women more often than men. If this is a potential problem for you, try thinking in terms of appropriate levels of intimacy, as depicted in Figure 3-1.

It is appropriate to reveal your inner thoughts, personal problems, deepest feelings, controversial beliefs, and other deeply personal aspects of yourself to your intimates—your most trusted family members and friends and, to a lesser extent, those you think of as close friends. Most people consider themselves lucky to have even six or seven such people in their lives at one time. These mutually supportive relationships are the sign of a well-balanced person and provide a safe place for expressing and sorting out your feelings and beliefs. Such relationships are probably essential to managing stress effectively.

The third level of relationships, at a further distance from the innermost you, in-

FIGURE 3-1: Emotional Distances: Putting Relationships in Perspective

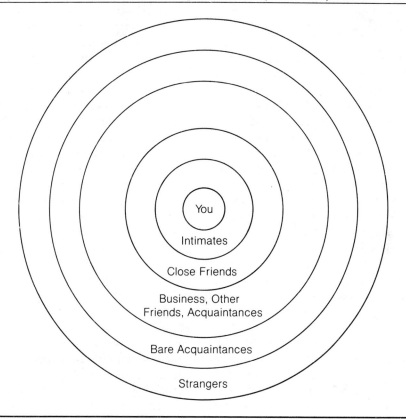

cludes work relationships and other friends and acquaintances. With these people you discuss current events and activities of mutual interest. The focus is on events and activities—not necessarily on your personal feelings about them, your evaluations of the people involved, personal problems they create for you, how they affect your intimate relationships at home, and other private matters. Nor is it wise to delve into your deep personal beliefs about the religious or political aspects of situations.

Why the distance in work relationships? For one thing, you avoid needlessly stepping on toes and alienating people. For another,

you avoid providing possible ammunition for future battles to people who haven't yet proven their trustworthiness. While you don't want to become paranoid, it is realistic to recognize that organizations are fertile ground for frequent power skirmishes, occasional battles, and even a rare all-out war. So why blab unnecessarily—about your past or current problems, for example? Finally, if you keep your distance at work from the very beginning, you avoid the problems inherent in becoming the boss of former buddies. As you can see, by filling your need for close, intimate relationships with people outside the work place, those in the first two levels of intimacy, you'll avoid a number of typical traps waiting for the unwary woman manager.

The fourth level of intimacy includes people you recognize, speak to, and perhaps conduct brief exchanges with, but whom you know little or nothing about. The fifth level is comprised of strangers. If you have a burning desire to blab and can't get to an intimate, it's usually better to tell all to a stranger you'll probably never see again than to let it all hang out with a business associate. Bartenders and passengers on public conveyances can attest to this phenomenon.

If you establish appropriate distances in your relationships, you will not alienate people. You will merely provide a framework for establishing the support network you need in order to be effective in your job and to advance in your career. Your support network is your power base, and as Figure 3-1 symbolizes, its inner core is you. This means you must be your own best supporter by continually giving yourself credit, acknowledging your own value, and taking care of your needs. The foundation of your support network, then, is made up of you, the keystone, along with your intimate and close friends. Let's explore ways of building upon this foundation with your work relationships.

ESTABLISHING A SUPPORT NETWORK

In *Networking*, Mary-Scott Welch gives this example of how *men's* ("old boys' ") networks operate [19, p. 16]: "When a job opens, a contract goes out for bids, a stock splits, a story breaks, or a rumor spreads . . . the old boys meet . . . and business gets done . . . . They'll have cut through all the resistance and red tape with ease, simply because they knew each other well enough to get in touch informally." *Your* support network consists of the relationships you've established—both inside and outside the company—that are based on mutual good will, trust, and willingness to help. They are business friendships that are mutually supportive.

Women are inclined to concentrate on proving themselves to their bosses when they first become managers. The *best* way to prove yourself to your boss is to develop your own interpersonal power and to build effective working relationships, starting with the people in your department. You must use your personal power and your ability to handle organizational game players in order to build a support network of workers, peers, and bosses—including your immediate boss, top management, and perhaps a mentor or two.

Your support network functions as your power base, which means it is an essential source of power for you. You'll probably be more effective in developing a power base if you understand the types of power people are attracted to. We've already discussed some ways power works within the organizational setup. Now let's take a closer look at one-on-one power—your power as other individuals perceive it. (See Chapter 4 for a discussion of personal (inner) power and Chapter 8 for a discussion of power needs as inner motivators.)

Developing Interpersonal Power

People tend to be attracted to powerful people, especially when they sense that the power is used constructively and may be used to empower them. And powerful people are almost universally respected. For these and other reasons you must gain some minimal level of power to be an effective manager. Interpersonal power refers to the power you possess as others perceive it, the one-on-one power you exert in dealings with others. If you were to list all the types and sources of interpersonal power you could think of, they would probably all fit into one of the following five categories of interpersonal power.

Reward/Punishment—Your ability to provide meaningful rewards to people or to punish them in some way. The rewards you offer may be either concrete, such as a choice assignment, or personal, such as recognition, acceptance, even a smile. Rewards can increase motivation and build long-term good will when used intelligently. Punishments may likewise be either concrete, such as withholding a salary increase, or personal, such as ignoring the person. They are the least effective sources of power. While recipients may try to please you in order to avoid the punishment, they tend to harbor resentment, passive resistance, and desire for revenge.

Position/Role—The power inherent in your position in the organization or your role in relation to another person. You may expand your role and the power of your position by using other types of power. Over the long term you must bring other types of power to your management position to succeed. The blatant use of your position power to achieve goals carries the same disadvantages as the use of punishment.

Skill/Expertise—Can refer to professional skills (such as those of an accountant, a lawyer, or a doctor), technical skills (such as computer or financial skills), managerial skills, social skills, or any type of skill that's useful or respected by the other person.

Information/Data—Your access to facts, figures, gossip, any information that an-

other considers necessary, helpful, or interesting and that is not readily available elsewhere. Your power may come from providing the information, from doling it out to a selected few, or from withholding it at times.

Charisma/Identification—The extent to which another is personally attracted to you or is able to identify with you as a fellow human being. (See Chapter 8 for a further discussion of the elements of charisma.) This area is one of the few power sources that has not been sex-role stereotyped. To make the best use of your charisma/identification power within the organization, stress your organizational role over your sex role. Stress the similarities you share with others rather than the differences.

The power you're able to gain in the position/role, reward/punishment, and information/data areas depends to some extent on your position within the organization. Your power in the skill/expertise and charisma/identification areas is dependent on your own resources [4].

How do you normally use the power you have? Do you use it in a direct or an indirect way? Women have traditionally relied on indirect uses of power: first influencing their parents to get what they want, then marrying well and influencing their husband's career and achievements, getting what they want through their husbands.

Such women tend to live vicariously through their husbands and later through their children, basking in the reflected glory of their achievements. In so doing they neglect developing their own sources of direct power and achievement. This syndrome often leads to the "empty-nest syndrome" when the children leave home. The problem can become a tragedy if the husband solves his midlife identity crisis by finding another (usually younger) mate, leaving the wife who sacrificed her own personal and career growth with little in the way of personal resources—that is, direct power. Direct power is based on your own power sources rather than those of a go-between. Instead of influencing a go-between to use his power in ways you think are desirable, you develop and use your own power to achieve your goals—or mutually agreed-upon goals in business or personal relationships.

Today more and more women are learning to use direct power more frequently. You must become comfortable with the use of direct power to succeed in a managerial role. So identify your major sources of direct power using the five categories to stimulate your thinking. Which areas do you need to develop further? How can you go about increasing your power in those areas?

Getting Workers on Your Side

To build a supportive work team, start getting answers to some key questions as soon as possible: Did one of my people want this job? Who are the slightly mean or vicious people in this group? What combinations of people usually share confidences, trade gossip, and influence the group's thinking? Who is allied with whom? Which people are most likely to become my supporters? Whom can I probably trust?

Select friends or supporters from the people you can probably trust. You can identify these people by careful observation during the first few weeks you are on the job. As a general rule, select individuals who seem to be basically positive and constructive in their approach to life. People who feel threatened much of the time and are frequently defensive are often unreliable supporters. You'll never know when they'll feel threatened by *you* and suddenly switch loyalties. Try to provide a supportive climate

for these people (see the discussion of defensive versus supportive climates in Chapter 7), but don't depend on them as reliable supporters. Bide your time when making decisions about whom to cultivate as supporters. Then focus special energy on developing good rapport with those people.

In the process be sure to give everyone a fair chance as well as a fair share of your attention. Just as you have avoided becoming buddies with coworkers, you must avoid playing favorites; try to give everyone a chance to shine. Confine most of your conversation to business-related topics. While you want to get to know your people and show concern for them as people, you can do this without close, emotional involvements. Keep it friendly but professional.

Establishing professional relationships requires special tact when some of your coworkers suddenly become your subordinates. You can avoid the worst aspects of this situation by not becoming close buddies with them as coworkers. Even so, it can be touchy. One way to prevent potential problems is to discuss your changed role with them in a friendly, sincere way. You can tell them how much you value their friendship. Although you haven't changed as a person, your role has changed. Therefore, your relationships will need to change somewhat. Point out that the other members of the department can make life difficult for them as well as for you if they sense you are playing favorites. Stress the need for teamwork, fairness, and good working relationships.

Keep your ears open, but evaluate what your workers tell you. Whether Jane is complaining about Jim's nasty attitude or singing the praises of Carol, ask probing questions of both Jane and others before making verbal or action commitments. Always ask yourself, "Why is he or she telling me this?" and follow up by getting other opinions or information—tactfully and discreetly, of course.

When your people aren't getting the results they should, look behind their reasons, especially if they're passing the buck. Ask yourself, "Is politics being used to cover up?" A related question is, "What methods are being used to impress me?" Sort out puffery from true achievement. See the discussion of handling political game players later in this chapter.

On the other hand, do your share in the relationship by being a fair, supportive boss. Be sensitive to human relationships as well as to the need for productivity by considering some of these suggestions: Show respect for subordinates by promptly responding to their telephone calls, memos, and requests. Don't keep them waiting outside your office or in meetings. Accompany unusual requests with an explanation.

Let your workers know, subtly and without bragging, that you have powerful connections by mentioning their names in work contexts. ("J. B. and I were discussing this problem the other day.") Then go to bat for your people when they deserve it, and always follow through on your commitments to them. Workers like having a powerful boss they can respect.

Help your workers achieve their goals, then give them credit. Handle their errors and shortcomings in private and avoid pinpointing the blame when discussing errors to others. Back your workers up whenever you can. Above all, aim for fairness and equity within your department; your actions should reassure people that they'll always get a fair shake.

Cooperating with Peers

In most organizations you must be generally accepted by your peers or colleagues in order to develop an effective power base and to climb the ladder. As you move to higher positions, you will find it increasingly important to get peer cooperation in order to achieve the objectives you set for your job. Managers who form strong peer alliances by sharing successes and helping peers are likely to be thought of as having leadership quality.

In the world of male managers, one way to operate, survive, and get ahead is to trade favors with peers: "You scratch my back and I'll scratch yours." In this system, managers keep mental track of the IOUs they hold for favors granted as well as those they owe to other managers. They try to cash them in wisely in order to achieve their highest-priority goals.

Here's an example of turning a negative into a positive by establishing peer solidarity: Bob Pirosky, Advertising Manager, refused to cooperate with Carrie in providing ads for one of her important customers. As a result, Lighthouse was in danger of losing the customer's business. If Carrie had gone to Jan Arguello, Vice President of Sales, to complain, she probably could have forced Bob to cooperate in the future, but she would have made an enemy. Bob would have "owed her one" in the negative sense and would have waited for her to stumble so he could cause trouble for her. Instead, Carrie went to Bob and worked the problem out with him, promising him that once they worked it out, the matter would go no further. Carrie would keep her mouth shut. In this way, she made an ally of Bob instead of an enemy. Now Bob owes her one in the positive rather than the negative sense—and he'll probably be more cooperative with Carrie in the future than he would have been if his boss, Jan, had instructed him to cooperate.

Trading favors signals that you're a team player. Here are some other positive signals: You share the credit for your achievements with others who have helped. You look for opportunities to offer information and constructive opinions and to touch base with your peers. You also look for opportunities to compliment them, focusing on concrete accomplishments, passing on others' praise of them, and individualizing your compliments. You ask for their advice in their areas of expertise. You avoid devious political tactics and, in general, appear more interested in the welfare of the firm than in feathering your own nest.

If you carry the team player idea a step further, you can show leadership. Take the initiative and find out what your colleagues' most pressing needs and wants are and what problems they're having in achieving their goals. You can learn a great deal *if*: (1) you're friendly and regularly available to chat; (2) you gain your peers' trust through showing supportiveness, solving problems, and keeping confidences; and (3) you listen well and ask probing but tactful questions. (See Chapter 6 for a discussion of listening and questioning skills.) Then do what you can to help your peers meet their most important needs.

Is Peer A having trouble relating well with his boss? Perhaps you can put in a good word for him at an opportune moment. If Peer A is present when you do this, so much the better. If not, let him know what you did, but tell him in a casual, tactful way. Does Peer B really want to find a job with a different type of firm? Help her make the right connections and she will become part of your external support network.

Although virtually all successful women managers gain the cooperation of their male colleagues, women cannot really be a part of the "old boy network" that is a tradition in the male world. Therefore, women need to develop their own equivalent of it—women's networks, both within the company and externally within a particular field or area of interest.

Since women managers are still relatively rare in most organizations, it may be necessary to have some sort of formal network to get things started. This might be a task-related group with a meaningful function to perform for the organization. One possibility is a women's task force to aid in the recruitment and selection of other women. New women that are hired can then be brought into the network. Another example is an ongoing series of meetings where women help each other gain insight into any problems in their current job situations. The group could encourage its members to support each other instead of siding with men against other women. Regardless of the form the women's network takes, its main goal would be to give its members support and to offer feedback and valuable information.

Virtually every major city now has a number of women's organizations that serve the function of providing a support network outside the company. In addition, there are many national women's organizations and networks. For more details, check your telephone directory, watch for newspaper articles that give information about such organizations, and check issues of magazines directed toward business and professional women that frequently include information on networks. See Appendix 2, Magazines for Career Women, at the back of this book. Also see Appendix 1, Networks: Women's Organizations, for a list of the national offices of women's groups that may appeal to you. Call or write for information about local groups in your area.

Supporting Your Boss

Your boss needs to know that he or she can depend on you. Show in every way possible that you will prevent and solve all but the hairiest problems in your bailiwick and that you recognize when to get the boss' input before blasting ahead on your own. Be alert to opportunities to make your boss look good, especially to his or her own bosses. Develop trust by reporting only to your boss, honoring the chain of command in all but the rarest, most extreme cases. Going over your boss' head to complain or get a decision reversed is usually political suicide.

Help your boss reach her or his objectives. You may have to probe tactfully to get a clear picture of what the boss is trying to accomplish. All too frequently bosses don't have clear, specific objectives. It's worth your while, because supporting your boss in achieving objectives is one of the best ways of winning his or her support in return.

If you think you can improve your boss' policies, procedures, or methods of operating, first gain his or her trust by focusing on what's good about departmental operations. Communicate your admiration and approval. Gain the boss' trust by showing you're a loyal team player. Then you can start suggesting ways to make "a good operation even better," one step at a time. If your changes are successful, give the boss credit, but be sure to file away memos documenting your role for use in promotion or raise negotiations. By giving your boss credit for successes, you lay the groundwork for acceptance of your future recommendations for change.

Consider documenting your boss' accomplishments as well as your own, passing on copies or accumulating information to produce at an opportune time. Look for opportunities sincerely to compliment, support, and touch bases with your boss in positive ways, as suggested in dealing with peers. Many of these same approaches are con-

structive in gaining the support of top management as well.

Becoming Visible to Top Management

Are you so in awe of the top people in a large organization, especially those who have some power over your life, that you avoid them or become tongue-tied in their presence? If so, refer to the relaxation and visualization exercises at the end of Chapter 4. Use them to become comfortable with powerful people, first through visualization and then in actual practice. Becoming visible to top management can put you on the fast track and may attract a mentor to your cause.

The most effective approach to impressing top management involves sensitivity, judgment, and balance. The impression you'll convey is that you're committed, deeply involved, and competent at your job, as well as friendly and good-natured in your dealings with bosses.

Getting to know the top people requires taking initiative and being assertive in a positive way. Look for opportunities to express sincere approval, admiration, and support of their programs and policies. If you can't sincerely support something, then stay quiet about it. If you have unique knowledge or information about why the program is headed for problems, relay it through proper channels in a manner that focuses on the benefit to management and the organization. On the other hand, avoid appearing pushy, being an automatic yes-person, or using manipulative flattery. Most executives aren't dense.

Avoid trivia in conversations with bosses. A little small talk may be necessary to get started, but quickly shift to larger issues that involve or affect the company. Your opportunities to initiate conversations may be brief—in the elevator or hallway. Stay prepared. Formulate your ideas on current issues as they come up, practice verbalizing them to friends, and be ready when you have an opportunity to respond to an inquiry or to initiate a conversation.

Take advantage of opportunities to become visible to top management. Join business and social clubs that provide contacts. Send copies of articles mentioning the executive's achievements or items of interest to him or her. Send notes of congratulations. Keep appropriate people informed of your activities and progress by sending copies of memos or articles.

Show that you would fit into top management through your dress, manners, and habits. Display the right reading material and other items in your office, using top managers as role models but not overstepping your bounds by displaying items reserved only for them.

Become associated with special projects and task forces, especially those that will include meetings with top managers. Then make the most of those meetings by being thoroughly prepared, asking intelligent questions (but not questions that will put a top manager on the spot), volunteering crucial information at opportune moments, and sharing credit with others. Be objective, keep your emotions under control, and stay cool under pressure to show you're executive material. (More on this in Chapter 4.)

Working with a Mentor

In most organizations, entrance to middle- and top-management positions is not determined by mere competence. It depends on acceptance by those who are most powerful and influential. This is one reason virtually all people who make it to the top have at least one mentor or sponsor from this powerful, influential group. This fact is consistently reported by researchers who have investigated how men and women make it to the top. Here are some typical questions that arise.

What Is a Mentor? A mentor is a more experienced person at a higher level in your organization who takes a promising younger person under his or her wing as a protégé. The mentor takes a *personal*, somewhat parental interest in the protégé, to some degree above and beyond the usual professional relationship. Male mentors are referred to in some organizations as godfathers or rabbis.

What Does a Mentor Do? Most mentors are especially helpful in the areas of self-presentation, positioning, and connecting—the essential aspects of promotability that are above and beyond technical competence. In helping you, a mentor can

Teach, advise, counsel, coach, guide, and sponsor

Give insights into the business

Serve as a sounding board for decision-making

Be a constructive critic

Provide necessary information for career advancement

Show how to move effectively through the system

Help cut through red tape at times

Teach the "political ropes" and introduce you to the right people

Stand up for you in meetings or discussions with his or her peers; in case of controversy, fight for you

Suggest you as a likely candidate when appropriate opportunities come along

Increase your visibility; single you out from the crowd of competitors surrounding you and argue your virtues against theirs

Provide an important signal to other people that you have his or her backing, helping to provide you with an aura of power and upward mobility.

Regardless of the appraisal system an organization uses and its formal attempts at objectively rewarding and promoting people, mentors still make a difference.

How Do You Get a Mentor?   If you can get a mentor to do for you even some of the things just listed, your chances of advancement are drastically improved. If mentors are necessary to the success of men in a large organization (as most authorities tell us they are), then they are probably indispensable to the success of women. After all, women have more barriers to overcome, less access to inside information, less training from childhood in areas essential for business success.

If you have the opportunity to relate to more than one, by all means do—as long as none is a political enemy of the others. Becoming the protégé of an appropriate mentor can be more difficult for a woman, however, than for a man. Mentors tend to identify with their protégés and see something of themselves in them. This means males tend to adopt males. Experienced women executives may feel the same way, but they are still rare in the business world.

Like any friendship, the mentor-protégé relationship cannot be forced: Either the chemistry is right or it's not. However, you can certainly take some initiative in becoming a likely protégé, in such ways as these:

- Be sure you know where you want to go and are fully committed to getting there. Good mentors want to feel their efforts are not wasted.

- Do everything you can to become a promotable manager, including projecting that image.

- Become visible within the organization.

- Show that you are eager and able to learn.

You can also take steps toward locating potential mentors, getting to know them, and increasing the likelihood of their adopting you. Examples of such actions include the following:

1. Identify the most powerful, secure, and upwardly mobile people in your organization. Which are the most likely candidates for mentor? Be sure they are respected and have influence.

2. Figure out ways to become acquainted with your candidates so you can see if a sense of rapport develops.

3. Seek their advice. Ask intelligent, thoughtful questions. Avoid acting helpless. Don't say, "I don't know what to do about this"; say, "I would appreciate your reactions to these two ideas I'm considering." Give the impression of a competent executive searching for input in order to make intelligent decisions. To avoid offending the person in case you don't follow the advice, use it as a takeoff for discussion of the problem and don't arrive at a clear-cut conclusion during the discussion.

4. Ask for further support if the relationship goes well. Use a direct approach at this point. Tell your potential mentor that you would like his or her help in

learning the ropes, developing your potential, contributing to the organization, and/or reaching your goals.

5. Communicate that you are fully committed to achieving your goals. It's especially important for women to do this, for many men assume a woman is not really committed to her career.

If you are still in college, look for a professor who might serve as a mentor. The teacher/student relationship can naturally deepen into that of mentor/protégé. Your professor can throw many opportunities your way and even help you to land a job.

As a student you can get an early start on both job-hunting and finding a mentor by enrolling in an internship program. Many business schools have them, especially those located near metropolitan business centers. Such programs involve part-time work in a business or government organization, and they give you an opportunity to apply the principles you learned in school and to gain firsthand experience of business operations. They frequently lead to full-time employment upon graduation.

What Are Some Dos and Don'ts? Here are some suggestions and precautions for dealing with potential and actual mentors:

1. Be sure your mentor gets her or his reward from the relationship. What does she or he want from it? The satisfaction of watching you grow? The knowledge that another key position is being filled by a competent person? A vocal supporter for his or her "team"? The mentor/protégé relationship should be a give-and-take one. Are you ready and able to give your mentor what he or she is looking for?

2. If your mentor's position is higher than your own manager's, you have to be careful how you use the reflected power. Avoid alienating your own boss or "cashing in your chips too soon."

3. Try to team up with a winner. If your mentor falls from power, you may fall also.

4. If your potential mentor is male, he may get the impression that sexual attraction is the basis for your interest in him. You may avoid misunderstanding by telling him directly that you are interested in being just friends and learning about the company and the job from him. (If you do become sexually involved with your mentor, you open the door to a whole new set of potential problems, discussed later in this chapter.)

5. Some excellent potential mentors will be reluctant to adopt you as a protégé because *they* want to avoid the sexual innuendo that might result. This is another good reason for the woman manager to establish a reputation in the organization as an above-board professional who "keeps her skirt clean."

6. Be aware that some male managers will take on a high-performing woman protégé just to show they can handle a "tricky" management situation and solve a problem for the corporation. Where will you be once this mentor proves his point?

7. Finally, know when and how to change the mentor/protégé relationship. If your mentor is not helping you to grow and move along as you think you should, it's time to look for one who will. If you find you have chosen unwisely and your mentor is insecure in his job or is threatened by you, you must look for another one. Even if you have chosen wisely and find an ideal mentor, the day will come when you must outgrow your dependency and become more autonomous. It's up

to you to be sure that the relationship moves from that of mentor/protégé to that of two professionally equal managers. If you don't outgrow the relationship, you'll almost surely get stuck in middle management. If you want to move on to top management, you must become more autonomous.

HANDLING POLITICAL GAMES

Battle-scarred veterans from all types of organizations have estimated that 75 percent of the managers who are forced out of their jobs fail because of organizational politics. Women are often more naïve and vulnerable to such treachery than men. When you move into a management job, you must assess your political savvy, for you will inevitably become the target of certain political game players.

The extent to which you become embroiled in their games depends on your attitude toward people and your personal power in foiling game plans. As a general rule, if you respect people and are reasonably direct and honest with them, most of them are likely to respond in kind. On the other hand, if you initiate power games by using devious political tactics, most people will respond with their own games. Unfortunately, no matter how straight you play, you can suffer extreme agony, and even defeat, at the hands of the few inveterate game players found in every organization. To avoid such agony, you must study the various types of games you may encounter so you can recognize what's going on. Of course, you don't want to overreact and become unduly suspicious, but neither do you want to play Little Red Riding Hood, just waiting to be eaten alive.

Let's explore the games most likely to be played by bosses, rivals, and workers. Then we'll look at some general strategies you can adopt for foiling the game plans of even the master players, while keeping your dignity intact and perhaps emerging in an even stronger position.

Recognizing Game Players: Bosses' Games

Most bosses are fairly straightforward. In many organizations those who go the furthest are people who are fair and reasonable in their dealings with subordinates (even though they may be pretty foxy with their rivals). Unfortunately, there are exceptions. Bosses' games are the deadliest, since they have the most power over your job security. In the early stages these games are designed merely to undermine you; later, in the "hardball" stage, the goal is to get rid of you. Let's consider first the "softball" games, those intended to undermine you.

Subtle exclusion is perhaps the most common game directed against women by males in power—both by bosses and rivals. For example, at meetings the men listen politely to your contributions, then continue the conversation as if you had said nothing. Later one of them may present a similar or identical idea phrased in a slightly different way, and it is accepted and perhaps adopted by the group. Of course you get no credit. Or they may fail to include you in planning and decision-making, meetings, business-related social functions, or business trips. The key to handling this game is to determine if the exclusion is an oversight, a test of your assertiveness, or the first step of an all-out war. Then develop your own game plan accordingly.

If it's an oversight or test of your assertiveness, you'll probably have to bring up the unpleasant fact that you're being excluded. You can easily fall into the role of shrew or nag unless you confront exclusion matter-of-factly without a trace of emotion. Keep your goal in mind (being included *and* accepted), stick to the facts, and assume that the exclusion is an "unintentional oversight." Project the image of a cool, rational, professional person; focus on the business reasons that make it important for you to be included. For example, at a meeting where your idea is adopted as the contribution of someone else, you might say, "Bob, I like the way we work together and bounce ideas off each other. You took my suggestion of . . . and gave it a slightly different twist, so we ended up with . . . "

If you decide the oversight means all-out war, consider setting up your own meetings, merely by-passing your boss or rival. Focus on strengthening your own support group.

Divide and conquer is an old game in which you and your peers are set up to be suspicious of each other or to fight among yourselves so you're less likely to form an alliance against the boss. Good managers encourage teamwork; so be on guard if your boss doesn't. Tactful questioning of peers can unearth this game, and peer solidarity can stymy it, even without forming an antiboss alliance.

Stealing ideas and credit is a particularly obnoxious game weak bosses play. You do the work or come up with the original idea, and the boss takes all the credit. To protect yourself, write memos to your boss that document your ideas and accomplishments—with one copy to his or her boss and one for the permanent file you keep on yourself.

Death on the vine refers to a game played with your plan or program. For some rea-

son the boss doesn't want to oppose your plan, but she doesn't want it implemented. So she says she'll go ahead with it, then plays a stalling game until it eventually dies. Whether you call her hand or back off gracefully will depend on the circumstances.

Now let's go on to the hardball games, those intended to get rid of you. First we'll review the most common hardball games bosses play; then we'll discuss some tactics for coping with them.

The setup is probably the most common game male bosses have used against women they were forced to accept under Affirmative Action rulings. It involves setting you up in an assignment or project where you are likely to look bad or fail completely. Then they fail to give you the support and resources you need to succeed. If you blow it, the boss tells others, "Let's face it; a woman just can't hack this job."

Abolishing the position is an especially devious way of getting rid of opposition. Instead of firing a person, the boss gets the job position eliminated, then "regretfully" lets the person go since there's no longer a job for him or her to do.

Kicking up is a game to get an unfavored subordinate out of a meaningful job into a meaningless one by giving her a promotion, a raise, and a fancy title, but little or no power or responsibility. Get full information about any job promotion offer, whether or not you suspect they may be trying to kick you up.

Threat of a bad reference is a game to force a subordinate to resign so the boss won't have to fire him or her. The person is promised a favorable reference if he or she resigns and threatened with a negative one if not.

Making life miserable may be played when the boss has inadequate grounds for firing someone he or she wants out. The tactics range from phrasing all communications in a negative tone to frequently transferring the employee from town to town, giving a family person a job requiring constant travel, transferring a city type to the "boonies," and other "legitimate" actions designed to make life miserable.

Preventing retaliation is a strategy of bosses for getting rid of people they have wounded in battle so they won't have to worry about past victims' getting revenge later. Your best protection from ruthless bosses—and rivals—who play power games to win is to stay out of their way and make sure they understand you are not a threat.

Defending Yourself in Hardball Games Before we move on to other types of games and ways of foiling them, let's discuss ways of handling this most difficult challenge: the boss who plays games designed to oust you. These games are difficult to counter without powerful contacts in higher management or a strong peer support group that can bring pressure to bear. Therefore, building a support network may be your most important defense. Another important preventive measure is to insist on specific, measurable goals and standards—for your job and for each major assignment (the boss' expectations for the end results). Make sure they're reasonable; then make sure you achieve them.

If all else fails, you will have to weigh several countermoves according to their chances for success: (1) confronting your boss with the situation and trying to work through the causes and possible solutions;

(2) going over your boss' head to find a solution or to ask for a transfer; (3) making the best of the situation for a while if you think the boss may be moved soon; (4) finding another job; (5) fighting the boss through legal action. If you see you're losing the fight within the organization, however, the best career decision is usually to find another job. Resort to outside legal action only if you decide that proving a point about principles and fairness is more important than your career.

Rivals' Games

Even though you signal that you are a team player, and even though you look for ways to cooperate with and help your peers, you'll run into an occasional game player who considers you fair game.

Discrediting is the most common game rivals play to belittle their competition (you) through direct accusation or innuendo. Even more deadly is the back-stabbing game, in which the rival pretends to be nice and tries to befriend you. This tactic is intended to disarm you and encourage you to furnish information that the rival will later use as ammunition against you. A milder form of discredit is to raise questions about your capabilities: Is she irreplaceable? Is she overloaded? Is she more of a specialist than a generalist?

Setup for a flareup is a strategy to provoke a rival into losing her temper, crying, or otherwise losing control. First the game player discovers your most sensitive areas. Then in front of others the game player innocently asks you a related, leading question designed to trigger your defenses. Your best protection is to keep quiet at work about sensitive areas, work on internally desensitizing those areas, and if you still feel your emotions going out of control, find a businesslike reason to exit—for example, "I must call New York in five minutes." See Chapter 4 for more suggestions on handling emotions.

Faint message is a technique used by peers who are obligated to pass on information to you but do so in an obscure way, hoping you won't grasp it and act on it. They might include it in a lengthy computer printout or long memo on other routine topics. Carried one step further, the rival actually double-crosses you by giving you incorrect information to lead you into mistakes.

Self-serving advice refers to the unfriendly tactic of giving advice that serves the advisor's own ends even when it has disastrous results for the advisee.

The case file is a devious tactic played by some rivals; some even keep files on everyone in the office. They jot down the dates and circumstances of any suspicious actions, for example, as well as reports, letters, and other documents containing errors or possible gaffes. Such file-builders hope to build a case against each rival and discredit him or her—or at least to protect themselves if attacked by another.

Workers' Games

Finally, there are games that tend to be played by workers—games that drain a manager's power unless she intercepts them.

Crisis creation may be played at several levels, but it becomes your problem when it's played by your subordinates. They create crises or exaggerate problems so

they can be assigned the job of resolving them. Their payoffs may include getting to work on a project they like, gaining visibility and recognition for playing rescuer, or becoming known as an indispensable problem-solver. To break up this game, give workers greater rewards and more attention for anticipating and preventing problems than for solving them. See Chapter 9 on problem prevention.

Indispensable is a similar game that is usually based on keeping such poor records that no one else can step in and replace the worker when he or she is out. Review all recordkeeping procedures, and require workers to prepare written procedures for all their recurring tasks.

Help the opposition right out the door is a strategy for removing rivals by finding a way to get them hired by other organizations. Since the more competent workers may be removed in this way, your department may be weakened as a result. Keep communication lines open with workers, and ask probing questions of any who mention leaving.

Highway robbery is a trick workers occasionally play in order to get a raise or other perks. Such workers know their services are critical for completing a key stage in a project, for example, so they threaten to change companies unless their demands are met. You may have to give in, but you can start building a file on such workers' tactics and errors. If you can justify firing them as soon as the project is completed, the lesson won't be lost on their coworkers.

Let her hang is a game based on the notion that if some people are given enough rope they will hang themselves. The game player would like to see you hang yourself, but instead of giving you something, he or she withholds things, such as information, feedback about your errors, or new developments.

Tell her what she wants to hear can have the same results as "let her hang," but it may have a different motive, such as a desire to avoid confrontation and unpleasantness. Feeling that the bearer of bad news will be unwelcome, this subordinate will turn it into good news, despite some reliable data to the contrary.

Social Games

Socializing with people from any level of your organization may be tempting. Sometimes it's harmless; sometimes it's extremely helpful for gaining useful information, cementing relationships, and making transactions more effective on the job. In general, avoid the traps discussed so far: becoming too personal or intimate, getting involved unnecessarily in other people's battles, and engaging in negative gossip (it often finds its way back to its victim).

You'll avoid most of the potential problems if you view all work-connected social functions and contacts as primarily business occasions and contacts. The office party, therefore, is *not* the place to let your hair down, drink until you're feeling no pain, have a ball, or otherwise let it all hang out. Confine those activities to parties with your close friends or other groups. While your work associates may enjoy your performance, you can be sure the decision-makers (and probably their spouses) are observing all your actions. So whether it's a casual drink after work, the company picnic, or the Christmas party, keep your professional image intact by carefully monitoring your behavior, as well as your escort (if unmar-

ried) and your attire. This approach will pay off in the long run.

During these functions, how does the promotable woman handle such questions as who pays the restaurant or bar tab, opens doors, or helps with wraps? She simply follows the same commonsense rules of etiquette she uses when socializing with a woman friend: The person who did the inviting pays the tab, or they agree to go halves. The person who gets to the door first opens it for the other. If one of them is struggling to get into or out of a wrap (or a car), the other helps out.

Foiling the Game Plans

We've covered briefly some of the political games business people play and a few tactics for countering those games. One reason people are sometimes intrigued with political games, however, is that their variations are endless, and each situation with its particular players is unique. Therefore, you'll need to adapt the following general strategies for foiling game plans to your unique situation.

Look for the Cause The first step in devising your own game plan is to look for the reasons behind the player's actions. What is he or she trying to accomplish or avoid? Is the game played at a conscious or unconscious level? Unconscious games are more difficult to counter because the player probably won't understand a direct confrontation. Is it really a game or just an oversight or misunderstanding? The latter may require only a tactful but direct confrontation. Is the game a test of your spunk or savvy? Or is it the first skirmish in an all-out war to discredit or remove you? The longer game players can keep you in the dark about their undermining activities, the better their chances of success. This means you must nip any war efforts in the bud without overreacting to mere tests, misunderstandings, or oversights. Figuring all this out is difficult for beginners and is a necessary part of gaining experience. Discuss problems with trusted mentors and more experienced friends.

Don't Take It Personally This is probably the most difficult—and the most important—key to foiling game plans. With experience and hindsight, you'll find it easier to realize that these people will inflict their games on anyone in your position—if they think they can get away with it. It has nothing to do with you as a person—in fact the game players don't really know you. They don't bother to get to know people on an authentic, personal basis, but only on a manipulative basis. Their main motive for learning about you is to discover how to pull your strings. So don't assume there's something wrong with you, become defensive, or rise to their bait. Keep your counsel and decide on your own game plan. (See the discussion on taking things personally in Chapter 4.)

Stay Goal-oriented Keeping your personal goals in mind can keep you from getting sidetracked with overemotional, ego-protecting responses. In each political situation, ask yourself, "How does this affect my personal goals? Company goals? What results do I want from this situation?" Then couch your responses in terms of company goals, if possible.

Develop a Support Network and Use It To succeed, political games must have the cooperation—whether knowing or unwitting—of people. Isolated victims are the most vulnerable. Therefore, a key to foiling game plans is the power base comprised of your network of supporters at all levels. To maintain balanced relationships, keep in mind the IOU system. Ask for supportive action selectively, where it will do the most good; then look for opportunities to repay the favor.

Be Knowledgeable Begin by knowing the basics: everything in the company manual and employees' handbook; company policies, strategies, goals, procedures, and rules; legal aspects of employee relations and company activities. You can limit game players' potential moves by knowing the score in these basic areas. Also learn as much as you can about the unwritten rules, and keep in touch with day-to-day events. Keep lines of communication open with as many people as possible, and keep your antennae up at all times. Never make the mistake of thinking you have it made so you needn't pay attention to political games. You're never immune.

Know Your Rights and Be Assertive In addition to knowing your basic organizational and legal rights, identify your personal rights and learn how to assert them effectively. See Chapter 5 for a wider discussion of asserting yourself.

Read Nonverbal Messages The most astute managers have learned to pick up and understand people's nonverbal messages. In fact, by merely taking a walk through the office, they can pick up reams of information. This skill is especially valuable in identifying and foiling game players. Few of them are such accomplished actors that they can totally control their nonverbal behavior in order to hide their emotions and ulterior motives. Body language, facial expression, and voice tone will often give them away. See the discussion on this in Chapter 5.

Document Transactions Follow up all important or questionable transactions with a written memo to the appropriate person, perhaps with copies to key people. Keep your copies on file where you can find them easily if you need them. They can be invaluable in backing up your case when you need to confront a player's game. Document your achievements also.

Observe Behavior Patterns   People's behavior patterns tend to be consistent. If you observe one person stabbing another in the back, you can be pretty sure that person would stab you in the back sooner or later.

Focus on the Leader of a Group Game   Sometimes a game is played by several people, especially among your peers or workers. When they band together to work against you in some way, it's usually most effective to determine who is the leader of the attack. Then focus your counterattack on the leader only; ignore the others. You have a better chance of winning a battle with one person than with several. If you are successful, the others will quickly get the message and lay off.

Stay in Command of Your Inner Resources   This ability goes hand in hand with not taking attacks personally. Together they furnish the power you need to transcend games. The exercises in Chapter 4 for relaxing, visualizing, and letting go of needs will enable you to command your inner resources. They'll help you to achieve a relaxed focus on your goals so your inner self, or subconscious, can pick up verbal and nonverbal clues to people's intentions. They'll enable you to put games in perspective and not take threats personally, as well as to respond in a relaxed but effective manner. Your key defense, therefore, is to maintain your self-confidence by commanding these inner resources.

STEERING CLEAR OF STEREOTYPED FEMALE ROLES

Changing your focus and taking steps to develop a support network will go a long way toward helping you make a successful transition to management. However, much of your good work can be wiped out if you allow yourself to fit other people's stereotypes about the ways women behave.

Handling Sexual Stereotypes

Perhaps the largest single problem women managers face stems from sex-role stereotyping. Most of the men you'll encounter will probably try to place you in some category they are familiar with. Most variations on this theme can be placed in one of the following four categories.

Mother or maiden aunt. Men look to her for nurturing. If she accepts the role, she will probably at times be nurturing and at other times critical and demanding. She tends to be subjective and judgmental.

Daughter or kid sister. Men have a paternal attitude toward her. They tend to overprotect her but not take her seriously. She in turn may play the role of big sister to her female subordinates. Her friendliness may turn to jealousy if her subordinate becomes a rival for her job.

Sexpot. Men tend to look to her for a little excitement and flirtation, either covert or overt.

Hard-hearted Hannah. Men learn that she refuses to fit into any of the first three categories. Her insistence on being her own competent self is interpreted as hardness. The men may leave her alone, especially when she most needs their assistance or cooperation.

Because of these stereotypes, women managers find it difficult to be themselves, to act naturally. They may feel compelled to *react;* rather than just *act* naturally. They tend to respond in one of two ways: (1) They accept the stereotyped role rather than fight it: This means limiting their range of behavior, including some of the effective behavior appropriate to career advancement. Or (2) they try to avoid stereotyped roles by constantly monitoring their behavior and attempting to eliminate any action that might reinforce such stereotyping. This also can lead to unnatural or self-conscious behavior at times.

Men tend to protect women stereotyped in the first three categories. This protection, though sometimes essential to survival, prevents the woman from fighting her own battles. It limits and handicaps her. Men tend to feel threatened by Hard-hearted Hannah and keep their distance. She may find herself without the help or cooperation essential to functioning, and perhaps surviving, when she needs it most.

Men often have problems in establishing themselves in new jobs, but they don't encounter these problems with the frequency and intensity that women do. Women often have to deal with these problems in every new situation, with new associates, and so forth. They are probably even more affected than men by the need for self-repression and the need to refrain from certain kinds of expressiveness and self-disclosure. Women may find it difficult to comfortably participate in the customary ways of relaxing and easing tension, such as various forms of business socializing and joking.

Dealing with sexual stereotypes, then, tends to create unnaturalness and tension for women managers. Here are some ways to handle this problem:

1. Separate conflicting role expectations— your own and other's. Realize that you can't exhibit opposite kinds of behavior at the same time. For example, you can't be both a "poor little me" helpless kid sister and a promotable woman. Keep the image you want in mind and act accordingly.

2. Don't automatically and unthinkingly fall into others' expectations about your role. Instead of fitting into a stereotyped role, rise above it by firmly identifying your own professional image, goals, and priorities; identifying organizational and departmental work goals; and communicating with others in terms of goal achievement. (See Chapters 6 and 13.)

3. Develop strong *outside* support groups that you can relax with and be yourself with.

4. Use stress-reducing techniques to relax and to keep in touch with "who you are" (see the exercises in Chapter 4).

Perceptions of the Woman Boss

Attitudes toward the woman boss are changing, but women still must overcome some preconceived notions about their suitability for the role. A 1982 survey of business college students revealed these attitudes [6]:

When asked whether their mental picture of a boss was initially a man or a woman, 79 percent of the males and 71 percent of the females said "a man."

When asked if women supervisors often have greater difficulty controlling their subordinates, 67 percent of the males and 61 percent of the females answered "yes."

However, when asked if they could work for a woman boss, 94 percent of the males and 99 percent of the females said "yes." And in response to whether women were too emotional to be good logical decision-makers, 81 percent of the males and 97 percent of the females said "no." This contrasts with a 1977 study by Dr. Donald Jewell, which revealed that a majority of both males and females considered women executives inferior to men in the areas of decision-making, handling emotions, and responding to criticism [12].

Your subordinates and peers may include former students of the 1977 class, as well as the 1982 and other classes. And they may have even more specific perceptions of the woman boss.

Male Subordinates Another 1982 survey, conducted by Dr. Alma Baron [2], revealed a discrepancy between what men say about female executives and what they really feel. While nearly half the 8,000 men who responded agreed that in time women executives will become commonplace, over half believed that women are not generally as career oriented as men. Only half the men believed that women make good executives, and 40 percent had distinct misgivings about the woman boss. They offered seven reasons: (1) Women lack confidence in the role. (2) Women lack clout—real power. (3) Women don't know how to play the game. (4) Women come on too strong, try too hard. (5) Men are awkward with a woman boss, don't know how to treat her. (6) Men feel they lose face when they are subordinate to a woman. This holdover of the traditional belief that women are inferior, at least in business acumen, was most predominant in men over 35. (7) When they perceive that the woman is only a token for Affirmative Action purposes, men feel they must pay the price by having to function under an unqualified boss.

Men who report to a woman are sometimes almost impossible to please. If their female boss has an objective, businesslike approach, she may be labeled as a Hardhearted Hannah, a castrating female. On the other hand, if the boss shows some warmth and concern for them on a personal level, she may be labeled a pushover, and they are quick to take advantage of her. The line between being too hard and too soft may be a very fine one. The woman manager must find the proper balance for her particular situation.

Male Peers Men on the same managerial level as the woman manager may feel threatened and resentful, especially if they are not particularly secure in their own jobs. As a result of their insecurity, the woman manager may get no information, help or suggestions from them, and she may finally realize that her male peers are sitting back and waiting for her to fail.

Perhaps a more common problem is merely oversight on the part of male peers, stemming from the fact that women traditionally have not been included in *informal* communication channels. For example, the woman manager may be excluded from a great deal of useful information that is exchanged in the men's room, in the locker room, on the golf course, and at the corner bar. Women need to know what's going on in the company—which way the wind is blowing. Some information is available *only* through informal channels.

It's sometimes easy to overlook what amounts to an invitation from a male colleague. If he says, "I'm (we're) going to lunch," that's probably your cue to say, "Good idea. I'll be right with you." Sometimes your only workable solution may be taking the initiative yourself. For example, when you see the men going to lunch, join them, if possible, even without a formal invitation. Your attitude should be casual and confident.

When the men head for the corner bar, you can ask to join them. This may lead to certain pitfalls, obviously, but there are ways to avoid them. Depending on your capacity, drink nonalcoholic beverages or have only one or two drinks. Insist quietly on paying for your own drinks or on taking your turn in buying an occasional round. Leave with the group, at least the first few times. Then relax and have a good time. If you're fun to be with, the group is more likely to want to have you around in the future. Your goal is for your male peers to be comfortable with you and to think of you as just another colleague.

In assessing your position with your male peers, your primary concerns should be whether you are (1) treated fairly, with an equal share of the work, responsibilities, and rewards, and (2) allowed to participate in the events and decisions that affect your job.

Male Bosses Bosses tend to fall into three broad types when it comes to stereotyped expectations of working women. The first is the *dinosaur* who has always believed that wives and mothers belong at home, that they simply aren't capable of coping as leaders in a "man's world." This type is easy to recognize and avoid.

The second type is the *two-headed monster* with one head professing sympathy for women's issues and supportiveness of women's career goals, and the other—whether consciously or subconsciously—thinking more like the dinosaur boss. He is probably the most typical and the most difficult type to deal with; it can be like fighting invisible smoke.

The *enlightened man* who is truly free of the traditional, stereotyped expectations of working women is rare and of course delightful to work for. With him you can move directly to dealing with the issues at hand.

Coping with the stereotyped ideas of bosses is especially difficult because they hold so much power over your career progression. We've already discussed some specific stereotypes and myths about women. The ones that may cause the most trouble when held by your boss are: Women are too emotional, they can't **"crunch the numbers"** (handle math, statistics, finance); they aren't good at decision-making—calculating risks, weighing rational alternatives, standing behind their choices; they aren't really dedicated to their careers—they'll probably quit when they start having babies; they can't take the hard knocks and roll with the punches—they take things too personally and can't handle criticism.

Female Subordinates Women tend to feel very strongly about their boss. They tend to think she is either one of the best or one of the worst. Here are some of their perceptions, both positive and negative:

Positive Traits of the Woman Boss

> She understands what it's like to be a working woman. For example, she knows I must have some warning if I am going to work late.

> She understands my problems. How can a man understand? Most of them have wives at home to worry about details.

> She understands better than a man what motivates people.

> She takes time to explain what she wants. She will tell me when I have done a good job, not just when I have made a mistake.

> She makes it clear that she cares about people, not just machinelike perfor-

mance. She has a way of bringing out the best in people.

Negative Traits of the Woman Boss

She's too moody and unprofessional.

She talks about me behind my back, when I can't defend myself. She doesn't level with me and tell me what she is thinking.

She doesn't help other women. You can't please her because in doing a good job you become a potential threat to her.

Female Bosses and Peers   Let's look at the two extremes you may encounter among female bosses and peers when it comes to stereotyped expectations of other working women. At one end of the spectrum the *queen bee* is usually a middle-aged or older manager who scratched and fought her way up in spite of the overwhelming odds against her advancement. She may have sacrificed much of her personal life and some of her femininity, leaving her pretty hard around the edges. She has enjoyed the attention of being a rare bird in the organization and does not welcome competition for the spotlight from bright, fresh-faced young women.

The best way to deal with her is to give her the respect she has earned; let her know you admire her achievements; ask for suggestions and information. Do *not* make the mistake of confiding in her. Don't tell her about your past or current problems, your personal life, or anything you would not want broadcast throughout the company. Remember, she is a fighter, and she will probably not hesitate to use such information against you when the time is ripe.

At the other end of the spectrum is the *liberated woman*, who is automatically biased in your favor. She believes career women should support each other and assumes you feel the same way. You would have to convince her that you were her enemy in order to alienate her. More and more career women are adopting this stance; most probably fall somewhere between the two ends of the spectrum.

Some Facts to Offset the Myths   The body of research concerning women's aptitudes and actual performance in new work roles is growing, providing a factual basis for repudiating some of the more damaging stereotyped ideas. For example, the Johnson O'Connor Research Foundation has been testing the aptitudes of both men and women since 1922 [18]. The test battery includes measures of sixteen primary aptitudes plus English vocabulary knowledge. On ten of these abilities there is no sex difference. Females have consistently scored higher than males on five of the remaining six abilities and on English vocabulary knowledge.

The five primary abilities in which women excel are (1) speed and accuracy in comparing pairs of numbers, (2) short-term memory for meaningless verbal material, (3) short-term memory for strings of numbers, (4) ability to identify detailed changes in a picture, and (5) finger dexterity.

On the other hand, men excelled in structural visualization, an aptitude for picturing solid forms in space from various angles. This ability is needed for such occupations as engineer, architect, and physicist. People who score high in this aptitude tend to deal with problems by visualizing them, while others tend to use abstract reasoning. A 1982 foundation report states that an abstract reasoning approach indicates an aptitude for such occupations as manager, teacher, and lawyer. In other words, even in the one area where women scored lower than men, the lower score indicates a higher aptitude for management.

Women not only have the aptitude for success as managers, but significant numbers of them are beginning to excel in this role. A 1979 study comparing the management styles of men and women showed that the woman boss scored higher than her male counterpart in (1) giving information, (2) strengthening interpersonal relations, (3) being receptive to ideas, and (4) encouraging effort [1]. Male bosses were (1) more dominant, (2) quicker to challenge others, and (3) more likely to direct the course of conversations. Since most successful organizations have moved toward a more participatory management style, one that is sensitive to worker needs and solicits their input in solving problems and reaching decisions, the performance strengths of the women executives may be even more valuable than those of the males.

On the other hand, this survey also revealed that employees have a higher expectation that female managers will promote happy relations. They are also more tolerant of men directing the conversation than they are of women.

Your Balanced Image   In dealing with men and women at every level of the organization, the woman boss will never please everyone. To find the highest level of acceptance and admiration, she must maintain a delicate balance in many areas, as shown in Figure 3-2.

Can you think of other areas where you as a woman manager must find a correct balance? If possible, discuss this with a friend or members of your study group. Add your characteristics to those shown in the figure.

Avoiding Secretarial, Clerical, and Housemaid Stereotypes

The stereotyped thinking of most businessmen tends to relegate any woman in the office to the traditional roles of secretary, clerk, or maid. If you allow yourself to be treated this way, you'll undermine your ability to perform your job and to advance to more responsible positions. Here are some suggestions for avoiding this trap.

1. *Think twice before letting anyone know you can type, take shorthand, or file.* Most male managers have little or no skill in these areas and don't use them on the job. If some of the male managers in your company practice one or more of these skills, such as typing their own letters or rough drafts of reports, should you do the same? Probably not, even though doing so is sometimes more efficient. Men can do these things without risking identification with secretarial and clerical roles; women usually cannot. (There are some exceptions, however. In many newspaper and publishing offices, for example, *everyone* types.) Banish such items as typewriters, filing cabinets, and shorthand pads from your office. Don't become known as a reliable source of files, papers, or extra copies. The planning and maneuvering all this may require is worthwhile.

2. *Avoid taking notes or minutes at meetings.* It's better to ask one of your associates to refresh your memory on some point than to take notes and risk projecting the image of a glorified secretary. Besides, you need to be free to observe the participants at the meeting because their nonverbal communication is much more revealing than what they actually say.

   Avoid letting the others make you the minutes-taker of meetings as well. If the same group meets regularly, then at the very least try to get an agreement that members will rotate the role of recording secretary. If you don't get such an agreement, or if the meeting is a one-time-only situation, and you get drafted, then take

FIGURE 3-2: The Delicate Balance of the Woman Manager

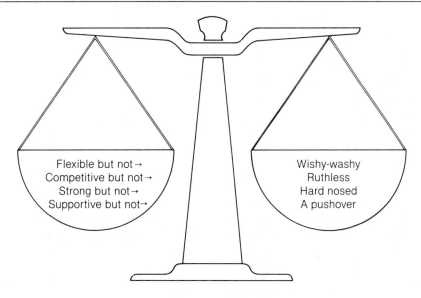

Flexible but not→
Competitive but not→
Strong but not→
Supportive but not→

Wishy-washy
Ruthless
Hard nosed
A pushover

Can you think of other areas where you as a woman manager must strike a balance?
If possible, discuss aspects of finding a good balance with a friend or with members of
your study group. Add your characteristics to those shown in the figure.

minutes as perfunctorily as possible. The minutes should be as brief and vague as you can make them. The idea you must convey is that you're *not* a secretary, let alone an efficient one. You want to shine in performing your *current* functions— not those of subordinates.

3. *Don't provide coffee or perform other "hostess" duties.* Bend over backward to avoid reinforcing the stereotyped female roles of servant, waitress, maid, or "office wife." Do not make or serve coffee, clean up the meeting room, call out for lunch orders, and bring "goodies" from home. If you're virtually ordered to perform such duties, try to get an agreement to rotate such chores so the men do their share. Do your part pleasantly but perfunctorily.

4. *Don't be caught dead doing knitting, crocheting, or needlework.* Add a shawl and granny glasses and you have the ladies' sewing circle transplanted to the conference room. Enough said?

5. *Don't automatically become associated with volunteer projects (unless it's a pet project of a top corporate officer).* The stereotype is that volunteer work is for women because they have nothing more important to do. Therefore, think about limiting visible volunteer work to corporate-wide charitable projects that can help you in your career plan. If you choose to devote some of your *personal* time to a charity, it may be best to keep this activity completely separate from your office activities until you're well established as a manager.

AVOIDING SEXUAL PROBLEMS

Nowhere is sexual game-playing more rampant than in the corporate world. As you climb the ladder, you'll need to be more watchful and tactful than ever because you'll be an increasingly attractive "catch." Here are some suggestions from your predecessors.

The Woman Is Usually the Loser in the Office Sex Game

The major fact to keep in mind is that as a woman you'll probably be the loser if you get involved in office sex games. Remember that you're operating in a male culture and playing by male rules. In *Games Mother Never Taught You*, Betty Harrigan has discussed sex games in great detail, along with some of the points that follow [11, pp. 287–315].

Although nearly all organizations profess to be against office sex, unofficially it's usually condoned for the men as long as they stay in control of the situation and are properly discreet. Don't make the mistake of thinking this liberal view of sexual affairs applies to you. You represent the target of the conquest and eventually the victim if you give in.

Office affairs are almost never a secret. Since sexual conquests of female employees are male status symbols, they would have no value unless the male made sure he got credit. However, if the man shows any sign of emotion or if there's any indication that the woman began the affair or will decide when it's over, the man loses status among his colleagues. If you try to change the rules of the game, therefore, you can expect a real battle from him.

The higher the level of the woman who is conquered, the greater will be the value of the status symbol. As you climb the corporate ladder, you can expect more determined efforts to get you into bed.

Corporate wives are off-limits and are kept in the dark at all costs about the sexual conquests of any of the husbands. This also goes for wives of important clients and associates in the same industry.

Many married executives conduct their lives on two levels, which might be dubbed "top level" and "bottom level." The top-level life is designed to preserve the appearance of the good family man, responsible executive, pillar of the community. The bottom level is designed to enhance the male ego through sexual conquest, to impress other males with his apparent sexual prowess, and to add some fun, variety, and excitement to his life through sexual encounters.

Men cooperate with each other in the balancing act of keeping the two levels properly separated so that the appearances so necessary for the top level remain untarnished. If you participate in the bottom level, you may be perceived as a threat to the top level once the affair is over. You will know too much about the bottom-level life of your former partner and perhaps about the lives of some of his colleagues as well. The safest way for men to handle this problem is to remove you from the scene; as a result, you may lose your job. Even if you get through this phase with your job intact, you may be automatically excluded from further promotions because you'll probably be branded "inferior."

Clients and suppliers are, generally speaking, included in the sex game along with people within the company. Your best bet may be to restrict your sex life to men in some completely different field.

To summarize: The objective of the office sex game is to increase the man's status with his peers and superiors. This is one of the ways he becomes "one of the boys" who make decisions about promotions and salaries. You may therefore increase the status of every man you have sex with and at the same time decrease your own status.

Get the Wives on Your Side

Get to know the wives and cement your position in the top level. It helps if the wives view you as a competent professional. It's even better if most of them like you as a person too. If you are happily married, be sure they know it and have opportunities to meet your husband. If you are not, it's even more helpful to get the wives on your side. Bring an appropriate man with you to any social occasion where wives are included, preferably a man who is *not* a business associate.

Your major focus and the message you want to convey is that you are not and will never be a candidate for an affair with any of the men in the company; you are a competent professional with a busy, satisfying personal life of your own.

Learn to Say "No" Gracefully

Given the fact that sex in the office is a losing game for you, how can you keep from playing? Here are some suggestions.

Don't allow men to use endearing terms without challenging them. These terms indicate possessiveness and can imply a personal relationship beyond normal business dealings. You can privately inform men who use them that terms such as "Doll," "Dear," "Darling," "Honey," and "Babe" have negative connotations for you and you're sure they don't intend to continue making you uncomfortable by addressing you in that manner.

Ignore innuendoes and subtle overtures. Pretend you don't get double meanings in this area. If the overtures become not so sub-

tle, change the subject to a job-related topic. Become more businesslike than ever.

If he persists, say you're not interested and give him a legitimate reason why you're not. Above all, avoid hurting his ego. The person with a hurt ego tends to lash back sooner or later. Your goal is to win as much professional respect and support from him as possible and still say "no."

Here are some possible responses: *If he's married,* tell him you appreciate his interest but you never go out with married men. *If he's not married,* tell him you would enjoy being with him, but you never accept social invitations from business friends. *If you're married,* tell him you'd like to join him but your husband would be hurt if he couldn't share the occasion. The underlying message you want to get across is that you like him but the answer to sexual involvement is "no" and will always be "no."

Have basically the same response for every man in the office, regardless of rank. The response is basically "no."

If a man in a higher position starts asking about your personal life, tell him about your career aspirations and plans. Give the impression that your career (or career plus husband) is your entire life. (See Chapter 5 for a further discussion and exercise on saying "no.")

If He Won't Take "No" for an Answer, Take Steps to Challenge Him

When does the office sex game become sexual harrassment? Lin Farley describes it as unwanted, unsolicited, and nonreciprocal male behavior that asserts a woman's sex role over her function as a worker [10]. It may be nonverbal, verbal, physical, or any combination of these. Certainly when the result is a threat to your job or career or a compulsion to leave the organization, the behavior may be considered sexual harrassment. Don't accept the victim role. Here are some specific steps you can take.

1. Keep a detailed record of what is said, when, and under what circumstances.

2. Let other people know about the situation—both friends of yours in the company and at least one superior you can trust.

3. Write a statement to be placed in your personnel file (without naming names at this point). Make an appointment with your Equal Employment Opportunity officer, and make a formal request for a record of your statement to be placed in your personnel file.

4. Formally request a job transfer and follow up on it.

5. Keep doing your job and maintain as much distance from him as you can.

6. Keep a file with copies of everything that's been written on the subject, a list of people who know about the situation, and the record of everything that was said. Get the advice of an EEO officer, a lawyer who specializes in discrimination cases, or some other *trusted* official on how to proceed.

The main thing to remember is that you needn't be afraid. There are things you can do. You *do* have some ability to handle these situations, and you *can* take steps in most cases to ensure that you don't have to leave or give in.

Retain the Best Aspects of Your Femininity

Here's where that important matter of balance enters the picture again. It's important for you to accept yourself and express yourself as a woman *and* as a competent manager. That balance will be a little different for each woman and each job situation. The extremes are what you want to avoid. On the one hand, do not try to be "one of the boys" by adopting some of the men's coarser behaviors, such as using foul language, pounding on the desk, or overindulging in alcohol. On the other hand, be careful not to come across as a "sexpot" because of the way you dress and behave.

We might view the range of behavior on a scale from 1 to 10, as shown in Figure 3-3. What you want to aim for is the "comfortable mean" signified by number 5: You enjoy being a woman *and* you know you have what it takes to be a competent manager.

FIGURE 3-3: The Executive Woman's Behavior: The Comfortable Mean

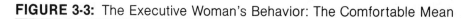

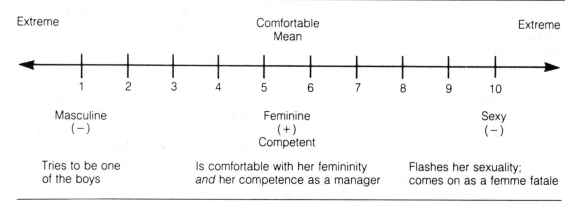

SUMMARY

When you become a manager, it's crucial to change your focus and your priorities in several ways: Concentrate on getting the work done through others rather than doing it yourself. Identify the true power structure within your organization. Learn about the customs and habits of the people you'll be working with. Project an image of being "your own person," and keep an appropriate emotional distance from work associates.

To be an effective manager, it's also crucial that you start at once to establish a support network among your workers, your bosses, and your peers. Get your *workers* on your side by gaining a reputation for fairness and objectivity and by keeping relationships on a friendly and professional level without close, emotional involvements. Collaborate effectively with your *peers* through sharing successes and helping them, by trading favors where appropriate, by attempting to work out differences directly before resorting to higher authority, and by becoming involved in women's networks, both within the company and externally.

Make the most of opportunities to work with *mentors* who can guide and sponsor you in your upward climb. You're more likely to find mentors by taking some of the initiative to develop the relationship yourself, even though such a relationship cannot be forced. If you're fortunate enough to find a mentor, be sure he or she gets something from the relationship too.

Avoid becoming known as a game player, but be aware of the typical office power games so you can be ready to recognize and intercept them. Games are played in the social arena too, so maintain a friendly but professional image in all business-related social activities. These social contacts can be useful and even crucial to success. Your goal is to keep them constructive without getting too personal or emotionally involved.

To be your own person, you must avoid becoming identified with other people's stereotypes of female roles. Some typical categories to avoid are mother or maiden aunt, daughter or kid sister, sexpot, and Hard-hearted Hannah. Focus on accomplishing results rather than fulfilling role expectations. Realize that most of the beliefs and stereotypes about women's ability to function effectively as managers are more myth than fact. According to some studies, women are better suited than men for top management.

Male peers who are insecure may feel especially threatened by competition with a woman manager. Others may exclude you simply from oversight. Be alert to opportunities to participate in their informal communication channels and even take some initiative at times to become one of the group.

Both male and female subordinates may have stereotyped ideas about (and offer some resistance to) a woman manager. The best way to cope is to be your best competent self, focus on results, and maintain a balanced image.

The stereotyped thinking of most businessmen tends to relegate any woman who happens to be around to the traditional roles of secretary, clerk, or maid. You can avoid reinforcing this type of thinking by (1) avoiding involvement in typing, shorthand, filing, or note-taking activities; (2) staying away from coffee-making, food-providing, and other "hostess" duties; and (3) leaving your needlework at home.

Being aware of sexual games and avoiding their particular traps will ease your transition to manager. Since the woman is almost invariably the loser in the office sex game, you need to be aware of the basic rules and be prepared to avoid problems. Your main protection is the ability to project a businesslike, professional image and to say "no" tactfully and consistently to all sexual overtures. Even if a powerful boss won't take "no" for an answer, you can take steps to successfully challenge him.

ADDITIONAL EXERCISE

EXERCISE 3-2: THE DAWSON CASE

Vickie Dawson had been secretary to the head of the Administrative Services Department for three years. Vickie's job would have been classified as administrative assistant in many companies because very few of her duties were secretarial and she frequently supervised the work of typists and stenographers.

When her boss took a higher-paying job with another company, Vickie was called into Vice-President Phil Crain's office and told that she would be the new department head. Phil suggested that she arrange a department meeting where he would formally announce her promotion.

At the meeting, Phil explained the departmental changes that had been made. Then he patted Vickie on the shoulder and said, "I know Vickie here will do as great a job as department head as she did as the top secretary in the department. And Vickie," he added jokingly, "you just let me know if any of these guys gives you a hard time."

The next day, Vickie started going through stacks of financial data to be analyzed, schedules to be worked out, and correspondence and reports to be prepared. This work had been piling up ever since the previous department head had started preparations to move. Vickie decided she would simply have to plow through the paperwork until she got caught up.

During her first few days on the job, several of the department employees dropped by to see Vickie. Bob, the Word-processing Supervisor and a good friend of Vickie's, came to talk about a salary increase. He said, "You know what budget problems I've been having since my youngest son entered college this fall. With two kids in college, I just can't make ends meet anymore. Bradley (the previous department head) didn't care about my problems, but I know you do, Vickie."

Olivia, the Reprographics Supervisor and also a good friend, dropped in to tell Vickie about the Thing-A-Thon fund-raising project she was chairing this year for the Heart Association. Olivia had been active in the association for several years; it was her main social activity outside the office. She said, "Vickie, I've just *got* to raise more money than that awful Imagene White did last year. If you'll just send a memo around to all the employees about it and let our department have about thirty minutes to meet each week for the next couple of months, I *know* I can go over my goal."

Ben, the Supply Clerk, came by to suggest an immediate change in the method of requesting and distributing supplies to the company secretaries. Vickie knew that the new system Ben was proposing would save him a little time each month. She also knew that the secretaries felt very strongly about being able to get supplies at a moment's notice. She told Ben she wanted to think about it. He said, "Frankly, Vickie, some of the men in the department don't think a woman has the guts it takes to stand up to people and make the changes that are needed around here. But I say that if the big boss upstairs is willing to give you a chance, so am I."

1. What are the major problems Vickie must deal with in her new job?

2. What attitudes, approaches, and specific actions do you think she should take?

3. Which items should receive top priority?

See the answer key for a discussion of these points.

REFERENCES

1. Baird, J. E., Jr., and P. H. Bradley. "Styles of Management and Communication: A Comparative Study of Men and Women." *Communication Monographs*, Vol. 46 (June 1979), pp. 101–111.

2. Baron, Alma. "How We're Viewed by the Men We Boss." *Savvy* (July 1982), pp. 15–18.

3. Blank, Raymond. *Playing the Game*. New York: Morrow, 1981. The author calls this a psychopolitical strategy for your career.

4. Cartwright, D. *Studies in Social Power*, pp. 150–167. Ann Arbor, Mich.: Institute for Social Research, 1959.

5. Collins, Nancy W. *Professional Women & Their Mentors*. Englewood Cliffs, N.J.: Prentice-Hall, 1983. This is a practical guide to mentoring for the woman who wants to get ahead.

6. Crittenden, W. F., and V. L. Crittenden. "Male and Female Students' Perceptions of Women in Management." *Collegiate News and Views* (Spring 1983).

7. Cunningham, Mary. *Powerplay*. New York: Simon & Schuster, 1984. Cunningham tells the story of her rise and fall at Bendix, her relationship with its president, William Agee, and the political treachery that plagued them.

8. Deal, Terrence E., and Allan A. Kennedy. "Who Has the Power in the Corporate Clan?" *Savvy* (June 1982).

9. Dubrin, Andrew J. *Winning at Office Politics*. New York: Ballantine Books, 1982. This is a hard-hitting on-the-job guide to political game-playing.

10. Farley, Lin. *Sexual Shakedown*. New York: Warner Books, 1978. Farley discusses typical forms of sexual harassment and gives suggestions for protection and remedy.

11. Harrigan, Betty. *Games Mother Never Taught You*. New York: Rawson Associates, 1977. Harrigan was one of the first to define the business game and its barriers for women. Her work is still essential reading.

12. Jewell, Donald O., ed. *Women and Management: An Expanding Role*. Atlanta: Georgia State University, 1977. This is a book of readings on the movement of women into managerial roles.

13. Jourard, S. M. "Some Lethal Aspects of the Male Roles." In *Behavior in Organizations*, ed. by R. E. Coffey, et al., pp. 61–68. Englewood Cliffs, N.J.: Prentice-Hall, 1975.

14. Korda, Michael. *Male Chauvinism! How It Works*. New York: Random House, 1973. Korda was one of the first men to write about male chauvinism, and his information is still valuable.

15. Kennedy, Marilyn M. *Office Politics*. New York: Warner Books, 1980. Claiming that 75 percent of all office firings are political executions, the author discusses seizing power and wielding clout through constructive use of office politics.

16. Merkin, Ann. "Choosing a Mentor." *Women's Work*, Vol. 3, No. 5 (November–December 1977), pp. 31–33.

17. Phillips-Jones, Linda. *Mentors & Protégés*. New York: Arbor House, 1982. The author discusses in detail how to establish, strengthen, and get the most from a mentor-protégé relationship.

18. *Summary of Findings on Sex Differences*. A monograph. Fort Worth, Tex.: Johnson O'Connor Research Foundation (650 South Henderson), 1982.

19. Welch, Mary-Scott. *Networking*. New York: Warner Books, 1980.

Chapter Four

Managing Stress

"For fast-acting relief, try slowing down."
Lily Tomlin

The manager's job is a demanding one, especially when she is aiming for visibility and promotion. It requires a high level of health and well-being. Some of the managers who fall by the wayside simply don't have the stamina to stay in the running. They can't cope with the stress. Others keep running at high speed until they literally drop dead. Women managers are not immune to the stress-related illnesses that plague male managers. Recent research indicates that women executives who adopt lifestyles and habits similar to their male counterparts tend to develop the same kinds of physical problems: ulcers, high blood pressure, and heart disease, for example.

Managing stress is essential for maintaining the high level of health and stamina you need in order to do your best in the short run. In the long run, it's a matter of life and death.

In this chapter you will have the opportunity to learn more about

1. The nature and impact of stress

2. Strategies for preventing and minimizing stressful situations, including taking full responsibility for your own health by planning for your nutritional needs,

getting adequate exercise, and controlling your environment to minimize stressful aspects

3. Practicing various relaxation and visualization techniques

4. Making the most of your sleeping hours to minimize stress

5. Using criticism and handling your emotions constructively

6. Experiencing feelings without acting them out.

 Getting Stress Under Control

"Jan? This is Carrie. How are things in San Francisco?"

Jan smiles as she cradles the phone to her shoulder and finishes signing the letters in front of her. "As hectic as ever, Carrie. How about things in San Diego?"

"Well, I thought I had everything going my way. I have excellent relationships with most of the people here—a good support network, a fine professional image, I think. And the reorganization I suggested was adopted and so far is working out fine."

"I sense a 'but' coming up," Jan responds.

"Yeah. Well, I've been having a little difficulty lately handling all the problems that seem to crop up. The last one just about did me in. You know Tom Jenson, the Production Manager? Well, the other day he barged into my office waving a handful of orders . . ."

T: Dickeson! Don't you ever learn? I've told you we've got to have at least nine weeks' lead time on orders for new styles of sweaters. Your people are promising delivery in six to eight weeks in some cases.

C: But it's only been a couple of weeks since you told me that, and I haven't had a chance to meet with the salespeople since then.

T: Only a couple of weeks? That was plenty of time for you to contact your people before they started showing the fall line. Don't you know how to communicate? Haven't you ever heard of memos or the telephone?

C: Of course I have. It's just that I've been so swamped trying to get everything ready for the fall sales campaign . . .

T: Oh, I get it: Other things are more important than cooperating with my department. Well, I'm not going to take the rap for losing these accounts when the orders aren't delivered on time. I'm telling Brockfield that if you can't do this job, I think he ought to get someone who can.

C: *(Near tears)* You've picked on everything I've done ever since I've been here. You've just been waiting for me

to slip up so you could pounce on me. Get out of here!

T: As if I didn't have enough problems, now I have to deal with an overly emotional female! Just forget it. I'll take it up with Brockfield. *(Walks out)*

"I just fell apart," Carrie continues. "I slammed the door shut after him and gave it a hard kick. When I sat down I was shaking with rage. Then I felt the tears coming—along with all these awful physical symptoms: heart pounding, stomach tied in knots, hands and knees trembling, pulse rapid. It was just terrible."

Wrinkling her brow, Jan asks, "Carrie, do you have such symptoms often?"

"More and more frequently lately. I love being married, but it seems so difficult to do everything I'm supposed to do since Murray entered my life. I guess it's time I took a look at my priorities."

"Yes. Listen, will you do me a favor? Make a schedule of your typical working day—from the time you get up until you go to sleep again at night. Include all your habits—activities, food, drink, cigarettes, everything, and send it to me. Then I'll get back to you."

Here's the typical working day Carrie records:

6:30 A.M.: Wake up, often tired and bleary-eyed. Shower, dress, grab a cup of coffee, sweet roll, and a cigarette.

7:15: Start the commute to the office.

8:00: Arrive at the office. Have a second cup of coffee and cigarette. (Coffee and cigarettes throughout the day.)

8:00–12:00 NOON: Handle problems, attend meetings, dictate correspondence, do whatever needs doing—always with too many interruptions, too little time and too much frantic activity.

12:00–2:00: Continue working if no business luncheon is planned, eating a sandwich at desk. Business luncheons usually include a cocktail or two, then rich food and wine.

2:00–? Continue working. Always find it difficult to find a "stopping place." Rarely leave the office before 6 or 7 P.M., and when I do, usually carry some work home that I just couldn't get around to. It's not unusual to stay until 9 or 10 P.M. to meet deadlines.

Evening: After the commute home, usually need a couple of drinks to unwind. Usually smoke a pack or two of cigarettes a day to help relieve tension. Sometimes have dinner at a restaurant; frequently pop a TV-dinner in the oven or open a few cans or packages for a quick meal. After dinner frequently work on an office project until bedtime, which may be well after midnight.

This pattern of living has taken its toll, and Carrie is just beginning to pay the price.

1. What do you see as the major problems here? _____

2. What connection do you see between Carrie's lifestyle and her job problems? _____

WHAT IS STRESS?

"Stress" as used here refers to significant disruptions in an individual's environment, whether the disruptions come from within (from unresolved hurts and fears) or from without (from pressures in her working, family, or social world). Even seemingly pleasant or neutral change, such as a job promotion or a vacation, *may* be a significant disruption for a particular individual and therefore create stress.

Career women may experience more disruptions than men for many reasons. For one thing, they may have more responsibilities. For example, when they accept the primary responsibility for the children and housework, there are simply more things going on in their lives—things they perceive as crucial. For another, women who have not resolved inner conflicts concerning their career role and their wife or mother role are subject to added stress. In addition women are likely to experience more stress than men in the process of establishing their credibility and advancing within an organization because of the stereotypes and other barriers discussed in previous chapters. In fact, an extensive study conducted in England revealed that women managers do in fact experience significantly higher levels of stress than male managers [5, pp. 10–12].

According to Margaret Hennig, there are now many women in their mid-30s to early 40s who have been deeply involved in their careers for fifteen to twenty years. "They have already worked harder in terms of hours and stress anxiety than the traditional 65-year-old man." Most are not willing to sacrifice family relationships in order to move up in their careers. Therefore, when they are faced with the additional stress of children and family in their mid-30s many are dropping out [12]. They are the victims of job burn-out—too much stress for too long with too little psychological nurturing in return, resulting in a loss of enthusiasm and drive.

You have a head start on preventing such burn-out because you've gained skills in establishing goals, priorities, and action plans, and therefore in balancing your life. We'll discuss other preventive strategies in this and later chapters.

Dr. Hans Selye of the University of Montreal, a leader in the study of stress, believes we respond to stress with some version of the fight-or-flight biologically based survival reaction [4]. When a person interprets a significant disruption as a threat, powerful hormones are released into the bloodstream, and the sympathetic division of the autonomic nervous system prepares the body for instant action—either to fight or to run for it. We almost never get so physical in an office. Instead we tend to squelch our emotional and physical reactions, which can eventually damage our mental and physical well-being. Later in this chapter we'll discuss alternatives to this squelching process.

Sources of Stress

What are some common sources of stress? Dr. Selye mentions (1) psychological upsets, (2) anxiety (from your reactions to life events), (3) overwork, (4) drugs (including medications), (5) chemicals (including additives and residues in food), and (6) excessive noise and air pollution. A survey of American working women revealed that one-third of them rate their jobs as very stressful and that managers were much more likely than other workers to describe their jobs that way. The most common job condition reported by the group who rated their jobs very stressful was "work load always too heavy," followed by pressure to work very fast, lack of authority to carry out responsibilities, tight time deadlines, and the threat of costly mistakes connected with actions they take or decisions they make [17].

The English study revealed similar sources of stress reported by women managers, with the addition of "lack of consultation and communication, perceived need to perform better than male peers, sex disadvantage in career advancement, career-related dilemma concerning whether to start a family, and office politics" [5, pp. 10–12].

The more predictable these disruptions are and the more control we believe we have over them, the less stressful they are for us. Disruptions are changes in the status quo. We all need *some* change in our lives, of course, to provide interest and challenge. Some people welcome and thrive on change; however, we all have limits to the degree of change we can tolerate within, say, a year, without ill effects.

Dr. Thomas Holmes and Dr. Richard Rahe have studied the life events that tend to create the most severe anxiety or psychological upset for people. (The resulting "social readjustment rating scale" is reproduced in Exercise 4-1.) They have ranked those events in order of severity (left-hand column) and given each an average mean value

EXERCISE 4-1: ASSESSING THE IMPACT OF TYPICAL DISRUPTIONS

Step 1. Read the list of forty-three life events listed below. Add other events that might disrupt your life in a stressful way.

Step 2. Rank all the life events (the forty-three listed plus any you added) in order of their potential disruptive impact on your life.

Step 3. Assign a mean value for the relative degree of disruption each life event would probably create (100 points for total disruption; 0 points for no disruption).

Step 4. Identify those events that have occurred in your life during the past year. Write them down along with the mean value you assigned each one. Add the mean values together. Compare your total mean value rating with the probability of illness findings shown at the end of the exercise. What is the probability of your becoming ill during the coming year based on this exercise? (Example: If your score is between 150 and 299, there's a 50/50 chance you'll become ill during the coming year.)

Your Ranking (Order of Severity)	Life Event	Your Value (Relative Degree of Stress)	Your Ranking (Order of Severity)	Life Event	Your Value (Relative Degree of Stress)
1	Death of spouse	100	27	Begin or end school	26
2	Divorce	73	28	Change in living conditions	25
3	Marital separation	65	29	Revision of personal habits	24
4	Jail term	63	30	Trouble with boss	23
5	Death of close family member	63	31	Change in work hours or conditions	20
6	Personal injury or illness	53	32	Change in residence	20
7	Marriage	50	33	Change in schools	20
8	Fired at work	47	34	Change in recreation	19
9	Marital reconciliation	45	35	Change in church activities	19
10	Retirement	45	36	Change in social activities	18
11	Change in health of family member	44	37	Mortgage or loan less than $10,000	17
12	Pregnancy	40	38	Change in sleeping habits	16
13	Sex difficulties	39	39	Change in number of family get-togethers	15
14	Gain of new family member	39	40	Change in eating habits	15
15	Business readjustment	39	41	Vacation	13
16	Change in financial state	38	42	Christmas	12
17	Death of close friend	37	43	Minor violations of the law	11
18	Change to different line of work	36		Other _____	
19	Change in number of arguments with spouse	35			
20	Mortgage over $10,000	31			
21	Foreclosure of mortgage or loan	30			
22	Change in responsibilities at work	29			
23	Son or daughter leaving home	29			
24	Trouble with in-laws	29			
25	Outstanding personal achievement	28			
26	Wife begins or stops work	26			

Total Mean Value Rating:	Probability of Illness Occurring Within One Year:
300 or more	80%
150 to 299	50%
149 or less	30%

that reflects the degree of disruption it tends to create in the lives of the persons studied (right-hand column).

Thomas and Rahe found that the number and severity of stressful incidents that occur in a person's life during a year's time can serve as predictors of the probability that the person will become ill within the following year. The probabilities are shown at the bottom of the exercise. Assess your own status by completing Exercise 4-1.

How can you use the results of Exercise 4-1 to prevent or cope with the stress that may occur in your life? A good beginning might be to put your scale where you can easily see it every day so that you become thoroughly familiar with the life events that are likely to create stress for you. Think about the meaning of events for you, and try to identify some of the feelings you experience. In this way you gain practice in recognizing stress buildup before it gets out of hand.

Identify constructive ways to handle negative feelings and different ways you might best adjust to the more important events (more on this later). Ask yourself if focusing on guilt, humiliation, or resentment over past actions or worry over possible future events has ever been helpful to you in the past. An honest evaluation usually reveals that the only positive things we gain from past disasters are lessons for future guidance. Otherwise, they're best forgotten. And the only positive approach to future events is to take action now to prevent them or cope with them. Mere worry only drags us down *now*; it causes us to ruin our enjoyment of the present because of a future event that may never occur.

Your goal is to anticipate life changes and plan for them well in advance. The more you learn about your psychological and physical reactions to stress, the more adept you can be at managing it. You'll be able to pace yourself when events start building up.

Symptoms of Stress

What symptoms do women under stress experience? The working women in the U.S. survey who reported they "always had pressure without adequate clout" listed fatigue, muscle pain, anxiety, anger, headache, depression, digestive problems, eyestrain, and insomnia, in that order. From 30 to 60 percent of the women experienced these symptoms; 12 percent even reported nausea and chest pain [17]. English women managers reported that the stress of their jobs led not only to these but to the following additional symptoms: "unable to cope well in conflict situations; general nervousness, tenseness; unable to sell self in competitive situations; make more mistakes; difficult to get up in morning; want to be left alone" [5, pp. 10–12].

Some illnesses that have been directly related to stress are hypertension, heart disease, cancer, ulcers, premature aging, and sexual dysfunction. Various illnesses that are closely related to mental states are also directly related to stress; some examples are headaches, asthma, insomnia, diarrhea, rheumatism, and back pain. We each have our own pattern of symptoms and illness when we are unable to cope effectively with the stress in our lives.

We also have our unique pattern of stress sources. The first step in gaining control of stress is to identify those situations in which you are aware of pressure, anxiety, or some other symptom that you experience when you are stressed. Exercise 4-2 is designed to get you started.

EXERCISE 4-2: SORTING OUT YOUR STRESSORS

Step 1. On a separate sheet of paper, draw yourself. Now symbolize in some way all the pressures and demands that you're aware of—use drawings, words, or other symbols. Then draw arrows, bridges, or other connections between the pressure and you that indicate (by their size, thickness, darkness, or other means) the intensity of each pressure, demand, or anxiety.

Step 2. Now list each item from Step 1 in one of the two columns below.

External Sources	Internal Sources
(Other people, situations, cultural factors, physical environment, etc.)	(Self-doubt, repressed anger, fears, anxieties, etc.)
_____	_____
_____	_____
_____	_____

Step 3. What personal actions or attitudes tend to feed into or maintain the stress sources you listed in Step 2? _____

_____

Step 4. For each pressure or demand shown in Step 2, list at least one way you can prevent its occurrence or handle it more effectively to prevent stress. (You may want to return to this step after you finish this chapter.) _____

_____

Step 5. Think of an illness you've had in the past. List the major stressful factors in your life during the year prior to the illness. _____

_____

Step 6. List payoffs for being ill. (Examples: Getting a vacation from work or class; getting sympathy from a loved one) _____

_____

Step 7. How can you take care of yourself and provide reasonable facsimiles of these payoffs without becoming ill? (Example: Allowing yourself to accept more love and attention from others and from yourself when you're well) _____

_____

Step 8. Do you see any patterns in the ways you respond to stress that may be harmful to your health? (Example: Interpreting a change as a defeat or sign of failure, or as proof that life is unfair, or as a trap) List. _____

_____

Do you see patterns that are constructive and may prevent illness? (Example: Interpreting a change as an opportunity to move into more appropriate activities, or as a sign that it's time to move on) List. _____

_____

An Overview of Stress Management Strategies

How do most working women cope with stress? The study of U.S. working women indicates that most of them use relatively constructive means, as shown in Exhibit 4-1.

In this chapter we'll discuss ways of avoiding the negative means of coping with stress and focusing on the more positive strategies and tactics for preventing and avoiding undue stress. Mastering techniques that work for you will give you high-level payoffs—such rewards as maintaining high energy on the job, living longer, and enjoying your life more fully.

Dr. Selye and many other scientists believe that we are born with a fixed amount of vitality or "vital energy" that we can draw on to respond to stressful happenings throughout our lives. (Some scientists call this vital-energy account the "immune response"; it can provide us with the necessary immunity to avoid or recover from illness.)

We can conserve our vital energy, but there's no way to increase it. It's there for us to draw on and eventually use up. When we don't use it effectively (for example, when we fail to pace ourselves or otherwise neglect our health), we get sick. When our total vital-energy account gets low, we show signs of aging. When it's all gone, we die.

Many medical experts believe we can cope effectively with stress by drawing intelligently on our vital-energy account. The degree of stress we experience depends on how we perceive and react to situations and how our bodies absorb the effects of stress. Therefore, an intelligent approach must deal with both psychological perceptions and physical health. Here is a two-pronged strategy:

1. *Anticipation and prevention.* You can anticipate problems (both physical and psychological) likely to create disruption and pressure and develop strategies for preventing, reducing, or postponing them so

EXHIBIT 4-1: Mechanisms Used by Working Women for Coping with Stress

	Percentage Who Often or Always Use	Percentage Who Sometimes Use
Positive or neutral means:		
Talk to a friend	56	37
Take action	50	45
Exercise	36	44
Blow off steam	33	54
Engage in hobby	27	47
Get away from it all	21	62
Negative means:		
Drink coffee or soda or eat more	42	40
Keep it to myself	35	46
Act as if nothing much happened	30	50
Smoke cigarettes	23	7
Drink alcohol	15	43
Apologize even though I was right	13	48
Take it out on others or blame others	8	51
Take drugs or medicine	8	22

Adapted from "Stress on Your Job—A Major National Survey," *Ms* (April 1984), pp. 83–86.

that you don't become "swamped." This process requires an assertive approach to taking responsibility for your physical well-being by adopting and maintaining a healthful lifestyle. It also requires an assertive approach to dealing with people that gives you more control over your life and helps you avoid becoming the victim of others' manipulations, games, and whims.

2. *Effective coping.* You can learn to turn off stressful thoughts so you can relax, and you can learn to handle your emotions constructively. When you're in a position of responsibility that calls for risk-taking and decision-making, you may occasionally be hit with an overload of disruption and the resulting pressure, no matter how well you anticipate and

prevent problems. The key to coping with this stress and the "churning hormones" of the fight-or-flight response is to become skilled at relaxation, visualization, and letting go. A quick technique for staying centered or in balance on the job is sometimes essential to regaining your perspective of the situation in order to handle it effectively. Regular periods of relaxation are also essential for maintaining a level of calmness, serenity, and stability that eliminates the need to overdraw your vital-energy account.

In this chapter we will focus on specific strategies and tactics for both preventing and coping with stress. However, in a very real sense, this entire book is designed to help you prevent problems that can lead to stressful situations.

STRATEGIES FOR PREVENTING STRESS

Reducing the number of problem situations that contribute to stress is the first step in stress management, because preventing is certainly less stressful than coping and curing. Here are some strategies for providing that ounce of prevention. We'll discuss the pound of cure later.

Using Time Management, Support Networks, and Assertion

Three major ways of preventing stress are managing your time well, developing an appropriate support network, and asserting yourself effectively. Time management is based on periodically listing major objectives and ranking them in order of priority. It also involves keeping a daily "To Do" list that is categorized and numbered according to priorities, delegating, and arranging "quiet times" for uninterrupted work. These and other techniques are discussed in detail in Chapter 13.

Developing a support network at all levels *within* the company is not only essential to survival as a manager, it's a source of help and comfort in preventing and coping with stress. A support network *outside* the company is also helpful. In Chapter 3, you saw the importance of support networks in preventing stressful problems. We'll also discuss their importance and use in the coping strategies section of this chapter.

Asserting yourself at the right times is essential for preventing problems that create stress. People who can comfortably stand up for their rights and express their preferences and desires are seldom victimized. They exercise a relatively high degree of control over their lives, and they are more secure and confident as persons. You'll learn more about this in Chapter 5.

Taking an Assertive Approach to Health

Donald Ardell, in his book *High Level Wellness* [2], takes a **wholistic** approach to health and stress management that recognizes the impact on your health of every aspect of your lifestyle. According to Ardell's theories, the lifestyles of many managers are more conducive to "low-level worseness" than to "high-level wellness." If you decide you're one of these and want to change, try making changes one step at a time. As soon as you're comfortable with one step, add another.

The basis for an assertive approach to health is the belief that "I am the cause of my health." Once we accept that fact, we don't surrender responsibility for our health to the medical system; we use this system when necessary on a client/customer basis. Only when we become accountable for our own health are we likely to avoid such high-risk behaviors as excessive eating, smoking, and drinking. Because these high-risk behaviors are forms of self-abuse, taking responsibility may involve a consciousness-raising program for building self-esteem and becoming more aware of and responsive to the body and its signals. After all, no one else can know your body and what it needs the way that you can, for each body is unique.

Taking an assertive approach to health also specifically involves (1) taking care of nutritional needs, (2) exercising regularly, and (3) controlling your environment.

Taking Care of Nutritional Needs A U.S. Senate Select Committee, in noting that the major diet-related problem in the United States is the deadly combination of overconsumption and undernutrition, reported:

> We have reached the point where nutrition, or the lack or the excess or the quality of it, may be the nation's number-one public health problem. The threat is not beriberi, pellagra,

or scurvy. Rather we face the more subtle, but also more deadly, reality of millions of Americans loading their stomachs with food which is likely to make them obese, to give them high blood pressure, to induce heart disease, diabetes, and cancer—in short, to kill them over the long term [quoted in 4, p. 5].

To meet your nutritional needs, Ardell has suggested the following practices:

1. Eat as many natural foods as possible, such as fresh fruits, raw vegetables, whole grains, low-fat cottage cheese and yogurt, onion, garlic (combined with or followed by fresh parsley, they leave no mouth odor). Eat plenty of high-fiber roughage (especially bran) every day.

2. Eat a balanced diet—no crash diets.

3. Avoid foods containing artificial colors, additives, preservatives, stabilizers, and other processed chemicals; also, foods containing nitrites (found in bacon, sausage, luncheon meats, and frankfurters).

4. Avoid refined, processed foods, including "enriched" foods. They usually have little nutritional value and many calories.

5. Avoid foods containing white sugar or white flour. Many degenerative diseases have been correlated with overconsumption of these foods. Avoiding them can be difficult since some form of refined sugar is added to a high percentage of our packaged, canned, frozen, and bottled food (for more information on this subject, see *Sugar Blues* by William Dufty [7]). Labels, however, reveal the contents in order of their proportion.

6. Minimize intake of salt, coffee, tea, alcohol, colas, and chocolate.

7. Concentrate on high quality in proteins. Many authorities believe Americans eat far too much beef and pork for their own

good. The right combinations of eggs, milk, fish, cheese, beans, legumes, brown rice, whole grains, and seeds can provide higher-quality protein for less money. They can also provide variety in your diet and improve your elimination.

Exercising Regularly Strangely enough, most people find they have *more* energy when they get some regular form of exercise. Most authorities recommend exercising at least an hour a day; a goal of twenty minutes should be your absolute minimum. Include bending and stretching exercises for flexibility, lifting and pulling exercises for muscle tone, and build up to some cardiovascular-stimulating exercises (aerobic exercise that will make you "huff and puff" but not get out of breath) for respiratory and circulatory health.

Busy managers often find it difficult to take time for adequate exercise. Often the only way is to give it top priority—"If I don't get anything else done today, I'm going to get some exercise." It also may help to keep reminding yourself, "If I take care of my body, it will take care of me." At least one expert claims you can maintain cardiovascular fitness and weight level with his specific aerobic exercise routine in as little as twelve minutes a day for three days a week [3]. If you spend at least twelve minutes on three other days doing exercises for flexibility and muscle tone, you'll probably get fair results. After all, anyone should be able to spare twelve minutes a day with Monday off for weekend recuperation!

Keep in mind, though, that each time you get a *thorough* workout, you reap many benefits; some of them are (1) using up calories at a faster rate for the next 4 or 5 hours; (2) slowing the aging process; (3) improving your figure; (4) keeping bones and muscles healthy and strong; and (5) preventing stress buildup.

It's best to find some forms of exercise you really enjoy, perhaps one that also provides some social interaction. Above all, don't think of your exercise regimen as a crash program. Move into it one step at a time and make it a permanent way of life. The older you get, the more you need it.

Controlling Your Environment Your environment has three aspects: the physical, the social, and the personal. The air you breathe, the water you drink, and the land around you make up the physical environment. The quality of the social environment depends on how economic, governmental, and cultural conditions affect your health and well-being. Your personal environment reflects the way you organize your living and working spaces, the kinds of friendships you create and maintain, and the kind of feedback about yourself that you invite by your actions. Here are some suggestions for developing sensitivity to all three aspects of your environment.

1. *Analyzing your physical environment.* Think about what interrupts, distracts, upsets, or prevents you from doing something constructive during the day. Then make a list of things, events, sounds, scents, and opportunities that could be *added* to your daily routine. Evaluate the positive and negative impacts of these things. Set goals that will help you structure space in ways that enhance your efficiency, effectiveness, well-being, and your continued progress toward achieving your major objectives.

2. *Reevaluating.* Periodically pause to get in touch with basic questions and purposes in your life. Then examine or reexamine the extent to which your personal and social environments hinder or enhance your progress toward your top-priority goals.

3. *Enhancing your personal environment.* Learn to arrange your personal environment to enhance the positive and minimize the negative elements in your life. Some possibilities: bottled spring water; air ionizer; soothing music; a deck or patio with greenery and flowers; reorganized closets, kitchen cabinets, or desk; a more relaxing commute; strategies for avoiding daily irritations like waiting in line or running too many errands.

4. *Turning your internal needs into preferences.* When you think in terms of *wanting* something to happen instead of *needing* it to happen, you retain a healthier perspective, are more likely to gain respect, and therefore improve your personal environment. Upgrading needs to preferences is often called "letting go." It's one of the most important coping strategies, as well as a good preventive strategy.

COPING STRATEGIES FOR KEEPING YOUR COOL

Even with effective prevention strategies, you'll probably have plenty of stress to deal with, from both within and without. Our "pound of cure" includes tactics for commanding your inner resources through living in the present, learning to relax, visualizing results, letting go of desperate needs, adopting "abundance thinking," and using your sleep time constructively. It also includes tactics for handling emotions constructively by learning not to take things personally, for putting criticism in perspective, for experiencing feelings without acting them out, and for talking things out with a trusted friend.

Commanding Your Inner Resources:
Your Personal Power

Commanding your inner resources is the key to dealing with stress, as well as reaching your goals, becoming an effective manager, and generally creating the life you want for yourself. It is your ultimate source of personal power. The three major steps are

1. *Deep relaxation*—focusing on the here and now, moving away from a focus on negative mind chatter, and moving into a state of deep relaxation

2. *Visualization* of the end results you want for virtually any situation that concerns you

3. *Letting go* of any tension-producing need to have the results you picture

Living in the Present This is the way to eliminate guilt, resentment, and worry from your life, as mentioned briefly in an earlier discussion. When you're feeling guilty or resentful, you're really living in the past. When you're worrying, you're living in the future. Acting in the here and now is the only way to change things. The key is to focus on the present moment and determine what, if anything, you need to *do*. Exercise 4-3 is designed to bring you into the present moment by helping you focus on the sensations your body is experiencing now. Practice it frequently when you're *not* under

EXERCISE 4-3: GETTING IN THE HERE AND NOW

Variation 1—Focusing on the Five Senses
Step 1. Take a few deep breaths.
Step 2. *Seeing.* Become intensely aware of what you see around you. Look at it in detail as if you've never seen it before. Pretend you just arrived from another planet. Notice colors, patterns, textures.
Step 3. *Hearing.* If the situation permits, close your eyes. What do you hear? Notice every little sound; identify it; describe it mentally.
Step 4. *Touching.* Now focus on your sense of touch—the feel of your clothes against your skin, the air on your skin, the floor under your feet, the chair under your seat if you're sitting. Describe the sensations to yourself.
Step 5. *Smelling and tasting.* If there are noticeable odors around you or tastes in your mouth, become aware of them; identify and describe them.

Did you notice that your focus moved away from your mind and its internal chatter about the past or future and into your body and what it was sensing in the present moment? Here's an alternate technique that may work better for you:

Variation 2—Progressive Muscle Relaxation
In this process, you alternately tense and then relax all the muscle groups in your body beginning with the toes and moving upward. Tense up the toes of your right foot, hold it, then quickly release them all at once. No-

tice the resulting feeling of relaxation in those muscles. Continue up your right leg, tensing and relaxing the calf muscles and the thigh muscles. Then do the left leg; next, progress up through the various muscle groups in the trunk of your body, then the right and left arms, and finally the neck and head. Pay special attention to the muscles of the jawline and between the eyes; both are places where we tend to retain tension.

---

stress, and you'll soon be able to use it quickly even in stressful situations.

Mastering Relaxation Techniques This is a more advanced approach to getting in the here and now, because the goal of these techniques is to cut through the tension created by negative mind chatter and to reach a deeply relaxed state. As with all the techniques for commanding your inner resources, these may be relatively difficult and time-consuming to master in the beginning. With practice, however, you'll be able to use your skills even in the midst of a stressful situation, and you'll be able to go into deeper states of relaxation more quickly.

The ultimate goal is to be able to move into a state of relaxation so deep that you would be producing alpha brain waves if you were having an electroencephalogram taken. Although biofeedback mechanisms are available for helping you develop this ability quickly, you can learn well enough without them. Research indicates that when you are in such a relaxed state, you can communicate more effectively with your subconscious. You can give it new messages, even messages that override key decisions about life you made long ago—viewpoints that no longer serve you. You can enlist the aid of your subconscious in reaching your goals and solving problems—so that your verbal and nonverbal actions are well integrated and your entire person is moving toward achieving what you decide you want in life.

You get double payoffs, therefore, for learning to relax deeply. The relaxation alone is an immediate antidote to stress. It enhances your sense of well-being, your health, and potentially your longevity. In addition, when you combine it with visualization—that is, mental imagery—it helps you create the life you want. But more about that later.

Four conditions are necessary for mastering the relaxation techniques provided here: (1) a quiet, calm place as free from distraction as possible, (2) a comfortable body position, (3) a mental focusing device to help you shut off your mind chatter (internal dialogue) and go deep within yourself, and (4) a passive attitude that lets you merely observe distracting thoughts, let them go, and bring your mind back gently to your focusing device. Keep in mind that you can't *make* relaxation occur; you can only *let* it occur.

Once you've found a quiet place, experiment with comfortable positions. (A favorite of many is sitting in a comfortable but firm chair with back perfectly straight, legs and arms uncrossed, feet flat on the floor, and arms resting on the thighs.) Then experiment with the techniques included in Exercise 4-4, Deep Relaxation. Discover the ones that are most relaxing for you.

Visualizing the Results You Want Once you're in a deeply relaxed state, you can talk to your subconscious and tell it what you want. Your subconscious (or inner self)

EXERCISE 4-4: DEEP RELAXATION

Deep relaxation begins with deep breathing. The goal is to slow down your breathing pattern. So start with one of the breathing techniques. Then move into one of the focusing devices. If you have trouble moving out of a focus on mind chatter and into a passive attitude, do an exercise for getting in the here and now.

Deep breathing—Variation 1. Breathe in through your nostrils, counting slowly as you do so; hold the breath, starting your counting over again; breathe out through your mouth, lips slightly parted, again counting. The actual process: Breathe in 1-2-3-4-5; Hold it 1-2-3-4-5; Breathe out 1-2-3-4-5. Each time you repeat the process, extend the time you take to breathe in, hold it, and breathe out. See how much you can extend it.

Deep breathing—Variation 2. Visualize yourself stepping onto the top of an escalator. As you breathe slowly in and out, watch yourself descending on the escalator into a deeper and deeper state of relaxation and count: 10-9-8-7-6-5-4-3-2-1.

The backward counting described in Variation 2 serves as a focusing device. Variations 3 and 4 also incorporate focusing devices.

Deep breathing—Variation 3. Close your eyes, take a deep breath, and enjoy the pleasure of feeling yourself breathe. As you breathe in, say quietly to yourself, "I am." As you breathe out, say to yourself "relaxed." Or say, "I am . . . calm and serene" or "I am . . . one."

Deep breathing—Variation 4. Focus all your attention at the tip of your nostrils. Quietly "watch" in your mind's eye the breath flowing in and out past the tip of the nostril. Count from 1 through 10 each time you breathe in and each time you breathe out. Continue counting from 1 through 10 each time you breathe in and out until you're completely relaxed.

Focusing device 1—Candle flame. Place a lighted candle about a foot in front of you and focus all your attention on the flame. As thoughts float by, notice them, let them go, and gently bring your attention back to the flame. This form of relaxed concentration can help you notice how your thoughts and senses keep grabbing at your awareness. The goal is to free your awareness from its identification with thoughts. We cling to our senses and thoughts because we're so attached to them. While focusing on the candle flame, you start becoming aware of that clinging and attachment and the process of letting go.

Focusing device 2—Centering. Focus all your consciousness into the center of your head. Visualize a point of light about a foot in front of your eyes. Now focus all your attention on the point of light.

Focusing device 3—Grounding. Visualize the center of the earth as a very dense place of rock or metal. Focus all your attention on the center of the earth, and picture a huge iron bar there. Next bring your attention to your spinal cord. Visualize a large cable or cord running from the base of your spine all the way to the center of the earth. Picture a big hook on the other end of the cord; now hook it into the center of the earth. Feel a slight pull toward the center of the earth and a slight heaviness of your body.

Focusing device 4—Your peaceful place. Think of a place where you usually feel especially serene, relaxed, and happy, such as the beach, the forest, or the lake. Picture yourself there. Reexperience in your mind's eye all the sights, sounds, smells, and tastes you experience there. Focus on your sense of touch, too—the sun, water, and air on your skin, the sand or earth under your feet. Bring in as much vivid detail as you can. Get in touch with the positive feelings you experience when there—your sense of well-being, confidence, serenity.

---

is amazingly competent at moving you toward the best results for you—if you'll only relax and let it do its work. It tunes in better to pictures and feelings, however, than to words. That's why visualizing results and getting in touch with the feelings you want to experience along with those results is so powerful.

What if you have difficulty "making pictures" when you close your eyes? Never fear. Everyone differs to some extent in the way they visualize. If you see no pictures at all, think of what it might be like if you *could* see the pictures you're thinking about. That's good enough.

When should you practice your visualization skills? Shortly before going to sleep each night is a time preferred by many people because it's a quiet time when they're ready to relax fully. To make the most of your personal power, practice deep relaxation and visualization at some time every day so that it becomes a deeply ingrained habit—a way of life that you can put to use almost automatically. If you do this, you will soon discover that you can use these skills—quickly, with your eyes wide open, and with no one the wiser—any time you're dealing with potentially stressful situations. You'll be able to stay centered or to regain your composure quickly even if you're taken by surprise.

The processes described in Exercise 4-5, Visualizing Results, are designed to enlist the aid of your subconscious in handling specific types of situations. You can adapt them to any kind of situation; just remember that important final step, letting go.

Learning to Let Go Have you ever observed someone sabotaging herself because she was trying too hard? You probably thought, "Why doesn't she relax a little?" Can you think of a time when you probably sabotaged yourself by trying too hard or caring too much? Why do people do this?

EXERCISE 4-5: VISUALIZING RESULTS

Step 1. Focus on the here and now and move into a deeply relaxed state by using any combination of techniques from Exercise 4-4.

Step 2. Select the visualization that applies to your situation from the ones listed below (or adapt one of them to fit your situation).

Step 3. Use one of the letting-go techniques from Exercise 4-6.

Visualization 1—Problem resolution. Deeply relax. Get in touch with your problem situation. If thinking of it or picturing it causes you to feel anxious, focus again on a relaxation technique. Repeat until you're able to picture your problem situation without feeling anxious. What do you want the end results of this situation to be? How do you want it to be resolved? Picture that happening—in vivid detail, bringing all your senses into play: colors, patterns, textures you see; sounds you hear; and things you touch, smell, and taste. Picture your interactions with the other person(s) involved, focusing on your specific feelings and the feelings flowing between you and others; for example, understanding, acceptance, warmth, good will. Focus on the pictures and feelings until you feel quite comfortable and secure with them. Now use a letting-go technique to release them.

Visualization 2—Goal achievement. Follow the process described in Visualization 1, but instead of focusing on a problem situation, focus on a goal you want to achieve. Picture yourself actually achieving the goal. Include all the people involved in helping you reach the goal; focus on the positive feelings flowing between you and them. Now let go.

Visualization 3—Evaluating goals. You can carry the process used in Visualization 2 a step further to help you evaluate possible goals. (For example, if you're not sure whether getting a master's degree should be merely one alternate activity for achieving a career goal or a goal in itself, picture yourself having achieved the career goal without the master's degree.) Picture all the consequences of having achieved the goal. How do you feel about each? Is anything missing? What? Would a different goal have led to better results?

Visualization 4—Handling stage fright. Use this process to overcome the "jitters" that accompany any type of presentation you must make before a group. For best results, practice the visualization several times before your presentation. Just before going to sleep the night before the presentation is an especially good time to visualize positive results. Follow the process described in Visualization 1, but instead of picturing a problem situation, picture yourself making a successful presentation. See yourself focusing on the major thrust of your message and getting it across in a clear, dynamic, persuasive way. See your audience understanding and accepting it. Get in touch with your positive feelings and theirs. Now let go.

Usually because they are too strongly attached to having the situation turn out just the way they want. They cling—perhaps desperately—to the idea or picture of certain end results. Therefore, they create a tension-producing need to achieve those results, often accompanied by fear that they won't.

Think of some situations in which you achieved the results you wanted—times when you moved relatively effortlessly toward your goal. Think of top athletes who have done that. Top achievement is usually a result of *relaxed concentration*. You fully intend to achieve certain results, and your mind and body are focused on the process of doing so. You *desire* those results, but you don't desperately *need* them, and you're not focused on fear connected with failure to achieve the results.

You prevent the self-sabotage caused by tension-producing needs when you add a letting-go step to the visualization process you use for goal-setting. Exercise 4-6, Letting Go of Results, offers several techniques for this final step of the personal power process. Remember, when you let go of your goal, you retain a clear picture of having it, but you release the needs and fears related to not having it. This process frees you to work toward your goal in a relaxed, confident way, which in turn makes it easier to gain the cooperation and support of others. However, you must truly become comfortable with the idea of *not* achieving your

goal. If letting go is accompanied by sadness, regret, or unwillingness, you need to work on your fear of failure (see Exercise 2-2.)

You can also adopt a viewpoint that there is abundance in the world. When you let go of your goal pictures, you "put them out into the universe." The view that there is abundance in the universe implies that everything that happens eventually works toward your benefit. Therefore, if you give a goal situation your best shot, you are confident of achieving it. If it doesn't turn out the way you pictured, then your deep inner self had the wisdom to know that those results were not best for you in the long run. That's the time to ask, "What lesson can I learn from this situation?" "What's my next goal?"

Abundance Thinking Do you approach goal achievement from a viewpoint of scarcity? Do you think, "Since there are not enough resources for everyone to have all they need, then the more I get, the less there will be for someone else"? Think of all the things that are perceived as scarce. Jot them down.

Most people list things like food, clean water, housing, education, health care, money, time, energy, love. Actually, all of these resources are in adequate—even abundant—supply if enough of us decide to manage them properly. According to a 1981 publication of the American Friends Service Committee, a supplement of seventeen bil-

EXERCISE 4-6: LETTING GO OF RESULTS

Step 1. Move into a state of deep relaxation (Exercise 4-4).

Step 2. Visualize the end results you want (Exercise 4-5).

Step 3. Let go of your pictures of end results by one of the following methods (or devise a similar method of your own for putting your goals out into the universe):

Variation 1—Hot air balloon. Picture a beautifully colored hot air balloon with a lovely passenger basket. It's tied to the ground with velvet ropes. Put the pictures of your end results into the basket—all the pictures and the feelings related to them. Untie the ropes and watch the balloon float away, up into the sky and away toward the horizon. As it floats out of sight, repeat to yourself, "Let go, let go."

If you experience discomfort or negative feelings, such as sadness, regret, or unwillingness to let go, turn to Exercise 2-2. Work on the fear of failure that is causing you to cling to the needed results until you are comfortable with letting them go.

Variation 2—Space capsule. Follow the process described in Variation 1, substituting a sleek space capsule for the hot air balloon. Picture all the latest technology and equipment for controlling the capsule; put your end results inside; lock it; watch it blast off and disappear into space.

Variation 3—Bottle at sea. Follow the process described in Variation 1, substituting a large glass bottle for the hot air balloon. Put your end results inside; place the cork in the bottle top; throw it into the ocean. Watch the tide carry it out to sea; see it disappear toward the horizon.

---

lion dollars a year could have insured adequate food, water, housing, health care, and education for every person in the world. In 1981 world governments spent this amount for arms—every two weeks [18]. If enough people decided it was essential, we could suspend the arms race for just two weeks a year and have adequacy; surely we could collectively choose to have abundance.

Abundance thinking reflects an individual or collective attitude. Take money—our creative energy becomes money; we can think of it as green energy. Or time—there are always twenty-four hours in a day; we have abundant time to achieve our top-priority goals once we clarify them and weed out the nonessentials. Or energy—all that exists in the universe is energy; the only problem is finding and using the best form of energy for each of our purposes. And love, which exists in our minds—the more love we give to ourselves and others, the more we tend to receive, and the more we have to give back again. The only limits are our fears that shield us from receiving love.

When you come from an attitude of abundance, you can move more freely toward your goals. Since there's plenty for everyone, your successes need not be built on someone else's failures; your having more need not mean that someone else has less. It's a win-win attitude: everybody can win.

Sleeping on It You can even use your sleep time to move you toward your goals. For years we've heard managers say, before making an important or difficult decision, "Let me sleep on it and get back to you tomorrow"—and for very good reason. Research studies increasingly point to the importance of sleeping, and especially dreaming, to our mental health and ability to function well during waking hours. Your subconscious mind is very powerful, and you can draw on its resources almost effortlessly by using the dream state to help you solve problems, resolve conflicts, and come up with new ideas.

Suppose Carrie Dickeson decided to combine visualization and "sleeping on it" to help solve the problem of getting sales orders to Tom Jenson's people. Just before going to sleep, Carrie uses deep relaxation and visualization to picture a positive solution to her problem. Next she expresses her wish in a concise statement: "I want a solution to the sales order problem." Another way of putting it might be "I'll discover a method for coordinating the sales orders." She tells herself that she will have a solution when she awakens. Finally she repeats her concise statement over and over as she drifts into sleep.

Here are the steps to take:

1. Just before going to sleep, use a deep relaxation and visualization process (see Exercises 4-4 and 4-5) to picture a positive solution to your problem.

2. Put your wish into a concise statement.

3. Visualize yourself waking up with the solution or ideas you want. Tell yourself you *will* have them in the morning.

4. Repeat your phrase as you drift into sleep.

5. Upon awakening, lie still and think about your subject. Write down any ideas that come to mind. The idea may come to you later in the day. Relax and be open to it.

This procedure can help you with any problem, including handling your emotions on the job.

Handling Emotions Constructively

Most women are blessed with the ability to express their emotions more freely than men. However, this blessing can become a curse to the woman manager who hasn't learned appropriate ways to express and channel her emotions in business situations. In fact, one of the most damaging and widespread stereotypes women in business have been stuck with through the years is that of the overly emotional female.

You've heard the comments: "Women are too emotional to be managers. They go to pieces in a crisis." (This overlooks the fact that nearly all mothers get their children through the numerous crises growing up entails without "going to pieces.") "You can't afford to hire a manager who might burst into tears in the crunch." "Women are just too flighty to handle a manager's job." "Women don't roll with the punches like men do." "A man can keep problems in perspective better than a woman."

A key factor that has led to these stereotypes is the different payoffs our culture tends to give to little girls and boys when they express emotions. Girls usually get payoffs of sympathy or approval when they cry, show fear, express sadness or other tender feelings, show sympathy for others, and nurture others. Boys frequently get disapproval or even punishment for such behavior. ("Big boys don't cry." "Don't be a chicken.") On the other hand, boys often receive approval, admiration, or at least acceptance for expressing various forms of anger or aggression. Such "masculine" expressions of emotion by girls, however, are usually met by disapproval or rejection.

In the male-dominated business world, therefore, it is generally acceptable to express anger or aggression within certain limits. However, a display of tears or fear signals you can't handle the game; that is, you can't handle real responsibility on the line where key decisions are made and where the real power is wielded. It's especially important to manage fear because some political game players can sniff out the nonverbal signs of fear like bloodhounds, and they'll quickly move in for the kill if it suits their purposes.

What should you do with your tears, fears, and anger? Squelch them? Pretend they aren't there? That approach just leads to more problems. We'll discuss several ways to prevent emotional buildup and to handle emotions you don't care to display on the job. You can control the viewpoint you take toward others' actions, including their criticism of your performance. When you choose to change viewpoints, your emotional reactions will also change. Also, through self-mastery visualization you can learn to absorb personal attacks and dissolve any negative emotional energy they carry. When negative feelings do intrude, you can learn to express them in ways that

are acceptable in the business world (see Chapter 5), to experience them without acting them out, or to release them through substitute acting-out or expressing them to a trusted friend.

Now let's look at some suggestions from people who have stopped being the victims of their feelings and have learned to use their feelings in ways that keep them in closer touch with themselves and others.

Avoiding the Tendency to Take Things Personally The tendency to view other people's actions and criticisms as a personal put-down stems from the fear of some sort of personal failure. Why do women seem to take these things more personally than men? Perhaps because men have generally been more single-minded about their career objectives. They are more likely to keep focusing on such questions as "What do I have to *do*, what do I have to *learn* in order to advance?" That focus makes it easier to keep things in perspective. When the intention to *learn* from our mistakes overcomes our fear of failure, we're less likely to take people's criticisms and actions personally.

It may help to view business as a game. First, what's your major objective in this game? Discovering the limits of your capability? Financial independence? Making a specific kind of contribution to the planet? Once you're clear about your major objective and let go of any tension-producing *need* to achieve it, you can relax and begin to enjoy the *process* of playing the game in order to achieve the objective. The actions of others become part of the challenge and complexity of the game, and you make your moves with your goals foremost in your mind. Your focus changes from avoiding the risk of failure and protecting yourself from failure to winning the game. Problem situations merely alert you to the need to take corrective action. You switch from agonizing over the fact that a problem was allowed to develop to getting on with the job of correcting the problem. Your ego is not on the line. After all, it's just a game.

In addition, when you learn to identify your rights (the rules of the game?) and to stand up for them, you're better able to view others' actions objectively. When you consistently assert your rights, you avoid the buildup of emotional resentment that leads to the "chip-on-the-shoulder" attitude that hampers some women. Assertion is discussed in Chapter 5.

Putting Criticism in Perspective Ask yourself about the qualifications of your critic on the subject at hand. Suppose you were to take a visitor on a tour of your department and explain major departmental goals, organization, procedures, and controls. He sees some potential problem with the way you're running things and suggests some ways you could improve the setup. The range of possibilities about his qualifications to criticize and advise you is shown on this scale:

1	2	3	4	5	6	7	8	9	10

Ignoramus   Expert

Let's look at the two extreme possibilities. Possibility number one is that your critic doesn't know a thing about running the business. In fact he's so ignorant that he doesn't know the difference between a work schedule and an organization chart. In that case, if you allow yourself to become upset because of the criticism of a business ignoramus, you are acting even more foolish than the person who criticized you.

At the other extreme, your critic may be one of the most renowned experts on business organization in the world. In that case, his observations are probably valid and his suggestions extremely valuable. In fact if you acted on those suggestions, you might be-

come a top officer of the company in a very short time. To be upset by such criticism, then, would be inappropriate and self-defeating.

Most of your critics' qualifications will lie somewhere between complete ignorance and incomparable expertise. The point is that if you automatically respond negatively to feedback, you are showing that you lack self-esteem in that area of your life. Such negative reactions not only waste your energy, they tend to sidetrack you from your major objectives and goals. When you are criticized, ask yourself: What are the qualifications of my critic? What validity does this criticism have? Are ulterior motives involved? Can I use this feedback to help me reach my goals and objectives [9, p. 192]?

Emery tells a story that further illustrates this concept.* He describes the autopilot and the inertial navigation system on the plane he flew to Hawaii. The plane's crew refers to the autopilot as George and to the inertial navigation system as Fred. The relationship between these two pieces of equipment is called a "closed-feedback mechanism" in engineering terms. Emery explains that this is just a fancy way of saying that Fred and George never get out of communication. They always supply each other with feedback; they don't make each other wrong; and they don't take anything personally. If Fred and George communicated with words rather than by mechanical means, their conversation on the trip to Hawaii would go something like this:

F: George, we're off course two degrees to starboard.

G: Okay Fred I'll fix it.

---

*Adapted from *Actualizations: You Don't Have to Rehearse to Be Yourself* by Stewart Emery. Copyright © 1982, by Stewart Emery. Used by permission of Doubleday & Company, Inc.

F: George, we're off course three degrees to port.

G: Okay Fred I'll fix it.

F: George, we're Dutch rolling.

G: Okay Fred I'll fix it.

F: George, we're forty knots below our airspeed.

G: Okay Fred I'll fix it.

F: George, we're 300 feet below our corridor.

G: Okay Fred I'll fix it.

This type of communication would continue all the way to Hawaii. Now, if Fred and George also happened to be human beings instead of machines, the conversation might go something like this:

F: George, we are off course two degrees to starboard.

G: Okay Fred I'll fix it.

F: George, we're off course three degrees to port.

G (Pause): Okay Fred I'll fix it.

F: George, we're Dutch rolling.

G: All right, Fred, I will fix it.

F: George, we're forty knots below our airspeed.

G: Will you knock it off, Fred! Gripe, gripe, gripe! All you ever do is gripe.

As a person, it's difficult for George to avoid the tendency to take the feedback as a personal affront. Yet this feedback is the essence of the Fred/George relationship that allows the safe arrival of the plane at Hawaii.

Do you welcome feedback? Ask yourself: Is it better for me to know what's going on in my department—the problems, conflicts, others' reactions—or not? If having all pertinent information, negative or positive, about what's going on in your area of responsibility is important to you, then your logical response to feedback will be, "Thank you. I'm glad you brought that to my attention. I'll look into it."

Sometimes people will criticize you in such a negative, hostile way that it's difficult to remain emotionally detached. It may be appropriate to tell such a person that you appreciate the feedback but you *don't* appreciate the manner in which it was given. At the same time, it helps to keep in mind that the hostility is the other person's problem. She or he would react that way to *anyone* who represents to him or her what you do at the moment. It's a part of the individual's own conditioning and working out of his or her own life story and really has nothing to do with you personally. And, if you *still* feel strong emotions, you don't have to act them out. You can choose to use self-mastery visualization or select a substitute acting-out method.

Self-Mastery Visualization Once you've gained some skill at deep relaxation and visualization, you can use similar processes on the job—quickly, with your eyes wide open—to maintain or regain your emotional balance during or after a perceived attack. Such an attack directs negative energy toward you and represents a force that uncenters you, knocks you off balance. Self-mastery visualization is a technique used by warriors of old to recognize this force and transform it into positive energy.

By visualizing yourself as a consistently centered, self-possessed person, you remain alert but serene. You are poised and proficient when confronting the attacker without the slightest hint of fear. The key to this approach: You accept the negative energy, channel it through you, and then dissipate it so that it never perturbs or harms you. You assimilate, absorb, and dissolve it. You don't need to ignore it, withdraw from it, or anesthetize or armor yourself against it. You see clearly, without hiding anything from yourself, all external forces and events—and you can use them to your benefit.

Practice the variations of self-mastery visualization shown in Exercise 4-7 to determine which work best for you. Use past or current situations for practice every day until transforming negative emotional energy becomes a habitual, natural process for you. Then use it as the first step in asserting yourself with anyone who behaves aggressively toward you.

Experiencing Feelings Without Acting Them Out As you master the techniques we've been discussing, negative emotions will become less and less a problem. Here's a strategy for constructively handling those that

do occur. Many male managers have learned to control their feelings by suppressing them and pretending they don't exist. This practice creates a number of negative side-effects.

Suppressed feelings don't go away; they tend to build up inside until they reach the "explosive stage." We tend to forget the incident that triggered the feeling and the fact that we suppressed the feeling. Therefore, our outbursts of anger, self-pity, fear, and so forth come as a surprise to us and are out of our control.

Suppressed feelings that simmer and fester within continue to create stress for us long after the stressful situation has passed. We then become vulnerable to stress-related

EXERCISE 4-7: SELF-MASTERY VISUALIZATION (Transforming Negative Emotional Energy)

Practice this process in a quiet place on your own. You may also practice with a partner; have your partner stand in front of you and shout negative comments. Respond with self-mastery visualization. Have your partner then test you by gently pushing against your chest or the small of your back. You should feel solid but lightly resilient. If you wobble, fall over, or have to take a step to regain your balance, you're probably uncentered. Keep using the image patterns, one at a time to *expand, direct, and dissipate* the negative emotional energy so you stay centered.

Step 1. *Deep relaxation* (see Exercise 4-4). After you gain skill, you can omit this step. Instead, start breathing deeply and slowly.

Step 2. *Negative energy source.* Imagine a ferocious, huge, very violent, angry man towering over you, shouting obscenities at you. The two of you are standing in a ten-foot-square room. His loud, booming voice is threatening. It shocks and unsettles you.

Step 3. *Expansion/visualization.* Imagine the room expanding and yourself expanding with it. The man, though, remains the same size. As you expand, he shrinks, and his body and voice become smaller and smaller, weaker and weaker. After a while, it's as though he's yelling at you from across a great hallway, then croaking at you from across the Grand Canyon. Then he's chirping at you from across a sweeping expanse of inter-planetary space, until he becomes a tiny, squeaking speck of dust disappearing amid a swirl of stars.

Key thought: When I am confronted by a personal attack or any threatening situation, I can expand my self-image to a universal dimension.

Step 4. *Directing and dissipating negative energy.* Imagine a door that opens into your interior universe. Now picture the negative energy of the ferocious man entering that door. As your universe expands, this negative energy becomes smaller, less significant, and finally unimportant.

Variation 1—Magic pot. Picture a magic pot in the center of your universe. The reason it's magic is because it has infinite capacity, yet no matter how much you put into it, it is always empty. Now imagine all the negative energy of the ferocious man going into the magic pot.

Variation 2—Polarity switch. Imagine a switch just inside the door to your interior universe. When the switch is up, the energy that comes in is positive; when it's down, the energy flow is negative. Now imagine yourself throwing the switch up to "positive" as the ferocious man's negative energy comes through the door. You have chosen to reverse the energy flow from negative to positive. Now see yourself using the positive energy to expand.

Variation 3—Power plant. Imagine that beside the door to your interior universe there is a power plant. Its wheels are turned by water to produce energy. The plant doesn't care whether the water is pure and clean or dirty and toxic. It merely uses the flow of water to produce energy. Now picture the negative energy coming from the ferocious man as a stream of water. As it moves through your power plant, it turns the wheels and produces positive energy. Use it to expand.

Variation 4—The wave. Picture the negative energy as a huge tidal wave rushing toward you, ready to engulf you. Now expand yourself to match the size of the wave; ride on its force to keep expanding until it becomes small and insignificant.

Variation 5—The lightning rod. Picture the negative energy of the ferocious man as a bolt of lightning and yourself as a lightning rod. Conduct the bolt of lightning through you into the ground. The lightning has no effect on you whatsoever. You are merely the conduit that conducts the energy from one point to another. Once the energy reaches the ground, it is absorbed and swallowed up by the earth.

illnesses, especially ulcers, high blood pressure, migraine headaches, allergies, asthma, and heart disease.

Denial of feelings as a way of coping with life takes us more and more out of touch with ourselves—the way we are, the true effects of people and events in our lives, all the facets of the ways we really respond to those people and events. Such denial will inhibit your personal growth and development as a creative, autonomous person. As a result, you'll find it more and more difficult to be clear about your values and therefore your goals and to evaluate situations and opportunities in the light of those goals.

It is important that we fully *experience* the feelings we have without judging those feelings to be good or bad. It may be inappropriate and self-defeating to *act-out* some of those feelings.

For example, in the second case described at the beginning of this chapter, Carrie felt frustration, then self-pity, then rage. She expressed her frustration and self-pity in ways that upset Tom Jenson, intensified her problems, and were therefore inappropriate and self-defeating.

How can you fully experience feelings so that it's not necessary to act them out? Here are some suggestions.

1. *Accept your feelings.* Be glad that you're able to experience the whole range of human emotions and that you're aware of being able to do so.

2. *Don't judge your feelings.* Tell yourself that a feeling is not right or wrong, good or bad; it just is.

3. *Let yourself fully experience a feeling.* Be aware of it in the present moment. Don't begin focusing on guilt (about past experiences associated with a similar feeling) or worry (about what will happen in the future). Stay in the here and now by fo-

cusing on your senses: Focus on what you are seeing, hearing, touching, and so forth.

4. *Choose not to act-out.* Tell yourself that you are choosing not to act-out your feeling because to do so would be inappropriate and self-defeating.

5. *Decide whether and when to give feedback.* You may decide it is appropriate to *tell* the person who triggered the feeling what you are feeling. If this is done effectively, it is not acting-out, and the feedback can be constructive to that person. (See Chapter 5 for suggestions on giving feedback constructively.)

6. *If you can't give feedback calmly, postpone it.* As a general rule, you don't have to respond immediately to anything. When your feelings are too overpowering for you to "experience them out" quickly, it's more professional to delay responding. You can act-out your feelings in privacy. Later, when you're ready to deal with the problem situation, you can do so without having to deal with explosive feelings at the same time.

   To postpone gracefully, it helps to have some "exit lines" in mind. Your exit line is what you say before you change the subject or excuse yourself from the scene. For example: "I'd like to check on a few things before I give you my answer (or respond to that, discuss that). May I get back to you at/on . . . ?" "Let me think about that for a while. I'll get back to you at/on . . . ." "I'm glad you brought that up. I must leave for a meeting (or appointment) now, but I want to talk with you about this as soon as I return."
   Use Exercise 4-8 to help prepare your own exit lines.

7. *Use substitute acting-out.* Tell yourself that you'll enjoy acting-out your feelings in an

EXERCISE 4-8: ARMING YOURSELF WITH BUSINESSLIKE EXIT LINES

Recall three situations in which you acted-out your feelings and got poor results. After noting each situation, make up an exit line that would have been appropriate. Keep these lines in mind for future use in similar situations. (Note: When you become skilled at self-mastery visualization, exit lines will become unnecessary.)

Tense Situation 1 _____

Exit Line _____

Tense Situation 2 _____

Exit Line _____

Tense Situation 3 _____

Exit Line _____

appropriate way later. Sometimes just telling yourself this can defuse the situation enough for you to deal with it effectively at the time it occurs.

You can visualize throwing darts at a picture of the person on a dart board. (Some people even have dart boards in their office for this purpose.) Other substitutes are

Any game that requires hitting a ball: Pretend the ball is the person or thing you resent and really smash it.

Jogging or walking: Pretend you're stepping on the person you resent (if you need to!).

Karate: Pretend your opponent is the person you resent (but don't get carried away!).

Any physical exercise: You can work off the bottled-up energy of unexpressed

feeling by reminding yourself while you're exercising that you're working out those feelings. Be aware of the situation and the resulting feeling you're now working out. You'll probably be free to rest peacefully once the tension and energy drain of unresolved feelings is eliminated.

Hitting a large stuffed doll: Try to knock the stuffing out of a large doll, animal, or dummy, using either your fists or a baseball bat.

A quick mental acting-out: Instead of visualizing the dart-throwing incident, you can picture yourself telling off the other person, kicking him or her in the seat of the pants, and so on. You may be able to work out the feeling in a few seconds and go on to deal with the situation calmly.

Expressing Feelings to a Trusted Friend
Another way of handling your emotions is to

talk them out with someone. The more stressful your job, the more essential it is to have at least one trusted friend that you can "let your hair down" with. It may be best if such friends are not connected with your job. Although business friends may understand the problems better than someone outside the company, you may feel it's risky to be completely open with them. True friends are rare: Most people are lucky if they have five or six at any one time in their lives. Someone who might serve as confidant(e) could be your husband, someone you live with, some family member or relative, or simply a friend. For the relationship to be mutually supportive, it should include aspects such as these:

You can be yourselves with each other.

You are interested in each other's well-being.

You really listen to each other.

You don't make judgments about each other's character, feelings, or behavior.

(To avoid making judgments, think in terms of behavior that works or doesn't work, that appears to be constructive or destructive, rather than what is right or wrong, good or bad. Deal more with what is rather than with what *should* be).

You confide in each other about the joyous events in your life as well as the problem situations.

You both feel more lovable and capable as a result of the friendship.

You can trust each other's judgment about revealing shared confidences.

Frequently you can gain insights into problem situations and learn more about yourself by discussing things with a friend. Such discussions can also be very helpful in "experiencing out" any leftover, bottled-up feelings you may have. This type of friendship can help both parties keep a balanced perspective on life. When things get rough, it can have a healing, therapeutic effect.

SUMMARY

"Stress" as used here refers to significant disruptions in an individual's environment, whether the disruptions come from within (from unresolved hurts and fears) or from without (from pressures in her working, family, or social world). Even pleasant or neutral change can be a significant disruption of a person's environment and therefore can create stress. The more predictable disruptions are and the more control we believe we have over them, the less stressful they are for us. We can manage stress effectively (1) by anticipating problem areas likely to create disruption and pressure and developing strategies for preventing, reducing, or postponing them and (2) by coping effectively through learning to command inner resources so we can relax and through handling emotions constructively.

To *prevent* stress, keep in mind these strategies.

1. Use time management techniques. Develop a support network of peers, bosses, workers, and people outside the company. Know when and how to assert yourself appropriately.

2. Take an assertive approach to health, based on the viewpoint: "I am the cause of my health." An assertive approach means not surrendering responsibility for your health to the medical system. Instead, use the system when necessary on a client/customer basis. Place a high value on your health and be aware of and responsive to your body and its signals. Avoid high-risk behaviors.

3. Take care of nutritional needs and exercise regularly.

4. Control your physical, social, work, and personal environments.

Here are some strategies for *coping* with stress and keeping your cool.

1. Learn how to command your inner resources by using specific techniques for (1) staying in the here and now, rather than dwelling on past guilt and grudges or future worries; (2) mastering techniques for reaching a state of deep relaxation; (3) visualizing the results you want; (4) learning to let go of tension-producing needs; and (5) using your sleep time to move you toward your goals.

2. Handle emotions constructively and avoid the stereotype of the overly emotional female by (1) avoiding the tendency to take criticisms or slights personally; (2) putting criticism in perspective by evaluating the qualifications and motives of the critic, the validity of the criticism itself, and how the feedback can help you reach your goals; (3) using self-mastery visualization to expand your self-image until negative emotional energy becomes insignificant, then to direct and transform the energy so it has a neutral or positive effect; and (4) experiencing your feelings without acting them out by accepting your feelings rather than judging them as good or bad, consciously choosing whether to act them out, giving feedback about your feelings in a calm manner, postponing feedback with businesslike exit lines when you can't give it calmly, and using substitute acting-out to release strong feelings. Remember that expressing feelings to a trusted friend can help you handle them constructively by getting them out in the open and gaining insights about yourself and others.

REFERENCES

1. Adams, Ramona; Herbert Otto; and Audeane Cowley. *Letting Go*. New York: Macmillan, 1980. This book elaborates on the letting-go process in commanding your inner resources.

2. Ardell, Donald B. *High Level Wellness*. Emmaus, Pa.: Rodale Press, 1977. The author gives an effective presentation of the wholistic approach to health with a number of self checks and an excellent annotated bibliography.

3. Bailey, Covert. *Fit or Fat*. Boston: Houghton Mifflin, 1983. A detailed guide to developing an aerobic exercise plan that takes into account your age and physical condition, this book includes explanations of body processes and dietary suggestions.

4. Benson, Herbert. *The Relaxation Response*. New York: Morrow, 1975. Dr. Benson discusses the various types of diseases and illnesses directly connected to stress and presents relaxation techniques to help decrease blood pressure, relieve stress, and prevent illness.

5. Davidson, Marilyn, and Cary Cooper. *Women Managers: Their Problems and What Can Be Done to Help Them*. Sheffield, England S14PQ: Manpower Services Commission, Training Division, Moorfoot, 1983. The authors are professors in the Department of Management Sciences at the University of Manchester (P. O. Box 88, Manchester M60 1QD). Their extensive research includes male/female comparisons of stress sources in the work, home and social, and individual arenas; effects of stress on work performance and psychosomatic symptoms; and comparisons of sources and effects on four levels of management.

6. Delaney, Gayle. *Living Your Dreams*. San Francisco: Harper and Row, 1981. This detailed guide describes how to use your sleep to solve problems and to help create the life you want.

7. Dufty, William. *Sugar Blues*. New York: Warner Books, 1976. Dufty presents scientific evidence for the connection between refined sugar and a host of diseases and chronic conditions. He also discusses the high sugar content of many foods we don't think of as "sweets" and gives suggestions for determining sugar content.

8. Dyer, Wayne W. *Your Erroneous Zones*. New York: Avon Books, 1981. Dyer discusses attitudes and behaviors that create problems for people, along with strategies for changing. Two of the best chapters give suggestions for dealing with fear and guilt.

9. Emery, Stewart. *Actualizations: You Don't Have to Rehearse to Be Yourself*. Garden City, N.Y.: Doubleday, Dolphin Books, 1982. This book offers some excellent insights into becoming more comfortable with yourself and your relationships, maintaining perspective, and handling criticism.

10. Gallwey, W. Timothy. *Inner Tennis: Playing the Game*. New York: Random House, 1983. This book might be titled "Inner Life." Gallwey discusses ways of rising above the "ego self," whose anxieties and fears cause us to suffer defeat in the game of life as well as tennis. He suggests ways to relax and let the "inner self" take over.

11. Lamott, Kenneth. *Escape from Stress*. New York: Berkley, 1975. The author discusses the nature of stress, the connection of stress with various diseases, and ways of letting go, including meditation, hypnosis, and biofeedback.

12. Rivers, Caryl. "Reaching for the Top." *Working Woman* (September 1983), p. 138.

13. Ross, Ruth. *Prospering Woman*. Mill Valley, Calif.: Whatever Publishing, Inc., 1982. This excellent guide to achieving a full, abundant life includes detailed suggestions for commanding your inner resources.

14. Seaman, Barbara, and Giddeon Seaman. *Women and the Crisis in Sex Hormones.* New York: Rawson Associates, 1977. This is the first book to bring together all the information and research on what hormones do to human health, including the pill, DES, and estrogen replacement therapy. It includes an excellent section on wholesome and healthful alternatives.

15. Shealy, C. Norman. *90 Days to Self-Health.* New York: Bantam Books, 1977. Dr. Shealy's book is full of all types of techniques for relaxing.

16. Simonton, O. Carl; Stephanie Matthews-Simonton; and James L. Creighton. *Getting Well Again.* New York: Bantam Books, 1978. The Simontons are a husband and wife medical team who have achieved amazing results with "hopeless" cancer patients at their clinic in Fort Worth, Texas, using the relaxation/visualization techniques with conventional medical therapy. See especially "A Mind/Body Model of the Development of Cancer" and "A Mind/Body Model of Recovery."

17. "Stress on Your Job—A Major National Survey." *Ms Magazine* (April 1984), pp. 83–86.

18. "World Hunger Actionletter." Ed. by American Friends Service Committee. *Ms Magazine* (August 1981).

Chapter Five

Asserting Yourself

"You can control your destiny without leaning."
Ellen Burstyn

The more positive and constructive your dealings with the people you work with, the easier your job as manager will be—and the more effective you will be. Understanding your own and others' behavior is crucial in getting along with people. During childhood, many women learn to be "too nice" (over-compliant or nonassertive) because they believe it pleases others or prevents problems. Every once in a while they may get fed up with being "walked on," rebel in an aggressive manner, and then return to a basically passive, indirect way of dealing with people. At both extremes, they give up control of how they will express their feelings. The cycle also creates further problems.

A basic and essential rule to follow in order to get along with people on the job requires **assertiveness** in your transactions. The rule: Go directly to the person(s) involved.

If you have a problem, foresee a potential problem or opportunity, need or want something, or merely want to give constructive feedback, go first to the person(s) most directly involved. State your case candidly and tactfully. Asking someone else to broach the subject or merely complaining or dropping

hints and "hoping" something will change or someone will pass along the word often creates problems of its own. This is a passive, timid approach. However, going over the person's head to get results is usually even worse. It may rightfully be viewed as an act of aggression, violating another person's rights. When you complete this chapter, you should have the assertiveness skills for handling problem situations.

In this chapter you will have the opportunity to

1. Become aware of ways in which communicating assertively can help you prevent problems, manage stress, improve your self-confidence, and become a more respected, effective manager

2. Define some of your basic rights and become committed to standing up for those rights

3. Identify assertive, nonassertive, and aggressive behaviors

4. Become more assertive in a variety of situations by applying the most appropriate techniques or combination of techniques

168

5. Learn how to change nonproductive behavior by changing your internalized **parent messages,** irrational beliefs, and self-statements through focusing on the payoffs for assertiveness, and trying out new behaviors

6. Become comfortable with behaving assertively in appropriate situations with your workers, other managers, and your bosses

---

 Recognizing Assertiveness Gaps

"Jan, you were right, as usual. I just wasn't managing the stress in my life. That seminar you recommended was just the ticket. You should see the changes I've made! And they're working."

"That's wonderful, Carrie. And you're looking wonderful, too, I might add." Jan smiles as she and Carrie settle into the restaurant booth for lunch during a break in the quarterly national sales meeting.

"Well, I'm off cigarettes, and I'm substituting spring water and herbal teas for some of the coffee and booze I used to drink. A healthy diet and making time for exercise has worked wonders—along with picking up some good time management techniques."

"Yes," says Jan, "they all seem to work together, don't they?"

"That's right, and you know, the skill that's been most helpful so far has been the relaxed concentration—it not only works to calm me down, but I'm convinced it's helping me solve problems and achieve my goals."

"I'm sure you need all the skills you can get to handle Tom Jenson. Any run-ins lately?"

"I thought you'd never ask," laughs Carrie. "Just the other day he came barging in with the same old complaint . . . "

T: Can't your people ever do anything right? They're driving my people crazy!

C: What's the problem, Tom?

T: You don't seem to be able to train them well enough to fill a simple order form correctly. If we don't get the information we need, how can you expect us to get the right orders to the customers on time?

C: Do you have copies of the incorrect orders so I can see who's leaving off what?

T: Well, no, not with me. I just know that nearly every day we have a problem with one of your orders and today we have a whole stack of them.

C: Tom, I'm glad you brought this matter up. It's important that I stay on top of this so your department gets the proper information. First, if you'll send me the orders you're having difficulty with today, I'll have someone in my office locate the information for you at once. Second, if you'll send me copies of incomplete orders you've received in, say, the past month, I'll analyze them to see who needs further training and in what areas. Then I'll set up a training session. Finally, let's work out a system where your people divert any incomplete orders to my office in the future so we can handle the problems before sending the orders back to you.

T: Well, I don't know. Maybe it will work. But you'll have to do something about this incompetence in your department.

C: Tom, I want to cooperate with you in every way I can to get the right orders to the customers on time. Can you meet with me at ten in the morning to go over a plan for diverting incomplete orders to the sales department?

T: Okay, we can give it a try.

Jan nods approvingly. "That's more like it. You played it cool—*and* you were assertive. By the way, I hope your seminar leader pointed out that being assertive can also prevent stress from building up."

"Yes, but I think I need some work on that. I'm doing pretty well with my people and my peers, but I'm still intimidated by my bosses. You know, they're all men who are old enough to be my father. Well, here's an example—I know I handled this one badly: George (San Diego Sales Manager George Rodriguez) was on the road most of the month and delegated the preparation of the department budget to me. Then John (John Brockfield, San Diego General Manager) called me one day."

J: Carrie, could you drop by my office tomorrow afternoon at two? Be thinking about ways to cut salary expense in your department. Everyone's going to have to cut salary expense by at least 10 percent.

C: Yes, John. (*To herself:* Oh boy, this is going to be a tough one. Well, I might as well look at all the possibilities I can think of. Maybe I can find a way to salvage our salary figure.)

"Well, Jan," Carrie continues, "I came up with several ideas during the following twenty-four hours. The first idea was to cut the commissions of the salespersons for the coming quarter—that would create a real morale problem, and we would probably lose some of our best people. That in turn would cause us to suffer a decrease in total sales by the end of the quarter.

"A second approach would be to lay off some of the salespersons and reorganize the territories covered by the others so all customers would have a rep—but that would mean that each salesperson would have to work overtime at no extra pay or that some customers would have to be neglected.

"A third approach would be to lay off some of the office personnel—but customer orders and servicing would be delayed, and we might lose some valuable accounts. The only positive alternative I could see was to convince Brockfield that a cut in the Sales Department's salary expense would only aggravate the budget problem. If we could maintain our salaries, we could help the region pull out of the slump. And if the sales staff knew they were being given special treatment, and why, I felt we could motivate them to achieve even greater sales.

"Well, I went into John's office the next day and . . .

J: Oh, yes, Carrie. You have a revised salary budget ready for me?

C: Well, yes, Mr. Brockfield, but . . .

J: Oh, good. You know, Carrie, everyone's pulling together on this like champs. It's good to have team players in a crunch like this.

C: Well, actually, I prepared three alternative plans, but I feel that none is satisfactory. If you would only let us retain our salary expense figure for this quarter, I'm sure we could . . .

J: Now, Carrie, I know you mean well, dear, but you people in Sales have to learn to be team players like the rest of us.

C: But, Mr. Brockfield, if you'll just . . .

J: Come on, now, Carrie. Bite the bullet. Which of the three alternatives do you think is best?

C: Well, none, really, as I said. Actually, I think if we could just . . .

J: Okay. Let me see what you have there. (*Picks up Carrie's working papers*) Hmmmm. I'd say the best approach is to lay off a few salespersons and a few clerical people. That way no one will be hurt too much. Sold, Carrie. Good work. I really appreciate your cooperation, dear, and I'll be sure to mention it to George.

C: Well, thanks, Mr. Brockfield.

"You see?" continues Carrie to Jan, "I just knuckle under to people like John."

Jan smiles. "Looks like your next training seminar will be on developing assertiveness skills."

---

1. What are the major differences in the way Carrie handled the meeting with Tom Jenson and the one with John Brockfield?

2. What actions and attitudes do you think were especially effective or ineffective?

3. How would you advise Carrie to handle the meeting with Brockfield? _____

4. What risks are involved in behaving assertively with the boss? _____

5. List some possible payoffs. _____

ASSESSING YOUR AWARENESS OF ASSERTIVENESS

It's obvious that Carrie was assertive in the first example and not in the second. But how do *you* know when *you're* being assertive? How do you decide on appropriate behavior? What do you base your decisions on? We'll discuss these questions in detail later.

First, let's briefly define assertion, nonassertion, and aggression as we'll use the terms in this book. Assertion is confidently expressing what you think, feel, and believe—and standing up for your rights while respecting the rights of others. Nonassertion is a reluctance or inability to express confi-

dently what you think, feel, and believe—allowing others to violate your rights without challenge. Aggression is expressing yourself in ways that intimidate, demean, or degrade another person—and going after what you want in ways that violate the rights of another.

Before we go into more detailed descriptions of behavior, let's establish a clear understanding of the foundation upon which assertive actions are based: human rights.

If your assertive actions are to be effective, they must be convincing. You must believe in what you're doing. This means you must be clear about your rights and the rights of others in the situation. Later, we'll discuss what other authorities say about rights; first, get in touch with what you (as your own authority) believe by completing Exercise 5-1. After you've formulated your own ideas about basic human rights, see how they compare with lists compiled by others. See Exhibits 5-1 and 5-2.

Has this brief discussion of rights helped you clarify what assertiveness is based on? Hopefully, you're already feeling more committed to standing up for your rights (and respecting the rights of others). Now test your understanding of the differences between assertiveness and other kinds of behavior by completing Exercise 5-2.

Descriptions of Assertion, Nonassertion, and Aggression*

To clarify the differences between assertive, nonassertive, and aggressive behavior, assertion trainers Patricia Jakubowski and Arthur

---

*Based on the work of Arthur Lange and Patricia Jakubowski, *Responsible Assertive Behavior*, copyright © 1976 (Champaign, Ill.: Research Press, 1976), by permission of Patricia Jakubowski.

EXERCISE 5-1: DETERMINING YOUR RIGHTS

Think about some basic rights you are entitled to. List them here. (If you're meeting with a group, you may want to jot down your own ideas first; then discuss them with the others. Perhaps the group can formulate its own list of basic rights.)

1 _____   6 _____

2 _____   7 _____

3 _____   8 _____

4 _____   9 _____

5 _____   10 _____

EXERCISE 5-2: IDENTIFYING ASSERTIVE, AGGRESSIVE, AND NONASSERTIVE BEHAVIOR

Indicate whether you think the response to each of the following situations is assertive (As), aggressive (Ag), or nonassertive (N). After you've completed the exercise, turn to the answer key to see how you did.

	Situation	Response
_____	1. Husband expects dinner on table when he arrives home from work and gets angry when it is not there immediately. You say:	I know you are tired and hungry and would like to have dinner immediately, but I have been doing some sculpting which is important to me. I will have dinner ready soon.
_____	2. You are having trouble writing a paper and don't know exactly what further information you need. You say:	I really must be dumb but I don't know where to begin on this paper.
_____	3. You are at a meeting of seven men and one woman. At the beginning of the meeting, the chairman asks you to be the secretary. You respond:	No, I'm sick and tired of being the secretary just because I'm the only woman in the group.

Situation	*Response*
_____ 4. A woman is being interviewed for a job, in the process of which the interviewer looks at her leeringly and says, "You certainly look like you have all the qualifications for the job." She responds:	I'm sure I am quite capable of doing the work here.
_____ 5. You're walking to the copy machine when a fellow employee, who always asks you to do his copying, asks you where you're going. You respond:	I'm going to the Celtics ball game . . . Where does it look like I'm going?
_____ 6. You are asked to serve on a committee. You respond:	I'm sorry. I'm not available to serve on that committee.
_____ 7. Man asks you for a date. You've dated him once before and you're not interested in dating him again. You respond:	Oh, I'm really so busy this week that I don't think I will have time to see you this Saturday night.
_____ 8. You are in a line at the store. Someone behind you has one item, and asks to get in front of you. You say:	I realize that you don't want to wait in line, but I was here first and I really would like to get out of here.
_____ 9. Employer sends a memorandum stating that there should be no more toll business calls made without getting prior permission. One employee responds:	You're taking away my professional judgment. It's insulting to me.
_____ 10. You'd like a raise and say:	Do you think that, ah, you could see your way clear to giving me a raise?
_____ 11. Student enjoyed the teacher's class and says:	You make the material interesting. I like the way you teach the class.
_____ 12. Your husband promised you that he would talk to your daughter about her behavior at school. The promise has not been carried out. You say:	I thought we agreed last Tuesday that you would have a talk with Barb about her behavior at school. So far there's been no action on your part. I still think you should talk to her soon. I'd prefer sometime tonight.

Situation	*Response*
_____ 13. A committee meeting is being established. The time is convenient for other people but not for you. The times are set when it will be next to impossible for you to attend regularly. When asked about the time, you say:	Well I guess it's OK. I'm not going to be able to attend very much but it fits everyone else's schedule.
_____ 14. In a conversation, a man suddenly says, "What do you women libbers want anyway?" The woman responds:	Fairness and equality.
_____ 15. You've been talking for a while with a friend on the telephone. You would like to end the conversation and you say:	I'm terribly sorry but my supper's burning, and I have to get off the phone. I hope you don't mind.
_____ 16. A married man persists in asking you out for a date, saying, "Come on honey, what harm can it do to go to lunch with me just this once?" You respond:	I like our relationship the way it is. I wouldn't feel comfortable with any kind of dating relationship—and that includes lunch.
_____ 17. At a meeting one person often interrupts you when you're speaking. You say,	Excuse me. I would like to finish my statement.
_____ 18. You have been pestered several times this week by a caller who has repeatedly tried to sell you magazines. The caller contacts you again with the same magazine proposition. You say:	This is the third time I've been disturbed and each time I've told you that I'm not interested in subscribing to any magazine. If you call again, I'll simply have to report this to the Better Business Bureau.
_____ 19. Wife tells husband she'd like to return to school. He doesn't want her to do this and says:	Why would you want to do that? You know you're not capable enough to handle the extra work load.
_____ 20. An employee makes a lot of mistakes in his work. You say:	You're a lazy and sloppy worker.

EXHIBIT 5-1: A Bill of Assertive Rights

1. You have the right to judge your own behavior, thoughts, and emotions, and to take responsibility for their initiation and consequences upon yourself. (This is your prime assertive right. The other nine rights listed here are derived from this one and serve to elaborate on it more fully.)
2. You have the right to offer no reasons or excuses for justifying your behavior.
3. You have the right to judge if you are responsible for finding solutions to other people's problems.
4. You have the right to change your mind.
5. You have the right to make mistakes—and be responsible for them.
6. You have the right to say, "I don't know."
7. You have the right to be independent of the goodwill of others before coping with them.
8. You have the right to be illogical in making decisions.
9. You have the right to say, "I don't understand."
10. You have the right to say, "I don't care."

In other words, you have the right to say "no" without feeling guilty.

Excerpted from the book *When I Say No, I Feel Guilty* by Manuel J. Smith. Copyright © 1975 by Manuel J. Smith. Reprinted by permission of the Dial Press.

EXHIBIT 5-2: Everywoman's Bill of Rights

1. The right to be treated with respect
2. The right to have and express your own feelings and opinions
3. The right to be listened to and taken seriously
4. The right to set your own priorities
5. The right to ask for what you want
6. The right to get what you pay for
7. The right to ask for information from professionals (doctors, lawyers, counselors)
8. The right to choose not to assert yourself

Adapted from Lynn Z. Bloom, Karen Coburn, and Joan Pearlman, *The New Assertive Woman* (New York: Dell, 1975), pp. 32–33.

Lange have developed excellent definitions of the three categories.

Assertion You assert yourself when you stand up for your personal rights and act in ways that express your thoughts, feelings, and beliefs in direct, honest, and appropriate ways that don't violate another person's rights. You assert yourself as much by your actions (if not more so) as by your words. By your actions and your words you convey to people: This is what I think. This is what I feel. This is how I see the situation. You convey this in a way that doesn't dominate, humiliate, or degrade the other person.

Assertion is based on respect for yourself and respect for the other person. You express your preferences and defend your rights in a way that also respects other people's needs and rights. The goal of assertion is to get and give respect, to ask for fairness, and to leave space for compromise when your needs and rights conflict with another person's. Such compromises respect the basic integrity of both people, and both get some of their wishes satisfied. This approach to assertion helps you avoid the temptation of using assertion to manipulate others in order to get what you want. It frequently leads to both people getting what they want because most people tend to become cooperative when they're approached in a way that respects both parties.

Nonassertion When you let others victimize you by failing to act in ways that express your honest feelings, thoughts, and beliefs, or when you express them in such an apologetic, unsure, or self-effacing way that others can easily disregard them, then you're allowing your rights to be violated through **nonassertiveness**. By such actions you tell others: I don't count for much: You can take advantage of me. My feelings aren't very important: Yours are. My thoughts aren't important: Yours are the only ones really worth listening to. I'm nothing: You're superior.

Nonassertion reflects a lack of respect for your preferences. In an indirect way it reflects a lack of respect for the other person's ability to take disappointments, to assume some responsibility, or to handle problems. The goal of nonassertion is to please others and to avoid conflict at any cost.

Aggression When you stand up for your personal rights and express your thoughts, feelings, and beliefs in ways that violate the rights of another person, you're behaving with **aggressiveness**. Such actions and words are often dishonest and usually inappropriate. Such behavior carries this message: This is what I think: You're stupid for believing differently. This is what I want: What you want isn't important. This is what I feel: Your feelings don't count. The goal is domination and winning—which means the other person loses. Winning is achieved by humiliating, belittling, degrading, or overpowering other people so that they become less able to express their preferences and defend their rights.

Examples of Assertive, Nonassertive, and Aggressive Responses

You ask for a long-overdue raise.

> **Aggressive:** "You've been ignoring the fact that I'm underpaid for what I do. I think you're taking advantage of my good nature."
>
> **Assertive:** "I've prepared this analysis showing that my job responsibilities and productivity have increased by more than fifteen percent since my last raise. I would like a fifteen percent raise based on these increases."
>
> **Nonassertive:** "Uh . . . I know things are tight just now, but . . . uh . . . do you think you could see your way clear to give me a raise?"

Your subordinate is habitually late for work.

> **Aggressive:** "Do you really think you can come dragging in late all the time and keep your job?"
>
> **Assertive:** "Let's discuss this problem of getting to work on time."
>
> **Nonassertive:** You send a memo to all subordinates regarding the need for punctuality, hoping the late worker will get the message.

A boss asks you to take on tasks that are not your responsibility and that you don't want to get saddled with.

> **Aggressive:** "Get someone else to do your dirty work."
>
> **Assertive:** "I realize you must find someone to do this, but I don't think it's part

of my job responsibilities and I don't want to take on tasks that will prevent me from doing my best with my own responsibilities."

Nonassertive: "Well, okay, I guess I can handle it."

To Assert or Not to Assert?

By now you have an idea of appropriate assertive behavior, and you know that you have a right *not* to assert yourself. How are you going to decide when to assert? In making this decision, keep in mind that the choice may involve the rights of others. If so, are you willing to compromise?

How will others interpret your nonassertiveness? The men you work with may interpret your behavior in ways you never intended. For example, many women use silence as a way of ignoring a situation, avoiding an embarrassing confrontation, or "rising above" unpleasant circumstances. For men, silence may signal consent, or they may interpret it as weakness—a sign that you'll have trouble in the tough business world.

Will assertiveness improve your relationships and your self-respect? This is a key factor to consider when you're deciding whether to assert yourself. Nonassertive behavior creates problems for many women. Aggressive behavior is less frequently a problem because most women have accepted the **socialization messages** they received in childhood and the cultural stereotypes of ways they should act. However, some women believe they must behave aggressively in order "to make it in a man's world." They feel they will become vulnerable and lose control if they don't. This viewpoint overlooks the fact that most people "go underground" in their relations with aggressive people. They find indirect ways to undercut the aggressor's control.

The most successful relationships are based on assertive behavior, and they help prevent and reduce the degree of stress you experience.

Will assertiveness prevent or reduce stress? This is another key factor to consider when you're deciding whether to assert yourself in your relationships (see Chapter 4). We teach people by our actions how we will and will not be treated and how we think, feel, and believe about certain matters. When someone violates our rights and we *don't* say anything, we teach them that it's okay to exploit, dominate, or manipulate us, and we therefore create stress in our lives.

What if you alienate another in the teaching process? If you've shown respect for that person while asserting yourself, then it's fairly safe to assume that a mutually beneficial relationship was impossible to begin with. In such cases it's best to lay your cards on the table early; otherwise, you are likely to get hooked into playing the other person's games. If you eventually decide to assert yourself and break up the games, your "friend" is likely to react much more negatively at this point than in an initial encounter. And you are more likely to have an emotional stake in the relationship the longer it continues, and therefore experience more upset when it runs into trouble.

In short, you prevent stress by asserting yourself in the beginning in any new situation or relationship. If you do, you are likely to find yourself surrounded by people who honestly accept, respect, and admire you—a true support network. Others pass on by, and you will probably find yourself with *fewer* enemies.

Strangely enough, people like most those people they respect, and you don't gain respect by letting yourself be dominated or manipulated. In fact people may pity you even while they take advantage of your nonassertion. This pity may eventually become irritation and even disgust. In the long run more people that you really want to be around will like you if you behave assertively. People who appreciate you for who you are and who support your growth and autonomy will respect your assertiveness, and you'll respect yourself more. As you feel better about yourself, more self-confident, you'll start getting more of the things you want in life. You'll prevent many of the problems that create stress, including the frustrations and resulting pressures created by nonassertion.

As you are deciding when to assert yourself, ask the following questions: (1) How important is this situation to me? (2) How am I likely to feel afterward if I *don't* behave assertively (rather than aggressively or nonassertively) in this situation? (3) How much will it cost me to assert myself in this situation?

Once you decide to assert, follow the advice offered by psychologist Wayne Dyer in *Pulling Your Own Strings:*

> Try to make all your assertive encounters happy, fun, and challenging experiences, rather than battlegrounds in which you place your humanity on the line. *Have fun* seeing how effective you can be. If you succeed in this, but don't invest your entire self-worth in the process, you need never again be a victim. Avoid plowing through with deadpan seriousness or "trying hard." Relax and enjoy the challenge [3, p. 89].

SELECTING THE BEST ASSERTIVE APPROACH

Situations calling for assertiveness can vary widely. Therefore, you need to become familiar with a number of different approaches to asserting yourself, so that you can select the most appropriate method or combination of methods for each type of situation.

We'll define ways of behaving assertively according to the following categories: (1) basic assertion, (2) assertion with empathy, (3) I-messages, (4) assertion with increasing firmness, (5) assertion that confronts broken agreements, (6) persuasive assertion in groups, and (7) **feedback assertion**.

These approaches should provide you with a broad range of practical, constructive actions to take in order to assert yourself in most of the situations you will encounter.

Basic Assertion

The direct, simple actions involved in standing up for personal likes, opinions, beliefs, or feelings are known as basic assertion [6, p. 14]. Basic assertion also involves expressing affection and appreciation toward another person. Here are some examples:

1. You're asked a question for which you have no ready answer. You reply: "I'd like a few minutes to think that over."

2. The person in the next room has a radio playing loudly. You say: "Your radio is disturbing me. Would you turn it down?"

3. Your boss keeps interrupting you while you're trying to make a point. You say: "Excuse me, I'd like to finish making my point."

4. A colleague makes a good presentation. You say: "I enjoyed your talk. Your descriptions were so clear."

Assertion with Empathy

Sometimes you want to express empathy along with your preferences or feelings. You want to show that you recognize the other person's viewpoint or feelings. The empathetic statement is followed by one that stands up for your rights [6, p. 14].

Assertion with empathy is often effective because people are more likely to accept your assertion when they feel you have some understanding and respect for their position. It's especially valuable in situations where you tend to overreact in an aggressive way. If you take a moment to try to understand the other person's viewpoint before you react, you're less likely to respond aggressively. On the other hand, your expression of empathy must be sincere in order to be effective. People can usually spot insincere expressions of empathy, and they resent such attempts to manipulate. Here are some examples of assertion with empathy.

1. The boss wants a time-consuming report submitted tomorrow. You say: "I know you need this report as soon as possible, but I have important plans for this evening and won't be able to work overtime."

2. A subordinate is trying to get you to serve as referee in his personality clash with a coworker. You tell him: "I can understand why you want help with this problem, but the two of you will have to work this out together on your own."

I-Messages

You are most likely to retain the goodwill of the person you're standing up to if you stick with your own thoughts, feelings, and beliefs and avoid direct or implied criticism of the other's thoughts, feelings, or beliefs. One way to do that is to think in terms of **I-messages**. In *Effectiveness Training for Women*, Linda Adams has described an I-message as

a statement that describes you; it is an expression of *your* feelings and experiences. It is authentic, honest, and congruent. And since I-messages express only your inner reality, they do not contain evaluations, judgments, or interpretations of others. Since you are saying what you really feel, your verbal and nonverbal expressions are in harmony. Your messages come through confidently and congruently [1, pp. 31–32].

Think about your own reaction to the **you-message** "You talk too loudly" versus the I-message "I have sensitive hearing." Let's look now at some specific instances in which I-messages can be effective.

Preventive I-messages let people know ahead of time what you will need and want. They can prevent many conflicts and misunderstandings. In order to send preventive I-messages successfully, it's important that you (1) know what you want, or need, in life and in specific situations, (2) decide to take personal responsibility for meeting your preferences, (3) express your preferences in an assertive way to the person whose cooperation you need, and (4) are willing to shift gears to listen if the other person becomes defensive. Here are some examples.

1. "I'd like to set up a time to meet with you to plan what we're going to do at the conference, so I'll feel prepared and less anxious when we get there." (Instead of a you-message: "You shouldn't wait until the last minute to plan what you're going to do at the conference.")

2. "I'd like us to figure out what needs to be done before the week is over, so we can make sure we have time to get it all done." (Instead of, "You need to manage your time better.")

3. "I'd like to know what we're going to discuss in our meeting tomorrow, so I can bring the necessary information with me." (Instead of, "You should send out an agenda.")

These I-messages all begin with "I'd like" to point out that they express your preferences. They may also be phrased as questions: "Could we set a time . . . ?"

Declarative I-messages help others know more about you. They are self-disclosures that tell people about your beliefs, ideas, likes, dislikes, feelings, reactions, interests, attitudes, and intentions. They let others know what you have experienced, what it feels like to be you. They describe your inner reality. Here are some examples.

1. "I'm excited about the project."

2. "I'm worried about completing the project on time."

3. "I'm looking forward to more business travel."

4. "I appreciate the time you've spent on this."

Responsive I-messages clearly communicate "no" when "no" expresses your authentic feelings. They also can clearly communicate "yes" when "yes" expresses your authentic feelings. In addition to saying "yes" or "no," you may also want to express how a request will affect you or the reason you are saying "yes" or "no." Here are some examples.

1. "I have decided not to."

2. "No, I can't have the report to you on Monday because I have another project that I want to complete first."

3. "Yes, I will be glad to tackle that project. It will give me a chance to learn more about . . . "

Assertion with Increasing Firmness

Frequently a simple statement of assertion made in a friendly manner will be effective. On the other hand, you'll sometimes have to deal with people who persist in violating your rights or ignoring your stated preferences. In such cases you can state your position with increasing firmness without becoming aggressive [6, pp. 16–20]. Here are some examples.

You have helped out a married male colleague, and he keeps insisting on taking you to dinner to "return your favor."

> *First response:* "That's very nice of you, but I never go out socially with business friends. You can return the favor by helping me out sometime."

> *Second response:* "No thanks. I really feel very strongly about not accepting dinner invitations from business friends, especially married men."

> *Third response:* "The answer is 'no.' Please don't ask me again."

A subordinate is repeatedly late in submitting an important periodic report. When you speak with him about it, he argues about the necessity of giving it top priority.

> *First response:* "I know it's time consuming to collect all the figures you need for this report, but it has top-priority status. I must receive it on time in order to prepare for the regular staff meetings."

> *Second response:* "You'll have to manage your activities so that this report gets done on time. Make certain you're not late in submitting it again."

> *Third response:* "If you can't manage your work so that the most important jobs are done on time, I'll have no choice but to reassign you to a position with less responsibility."

In these cases the third responses were appropriate because the earlier assertions were ignored. They would have been inappropriate if they had been the initial responses.

In the second situation a **contract option** was offered. The speaker said what her final assertion would be and gave the listener a chance to change his behavior before that occurred. Some people will believe you're serious about standing firm only when you reach the contract-option point. The option should be said not as a threat, but merely as a fact. Therefore, it's important to be calm and rational when delivering this type of assertion, speaking in a matter-of-fact tone of voice. You simply give information about the consequences if the problem is not satisfactorily resolved.

Assertion that Confronts Broken Agreements

When another person fails to keep his or her agreements with you, **confrontive assertion** is appropriate. This involves describing specifically and nonjudgmentally what the other person said he or she would do, what he or she actually did do, and what you want [6, pp. 16–20]. Again it's important to express yourself in a matter-of-fact tone of voice with nonevaluative language. Here are some examples.

1. "I thought we agreed that my department will receive two additional personnel assistants, and I confirmed that in my memo of June 2. Yet the new budget shows no provision for new assistants. I would like for you to revise it to provide for them."

2. "I agreed that you could use the services of my secretary occasionally as long as you check with me first. She said you asked her to do some work yesterday, but you didn't mention it to me. I'd like to find out why you did that."

The confrontive assertion normally involves more two-way interaction than is shown here. You'll usually want to learn more about the circumstances of the broken agreement in order to solve the problem it has created. It's important to avoid a critical, accusing attitude, which usually results in an aggressive confrontation that judges the other person and attempts to make him or her feel guilty. For example: "You broke your promise! Obviously I can't depend on your word and will have to get everything in writing from you from now on."

Persuasive Assertion in Groups

We've been discussing types of assertion that apply mainly to one-on-one transactions. Now let's look at ways to assert yourself in group situations. To have the greatest impact when expressing honest opinions in task-oriented groups such as staff meetings and committee meetings, you can learn to use timing and tact [6, pp. 16–20].

Timing involves not only choosing the right time to express an opinion but avoiding taking up too much group time by expressing your opinion too frequently. Therefore you need to decide which of the agenda items being discussed at a meeting have top priority for you and are worth taking a stand on. Otherwise you may end up talking far too long about nearly every topic that's brought up. If the other group members decide that you just like to hear yourself talk and that you need to be the center of attention, they'll be likely to ignore your opinions on the issues that are really important to you.

Probably the best time to state your opinion on an issue is after a third or a half of the committee members have already expressed their positions. By then you have a sense of the group's position, and you can respond to the points that have been raised. It's unlikely that the group has made up its mind on the issue, so your position has a good chance of influencing the group's decision.

When you express your opinion on your top-priority item, state it as clearly and concisely as possible without belittling yourself.

Nonassertive: "Well, I've been known to be wrong before, but it seems like maybe we should think of some other ways of doing this."

Assertive: "This approach to marketing the product involves some high-risk factors. I think it would be a good idea to consider some other approaches that could reduce our risks."

To have the greatest impact, assertive words must be accompanied by assertive body language: Look directly at the various members of the group. Speak with appropriate loudness and firmness. And use your hands in a relaxed way to make reinforcing gestures. Of course, you must do your homework before the meeting so you know what you're talking about (see Chapter 6).

Tact is extremely important when your viewpoint differs from that of the majority of the group or from that of an influential member. Find something that you honestly think is good about the opposing viewpoint and acknowledge that before stating your viewpoint. For example:

1. "I agree that we need to expand our market in the southern region. However, if we expand too rapidly, we won't be able to deliver the goods on time, and eventually we may lose more customers than we gain."

2. "That's a good analysis of our internal budget problem, but it doesn't take into account the role that our competitors play in the problem."

Assertion That Gives Feedback

Assertive managers are able to give feedback that clarifies their thinking, feelings, opinions, and understanding of what others have said and done. We'll discuss constructive approaches to giving feedback, including suggestions for describing others' behavior specifically and nonjudgmentally and for expressing your feelings appropriately.

Giving Feedback That Clarifies You can develop skill in giving feedback that clarifies situations and keeps communication lines open. Your feedback can help build and maintain good relationships rather than destroy them when you use a constructive approach such as we discuss here.

Give regular feedback so that the receiver gets at least as much positive as negative feedback. Give negative feedback early, before a situation builds to the point that strong emotional reactions may be involved. Approach situations in a spirit of helpfulness and willingness to solve any problems.

Let's take those most difficult situations in which you need to assert yourself by giving someone feedback about how their behavior is affecting you. Such feedback assertion should clarify your viewpoint and help resolve the problem situation. For best results include these four basic aspects:

1. *When you* . . . (You nonjudgmentally describe some specific behavior of the other person.)

2. *The effects are* . . . (You describe as specifically as possible how the other person's behavior *concretely* affects your life—the practical problems it creates.)

3. *I feel* . . . (You describe the feelings you experience as a result; avoid the expression "you make me.")

4. *I prefer* . . . (You describe what you want—preferably after giving the other person a chance to state what she or he thinks might be done.)

The first three parts of the message can be given in any sequence using any words that express the ideas shown here. Here's an example of this type of feedback message: "When I don't get the information I need from you about the number of orders your department has processed each day, I'm unable to make appropriate work schedules for the next day. This has happened twice in the last two weeks, and I'm getting frustrated. What procedures can we work out to make sure I get the information I need each day?"

Now test your initial understanding of feedback messages by evaluating this example: "When you don't send me information about the number of orders your department has processed each day, you really frustrate me. I'd like you to be more reliable."

In that example, the speaker hasn't stated what effect the problem behavior has on her life. By the way she expresses her feelings, she puts herself in the position of a helpless victim. Instead of asking for a preferred type of behavior that is specific and objective, she makes a vague request that implies a condemnation of the receiver's character.

Here are some general suggestions for giving feedback constructively in situations where tension has been building: First, focus on your viewpoint by analyzing what it is that's really bothering you and how you feel when it occurs. Form this into an I-message that incorporates the first three elements of feedback assertion just listed. Find an appropriate time, and state your I-message to the other person. Describe accurately and completely enough to give a clear observable picture, but don't talk too long (a response known as "overloading") or introduce a great deal of evidence (sometimes called the "court room technique").

Next, focus on the receiver's viewpoint. Ask the other person how she or he sees this situation and listen with an open mind, as nonjudgmentally as possible. Acknowledge what the receiver says (for example, "You feel that . . ." or "You think we should do

. . ."). Avoid the tendency at this point to defend your position by reiterating your point and trying to prove it. Instead focus your energy on understanding the other person's viewpoint while not losing sight of your own.

Once you are sure you clearly understand the other person's viewpoint, you may want to come back to your position but almost as if you are approaching it from the other person's side. For example, "So the way you see this is that I am making it very difficult for you to cooperate by expecting too much too soon? Is that right?"

Finally, reach an agreement. When both viewpoints are adequately clarified, determine whether some action needs to be agreed upon or whether communicating thoughts and feelings is all that's needed for now. For example, "How are we going to do this from now on?" or "I think it's enough for now if we just understand each other's viewpoints and feelings about this." Establish a feeling of closure by expressing how you feel *now* at the end of this discussion and asking the other person how she or he feels now. Accept these feelings without trying to change them. For example, "I feel relieved for having shared my thoughts and feelings, but I'm worried that you may resent my telling you this," or "I do feel a little defensive, but I think I'll get over it. I appreciate your letting me know about this."

Now that you've had an overview of giving feedback assertively, we'll look at the two most common barriers to doing so effectively and at ways to overcome them.

Giving Feedback Specifically and Nonjudgmentally Most people give feedback about problem behavior in vague, accusatory language and therefore trigger a defensive reaction from the listener. Here are some suggestions for giving another person specific feedback about his or her behavior and the effects it has on your life.

1. *Be specific.* State exactly who did what, when, where, and to whom or what it was done. If appropriate, give a detailed but brief step-by-step replay of exactly what happened. Don't bog down in detail. Keep your purpose clearly in mind.

2. *Paint an observable picture.* Describe the situation so that the listener can see a picture of what you saw, as if he or she were a disinterested observer watching the situation.

3. *Clarify your statements.* Be exact and accurate. Avoid the tendency to exaggerate behavior that bothers you by using all-or-nothing expressions such as "never," "always," and "every time." To describe behavior accurately, it's important to be exact by using phrases such as "three times this month," "every day this week," "sometimes," "often," "occasionally."

4. *Use nonjudgmental words.* When people discuss behavior that offends them, they're prone to use judgmental words such as "sloppy," "lazy," "inconsiderate," and "stupid." These words not only judge a person's behavior, they are frequently used to overgeneralize about a person's character traits. Because they tend to put down a person and imply he or she is wrong, they are aggressive rather than assertive. They usually trigger defensive or guilty feelings. In addition they give little or no information that can help the listener identify specific behavior that will be acceptable to you, as these examples reveal:

Nonspecific, judgmental feedback: "I would appreciate it if you would at least be considerate and polite in your dealings with me."

Specific, descriptive feedback: "When you came over to my desk yesterday, you spoke in a very loud voice and demanded the Carter Company invoice. When we were unable to furnish it, you called us incompetent . . ."

Nonspecific, judgmental feedback: "We have a problem with your invoicing unit."

Specific, descriptive feedback: "During the last three weeks, your invoicing unit has not informed us of delays in their invoice-processing. We have received several telephone calls from angry customers because of these delays . . ."

Expressing Feelings Effectively Most people have difficulty identifying and expressing their feelings appropriately, but this skill can also be mastered. Even in business situations it can be important to communicate your feelings about another's behavior. Doing so increases the impact of your feedback message. The listener is more likely to get it and to remember it. To be effective, however, your message must also make clear that you take responsibility for your own feelings.

When people first attempt to communicate their feelings, they are likely to make such statements as "You make me angry when you accuse me like that." This you-message implies that the other person is responsible for your angry feelings, and that you're blaming the other person for your feeling and accusing him or her of causing it. This further implies that the other person can control the way you feel, which places you in a weak, helpless role.

"When you called me incompetent, I felt angry" may appear to be an almost identical statement to the one above. But in fact it is a quite different I-message in which you take responsibility for your feelings. You have the ultimate control over how you choose to view an accusation (or any other event) and therefore over how you will feel when it occurs. The way you phrase your messages about your feelings may seem unimportant. However, each time you phrase them in language that blames someone else for them, you are telling *yourself*—as well as others—that you are a victim controlled by others' actions.

Stating feelings directly and honestly is difficult for many people. They find it much easier to (1) state an evaluation of the other's behavior, (2) state the solution they want to the problem, or (3) imply their feelings indirectly. Many people expect a listener to be a mind-reader, or more specifically a feelings-reader. Here are some suggestions for avoiding those traps.

1. *State feelings, not evaluations.* Imply that your underlying attitude is "I'll tell you very directly what I'm feeling in response to your behavior, but I won't judge your behavior." This attitude carries a quite different message from one that implies "I'm going to tell you when you're good or bad, based on your behavior toward me."

2. *State feelings, not solutions.* When you state solutions to the problem instead of expressing your feelings about it, you imply that you're superior to the other person. You are able to figure out the problem and a solution without even discussing it with him or her. This approach also implies a lack of trust, that you don't expect the other person to be able to figure out an acceptable solution to his or her own problem behavior. Also, stating a solution before discussing the problem omits vital problem-solving steps. You haven't agreed on a definition of the problem, much less a solution that is acceptable to both of you. The problem may now become one of enforcing the solution! People may resist your high-handedness even if they agree with your solution.

3. *State feelings directly.* Simply say you are hurt, pleased, happy, annoyed, or frustrated. Don't imply your feelings by your voice tone, emphasis, sarcasm, or other indirect means; and don't expect people to infer them from your cutting remarks, questions, denials, or cloaked messages. For example, instead of saying directly; "I really become annoyed when you borrow my directory and don't return it," you say, "If people in this office would be more thoughtful, it sure would make it a nicer place to work." Such indirect messages usually communicate only a vague, underlying negative feeling. They are often interpreted by receivers as a generalized rejection of them as persons rather than as a specific reaction to a specific event. Instead of thinking, "She's upset because I didn't return her directory," the other person tends to think, "She doesn't like me; I wonder why."

Now you have the tools to give feedback assertively in problem situations. Even if the feedback doesn't lead to your preferred solution of a problem, it can help you become more open and direct with your thoughts and feelings. As a result, people are more likely to learn they can trust you. They know "where you're at," for better or worse. They tend to become more open in their dealings with you and with others in the work group.

You can enhance this openness and trust by using feedback assertion about constructive behavior, too. Here's an example: "Thank you for getting these reports to me on time every week. That makes it easy for me to be well prepared for staff meetings. I feel happy when I get that kind of cooperation. Keep up the good work." Feedback assertion helps you build an atmosphere for dealing with all kinds of behavior and at the same time minimizing defensiveness. Exercise 5-11 at the end of this chapter is designed to help you learn more about giving effective feedback, especially about describing behavior nonjudgmentally.

Combinations for Maintaining Assertiveness

You'll probably be surprised at how readily others accept and respect your assertiveness. You must be prepared, however, for the occasional "tough cookie" who responds aggressively by coming back with verbal attacks, demands, or put-downs. Think about appropriate combinations of techniques you can use as shown in this example of dealing with a person who won't take "no" for an answer.

Assertion with empathy to show that you have actually received the other person's message can be used initially: "I understand that your work is important to you and therefore you think it's unfair that I don't give your work top priority, but we can't complete it before Thursday."

Repeated assertion, in which you firmly repeat your original point while still responding to *legitimate* points made by the other person, can be used when the other person persists. The repetition helps you avoid becoming sidetracked by justifying your personal feelings, preferences, or opinions or arguing about irrelevant issues: "I must use my own judgment about the priorities I assign to the work that comes into my department." Or: "I understand the importance of this work to you, but we still must complete two other projects before we start yours."

Active listening questions (see Chapter 6 for more on this) about the other person's assumptions or positions can help clarify while you remain firm: "Are you saying that I should ignore everyone else's requests except yours?" Or: "Do you think that just because I don't grant this request that I don't want to cooperate with your department?" Or: "Are you angry because there's other work ahead of yours?"

Feedback assertion can be used if the discussion reaches an impasse: "I'm getting irritated. When I tell you we can have your project completed no earlier than Thursday and you keep insisting that we complete it by Tuesday, I begin to think you're trying to interfere with the way I run my department. I would prefer not to take up any more time discussing this."

NONVERBAL MESSAGES: ACTIONS SPEAK LOUDER THAN WORDS

Regardless of the assertive approach you select, you must learn to communicate your message nonverbally as well as verbally. One reason it's so important to be convinced of your rights is that your true convictions will come through in your nonverbal behavior. Many nonverbal aspects are virtually impossible to consciously control. They reveal how you really feel about a situation or person. They have far more impact than the verbal part of your message. Research indicates that our words, our vocal expression or tone, and our facial expression have the following impact on a listener's perception and decoding of a message [8, p. 44]:

Impact of words (verbal impact)	7%
Nonverbal impact	93%
Vocal expression	
or voice tone 38%	
Facial expression 55%	

If a speaker's facial expression or voice tone conflicts with what he or she says, the listener will normally accept, remember, and act on the nonverbal message. This makes sense when you consider that feelings have much more influence on actions than rational, logical thoughts do. People are more likely to act on their feelings. (So when you get conflicting messages, pay more attention to the nonverbal portion of the message.)

Types of Nonverbal Communication

Nonverbal communication takes many forms besides vocal and facial expression. The clothing people wear, the way they establish and observe territories and status symbols, whether and how they shake hands, and their body positions and postures can speak volumes.

Facial Expression High-status, assertive males tend to be more impassive than most women are. They are more "poker-faced" in business situations and thus express less emotion. They also smile less often and less broadly than women.

Voice Tone and Expression Most people equate a strong, deep male voice with power and authority. While most women neither want nor could have such a voice, you can almost certainly improve the assertiveness level of your voice. You can work to make your voice firm, strong, relaxed, self-confident and appropriately loud, forceful, low-pitched, and well-modulated.

Many women retain the voice pitch and tone of a little girl throughout their lives. Voice pitch can be lowered with practice. We all have a range, from high to low, that is comfortable for us. Record your voice on a tape cassette and play it back. Now record yourself as you practice speaking at a deeper pitch; as you practice, think of yourself as an extremely important, powerful leader. Can you detect the difference in your playback? When you listen to your playbacks, be alert for voice tones that are apologetic, tentative, meek, imploring, whining, prissy, nagging, or schoolmarmish. If you make a practice of taping your telephone conversations, you may pick up some voice patterns you'll want to change.

Some women speak so softly it's difficult to hear them from more than a few feet away. A stronger, louder voice is essential to an assertive image, so practice until you're comfortable speaking so a person twenty feet away can easily hear every word.

High-status male executives are usually somewhat less expressive in their voice modulation, as well as in their facial expression, than low-status women workers. This is one way they project a more self-possessed, rational image—one of cool moderation, carefully revealing only what they intend another to know. While an expressive, well-modulated voice can be a real asset, it can signal low status if it's overdone.

Clothing and Grooming Your appearance tells people a great deal about your attitude toward yourself and others, your competence, and your role in the company. Your clothing and grooming signal how well you fit in with the company image and with others in the company. (See Chapter 2 for a discussion of appropriate dress.)

Eye Contact The eyes are considered by many to be the most important means of nonverbal communication. Often they are a clue to thoughts and feelings the sender may be trying to hide. In normal conversation you glance at a person for about a second and then glance away to show the speaker you're listening but not staring. If you avoid eye contact, it will probably be interpreted as a sign of low self-esteem, weakness, or guilty feelings. A longer meeting of the eyes is uncommon and therefore can have special importance, indicating anger, challenge, or sexual attraction, for example. Research also indicates that people tend to maintain a higher degree of eye contact with those they believe will be approving or supportive of them.

Use of Space and Territories The way space is used is also a means of nonverbal communication. Humans, as well as other animals, tend to lay claim to and defend a particular territory. There is a psychological advantage to meeting with someone in your own territory. Lawyers like to hold important meetings with adversaries in their own offices just as athletic teams prefer to play on their "home" court or field.

In *Organizational Communication*, Gerald Goldhaver expands this concept and identifies three principles relating to territory and status in an organization [4, p. 150]. People with high status (1) control a larger **territory** (space, subordinates, decision-making authority, and other aspects of power) than people with lower status, (2) protect their territory better, and (3) invade the territory of lower-status employees more readily. Look at the people in your organization. The higher their status, the larger their office is—and the more private it is. As executives move up, their territory is better protected by the number of stories in the building, the length of hallways, and the presence of walls, doors, receptionists, secretaries, and other barriers to immediate access.

Executives usually presume familiarity with subordinates by casually dropping by their desks or offices. And executives usually feel free to sit down without being asked, implying that they are relaxed and intend to stay awhile. Most subordinates, on the other hand, would hesitate to invade the territory of their boss in this way. The larger the gap in status between the executive and the subordinate, the freer the executive tends to feel to invade and the more hesitant the subordinate is to do so.

Male peers and subordinates may attempt to subtly dominate you through such territorial moves. Unless you're aware of the significance of such actions, you may unconsciously respond with submissive behavior. Your most effective defense is to mentally "hold your ground." You can also signal your own sense of status in any number of ways, including: (1) rising and moving casually around your office during the conversation, (2) excusing yourself on the pretext of keeping an appointment, (3) setting up a barrier to screen visitors to your office or desk, (4) assuming the same familiarity with peers by dropping by their offices.

Status Symbols Nonverbal status symbols trigger strong feelings because they can satisfy or frustrate ego needs. People are usually quite sensitive to the messages implied by the ways managers handle status symbols such as these: their names on routing slips, lists, directories, organization charts, office doors, and stationery; the size and location of their offices; their furniture and equipment; their secretarial and clerical support and their access to other company resources. The more visible such status symbols are to others, the stronger are the feelings likely to be attached to them, especially if they're taken away.

A Handshake In our culture, a handshake is almost universally obligatory for men when they are introduced, and frequently when they meet or say goodbye. Women have traditionally used the handshake selectively and at their own option. Psychologist Albert Mehrabian, in *Silent Messages*, says that a person's general level of preference for handshakes reflects how positively he or she feels toward others [8, p. 7]. A firm handshake indicates a greater liking and warmer feelings, but a prolonged handshake is considered too intimate for most situations. A loosely clasped hand is usually interpreted as a sign of aloofness and unwillingness to become involved. A downright limp, cold handshake is repugnant to most people and is taken as a signal of an unaffectionate and unfriendly nature as well as an unwillingness to become involved in any way.

When a businesswoman volunteers a firm, friendly handshake in appropriate situations, it is usually interpreted as a sign of professionalism, assertiveness, and strength. Any time you're introduced to someone or encounter someone you haven't seen for awhile, initiate a handshake. Use it to congratulate and to seal agreements.

Body Position and Posture Through your body language you signal either weakness or dominance and status. Dominant postures also convey a sense of personal power or fearlessness. According to Mehrabian, "In our culture relaxation-tension is a very important way in which status differences are subtly conveyed" [8, p. 115]. Mehrabian's research into the significance of relaxed, as opposed to tense, body positions indicates that males in our culture assume more relaxed postures than females do. This pattern predominates in a variety of circumstances, whether the men are in the presence of women or other men. Dr. Diane Warshay has studied these power postures and ways

women can respond to them (as shown in Exhibit 5-4). She stresses the importance of responding with a message of strength, since most men know the signs of weakness and look for them (though not necessarily at a conscious level).

Research by John Malloy [7] indicates that the most effective power stance for both men and women is almost military, spine and head erect and straight, feet slightly spread, arms at sides with fingers lightly cupped. He also discovered that standing with one or both hands on the hips is a power stance for a man but a nonpower stance for a woman.

Malloy also found that upper-middle-class males (most top executives fall into this category) have somewhat different body postures than lower-middle-class males. A key difference is the angle of head and shoulders—the upper-middle-class head is more aligned with the spine—neck back and head erect. "Lowers" stoop their shoulders more, which throws their heads forward and downward, as shown in Exhibit 5-3.

EXHIBIT 5-3: Head Positions Signal Status

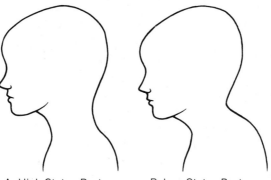

A. High-Status Posture   B. Low-Status Posture

Based on research by John Malloy [7].

These head angle differences are also found in females of both classes. The walk of the "uppers" is different, too—shoulders are straight, head aligned, eyes forward, arms in toward body, fingers lightly cupped, walk almost military with even strides of about twelve inches. The most powerful individuals walk with the relaxed power of a panther—unhurried, smooth movements, but ready to spring. "Lowers" walk with the shoulders and body rolling more, hips swinging, arms swinging out, head thrown more forward and downward, and long or erratic strides.

Developing New Nonverbal Messages

Managers who are most effective tend to engage in nonverbal behavior that conveys self-confidence, liking, involvement, and interest in others. People who are relatively outgoing, friendly, and approachable are more likely to take charge of situations. Managers tend to be dominant persons who have controlling and relaxed styles.

The nonverbal behavior of women tends to convey more liking than that of men, but also more tenseness and submissiveness. Women's nonverbal behavior also reflects a greater measure of empathic and affiliative tendencies [8, p. 67]. As a woman manager, you'll want to develop and project the tendencies and behaviors you already express that are typical of effective managers. It's also wise to become aware of necessary traits that you're *not* projecting.

Are you projecting an assertive, powerful image through your body language? Watch the high-status business executives you know. Then observe low-status workers. You may want to consciously practice some of the nonverbal behaviors that signal personal power and strength.

Exhibit 5-4 can help you identify new responses to male power postures, and Exhibit 5-5 can help you identify other nonverbal behaviors you may want to modify.

The good news is, you can change the way people perceive you by consciously changing your nonverbal messages. When you send high-status messages, people peg you at that level whether you're actually there or not [9]. Any time you try out new assertive verbal messages, it's important to practice the nonverbal actions that must accompany your words. While the new ways of behaving may seem difficult and awkward at first, with practice they'll become a natural part of you. So practice before a mirror and with friends at first, use videotaping and cassette recording where you can, and soon you'll have a new power image.

How can you be sure your nonverbal messages match your verbal ones? Perhaps most important is being very clear about what you *intend* to communicate. Before the anticipated confrontation, periodically relax and focus on your intended message (see Exercise 4-5). Visualize coming across assertively, both verbally and nonverbally, behaving naturally and appropriately, and achieving your intended goals. When the time comes to assert, your subconscious mind will take over the nonverbal aspects if you'll let it. Relax, keep your ultimate goal in mind, and play it by ear. (See Exercises 5-3, 5-4, and 5-5.)

USING YOUR ASSERTIVE SKILLS ON THE JOB

By now you should be clear about your level of assertiveness and how it's affecting your life. Later we'll discuss some specific steps you can take to change nonproductive be-

(Continued on p. 195)

EXHIBIT 5-4: Nonverbal Power Postures

Male Power Postures	Female Weakness Postures	Alternative Female Responses
The Power Position: A woman walks into a man's office. He leans back in his chair, puts his hands behind his head, spreads his elbows wide, and straightens his knees. The message is that the woman is inferior.	The woman clasps her hands, leans forward. If seated, she crosses her legs and looks slightly downward.	Assume a relaxed posture. Put your fingertips together with your hands pointed upward, a gesture called "steepling." Stand over his desk. Sit on his desk.
The Power Stance: A man approaches a woman's desk where she is seated, and he talks to her from above. Or, a man who is much taller than a woman moves close to her during a conversation.	The woman remains seated, straining to look up at the man during the conversation. The woman throws her head back in order to look up at the man.	Move casually back and then stand up. Step back. Find an excuse to casually move far enough away that your gaze seems to be level with his.
The Power Touch: A man puts his arm around a woman to discuss an office procedure. (People can show their power by acting in an intimate way with someone who wouldn't act in an intimate way with them.)	The woman touches her hair, wets her lips, smiles.	If you're standing or walking, step back and turn toward him in a relaxed way as you continue to talk, listen, and/or walk along, forcing him to drop his arm. If you're seated, turn in your chair and/or get up. If he repeats the touch, fold your arms and move away. If he persists, tell him he's invading your personal space.

EXHIBIT 5-5: Nonverbal Behaviors Signaling Nonassertiveness, Assertiveness, or Aggressiveness

	Nonassertive Behavior	Assertive Behavior	Aggressive Behavior
Facial expression	Smiling often, broadly; relatively animated, expressive	Relatively impassive; less smiling	Tight with anger; jaw and brow tense; sneering or scornful; patronizing; come-on smile, manipulative
Voice tone	Relatively expressive, sometimes apologetic, tentative, meek, imploring, whining, or prissy	Relatively impassive; objective, self-confident, firm, decisive	Angry, sarcastic, sneering, flippant, nagging, scolding, scornful; extremely loud; menacingly low

EXHIBIT 5-5: Continued

	Nonassertive Behavior	Assertive Behavior	Aggressive Behavior
Voice pitch	High, little-girl quality	Relatively low, forceful	
Hands	Playing with hair or earrings; nervous movements, mannerisms; primly folded in lap.	Still or purposeful, smooth movements; hands at sides, fingers lightly cupped.	On one or both hips; pointing or shaking finger
Eyes	Cast downward; little contact while speaking; watching speaker intently; avoiding direct contact	Frequent eye contact while talking; steady, firm, decisive gaze; casual, relaxed observation while another is talking	Staring—angry, challenging; or cold, expressionless
Head	Tilted, nodding, moving from side to side, up and down; ducked	Still, straight	Stiff, erect
Posture	Slumped, stooped, but tense; or ramrod tense, at attention, nervous	Almost military but relaxed; head and spine straight, erect, feet slightly apart, well-grounded, arms at sides	Tense—knees locked, feet spread widely apart, firmly planted; fists clenched
Positions	Hesitantly standing; sitting forward tensely; knees and feet together; arms folded tightly in lap; other balanced, tense positions; vigilant	Asymmetrical, expansive positions—arms on sides of chair, sometimes leaning to one side in relaxed way; leaning back, clasping hands behind neck; males: turning chair around and straddling it or putting feet on desk; casually turning one's back on another to get something	Tensely, forcefully leaning forward; pointing fingers; pounding desk
Movements	Small, controlled, tense; covering face with hand; fiddling with an object; rhythmic shaking of leg or foot	Expansive, relaxed, free; pressing fingertips together in a steeple; staring through them; free of nervous mannerisms	Waving arms angrily; closely towering over another; invading another's personal territory without asking
Other patterns	Allow others to interrupt; won't turn back on another	Not allowing others to interrupt; "competitive turn-taking" at interrupting	Interrupting others frequently; passing an acquaintance, making eye contact without speaking or smiling; failing to step aside when on a collision course with someone

EXERCISE 5-3: NONVERBAL POWER POSTURES AND RESPONSES

If you can, do this exercise with a partner. If not, practice the postures in front of a mirror until you become comfortable with them.

1. Practice the male status or dominance postures (described in Exhibit 5-4) that you would like to work on.

   (a) As you talk with your partner, deliberately use expansive gestures. Then try small, controlled movements. Compare how you feel while using each type of movement. Get feedback from your partner (or your mirror) on the impression you make in each mode.

   (b) Practice walking and sitting taller. Think of yourself as actually being the height you would like to be in business situations. Then draw yourself up, beginning at the base of your spine and continuing to the top of your head, to your full height. Now go back to your regular height. Next try slumping or bending. Compare the different ways you feel in each posture. Get feedback from your partner on the impression you make.

   (c) As you talk with your partner, consciously relax. Move around in a relaxed manner, occasionally turn your back on your partner, and then face her or him again. Next, practice tense movements in a vigilant manner as you talk. Compare the differences in the way you feel in each mode and get feedback from your partner on the impression you make.

   (d) As you talk with your partner, sit in a relaxed manner with legs crossed, leaning back slightly, and slanting sideways a little, with arms asymmetrically placed (for example, one arm on the table and the other in your lap or on the chair arm). Now change your posture so that you are leaning forward in your chair and carry on a discussion while in this posture. Compare how you feel in each posture and get feedback from your partner on the impression you make.

2. Practice the female postures (described in Exhibit 5-4) with your partner.

   (a) Have your partner play the male role and you play first the female weak role and then the alternative female role.

   (b) Compare the way you feel in the female weak postures with the way you feel in the alternative female postures.

   (c) Get the feedback from your partner on the impression you give in each posture. If some of the improved postures seem awkward, practice them some more until they become more natural.

   (d) Switch roles with your partner. You now play the male role while your partner plays the female role.

EXERCISE 5-4: NONVERBAL AWARENESS

This activity will help you to get a feeling for the differences between assertive, nonassertive, and aggressive postures and gestures and the impact of these movements on the way you feel about yourself and others [2, pp. 154–56]. Do it with a partner, if possible (see Exhibit 5-5).

Nonassertive behavior: Think of a situation in which you have trouble asserting yourself. Close your eyes for a few seconds and picture yourself being nonassertive. Now stand up and *without words* act-out the way you behave in that situation. Move around doing the things you would normally do and thinking the things you would normally think or say. Fully experience the situation and your actions. Then sit down. Close your eyes again and recall how you felt acting nonassertively. Now erase the memory from your mind.

Aggressive behavior: Think of a situation in which you would probably overreact, perhaps something you have been feeling angry or frustrated about for a long time. Close your eyes for a few seconds and picture yourself behaving aggressively. Now stand up and *without words* act-out the way you would behave in that situation. Fully experience the situation and your feelings as you move around. Then sit down. Again close your eyes and recall how you felt when you were behaving aggressively. Now erase that memory from your mind.

Assertive behavior: Think of a situation in which you are comfortable asserting yourself (or a situation in which you think you could become comfortable behaving assertively). Close your eyes for a few seconds and picture yourself behaving assertively. Now stand up and *without words* act-out the situation in an assertive manner. Fully experience the situation and your feelings as you move around. Then sit down. Again close your eyes and recall how you felt when you were behaving assertively.

Comparison and feedback: Discuss the exercise with your partner.

1. How did you feel in each role?

2. How did each type of behavior make you feel about yourself? About others?

3. Which role were you most comfortable with? Least comfortable with?

4. Which role was the easiest to get into? The most difficult?

5. How did your partner perceive each of the roles?

6. What suggestions does your partner have for a more effective expression of assertiveness?

Replay: Take the assertive role again. Incorporate your insights and your partner's suggestions as you act-out without words.

EXERCISE 5-5: NONVERBAL AND VERBAL AWARENESS

With a partner or by yourself, say each of the following statements in three ways: assertively, nonassertively, and aggressively. Be aware of how your nonverbal behavior changes the message. If you are doing this exercise with a partner, ask her or him to identify the kind of behavior you are acting out. Ask for feedback about the effectiveness of your assertive behavior [2, p. 156]. Add your own list of statements to practice.

1. "That's all right."

2. "I'd rather do it myself."

3. "I didn't say that."

4. "I don't care to go."

5. "Please don't do that."

6. "Can you take my place?"

---

havior into effective behavior that gets the results you want. First, let's survey some ways you can use assertive skills to become a more effective manager.

To Manage Your Workers

Women managers generally must develop a little toughness in order to be firm. Toughness, the ability to dish it out and take it without complaining, is expected of good managers. Only you can decide the best place on the scale for you in dealing with your particular group of workers:

1	2	3	4	5	6	7	8	9	10
Soft				Firm					Hard

Here are some steps you might take to develop the appropriate degree of firmness.

1. Get to know your subordinates.

2. Think through the personalities and the requirements for full productivity.

3. Anticipate the various types of situations you will encounter and the decisions you'll have to make.

4. Decide where you will draw the line in each type of situation. Stick to it, unless you discover valid reasons for changing your mind. If this occurs, ask yourself if you are rationalizing the switch in positions as valid when it is actually based on insecurity or fear.

Being Firm and Fair Your workers want you to be assertive. They admire a sense of fairness that includes equal rights for all. Most of them will resent seeing a coworker getting away with something. Some will see if they can get away with it too. Therefore, it's important to assert your rights and the company's rights. Your workers expect that and will generally approve it. Even when they are the ones being "called on the carpet," they will usually agree with the idea that "It's not fair to your coworkers for you to behave this way," or "It's not fair to the others for me to condone this."

Giving Criticism or Feedback on Performance When it's necessary to confront workers with poor results or unacceptable actions, use a problem-solving approach assertively. Focus on what can be done next, how to solve the problem, and how similar problems can be avoided in the future. Where possible, tie desirable behavior to achieving objectives a worker has helped to set for his or her job, or tie the behavior to departmental or company objectives.

Avoid the trap of comparing or implying comparison of one subordinate with another. Focus on the worker's own performance according to the standards and objectives the two of you have previously agreed upon.

Focus on *behavior*, not attitudes or personality traits that produced the behavior. Give **feedback** as soon after the behavior occurs as possible. If performance needs improvement, give the feedback in private. Be prepared to make suggestions or give instructions on how performance can be improved.

Dealing with Tardiness If a worker's tardiness is a potential problem, it's best to nip it in the bud. Try a variation of feedback assertion. Confront the worker and describe in nonjudgmental terms the specific behavior that is creating the problem: "I noticed that you arrived at 8:40 on Monday, 8:50 on Tuesday, and 8:45 today." Ask whether there is some problem. If there is a legitimate problem, let the worker know you will appreciate being informed of such problems at the time so you will be able to plan accordingly. If there is no legitimate reason, mention the effect tardiness has on your work and on the others in the department and the kinds of feelings it triggers. You might want to point out that it's unfair to permit some people to violate agreed-upon work hours while their

coworkers are careful about keeping this agreement. Make it clear that you expect the worker to honor this agreement in the future.

Dismissing Workers Sometimes, after you have taken all the usual steps of discussing performance problems, coaching, giving deadlines for improvement, and searching for alternatives (see Chapter 12), you must dismiss a worker. Every situation is different, and you will have to decide how to handle each according to its own peculiarities. Here are some suggestions to consider.

1. Be cordial but get straight to the point.

2. Give specific reasons why. Discuss performance and behavior, not personalities, attitudes, or personal characteristics.

3. Give a specific termination date and tell the worker how much termination pay she or he will receive.

4. Answer questions.

5. If asked for suggestions about what the worker might do next, be prepared to respond helpfully. Think of the dismissal as an opportunity to support a worker in finding a more appropriate niche. Help the worker see the dismissal as a learning experience and a growth opportunity.

To Deal with Peers

It is essential to be able to assertively ask for favors from peers and colleagues. Trading favors is an important factor among male colleagues in getting things done, taking advantage of opportunities, and moving on up the ladder. Grant as many favors as you can. But be assertive about refusing to grant those that are inappropriate.

Also be ready to handle some common problems assertively.

Someone takes credit for your ideas. Confront the person in private. Tell him or her you don't want it to happen again.

You are hesitant to speak up at meetings. Be prepared for the meeting. Review your facts, then be positive about expressing yourself ("I think . . . I believe . . ."). If you find yourself thinking negative thoughts ("They'll think this is silly," "I'm no good at expressing myself at meetings"), stop that train of thought by saying "stop," then "calm," and deliberately relaxing your muscles for a few seconds. If you are alone, say the words aloud.

You are by-passed at meetings. The meetings consist of a dialogue between a few people speaking mainly to each other. Even though you speak up, your opinions are generally ignored. Try feedback assertiveness. Describe the behavior nonjudgmentally. For example, "I have been listening to this discussion for the past twenty minutes and only three people have spoken, mainly to each other. Prior to that I contributed my opinion a couple of times and it received little or no comment. I've had the same experience at other meetings. I would like to contribute to this committee, but I feel frustrated in my efforts to do so." Then be prepared to make specific suggestions for increasing your level of participation. If you are stumped for suggestions, at least ask the group what can be worked out to increase participation by all members. Here are some possible suggestions.

1. "Perhaps each speaker could remember to speak to everyone by looking at each of us."

2. "If each speaker would pause after making a point, we can ask questions or get clarification without interrupting."

3. "Perhaps the chairman can stop the discussion before going on to a new item and ask for contributions from others."

4. "If members would listen carefully to all input and formulate appropriate questions about statements that need clarifying, perhaps more of us could make a real contribution."

A peer is keeping you from doing your job. First, go to your colleague and confront him or her with the problem. Be as tactful and as candid as possible. If this doesn't get results, let the boss know what's going on.

To Hold Your Own with Your Boss

Your boss may be the person you have the most difficulty with in asserting yourself. However, you must learn to be assertive with your boss in order to gain his or her respect and to communicate your wants, goals, and requirements. You must be able to assert yourself in every area, from requesting office space and equipment comparable to that of your male peers to requesting a promotion and raise. No one person has the power that your boss does to implement or block your immediate career goals. Dealing assertively with this important person can be a real bonus to your career. Here are examples of typical problem situations that can be handled in an assertive way.

Your boss takes credit for your ideas. Start putting your ideas in writing. Send your boss a memo with a copy to his or her boss.

You have difficulty saying "no" to your boss. If you feel you want to say "no" and should say "no," be prepared to give your boss a reason, preferably without going into a lengthy explanation. Practice your refusal mentally when you are calm. Picture yourself being calm when you say it.

You have difficulty asking for a promotion or a raise. Read Chapter 14 for information about preparing your facts and picking the right approach. If you are nervous, rehearse with a friend. Have your friend offer all the objections and responses you fear. Practice handling them until you're comfortable.

Your boss makes a decision affecting you that you disagree with. Not only that, you are convinced that if you carry out the decision, the results will be disastrous. Counter with another suggestion or slant your boss' suggestion differently: "That ties in with something I had in mind." "What would you think if we did it this way?" "Perhaps the most *professional* way to handle it would be . . ."

You are excluded from a meeting or a trip you think you should attend. Write a memo saying you understand there will be a meeting (or trip) concerning (topic) on (date). Tell your boss you have some ideas on this subject or that you think the experience will help your job performance, and ask whether it is all right for you to attend.

You're uncomfortable calling your boss by his or her first name. If your boss and your peers use first names, you should too. It's important for your assertive stance that you think of yourself as basically equal to your boss as well as to your peers. Being on a first-name basis can help you feel equal and reduce the possibility of being intimidated or dominated.

Your boss tries to compare you (or your behavior) with others. Confront the issue. Wayne Dyer [3, pp. 85–89] suggests some assertive strategies for dealing with this.

Remember that the boss' comparison has nothing to do with you as a person. He or she would do the same to any subordinate willing to take it.

Say, "You are using other people's examples as reasons why I should be a certain way, but I am not any of those other people."

Use sentences that begin with "you" to indicate that you are not internalizing the boss' efforts to compare you: "You think I should be more like Bob?" "You think I should do things the same way as Jim?" Be sure to sound incredulous and bewildered.

Give an honest evaluation of what you see going on: "You are comparing me with someone else so that I will stop trying to do what I believe in."

Ask yourself "What do I want from this encounter?" rather than "Who does he think he is, telling me I should be like someone else?" In this way you can avoid becoming angry. You start focusing on getting what you want rather than on the boss' behavior.

Ask yourself "Does he need to feel powerful, understood, important, effective?" If you can see what the boss needs out of this encounter, you are more likely to see an appropriate way to let him (or her) "save face" while you still assert your rights.

If your boss later makes comparisons in spite of what you have done, confront the issue again—and again, if necessary. It's important to be persistent and consistent.

Your boss overloads you. If your boss asks you to take on an unreasonable amount of work, it's important for you to assert your rights and communicate your situation. "I know there's a lot to be done, but I'm overloaded right now. Let's discuss what your top priorities are and I'll work on those first."

You're afraid you aren't pleasing the boss. Many women are caught in the "trying to please trap." They depend on others, especially authority figures, for approval of their behavior, decisions, or ideas. Your boss will respect you if you are clear about what you want in your life and in your career. If you please yourself, you're likely to gain the respect of your boss. Keep cooperation and achievement on an objective level: company goals, department goals, your personal job goals. Find a boss you can honestly admire and respect enough to support and be reasonably loyal to. Then focus on achieving your professional goals, not on pleasing the boss.

You get a new boss. When a new administration takes over a company, they frequently bring in some of their own staff. You may suddenly find your job in jeopardy. Consider meeting with your new boss. Before the meeting, review your achievements and update your objectives. Tell your new boss you have heard about possible layoffs and you would like to discuss why you think it would be a mistake to let you go. Tell him or her what you have accomplished in specific, measurable terms and provide documentation. Then lay out future plans for you and your department. Avoid becoming defensive or belittling anyone in the company.

You feel your boss is behaving incompetently or unfairly. If you believe your boss is not handling matters competently or is dealing unfairly with you, discuss the situation with the boss. Present the problem as you see it and be ready to give possible solutions. Try to work it out. If you get nowhere, seriously consider talking to the appropriate superior on up the ladder. Decide whether or not it's best to inform your boss in advance of your intention. Either way, try to time your moves so that your boss doesn't have a chance to influence *his* boss' attitude before you give your side of the story.

When you talk with your boss' boss, be clear about why you are asking for the meeting and what you want as a result of it (that is, the action that you want). Give a brief overview of the situation, the major problem, and your major concern. Don't get bogged down in details. Let them come out as needed in response to the executive's questions. Remain objective and stick with facts. Avoid bad-mouthing your boss, but be frank about the facts. Stress what's "for the good of the company."

Your boss dismisses you. Ask the boss to give you adequate reasons for the dismissal. If he or she cannot, get your files in order. Be prepared to document your case and go to your boss' boss. Bring along a complete file of ideas you have given your boss as well as letters and memos recording your achievements.

If the boss *does* give you adequate reasons for your dismissal, make your departure as gracious and positive as possible. Tell your boss how much you have learned from this experience. Ask for a letter of recommendation. View your dismissal and its causes as a learning experience and possibly an opportunity for a new direction in your life. Analyze your behavior to determine if you want to make any constructive changes.

CHANGING YOUR THINKING AND BEHAVIOR

You've had a chance to become aware of your current attitudes and actions in the area of assertiveness, as well as to see some ways in which assertiveness enhances a manager's effectiveness. What aspects of your behavior do you want to change in order to enhance your *own* effectiveness? The rest of this chapter is devoted to guiding you through the change process.*

---

*An understanding of transactional analysis can help you in every area of the change process. **Transactional analysis** (TA) is a comprehensive approach to becoming aware of the subtleties and meanings that underlie people's behavior, interactions, motivations, and games. It offers a model or framework for understanding yourself and others and for changing nonproductive behavior.

If you're dissatisfied with your level of assertiveness, it's best to work on changing your thinking and behavior in one area of your life at a time. Begin with situations where little is at stake: interactions with strangers and acquaintances who have little impact or significance in your life. (If you blow it, it doesn't really matter.)

Don't *condemn* your ineffective behavior or actively try to squelch it. This kind of attention tends to reinforce it so that it becomes more deeply entrenched than ever! Simply notice it and start *substituting* assertive behavior. Build on the strengths you already have: You're behaving assertively in some types of situations already. Spend more time in these kinds of activities. Gradually expand that assertive behavior to similar kinds of situations.

Take it one step at a time, and you'll find that a small success in one area of your life will provide incentive to make changes in other areas. You'll gain confidence in asserting yourself in more and more significant situations where the stakes are higher.

Many psychologists believe that behavior is learned through (1) modeling, (2) association, and (3) payoffs. *Modeling* is copying the behavior of your parents and others. *Associ-ation* refers to the external and internal messages and experiences that you associate with your behavior. Messages from parent figures have a significant impact. These messages, along with your interpretations of them and the feelings you experience, lead to both rational and irrational beliefs, which determine what you say to yourself in stressful situations. *Payoffs* are the rewards you got from parents and others that reinforced the behavior, the "something pleasant" you got or the "something unpleasant" you avoided as a result of the behavior.

You can learn new, more productive behavior in exactly the same way you learned the old, now nonproductive behavior. The basic change process is described in Exhibit 5-6. We'll discuss each step generally and its affect on your life specifically. Then you'll put it all together to deal with a situation you want to change.

Role Models

Copying the behavior of role models is easy for most of us. Although you may have trouble finding numerous female role models, you can surely find plenty of male managers

---

EXHIBIT 5-6: The Change Process: From Nonproductive to Assertive Behavior

1. Identify the problem situation clearly and specifically and decide exactly what your goal is. State your current behavior and your desired behavior. Determine how much control you have over these outcomes. (Does the outcome depend mostly on your behavior or on another person's?)

2. Look for, or think of, *role models*, both male and female, who handle similar situations well. Pick up verbal and nonverbal cues from them, and absorb their attitude and style as they go about dealing with these situations.

3. Identify any *parent messages, irrational beliefs,* and consequent *self-statements, feelings,* and *anxiety* about what would happen if you acted assertively.

4. Dispute and challenge nonproductive parent messages, irrational beliefs, and self-statements about your rights and behavior in this situation. Eliminate them by substituting more rational, productive ones.

5. Identify the *payoffs* you get from the old and the new behavior.

6. Identify your *personal rights* in the situation and act on these convictions.

to learn from. Of course you'll retain your own personality and autonomy. You'll simply be picking and choosing certain actions and approaches others use that you think will work well for you too.

Parent Messages

All of us operate at times on parent messages that we internalized in childhood. But we're frequently unaware of these messages and their impact on our behavior. When you become aware of the parent messages underlying your nonproductive behavior, the behavior changes you make are likely to be more profound and long lasting than when you remain unaware.

Take shyness, for example. Its root cause is an excessive concern that you'll be evaluated, plus an assumption that the evaluation will be negative and that you'll be rejected in some way. Dreading or fearing rejection, the shy person hangs back, "freezes," becomes self-conscious, and won't risk taking assertive action. Simply developing and practicing relevant verbal and nonverbal skills can do much to remedy shyness—for example, practicing assertiveness, public speaking, and social skills.

Such behavior change will be longer lasting, however, if you look at underlying causes and make changes at a deeper level. That means becoming aware of parent messages you internalized, such as "You must achieve, you must compete, you must win to be okay." The implied message is, "If you fail, it's because you're a loser, not okay, didn't try hard enough." The cure for nonproductive parent messages is to refute them in your own mind now and make new messages to yourself. Then focus on your strengths, keep substituting your new messages, and spend more time being involved with activities and people that enhance your feeling of self-worth. Exhibit 5-7 and Exercise 5-6 list common messages parent figures stress to children through verbal and nonverbal communication. The messages in Exhibit 5-7 are followed by explanations of how children frequently interpret them, the effects such interpretations can have on their rights and their assertive behavior, and alternate messages that are more realistic and workable. Exercise 5-6 lists only the parent messages, not the effects or alternates. See whether any of these messages, or similar ones, are affecting your viewpoints and actions.

Irrational Ideas

Irrational ideas are often the basis for nonproductive behavior; they frequently give rise to emotional reactions to situations. If we irrationally believe that it would be "awful" and "catastrophic" to fail to accomplish a major goal or to be rejected by a significant person in our lives, then we will feel anxious, depressed, or guilty. Another irrational idea is that it's terrible if others treat us unfairly and those who do so should be blamed and severely punished. This idea leads to intense anger when others behave unfairly toward us.

The key difference between irrational and rational ideas is that irrational ideas are based on the belief that "I need" or "I must," while rational ideas are based on the viewpoint that "I want" or "I prefer."

Here are some irrational beliefs and alternative messages that are especially significant for women[2].

If I stand up for my rights, others will get mad at me.

Alternate belief: If I stand up for my rights, people may get mad, they may not care much one way or the other, or they may

EXHIBIT 5-7: Parent Messages That Affect Assertion

Parent Message	Effect on Rights	Effect on Assertive Behavior	Alternate Message to Enhance Enlightened Self-Interest and Assertiveness
Think of others first; give to others even if you're hurting. Don't be selfish.	I have no right to place my needs above those of other people.	When I have a conflict with someone else, I will give in and satisfy the other person's needs and forget about my own.	To be selfish is to place your desires before everyone else's, which is undesirable human behavior. However, all healthy people have needs they strive to fulfill. Your needs are as important as other people's. Try a compromise when needs conflict.
Be modest and humble. Don't act superior to other people.	I have no right to do anything which would imply that I am better than other people.	I will discontinue my accomplishments and turn aside any compliments I receive. When I'm in a meeting, I will encourage other people's contributions and keep silent about my own. When I have an opinion which is different from someone else's, I won't express it.	It is undesirable to build yourself up at the expense of another person. However, you have as much right as other people to show your abilities and take pride in yourself. It is healthy to enjoy one's accomplishments.
Be understanding and overlook trivial irritations. Don't be a nag or shrew and complain.	I have no right to feel angry or to express my anger.	When I'm in a line and someone cuts in front of me, I will say nothing. I will not tell my girlfriend that I don't like her constantly interrupting me when I speak.	It is undesirable to deliberately nitpick. However, life is made up of trivial incidents, which are sometimes irritating. You have a right to your angry feelings; if you express them somehow as they occur, they won't build to an explosion.

Based on the work of Patricia A. Jakubowski, "Assertive Behavior and the Clinical Problems of Women," in *Psychology for Women,* ed. D. Carter and E. Rawlings, copyright © 1982 (Springfield, Ill.: Charles C. Thomas, Publisher, 1982). Used by permission of Charles C. Thomas.

like and respect me more. When I assert a legitimate right, chances are the results will be at least partially favorable.

If people do get mad at me, it will be terrible. I will be shattered.

Alternate belief 1: I can handle other people's anger without feeling devastated.

Alternate belief 2: When I stand up for a legitimate right, I don't have to feel responsible for another person's emotional reaction.

EXERCISE 5-6: EXAMINING PARENT MESSAGES

Did you receive any of these messages as a child? If you did, how did you interpret them? Write your responses in the appropriate columns; then think of alternate messages. Finally, list any other parent messages that might be affecting your assertiveness, along with their effects and alternate messages. You'll want to keep your new messages in mind when it's time to assert yourself. Return to your list occasionally and review it for reinforcement.

Parent Messages	Effect on Rights	Effect on Assertive Behavior	Alternate Message
Be perfect.	_____	_____	_____
Hurry up. (And grow up. And get out of my hair.)	_____	_____	_____
Please me. (Act in ways that are important to me at the expense of your growth or desires.)	_____	_____	_____
Try hard. (And make me proud. And never notice that you've made it.)	_____	_____	_____
Be strong. (Don't be afraid. Don't be sad. Don't cry.)	_____	_____	_____
Other Parent Messages			
_____	_____	_____	_____
_____	_____	_____	_____

If I am honest and direct with people and say "no," I will hurt them.

Alternate belief 1: People may or may not feel hurt if I say "no" directly.

Alternate belief 2: Most people are not so easily shattered that they can't handle another's honest, straightforward message.

If the other person does feel hurt when I say "no," then I am responsible.

Alternate belief 1: Although they may be surprised and perhaps a little embarrassed when I say "no," most people are not so vulnerable that they will be devastated by it.

Alternate belief 2: I can let people know I care for them at the same time that I am saying "no."

Alternate belief 3: The other person's hurt or angry feelings may be his or her own problem.

It's selfish and bad for me to turn down others' valid requests. They will think I am mean and won't like me.

Alternate belief 1: Even valid requests don't necessarily warrant my time and energy.

Alternate belief 2: I can find myself continually carrying out other people's priorities rather than my own.

Alternate belief 3: It's okay to take care of my own needs before the needs of others.

Alternate belief 4: The more decision-making power and visibility I have, the more critics I will have. This is true for all managers, executives, administrators, and other leaders.

I must be extremely cautious about making statements or asking questions that might appear "dumb."

Alternate belief: No one is perfect and no one knows everything—even about his or her area of expertise. Asking apparently "dumb" questions at times reflects confidence and competence. ("I figure if I don't understand it, something must be wrong.")

People label women who stand up, speak out, and fight back. They will call me a nag or a shrew. They will say I am grouchy or difficult.

Alternate belief: When I am direct, honest, and stand up for my rights appropriately, others are likely to respect me. Those who don't would probably not respect my nonassertiveness either; rather, they would probably use my timidity, fear, or anxiety to manipulate me and take advantage of me.

Nonproductive Self-Statements

What you say to yourself just before, during, and after an incident is based on your parent messages and beliefs. It has a very important influence on your behavior. Exercise 5-7 gives you an opportunity to become aware of these "self-statements" [6, pp. 141–44]. Examples of nonassertive self-statements are "They'll think I'm dumb"; "I'll probably blow it." Examples of assertive self-statements are "I'll relax and let my best self handle this"; "I can do it."

Compare the two sets of self-statements that you listed in Exercise 5-7 for differences in negative/positive, destructive/constructive, and distorted/realistic content. Most statements that lead to nonassertive or aggressive behavior have one or more of these characteristics [6, pp. 141–44]:

1. Draws conclusion when evidence is lacking or even contradictory: "He said there was no need to discuss next year's vacation now. I'll bet he's planning to let me go before the first of the year."

2. Exaggerates the meaning of the event: "I never though I would get the news that I was a failure in front of the copy machine on a Monday morning."

3. Disregards some important aspect of the situation: You overlook the fact that the boss has a hangover and is running behind on current projects.

EXERCISE 5-7: SELF-STATEMENTS: CHANGING FROM NEGATIVE TO POSITIVE

Step 1. Think of three or four incidents in which you behaved nonassertively with poor results. List them in the lefthand column. What did you say to yourself about these situations at the time? Write your comments in the right-hand column.

Nonassertive Incidents   Self-Statements

1 _____ _____

2 _____ _____

3 _____ _____

4 _____ _____

Step 2. Now think of three or four incidents in which you behaved assertively with good results. Write down what you said to yourself about those situations.

Assertive Incidents   Self-Statements

1 _____ _____

2 _____ _____

3 _____ _____

4 _____ _____

Step 3. Now go back and change the nonassertive self-statements in Step 1 to assertive ones.

---

4. Oversimplifies events as good or bad, right or wrong: "He's had it in for me ever since we lost the Acme account. He probably thinks it's all my fault."

5. Overgeneralizes from a single incident: "It's terrible to be a failure at 35. I'll bet no one will want to hire such a failure."

Negative self-statements can cause you to cycle down into a state of anxiety. One way to break the cycle is to stay in the present moment and deal with current reality by asking yourself questions such as these: What is my anxiety level (on a scale of 1 to 10)? . . . What am I doing (verbally and nonverbally)? . . . What am I feeling? . . . What am I thinking? . . . What do I *want* to be thinking, feeling, and doing? . . . What thoughts, opinions, desires, or feelings do I want to express in this situation? . . . What do I want the other person to know? . . . What thoughts are keeping me from doing what I want? . . . What do I think is appropriate to express? . . . How can I go ahead and express what I want?

Addressing these questions can help you change your pattern of irrational or self-defeating thinking, become aware of your thoughts, and stop them in midstream. Then you can make your thoughts more rational and workable by using *constructive* self-statements:

Before the event: "I know how to deal with this even though it's upsetting." "Easy does it! Remember to keep your sense of humor." "I'm not going to let him get to me." "I'll look for the positives and not assume the worst."

During the event: "Getting upset won't help." "My anger (or anxiety) is a signal of what I need to do; it's time to instruct myself." "Keep your cool."

After the event: "Don't take it personally." "Can I laugh about it? Is it really so serious?" "Don't let the bullies get you down." "I can win this game if I play my cards right." "I handled that one pretty well!"

Now, in order to assert yourself appropriately, practice making new, more constructive self-statements. Also, when your anxiety level is high, remember to use an effective relaxation technique or self-mastery visualization (see Chapter 4). Excuse yourself as soon as possible and find a private place to relax and get things in perspective.

Payoffs

Many women are comfortable with the "security" payoffs nonassertiveness helps them hold onto. They're either unaware of the higher-level payoffs assertiveness brings, or they're afraid to risk losing what they're sure of.

In other words, although they are not satisfied with what their current behavior is getting them, at least they know more or less what to expect. They fear they may lose more than they gain if they begin asserting themselves. When women begin realistically to weigh what they gain against what they lose, however, the risks of assertiveness become more attractive. Here are some typical comments.

"My boss will protect me, but I never develop the confidence of standing on my own two feet."

"I avoid rejection, but I give up lots of opportunities to learn and grow."

"I was driving down the street listening to the car radio. Someone said, 'If you are not being rejected at least once a week, you are simply not trying.' What a revelation! Most men risk rejection all the time. That's when I started coming out of my protective shell."

"At first it was scary coming out of my cocoon. But at least my achievements are my own now. There's no way I would go back again."

"I *like* myself better when I speak out and stand up for my rights. It may be more trouble at the time, but it feels so good afterward. I no longer have to deal with conflict over what I should have said and done."

"Sure, some people don't like having their hands called, but I've been surprised at how many of them show increased respect and eventually like me more than before."

Let's focus for a moment on those situations in which you have behaved nonassertively, with poor results. Understanding *why* you acted that way—what payoffs you get from such behavior—can help you decide to assert. We only repeat behavior that brings us some reward or payoff. (Sometimes we even perceive negative attention as a payoff, though usually at a subconscious level.) Exercise 5-8 can help you identify the payoffs you get from nonassertion.

Here are some payoffs other women report; see how they compare with yours: avoiding risk, getting approval (avoiding losing another person's approval), playing it safe, not rocking the boat, avoiding a scene or hassle, being able to blame someone else if things don't work out, being polite, being helpful, avoiding rude or aggressive behavior. These payoffs obscure the greater rewards assertiveness can bring. If you focus on "safety payoffs," you forget that standing up for your rights can pay off in increased respect *and* goodwill from others.

Whenever you find yourself *not* taking assertive action because of fear, ask yourself, "What am I getting out of this?" You know the typical payoffs to look for.

Now for the other side of the coin: situations in which you *are* assertive and the payoffs you get. Identify them by completing Exercise 5-9.

When you examine the feelings you've had after behaving assertively, do they include feeling stronger as a person? You have many strengths and many assertive experiences in your background. When you operate from those strengths, you're most effective.

Now you have the tools and the framework for deciding when and how to assert yourself effectively. Exercise 5-10 gives you a chance to apply the step-by-step change process as we've discussed it. You can also select appropriate exercises from those presented at the end of this chapter for practicing new behaviors and rehearsing anticipated situations. Build on your successes. Take time to notice your growing sense of strength and self-confidence. And above all *enjoy* being the creator of your own life.

EXERCISE 5-8: PAYOFFS FOR NONASSERTIVENESS

Describe recent situations in which you found yourself not taking assertive action because you feared the consequences. Ask yourself, "What did I get out of that behavior?" Then describe the payoffs. (Example: "I avoided alienating him/her.") If your first answer is "nothing," recall your feelings afterward, both positive and negative, and any thoughts they led to.

Nonassertive Situation 1 _____

Payoffs _____

Nonassertive Situation 2 _____

Payoffs _____

Nonassertive Situation 3 _____

Payoffs _____

EXERCISE 5-9: PAYOFFS FOR ASSERTIVENESS

Describe recent situations in which you took assertive action. Ask yourself, "What did I get out of that behavior?" Then describe the payoffs. Record the feelings you had about yourself afterward and the feelings you think other people had toward you and the situation afterward.

Assertive Situation 1 _____

Payoffs _____

My Feelings _____

Other People's Feelings _____

Assertive Situation 2 _____

Payoffs _____

My Feelings _____

Other People's Feelings _____

EXERCISE 5-10: APPLYING THE CHANGE PROCESS TO YOUR LIFE

Briefly describe an activity or situation that you want to handle assertively. Then respond to each of the instructions listed below.

Your Problem Situation _____

The Change Process

1. Identify your goal, your current and desired behavior, how much control you have.

1 _____

_____

_____

2. Identify role models, their verbal and nonverbal actions, attitudes, and style.

2 _____

_____

_____

3. Identify parent messages, irrational be-   3 _____
   liefs, self-statements, feelings, and anxiety level.   _____

   _____

4. Dispute and challenge the nonproductive   4 _____
   responses you listed in number 3. List
   here new responses that you will substi-   _____
   tute for the old ones.
   _____

   _____

   _____

5. Identify payoffs from old behavior and   5 _____
   from new behavior.
   _____

6. Identify your personal rights.   6 _____

7. With a partner, practice new verbal and   7 _____
   nonverbal behaviors you'll use.
   _____

   _____

8. Visualize yourself behaving assertively in   8 _____
   this situation, using the process described
   in Exercise 4-5.   _____

   _____

SUMMARY

The concept of assertiveness as discussed here is based on standing up
for your rights while respecting the rights of others. In order to assert
yourself convincingly, you must be aware of and committed to those
rights. When you let others victimize you because you don't express your
honest feelings, thoughts, and beliefs in a confident way, you're behaving

nonassertively. When you violate the rights of others by overreacting, or by overpowering or belittling them, you're behaving aggressively.

Appropriate assertiveness actually improves your relationships with others, gains you respect, and increases your self-respect. Because it's based on honest communication, assertion prevents some of the human relations problems that create stress. It also reduces stress that does occur because it enables you to handle problem situations productively, which leads to self-confidence and tranquility.

When you acquire skill in basic assertion and in a variety of assertive approaches—assertion with empathy and with increasing firmness, assertion that confronts broken agreements and is persuasive in groups—as well as I-messages, active listening, and giving feedback, you'll be in a better position to handle any type of situation. To back up and reinforce your verbal assertiveness, you'll find it helpful to practice nonverbal behaviors that signal assertiveness.

Here are some suggestions for becoming more assertive. Find role models to selectively emulate. Become aware of nonproductive parent messages and irrational beliefs and replace them with more productive, rational ones. Examine self-statements that trigger uncontrollable emotions and raise your anxiety level or otherwise inhibit assertive action and change them to positive statements. Identify the payoffs you get for nonproductive versus productive behavior. Confirm your personal rights in each situation.

Finally, you must practice your skills, taking one situation at a time and beginning with low-risk, simple transactions. Eventually you'll find it easy to assert yourself with your workers, your peers, and even your boss. The result will be a more effective management style. The ultimate payoff: You increasingly become the active creator of what you have in your life.

Additional Exercises

EXERCISE 5-11: GIVING FEEDBACK MESSAGES

Read the following story:

You have a new apartment-mate, Lois. You have been sharing an apartment for about a month now, and things have been going fairly smoothly. However, two or three times you have come home from the office to the following scene: In the entry hall, Lois' coat is thrown over the chair; her shoes are lying in the middle of the floor; and her briefcase is on the floor, leaning against the wall. In the living room, the newspaper is spread all over—part of it on the floor and the rest of it on the tables and the sofa. Various articles of clothing are also scattered around the room. Lois, wearing an old robe, is sitting in the easy chair with her feet propped up on the arm of the sofa. She's drinking a can of beer and eating a package of peanuts. A few peanuts and an empty beer can are on the living room floor. The television is playing loudly.

Now it's Friday. This morning a man you've been interested in getting to know better called you at the office and asked you out to dinner. You agreed and suggested he come by your apartment about 7 p.m. for a before-dinner drink. You rush home from the office and reach your apartment at 5:30. As you enter, you see a repeat of the previously described scenario. You decide that the time has come to give Lois some feedback about her behavior.

You say; "Lois, I want to talk with you . . . "

Now you finish the statement. On a separate sheet of paper, write what you would say to Lois. (If you're doing this exercise as part of a class activity, your instructor may ask you to complete the message and then exchange papers. If so, don't sign your name on the front of the paper. Instead turn the paper over and print your initials in the upper righthand corner.)

WITH A PARTNER

NOTE: These exercises may be used for videotaping; see also Exercises 5-3, 5-4, and 5-10.
Before doing exercises with a partner, study Exhibit 5-8, which is designed to help you give feedback in ways that will be most helpful to your partner.

EXHIBIT 5-8: Guidelines for Giving Feedback During Exercises with a Partner

1. Start off with the strengths of the performance. Specify exactly which behaviors were positive.

Verbal Behaviors

Was the statement direct and to the point?
Was the statement firm but not hostile?
Did the statement show some consideration, respect, or recognition of the other person?
Did the statement accurately reflect the speaker's goals?
Did the statement leave room for escalation?
If the statement included an explanation, was it short rather than a series of excuses?
Did the statement include sarcasm, pleading, or whining?
Did the statement blame the other person for the speaker's feelings?

Nonverbal Behaviors

Was eye contact present?

Was the speaker's voice level appropriately loud?

Was the statement filled with pauses?

Did the speaker look confident or were nervous gestures or inappropriate laughter present?

Was the statement flat or expressive?

2. After all positive feedback has been given, offer feedback suggestions.

Describe the behavior, rather than give a label. Be objective rather than judgmental.

Offer a possible way of improvement. This should be expressed in a tentative rather than absolute manner. Do not impose a suggestion.

Ask the group member for a reaction to the suggestions, allowing the member to accept, refuse, or modify the suggestion.

Note: Stick to the basic assertive problem and do not get involved with long and complex descriptions of the history of the problem or the anticipated negative reactions of the other person.

Reprinted from Arthur Lange and Patricia Jakubowski, *Responsible Assertive Behavior,* copyright © 1983 (Champaign, Ill.: Research Press, 1983), p. 195. Used by permission of Patricia Jakubowski.

EXERCISE 5-12: VOICE LOUDNESS

The purpose of this activity is to make you aware of the full range of loudness available to you and to contrast it with the range of loudness you are accustomed to [6, pp. 76–77].

Say the word "yes" and ask your partner to respond at the same loudness level. Repeat back and forth for a minute or two. Then vary the loudness of the word "yes" from very quiet to as loud as possible. Your partner should match your loudness level with "no" each time. Switch roles.

Is your present range of loudness wide enough? How much loudness control do you use? (How well are you able to match the loudness level of your partner when you are answering "no"?)

EXERCISE 5-13: MAKING AND REFUSING REQUESTS

This activity will give you an opportunity to practice discriminating between effective and ineffective refusals and requests. Here's your chance to practice standing up for some of those personal rights you identified earlier [6, pp. 102–03].

1. Create a role-playing situation in which a fellow worker, friend, or roommate makes a reasonable request of you that you want to refuse.

2. With your partner playing the role of the other person, you respond to the request with a simple "no"; then switch roles so that you play the person making the request.

3. Is saying "no" all you wish to communicate? What else do you wish the requester to know? Is the additional message an excuse that avoids the real issue?

4. With your partner, again act-out the scene, this time intentionally offering excuses that avoid the real issues. The "requester" should persist and confront the "I can't" responses either with solutions or with alternatives that still include a request.

   (a) Are the "I can't" responses easier to give? Are they satisfactory?

   (b) How does the fear or wish to avoid being selfish or hurtful to others affect your responses?

5. Identify your thoughts and beliefs that led you to avoid *making* requests and refusing requests. Write them down. Which beliefs are rational or faulty? What are some alternatives to those beliefs?

6. If you are not comfortable making and refusing requests and you wish to work on that, identify specific situations and work on them when you do behavior rehearsal with a partner.

7. With your partner practice making and refusing requests in an honest and direct way. Emphasize "I don't want to" or "I won't" messages rather than "I can't."

Explanations and expressions of concern for the requester are appropriate if they are said in a direct, honest way that doesn't put down the other person. Practice making requests without apology or low expectation of getting what you ask for.

EXERCISE 5-14: MAKING STATEMENTS WITH AND WITHOUT EXPLANATIONS

In this activity you will have a chance to discriminate between *wanting* to explain your behavior and *having* to explain it, and to practice making statements with or without explanation [6, pp. 104–06].

1. Think of a situation in which you have avoided taking action because you are afraid you didn't have a good explanation for your behavior.

2. Think of a situation in which you *have* taken action but you felt obligated to give a lengthy explanation (perhaps untrue) to justify your behavior. The following are examples that might help you think of your own:

   (a) Leaving a shop without buying anything after a salesperson has spent a great deal of time and energy trying to make a sale.

   (b) Canceling or changing plans.

   (c) Returning merchandise.

3. Think of a situation in which you normally feel a need (as opposed to a preference) to give a lengthy explanation. Act-out the scene with your partner; then switch roles and respond while your partner gives a lengthy explanation from her own scene.

4. Reenact the scene *without* the lengthy explanation. Compare the effect on both you and your partner.

EXERCISE 5-15: DEFINING YOUR OWN BEHAVIOR—OR THE OPPOSITE OF TRYING TO PLEASE

This activity will help you to recognize when your behavior is misperceived or misinterpreted and when incorrect motives or meanings are attributed to your behavior, and it will enable you to practice direct and nondefensive ways of responding to such redefinitions [6, pp. 111–12].

1. Think of a situation in which someone has redefined the meaning of your behavior and you did not respond assertively. Here are some examples to help you get started:

   (a) You refused a friend a favor and he or she defined the refusal as a personal insult or rejection.

   (b) You spent time with a friend and another friend reacts jealously and takes it as a personal put-down.

   (c) You arrived late and someone assumes the meeting is not important to you.

2. With your partner create a role-play situation in which your partner will redefine your behavior.

3. Act-out the scene several times, trying various responses to the other person's redefinition. Compare your feelings and the effectiveness of the various ways of responding to the situation. Switch roles.

4. Optional additions:

   (a) Express irritation or concern toward a partner who has redefined your behavior.

   (b) Have your partner persist in redefining your behavior in the situation. Try out various ways of dealing with that.

REFERENCES

1. Adams, Linda. *Effectiveness Training for Women.* New York: Wyden Books, 1979. A good book for women. It has a special focus on making decisions about what is and what is not your problem and eliminating worry and guilt over other people's problems.

2. Bloom, Lynn Z.; Karen Coburn; and Joan Pearlman. *The New Assertive Woman.* New York: Dell, 1975. One of the most valuable assertiveness-training books written especially for women.

3. Dyer, Wayne W. *Pulling Your Own Strings.* New York: Thomas Y. Crowell, 1983. Although not advertised as an assertiveness-training text, this book is the best one in the field.

4. Goldhaver, Gerald. *Organizational Communication.* Dubuque, Iowa: Wm. C. Brown, 1984. A comprehensive guide to organizational communication. The chapter on use of space and territory is especially valuable.

5. Lange, Arthur, and Patricia Jakubowski. *The Assertive Option.* Champaign, Ill.: Research Press, 1984. An excellent book for anyone who wants to become more assertive. Written for participants in assertiveness-training groups.

6. Lange, Arthur, and Patricia Jakubowski. *Responsible Assertive Behavior.* Champaign, Ill.: Research Press, 1983. An excellent manual for trainers. It includes all aspects of assertiveness, as well as numerous exercises.

7. Malloy, John. *Live for Success.* New York: Perigord Press, 1981.

8. Mehrabian, Albert. *Silent Messages.* Belmont, Calif.: Wadsworth, 1971. An excellent review of the major research findings on nonverbal communication, with practical applications.

9. Parlee, Mary. "Women Smile Less for Success." *Psychology Today* (March 1979), p. 16.

10. Smith, Manuel J. *When I Say No, I Feel Guilty.* New York: Bantam Books, 1983. A helpful discussion of defining your rights.

Chapter Six

Communicating Effectively

"If you can't be direct, why be?"
Lily Tomlin

Most work problems can be traced back to a failure in communicating. Every skill you gain will be either enhanced or undermined by your ability to communicate effectively. You use all your personal and managerial skills to get work done through leading your team, gaining the cooperation of your peers, and inspiring the support of your bosses. This leadership process relies on your skill at communicating effectively, which links everything together. Your communication skill is the key to personal and managerial success—it's a basic linking tool.

As a woman, you probably have an advantage over your male peers when it comes to listening and speaking effectively. From the time we were little girls, most of us were encouraged to tune in to other people's feelings and messages and to interact empathetically with them. Most of us were constantly reinforced in our verbal attempts and in our efforts to develop interpersonal skills—probably to a much greater extent than our male counterparts were. Here is a strength, then, that you can capitalize on.

The only *new* communication skills you may need to develop involve *adapting* your messages to the special requirements of your new management role. We've already dis-

cussed communicating assertively, perhaps the most important adaptation the typical woman manager must make. Now we'll turn our attention to sharpening the listening and speaking skills that are especially appropriate to you as a manager.

In this chapter you will have the opportunity to learn more about

1. Viewing communication as an ongoing process

2. Sending messages that get the results you want

3. Listening for the total message and overcoming some listening barriers

4. Developing active listening skills that support your leadership role

5. Arranging business meetings that achieve specific objectives

6. Conducting meetings that are group centered instead of leadership centered

7. Using the jitters constructively when making presentations and talks

8. Preparing and giving talks that get the results you want

9. Determining when to send oral or written messages

10. Writing effective proposals

 A Focus on the Message

"Carrie, Jan here. How did Brockfield react to your second-round proposal?"

"Jan, he went for it! When I stayed focused on my goal and my right to present my case and argue for its merits, John actually stopped talking long enough to really listen."

"Well, you must have prepared an excellent case. John gets arguments all the time, and he prevails unless someone convinces him of the logic and payoffs of a different approach."

"Jan, the more I thought about it, the more I knew that the only positive alternative to our budget problem was to avoid layoffs in the Sales Department so we could put forth maximum effort to help the region pull out of the current slump. If I could convince John of this—and in turn convince my people of the payoffs to them and the company for achieving a higher level of sales and customer service—then my department would get a lot of credit for pulling the region out of the slump."

"Sounds like a good plan, Carrie."

"It's the same one I had when I met with John before, but I let him overpower me so that he never heard it. So, like my seminar leader suggested, I kept my goals and rights up front in my mind and made an appointment with John to discuss the problem again. My goal was to convince him that the salary expense budget for the Sales Department should not be cut. This

time I persisted. I talked about the end results of the layoff solution he had chosen last week—for my department, for our region, and for the company as a whole. Then we got down to the nitty-gritty . . . "

J: Carrie, I still think the best approach to this problem is for you to lay off a few salespersons and a few clerical people. That way no one will be hurt too much.

C: You're right John, the sales people would be in a better position than if we took all the decrease from that area, and the same is true of the clerical people. The problem is that morale would be lower throughout the entire department, not just part of it. Not only will sales drop, but customer service will suffer too.

J: Look here, Carrie, you've got to make your cuts just like every other department. Everyone's going to be treated equally in this situation.

C: I agree with the goal of fair treatment for everyone, John, but each department is different and what's fair for one is not necessarily fair for another. A significant increase in sales volume could solve the current budget problem. I can give you that increase if you give me the salary funds I need.

J: Carrie, I know you mean well. Sales people tend to be optimistic, but you can't expect to work miracles.

C: John, you can't deny the Sales Department *is* the key to increasing revenues for the company. I don't promise miracles, but I think that when my sales people understand that they're not being cut back because this branch is depending on them to pull us out of this slump, they'll get in there and do the job.

J: The problem is . . . I can't appear to be playing favorites. The other department heads are taking cuts.

C: I know you don't play favorites, John, and so do they. I think they will go along with the idea if you tell them why the Sales Department is maintaining its salary expense and what you expect in return. If you think it would help ease the tension with the other departments, you could put it on a trial basis for one month.

J: Okay, I'll give it a try for a month. We'll see whether sales increase or not.

C: Thanks. I'll do my best to make you glad you did.

"I think you handled that beautifully, Carrie. Now—have you marked June 1 on your calendar?"

"You bet. I wouldn't miss that national sales meeting in San Francisco for anything. I hope you're lining up the best sourdough bread, Irish coffee, and other goodies for us."

Jan smiled. "I have a better goodie than that for you. I want you to report on the Spring Fashion Preview you put on last November. The buyers are saying it's the best one we've had. I'd like you to tell the other Regional Sales Managers about it. They can use the tips, and the visibility won't hurt you. Our top executives and most of the board of directors will be there too."

"Say, I'm impressed! What an honor. Sure, Jan, I'd love to do it. I'll start working on it right away." Pulling a scratch pad toward her, Carrie starts to write. "Now, how long should the presentation run? . . ."

A few weeks later, Brian, Carrie's assistant, enters her office carrying several large charts and a few five-by-eight note cards. "Here's the stuff for your speech,

Chief." He holds up the note cards. "Brief outline of main points plus opening sentence and first sentence of conclusion." Then he holds up the charts, one by one. "I think Graphics did a pretty good job, don't you? A few simple items on each chart, large and bold—even those old codgers on the Board who are half-blind should be able to see these."

"Good job, Brian. Now, listen while I go over my part of the presentation. Tell me if there's anything you don't understand or any parts that drag."

A few days later in San Francisco, shortly after her presentation, Carrie relaxes in the hotel coffee shop with Jan.

"Congratulations, Carrie. You did a good job of explaining how you made your Spring Fashion Preview so successful. Your talk was well organized, and the visuals were great."

"Thanks, Jan. Some day I hope to make presentations that are as smooth and professional as yours. I'm not too happy about my talk today. Actually, I left out some key points."

"Oh, I do that too, Carrie. But I don't worry about it. I nearly always have time to ask for questions afterward, so someone asks something that triggers my memory—if it's really an important point. Talks can be more spontaneous and interesting to the group when some of the facts come out that way. People like to get involved in the talk."

"My main problem is nervousness. It doesn't go away once I start talking, either. It either gets worse or it comes and goes. I always seem to end up cutting my talk short and practically running for a seat. I just can't take being in the spotlight one more minute!"

Jan smiled gently. "I guess we all tend to get the jitters when we make these more formal types of talks."

"You sure don't! How do you stay so cool and calm, Jan?"

"Oh, I get my share of the jitters. But I make sure I'm well prepared, without memorizing my talk. Then I just keep focusing on getting my message across. Part of my preparation is getting clear about the main points I want to get across—what it is I want the people to come away with. Then any time I start feeling nervous—before *or* during the presentation—I just focus on my message. I picture the message going across from my head to their heads. In fact, if I get anxious in the days before the talk, I focus on that picture during my deep relaxation times."

Carrie thought for a few moments. "I like that idea. But sooner or later I always start worrying about how I'm coming across. That's when I lose my cool."

"I know. But I think you'll find it's impossible to concentrate totally on two things at once. So if you concentrate totally on the *message*, you can't focus much on *yourself* or what people think of you."

"Well, Jan, so far every one of your suggestions has worked for me. I can hardly wait for a chance to try this one."

---

1. Why was Carrie able to get what she wanted in her "second round" with Brockfield? _____

2. What specific assertive techniques did she use? _____

3. What were probably the strong and weak points of Carrie's presentation at the national sales meeting? _____

4. Can she apply Jan's suggestions to situations other than formal talks? Explain.
_____

THE COMMUNICATION PROCESS

You can improve your verbal and nonverbal communications if you think of communicating as a process rather than as a series of isolated events. Consider your receiver's personality, experience, and feelings, and your previous transactions. Watch and listen for feedback that indicates the reaction to your message; otherwise you won't know how it was perceived, understood, and accepted. Feedback from the receiver constitutes a new message to you and closes one cycle in the communication process.

Models of the **communication process** can help us to better understand what happens when we communicate (see Figure 6-1). The essential elements of the process include a sender, a message, a receiver, and feedback from the receiver to the sender. This feedback may be present even if it consists merely of silence [4, pp. 1–4].

The communication process starts with thinking—the formation and framing of an idea in the sender's mind. This idea is then **encoded**—that is, the thought is put into some form for possible communication. We think in terms of language and express our thoughts in verbal forms—speaking and writing. We also experience feelings that we express (or encode) in both nonverbal and verbal forms. Nonverbal forms of expression include physical touch, visible movement of some part of the body, crying, and the creation of symbols such as music, pictures, and sculpture.

Next, we **transmit** our message to the receiver—by the spoken word, the written word, nonverbal language, or by some combination of the three. The message is transmitted to the receiver through some **medium**—for example, it may be transmitted through the telephone, telegraph, radio, television, a letter, a report, or a face-to-face encounter.

The receiver actively enters the process when she or he perceives the message by means of the senses (seeing, hearing, smelling, tasting, touching). The receiver then **decodes** the message by translating it, interpreting it, or organizing it to fit into her or his background of experience.

The next step is for the receiver to understand the message, then accept it, and finally have it lead to some sort of action or behavior. This feedback gives clues to the sender about the impact of the message upon the receiver.

As Figure 6-1 indicates, various factors either facilitate the communicative process or form barriers to it at each step. The ma-

jor purpose of this chapter is to help you identify ways to overcome barriers and facilitate the process.

Some of the key barriers created by typical female speech patterns (or stereotypes of those patterns) in business situations are shown in Exhibit 6-1. Identify those patterns that may be holding you back. Recall your past conversations; ask trusted friends for feedback; tape-record some of your conversations.

Then decide on alternate speech patterns that will facilitate understanding and acceptance of the meaning and image you want to convey to your business associates. (The second column in Exhibit 6-1 offers sugges-

FIGURE 6-1: A Model of the Communication Process

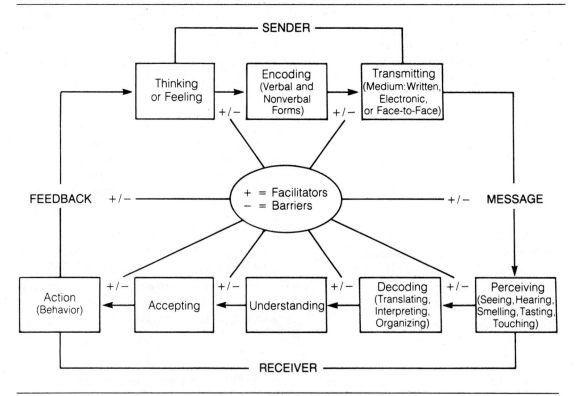

EXHIBIT 6-1: Key Communication Barriers and Facilitators for Women Managers

	Typical Barriers for Women: Speech Patterns/Stereotypes	Facilitators in Male Business Culture: Alternate Patterns	Barriers Created by Overcorrection of Female Speech Patterns
Gossip	Always ready to participate; indulges in idle, even malicious, gossip	Well-informed, alert; listens but rarely participates	Ignores all gossip
Content	Focus on trivia, chit-chat	Focus on relevant topics (business, politics, etc.)	Business talk only
Quantity	Babbles on too much; or keeps silent rather than "create conflict"	Usually speaks with a purpose or keeps her counsel; takes a stand on relevant issues	Every word carefully monitored; lacks spontaneity
Quality	Emotion-charged words ("just love it, so sweet, too gross")	Objective, operational words ("appreciate, thoughtful, inappropriate, effective")	Never expresses feelings
Reactions	Chip-on-shoulder, "women's lib," angry reactions; or gives in easily; backs off from conflict	Assertive, problem-solving responses	Swings from rebellion to submission or vice versa
Clarity	Vera Vague ("the nicest meeting, a super group")	Clear, specific descriptions ("well-organized meeting, top-performing team")	Overdoes details and explanations; tedious, boring
Logic	Illogical (Gracie Allen type); disconnected conclusions, idea-hopping	Coherent, connected, provides closure	Computerlike logic
Credibility	Tentative, overpolite, uncertain, indecisive ("We'll be able to do this?" "This is a sales problem—isn't it?" "Could I please see that for a second when you're through with it?" "I sort of think we should wait a little while?")	Confident, assertive, decisive ("We can do it!" "This appears to be a sales problem." "I'd like to take a look at that too." "I suggest we wait till the progress report comes in.")	Arrogant; overbearing
Interrupting	Avoids; thinks it's impolite; men may assume she has nothing to say	"Competitive turn-taking"; holds ground if peer overdoes it	Constantly interrupts; never gives ground
Profanity	Responds with disapproval, shock, embarrassment	Treats it as normal language; if male apologizes, responds, "I'm used to shop talk."	Starts swearing too
Jargon (military, sports, business)	Unclear of meanings of many words; rarely uses	Relies on jargon to create a sort of fraternity	Uses jargon to impress and intimidate "outsiders" who don't understand it

tions.) After all, the male-dominated business culture does have its own patterns of speaking and listening. On the other hand, some men carry the cultural pattern to the extreme—and women attempting to adapt may do this too. So watch out for the types of overcorrection shown in the third column of Exhibit 6-1.

Perhaps the most common, and damaging, female speech habit is that of phrasing statements tentatively. Women often phrase statements as questions by the inflection they place on the last word or two. ("I'd like to have the printout, tomorrow?" Or they pepper their statements with such conditional words as "I guess," "maybe," "sort of," "kind of," "a little," "pretty much," "if you don't mind," "when you have time." Carrying politeness to the point of subservience undermines your credibility.

Frequent "tag-on" questions can also wreck credibility; for example, saying "Right?" "Don't you think?" "Isn't it?" after you make statements. When the tag-on is directed at a man in a meeting, other men may think you're asking his permission or that the idea was originally his.

A major factor in facilitating communication—a factor not shown in Figure 6-1—is the timing and quality of the feedback. Feedback may be verbal or nonverbal, immediate or delayed. The most effective feedback is usually immediate and both verbal and nonverbal—in a face-to-face conversation, for example, where you can both see and hear the receiver's total reaction as soon as you send the message. When you telephone your receiver, you sacrifice the advantage of observing facial expressions and other body language. And when you send the receiver a written message, you further sacrifice the immediacy of the feedback as well as all its nonverbal aspects, including voice tone and inflection.

Obviously both verbal and nonverbal forms of communication are necessary to ef-fective communication. Verbal forms are most helpful when you want to send logical, **analytical messages.** Let's look at what you do when you analyze: You break down messages, such as reports, into parts. Then you examine each part to see how it relates to a particular situation or problem.

On the other hand, how do you "analyze" the boss' mood or a worker's frown in response to your suggestion? These nonverbal forms of communication are most helpful in **synthesizing** a variety of messages. If you're smart, you'll use these nonverbal messages—along with the verbal ones—to make sense of company politics, the sphere the company operates in, and the "big picture." You'll put it all together (synthesize it) to understand the relationships between parts and to build mental models of the world. Whenever you're deciding on an action, use your model to anticipate outcomes. Let's look at verbal forms of communication in more detail.

WAYS OF LISTENING AND SPEAKING

Even the most fluent women must adapt their talents to the language of business, both spoken and written. Let's concentrate first on the spoken word: developing some basic skills, listening, conducting meetings, and making presentations.

Sharpening Your Basic Skills

The spoken word can be a powerful tool for gaining and using personal power. Therefore, it will pay to continually sharpen your skills in persuading people and in getting through to them with clear instructions, questions, and responses. Keep developing skills in tuning in to the other person's viewpoint and gearing your messages accordingly. And remain aware of your responsibility as boss for taking the initiative to establish lines of communication with your people and to keep the lines open. Let's review some suggestions for sharpening these basic communication skills.

Practice Empathy   To be aware of what your listener will value as a payoff, try to put yourself in his or her shoes. How is your listener likely to feel about your message? What pressures is he or she under? How calm and confident is he or she feeling? What kind of relationship do you two have? If the topic is controversial, is there anything the two of you *can* agree on to begin with?

Develop the Art of Persuasion   Remember that people usually base actions more on feelings, opinions, and beliefs than on logic and reason. A rational approach is one that considers all the variables, and in most situations there are many variables we cannot be sure of. True rationality also considers people's emotions and other "illogical" factors. Here is a five-step sequence for persuasive communication.

1. Establish rapport. Communicate to the listener, in both words and actions, that you see the problem or situation from his or her viewpoint, too.

2. Introduce your proposal or idea and suggest how it can help generally.

3. Try to determine what your listener's problems are and what payoffs are important to him or her by using good questioning techniques (see the discussion that follows).

4. Follow up with details to convince. Provide the listener with evidence that your proposal can help. Maintain your credibility by avoiding too many strong adjectives, adverbs, superlatives, euphemisms, or worn out phrases; words that imply a certain knowledge of future events; and inappropriate surprise or amazement.

Watch Word Choice   Be yourself and use language you are comfortable with, but modify it to fit the situation and your listener. Choose familiar nontechnical words when talking with people who might not understand technical terms or business jargon. Make this your goal: words and statements that are as short, simple, direct, familiar, and concise as is appropriate for the listener and the situation.

Use Specific Language   Another barrier to complete communication is the use of vague, abstract, general language. The more specific your message is, the more likely the listener is to interpret it correctly. You have a picture in your mind of what you're trying to get across. The more specific the language you use to describe that picture, the more likely the listener will be to get the same picture in his or her mind. Let's look at some comparisons:

General: We have got to get on the ball.
Specific: Everyone in the Field Audit unit must increase his or her production by at least 5 percent.

General: You can bring me the stuff now.
Specific: I'm ready to go over the Western Region account files now.

General: Some people are taking advantage of my good nature.
Specific: Both Jim and Bob have been leaving twenty or thirty minutes early several times a week for the past month.

General: It's time I got what I deserve for all the hard work I do.
Specific: Since I achieved all the objectives we agreed upon—and even exceeded two of them—I think I deserve a $4,000 a year raise.

Notice that in order to be specific, it's important to use the names of things ("the Western Region account files"), names of people, and numbers where possible. Watch how you use indefinite words such as "there," "that," "this," "it," "thing," "whatchamacallit," "dilly." Even when you use "he," "she," or "they," be sure you are clear about exactly whom you're referring to.

Use the Active Verb Form   Active verbs generally signal a willingness to assume responsibility, a sense of being in control, and an assertive, positive approach. Active verbs are also more specific. They give more information and help the listener form a picture in his or her mind of someone doing something, of action taking place. Compare the active and passive forms:

Active: I will achieve the objectives by May 1.

Passive: The objectives will be achieved by May 1.

Active: On the basis of my investigation, I believe that the CRP is the best buy.

Passive: The investigation has led to the conclusion that the CRP is the best buy.

Don't Focus on Rules   The typical bureaucrat uses a variation of the logical approach when he or she keeps falling back on company rules or company policies as the reasons for decisions and instructions. Although some people will seem to go along, you'll get more cooperation if you communicate the *reason* for a policy or rule and the *payoffs* for following it. This approach conveys consideration of people as human beings rather than viewing them as cogs in the machinery. At times it's more productive to put people's feelings ahead of following the rules or even to allow them the freedom to make their own decisions.

Prepare Key One-Liners   Condense your thoughts and opinions on key issues, new proposals, and other company matters and be ready to express them at appropriate times. This is one way to stay prepared, avoid being caught with "egg on your face," and come across as an intelligent, well-informed, decisive, and assertive manager. Keep on top of issues that may come up in meetings or in chance encounters where you may have only a few minutes to communicate. Formulate your position and phrase it in one clear sentence. Write down these key one-liners and keep them up front in your mind.

Avoid False Assumptions   One of the most common barriers to communication is false assumptions about yourself or your listener. People frequently assume that the listener knows more about the content of the message than is actually the case. We can become so involved in a situation that it's easy to forget how unfamiliar a listener may be with important details. We therefore leave gaps in our messages, causing the listener in turn to act on incomplete information.

Allow for Face-Saving   The listener may or may not be aware of gaps in a message. Someone who is aware may be unwilling to ask for more information for fear of appearing ignorant or stupid. As the speaker, then, it is often crucial that you make sure your message is clear and complete. For example, you can say, "Let's review. Will you give me your interpretation of what I just said so I can be sure I have covered everything?"

On the other hand, when you are the listener, don't resort to face-saving tactics when you are unclear about a message. Feeling free to say you don't understand can be a sign of confidence. Certainly no one signals a lack of confidence more clearly than the person who is pretending to understand.

Provide Closure   Have you ever talked with someone who jumped from one topic to another, perhaps switching back and forth among topics? Some people even interrupt themselves in midsentence to digress to other topics, confusing and frustrating their listeners.

Listen to yourself. Do you usually stick with the topic until discussion of it is complete before moving on to another matter? If you find it difficult to stay aware of your conversational patterns, tape-record yourself. Telephone conversations are good ones to record because the listener doesn't have to be aware of what you are doing. When you play back the conversation, make notes on speaking habits and patterns that need improvement. Do this periodically until you have cleared up any poor speaking habits.

Maintain Relationships Keep communication lines open and let your people know you're interested in them as people through the appropriate use of small talk. You don't need to slip into "typical woman talk," but you can be warm and friendly while maintaining an air of professionalism. Consider using brief references to interesting current events or to the listener's interests, hobbies, family, home, pet, or vacation or holiday activities. By giving people this type of personal attention in the hallway, on the elevator, during breaks in meetings, and in other routine encounters, you can maintain relationships with little or no extra time cost. The manager who discusses *only* business can get the reputation of being more a machine than a person.

Take Initiative In addition to taking the initiative to maintain personal relationships with people, you must also let them know what's going on in the company and what you're thinking—if you expect them to let you know what *they're* thinking. Although some details may have to be kept confidential, you should communicate as much as possible about every phase of the group's

operations to as many people within the group as possible. Take stock. Are you expecting your people to read your mind? Maybe they *should* know you need that report by Friday, but chances are they don't.

Get the Feedback You Need The key to getting feedback is letting people know you're open to it. Your people will give you the feedback they think you want, not what you need, unless you can accept criticism from them, help them bring facts and ideas into proper focus, and ask them for data properly.

When you ask for data, let people know why you need it and what you plan to do with it. In that way you're more likely to get exactly what you want in the best form for your purposes.

Helping your people bring their ideas into focus is the key to getting good feedback when you meet to discuss problems, plans, or the progress of projects. Draw out all the ideas and approaches your people have been thinking of. Don't just have a vague discussion. Get people to focus on specific questions: What are we going to do? What other information do we need to get? Who is going to do what and when? At the end of the discussion, ask for a summary. Once you get it, ask for a one-page memo itemizing what has been covered and agreed upon.

Accepting criticism from your people without resentment is necessary if you want honest feedback that helps you lead your team to top performance. If you ignore or punish critical feedback, you'll probably become isolated from the effects of your decisions and therefore make increasingly poor decisions. The subordinate who is willing to tell you that you're going in the wrong direction may be far more loyal than the one who keeps telling you how wonderful your decision is. Such honesty may also indicate strength and self-confidence.

A major obstacle to getting constructive criticism from people is a lack of clearly stated, specific objectives. This lack prevents a subordinate from intelligently discussing how your decision affects departmental performance. Another major obstacle is fear that you will react badly. You can help your people overcome this obstacle by training them through example.

Listening for the Total Message

Saying the right things to the right people at the right time requires good listening skills. For example, the ability to determine when it's best to just listen and when it's best to become actively involved in a situation is important to the effective manager. Most managers can profit from spending some time on improving their listening habits and skills. Speaking and listening skills can work together to increase your personal power.

The ability to communicate empathy, encouragement, and acceptance of the speaker depends mainly on what you *don't* say. The ability to phrase questions effectively as well as to identify and follow up on the speaker's key points depends on your level of verbal skill. So does the ability to help the listener identify, analyze, and express her or his thoughts, beliefs, ideas, and behavior patterns. Finally, you must depend on your own judgment about the degree of personal involvement that is appropriate to your role as listener and as manager.

Exercise 6-1 provides you with an opportunity to review some of your listening habits. After you have completed it, take a look

EXERCISE 6-1: REVIEWING YOUR LISTENING HABITS

Place a check mark in the column that best reflects your habits.

	5 Always	4 Usually	3 Often	2 Seldom	1 Never
1. If I cannot pay attention to the person speaking to me, I end the conversation or postpone it to a time when I can pay attention.	___	___	___	___	___
2. I look at the person who is talking to me.	___	___	___	___	___
3. I maintain almost constant eye contact when someone is talking to me (instead of reading or looking at other things on my desk or at other people who are passing by).	___	___	___	___	___
4. If I remain in a conversation, I concentrate on what the speaker is saying even though it may not be of great interest to me at the moment.	___	___	___	___	___

	5 Always	4 Usually	3 Often	2 Seldom	1 Never
5. I listen to a person's ideas and facts, but at the same time I listen for the person's feelings and emotions.	___	___	___	___	___
6. I notice the speaker's body language and integrate it with the verbal message.	___	___	___	___	___
7. I allow the speaker to finish a complete thought without interruption.	___	___	___	___	___
8. I concentrate on what a speaker is saying even in noisy, distracting surroundings.	___	___	___	___	___
9. I listen for facts and information that other people can offer and that I do not possess.	___	___	___	___	___
10. I am not distracted by the way a person delivers a message.	___	___	___	___	___
11. If a speaker uses words that bring certain prejudices to mind, I try to be aware of prejudiced feelings and suspend them until I've got the full message.	___	___	___	___	___
12. If the speaker seems inappropriately dressed or speaks with an accent different from mine, I listen intently to what that person has to say anyway.	___	___	___	___	___
13. If a speaker makes a statement that is not clear to me, I speak up and ask questions.	___	___	___	___	___
14. If the speaker answers my questions and I still do not understand an important point, I ask the person to explain the point again.	___	___	___	___	___
15. After I have learned what I want from a speaker, I still give him or her my undivided attention until the conversation is over.	___	___	___	___	___
16. I keep my mind focused on what the speaker is saying (instead of thinking about what I am going to say next or letting my mind wander to other topics).	___	___	___	___	___

at your overall pattern of listening behavior. What areas most need improvement? How do you plan to change your habits in that area? Make changes one step at a time.

Developing the Art of "Being with" Another Person Perhaps the first step in improving listening skills is becoming aware of the importance of simply "being with" another person. This is an art that can be especially important in listening to subordinates.

When you meet with subordinates on a one-to-one basis, it's important to give them your full attention. First, put everything else aside and concentrate on merely being with that person—without adding anything to or taking anything away from the experience of just being there together. Take in everything the person has to communicate, both verbally and nonverbally. It may help if you think of yourself as an empty sponge being filled with that person's message. Take it all in and absorb it as fully as possible. Don't try to evaluate it as good or bad, right or wrong. It just *is*. Let the person know you are taking in the message. If parts of it are unclear, ask questions or feed it back in your own words to check for understanding. Once you are sure of the message, you can evaluate its validity and appropriateness, its effects on achieving objectives and cooperating as a group, and other factors. Absorb first; evaluate later.

Encouraging People to Talk Drawing people out of themselves requires the use of some specific skills in addition to the ability to provide a supportive atmosphere. The first step is to put people at ease by acting relaxed yourself and giving sincere compliments. Remember to smile when it's natural and comfortable to do so. Once the speaker is relaxed, encourage talk by drawing him or her out. For example, make an opening statement that stimulates conversation: "That was the most complex set of specifications

we've ever attempted!" Or ask an effective lead-off question: "How did you ever unravel that set of specifications?" Once the person starts talking, make encouraging listening responses ("Um-hum." "Yes?" "Right!" "Tell me more."), make supportive remarks, and ask questions at appropriate intervals. Maintain regular eye contact (no glazed-over or blank stares).

Avoid the habit of assuming you know what the other person is going to say after the first few words of a statement and finishing the sentence for him or her. If the speaker is too unassertive to give the correct ending, you may never know what he or she really intended to say. And don't tune out because you think you know what the speaker is going to say. While you're daydreaming, you may miss something important.

Getting others to talk can bring rich benefits to you. It helps keep the other person at ease as he or she becomes engrossed in verbalizing thoughts and experiences. It can start the person to thinking about a topic you want emphasized. You give the person an opportunity to show what he or she knows and understands. You bring out facts you might not otherwise find out about, and you get the opportunity to communicate that you understand his or her situation.

Phrasing Questions Appropriately Another key to drawing people out and to pinpointing information you need is skill in phrasing questions. Open questions are phrased so that they cannot be answered "yes" or "no": "What do you think about this decision?" "Why are you late so often?" Use open questions when you want to encourage talk. Open questions usually begin with some variation of the "Five W's" of journalism fame (who, what, where, when, and why). Closed questions, on the other hand, frequently begin with some variation of the "be," "do," or "have" types of verbs. They are phrased so that they *can* be answered "yes" or "no" or with a specific bit of data: "Do you feel this is fair?" "How many units did you sell that year?" Use them when you want to zero in on a specific response. More examples of open and closed questions are given in Exhibit 6-2. See Exercise 12-5, Interviewing Techniques, for applying open questions to job interviews.

Focusing on Important Aspects You can guide a conversation so that the most important facts come out and the key issues are explored. Listen for key thoughts and follow up by further questioning and discussion. A key thought is an idea, opinion, or experience that is expressed by the person talking and appears to the listener to have an important bearing upon the matter being discussed, even though it may be hidden in casual comments or very brief references. Become alert to the underlying meanings of the speaker's words, so you can note key thoughts and return to them.

Learn to distinguish between the content and relationship levels in conversations. **Content level** refers to the topic being discussed, the verbal content of the message. **Relationship level** refers to predominantly nonverbal messages about the way one person values or accepts the other person; it is based mainly on feelings. We *feel* comfortable, free, anxious, or guilty in a relationship, for example, and the other person's

messages of acceptance or nonacceptance can trigger these feelings. Messages at the relationship level usually contain the best clues to key thoughts and the important aspects of a situation.

Communicating Acceptance Let people know that you accept not only the facts they present but the feelings and opinions they convey. If you accept only facts, you limit your acceptance, placing conditions on it. Since people's feelings and viewpoints are what help to make them unique, you seem to be rejecting their individuality when you accept only the messages that *don't* include opinions and feelings. When you communicate acceptance at a relationship level, people feel trusted and respected.

On the other hand, when people feel rejected, they often respond by pushing harder, trying to prove that their feelings and opinions are justified. Messages at the relationship level tend to become pressured, accusatory, and defensive. The speaker may withdraw and withhold information. Therefore, it's worth sharpening your skills at communicating acceptance so your people can relax and give acceptance in return. When they feel free to listen to your messages, accept them, and act on them, they may allow other, perhaps deeper, feelings to surface.

EXHIBIT 6-2: Open and Closed Questions

Open	Closed
Who is in favor of the reorganization?	*Are* most of the accounting people in favor of the reorganization?
What information did you get?	*Have* you got the information?
Where is the best place for the new machine?	*Is* this the best place for the new machine?
When did you first notice the communication problem?	*Has* the communication problem been bothering you for long?
Why do you dislike the new schedule?	*Will* the new schedule interfere with your Baker project?

Avoid the trap of thinking that acceptance of another person's opinions and feelings is the same as *agreement* with them. It's not, necessarily. Agreement is an alliance with the other person in his or her position that implies you feel basically the same way. Acceptance is merely an understanding that a person feels a certain way about a topic without condemning or denying the person's right to feel that way. To be a supportive listener, you must be able to accept people's feelings and opinions, whether you agree or not. When you and your people *share* feelings, opinions, and experiences rather than try to prove they're good or right, you have a chance to begin understanding one another.

Until people feel they can trust you, they tend to express themselves indirectly, perhaps by sending out trial-balloon problems. They present you with small, relatively innocuous problems. If you accept the total message and express acceptance of the total person, then she or he will probably feel safe enough to discuss more basic, meaningful problems with you. Effective listening, therefore, is essential to communicating at progressively deeper levels.

Some typical responses that can communicate nonacceptance of a person's feelings, thoughts, and actions are shown in Exhibit 6-3, which is based on the work of psychologist Dr. Thomas Gordon. The responses illustrate the difficulty of merely listening, be-

EXHIBIT 6-3: Responses That Can Communicate Nonacceptance

When You Make This Response:	Are You Implying This Message?
Ordering, demanding: "You must try . . ." "You have to stop . . ."	Don't feel, act, think that way; do it my way.
Warning, threatening: "You'd better . . ." "If you don't, then . . ."	You'd better not have that feeling, act, or think that way.
Admonishing, moralizing: "You should . . ." "It's not proper to . . ."	You are bad if you have that feeling, act, or think that way.
Criticizing, blaming, disagreeing: "You aren't thinking about this properly . . ."	You are wrong if you have that feeling, act, or think that way.
Advising, giving answers: "Why don't you . . ." "Let me suggest . . ."	Here's a solution so you won't have that feeling, act, or think that way.
Praising, agreeing: "But you've done such a good job . . ." "I approve of . . ."	Your feelings, actions, and opinions are subject to my approval.
Reassuring, sympathizing: "Don't worry . . ." "You'll feel better . . ."	You don't need to have that feeling, act, or think that way.
Persuading, arguing: "Do you realize that . . ." "The facts are . . ."	Here are some facts so you won't have that feeling, act, or think that way.
Interpreting, diagnosing: "What you need is . . ." "Your problem is . . ."	Here's the reason you have that feeling, act, or think that way.
Probing, questioning: "Why . . .?" "Who . . .?" "When . . .?" "What . . .?"	Are you really justified in having that feeling, acting, or thinking that way?
Diverting, avoiding: "We can discuss it later . . ." "That reminds me of . . ."	Your feelings, actions, and opinions aren't worthy of discussion.
Kidding, using sarcasm: "That will be the day!" "Bring out the violins . . ."	You're silly if you persist in having that feeling, acting, or thinking that way.

ing with a person, and showing acceptance. Some of them may be appropriate and even constructive messages at certain times, but not when your major goal is to communicate acceptance at a relationship level. The receiver of one of these messages may become defensive and never allow you to hear anything deeper than the trial-balloon problem.

Developing Active Listening Skills This prepares you for a deeper level of involvement with the speaker once she or he feels accepted and trusts you. In *Effectiveness Training for Women*, Linda Adams has described active listening in this way:

> Active Listening is a special way of reflecting back what the other person has said, to let her or him know that you're listening, and to check your understanding of what she or he means. It's a restatement of the other person's *total* communication: the *words* of the message plus the accompanying *feelings*. To shift gears to Active Listening, you must temporarily put yourself in the other's position, try to get a sense of the other's thoughts and feelings, and then share your understanding with the other to check its accuracy [1, pp. 36–37].

This active listening sequence consists of these steps:

1. You receive the other's message, verbal and nonverbal.

2. You translate the message and get your sense of what the other is trying to communicate.

3. You feed back your understanding of the other's message, saying in effect: "Here's my understanding of what you're feeling or experiencing. Am I right?"

4. The other person then reacts to your active listening response, confirming or clarifying your understanding of her or his message.

Here's an example of active listening in a business situation:

You (*I-message*): I think you did a good job with that presentation, but I disagree that we should expand our product line just now. It would overextend our production facilities.

Peer (*resistance to message*): That's a pretty pessimistic point of view. I'm really surprised to hear you say that.

You (*shifting gears to active listening*): I see you are upset about what I said. I'm interested in knowing more about why you feel the way you do.

Peer: I believe we could put on a night crew and make better use of our production facility.

You (*active listening*): It's important to you to expand as rapidly as possible, right?

Peer: Yes, and one reason it's important is because the market is ready for our product now. It may not be so favorable a couple of years from now.

You (*another I-message*): I see your point; however, we've built our reputation on providing top-quality products and excellent service. I'm concerned about the effect rapid expansion would have on that.

By shifting gears to active listening after an assertion, you can constructively explore *value* differences. Avoid assuming what the other's *motives* are, however. Frequently you can cool down a potentially volatile argument without either party backing away from her or his own feeling. You encourage rational discussion of controversial issues.

Determining the Right Degree of Personal Involvement How "actively" you listen will depend on the degree of personal involvement you think is desirable or necessary in the situation. One trait of a good listener is the ability to distinguish those times when the speaker doesn't want you to do anything except understand from times when the speaker is seeking guidance or action on your part. Let's explore three progressively deeper levels of listening.

Level 1: Listening to interpret and give feedback: In order to make sure you understand what the message is and to let the speaker know you understand, you can restate what you think you have heard, as in this exchange between a manager and a worker:

W: This problem has occurred several times, and I think I should change the way I handle these transactions.

M: You're considering rewriting the procedures?

W: Well, I think I should. I just don't like having people jump all over me.

M: You are really tired of being pressured to have the information in the form the Accounting Department wants it?

W: Yes, I want them to stop bugging me, and I'm going to tell them that, too. I'm tired of people thinking I'm a patsy and that they can take out their resentment on me.

M: You think people are in the habit of hassling you, but this time you're going to see that they stop it.

W: That's right . . .

This type of active listening can encourage the speaker to come to his or her own conclusions. You can restate the *content* of the message back to the speaker; you can also notice feelings and check them out.

Level 2: Listening for behavior patterns: A pattern of behavior indicates a readiness to respond in a typical way to certain types of situations. Our patterns of behavior are determined by the basic underlying feelings we have about ourselves—for example, "People are always

jumping on me," "I always get what I really want in the end," "People are always becoming envious of me," "No one really cares about my feelings." These decisions people make about themselves, frequently in early childhood, largely determine how they are going to react in certain situations. If you can listen and give feedback at this level, your interaction with the other person can become more meaningful. If people can reevaluate these childhood decisions in light of current reality they often redecide and consequently change their behavior.

Level 3: Listening for deeper insights and guidance: At a deeper level of listening and involvement you look for deeper insights the speaker touches on, such as a desire for change, intentions, causes, and solutions.

W: This seems to happen to me frequently.

M: And you would like to change that?

When you assume a guidance role as a listener, you will sometimes need to decide which avenue toward a deeper insight to pursue. For example, if a subordinate tells you about what other people do to him, you can focus on the others or you can focus on the part the subordinate plays in the situation.

W: People are always pressuring me.

M: People expect too much from you?

In that response, the manager focused on "them," not on the worker. Contrast it with this:

M: You have difficulty handling other people's demands?

Here the manager focuses on the speaker.

It's usually more productive to focus on the speaker's role so that she can pursue ways of gaining control over herself and her life, regardless of other people's behavior. This focuses on what she can control rather than on her helplessness. If you want to be less directive, you can feed back both aspects and let the speaker pursue what is most relevant to her at this point. For example:

M: People expect too much from you and you have difficulty handling the demands?

Although some guidance can be helpful, it's important to avoid directing the flow of communication. When the speaker takes the lead and arrives on her own insights, the resulting conclusions and decisions will have the most meaning for her and she is most likely to act on them. Your role as an active listener can be more productive if you facilitate this process rather than direct it.

Aim for an underlying attitude that asks ("Is this the way you feel?") rather than tells. If you have difficulty interpreting the speaker's total message, ask, "Is that right?" or "Does that seem to fit?" If your feedback is not accepted by the speaker, ask what he or she *does* mean. Focus on getting the total message, never on proving you're right in your interpretation or explaining why you interpreted in a certain way.

Being an active listener gives you a chance to communicate understanding and acceptance of a person's ideas and feelings, and it gives the speaker an opportunity to correct you if you have misunderstood. When you use this skill, your people will feel more comfortable about bringing ideas and problems to you and sharing deeper thoughts and problems. They'll be able to talk through their feelings and subsequently to solve many of their own problems. Test your listening skills by completing Exercise 6-3 at the end of this chapter.

Arranging and Conducting Meetings

In many organizations attendance at meetings where little or nothing is accomplished is the biggest time-waster for managers. When you are in charge of conducting meetings, you have an opportunity to turn them into time-savers. You also have a chance to build group morale and team spirit through meetings that are well planned and group centered.

Exhibit 6-4 summarizes some of the differences between traditional leadership and group-centered leadership of meetings. In conducting meetings, as in other aspects of managing, your goal as the leader is to reach the optimal balance between accomplishing the tasks at hand and meeting the needs of individual members and of the group as a whole. A major barrier to adopting group-centered leadership is the manager's fears of appearing weak and inadequate to the group members. Many managers fear the risks of sharing planning and decision-making with the group. Dealing openly with group conflict and emotional behavior is also viewed as risky. Doing so does indeed require courage and commitment. The payoffs include a high level of worker motivation and participation, plus strong support and commitment to your plans and projects.

To turn your meetings into time-savers that accomplish specific goals, you must be able to decide when a meeting should be called, how long the meeting should last, and who should attend. You must also prepare people to participate by briefing them and by distributing an effective agenda. You must be able actually to conduct the meeting so that people participate and necessary actions are taken. It's wise also to develop skills in contributing as a group member when someone else is conducting the meeting.

EXHIBIT 6-4: Meetings—Gaining Support and Commitment (A Comparison of Old and New Approaches)

Traditional Group Leader	Group-centered Leader
Leader is in control of her group; her authority and responsibility are acknowledged by the group. She directs, polices, leads them to the best decision.	Group takes responsibility for the meeting; it is *their* meeting. Leader assists all members to contribute to group activities.
Leader focuses her attention on the purpose of the meeting and keeps the group focused on the task at hand. Leader performs all the functions necessary to arrive at the best decision.	Responsibility for reaching a decision lies with the group. All participate and the decision belongs to all. Leader serves the group and helps it achieve the purpose of the meeting.
Leader sets limits, uses rules of order to keep the discussion within strict topic and time limits set by the agenda.	Members are brought into the planning of the meeting, setting goals and methods of achieving them, developing an agenda, and assigning tasks.
Leader encourages objective, logical thinking and discourages the expression of emotions. Leader explains the disruptive effect of emotions.	Feelings, emotions, and conflicts are accepted as realities that may be as important to address as the task agenda.
If a member's behavior becomes disruptive, it is the leader's responsibility to take the member aside to discuss the behavior and its effects.	Disruptive behavior is a group problem and must be solved within the group. As the group moves closer to the goal of mutual trust, members start monitoring their own potentially disruptive behavior.
The needs of individual members are less important to the leader than the need to arrive at a task decision.	Leader helps members to realize that the needs, feelings, and purposes of each are important; that they are a unique group, and that they can continue to grow as such.

Adapted from Leland P. Bradford, *Making Meetings Work* (La Jolla, Calif.: University Associates, 1976), pp. 20–25.

Deciding When to Meet A universal complaint in large organizations is that too much time is wasted in meetings. We have all been to countless meetings where little or nothing was really accomplished, where business that took an hour or so to complete could have been handled in ten minutes with good planning and execution, where people didn't participate or go away committed to the plans made, and so forth.

How can you avoid the traps that seem to lure so many managers into arranging and conducting such poor meetings? Certainly the first step in avoiding wasted time in meetings is to learn to decide when and when not to call a meeting. Let's look at the most common reasons for meetings.

To report or share information—for quick, direct presentation of reports or information, instructions, or assignments by individuals

To solve a problem or make decisions—to draw on the thinking of the various people or units of an organization, to clarify an issue or problem, and to form this thinking into a solution or decision

To develop or create—to create new ideas or to develop and expand as yet undefined concepts, strategies, theories, and so forth (This type of meeting works best when the leader serves as the facilitator of creativity and asserts minimum control.)

Calling a meeting is usually *not* a good idea when

You have inadequate information or preparation to deal with the issue

You need to decide on personnel matters—hiring, firing, or salaries

You could communicate better by one-to-one discussion, telephone, or memo

The topic is confidential

The issue is low priority, and therefore you can handle it yourself or delegate it

You have already decided what you're asking the group to help decide

Some people in the group are angry and hostile but will cool down with time (Don't run scared, but be aware of feelings and of good timing.)

When you are deciding whether to call a meeting and how to go about it, ask yourself such questions as these: Is a meeting actually the best way to accomplish the business at hand? Do I need group participation? Do I need to brief people on action plans that require cooperation among them?

What outcomes do I want from this meeting? What's the major purpose for calling it? What are my goals for it? What are the group's goals for it?

Who needs to participate? What is the best way to involve them in planning and in preparing for the meeting? A recurring theme in this book is the importance of involving people in planning and decision-making. Since there are so many payoffs for doing so—such as a higher level of interest, enthusiasm, and motivation; improved communication and cooperation; access to a larger pool of ideas and information; increased commitment to the achievement of

goals—involve people in planning your meetings and in determining what outcomes you want. If it is not feasible to get this input beforehand, at least get it at the beginning of the meeting.

What agenda items, activities, people, and materials will best help us achieve the results we want from the meeting?

How can I get maximum feedback from the participants about their thoughts, ideas, beliefs, opinions, feelings, and suggestions? If you assume that a meeting you have held went well because no one complained, you are missing the boat. Take the initiative to get feedback from all participants on their reactions to the meeting so you can make appropriate changes and so people can see that they have a real influence on the meeting process.

What is the best procedure for assuring followup of the agreements, decisions, and action commitments made at the meeting? When the meeting is over, everyone should be clear about who will do what and when it will be done. You should be clear about your procedures for checking to see that commitments are carried out on schedule.

Developing an Agenda Once you decide that a meeting actually needs to be held and determine the major purpose of the meeting, you are ready to develop an agenda. It's surprising how many meetings are called without an agenda and how many people show up at meetings without really understanding why they are there, much less being well prepared to contribute. Therefore it's important to prepare an agenda and to see that everyone who will be attending gets a copy of it ahead of time.

Consider keeping a folder of agenda items; then instead of calling regularly scheduled meetings, wait until you have enough agenda items to justify a meeting (or one item that is important enough).

The first item on any agenda should be a brief review of the purpose for the meeting. The group should rank the agenda items in order of importance. By *setting priorities,* the group can decide the amount of time that can be devoted to each item. They may then want to set tentative time limits for each item. Also, when members suggest or submit agenda items, have them include time estimates.

It is much more effective to state the agenda in terms of what you (or the group) want to achieve or what you plan to decide, rather than merely listing the subjects to be covered. One way of doing this is to state agenda items as *questions to be resolved.* This format has the added advantage of encouraging people to think ahead about the goals of the meeting and to prepare more effectively for achieving those goals.

For example, instead of stating an agenda item as "XYZ product," state it as "Should we add XYZ product to our line?" Instead of listing "Profit goals," ask, "How can we increase profits by 10 percent next quarter?" Your agenda items should be clearly worded, brief, specific, and if possible listed in the order in which they will be covered. Exhibit 6-5 presents two versions of an agenda for a meeting of a committee formed to select a consultant. Assume you are a member of the committee and compare the way you respond to each version.

Perhaps the major advantage of phrasing agenda items as decision questions is that discussion at the meeting is more likely to be results oriented. It is therefore easier to keep the discussion focused on possible solutions to problems. Practice writing results-oriented agenda items by completing Exercise 6-2.

A common problem is trying to squeeze too much into one meeting. If your agenda is too long, prioritize and eliminate some of the items. In some instances an alternative is to divide the items or activities among small groups, which then can report results to the entire group for action.

EXHIBIT 6-5: Sample Agendas for a Meeting to Select a Consultant

Action Statements	Results-oriented Questions
1. Establish criteria for selection.	1. What should be the criteria for selection?
2. Screen proposals and résumés of all candidates.	2. Which three candidates have the personal qualifications that best meet our criteria?
3. Choose three possible candidates.	3. Which three candidates submitted proposals that best meet our criteria?
4. Compose a letter of invitation for on-site visit by prospective candidates.	4. Are the top three candidates—using their personal qualifications as the deciding factor—the same as the top three using the quality of their proposals as the deciding factor? If not, would any of the personally qualified candidates be able to submit and implement a revised proposal?
5. Formulate questions for on-site visit.	5. What shall we include in the letter of invitation for on-site visits by prospective candidates?
	6. What questions shall we ask the candidates when they arrive?

EXERCISE 6-2: PREPARING ACTION AGENDA ITEMS

Change these agenda items to results-oriented questions. Check your responses with the answer key.

1. Sales targets _____

2. New XYZ product _____

3. Layoff policy _____

4. Next meeting date _____

Briefing Speakers, Resource Persons, and Members   Decide who should participate in the meeting and brief them on what parts of the meeting they will be participating in and what they will be expected to contribute. Try to brief participants at least several days before the meeting, not at the last minute. Then agree on what they will do, when and for how long, who will be attending the meeting, and what results you are after. If possible, brief people in person and follow up with a memo or letter, incorporating these suggestions.

1. Keep introductions short. Long introductions tend to put distance between the person being introduced and the group. Aim for a short, warm welcome and, if appropriate, provide a handout that gives the speaker's background and qualifications.

2. Make sure speakers and resource people are clear about time limits. Consider putting a large clock or watch where the speaker can easily see it. If appropriate, mention during the introduction that this will be a "fifteen-minute presentation."

3. Be clear about your purpose for having a speaker. Is it to stimulate the thinking of the group and get their inputs? If so, consider having at least two resource persons as speakers so that alternatives can be more openly and fully identified.

Deciding on Appropriate Time Limits and Group Size   Generally, effective meetings last no longer than an hour and a half. With good planning, short, relatively simple problems can usually be solved in less than one hour. Aim for this goal. Ask yourself, "Can the purpose of the meeting be accomplished with a 'crisp conference' of the twenty-minute variety?" Often everyone concerned is extremely grateful for leadership toward this type of conference.

It's important to provide for variety in regularly scheduled meetings. In order to keep people stimulated, alert, and thinking, consider changing the meeting time, place, or plans from time to time. Get feedback and suggestions from participants. If the meeting must last for several hours, consider some procedures for having people change seats so they won't get stuck in a rut.

Groups of more than fifteen people have difficulty achieving goals effectively. It becomes difficult for all members to relate to each other and for the leader to interact with every person. Group action becomes unwieldy and awkward, especially for a decision-making meeting. If you must have twenty-five or more people, consider dividing them into small groups.

You might also consider having a representative from each subgroup or unit attend the meeting instead of the entire group or unit. Keep the group small and tight, but urge unit representatives to determine the point of view of most of the people in their unit and to vote accordingly. Also, consider asking people to attend only the part of the meeting that they can contribute to or that they need to receive information from.

Providing Optimal Room Arrangements
Try to hold meetings in rooms that are well designed for them. Provide for adequate space but not a space so large that the group rattles around in it. The room should have adequate air and light. Crowded, narrow, smoky, dim, or overheated rooms tend to promote tension, irritability, or drowsiness.

Arrange seating to facilitate optimal eye contact among all group members and so that members will have maximum eye contact with each other. The best setup is a single row of chairs in a semi-circular or U-shaped arrangement.

Conducting Effective Meetings Once you have prepared adequately for a meeting, it becomes much easier to conduct it in an effective way. Let's look first at the importance of timing.

Begin your meetings on time even if some people are late. This is especially important for regular periodic meetings. If you wait for latecomers, people who are on time soon realize they will waste *their* time in the future if they are prompt. So they start arriving late, the chronically late ones arrive even later, and starting times lose their meaning. If some people arrive early, try to arrange some constructive reading, activity, or discussion for them, so that they don't feel they are wasting their time while waiting for others to arrive.

Throughout the meeting, be aware of the time factor. Stick to the agenda unless the group votes to digress from it. Try to get a satisfactory answer to each question on the agenda and provide for necessary followup.

Consider making a short meeting double as a coffee break to save time. For longer meetings make coffee available throughout the meeting to avoid coffee breaks, especially if activities are planned that include some moving around.

If you have planned properly, started the meeting on time, and remained aware of the time factor throughout the meeting, you should be able to end the meeting on time. It's important to make every effort to do so. If you regularly have problems with overly talkative people getting off the subject and dragging the meeting on, consider setting your meeting time for just before lunch or closing time.

Just as important as proper timing is the way in which the group achieves the meeting goals. After you clearly state the purpose of the meeting, express your ideas about it as positively as possible. Indicate that the meeting can lead to successful results. If a solution or decision is needed, focus on the importance of the problem and the challenge, as well as the benefits, of resolving it. For maximum impact, include others in this initial discussion (more about energizing the meeting later). Move along crisply in your explanation. Don't dawdle or ramble. Try to make the pace of the meeting relaxed but lively.

Make frequent summaries during the meeting. A brief one- or two-line summary after each step helps everyone remember what has taken place. At each step of the way—including the written followup—stress the positive aspects of the meeting. This doesn't mean you should ignore differences or sweep problems under the rug, of course. If the group confronts and handles them, focus on the resulting benefits rather than on the differences.

Be sure to make adequate arrangements for recording what happens at the meeting. Using a flip chart and felt marking pen to record ideas and posting them can be effective for some meetings. Participants get to see their inputs recorded and have access to them throughout the meeting so they can fully experience the feeling of participating and influencing results.

A "solution wheel" can be a permanent visual aid for decision-making meetings (see Figure 6-2). It can be prepared either on poster board or as a transparency for the overhead projector. Once the items on the wheel are prepared, a cover for the wheel is

FIGURE 6-2: The Solution Wheel

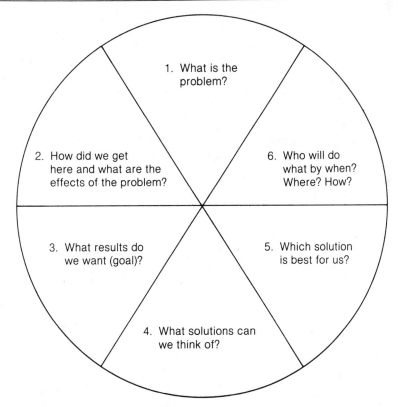

Using the solution wheel: Make a cover the same diameter as the solution wheel, but cut a pie-shaped opening from it that is large enough to reveal one step at a time. Rotate the cover wheel as the meeting progresses to show the step the group is working on.

Adapted from Frank Snell, *How to Hold a Better Meeting* (New York: Simon and Schuster, 1974), pp. 109–22.

made. The cover has a pie-shaped cutout. When it is laid on top of the wheel, only one item at a time is revealed. As long as the group is determining the problem, the wheel remains on item 1. Once they have agreed on the problem, the wheel is then moved to item 2. The use of the solution wheel helps (1) to keep the group focused on the question under discussion, (2) to avoid needless digressions and confusion, and (3) to keep all members informed about what has been accomplished and what still needs to be done.

Keep the meeting energized. The way a discussion is initiated at the beginning of a meeting is most important to the liveliness of the meeting. Plan in advance how you will get things started and keep them moving. Include others in the planning so they can be prepared to take responsibility and to help. It's up to you to promote the initiating of contributions by all members; otherwise the group can quickly become passive and uninvolved. Be sensitive to the appropriate time for initiating further exploration

of a new direction, and ask how the group feels about moving on.

The main energizing force in a meeting is the initiation of new topics and ideas by members and their general participation. Sometimes the group needs to move on but finds it is stuck. Techniques for energizing and moving the group are (1) introducing a novel idea, (2) expressing a feeling, (3) saying something in a humorous way, (4) devising an activity that involves all members and restores the momentum of the group, (5) taking a short break. Exhibit 6-6 contrasts behavior that energizes a group and behavior that tends to have the opposite effect.

The goals of a meeting can be sabotaged by persons or cliques who are attempting to carry out their own **hidden agendas.** A hidden agenda consists of personal goals that individuals do not reveal to the group spontaneously for fear of rejection. When these hidden individual goals are in opposition to the group's common goals, the meeting can be sabotaged. It's up to you as the leader to

EXHIBIT 6-6: Energizing Versus Deadening Behaviors

Behavior That Helps the Group Achieve Task Goals	Behavior That Tends to Deaden Meetings
Identifying objectives	Avoiding eye contact
Speaking appropriately loudly and assertively	Using closed body language
Offering ideas	Speaking softly and hesitantly
Asking key or clarifying questions	Making unnecessary apologies
Keeping a clear focus on the task	Unnecessarily qualifying all statements
Summarizing the discussion	Asking nonessential questions
Behavior That Encourages People to Participate	Generalizing, rambling, getting off the track
	Moving the group away from the heart of the matter
Active listening	Monopolizing the discussion
Direct eye contact	
Encouragement of participation	
Supporting others	
Soliciting ideas and responses from others	

deal with this problem. Hidden goals might include playing power politics, impressing the boss, getting revenge, making another member look bad, or playing the comedian. Some techniques that are commonly used include monopolizing the discussion, asking for clarification on all points, and agreeing with everything the boss says.

Someone with a hidden agenda may come to the meeting committed to one particular solution to the problem and determined to persuade the group to that solution—regardless of the facts, others' opinions, and alternative solutions that are presented.

Frequently the members with a hidden agenda use strategy to manipulate the group. For example, they will listen attentively to the discussion, waiting for the best time to try to achieve their own purposes. Then, at the opportune moment, they pretend their input is spontaneous, something "I just thought of." If other members become aware that some strategy is being used on them, they may become defensive, and open communication and trust may be blocked. This defensiveness is intensified when the manipulative member is also a powerful member.

When you are dealing with a hidden agenda, the main thing to keep in mind is that individual members' goals do not represent the group's goals. Keep returning to group goals and group input. Try to see that less assertive members are not intimidated by the member with the hidden agenda. Encourage quiet members to state their opinions and offer their suggestions.

In order to encourage participation by all, and block hidden agendas, you must differentiate between criticizing and evaluating a person and that person's ideas or specific actions. Business meetings, as well as business situations in general, are no place to indulge in criticism of personal traits or characteristics. Feelings and attitudes may need to be aired, but they also need to be respected. It is up to you to be alert to personal attacks

and to insist, if necessary, that the discussion be confined to an evaluation and exploration of effective versus ineffective ideas and actions.

You might even consider structuring seating arrangements to help foil persons with hidden agendas. If you anticipate cliques getting together to obstruct progress, consider physically breaking them up by seeing that they are seated apart from each other. Likewise, you can see that people who are personally hostile toward each other sit apart.

Finally, provide closure to the meeting so that members leave feeling that something has been accomplished. Some ways of providing closure are to (1) summarize what has been done, integrating the viewpoints that have been expressed into a unified whole as nearly as you can, (2) review what steps will be taken next, and (3) review action commitments—who is to do what by when. After the meeting, send a confirming memo of decisions made, assignments, responsibilities, and deadline dates for action.

Contributing to Meetings as a Member
When someone else is arranging and conducting a meeting, your input, preparation, and attitude are also important. If you approach meetings with the attitude that they are all a waste of time, they probably will be. If you approach them with the idea of making the most of them and contributing to the group's goals, meetings are more likely to be productive for you.

There is sometimes a fine line between cooperation and conformity in groups. When members don't feel free to openly express opinions, the group is in danger of overconforming and of indulging in groupthink. **Groupthink** occurs when members of a group appear to think as one and any deviation by one member results in severe negative sanctions by the others. In such an atmosphere, creativity and innovation are squelched. Both as a leader and as a member, you have a responsibility to point out situations in which you believe groupthink is operating.

As a group member, you are also responsible for

Being sure you understand the specific purpose of the meeting

Preparing adequately to contribute to the meeting

Expressing views that reflect some thought and preparation

Making and asking for suggestions

Clarifying and asking for clarification

Asking others' opinions

Even when you are not the leader of the meeting, it is still your responsibility to see that time is not wasted. Don't sit by and watch everyone's time being frittered away. Speak up. If you don't get an agenda, call the group leader and ask what needs to be accomplished at the meeting. Try to get specific questions that need answering. Suggest that sending agendas to all concerned might help everyone prepare and stay on track.

Once the meeting has started, if you see the leader letting the group jump to a new topic before resolving the question under discussion, ask, "What have we decided to do about the item we have been talking about?" You don't want to give the impression that you're trying to usurp the leader's position, but you can still put your knowledge of effective ways of arranging and conducting meetings to good use. Simply ask appropriate, probing questions at the right times.

Making Effective Presentations and Talks

Your participation and leadership in meetings frequently involves informal talking and interaction. Occasionally, you will have opportunities to make formal presentations and talks. The ability to make effective formal presentations is one of the most important assets a manager can develop. Since so many people shy away from formal speeches, the person who is comfortable with them obviously has an advantage over competitors for promotion to higher-level positions.

Using the Jitters Constructively   The largest barrier to effective formal presentations is stage fright or fear of speaking. Therefore, controlling the jitters is really the key to becoming an effective platform speaker.

Your mind is incapable of totally concentrating on two concerns at once. Therefore, if you can focus all your conscious thoughts on getting your main message across, you *cannot* focus on worries about what people think of you personally. Try thinking of yourself as merely the medium or vehicle for sending the message. In the story at the beginning of this chapter, Jan focused on getting her message across. By doing so, she freed her inner self, allowing it to help her.

Your inner self is amazingly competent; but if you're like most people, you don't believe it is. You think you must put forth great effort to be "good enough." These great, intense efforts actually sabotage your movement toward achieving your goals. This doesn't imply that you should stop learning, growing, and preparing for new kinds of activities and roles. It *does* mean that when it is time to actually perform, you forget yourself, keep your attention focused on the end result you're after, and at the same time let go of any burning, intense need (as opposed to relaxed intention) to achieve that result. See Exercise 4-5, Visualizing Results—Visualization 4, Handling Stage Fright.

An essential step in overcoming stage fright is to recognize it, face it squarely, and examine it. What do you fear will happen as a result of giving a talk?

A loss of esteem because of giving a poor performance?

The repetition of a traumatic experience? (If you've ever given a speech that you consider a disaster, you may have programmed yourself to connect speeches with disaster.)

Poor response from the audience leading to embarrassment? For example, not coming across the way you want to? People not laughing at your jokes? People leaving or nodding off? People asking embarrassing questions? People not asking questions when they should?

Amateurish performance because of your inexperience or because you're too introverted? (Do you believe only true extroverts make good speakers?)

Mediocre performance because you're not a podium star, dynamic and charismatic?

If you're a victim of any of these fears, it's up to you to develop a new set of attitudes that are more productive. First, keep in mind that the symptoms of stage fright are normal. Even the "podium stars" experience them. Anxiety can be a positive motivating force: It indicates you're concerned about doing a good job. The key is to control it so it doesn't become debilitating.

Next, focus on the fact that good speakers are made, not born. Public speaking is a skill you can master reasonably well with a little knowledge and a lot of practice. Granted, you'll probably never be a star or a silver-tongued orator. But, there are very few of these people in the entire world, so don't compare your performance with theirs.

Approach public speaking as a challenge rather than as an insurmountable barrier. Think of it as an exciting experience with many potential payoffs and many opportunities to learn. Then analyze your effectiveness and the results of your talks with the goal of constantly learning and improving.

Ineffective behaviors then become learning experiences rather than disasters or defeats or embarrassments. And you're miles ahead of your shy peers, still cowering in the corner.

In addition to developing a new set of attitudes, there are specific steps you can take that will help you overcome stage fright during your talk.

1. Be well prepared.

2. Just before your talk, do some relaxation exercises. Meditate, ground yourself, visualize, do deep breathing.

3. *Before* the talk, try looking at a friendly face in the audience and focusing on it. *During* the talk, make eye contact with people in all parts of the audience, occasionally returning to the friendly face. A high level of eye contact can help you speak conversationally and spontaneously as well as give you feedback about how your message is getting across. According to research findings, it also increases the likelihood that people will perceive you as credible, well qualified, and honest.

4. For some people it is most effective to visualize the audience as basically open and friendly. They tell themselves how warm and supportive they feel toward people in the group and that people in the group return that feeling and support them.

5. You can combine such messages to yourself with ones concerning the importance of the *content* of your speech. Focus on the importance of conveying the "meat" of your message to the group. Be clear about the major points you want to get across and the results you want.

6. Know your opening sentence and the first sentence of your concluding remarks like the back of your hand so you can easily

get into your speech and later move into your conclusion.

7. Keep in mind that mixing up words, skipping over points, forgetting the next point, and pausing to remember are all normal behaviors in everyday conversation. They can actually enhance your speech, making it come across as natural, conversational, and spontaneous. You can always mention the forgotten point later. Chances are, it will come up in the question-and-answer period and you can convey it in an even more interesting way then. If you have done a reasonably thorough job of preparing, you can relax and let your inner self take over. Your biggest enemy is *not* forgetting or stumbling; it's your expectations of perfection and the resulting tension and rigidity.

Preparing and Giving Talks That Get Results Talks that hold people's attention and get results are designed to appeal to both the logical and the psychological requirements of listeners. In order to make sense of a talk and to accept the speaker's credibility, most people need to grasp a logical progression of ideas, beginning with an overview of what

the talk is about, moving on to major points that are rational and backed up by facts, and ending with a summary or wrapup of what was covered.

You can deliver a talk that's accepted as credible yet still fail to persuade your listeners or to inspire them to action unless you also meet certain psychological requirements. You must determine what personal needs your listeners can satisfy by adopting your ideas and suggestions, show them the payoffs they will get, and touch their emotions. Only when people experience an emotional response to a talk are they likely to remember it and act on it. Exhibit 6-7 shows how talks can be structured to appeal to both logical and psychological requirements.

Now let's look at specific techniques for making the most of each aspect of the effective talk, beginning with determining the *purpose* of your talk. Decide exactly what end results you want from the talk. When the talk is completed, what do you want the effects or the outcome to be? What are you trying to accomplish? The answer to such questions as these will determine the title of your talk. Your purpose should be made clear or, where appropriate, intriguing, in both your opening and your closing remarks.

EXHIBIT 6-7: Structuring Talks to Meet Logical and Psychological Needs

Logical Aspects	Psychological Aspects
1. Introduction	1. *Attention:* Catch the interest or attention of your audience.
	2. *Need:* Show how listeners can meet certain needs or gain rewards by focusing on the information you will give them.
2. Body	3. *Satisfaction:* Make a few clear major points, tying in to satisfaction of needs or desires mentioned earlier.
	4. *Visualization:* Illustrate your points. Show how listeners can apply your ideas. Help them picture themselves in specific actions or situations and enjoying the resulting benefits.
3. Conclusion	5. *Action:* Summarize and wrap up your points. Touch listeners' emotions. Where appropriate, make a specific and concrete recommendation—a call for action that will fulfill the need mentioned earlier in your talk.

Don't try to achieve too many purposes or cover too many topics in one talk. The biggest mistake amateur speakers make is trying to cover too much ground and talking too long. Audiences generally cannot absorb more than two or three major points at one sitting, and they cannot pay attention to a speaker for more than about twenty minutes. If you must fill a longer time slot, plan some type of active audience involvement—an exercise, a game, a small group role-playing situation, a self-check or other type of quiz, for example.

A basic rule is to always talk on topics and cover points that you know enough about and enjoy enough to be comfortable with. Audiences immediately detect the degree of authority and the amount of enthusiasm and enjoyment you have about the topic you are speaking on. It is therefore wise *never* to accept a speaking assignment on a topic that bores you.

On the other hand, it sometimes works well to accept a speaking assignment on a topic in which you are quite interested but lack adequate knowledge. The key to success here is doing your homework and gaining adequate background knowledge to speak with authority. The advantage is that you learn a great deal about a topic in a short period of time. In addition, you tend to be more enthusiastic about a topic you've just learned about, and your enthusiasm comes through to your listeners. Also, you tend to speak at a level the lay audience can identify with since you have not yet gained a high level of sophistication.

One more word of warning: Never accept a topic or include points in your talk that conflict with your convictions or that you don't thoroughly understand, unless your purpose is to share conflicts or explore unknown territory as a group.

Plan an *attention-getting opening.* Your opening is the most important part of your talk. If you don't arouse the interest of your audience in the beginning, they may tune you out, and you may never have another chance to get them with you. The opening should catch immediate attention and arouse interest. It may even be startling or surprising, but it should lead into or suggest the theme of your speech and not be totally "off the wall." Exhibit 6-8 shows some examples of attention-getters that can give you ideas for your own openings.

Once you get your listeners' attention, give them an overview of what you're going to cover in the talk. If it involves mystery and surprise, set the stage. Either way, your introduction should prepare listeners to understand and accept the main points that come next.

Now decide on *a few clear points and how to illustrate them.* Generally limit your main points to three or four and provide adequate illustrations, both verbal and nonverbal—examples, supporting facts, explanations, pictures, charts, models, demonstrations, or applications of each main point. The only way to make a lasting impact on listeners is to *develop* a few major ideas. When you merely touch on major idea after major idea, none of them is likely to stick in the minds of your listeners.

Remember to provide for the logical needs of listeners by giving supporting facts, citing reference sources, and so forth. Also remember that feelings trigger action, so express your feelings, convey others' feelings, and appeal to listeners' feelings, where appropriate. If your talk is a persuasive one, show how your proposal will satisfy a need. Help listeners visualize themselves enjoying specific benefits and payoffs from doing what you ask.

A common mistake in preparing the body of the speech is failure to develop a good organizational plan and to communicate it to listeners. Communicate your organization of major points by stating a point clearly, then

EXHIBIT 6-8: Attention-Getters for Opening a Talk

1. A startling question or a challenging statement

   "Have you ever killed a man?"

   "Within two years you could be spending your winters in your own sunny villa by the sea."

2. An appropriate quotation, illustration, or story

   "All the world loves a lover."

   "Nuclear power plants are awe-inspiring monuments to man's manipulation of nature. As I was driving through the peaceful rural countryside recently, the sight of a huge monolithic white tower belching white steam startled me. It seemed so at odds with the quiet green pastures and grazing cattle."

   "When I was a little girl growing up in the rough, tough, he-man state of Texas, it never occurred to me that I might someday be a business executive. I remember walking to the local movie theater every Saturday and watching my heroines Ginger Rogers and Rosalind Russell playing sophisticated secretaries."

3. An exhibit: some appropriate object to use or to display, such as a picture or a sample

   Here's an example of using an object that created such a startling, exciting effect that the audience was spellbound throughout the five-minute talk: The speaker walked briskly over to a nail projecting from the wall. He was carrying several one-dollar bills in his hand. As he reached the nail, he impaled three or four dollar bills on it, saying "Bucks, bucks, bucks. Do you realize how many dollars are wasted every day simply because people do not communicate effectively with one another? Why, just last week a whole boat-load of bananas rotted in the hold of a ship in the harbor of Managua, Nicaragua, just because no one got the message through to unload them." The speaker moved from this specific incident of waste caused by lack of communication to the generalized effects of noncommunication among computer programmers.

4. A generalization that is attention getting and ties in with what follows

   "People love to hear their own names spoken."

developing it fully, and finally summarizing it. Be especially aware of letting listeners know when you are leaving one point and moving on to the next: "That gives you an idea of what the XYZ Model can do for your customers. Now let's take a look at how it can increase your sales volume next quarter."

Effectively illustrating or reinforcing your points through *visual aids* is a skill worth developing because it can contribute so much to the success of your talk. Keep visual aids simple—only a few words, figures, or items on each one. Use your visuals to reinforce points, not to tell whole stories. Make them large enough for everyone to easily see: Determine the maximum distance a viewer will be from the visual, pace it off, and check it out. Use heavy lines with plenty of contrast, and use color to advantage. (If you use handouts, distribute them *after* the talk as a rule; otherwise your listeners will focus on reading instead of listening to you.) Pointing to the items on your visuals as you discuss them can help you move and gesture naturally, relaxing and directing your tension.

The most helpful type of visual aid in most business situations is an appropriate graph or chart; they're especially effective for presenting quantitative information. Charts display information for quick comprehension. Graphs can show trends, fluctuations, relationships, and proportions more vividly than words alone could ever do.

Be sure your chart or graph is aptly labeled and the contents of any lines and columns are clearly identified with headings.

Play around with the form it will take by making rough pencil sketches of key parts of it, using two or more different setups. Then choose the one that will best meet your recipients' needs and your purpose. Most computers have the capability to produce graphs, and most large organizations have graphics technicians.

Your discussion should expand on the data in the chart or graph by (1) explaining what it means, (2) pointing out implications for situations, problems, or decisions being considered, (3) analyzing it in some other way (for example, showing how it supports conclusions or compares with something else), (4) making clear how it ties in with other information.

Deciding on the type of graph to use is easy when you understand the purpose of three basic types of graphs: (1) broken line, (2) bar, and (3) pie (see Figure 6-3). **Broken-line graphs** are best for showing progress over a period of time. They're excellent tools for showing trends or fluctuations. For example, you might show how sales have gone up and down (fluctuated) during the months of the past year, or you might show how the overall sales trend for your company has been upward during the past five years.

Bar graphs are the most effective means of grouping data when your main purpose is to help the reader make comparisons of figures which represent something that occurred at the same time or during the same period of time. They're appropriate for comparing the total sales of each of four sales representatives in a region or the total production of each of a company's five manufacturing plants, for example.

Pie graphs are best for showing the proportion of each of the items in a group to the whole amount. They're an excellent means of showing how each of the major items of a budget, for example, compares with the others and with the total budget. Pie graphs can also be used to show how each type of tax a company pays fits into its total tax picture.

For practice at choosing the best graph and constructing and interpreting graphs, see Exercises 6-4 and 6-5 at the end of this chapter.

Finally, plan to climax your talk with a *clear conclusion* that will reinforce the results you want. One of the most common mistakes beginning speakers make is failing to clearly conclude their talks—to wrap them up. Sometimes they merely stop talking and sit down, as if they can hardly wait to get the ordeal over with. At other times they give rather vague, "inconclusive" conclusions. Listeners aren't sure whether the speaker is trying to wrap up the talk, and

FIGURE 6-3: Basic Types of Graphs

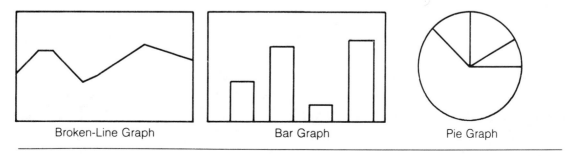

Broken-Line Graph   Bar Graph   Pie Graph

they have difficulty pulling all the parts of the talk together in their own minds. If you're going to devote time and energy to preparing and giving a talk, don't drop the ball at the conclusion! Use it to leave a good last impression and to insure a strong listener response by touching their emotions. Make your conclusion agree with your opening. Summarize your main points, tying them in to what your talk means for the listeners—the bottom line. Exhibit 6-9 shows examples of effective conclusions.

Now you're ready to rehearse, keeping in mind the goals of *comfort and spontaneity*. You need to rehearse your talk several times in order to feel comfortable with it. Your goal should be to prepare and rehearse just enough to feel adequately prepared and to come across as adequately prepared, but not so much that your talk seems to be "canned," mechanical, or lacking in spontaneity.

To achieve spontaneity, it is essential that you observe two rules: (1) Never memorize your talk. (2) Never read your talk. When you memorize or read a talk, you form an insurmountable barrier between the real you

and your listeners. Your words tend to simply travel mechanically through your brain and out your mouth. They don't come in contact with your inner self. Audiences immediately sense this and tend to tune out. It would be better to send them a written report ahead of time and then chat informally about certain aspects of it when you meet. Reading or giving a memorized speech are both poor ways to communicate. When you have a group of people together, take advantage of the opportunity to interact with them and to get a message across from your inner self that has a chance of engaging the inner selves of your listeners.

To retain this spontaneity, make a brief outline of your talk. (The first sentence of your opening and of your closing are the only ones you write in full.) Write only a few words for each main point and supporting points and put them on a 5 × 8 index card. Your goals are to (1) see your notes easily from the lectern or podium, (2) find your place easily as you move from point to point, and (3) use the notes unobtrusively. Lay them down in one spot and leave them

---

EXHIBIT 6-9: Ways to Conclude a Talk
_____

1. A summary of points made and how they lead to a general conclusion

   "Now we have seen how the XYZ model gives your customers 20 percent more storage capacity and will process information twice as fast as any current model. We have also seen that by focusing first on the 30 percent of your customers whose present equipment is depreciated out, you can increase your sales volume by $200,000 to $500,000 during the next quarter. The resulting $2,000 to $5,000 boost in your income will buy lots of goodies! Therefore, I know you'll want to focus most of your energy during the coming quarter on sales of XYZ."

2. An appeal for definite action

   "Let's show the Board of Directors that we're tired of the situation and we're not going to stand for it any longer! Fill out your proxies now if you can't attend the annual stockholders' meeting, and vote against proposition B."

3. A pointed story, quotation, or illustration that fits and packages the subject

   "I was watching a little robin building her nest the other day, and I was taken by her persistence and determination . . . and so we can eventually build the best sales organization in the fashion industry, step by step, with persistence and determination."
_____

there. Glance at them only briefly and occasionally as you move from one point to the next.

Here are some further suggestions for rehearsing your talk.

1. Be sure you are familiar with your illustrations, anecdotes, and facts.

2. Know the basic sequence of thought.

3. Talk about the subject to others so that you become accustomed to spontaneously verbalizing your ideas about it.

4. Make a tape recording of your talk using your note cards. Play it back and note areas where improvement is needed. Incorporate improvements in the second rehearsal. Don't over-rehearse.

5. Before and during rehearsal, keep in mind the sources of your enthusiasm and conviction in order to maintain them.

6. During rehearsal, pretend you are actually talking to your audience and concentrate on your message and the importance of getting it across to your audience rather than concentrating on yourself.

Some people find the following procedure to be effective for rehearsing: In the first rehearsal, cover the first major point. In the second rehearsal, cover the first and second major points. In the third rehearsal, cover the first, second, and third major points.

During the rehearsal period, remember to follow the suggestions we discussed earlier for handling the jitters. Practice them, especially when you feel yourself getting nervous as you rehearse. Use a relaxation exercise, visualizing success, several times before you actually give your talk. At the very least use the visualization technique once before the talk, preferably the night before.

As you go through the preparation, delivery, and evaluation phases of giving a talk, keep in mind the value of this skill you're developing. It will help you gain visibility as a promotable woman, especially since so many of your peers avoid speaking opportunities. And remember to pat yourself on the back each time you conquer one more little fear.

WHEN AND HOW TO WRITE

Most of your managerial communications will be oral rather than written. However, the ability to write clear, action-oriented letters and reports is almost as rare as the ability to deliver effective speeches. Therefore, sharpening your writing skills and adapting them to business situations will certainly enhance your promotability. Your written messages can create visibility for you among the higher-level decision-makers and showcase your ability to think, reason, analyze, and make decisions as well as your level of sophistication and political savvy. Knowing when to document actions and agreements, for example, and when and how to use such documentation can be crucial to your survival and your advancement within the corporate environment.

Determining When to Write

Determining when to talk to someone face to face, when to make a telephone call, and when to write is every bit as important as developing a well-written, well-organized message. It pays to keep your eyes and ears open and to develop your awareness of the most effective ways to communicate in your organization. Since every organizational environment has its own peculiarities, you must use your own experience and judgment in determining how to communicate best.

A mentor can be invaluable in developing this ability, for there is often no substitute for years of experience in dealing with the communication requirements of the unique personalities and circumstances of an organization. There are, however, some general principles for determining when and how to communicate.

Sometimes it's best to communicate orally, in a face-to-face situation, especially when your message involves some break with custom, tradition, or usual procedures. People tend to become very touchy about such changes and often misinterpret the reasons for them. They frequently fail to understand such messages because they are not expecting a change; they may glance at the message and assume they know what it says without grasping the change. So whenever your message involves something basically different from the routine, it's usually best to communicate it first in a face-to-face conversation where you can fully explain and get feedback about how well it is understood. Then you may want to follow up with a written version of your message.

When deciding whether to write, ask yourself, "Is this the most effective way of communicating this message to this person?" "What are the advantages and disadvantages of writing, of talking face-to-face, of telephoning?" Most important, ask yourself if you are writing because it is easier for you to approach or respond to a difficult situation by writing than by eyeballing the person and asserting yourself. Face-to-face assertion requires more courage than a telephone call or a letter. An assertive telephone call requires more courage than an assertive memo.

If you decide to take the easy way out, at least be aware of what you are doing. Keep in mind that you may be merely postponing the necessity for face-to-face assertion. You may even be worsening the situation; initiating an assertive stance in writing may be interpreted by the receiver as more threatening than initiating it in person. The receiver may wonder if the reason for writing is that you are "building a case" against him or her with written documentation. You also run a greater risk that the receiver will misinterpret your statements because you have no opportunity to give nonverbal messages or to further explain.

Since you can't get and give nonverbal messages or immediate feedback through written communication, you'll probably use oral messages most of the time. *Do* use written messages, however, to protect yourself, to confirm and document agreements and actions, to save time and money, and to build goodwill.

Protecting Your Interests   There is a great deal of truth in Dean Acheson's rule of the bureaucracy, "A memo is written not to inform the reader but to protect the writer." Organizational politics are an inescapable fact of life. Determine those times, situations, and people that pose possible future problems for you. Then determine the appropriate ways of documenting your actions and theirs. Again, a mentor can be invaluable in suggesting appropriate ways and times for protecting yourself through documentation.

Confirming Oral Agreements and Transactions   Whether you are the sender or the receiver, consider documenting all assignments, projects, agreements, and other transactions. Be sure the concepts involved in the project or transaction are explained fully enough that you both have an understanding of what is entailed. Then put it in writing. Since it's easy for one or the other of you to forget exactly what you originally agreed to, documentation will tie it down. Any significant changes should also be communicated orally and in writing. Important insights and new ideas about a project should be discussed and documented before they're incorporated into a subordinate's work or a boss' expectations.

Documenting Your Ideas and Proposals Use memos to document *any* new idea you have. If your boss or peers tend to take credit for your ideas, don't breathe a word of a new idea to anyone, including your boss, until you have it in memo form directed to your boss with a copy to his boss and any other appropriate people you can think of. Since good new ideas are in short supply and are held in high esteem in most companies, they tend to be stolen. You might as well get all the credit you can for any new idea you may have. (The information about writing proposals that follows can help you implement your ideas.)

Saving Money Sometimes long-distance transactions are just too lengthy, complex, or low priority to justify the travel necessary for face-to-face communication or the expense of lengthy long-distance telephone calls. Written messages will fill the bill here.

Conducting Routine Business Transactions When you're sending routine letters, memos, and reports that all parties are familiar with and understand, you can probably do so without an oral preface or followup.

Building Goodwill In addition to the more obvious routine business that can be handled by written communications, don't overlook the opportunity to send written notes of congratulations to business associates who earn promotions or win recognition. Thank you notes for special favors and notes remembering birthdays and company anniversary dates are also cordial and thoughtful.

Whatever you do, don't send a letter or memo that is written while you are angry. Write it if doing so makes you feel better, but

sleep on it at least one night. Then ask yourself whether it really achieves your goals most effectively.

A final word to the wise that applies to all types of written communications: Limit them. Don't swamp people with paper. If you must send a written message that is especially important, make it stand out. Consider developing special signals for urgent or special messages, such as different paper, a special color, a special mark or heading, or a similar signal. If you reserve these special signals for really important messages, you have a good chance of regularly getting quick results from them.

Writing Convincing Proposals

If you can effectively formulate and present your ideas, suggestions, solutions, analyses, and recommendations in the form of a proposal for action to your boss (and perhaps to his bosses), you can gain favorable visibility. A proposal is a special type of report proposing that certain actions be taken, such as purchasing new equipment, contracting for services, implementing new procedures, reorganizing a department, or making a new product.

Writing a proposal, as opposed to merely discussing it orally, can help you shape your thoughts and think through the ramifications of a request or idea. By putting it in writing, you show you have covered all points, and you provide documentation for your boss and others to refer to when considering the action they'll take on your proposal. If you write it well, you show people you have good reasoning and planning skills as well as communication skills, including that tough one, writing ability.

Writing an effective proposal requires careful preparation, as illustrated in the four-step PREP plan shown here.* "PREP" not only stands for preparation, but it's an acronym for the four steps:

P = Person who will receive the report

R = Results you want the report to have

E = Essential Information that must be included

P = Presentation of the information for best results

By adequately covering these four aspects of report preparation and by applying the best business writing skills, you can produce a proposal that gets the results you want. Here are specific suggestions to help you cover all bases when writing proposals and other reports.

Person: What persons will receive the report? If the situation is complex, important, or touchy, jot down key points so you can clarify them, grasp interrelations, and keep them in mind as you write. Ask yourself questions such as these:

1. Will several different categories of persons receive this report? If so, do they have different needs and uses for the report? Do I need to prepare more than one version of this report?

2. What sort of personal relationship, if any, do I have with the receiver? What past transactions have we had?

3. What do I know about his or her field of experience, approach to life, psychological needs, "games" he or she plays?

---

*Adapted from Norma Carr-Ruffino, *Writing Short Business Reports* (New York: McGraw-Hill, Gregg Division, 1980).

4. How is the receiver likely to misinterpret messages? What mistakes is the receiver likely to make in carrying out instructions, suggestions, or requests?

5. What is the receiver's position in relation to mine—up, down, or lateral?

6. Did the receiver request this report, or am I initiating it?

7. What is the receiver's general attitude about the subject?

8. Am I making a request or recommendation? If so, how will the receiver benefit from taking this action?

Results: What results do I want this report to have? Jot down the key results and keep them in front of you as you write. These questions can help you identify the results you need to aim for:

1. What effect, outcomes, or reactions do I want?

2. What are my purposes or goals? To help the receiver do the job? To help the receiver get necessary facts or understand the situation? To help the receiver make a decision? To save the receiver time and effort?

3. Am I writing this report in order to persuade the receiver to do something, change the receiver's viewpoint, establish or maintain a positive working relationship?

Essential Information: What information and ideas must I include to get the results I want? Brainstorm. Jot down key words for everything that pops into your head. Don't write complete thoughts. Don't evaluate or edit yet. Don't organize the items yet. Be sure you cover all bases by asking yourself these questions:

1. Do I need to cross-check the information to be sure it is correct?

2. What information does the receiver have on the subject already?

3. Will the receiver remember it, need it, have problems looking it up?

4. What background information should the receiver have?

5. What information must I include?

6. What information can be omitted?

7. What questions might the receiver have as he or she reads this report? Can I include the answers? If not, have I recognized and discussed the questions in the report?

8. Do I need to review this report with the receivers at a later date? Follow up to see if instructions, requests, or suggestions were acted on? If so, have I provided for this in the report?

Presentation: How can I best present the essential information for the persons receiving the report to get the results I want? What is the best order of presentation for the report as a whole? Is this report analytical or is it informational? If it is analytical, will the receiver probably react negatively to the recommendations? If so, present recommendations *after* the discussion. If the receiver will probably react favorably or routinely to the recommendations, put them at the beginning, in this sequence:

1. Subject line, title, or paragraph establishing purpose of report

2. For analytical reports: recommendations and summary of conclusions
   or
   For informational reports: summary of most important points

3. Background information, if essential to understanding of discussion

4. Findings or further discussion of points (Use subheads for easy reading.)

5. Additional details, if any

Next ask yourself some key questions to determine the best way to present your findings or main discussion.

1. What is the best logical or psychological order for presenting the findings or discussion of facts? By order of importance? Size? Geographical location? Alphabetical sequence? Time sequence? Other?

2. Does the reader need to compare one set of facts with another (or others)? Have I organized them for easiest comparison? (By decision-making factors or criteria rather than alternative by alternative?)

3. Is it important for the reader to follow my thinking process? If so, how can I best present the facts and ideas to achieve this goal?

4. Can some of the information be understood more quickly and easily if it's presented in the form of a table, chart, or graph?

5. What information can I block in (itemize) and number?

Now go back and organize the items you jotted down earlier under "Essential Information." Gather any additional information you need. Evaluate and edit. Verify and cross-check information, where appropriate. Number all items of essential information in the order you want to present them. Now dictate a rough draft of the report from these brief notes. When you proofread, ask yourself whether you need to:

1. Be more specific, concrete?

2. Use more action verbs?

3. Use shorter words, sentences, paragraphs?

4. Add transitional words and phrases for coherence?

5. Add subheads that help tell the story?

Finally, decide the best way to transmit and sell your proposal. Is the receiver likely to respond more favorably to an oral presentation followed by the written report or vice versa? If you plan an oral presentation, who should be included? If you present the written proposal first, should you deliver it in person or route it through regular mail channels? Once you've developed a good proposal, follow through to give it the best chance for success.

SUMMARY

You can improve your communication skills if you think of communication as a process rather than as a set of isolated events. You can build on your talent for communicating well by adapting your skills to the business world. By practicing empathy and developing the art of persuasion, you can gain the trust of others. By watching your word choice, using specific language, and selecting active verb forms, you can get clear messages across. When explaining rules, focus on payoffs for the person affected. Prepare key one-liners to express your viewpoint quickly on key issues. Keep communication lines open by avoiding false assumptions and allowing for face-saving by others. Increase your credibility by providing closure to your conversations instead of jumping and rambling. Take the initiative in using good communication techniques to maintain relationships. Structure those relationships so that you get needed feedback concerning your actions and messages and those of your people.

The ability to determine when it's best to just listen and when it's best to become actively involved in a situation is important to the manager. So are listening skills. The art of "being with" another person involves concentrating on that person and his or her message without adding to or taking away from it. It's important to distinguish between evaluating the content of the message and evaluating the person's feelings or beliefs. While being with another person requires accepting the speaker's message and feelings, it doesn't necessarily require agreeing with the speaker. Developing active listening skills involves restating the content of the speaker's message, noticing feelings and checking them out, listening for behavior patterns, and looking for deeper insights.

Meetings are notorious time-wasters in many organizations. Effective managers turn them into time-savers that build group morale and team spirit. One way of accomplishing this is to make them as group centered as possible. The goal is to reach an optimal balance between accomplishing the tasks at hand and meeting the needs of individual members and the group as a whole.

Call meetings only when they'll be the best way of accomplishing specific purposes. Develop a results-oriented agenda that phrases items in question form, and set priorities for handling the agenda items.

Prepare well for each meeting by briefing any speakers, resource persons, and members that will participate, deciding on appropriate group size and time limits, and selecting the room arrangement so that members have maximum eye contact.

Conduct your meetings for maximum effectiveness by beginning and ending on time and keeping the group on target so that the meeting goals are met. Make frequent summaries during the meeting and stress the positive aspects of what is occurring. Consider using a solution wheel to keep the group focused on each step in a problem-solving meeting. Keep the meeting energized by behaviors that help achieve task goals and that encourage people to participate. Look for hidden agendas and intervene where necessary. Provide for closure by summarizing what has been done, reviewing steps that will be taken, integrating viewpoints, reviewing action commitments, and providing for a record of the meeting along with written followup.

The ability to make effective formal presentations can be one of your most important assets in winning promotions because so many of your competitors will shy away from such activities. You can overcome the greatest barrier to effective speaking, stage fright, by focusing on the main message you want to get across and using relaxation and visualization techniques.

Prepare your talk by paying attention to both the psychological and the logical needs of your listeners. Plan an attention-getting introduction that hooks into your listeners' needs or desires; a body that gives necessary details and clarifies the major points, including how listeners' needs can be met; and a clear conclusion that wraps up the talk and focuses on the results you want to achieve. Use visual aids to reinforce the main points of your talk. Graphs and charts are especially helpful for presenting statistical information.

If a message is really important or involves a deviation from the routine, try to deliver it orally, even though you may want to follow it up later with a memo or report. Consider sending written messages for (1) confirming oral agreements and transactions, (2) protecting your interests by providing written evidence for your files, (3) conducting routine transactions and sending routine reports that all parties are familiar with and understand, and (4) conducting long-distance transactions that are too lengthy, complex, or low priority to justify travel or long-distance telephone calls. Avoid writing as a copout when you should really assert yourself in a face-to-face meeting.

Good written communications are one way to gain favorable visibility and win promotions. The higher you go, the more important they become. Skill in preparing effective proposals is especially important. Use a

PREP checklist to help organize and present your data effectively by considering the persons who will receive the proposal, the results you want, the essential information to include, and the best sequence and format for presenting it.

ADDITIONAL EXERCISES

EXERCISE 6-3: SPEAKING/LISTENING EXERCISE

From the following list of topics (or any other topics your instructor may add), select the three you feel most strongly about, regardless of whether you agree or disagree with the statement. List them on a piece of paper, putting the topic you feel most strongly about first with the word "agree" or "disagree" after it, and so forth. Your instructor will assign you a discussion partner.

You and your partner should decide which one of you will be Speaker first. The other partner will be Listener during the first round. For the second round, you will switch roles.

When you are Speaker, you will talk to your partner for from three to five minutes about the topic you have chosen. Discuss the reasons you agree or disagree with the topic statement. Concentrate on getting your message across. Notice any barriers you experience to communicating effectively.

When you are Listener, concentrate on just "being with" your partner and taking in everything she or he has to say, both verbally and nonverbally. Notice any barriers you experience to listening. Do not talk. You can, however, use nonverbal responses such as head nods and facial expressions.

Controversial Topics for Discussion

1. Abortion should be banned.
2. Interracial dating and marriage should be avoided.
3. Pornographic movies should be banned.
4. Gambling should be legalized in all states.
5. Prostitution should be legalized in all states.
6. Capital punishment should be abolished in all states.
7. Homosexuals should have equal rights.
8. The federal government should rescue large corporations that are floundering.
9. Blondes have more fun.

10. Every adult should have a guaranteed income.
11. An "open" marriage is a happier marriage.
12. Oil companies need tax advantages, such as depletion allowances.
13. "Oil sheiks" have the right to acquire American land, banks, and other assets.
14. We need more nuclear power plants.
15. All pesticides and herbicides should be banned.
16. Both men and women should be drafted for the armed services.
17. Advertising helps the average American consumer.
18. Your doctor knows best.
19. Gasoline should be rationed.
20. The average American diet is mostly junk food.

EXERCISE 6-4: CHOOSING THE BEST GRAPH*

Decide whether you would use a broken-line, bar, or pie graph to illustrate the following data. Check your responses with the answer key.

1. The number of women employed in business organizations from 1900 to the present

2. Total sales from each of the five district offices of Acme Company

3. Money spent by your department last year for overhead, salaries, supplies, and miscellaneous expenses

4. The percentage of women in management during the past twenty-five years and in the next five years

5. A comparison of a company's net profits with expenses and cost of sales over the last five years

6. A breakdown by neighborhood of homeowners in Central City

7. Figures showing how sales have gone up and down during the past ten years

8. The portion of a company's taxes that went for federal income tax, state taxes, and local taxes

*Adapted from Norma Carr-Ruffino, *Writing Short Business Reports* (New York: McGraw-Hill, Gregg Division, 1980).

EXERCISE 6-5: CONSTRUCTING AND INTERPRETING A GRAPH*

As Marketing Manager for Lighthouse Designs, you want to include in a report to the President the total sales of ski wear for this year as well as last year. So that the President can grasp this information at a glance, prepare a preliminary draft of a graph that illustrates the data shown in the table.

	Total Sales of Ski Wear	
	This Year	Last Year
January	$125,000	$140,000
February	90,000	105,000
March	60,000	70,000
April	12,000	16,000
May	7,000	5,000
June	8,000	4,000
July	13,000	12,000
August	160,000	80,000
September	210,000	190,000
October	190,000	225,000
November	175,000	215,000
December	140,000	175,000

Then, suppose you were the reader of the report containing the graph you made from the data. Would you agree with the following statements about the information shown in the graph? Why or why not? Check your responses with the answer key.

1. The company sold more ski wear last year than this year.

2. The company will sell less ski wear next year.

3. Summer vacations cause a reduction in sales of ski wear.

4. The company is losing money on ski wear.

5. For the past two years the Marketing Manager has loved the fall months, at least for business reasons.

6. Sales of ski wear were generally unchanged in June, July, and October. Check your responses with the answer key.

---

*Adapted from Norma Carr-Ruffino, *Writing Short Business Reports* (New York: McGraw-Hill, Gregg Division, 1980).

REFERENCES

1. Adams, Linda. *Effectiveness Training for Women.* New York: Wyden Books, 1979.

2. Beegle, Bernard B. "The Message That Is Sent Without Words." *Supervisory Management* (February 1971), pp. 12–14.

3. Bradford, Leland P. *Making Meetings Work.* LaJolla, Calif.: University Associates, 1976. A detailed discussion of the group-centered approach to conducting meetings.

4. Carr-Ruffino, Norma. *Writing Short Business Reports.* New York: McGraw-Hill, Gregg Division, 1980. A step-by-step guide to effective business writing, with a special emphasis on writing proposals, memo reports, and letter reports.

5. Jellisco, Jerold M. and William J. Ickes. "The Power of the Glance: Desire to See and Be Seen in Cooperative and Competitive Situations." *Journal of Experimental Social Psychology,* Vol. 10 (1974), pp. 444–50.

6. Mintzberg, Henry. "Planning on the Left Side and Managing on the Right Side." *Harvard Business Review,* Vol. 54, No. 4 (July–August 1976), pp. 49–58.

7. Snell, Frank. *How to Hold a Better Meeting.* New York: Simon and Schuster, 1974. Snell focuses on getting maximum results in minimal time in business meetings. The discussion on using the solution wheel is especially helpful.

8. Taetzsch, Lyn and Eileen Benson. *Taking Charge on the Job.* New York: Executive Enterprises Publications, 1978. This book includes some suggestions that are especially helpful to new women managers.

Developing Management Skills

In Part 1 you laid the foundation for success as a promotable woman by developing personal skills that are required of effective managers. We've already discussed many business applications for those skills. Now you're ready to expand your knowledge to the more technical, traditional management functions.

The skill and knowledge areas we'll discuss in Part 2 are important for *all* managers. As we cover these basics, we'll focus on the aspects that most often create problems for women managers. You'll have a chance to (1) develop your own management style, (2) enhance the motivation of your people, (3) solve problems and make decisions with confidence, (4) develop performance plans and organize for productivity, (5) overcome any fears you may have about handling company financial matters, (6) build an effective working team, (7) get more done with less effort and use your highly developed skills to get that next promotion!

That's a challenging list, but you'll have plenty of support in the form of explanations, examples, and exercises in every chapter.

Chapter Seven

Developing Your Management Style

"No matter how lofty you are in your department, the responsibility for what your lowliest assistant is doing is yours."

Bessie Rowland Jones

This entire book is about developing management skills and, in the process, developing your own management style. Everything you believe and do has an effect on your management style and contributes to it. In this chapter, we will focus specifically on several theories and philosophies of management so that you can have a better sense of the implications and possible effects of *your* beliefs and attitudes in various business situations. We will also discuss using your management style to lay the groundwork for building a productive team of workers.

In this chapter you will have an opportunity to

1. Assess your current management skills and style

2. Learn more about the elements of an effective management style

3. Investigate some theories and philosophies of management and determine which ones best correspond to your style

4. Identify ways of providing a challenging yet supportive climate where subordinates will excel

5. Learn how to develop the one skill that is indispensable for good management—providing structure

6. See how performance planning skills can help you implement your management style

7. Consider ways of using the leadership traits you already possess through taking command of your inner resources

8. Establish your own authority and management style when you take over a new job position

9. Relate successfully to subordinates on a one-to-one basis while at the same time building a top-performing team

10. Handle conflicts in positive ways and facilitate the satisfactory resolution of conflicts

Different Strokes

Carrie has been Assistant Sales Manager at the San Diego branch for over a year now. The major duties her boss has delegated to her are supervising the customer accounts clerks and handling budgets, reports, and other paperwork. George Rodriguez, her boss and the Sales Manager, spends most of his time working with his sales people and dealing with large customer accounts. One day John Brockfield, General Manager of the San Diego branch, asks Carrie to drop by his office.

"Well, Carrie, come in, sit down. I see from these reports that the customer accounts have never been in such good shape. Those detailed job procedures you worked out must have done wonders. Congratulations!"

"Thanks, John. It's been an interesting challenge, figuring out ways to improve our performance in that area. And I think the clerks really needed someone to pay close attention to their work. So many of them are just out of high school or working part-time—they need the help."

"Well, are you ready for another interesting challenge? We would like you to step into the Sales Manager's position. George has accepted the General Manager's job at the Dallas branch."

"*Am* I? Not before tomorrow!"

A few weeks later, Carrie is discussing her job with her husband Murray:

"I just hope I can do as well with this assignment as I did with the last one. I've been analyzing the sales people's tasks and responsibilities, and I'm taking turns accompanying them as they call on customers. I've even tried my own hand at

selling again just so I can keep in touch with what they're doing."

"Well, I hope they appreciate your dedication," responds Murray.

"That will take time, I guess," replies Carrie. "Anyway, I'm working out some detailed job procedures I think will provide the sales reps with clear, precise ways of achieving the results I want. This should be really helpful, too, to our new people."

"How about the old hands?" Murray asks. "Will they accept these new procedures? What kind of group do you have, anyway?"

"Oh, the group. Well, I have twenty-one men and two women. Most of them have been with the company more than five years. In fact, a number of the salesmen have been with us fifteen or twenty years and have been quite successful. I'd guess that some years their commissions amount to more than the Sales Manager's salary. Anyway, these procedures are not that different from what the good reps are doing already. And there's always room for improvement, right?"

"Well, Carrie," Murray smiles, "you know your people. I'm sure you're on your way to being a great Sales Manager."

That same evening two of the older salesmen, Frank Andreini and Ken Cypert, are chatting over a before-dinner drink.

"I don't know about this Dickeson dame," says Frank. "You know, Rodriguez wasn't that great a manager, but he stayed out of our hair and took care of the administrative work."

"She seems okay so far, but I'd feel more comfortable with someone like you as manager, Frank. Why didn't you take that job five years ago when they offered it to you?"

"You know better than that, Ken. An old drummer like me would never be happy behind a desk. I've got to be on the road and making sales. Besides, I make more money this way over the long haul."

Within the next few weeks, Carrie completes the detailed job procedures and makes sure all the sales people have copies. She checks with them to be sure they understand what she wants them to do and how she wants them to do it. Then she makes regular checks to see that the sales people are actually following proper procedures. After three months on the job, her boss, John Brockfield, says one day:

"Carrie, I know you're putting forth a great deal of effort in your new job."

"Yes, John, and it's quite a challenge, as you said it would be."

"How do you feel about the way things are going in your department?"

"Frankly, John, I had hoped to be making more progress. It seems as if I'm losing ground with my people instead of gaining."

"I agree, Carrie. What do you think is the root of the problem?"

"I wish I knew! I'm doing the same kinds of things that were extremely successful when I was supervising the Customer Accounts. Somehow my management style just doesn't seem to be working with the sales reps. The office people seem to accept my leadership fairly well, but I'm having problems with the sales people—problems ranging from indifference to outright hostility."

---

1. How would you describe Carrie's management style? _____

2. Why do you think it was effective in the past? _____

3. Why is it causing problems for her now? _____

4. How do you think she should change it? _____

ASSESSING YOUR MANAGEMENT SKILLS AND STYLE

First, let's take a broad overview of management style by reviewing the manager's functions, roles, and style elements. Then you'll have a chance to assess your own management skills and style.

The Functions and Roles of a Manager

What is management style? It's how you do what a manager does. What does a manager do? Traditionally managers plan, organize, staff, direct, and control. Although these terms are valid, they are sometimes difficult for new managers to translate into daily activities. An overview of nine general competency areas and related activities is shown in Exhibit 7-1.

Joseph Steger of Rensselaer Polytechnic Institute's School of Management and his associates have defined the managerial functions in terms of the day-to-day activities of managers, as well as the roles they fulfill in interacting with others and the *ways* in which they carry out these activities [10, pp. 21–23].

Steger says these six functions are present in every manager's job—but in varying degrees, depending on the job situation:

1. *Persuasive Communication*

   Serving as a spokesperson for your group

   Selling or extolling your group's value to top management and colleagues as well as customers, suppliers, and others outside the company

   Selling the goals of top management to your subordinates

   Convincing others to comply with, or at least accept, your wishes

EXHIBIT 7-1: Management Functions and Skills: Nine General Competency Areas and Twenty-eight Specific Performance-Related Activities

A. Planning and Controlling Organizational Performance
    1. Establishing overall direction and priorities
    2. Planning strategy
    3. Planning operations
    4. Using planning and control techniques and systems
    5. Establishing policies and guidelines
    6. Evaluating organizational performance

B. Organizing the Work of an Organization
    7. Structuring/aligning resources
    8. Delegating effectively

C. Selecting and Developing Personnel
    9. Determining the requirements of a job and assessing personnel
    10. Developing subordinates' knowledges, skills, and abilities

D. Exercising Leadership and Managing Human Performance
    11. Understanding human behavior on-the-job
    12. Applying appropriate leadership strategies
    13. Motivating employees effectively
    14. Building team effectiveness
    15. Selecting and implementing appropriate organizational communication techniques
    16. Managing change
    17. Evaluating subordinate performance

E. Handling People Outside One's Own Work Group
    18. Working effectively with bosses, peers, and users of organizational outputs
    19. Handling issues and complaints that come from outside the organization

F. Solving Problems and Making Effective Decisions
    20. Making decisions in an effective, accurate, and timely fashion
    21. Solving problems effectively

G. Identifying Concerns Specific to Federal Sector Management
    22. Implementing federal sector-specific programs
    23. Assessing the implications of trends in federal management

H. Assessing Implications of General Management and Environmental Trends
    24. Applying the principles of management science theory (systems and subsystems)
    25. Assessing the impact of external trends which can affect any organization

I. Managing Oneself
    26. Understanding and managing your own behavior
    27. Developing your own technical and managerial knowledge and skills
    28. Coping with stress

SOURCE: U.S. Department of Defense

2. *Administration*

Performing tasks according to already-established rules

Establishing and using management tools that are necessary to accomplish specific tasks

Performing administrative tasks that range from establishing procedures to making appointments and are essentially short range in nature

3. *Technical Professionalism*

Applying expertise and training in your field

Knowing exactly what's required and the language of the trade so that you can ask important questions and give directions, even though you leave much of the detailed work to your subordinates

4. *Leadership and Power*

Exercising as strong an influence as is appropriate in each situation

Directing and giving orders without necessarily needing either to justify them or to convince others of why they must be done

5. *Training and Development*

Giving informal on-the-job training and encouragement to help subordinates live up to their capabilities

Providing opportunities for further training or study

6. *Planning and Objective-Setting*

Looking ahead, determining what needs to be done, and assessing the best way to do it

Pooling information from a wide variety of sources and using it effectively to set and achieve objectives and to make full use of human resources

Central to your management style is how you interact with others as you carry out these functions. At various times you must motivate, direct, and evaluate your people as you're communicating, leading, training, and setting objectives. Let's look at the roles you fulfill.

As a motivator you structure work situations so that you encourage or inspire enthusiasm or interest. If you are successful, others achieve their fullest potential on the job and

cooperate with you to meet company objectives.

As a director you help workers set their objectives and achieve them.

As an evaluator you assess and appraise situations after taking in the available information.

Elements of an Effective Management Style

The *way* you convey these managerial functions and the *way* you deal with people as motivator, director, and evaluator depends on your management style. This may be broken down into a number of elements. Here's the breakdown developed by Dr. Steger and his associates.

1. *Objectivity.* Observing situations, evaluating them and responding to them in a logical, factual way. Being aware of personal biases and taking them into consideration without letting them control decisions.

2. *Presence.* "Looking the part," including appropriate dress, speech, and manners. Grasping the social and role subtleties of each situation.

3. *Leadership style.* Exerting influence in appropriate ways; using power and consideration effectively. The use of power can range from an authoritarian to a democratic approach, although the "best" approach will depend on the situation. Consideration involves understanding and taking into consideration the people around you and their jobs, as well as the emotions and reactions of these people.

4. *Risk-taking.* Being comfortable with taking risks commensurate with the expected outcome of the risk.

5. *Work pace.* Getting the right things done efficiently; setting an appropriate work

pace for employees; timing actions properly.

6. *Humor.* Providing and appreciating wit and humor at the right time and place.

Exercise 7-1 is designed to help you determine your strengths and weaknesses in the functional skills and in the role/interaction skills. To make this exercise even more valuable, ask some of your workers, peers, and bosses to use the form to give you feedback about how they view your skills.

As you look over Exercise 7-1 to assess the strengths and weaknesses of your management style, decide which areas call for further training. As Exhibit 7-2 indicates, it's much easier to improve your functional and interaction skills in some areas than in others. The exhibit indicates the ease or likelihood of successfully training people to perform various functions in the roles of motivator, director, or evaluator.

For example, training in techniques of administration (rated "H") has a high probability of being effective whether its purpose is to motivate, direct, or control. Administration can be learned rather easily since the

EXERCISE 7-1: SELF-ASSESSMENT OF MANAGEMENT SKILLS

Place a checkmark in the space that best indicates your performance in each area.

Functions	Usually/Excellent	Often/Very Good	Sometimes/Adequate	Rarely/Weak	Never/Poor
Persuasion					
1. Frequency of my efforts at persuasion	___	___	___	___	___
2. Success at getting my points across	___	___	___	___	___
3. Success in sharing my viewpoint	___	___	___	___	___
4. Frequency with which subordinates agree with me on what to do and how to do it	___	___	___	___	___
5. Boss' evaluation of my department and its performance	___	___	___	___	___
Administration					
1. Ability to set priorities for paperwork	___	___	___	___	___
2. Frequency with which I meet deadlines	___	___	___	___	___

	Usually/Excellent	Often/Very Good	Sometimes/Adequate	Rarely/Weak	Never/Poor
3. Initiative and ability in providing appropriate rules and procedures	___	___	___	___	___

Technical Professionalism

1. Frequency with which I suggest approaches that might be effective or profitable	___	___	___	___	___
2. Adequacy of my knowledge of the field	___	___	___	___	___
3. Quality of my training compared with others in the company	___	___	___	___	___
4. My level of understanding of technical reports and of suggestions I am given	___	___	___	___	___

Leadership and Power

1. Frequency of making decisions and seeing that they are implemented	___	___	___	___	___
2. Ability to make demands when necessary	___	___	___	___	___
3. Ability to make decisions that involve possibly unpleasant results or side effects	___	___	___	___	___
4. Ability to handle confrontations	___	___	___	___	___
5. Ability to enforce discipline when necessary	___	___	___	___	___
6. Frequency with which people respond to my demands	___	___	___	___	___

Training and Development

1. Knowledge of the strengths and weaknesses of my subordinates; ability to draw on strengths and offset weaknesses	___	___	___	___	___
2. Ability to provide developmental opportunities and experiences for subordinates to help them develop capabilities	___	___	___	___	___
3. Knowledge of capabilities of subordinates and ability to capitalize on them	___	___	___	___	___

4. Frequency with which I encourage subordinates to continue with their own training   ___ ___ ___ ___ ___

Planning and Objective-Setting

1. Frequency with which I achieve objectives   ___ ___ ___ ___ ___

2. Frequency with which my plans backfire   ___ ___ ___ ___ ___

3. Ability to foresee results of my actions   ___ ___ ___ ___ ___

4. Ability to get adequate information for planning, decision-making, and implementation   ___ ___ ___ ___ ___

5. Ability to set long-range goals and achieve them   ___ ___ ___ ___ ___

6. Ability to set short-range goals that dovetail with long-range ones   ___ ___ ___ ___ ___

7. Ability to plan what my work group will need in order to grow in the years ahead   ___ ___ ___ ___ ___

Interactions

Motivator

1. Frequency with which people react favorably to my suggestions, presentations, and requests

   Subordinates   ___ ___ ___ ___ ___

   Peers   ___ ___ ___ ___ ___

   Boss   ___ ___ ___ ___ ___

   Customers   ___ ___ ___ ___ ___

   Others   ___ ___ ___ ___ ___

2. Frequency with which subordinates are willing to put in extra time on one of my projects, when necessary   ___ ___ ___ ___ ___

3. Subordinates' attitudes toward their tasks   ___ ___ ___ ___ ___

4. Others' opinions of my performance as a motivator

   Subordinates   ___ ___ ___ ___ ___

   Peers   ___ ___ ___ ___ ___

   Boss   ___ ___ ___ ___ ___

   Customers   ___ ___ ___ ___ ___

   Others   ___ ___ ___ ___ ___

	Usually/Excellent	Often/Very Good	Sometimes/Adequate	Rarely/Weak	Never/Poor

Director

1. My ability to achieve goals | —— | —— | —— | —— | —— |

2. My willingness to make decisions | —— | —— | —— | —— | —— |

3. Frequency with which I develop the right plan of action for a particular job or task | —— | —— | —— | —— | —— |

4. Clarity of my goals and action plans | —— | —— | —— | —— | —— |

5. Frequency with which I procrastinate in making decisions and in initiating action | —— | —— | —— | —— | —— |

6. My willingness to take risks in decision-making | —— | —— | —— | —— | —— |

7. My willingness to make decisions when the consequences could be unpleasant | —— | —— | —— | —— | —— |

8. The level of my commitment to my decisions | —— | —— | —— | —— | —— |

9. Others' opinions of my performance as a director

   Subordinates | —— | —— | —— | —— | —— |

   Peers | —— | —— | —— | —— | —— |

   Boss | —— | —— | —— | —— | —— |

   Customers | —— | —— | —— | —— | —— |

   Others | —— | —— | —— | —— | —— |

Evaluator

1. My ability to analyze projects | —— | —— | —— | —— | —— |

2. My ability to understand and use the strengths of my subordinates effectively | —— | —— | —— | —— | —— |

3. The level of my preparation to make major decisions | —— | —— | —— | —— | —— |

4. The quality of the rationales for the decisions I make

5. Others' opinions of my performance as an evaluator

Subordinates   ___ ___ ___ ___ ___

Peers   ___ ___ ___ ___ ___

Boss   ___ ___ ___ ___ ___

Customers   ___ ___ ___ ___ ___

Others   ___ ___ ___ ___ ___

Now return to the discussion on page 267.

EXHIBIT 7-2: Probabilities of Acquiring Various Managerial Skills Through Training

Managerial Functions	Relational Factors (Interaction Roles)		
	Motivator	Director	Evaluator
Persuasive communication	L	L	H
Planning and objective-setting	H	L	H
Administration	H	H	H
Leadership and power	L	L	L
Technical professionalism	M	L	H
Training and development	H	M	H

H = High probability of training being effective

M = Medium probability

L = Low probability

rules and regulations upon which administrative actions are based are usually already established. In contrast, persuasive communication as a motivator or as a director is ranked "L." It is difficult to learn because it's relatively general in application, and it depends heavily on innate personality traits and situational factors. Persuasive communication as an evaluator is easier to learn because it can be based on meeting specific objectives and the resulting rewards.

As a rule, the skills that are most difficult to learn through training are those that involve high levels of interpersonal ability. Understanding the relative ease or difficulty of acquiring various types of managerial skills can help you set realistic training goals and time targets for yourself and your people as you work on improving management style.

As many of the items in Exercise 7-1 indicate, your management style is the way you function and relate to people at all levels within the company. It is also reflected in your dealings with people outside the company. Figure 7-1 shows how effective managers ideally relate to their subordinates, peers, and superiors in the organization and to customers and clients on the outside.

Now that you have an overview of the elements of management style and your current strengths and problem areas, we'll delve more deeply into the attitudes and viewpoints that make up your management philosophy.

Determining Your Philosophy of Management

Whether you realize it or not, you have a philosophy of management. Your philosophy is revealed most clearly in the way you view subordinates in general. Exercise 7-2 can give you a rough idea about which

of two typical, but opposing, management philosophies you are more oriented toward. In the next section of this chapter, we'll discuss these two extremes, known as Theory X and Theory Y, and other philosophies that incorporate aspects of both.

BASIC PHILOSOPHIES OF MANAGEMENT

The elitist, autocratic management philosophy espoused by most bosses until nearly the middle of this century is now called Theory X. During the last fifty years, more and more managers have leaned toward a democratic, participative philosophy that is often referred to as Theory Y. Because this new approach is somewhat idealistic, managers who adopt it are sometimes disappointed in its results. In some cases productivity falls

FIGURE 7-1: Major Thrusts of Effective Managers

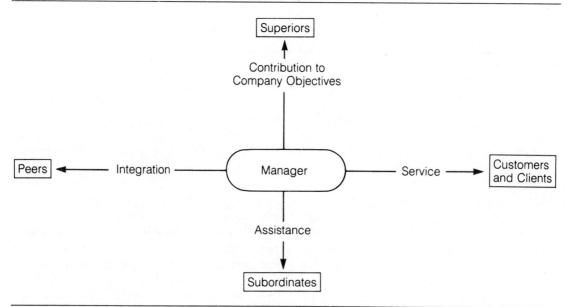

EXERCISE 7-2: HOW DO YOU VIEW SUBORDINATES?

As you read each of the following statements, place a checkmark in the space that best reflects your thinking. Check the answer key and read the next section for an interpretation of your responses.

	Strongly Agree +2	Agree +1	Undecided 0	Disagree −1	Strongly Disagree −2
1. Workers tend to be more highly motivated when they help to set the goals for their jobs and to determine how to meet those goals than when the boss makes all the decisions.	___	___	___	___	___
2. Basically, people don't like to work. They'll try to get out of work whenever they can.	___	___	___	___	___
3. Most workers have the brain power to contribute a great deal more to their jobs than they are now permitted to do.	___	___	___	___	___
4. Most workers prefer a boss who gives them specific directions about exactly how and when to do various tasks.	___	___	___	___	___
5. Most workers would not only accept more responsibility, they would seek it, if they felt the payoff was high enough.	___	___	___	___	___
6. Most workers perform well when the boss is around but tend to let up when left on their own.	___	___	___	___	___
7. Most people would work, even if they didn't need the money, providing the work fulfilled their needs for a sense of purpose and achievement.	___	___	___	___	___
8. The main thing most people want out of their jobs is a regular paycheck along with some good fringe benefits.	___	___	___	___	___
9. Nearly all workers are capable of using imagination, ingenuity, and creativity when they recognize opportunities and payoffs for doing so.	___	___	___	___	___
10. Most people who think they want to be a manager actually just want the privilege and prestige of the job, not the responsibility and challenge.	___	___	___	___	___

far below a satisfactory level. Recent philosophies that incorporate aspects of both Theory X and Y, depending on the situation, are Theory Z, Fiedlar's contingency theory, and Likert's approach.

Theory X and Theory Y

In *The Human Side of Enterprise* [8], a management text that has been used for the past twenty years in business schools throughout the country, Douglas McGregor describes two predominant but opposing philosophies of management—Theory X and Theory Y. **Theory X** is based on three key assumptions about people.

1. The average person has an inherent dislike of work and will avoid it if possible.

2. Most people will not strive to achieve organizational objectives unless they are coerced, controlled, directed, and threatened with punishment.

3. The average person prefers to be directed, wishes to avoid responsibility, has relatively little ambition, and wants security above all else.

During the nineteenth century and the early part of the twentieth century, Theory X was the predominant management philosophy. It still exists in some companies, though usually in a modified form. Managers who believe the assumptions of Theory X rely on a "carrot-and-stick" approach to get workers to perform. They reward workers for exceptional performance and punish them for poor performance. Workers with a Theory X manager are motivated externally.

A Theory Y manager, in contrast, structures the job environment to enhance motivation from within. **Theory Y** is based on six assumptions about people.

1. The use of physical and mental energy in work is as natural as play or rest.

2. External control and threats are not the only ways to motivate workers to meet organizational objectives. A person who is committed to the objectives will exercise self-direction and self-control.

3. Commitment to objectives is a motivator and is a function of the rewards of achievement.

4. Under proper conditions, workers learn not only to accept but to seek responsibility.

5. The capacity to exercise a relatively high degree of ingenuity and creativity is widely distributed in the population.

6. The intellectual potentialities of most people are only partially utilized in modern organizations.

Assumptions 2, 3, and 4 of Theory Y depend mainly on the manager's ability to achieve company/worker **goal congruence.** The manager achieves goal congruence by showing workers that when they help the company to achieve some of its specific goals they also achieve some of their own specific personal goals. In order to motivate a worker to action, the reward for achieving company goals must meet some need that the worker feels—a need that the worker is willing to spend significant time and energy in order to satisfy. The worker's goals and the company's goals must be congruent in some way. (We'll discuss various types of needs and their motivating aspects in Chapter 8.)

Theory Y managers not only achieve goal congruence in motivating workers, but they encourage workers to participate in making plans, organizing work flow, solving problems, and making decisions that directly affect their job responsibilities. These managers encourage workers to suggest ways to improve any aspect of company operations. Workers have a relatively high degree of autonomy in performing their jobs and a high level of motivation to contribute to company goals.

In contrast, Theory X managers tend to tightly control all aspects of workers' jobs. These managers try to perform all the management functions themselves and instruct workers about how to carry out managerial plans and decisions. The motivation of workers to contribute to company goals tends to be low under these conditions.

McGregor's thesis is that Theory Y managers will experience greater success and their workers will be more productive and highly motivated than those of Theory X managers.

What if you are oriented toward Theory X? According to McGregor, you don't need to adopt all the assumptions of Theory Y in order to improve your management style. He urges managers to be open to assumptions about people that are more constructive than those of Theory X, which tend to limit a manager's approaches to dealing with subordinates [8, p. 245].

Theory Y appears to be the answer to the problem of getting from workers a high level of involvement, commitment, and performance on the job—if companies and jobs are structured to implement its basic assumptions. In actual practice, however, attempts to implement Theory Y are often disappointing. From your own experience with people, what problems do you foresee in trusting people to exercise self-direction and self-control in situations where they have apparent reason to be highly motivated?

We've seen that Theory X reflects an authoritarian approach and Theory Y a participative approach. Both tend to be rather fixed and rigid. A more flexible approach has been called "Theory Z."

Theory Z

The situational approach known as Theory Z came about because workers who have learned to function efficiently in a Theory X environment frequently have difficulty in adjusting to a Theory Y environment and taking advantage of its opportunities. Just as students in a highly structured, autocratic school system learn to get by with as little work as possible in order to make the grades they want or need, so workers learn to play that game. Why should they knock themselves out for little or no additional payoffs, they reason.

When they are placed in situations where there actually is a large additional payoff, such as chances for advancement, recognition, profit-sharing, or some other appropriate reward, they find it difficult to shed old thought patterns and work habits. Therefore, if managers remove some of the controls, the work suffers. On the other hand, the continued presence of elaborate controls tells workers that nothing has really changed. One of the barriers to implementing Theory Y, then, is the attitude of workers who have years of experience in—and conditioning by—a Theory X environment.

Theory Y requires a fairly high level of personal interaction between managers and workers in order to accomplish goal congruence and participation in decision-making. In some work situations, achieving and maintaining this level of interaction may be prohibitive because it's so time consuming and expensive. Some organizations may be so large that the time-lag required to get participation is too long and productivity suffers. In addition, opportunities may be lost or greatly decreased if certain decisions are delayed while employee input or consensus is sought. The nature and circumstances of some companies may require an almost dictatorial approach at certain times in order for the company to survive or prosper in the short run.

As a practical matter, therefore, many managers who are philosophically oriented toward Theory Y have adapted to the circumstances in which they find themselves. This situational approach, **Theory Z,** is the philosophy arrived at after working through Theories X and Y. Theory Z managers analyze the entire organizational system. Then they use Theory Y as extensively as possible in order to achieve goal congruence. They use Theory X to the extent necessary to achieve the company's objectives.

Theory Z managers take into consideration these factors:

The size and peculiarities of the organization

The degree of interaction between manager and manager, manager and worker, and worker and worker

The background, experiences, and resulting attitudes of workers toward Theory X and Theory Y approaches

The extent to which goal congruence is being accomplished

The current state of the system—whether it is in crisis, ailing, or healthy and growing

Another situational approach to implementing Theory Y has been developed by Fred E. Fiedlar.

Fiedlar's Contingency Theory

In *A Theory of Leadership Effectiveness,* Fiedlar suggests that leadership involves the exercise of influence over workers in the performance of a common task [3]. In fact, your effectiveness as a manager is determined by measuring how well your group performs. In Fiedlar's view, how far you as a manager can go in implementing Theory Y will depend on (is contingent upon) the amount of influence you have over your subordinates in three areas.

1. *Leader/follower relations*—The degree of mutual respect and friendliness between the manager and workers. The more positive such relationships are, the greater influence the manager will have.

2. *Position power*—The degree to which power is inherent in the position of leadership, regardless of leader/follower relations. The more actions (both positive and negative) the manager has the power to take, the more influence she will have over workers.

3. *Task structure*—The degree to which workers' tasks can be defined and provided with procedures and controls. The more structured a task is, the greater is the manager's influence over subordinates. A manager can more easily hold workers accountable for their performance when tasks are structured than when they are ill defined or vague.

Fiedlar states that a Theory X, or strong task orientation, works best in situations where managers have either very little influence or a great deal of influence. In other words, in situations where the manager (1) is extremely well liked by subordinates, (2) has a lot of power, and (3) is directing well-defined tasks, a Theory X or task orientation is most effective: The manager has everything going for her and nothing to lose by focusing on the task. Likewise, in situations where the manager (1) is disliked by her followers, (2) has little power in the company, and (3) is directing an unstructured, sketchily defined task, a Theory X or task orientation is also effective: The manager lacks the influence necessary to lead her subordinates to an acceptance of goal congruence and a high level of commitment and responsibility.

Theory Y, or a strong human relations orientation, works best when the manager has moderate influence. In other words, in situations that represent some middle ground between the extremes where Theory X is best applied, the most effective management approach will be some degree of Theory Y or human relations orientation.

Fiedlar's contingency theory is based on fifteen years of research that encompasses thirty-five different studies involving sixteen hundred groups of workers. He arrived at these conclusions about management style and leadership effectiveness:

How effectively a work group functions depends on how well the manager's style fits the particular group and work situation. A particular management style might be extremely effective in one situation and ineffective in a different situation.

How much influence a manager is able to assert varies from one group situation to another. It depends on the manager's relationship with the workers, power within the company, and the structure of the tasks to be performed. Therefore, which management style will be most effective in a particular situation depends on the degree to which the group situation enables the manager to exert influence.

Since management effectiveness depends not only on the manager's style but also on the group situation, companies have two alternative ways to improve a managerial "fit": (1) They can design the selection and training of managers to fit specific group situations. This is usually the most workable approach. (2) They can design group situations to fit the managers' styles. Where a good fit exists, companies can se-

lect new workers who fit into the group situation. They can also continue the policies and procedures the manager is comfortable with.

Likert's Approach

Another way of viewing management style has been put forth by Rensis Likert in *The Human Organization* [7]. Likert describes four categories of leadership style: (1) exploitative/authoritative, (2) benevolent/authoritative, (3) consultative, and (4) participative. Most managers today adopt some variation of the benevolent/authoritative, consultative, or participative styles. Leaders who attempt the exploitative/authoritative style were numerous in the past but have difficulty attracting and holding followers now.

Likert's categories of leadership have the following characteristics.

1. Exploitative/Authoritative

   Leader doesn't trust subordinates

   Communication entirely formal

   Motivation through coercion and occasional reward

   Leader focused almost totally on production

2. Benevolent/Authoritative

   Leader shows condescending trust and confidence in subordinates

   Communication mostly formal

   Motivation through reward and some coercion

   High focus on production, some focus on workers as people

Some delegation, but control remains at the top

3. Consultative

Leader has substantial confidence in subordinates

Leader wants to retain control of decisions

Communication less formal

Motivation through reward and coercion

Some involvement in decision-making by subordinates

Fairly high concern for both production and people

Control diffused to middle and lower management

Ultimate responsibility remains at the top

4. Participative

Leader has complete trust and confidence in subordinates

Communication both formal and informal

Communication channels open, both upward and downward

Motivation through reward system developed jointly by leader and follower

Extremely high concern for both production and people

Reliance on teamwork to meet human needs

Responsibility for results lies with management

Minimal emphasis on control

Participation is used to obtain results

The first two categories in **Likert's approach** correspond with Theory X, and the last two correspond with Theory Y. Likert in-

dicates that the closer a manager's style comes to the participative model, the more likely the work group is to experience long-term success.

PERSONALITY TRAITS OF EFFECTIVE MANAGERS

Research and common sense both tell us that a wide range of management styles can be effective, depending on the work situation. They also tell us that we will find certain traits and actions generally more effective than others in our dealings with people. In this section we'll examine some research findings and expert's opinions regarding the personality traits of effective managers.

Using Your Personal Experiences as a Guide

You already have at least an intuitive sense of what personality traits, attitudes, characteristics, and actions are effective or ineffective for managers in various situations. Exercise 7-3 is designed to help you make full use of that knowledge. Complete Exercise 7-3 on page 279 before reading further.

The exercise has been completed by many groups of managers and manager trainees around the country. When groups develop a composite list of the traits and actions of their best bosses, they almost invariably reveal that good bosses set a good example; insist on high standards; encourage workers to learn, grow, and excel; believe workers can succeed; and stand behind them. This pattern of challenge and support seems to be common to managers who are perceived as good bosses. Later in this chapter, we'll discuss ways of developing a supportive climate as well as specific ways of providing challenge and support.

EXERCISE 7-3: ANALYZING TRAITS OF YOUR WORST AND BEST BOSSES

WORST BOSS: Relax a few moments, close your eyes, then recall all the bosses you've ever had. Does one boss stand out in your memory as the worst? (If not, then concentrate on the worst aspects of all your bosses.) Think about specific actions, personality traits, characteristics, attitudes, and habits that made this boss so poor. Remember exactly how you felt about each of these items, the effects they had on you, and how you responded. Fully tune in to that time in your life and the specific items you remember. Then open your eyes and list all the traits, actions, and so forth that you can recall.

Personality Traits, Characteristics, Actions, Attitudes, and Habits of the Worst Boss

_____

_____

_____

_____

_____

BEST BOSS: Now repeat the process, but this time focus on the best boss you've ever had.

Personality Traits, Characteristics, Actions, Attitudes, and Habits of Best Boss

_____

_____

_____

_____

_____

The Golden Mean of Management Styles

As you searched your memory for the traits that made your best boss great and your worst boss awful, were you tempted to look for a "magic bag of traits" that you could acquire in order to become a successful manager? Many people have been lured by this enticing prospect. In fact, R. M. Stogdill sifted through over twenty-five thousand books and articles—"all the competent research directly relevant to the subject" of leadership—in an effort to discover the magic traits [11]. Although he failed to come up with a miracle package of traits, he found a common theme that can serve as a guide for effective actions.

First let's look at how Stogdill defines "leadership": "A leader gets followers to do something more than his formal authority can require them to do. Leadership is an interpersonal relation in which others comply because they want to, not because they have to." Stogdill adds that tests designed to measure different aspects of personality have not proven very predictive or useful for selecting leaders.

Research indicates, however, that leaders tend to be (among other things) more intelligent, persuasive, self-confident, industrious, dependable, and humorous than their followers. But none of these qualities seem to be absolutely necessary for leadership, and all of them put together may not be sufficient.

Leadership has little meaning except in relation to some task or goal, says Stogdill. A figurehead is not a leader: Leadership is always associated with the attainment of group objectives. Stogdill defines two extremes of leadership.

1. *Work-oriented leadership,* in which the manager focuses almost entirely on getting tasks accomplished and increasing the level of productivity. Some variations are authoritative, directive, and structured leadership.

2. *Person-oriented leadership,* in which the manager focuses almost entirely on maintaining constructive relationships with workers. Some variations are democratic, permissive, and participative leadership.

The golden mean between these extremes could be called "structured leadership" (see Figure 7-2). It is work oriented but not autocratic or restrictive. Its essential characteristic is that the leader lets followers know what is expected of them. Paradoxically,

FIGURE 7-2: Leadership Styles

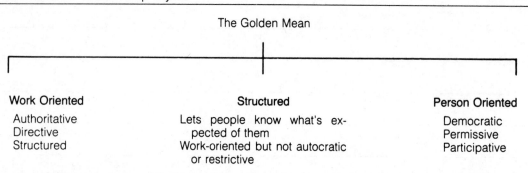

The Golden Mean

Work Oriented	Structured	Person Oriented
Authoritative	Lets people know what's expected of them	Democratic
Directive	Work-oriented but not autocratic or restrictive	Permissive
Structured		Participative

making clear to people what they are expected to do tends to *increase* their freedom of action.

The most effective leaders not only clarify job objectives, but they are also considerate; they look out for the welfare of followers. In other words, the ideal leader combines the work-oriented and person-oriented styles of leadership. Structure, however, appears to be more important than consideration. Members of a group tend to perform best with a moderate degree of structure, rather than with a great deal of it, but they prefer too much structure to none at all. Thus the leader should have enough authority to establish and maintain some structure for the role each person in the work group is expected to fill and the tasks each worker is to perform.

The only style of leadership that favors cohesiveness, satisfaction, *and* productivity is the structured style, in which job objectives, standards, and controls let people know what is expected of them. This style helps establish a pattern of challenge and support. The effective leader challenges workers by letting them know what's expected of them. She or he also supports them by showing consideration for them as persons, concern for their welfare, and a willingness to go to bat for them at appropriate times.

The Golden Mean and Performance Planning

We see here the importance of performance planning (as discussed in Chapter 10) in developing and maintaining an effective management style. Isn't it interesting to discover that out of thousands upon thousands of books and articles written on the subject of leadership—writings that reflect a vast amount of research—the most important factor turns out to be letting people know what's expected of them?

All managers have expectations of the people they manage. Many managers, however, are quite vague about what those expectations are; they have no idea what specific results they're looking for. How then can their workers possibly know how they will be measured at the end of the year? All they can do is guess and flounder. Workers who have the chance to help determine exactly what is expected of them in measurable terms are more likely to meet the manager's expectations. Their success, productivity, and sense of achievement and satisfaction mean success for the manager too.

Performance planning (also called management-by-objectives or MBO) is a tool for implementing Theory Y and in fact rests on the basic assumptions of Theory Y. It assumes that people will want to work to achieve certain personal goals and that those personal goals can be achieved through meeting certain company objectives. It also assumes that people are capable of constructive input into the objective-setting process and want to participate in it. It further assumes that people are capable of adequate self-direction and self-control to meet those objectives—in other words, that people are able and willing to make necessary decisions and evaluations to implement their objectives.

Characteristics of Top Achievers

Sidney Lecker, a New York psychiatrist, did an extensive study of highly successful executives and entrepreneurs [6]. He found an interesting set of attitudes and traits that were common to these leaders. People with what Lecker calls "the money personality" exhibit certain characteristics. They

1. Are persistent and don't wilt with failure, rejection, or time

2. Are unafraid of bigness

3. Set simple objectives

4. Identify key data and actions for meeting objectives

5. Can carry complex, abstract ideas through to realization

6. Search for facts and weigh them

7. Take calculated risks

8. Take total responsibility

9. Have no guilt or fear about success

10. Love the *process* of success; seeking, achieving, savoring it

11. Are in command of inner resources: intelligence, creativity, and emotional strengths

Lecker notes that most people share many of these traits but don't use them as fully as the top achievers. Item 11, the ability to fully tap inner resources, is the key factor to success. Once people take command of their inner resources, Lecker says, "They experience more success and less stress than others who live less challenging lives" [6, p. 126]. In other words, the traits are not as important as the ability to use them.

In fact, if you think of leadership as an activity rather than as a set of personal traits, then you can focus on *acting* rather than on wondering whether you have the right traits. You can let your subordinates know your career goals and find out about theirs. If you and they are going in the same direction, you can let them know you will help them get there. That's one way leaders get followers. Once again, we see how the MBO process is tied to leadership. In fact, notice how many of the characteristics that Lecker mentions are connected to actions typical of the manager whose approach to planning, organizing, staffing, directing, and controlling is based on performance planning.

Charisma

Our actions reveal our philosophy and personality traits, but the *way* we do something is frequently more important than *what* we do. Top leaders of organizations usually have a type of charisma, a brilliance or personal magnetism, that attracts people. Max Gunther interviewed many prominent psychologists and psychiatrists and found that most of them believe the quality of charisma can be developed. He has described six major components of charisma [5, pp. 12–14].

1. *Energy exchange.* A charismatic person gives off energy to other people. The major reason people are drawn to a person with charisma is that they go away with a sense of higher energy than they had before the encounter. This experience sharply contrasts with encounters with weak people who are always trying to get others to love them, cheer them up, or support them—who want to feed off others' mental or emotional energy. You can train yourself to become an energy giver, although doing so usually takes practice and enormous effort at first. The process can become painless and even enjoyable. The more you enjoy it, the bigger your energy reserves tend to become. Some people have developed their abilities to give energy through meditation and visualization [13].

2. *Physical appearance.* Although one need not be beautiful in order to be charismatic, it is essential to look interesting. Imaginative grooming, vibrant good health, and superb posture all contribute to the look.

3. *Independence.* Charismatic persons do not depend on others for their sense of well-

being and self-esteem. People who are *anxious* to be liked are never charismatic.

4. *Verbal ability.* Magnetic people are highly articulate and skilled in the art of swaying people with words. Whether they use that ability constructively or manipulatively is a matter of values and ethics.

5. *Acceptance of admiration.* People with charisma are comfortable when others openly admire them, and they accept homage as a completely natural phenomenon—as simply part of the environment.

6. *The look of serenity.* Charismatic leaders have doubts like anyone else, but they tend to keep them to themselves. They discuss their worries only with close confidants. Once they make a decision, they go confidently ahead and implement it without hesitation even though they may have some serious doubts. They commit themselves to implementing the decision, and they maintain the look of perfect serenity during the entire process.

To summarize: A charismatic person is strong, decisive, and self-confident. These qualities are worth developing because they'll contribute to an effective management style. With such leadership qualities, you'll be in a good position to provide the challenge and support your people need. We'll discuss some ways of providing a supportive climate for your people here and other ways of providing both support and challenge later in this chapter.

DEVELOPING A SUPPORTIVE CLIMATE

As manager or supervisor, you have more impact than anyone in your work group on the type of environment or climate that prevails. Your philosophy, your attitude, your approach to handling your responsibilities— that is, your management style—creates the work environment. It can be challenging or dull, supportive or defensive.

When people analyze the best work environment they've ever experienced, most discover it was challenging yet supportive—an environment in which they felt the need and desire to upgrade their skills and performance and at the same time felt free to take the risks involved in attempting new learning, new roles, and new assignments. They believed their manager was on their side and would back them up in their attempts to grow and learn.

As a result of an eight-year study, J. R. Gibb contrasted the characteristics of managers that tend to create either a defensive or a supportive work climate (see Exhibit 7-3). He found that in a defensive climate people are more likely to feel the need to defend their actions, beliefs, feelings, and motives than they are in a supportive climate. Such defensiveness creates a barrier to open, candid communication. In a supportive climate people don't feel threatened by the boss and are more likely to speak up and to take risks.

As you contrast the behaviors Gibb identified, think of your experiences and how you've reacted to such behavior.

Norma Carr-Ruffino has further interpreted these characteristics of behavior from a transactional analysis viewpoint [2, pp. 19–20]. TA deals with the ego state—Child, Parent, or Adult—of each party in a transaction.

Evaluating Versus Describing

When workers perceive that the boss is evaluating or judging them, they tend to become defensive. But if the manager is also supportive, this support will reduce or neutralize

EXHIBIT 7-3: Behavior Characteristics of Supportive and Defensive Climates

Defensive Climates	Supportive Climates
We tend to become defensive toward someone who seems to be	We tend to communicate openly with someone who seems to be
1. Evaluating our behavior	1. Describing our behavior
2. Trying to control us	2. Cooperating in solving a problem
3. Trying to manipulate us	3. Acting spontaneously
4. Indifferent to our welfare	4. Concerned with our welfare
5. Considering herself or himself superior to us	5. Considering herself or himself equal to us
6. Knowing it all	6. Open to others' ideas

Adapted from J. R. Gibb, "Defensive Communication," *Journal of Communication*, Vol. II, No. 3 (September 1961), pp. 141–48.

the defensiveness. For example, when your approach is one of seeking help to solve a problem, when you behave spontaneously, when you treat a worker as your equal or show that you understand the worker's viewpoint, then the worker is more likely to accept your apparent judgment of his or her behavior without becoming defensive. In other words, the six sets of behavior identified by Gibb work together and are dependent on each other for maximum effect on the work environment. How defensive the worker's response is depends on the overall work climate that currently exists and that existed in the past.

Evaluative messages that are especially likely to arouse defensiveness in workers are those that appear to place blame, to fit people into categories of good or bad, to make moral judgments about the worker or others, and to question the value of others' ideas. In the terminology of transactional analysis, these evaluative messages frequently come from the Parent ego state and arouse the most defensiveness when the transaction is directed from the Parent ego state of the manager to the Child ego state of the worker.

Descriptive messages, in contrast, come from the Adult ego state, and the transaction usually involved is from Adult to Adult. The worker tends to perceive these messages either as genuine requests for information or as neutral messages (as opposed to messages conveying values that conflict with the values of the worker). Messages that do not ask the receiver to change his or her behavior or attitudes are most likely to be perceived as supportive.

Controlling Versus Problem-Solving

A manager may control a worker through a legalistic insistence on attending to detail, conforming to norms, and obeying restrictive rules, regulations, and laws. Control may also take the form of gestures and facial expressions as well as such simple acts as receiving a visitor from behind a large, imposing desk.

Workers will usually resist a message that they perceive is being used to control them in some way—to influence their behavior, restrict their activities, change their attitude.

They may view attempts at control or change as signs of some sort of personal inadequacy—wrong or inadequate attitudes, inability to make effective decisions, ignorance, immaturity, lack of common sense. A worker who also perceives that an attempt to control is guided by hidden motives will increase his or her resistance.

The manager who communicates the wish to work with employees in defining a mutual problem and seeking its solution reflects a problem-solving orientation. When employees perceive that the boss is not going to impose a predetermined solution, attitude, or method on them, they are free to set their own goals, make their own decisions, and evaluate their own progress. At the very least, they will be able to share with the boss in doing these things. In order to communicate your willingness to take a problem-solving approach, you as a manager must do more than merely *say* that you have no wish to exercise control: Your nonverbal communications and ensuing actions must back up the verbal message.

Manipulating Versus Acting Spontaneously

A worker who believes the manager is playing a game with unclear and varied motivations will become defensive. He or she may perceive the hidden motivation to be larger than it really is and may resist being victimized by it.

Managers who are perceived to be playing a role, feigning emotion, toying with the worker, withholding information, or taking advantage of special sources of information are especially resented. And the resentment increases when the manager seems to be trying to make the game appear spontaneous.

In contrast, spontaneous messages—those that are interpreted as being free of deception, as having uncomplicated motivations, as being straightforward and honest, and as being authentic responses to a situation—are likely to arouse minimal defense in workers.

Being Indifferent Versus Being Concerned

Indifference usually indicates a lack of concern for the welfare of the worker. We all like to be received as persons of value having special worth and deserving of concern and affection. Messages that communicate little warmth or caring sometimes also communicate rejection.

Messages that communicate empathy and respect for the worker, however, are especially supportive and reduce defensive reactions. When you as a manager indicate that you are able to identify with the worker's problems, share his or her feelings, and accept his or her emotional reactions at face value, you provide reassurance to the worker.

Considering Yourself Superior Versus Considering Yourself Equal

If you communicate that you think you are superior in position, power, wealth, intellectual ability, physical characteristics, or some other way, you arouse defensiveness. Your subordinates are likely to feel inadequate and threatened. They may think you will try to reduce their power, status, or worth, and they may react by not hearing what you say, by hearing only part of your message, by distorting or forgetting it, or by competing with or becoming jealous of you.

Obviously, differences in talent, ability, worth, appearance, status, and power often do exist. But when you communicate that you attach little importance to these differences, you reduce the worker's defensiveness. If you communicate trust and respect and a willingness to enter into mutual planning and problem-solving, you can establish an atmosphere of equality.

Knowing It All Versus Being Open to Ideas

If you seem to know all the answers, to require no additional information, and to regard yourself mainly as a teacher rather than as a coworker, you will tend to threaten your subordinates. If you act as if you need to be right, want to win an argument rather than solve a problem, or see your ideas as truths to be defended, you are unlikely to have your ideas or your approach fully accepted.

On the other hand, when you have a high degree of tolerance for workers who disagree with you, appear to be investigating issues rather than taking sides on them, to be problem-solving rather than debating, and to be willing to experiment and explore, you are more likely to communicate that the worker will have some control over the joint venture or the investigation of the ideas.

In TA terms, the person who seems to know it all is probably coming from the Parent ego state and is communicating from Parent to Child. When a manager comes from the Adult ego state and the transaction is an Adult-to-Adult one, she is then generally searching for information and ideas and does not resent the help or participation of her employees.

The business manager who arouses defensiveness makes it difficult, if not impossible, to communicate her ideas clearly and to solve managerial problems effectively. Effective business managers can listen without engaging in premature criticism or evaluation. They are open to their workers' ideas and information, even though they may make the final decisions.

This supportive approach results in a relaxed atmosphere where workers feel free to communicate openly. If the manager also expects top-quality performance from her workers and encourages them to achieve it, then the climate is also likely to be a highly motivating, productive one. See whether you can identify some of the behaviors that tend to produce a supportive climate by completing Exercise 7-4, on page 287.

So far we've discussed philosophies of management, ideal attitudes and traits of managers, and ideal working environments. Now we'll turn to some practical applications of these ideas.

ESTABLISHING YOUR AUTHORITY AND MANAGEMENT STYLE

You'll want to select specific management techniques that reflect your philosophy and style when you establish yourself as the boss in a new situation and start building a top-producing team of workers.

In Chapter 3 we discussed the transition from worker to boss in some detail. Refer again to that chapter now that you have more information about management style and techniques of managing.

Each time you take a new management position, you will be replacing a boss who has had a distinct impact on the group—for better or worse. The approach you use to establish your own impact will depend somewhat on whether the previous boss led the group to good performance or to poor performance.

Replacing a Successful Boss

Following the act of a good boss can be tricky because the group may be highly critical of *any* replacement and feel no real need for

EXERCISE 7-4: IDENTIFYING BEHAVIOR CHARACTERISTICS OF DEFENSIVE AND SUPPORTIVE CLIMATES

Each pair of statements reflects behavior that is characteristic of one of the categories of defensive and supportive climates shown in Exhibit 7-3. Identify the appropriate category and write its name in the space provided. See the answer key for an interpretation of your response.

1. (a) "Your petty cash account is short again. You'll have to get my approval for all petty cash expenditures in the future." _____
   (b) "Let's go over your petty cash procedures and see what we can do about these shortages." _____
2. (a) "My proposal is based on some sophisticated concepts you may not understand." _____
   (b) "Please let me know if I'm communicating my proposal to you in an effective way." _____
3. (a) "John, this report is well done. As soon as these minor errors are corrected, it will be ready to go." _____
   (b) "I'm disappointed to see your poor proofreading habits are resulting in errors in your reports." _____
4. (a) "This project must be finished by Friday, no matter what!" _____
   (b) "Joe, how's your schedule this week? Our reputation with the Morton Company depends on finishing their project by Friday." _____
5. (a) "These are my instructions, and I expect you to follow them precisely." _____
   (b) "I've worked out some instructions for this job. Let me know if you have any questions or suggestions." _____
6. (a) "Well, Joan, I'll have to think about your request; I have a lot of other things to consider before I make my decision, you know." _____
   (b) "Joan, as soon as I get the new production schedule, I can let you know about taking next Friday off." _____

Adapted from Norma Carr-Ruffino, *Writing Short Business Reports* (New York: McGraw-Hill, Gregg Division, 1980), pp. 22–23. Copyright © 1980 by McGraw-Hill, Inc. All rights reserved. Reproduced with permission.

new leadership. It's usually best to keep a low profile for a while in these situations. Postpone as many decisions as possible, even those in your previous area of specialization where you feel more than competent. Flashy decisions in one area may only underline your weakness in other areas. So wait awhile on all decisions, where possible.

Consider keeping your plans to yourself until you are ready to make your move; then do it with your own dramatic flair. Meanwhile, get to know the abilities, resources, personalities, and quirks of your people and give them a chance to know yours. You will probably need at least a month to learn the game and the players in each new situation.

Your reorganization plans must go beyond what management indicates it wants done if you intend to really stand out in your new position. You'll need to use your creativity and sense of innovation. Sit down and go over the job and how your predecessor handled it. Ask yourself what there is about the current situation, your responsibilities, and the goals you are trying to achieve that suggests ways to do the job better. How can it be carried out more effectively? Which people can do what functions the best? Is the best combination of people being used? Are they overpaid or underpaid? Write down the things you think you can and should achieve.

Let the group know you think they've been doing a great job. Look for and applaud every positive aspect of the group and its performance. When you announce your new plans, reinforce that theme. Then show how the group can do even better. Invite them to join you in the search for ways of achieving better results—for their own sakes.

Next establish yourself as leader and consolidate your position. Consider holding a weekend planning meeting at a resort. If your operating budget is tight, at least try for an extended lunch or dinner meeting—anything you can manage that will break the usual routine. This helps you to set the stage and the agenda so that *you* become the producer and director of the show. Consider assigning topics ahead of time for study and reports. Start with your own report about what the operation looks like to you. Encourage discussion and criticism of your views, including mention of the group's strengths and weaknesses, its possibilities for improvement, and possible opportunities and goals. Try to get some agreement on areas for further study or action. Before the

meeting is over, make assignments accordingly.

This sort of meeting should be a turning point. People have been operating more or less in their old ways. Now they will be going your way. Now you are truly their boss, not just a figurehead. Step by step you can reveal and implement the ideas you've been working on since you moved into the position. Whatever training, development, or promotion programs you decide on, be sure to implement them person by person. If each program is seen as a reward to each person who accepts your leadership and joins your team, everyone will soon realize that excellent personal performance will pay off for them.

Replacing an Ineffective Boss

Following a loser can pay off handsomely for you if you succeed, but it's a tough assignment. You are, after all, inheriting a failure situation. The greatest barrier to success may be your own attitude. Since you are so aware of the liabilities, you may overlook the assets. Remember that the real problem is the failure of the unit or department to give other groups whatever goods, services, and support they expect and need. Your first step therefore is to question key people at every level in the groups that depend on yours for any goods or services. Get the answers to two key questions: (1) What do you expect from my group? (2) How have we failed you up to now? During this step, just listen. Be respectful of any ideas and suggestions submitted, but don't commit yourself yet.

The next step is asking your own people the same questions. See what discrepancies exist between their expectations and those of other groups. Which expectations are realistic or unrealistic? Look first for the simplest solutions, such as physical or mechanical rearrangement. Then decide on the most appropriate problem-solving approach. Remember that when you reach a solution, it's going to mean change—change that some people in your group may be hostile toward.

Once you are reasonably sure just what changes need to be made, don't delay. Move! The people in your group will never again be so open to change as they are in the beginning. Everyone knows the previous situation was unsatisfactory, so get the changes over with now. And make them as sweeping as necessary. Personnel changes are of course the touchiest. See if people's talents are being misused. Change within the unit where possible. Next, look within the company for people you might recruit for your department. Then look for appropriate slots to transfer the people who are not working out well in your department. When no slots can be found, you will have to bite the bullet and do the necessary firing.

It is almost certain that at least one worker will defy you, no matter how well you carry out your changes. Don't back down, or your authority may never be accepted. Handle challenges to your authority assertively now, or you will find yourself continually having to deal with them. Pick an issue where you know you are right; then make it a matter of "you or me." *Don't* suggest going to a higher authority. But if the subordinate suggests it or does it, make it clear that only one of you is going to come away with a job.

Building a Top-Performing Team

In Chapter 12 we will discuss evaluating and ranking subordinates into three groups: promotables, a middle group, and marginal performers. We will also discuss the necessity for weeding out the weak links so that you are constantly upgrading your group. Perhaps more crucial to building a team is the question of how to *keep* your good people—the promotables and the middle group.

A good way to start is to question them about their ambitions. If they are not sure what their ambitions are, find out (1) whether they are happy with what they are doing and (2) what they picture themselves doing in a few years.

Next inform them about new hires ahead of time. Make it clear why new people are needed and what they will help the group to achieve. If you're dealing with professionals, make it clear that the credentials of the new hires are indisputable, at least equivalent to those of the others in the group. You can defuse resentment from your good people by what you tell them ahead of time when you recruit new employees. This means giving them the real business reasons behind the decision, the detailed logic of the move.

If you consider your own people as well as outsiders for a position, be as open and honest with them as you can. Tell them when they can expect a decision. When you have made a decision, call in all the people involved and tell them first, tell them why, and ask for their help in making it work. Make sure those who aren't selected know that this decision in no way hurts their future with the company.

Deal constructively with team members who want to switch jobs. In spite of your best intentions, you will probably find that periodically one of your good people comes in to tell you that he or she is thinking of finding a better position. The best way to handle this is to discuss the situation as frankly, honestly, and realistically as possible. Point out opportunities for learning, fringe benefits, working conditions, recognition, and other job factors that the subordinate may be overlooking. As honestly and professionally as you can, help the subordinate analyze the chances of getting something better somewhere else.

Structure the job situation to keep your good people motivated. (We will be discussing ways to do this in Chapter 8.) In addition, check to see whether you are running a tight ship. Everyone should have plenty to do and plenty of challenges. The more bored people get, the less they want to do; and the less they do, the more their boredom increases. That vicious cycle is a real source of dissatisfaction. Next, be sure you are using job rotation and job enrichment as effectively as possible. Let people test their wings by giving them special projects and assignments to see if they would really be happy and effective in a new position (see Chapter 12).

If you have stars who are growing so fast that they no longer fit in your group, promote them out of your group. If you don't, you will probably lose them anyway—to another company. It is better for you to lose their outstanding services to another group *within* the company and get the credit for helping them along their career path. If you can't move them out, then give them as much real responsibility as possible. Challenge them all you can.

When you get right down to it, the best tool you have for keeping your best people is your willingness to give them something to manage.

Relating Successfully to the Members of Your Team

As team leader, you set the tone and pace of the group. Your relationship with individual members and with the group as a whole forms the foundation on which your team is built. Your success as a manager ultimately depends on the little daily activities you are involved in with your team members, the way you handle these encounters, and the resulting relationships. Here are some sug-

gestions to keep in mind as you work with your people on a day-to-day basis.

Providing Challenge   One of the most valuable contributions you can make is providing the right level of challenge for each of your subordinates at all times. Your *attitude* toward tasks, projects, and assignments is the key: If you view them as challenges rather than as threatening situations or mere drudgery, your subordinates are more likely to view them in a positive way too. Some sources of challenge are

A clear picture of the end results that are expected

Latitude to try out one's own ideas in carrying out the task

Deadlines to be met

A chance to learn something new, to stretch one's capabilities

Awareness that results will be evaluated

A chance to enhance promotability

A sense of competition with others or with oneself

A chance to increase visibility

Making a commitment to another or others to perform

An opportunity to gain recognition or praise

Giving Support   As we discussed earlier in this chapter, you support other people through your attitude and your verbal and nonverbal messages that they are capable and worthwhile individuals. Some ways of providing support are

Providing the necessary tools to meet the challenges of a task—the necessary authority, equipment, budget, information, staff support, supplies, and so forth

Giving appropriate training and coaching

Evaluating performance objectively and fairly

Serving as mentor

Recognizing workers' achievements, ideas, innovations, and projects and fighting for raises and promotions as rewards

Backing up workers in well-meaning decisions and actions, including those that don't work out

Taking a constructive, problem-solving approach to mistakes and viewing them as part of the learning process. For example, when discussing a way to improve performance, say: "This will give you a chance to follow through on the valuable know-how you picked up last month."

Letting workers know you think they can do the job, you will give them appropriate help to do it, and you are pulling for them to do it

Giving credit by remembering whose idea led to what successful result. Consider asking people who make offhand suggestions to outline them on paper for you. This helps them think through the idea more thoroughly, and it helps you recall who made each suggestion. If necessary, keep a file folder or card file of ideas and suggestions made by people. If you still lose track of the source, ask! When in doubt, give more credit than may be due, not less.

Keeping Lines of Communication Open
Virtually none of the other suggestions given here will work if you don't establish an environment where people feel free to come to you with their ideas, comments, questions, and problems. This doesn't mean that you should let them "dump on you" or that you should play the role of mother-confessor or psychiatrist. It does mean realizing that the best way for you to prevent or handle problems effectively is to know all the significant things that are occurring. The communication channel between you and each of your people should be two-way. It is crucial to determine what information they need and want in order to succeed and to give it to them.

Watching Offhand Remarks It's best to assume that there is no such thing as an offhand remark. Get accustomed to the idea that *everything* you say is likely to have an impact on your people. Be especially careful of sarcasm and joking remarks. Light humor is fine and can help relieve tension and pressure. Just be sure that everyone within hearing *knows* how you mean the remark. If it could possibly be interpreted as a put-down, better keep it to yourself. In some situations, however, your offhand remarks can be an asset, when you use them constructively—to share tidbits of information, for example.

Sharing Nuggets of Information Everyone likes a chance to hear "the inside dope." To let your subordinates know that they are an important part of the team and to keep them highly motivated, share bits of information with them. This can be done casually and on a one-to-one basis: "By the way, the XYZ division will be adding a new branch in July." Be aware of opportunities to share bits of news with your subordinates. Spread your nuggets around from time to time so that all your subordinates have a chance to feel special. You don't need to announce plans prematurely, of course; just selectively use your inside track on information to best advantage.

Differentiating Between "Wishes" and Requirements Here again, get used to the possibility of people carrying out your most casually mentioned desire. "It would be nice to have the project finished by Wednesday" can lead to a subordinate's dropping activities that have higher priority in order to grant your stated wish.

Recognizing Efforts It's easy to overlook efforts. For example, your group as a whole may have failed to meet certain objectives while someone or some team *within* the group really pushed and did make the targeted contribution to the effort. In discussing the situation with the entire group, it may be easy to generalize and overlook individual successes. People tend to be very sensitive about recognition of their efforts, so stay aware. Recognize contribution and special effort every time you get the chance.

Maintaining Awareness and Honesty Your subordinates want a boss who knows what's going on and faces problems and conflicts squarely. Never act as if you are unaware of problem situations; you will only damage your credibility. Although it is not necessary to go into detail or announce decisions prematurely, it is important to acknowledge that problems exist, if indeed they do, when communicating about a situation.

Giving Individual Attention Show your people that you recognize their uniqueness by really listening to them.

Getting Participation Nothing is more important for successful management than allowing, and in fact asking, people to participate. The more effective participation you can enlist and use successfully in problem-solving, objective-setting, decision-making, planning, organizing, directing, controlling, evaluating, implementing—you name it—the stronger your unit will be and the more you will shine as a manager.

Setting the Pace It is up to you to set the pace, the standards, the example of desirable behavior and performance in your group. Watch the signals—both positive and negative—that you give by your behavior.

For example, when you arrive early in the morning, you signal to both your subordinates and your superiors that you are enthusiastic about your job. On the other hand, if you stay much later than your colleagues, you may be signaling that you're unable to handle the job within the usual number of hours. The habit of propping your feet on your desk may signal to others that you are less than hard working and highly motivated. Also, if you take long lunch hours and other breaks, be sure you signal that you were doing business. This doesn't mean you should "explain" or "report" to your subordinates; it just means it's a good idea to signal the exact message you want them to get.

Resolving Conflict Within the Team

As team leader you are also responsible for constructively resolving conflict between and among team members. A constructive approach involves these steps:

1. Seeing conflict as an opportunity to look at all sides of an issue and to get at the heart of problems

2. Identifying types of competition among team members and guiding it into constructive channels

3. Openly airing the views of the people involved in the conflict in a group meeting

4. Isolating the real cause of the conflict: determining whether it is faulty communication, resentment of another's behavior, conflicting goals, conflicting choice of solutions, or some other root cause

5. Determining the resolution strategy of each party to the conflict: Is it competitive, collaborative, sharing, avoidant, or accommodative?

6. Reaching a resolution that is best for the organization and for all parties, one that provides control for the possibility of creating a related and more intense conflict in the future

We will discuss each step in detail.

Seeing Conflict as Opportunity Perhaps the most common way of viewing conflict is to see it as undesirable, something that should be avoided. From another perspective, however, conflict may add force, energy, and more intense interest in the idea or situation in question. When conflict is handled constructively, opposing opinions and ideas are discussed openly. This airing of ideas can lead to creative and innovative approaches.

If you view conflict as a natural and healthy aspect of group effort, your subordinates are more likely to be open about their opinions and ideas. Conflicts among your people will surface, and it will be possible to discuss problem situations at a stage when candid discussion is most helpful in defining the source of problems and in developing alternate solutions. In other words, people can air their differences at an optimal point in the problem-solving process—before the creative, brainstorming phase.

Also, if people can discuss their differences as soon as they surface, negative emotions they feel in connection with the conflict are more likely to be dissipated. When people keep their differences bottled up inside, along with accompanying negative emotions arising from squelched opinions, their resentments tend to fester and grow. When people harbor such resentments, they tend to block the process of cooperating to arrive at a problem solution and carry it out. As a manager, therefore, your key to avoiding *ongoing* conflict lies in accepting *initial* conflict among workers and airing it as openly as possible.

As leader of your group, you have the greatest influence on how conflict is handled. If you are watchful for signs of differences of opinion and see that they are considered and respected, you will teach your people by your actions that conflict can be constructive.

Constructively Handling Competition Among Members To handle competition among your subordinates in a constructive way, you should first identify the kind of competition that is involved. Let's look at three major categories: (1) friendly competition, (2) constructive group action, and (3) destructive politics.

Friendly competition occurs when participants, knowing that others are being considered for promotion to the jobs they want, intensify their efforts. They may develop personal, innovative approaches to their jobs as well as additional skills and traits needed for the promotion. They may set more challenging objectives and higher standards for themselves. When a competitor is promoted, the others are generally able to work cooperatively with their former rival. As a manager, you should *encourage friendly competition: It creates challenge and interest.*

Sometimes employees need to unite in *constructive group action* if they are to promote their individual interests and also meet organizational objectives. Subordinates may also need to team up with their peers to prevent action by another that would prevent them from adequately meeting their own job objectives. For example, one unit or department may be so successful in getting the lion's share of the budget that the other units or departments are shortchanged. They may have to unite to get their fair share. As a manager, you should *encourage this type of political action: It helps build the group into a top-producing team.*

Total concentration on the process of promotion rather than on the job at hand is a warning sign of *destructive politics*; for example, attempts to block a qualified peer's promotion, teaming up with peers to stop a front runner, automatically siding with friends against enemies, and logrolling (you scratch my back, I'll scratch yours, even if the company suffers in the process).

As a manager, you should *let your people know that you will not tolerate this destructive kind of company politics.* If you know one of your subordinates is involved in that kind of behavior, nip it in the bud. You want word to get around: "That sort of thing just won't work with the boss. It's more likely to result in being demoted or fired than in promotion."

Reward cooperation among competitors. Look for instances where subordinates bring in competitors on projects and where they cooperate with competitors in meeting objectives and in developing constructive, innovative approaches to implementing objectives. Make sure these people are recognized and rewarded for working as a team.

Airing Opposing Views Here are some suggestions to keep in mind as you lead the group in a discussion of differences of opinion.

1. Provide a supportive atmosphere for airing differences and reaching solutions.

2. Provide incentives for resolving the conflict. Each side must understand that more is to be gained by resolving the conflict than by continuing it.

3. Establish ground rules. Make sure that each side has equal time to present its views. Take steps to see that the most powerful or aggressive people don't dominate the situation unfairly.

4. Make sure that the parties to the conflict are ready to sit down and try to resolve it. Until they are, everyone will be wasting time.

5. Establish an atmosphere that is supportive of openness. Allow for expression of feelings without attack. Accept the feelings that are expressed. Reassure the parties involved that open communication is encouraged. Be noncritical and nonevaluative.

6. Listen, clarify, summarize, and give feedback. Encourage and support subordinates. Try to find mutual feeling and common ground. Look for opportunities to reduce tensions. Your goal should be to strengthen the personal relationships between the parties or at least to avoid their deterioration.

Isolating the Cause of the Problem Once conflicting opinions and ideas have been adequately discussed, your function is to guide the parties to a satisfactory resolution of the conflict. In order to do so, you must first be aware of the sources or causes of the conflict. Look at four main areas: (1) faulty communication, (2) resentment of another's past behavior, (3) conflicting goals, and (4) conflicting choice of solution.

Conflicts resulting from *faulty communication* are often more imagined than real. First look for signs of faulty perception, misunderstanding, or oversensitivity. The best way to reduce imagined conflicts is to encourage frequent discussion of problems.

Constructive discussion of a problem may be jeopardized because you or one of your subordinates is harboring *resentment of another group member's past behavior.* See whether such resentment can be brought out in the open. Try to get the person who resents the behavior to state the objection and describe the behavior specifically. Frequently the first objections brought up do not get at the heart of the problem. Conflicts based on unvoiced resentment need to be explored in an atmosphere in which feelings are respected so that true feelings can come to the surface.

Problems that arise because of *conflicting goals* are often the most difficult to resolve. Try to get each party to the conflict to pinpoint the specific goals she or he wants to see as an outcome of the situation. Then see whether they can agree on some common goal, such as increased productivity or even the survival of the company.

Sometimes everyone agrees on the major goal to be achieved in a situation, but two or more factions espouse a *conflicting choice of solutions* to best achieve that goal. When this happens, be sure the conflicting approaches are thoroughly discussed and understood by all. If conflict persists, search for alternate courses of action that perhaps incorporate the best aspects of the conflicting solutions.

Determining the Resolution Strategy of Each Party It is important to know how each party to the conflict is trying to resolve the problem. An awareness of strategies for conflict resolution can help you make sure that individuals' concerns or feelings are not squelched, ignored, or avoided. It can also help you equalize power in the situation. Kenneth Thomas [12] has identified five basic strategies for resolving conflict.

1. *Competitive.* A win/lose approach in which one party attempts to dominate the other(s) and to win sympathy for his or her concerns at the expense of the other(s)

2. *Collaborative.* A cooperative approach in which all parties try to integrate their concerns so that all are fully satisfied

3. *Sharing.* A give-and-take approach that seeks to find a solution somewhere in-between the desires of all parties, giving each party moderate but incomplete satisfaction.

4. *Avoidant.* A head-in-the-sand approach characterized by an indifference to the concerns of other parties and to the conflict itself. Behaviors might include withdrawal, isolation, evasion, flight, and/or apathy.

5. *Accommodative.* A nonassertive approach characterized by appeasement. One party tries to make peace by giving in to the other's concerns without taking care of his or her own concerns.

Reaching a Resolution Determine what each party sees as a possible solution and whether there *can* be a solution that will satisfy the concerns of all parties. Explore possible alternatives that the parties have not considered. The solution that is adopted should (1) be best for the organization (2) be best for *all* parties, and (3) provide control for the possibility of creating a related and more intense conflict in the future. Your role is to guide subordinates in selecting the solution that best meets these criteria and negotiate differences in reaching a solution that all can live with. See Chapter 9 for a detailed discussion of the entire problem-solving process.

SUMMARY

Your management style is how you perform your functions and how you interact with others in the various roles the manager plays. Traditionally, the management functions have been identified as planning, organizing, staffing, directing, and controlling the operations of the organization. Another way of categorizing them—a way that may be more meaningful in terms of day-to-day activities—is (1) persuasive communication, (2) administration, (3) technical professionalism, (4) leadership and power, (5) training and development, and (6) planning and objective-setting. As you perform these management functions, you are also interacting with your people as a motivator, a director, or an evaluator at appropriate times.

Each of us has a management philosophy that contains elements of one or more of the well-known philosophies. Theory X is a traditional, authoritarian view of management based on the belief that people are inherently lazy, unambitious, and limited. Theory Y is a participative approach based on the belief that people will exercise self-direction and self-control on the job if they see that they are meeting their own personal needs and goals through meeting the company's needs and goals. A Theory Y manager believes people are capable of exercising a relatively high degree of ingenuity and creativity. Theory Z is a situational approach to managing people. It implements Theory Y to the extent that it is workable in achieving goal congruence and Theory X to the extent necessary to achieve the company's objectives.

Fiedlar's contingency theory is another situational approach to implementing Theories X and Y, based on leader/follower relations, position power, and task structure. Fiedlar found that situations that represent either extreme in these categories are best suited to a Theory X approach, and situations that represent some middle ground are best suited to a Theory Y approach.

The golden mean of management styles was developed by Stogdill on the basis of extensive research showing that many types of managers can be successful, as long as their style is suited to the situation and people they are managing. Both work-oriented (Theory X) and people-oriented (Theory Y) types of managers can be successful *as long as* they let employees know what's expected of them (provide structure). MBO is a tool for implementing Theory Y. It can help overcome some of the problems inherent in Theory Y by providing adequate structure to the job situation.

The traits and attitudes of effective managers are quite diverse. However, certain characteristics have been found to be typical of successful executives and entrepreneurs. The key trait is the ability to fully tap inner resources in order to make full use of the other traits. Also, top leaders usually have a type of charisma; they give off energy to other people.

We know too that developing a supportive climate is extremely important to building a top-producing team. Such a climate enhances open communication, motivation, and a cooperative team spirit.

Although analyzing your management philosophy and style is helpful, the key to effectiveness is your ability to integrate these ideas, traits, and concepts into your day-to-day activities as a manager. You must be able to establish your authority and maintain your style when you move into a new management position, build a top-performing team, and relate successfully to your team members.

As team leader you are responsible for guiding your team members in resolving conflict. A constructive approach involves seeing conflict as an opportunity to root out problems, air viewpoints, promote understanding, ease tensions, expand alternate solutions, and emerge with a stronger team.

REFERENCES

1. Blake, Robert R., and Jane Srygley Mouton. *The Managerial Grid.* Houston: Gulf Publishing, 1980. See especially p. 10. The authors expand on the idea of a work-oriented versus a people-oriented management philosophy, along with the effects and impact of each.

2. Carr-Ruffino, Norma. *Writing Short Business Reports.* New York: McGraw-Hill, Gregg Division, 1980. A step-by-step guide to writing effective letter and memo reports. A focus on tuning in to your reader, getting results, getting and using essential information, as well as organizing and presenting the material for maximum effectiveness and impact.

3. Fiedlar, Fred E. *A Theory of Leadership Effectiveness.* New York: McGraw-Hill, 1982. Fiedlar gives a complete explanation of contingency theory, his research results, and practical applications.

4. Gibb, J. R. "Defensive Communication," *Journal of Communication*, Vol. 11, No. 3 (September 1961), pp. 141–48.

5. Gunther, Max. "Charisma." *Journal of Communication*, Vol. 29, No. 2 (Spring 1979), pp. 52–54.

6. Lecker, Sidney. *The Money Personality.* New York: Simon and Schuster, 1983. The results of a psychiatrist's research on traits common to top executives and entrepreneurs.

7. Likert, Rensis. *The Human Organization.* New York: McGraw-Hill, 1981. Likert explains his application and adaptation of Theory X and Theory Y and describes other aspects of a workable management philosophy.

8. McGregor, Douglas. *The Human Side of Enterprise.* New York: McGraw-Hill, 1960. This classic management text fully discusses the Theory X and Theory Y approaches to management, the implementation of Theory Y, and some case results.

9. Ouchi, William G. *Theory Z: How American Business Can Meet the Japanese Challenge.* Reading, Mass.: Addison-Wesley, 1981. Ouchi describes how Japan, using a situational approach to management, has achieved the highest level of productivity in the world. He suggests ways that American companies can adapt Japanese strategies. He includes case histories and philosophies of American companies that have successfully adopted a Theory Z approach as well as a discussion of the use of quality control circles.

10. Steger, Joseph. "Are You an Effective Manager—The Self Assessment May Help You Find Out," *MBA Journal* (1978), pp. 3, 21–23.

11. Stogdill, R. M. *The Handbook of Leadership.* New York: The Free Press, 1974. The results of a review of over twenty-five thousand books and articles on management and leadership. A search for the answer to the question of what makes a good manager or leader.

12. Thomas, Kenneth. "Conflict and Conflict Management." *Handbook of Industrial and Organizational Psychology.* Edited by Marvin D. Dunette. Chicago: Rand McNally, 1981.

13. Wallace, Amy, and Bill Henkin. *Psychic Healing Book.* New York: Dell, 1978. Discusses personal energy, its source, and its use. Gives practical exercises and methods for increasing your energy level, controlling your energy, and transmitting energy to others.

Chapter Eight

Providing
A Motivational Climate

"High performance is a cause of high satisfaction, not a result of it."

Lyman Porter

When you have developed the skills needed to plan for results and adapt your management style so that it is appropriate and effective in the various situations you may choose to work in, you will have gone a long way toward providing a motivational climate for your people. In this chapter we'll discuss some additional specific actions and attitudes that affect the motivation of your subordinates.

In the final analysis, motivation comes from *within* a person. Therefore, you cannot truly motivate people: You cannot really control another person's inner drives and attitudes. What you *can* do is help subordinates channel their attitudes and inner drives by showing them how they can satisfy their needs and desires through working productively toward organizational objectives. You can take specific actions that encourage and enhance each person's inner motivation to perform well. Even though you cannot directly motivate another person over the long term, you can provide a climate in which motivation is encouraged, enhanced, and nurtured.

In this chapter you will have the opportunity to

1. Understand the needs, both innate and socially acquired, that drive people

2. Understand the role of expectations in worker motivation

3. Learn how a manager can help to align worker and organizational needs and goals

4. See how motivating factors can be built into a job rather than tacked on

5. Recognize ways in which socially acquired motives both drive and inhibit women

---

 Firefighting Strategies

John Brockfield has been explaining the situational approach to management to Carrie. Now he says, "What you were doing is perfectly logical and understandable, Carrie—you were repeating behavior that had been successful in the past. The clerical staff you were dealing with were nearly all young and inexperienced, and the work they were doing was highly structured. So a relatively directive, controlling management style worked well. The workers didn't mind the attention you gave them—in fact it tended to motivate them to increase their productivity."

"Yes, that makes sense." Carrie murmurs.

"But that bunch of sales people you've got is a very different crew. Most of them are already highly motivated. They're skilled, experienced professionals, and their work is very unstructured. They generally have to figure out for themselves the best way to handle their various accounts. They have to establish the right relationship with the different buyers, and that frequently involves a delicate balance."

"I see," Carrie responds. "And they naturally resent a newcomer—especially a young, female boss—like me coming in and trying to tell them how to do their jobs."

"Right. So what's your next step?"

Carrie thinks that one over. Finally she says, "Well, John, it seems to me that I need to talk with all the staff at our next meeting. I'll ask them how the procedures are working out and encourage them to vent any feelings they have about that—and anything else connected with their jobs, for that matter. Then I'll let them know that I respect and appreciate their skills. My message will be that I'm here to assist and support them, but as long as they keep getting the results we're looking for, how they go about getting those results is basically up to them."

"Sounds like a good plan, Carrie."

Carrie feels good about moving toward a solution to her problem with the sales staff as she enters the restaurant down the street from the office. As she waits in a booth for her friend Audrey Frank to join her, Carrie hears a familiar voice in the booth behind her. "Why, it's Lin Leslie, our new Customer Accounts Supervisor," she thinks.

"It's good to get away from that place, Pete, even if it's just a business lunch."

P: How's the new job going, Lin?

L: Fairly well, Pete. However, it was a lot easier being an Accounts Clerk than a Customer Accounts Supervisor. I had a lot fewer headaches in my old job. I like the feeling of doing something more important than being just a clerk, but trying to motivate these clerks to perform is a heavy responsibility.

P: Yeah. I guess that's the hardest part of a manager's job, isn't it?

L: It sure is! If I could just figure out how to get people to move! To take some responsibility! To take pride in their work!

P: True. You can try to light a fire under some people and they *still* don't do much.

K: It gets very discouraging sometimes. People nowadays just don't seem to care as much as I did when I was learning the business.

Carrie decides it's best to keep quiet and moves to a table in the corner. After a quick lunch with Audrey, she returns to the office. Stopping by the employee's lounge, she overhears another conversation between two of Lin's clerks.

R: I guess we should get on back to work. We've been gone nearly an hour.

J: Why rush? The sooner we go back, the longer we'll have to sit there and work.

R: Yeah, but old Eagle-Eye Leslie gets upset when we're late, you know.

J: Don't worry. She had one of her "business lunches" with a Maxi-Mart rep today. She won't be back before two. We can take it easy this afternoon. She'll have her mind on Maxi-Mart.

R: Good. I don't want her getting mad at me, though. I really need a raise. Maybe if I stay on her good side, I'll get one next month.

J: Don't count on it! I thought sure she would recommend me for one last quarter and I got nothing. Zero.

R: I overheard Dawn telling someone on the telephone that she got a raise. I don't understand that. She doesn't do much.

J: It beats me. I don't know what Leslie expects. I knocked myself out last quarter trying to impress her and do a good job. It sure didn't do me any good. I'm going to try to stay on her good side, but I'm sure not going to kill myself working around this place anymore.

R: I tried to find out what I need to do to get a raise, but she just said, "Do your job and do it right."

That night after dinner Carrie snuggles against Murray's arm as they continue sharing the events of the day. "Sometimes, it's downright discouraging, Murray. I feel like a firefighter—about the time I see a way to get the fire under control in the Sales area, I stumble onto another one in the Customer Accounts area."

"Well, maybe that's what management is all about," he sighs. "The main thing is, you're hanging in there and you're handling it. I have a feeling that each time you learn to deal with one of these problems, you're also learning how to prevent it or cope with it more readily in the future."

"Now that's a viewpoint I like!" laughs Carrie.

1. Explain how you think Carrie's original management style affected the motivation of the clerical workers she supervised. _____

2. Explain how you think it affected the motivation of the salesmen. _____

3. What do you think is the source of Lin Leslie's motivational problem with the clerks she supervises? _____

4. If you were Carrie, would you bring up the problem to Lin? If so, why and how?

5. What advice would you give to Lin?

MOTIVATING THROUGH PERSONAL POWER INSTEAD OF POSITION POWER

Why aren't most employees really committed to their work and to the company's objectives? One reason is that most managers rely on the power of their positions rather than on their own ability to lead people. Although this use of power may be subtle and kept in the background, its effect is coercive. **Position power** stems from beliefs about the innate rights of the organization—beliefs that place the organization and its management on the side of the owners' interest and opposite to the employees' interests. As management expert Douglas Sherwin puts it, position power "is the root of the managing group's attitude as enforcer, driver, superior, privileged, and causative" [7, p. 672]. This somewhat arrogant attitude frequently triggers negative responses from employees.

Employees will generally *accept* (if somewhat grudgingly) the organization's concept of position power because they must accept it in order to earn a living. As a result, however, they think of work as a means to an end rather than a worthwhile end in itself. Since people commit themselves to ends, or goals, not to ways of achieving the goals, employees often fail to commit themselves to the work itself. The key to exercising leadership is the ability to understand the psychological needs (and therefore personal goals) of individual workers and to help them satisfy their needs through their own actions.

An essential part of this process is identifying how the actions that help achieve the goals of the organization also achieve the personal goals of a particular worker. This type of leadership replaces position power and is made possible by disregarding it. This doesn't mean that as manager you must keep a low profile, that you should serve merely as a facilitator. Nor does it mean that your decisions should always be made by vote, caucus, or democratic process. You must be tough when necessary and perform your functions with firmness.

Since such leadership requires understanding people's needs, a study of motivational theories will be helpful, for people are motivated to act in ways that help them satisfy their needs.

in somewhat different ways. For a few, salary may meet a purely physiological need to survive: "Will I have enough to eat in order to stay alive?" Most people would probably see salary as meeting a security need: "How can I ensure that I'll be able to survive safely in the future?" Other job factors often considered necessary for meeting safety and security needs are working conditions and company policy. These factors would fall into Category A for most American workers, but they're Category B factors for some, especially for workers in developing countries.

On the other hand, a certain percentage of Americans are motivated to high performance by rewards that fulfill the need for acceptance, to belong to a group. The factors of "relationship with fellow employees" and "kind of supervision received" are frequently interpreted as meeting these needs. Others have overriding needs for ego reinforcement in the form of recognition or status. "Recognition" and "opportunity for advancement" are often interpreted as meeting those needs.

According to psychologist Abraham Maslow [6], the need to discover and make the best use of one's talents is the highest-level need. The factors of "responsibilities assigned," "on-the-job achievement," "opportunities for personal growth," and sometimes "opportunity for advancement" are often interpreted as meeting this self-actualization need.

RECOGNIZING INNATE MOTIVATORS

Before reading further, see what motivates *you* by completing Exercise 8-1 on page 303. By understanding your own motivational priorities, you'll be in a better position to understand what motivates other people.

Different people will interpret job factors

Maslow's Hierarchy of Needs

Probably the best-known motivational theory in the United States is the theory developed by Abraham Maslow. Believing that people act in order to satisfy certain needs, he developed a hierarchy containing five levels of needs (see Figure 8-1). According to

EXERCISE 8-1: IDENTIFYING MOTIVATIONAL PRIORITIES

Determine whether each job factor belongs in Category A or Category B and place a checkmark in the appropriate space. Then rank the items you checked in Category A according to their relative importance. Do the same for Category B. After you've read this section of the chapter, compare your responses with those shown in the answer key.

Category A: Factors That Produce Satisfaction or Dissatisfaction: You expect the job to provide an adequate quantity or quality of this factor. This factor does not cause you to work harder—either to obtain it or as a result of having it present. If it isn't present, however, you will look around for another job.

Category B: Factors That Motivate: You are willing to put forth additional effort and commitment as a result of having this factor present or in order to obtain it.

Factor	*Category A*	*Category B*
Adequate salary	————	————
Responsibilities assigned	————	————
Relationship with fellow employees	————	————
The work itself	————	————
Opportunity for advancement	————	————
Working conditions	————	————
On-the-job achievement	————	————
Kind of supervision received	————	————
Recognition	————	————
Company policy	————	————
Opportunities for personal growth	————	————

FIGURE 8-1: Maslow's Hierarchy of Needs

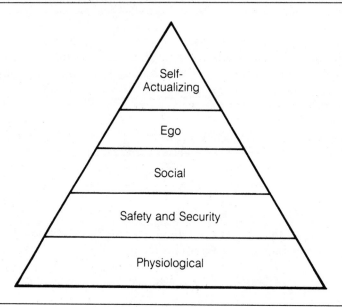

Adapted from Abraham H. Maslow, "A Theory of Human Motivation," *Psychological Review*, Vol. 50, No. 4 (July 1943), pp. 370–96.

Maslow, only when needs at the lowest level of the hierarchy have been satisfied does a person feel an active need at the next level.

At the base of **Maslow's hierarchy** are *physiological needs* basic to physical survival—adequate food, water, and air as well as protection from the elements through adequate shelter and clothing. A person who is hungry and has no access to food will do almost anything to satisfy the need for food. Obviously, the way to get that person to do something is to offer food (or money for food) as a reward. Until the need for food, clothing, and shelter has been met, an individual will feel little or no motivation to satisfy the need for safety and security.

Security and safety needs drive people after their physiological needs have been satis-fied. These are the needs to know that we can meet our physiological needs and do so in relative safety. Until we feel that our physical safety is adequately secure, we won't spend much time worrying about social needs, on the next level of the hierarchy.

Social needs are the needs we all feel at times to be liked, loved, and accepted. The need to belong to a group—whether to a family, peer, work, community, or some other kind of group—is also a social need. People who have not satisfied this need through family or social groups may be highly motivated to belong to a work group where they will be liked and accepted. Until social needs are met, they won't pay much attention to ego needs. In fact, if increased status makes them feel isolated, they may consider it more a punishment than a reward.

Ego needs are needs for respect, for recognition, for increased status, and for acknowledgment and appreciation of our work, our achievements, and our contributions. A person who feels that his or her physiological, safety and security, and social needs are being satisfied tends to focus on ego needs and is motivated by rewards that satisfy them. People operating at this level are more concerned with the favorable attention their actions, achievements, or contributions bring to them than they are with any personal satisfaction or growth that might be involved. Their rewards, then, are attention, applause, recognition, and fame.

Self-actualizing needs are needs for continuous personal growth and development, for the utmost achievement a person is capable of, for the full development of a person's potential capabilities. People operating at the highest level of Maslow's hierarchy are more concerned with personal satisfaction and growth than with popularity or recognition. They are even willing to pursue an unpopular course of action and perhaps alienate their peers if they feel such action plays an important enough role in their personal development. Self-actualization needs are never fully satisfied; the pursuit of **self-actualization** is a lifelong one.

Major Motivators of American Workers

Most workers in the United States have come to expect that at least the first two and possibly the first three levels of needs in the hierarchy will be satisfied through their jobs (Category A in Exercise 8-1). Many of them also expect some satisfaction of ego needs for appreciation and respect. If physiological and safety and security needs are in fact not met through their jobs, workers tend to be dissatisfied and will complain a great deal, look for other jobs, or find alternative ways to meet those needs (such as living on government subsidies). They will not be motivated to work harder in order to satisfy those needs because they can be readily satisfied by switching jobs or seeking government aid. Their focus is on the social, ego, or self-actualizing needs, and only rewards that satisfy the appropriate higher-level need will motivate them to greater commitment and productivity.

If you are to help people meet their needs through achieving company objectives, you must determine at what level each individual is operating and gear the handling of rewards accordingly. We'll discuss suggestions for doing this in the last section of this chapter.

RECOGNIZING SOCIALLY ACQUIRED MOTIVATORS

Another approach to motivation has been developed by psychologist David McClelland [5] and others over the past twenty years. Maslow's hierarchy implies that all humans are born with the lower-level needs as well as the potential to develop the higher-level needs in a step-by-step progression. McClelland takes issue with this viewpoint by suggesting that many human needs are socially acquired, rather than innate, and therefore vary from culture to culture. The rewards a child gets for excelling at studies, winning a fistfight, or shooting birds, for example, depend on cultural values. Such values and the resulting rewards help shape the needs we develop in childhood. McClelland also questions the adequacy of the concept of self-actualization. He indicates that the kinds of rewards that actualize a person's potential vary more widely from society to society and from person to person within one society than Maslow's work recognizes.

According to McClelland, needs for affiliation, power, and achievement are prime motivators. We can see some similarity in his affiliation need and Maslow's social or belonging need. We can also better understand McClelland's power and achievement categories by relating them to Maslow's ego and self-actualization needs, keeping in mind that McClelland's needs reflect cultural values and an expectation–reward–learning process rather than an inherent progression of need levels. Before we discuss these **socially acquired needs** in detail, take time to complete Exercise 8-2.

Now let's look at the key actions that help you determine whether a person's primary needs are for affiliation, power, or achievement. Remember, many of the actions described under each category are exhibited by all of us at one time or another; therefore the behavior alone doesn't necessarily indicate a primary need. For example, most of us seek the company of others at times, and such behavior doesn't necessarily indicate a strong affiliation need. When a person places special emphasis on being with others along with other affiliative behavior, however, we can assume a high affiliation need.

Affiliation

The stories written by most people in response to an exercise like 8-2 reflect affili-

EXERCISE 8-2: ANALYZING YOUR SOCIALLY ACQUIRED NEEDS

First read the questions that follow. Then study Figure 8-2 for ten or fifteen seconds. Finally, close the book and—without looking at the picture again—spend no more than five minutes writing an imaginative story based on the picture. Relax and be creative instead of merely describing the picture. Your story may include anything that occurs to you, but here are some questions that you may want to answer in it.

1. What is happening? Who are the people?

2. What has happened in the past that has led up to this situation?

3. What is being thought? What is wanted? Who is doing the thinking, the wanting?

4. What is going to occur next? What will be done?

After you've finished your story, read the discussion of socially acquired motives. Then analyze your story to determine the predominant motivational need it reflects.

ation needs. They focus on thoughts about relations with other people. When people with high **affiliation needs** are relaxing or daydreaming, they tend to think about the quality of their personal relationships. They might recall with pleasure the experiences they have had with some people and worry about problems with their relations with others. Persons with high affiliation needs tend to place *special emphasis* on (1) seeking out others to gain confirmation for their own beliefs or to relieve the stress of their own uncertainties, (2) seeking the company of others and taking steps to be liked by them, (3) trying to protect a favorable image in interpersonal relations, (4) smoothing out disagreeable tensions in meetings with others, and (5) helping and supporting others and wanting to be liked in return.

Here is a story that reflects needs that are predominantly affiliative:

This business woman is pausing in the midst of a busy day to think about her family. She's remembering the picnic at the beach they enjoyed so much last evening. She's concerned about having enough time and energy to devote to her children, who still need a great deal of attention and guidance. She decides to plan more family outings like the beach picnic, even if it means delaying some of her professional ambitions for a while.

As you can see, this story reflects thoughts about people. It could just as easily reflect affiliative needs by focusing on relations with people at work, as long as positive, constructive relationships are seen as an end in themselves and not merely as a means to other ends that reflect an achievement or power orientation.

FIGURE 8-2: Basis for an Imaginative Story

Power

People with high needs for power spend more time thinking about how to get and use power and authority than other people do. They tend to place *special emphasis* on (1) winning arguments, (2) persuading others to accept and implement their viewpoints or action plans, and (3) prevailing or winning.

People with high **power needs** feel uncomfortable without some sense of power. McClelland describes two aspects of power [5, p. 107].

1. *Power that is concerned with dominance and submission.* Persons who focus on gaining this kind of power are determined to have their own way and to have a strong impact in controlling others. They tend to view life as a win-lose game, especially when they feel threatened. If they are charismatic, their followers tend to feel submissive, loyal, devoted, and obedient to this type of leader's will. Their power needs are related to ego needs.

2. *Power that is more socialized.* People who focus on this aspect of power tend

to use persuasion and inspiration to actively lead people to higher levels of strength and competence in reaching their goals. These leaders help people form and attain goals. If they are charismatic, their followers tend to feel more powerful, confident, energetic, and inspired as a result of the association. Such power needs are related to self-actualization needs.

In actual practice, managers balance the two aspects of power. Even leaders with socialized power needs must take initiative in helping their groups form goals, or they are not really leaders. The balancing act involves deciding how much initiative to take, how persuasive to be, and at what point enthusiasm for certain goals becomes personal, authoritarian insistence that the goals are the right ones regardless of what others in the group think. McClelland says that a firm faith in people as originators of ideas and directors of the courses of their lives can help managers maintain a proper balance.

Here is a story that reflects a high power need:

The woman is a top-level executive in a growing firm. Her family looks to her for guidance and inspiration just as people in her company do. She is preparing her presentation for the annual stockholders' meeting tomorrow. She must convince the Board of Directors that her proposal is essential to maintaining the company's present growth rate. If she is successful and her plan works as well as she expects, she will probably be promoted before the next annual meeting.

This story focuses on the rewards of power. Any mention of people or problem-solving is done in terms of power roles.

Achievement

People with high **achievement needs** tend to place *special emphasis* on (1) taking personal responsibility for finding solutions to problems, (2) setting moderate achievement goals and taking calculated risks, and (3) seeking concrete feedback on how well they're doing.

Here is a story that reflects a high achievement need:

The woman is a staff specialist and is quite good at what she does. She has been working on a project and is relaxing from her efforts for a moment. She is thinking how proud her family will be when she tells them about the difficult problems she solved and the extra effort she expended in order to complete this project on time. She will have special cause to celebrate the completion of the project this evening. It was her brainchild from start to finish, and test runs have already indicated its workability.

The Effects of Socially Acquired Motives on Women

These three motives—affiliation, power, and achievement—are acquired by people in response to the actions and attitudes of their parents and others. The effects of this socialization process have special significance for women. The process can help us understand some of the typical differences between men and women—differences that are not necessarily innate and that can affect managerial effectiveness. For example, if you're uncomfortable with assuming a power position, you may be able to overcome this barrier to upward mobility more readily if you understand the source of your discomfort. Such insights can also help you guide other women over barriers.

We start acquiring these needs in early childhood as an outcome of actively trying to cope with our environment. Because the process begins so early, by the time we reach adulthood it is operating mostly at an unconscious level. The process begins at birth when we start coping with the problems of satisfying our hunger and getting adequate attention. It continues as we cope with the problems that accompany learning and growing. An immediate outcome of this coping behavior is that it tends to be pleasantly rewarding or neutral or to have unpleasant effects, which in turn affect our long-term patterns of behavior and need.

Getting Rewards and Reducing Anxiety We frequently experience either reward or anxiety as a result of the way others respond to our behavior. These early experiments are powerful influences in shaping our long-term behavior patterns. When a reward follows an act, it reinforces the behavior and increases the probability that it will be repeated. When as a child your active, problem-solving behavior led to satisfying results, you learned more than just how to cope or solve a problem. You also learned to repeat the *type* of behavior that led to success. When some of these types of behavior were consistently rewarded over a period of time, you learned to rely on them. As a result of this learning process, you developed your own pattern of affiliation, power, and achievement needs and motives.

The other force at work in the learning process is the reduction of anxiety. We tend to repeat the kinds of behavior that result in a reduction of negative states or unpleasant tension. If being warm and friendly paid off by relieving your pain and anxiety, for example, the warm, friendly behavior was reinforced and the foundation for a lifelong affiliation need was strengthened.

Effects of Socialization on Women's Managerial Effectiveness An analysis of socially acquired motives can perhaps shed some light on the assets and liabilities that women bring to the managerial role. It is safe to say that most women have received the greatest rewards and reduced more anxieties through affiliative behavior than through power and achievement-oriented behavior. In general, women therefore have an edge over men in sensitivity to people's feelings and in establishing warm, supportive relationships.

Some women also have received strong and consistent rewards for achievement-oriented behavior. The fact that until adolescence girls consistently get better grades than boys indicates at least some achievement orientation of girls at an early age. Until recently, however, nearly all girls responded to quite different messages during adolescence and early adulthood—such as "Don't be an intellectual," "Don't excel in academia," "Start looking for a nice boy to settle down with." As a result, even girls who were previously oriented toward achievement found out that their greatest rewards came as a result of affiliative behavior, and they responded accordingly. Many channeled their achievement-oriented behavior into keeping the neatest house on the block, having the most successful husband in the group, raising the brightest, most attractive children, belonging to the most exclusive, desirable clubs and groups. They aimed at basking in the reflected light of their husband's and children's successes rather than in their own.

Very few women have found significant rewards or anxiety avoidance through power-oriented behavior. Quite the opposite, most women have experienced some degree of censure and anxiety-producing feedback when they have attempted to take charge, win arguments, prevail, and so forth—especially with men. Some studies indicate that the few women who make it to top management have usually enjoyed special relationships with their fathers. These women had relatively strong fathers who supported and encouraged them to excel and take charge. In most cases the father served as role model and mentor in a way that is common in father/son relationships but extremely rare with daughters.

Most women bring to the job a lifetime of experiences that have discouraged the very power-oriented behavior that is essential to becoming a top-level executive. Since this behavior is learned, however, there is no reason you cannot make new decisions about certain values and behaviors that will help you attain the job positions you desire. You might well keep in mind that *someone* must lead and must occupy these power positions. It is possible that women can more easily combine affiliative with power-oriented behavior to become more humane, effective leaders than men.

How have interactions with others affected your needs, your perceptions of rewarding and anxiety-producing situations, and therefore your own motivational patterns? Exercise 8-3 gives you a chance to examine these factors. The purposes of the exercise are to help you identify *patterns* of behavior and how they developed as you grew up and to give you some insights into the effects of your early experiences on your current motivators. How can you use your insights to motivate the people who work for you? We'll focus on that topic next.

RECOGNIZING THE MANAGER'S ROLE AS A MOTIVATOR

We've examined two major theories of motivation that are based on the assumption that certain needs impel people to behave in

certain ways. The theories of Maslow and McClelland deal with innate and learned needs that people bring to the job situation, and they can help you understand what you (and others) want as well as how you (and others) developed that pattern of wants. Now let's look at some theories that deal more directly with the job situation itself and the manager's role in enhancing worker motivation. These theories examine the roles of expectations and guidance.

Expectancy Theory

Since people's needs determine what is rewarding to them, they behave in ways they think will lead to those rewards. The actual behavior depends on a person's thinking, "If I act this way in this particular situation at this particular time, I will get a reward that I want."

According to **expectancy theory,** merely having a particular motive or needing a particular reward is not enough to turn a readiness to behave into behavior and performance. Where motivational theories such as Maslow's and McClelland's help us identify what people *want*, expectancy theory helps us understand how desire leads to *action*. Before people will act, they must generally expect two things.

1. If they try to perform, they will actually be able to perform. It *is* possible to do what they are trying to do in this particular situation, and they have the ability to do it.

2. If they perform, they will get the reward they want.

Another aspect of expectations (although not a part of formal expectancy theory) is the expectation of the manager concerning each worker's abilities and potential. Look at the

EXERCISE 8-3: IDENTIFYING SOURCES OF REWARD AND ANXIETY

As you read through each list of behaviors, respond only to the items that "ring a bell." Recall the period of your life in which the behavior was significant. Finally, determine whether you experienced some type of reward or payoff for the behavior. If you did, put an "R" in the appropriate space. If you experienced anxiety as a result of the behavior, write "A." If the results were neutral, write "N."

Don't overanalyze or try to respond to every type of behavior in every life period. First get the high points; then review your responses, looking for patterns and insights.

R = Reward
A = Anxiety
N = Neutral

	Life Period			
	Early Childhood	Elementary School	Adolescence	Young Adulthood
Power-oriented Behavior				
1. Taking over in a situation	_____	_____	_____	_____
2. Arguing a point	_____	_____	_____	_____
3. Trying to persuade others to do what you want	_____	_____	_____	_____
4. Telling others what to do	_____	_____	_____	_____
5. Getting others to follow your lead	_____	_____	_____	_____
6. Breaking a rule when it interferes with a "valid goal"	_____	_____	_____	_____

Other power-oriented behaviors you have experienced:

7. _____	_____	_____	_____	_____
8. _____	_____	_____	_____	_____
9. _____	_____	_____	_____	_____

Achievement-oriented Behavior

1. Initiating and completing projects	_____	_____	_____	_____

(Continued on next page)

	Life Period			
	Early Childhood	Elementary School	Adolescence	Young Adulthood
2. Figuring out what was wrong	———	———	———	———
3. Figuring out how to fix things	———	———	———	———
4. Making good grades	———	———	———	———
5. Taking "hard subjects" as electives	———	———	———	———
6. Doing well in or liking math or science courses	———	———	———	———
7. Doing well in or liking courses in shop, drafting, or other "male-oriented" vocations	———	———	———	———
8. Doing well in or liking football, baseball, or other "male-oriented" sports	———	———	———	———
9. Working or playing on your own	———	———	———	———
10. Asking how you are doing	———	———	———	———
11. Trying to find out how you are being evaluated	———	———	———	———
12. Competing with others	———	———	———	———
13. Trying to do better and better	———	———	———	———

Other achievement-oriented behaviors you have experienced:

14. _____	———	———	———	———
15. _____	———	———	———	———
16. _____	———	———	———	———

Affiliation-oriented Behavior

1. Doing as you are told	———	———	———	———

(Continued on next page)

	Life Period			
	Early Childhood	Elementary School	Adolescence	Young Adulthood
2. Following the rules	———	———	———	———
3. Making lots of "nice" friends	———	———	———	———
4. Participating in the "right" group	———	———	———	———
5. Cooperating with others	———	———	———	———
6. Doing things to please others	———	———	———	———
7. Helping others	———	———	———	———
8. Putting others' wishes ahead of your own	———	———	———	———
9. Patching up quarrels or disagreements	———	———	———	———
10. Dating "nice" boys	———	———	———	———
11. Understanding others' feelings	———	———	———	———

Other affiliation-oriented behaviors you have experienced:

12. _____	———	———	———	———
13. _____	———	———	———	———
14. _____	———	———	———	———

situations where the worker respects the manager and is influenced by the manager's attitudes and actions. If the manager has reasonably high expectations for the worker's performance, the worker tends to rise again and again to the occasion. The manager's expectations reflect confidence in the worker's ability and therefore esteem for the worker. The worker's self-esteem and self-confidence are enhanced, and the manager's expecta-tions create a self-fulfilling prophecy of worker achievement.

In effect, such managers help workers picture themselves functioning in certain roles, meeting certain goals, and receiving certain rewards. Three essential steps to maintaining a high level of motivation are (1) having the appropriate self-image, (2) setting appropriate goals, and (3) applying the necessary self-discipline to overcome barriers and to reach goals. Managers can enhance workers' motivation by helping them through each of these steps.

The Path-Goal Approach

The manager who can understand and take effective action based on people's needs *and* their expectations is probably using some variation of a **path-goal approach** to motivation. Effective managers are able to show their workers how meeting their job objectives will satisfy their needs and help them obtain some of the rewards they want most. (We described this in Chapter 7 as achieving goal congruence.) The manager's behavior will have a motivating effect on workers to the extent that such behavior (1) makes satisfaction of workers' needs dependent on effective performance (that is, challenges workers in appropriate ways) and (2) provides a supportive work environment by providing the coaching, guidance, support, and rewards necessary for effective performance.

More specifically, managers can increase (1) workers' motivation to perform, (2) their job satisfaction, and (3) their acceptance of the manager by taking the following kinds of action [2, p. 327]:

Recognize and arouse workers' needs for results over which they have some control.

Increase personal payoffs to workers for attaining job goals.

Make the path to such payoffs easier to travel by giving effective coaching and direction (see Chapter 12).

Help workers clarify their expectations.

Minimize frustrating barriers.

Increase opportunities for personal satisfaction dependent on job performance.

As you can see, the manager's skill in identifying appropriate rewards is a key to making the path-goal approach work. Here are some general principles of motivating through reward.

1. Identify the precise behaviors that you are rewarding.

2. Reward the desired behaviors as soon as possible. Be specific in communicating what you are rewarding and why.

3. When a new behavior is being developed, reward it in some way every time it occurs until it is firmly established.

4. When a new behavior is being developed, the learner must perceive that the reward will be worth the risk and effort.

The ideal management style for implementing the path-goal approach is the participative style described in Chapter 7, but other styles can be effective in certain situations. When the demands of the tasks are ambiguous or when organizational procedures, rules, or policies are not clear, *directive leadership* provides the necessary guidance and psychological structure for workers. When workers are performing stressful, frustrating, or dissatisfying tasks, *supportive leadership* can offset their dissatisfaction.

Achievement-oriented leadership strives for higher standards of performance to meet challenging goals. When workers are performing ambiguous, nonrepetitive tasks, the higher the achievement orientation of the leader, the more confident the followers will be that their efforts will pay off in effective performance.

Regardless of management style, the path-goal model is one in which the manager focuses on results, with a balanced emphasis on the objectives of the organization and the personal goals of the workers.

PRACTICAL APPLICATIONS OF MOTIVATIONAL THEORY

The path-goal approach is a good start toward bridging the gap between understanding pure motivational theory and making theory work on the job. In this section we'll focus on applying motivational theory to constructively select, train, and direct people and to organize work. To get the best results, the manager must try to find the best match between the requirements of the job, the needs of the persons who'll be doing the tasks, and the working climate (that is, the organizational structure, the management styles of bosses, and related factors). Then the manager must choose among several alternative approaches in order to achieve two distinct goals:

1. To build a highly motivated team by such actions as hiring people that fit and counseling misfits into other jobs or companies

2. To structure a motivational work environment by reorganizing job descriptions and tasks to take better advantage of the needs, interests, and drives of the people in the work groups and by modifying the working climate to achieve a better fit with the types of workers involved

Matching Jobs to Workers' Motivational Patterns

Of all the actions you can take, the one that will have the most dramatic effects on the motivational environment of your group is matching the right person to the right job. You can get the right match by hiring people that fit the job and the group, by transferring people within the group to achieve a better fit, and by reorganizing jobs for a better fit. (Counseling misfits into other jobs or companies is discussed more fully in Chapter 12.) Let's look first at the kinds of jobs that are suited to people with high affiliation, power, or achievement needs.

Affiliation Motives = Coordinators, Integrators People with strong affiliation needs make the best coordinators and integrators. Place these people in jobs that require coordinating the work of others, such as specialists, or the work of departments. Such people are ideal also in jobs that require integrating the goals of various persons, units, or departments with organizational goals, as well as teaching and coaching others, and performing services that require directly helping others.

Power Motives = Upwardly Mobile Managers Anyone who is expected to move beyond the ranks of first-line or middle management must have a fairly high power need—at least in most organizational settings. The competition at higher levels is usually so stiff that people with less than a strong need to lead, influence, and prevail soon grow tired of the battle. The climb up the ladder usually requires skill and interest in organizational politics and skirmishes. Persons who enjoy the process are most likely to survive and come out on top.

Achievement Motives = Staff Specialists, Commission Salespersons, Professionals The salesperson on commission and the owner-manager of a small business are good examples of the person with a high achievement need. They are in a perfect position to see whether their performance is improving and to reap the rewards of that performance. Other job situations in which people are responsible for specific projects that require problem-solving skills are engineers, builders, and certain staff jobs requiring specialized expertise (such as computer specialists). Professionals such as accountants, lawyers, and doctors usually have high achievement needs.

Listening for Clues Pay special attention to people's thoughts and feelings and try to tune in to what motivates them [4, pp. 105–10]. How do workers talk about their experiences? What kinds of things seem to give them the most satisfaction? What do they think about when they are involved in their work? Detailed suggestions for analyzing the jobs or tasks to be accomplished and for identifying patterns of behavior of the people who might fill these jobs are shown in Exhibit 8-1.

Recognizing Multiple Orientations As you go about making the job/person fit, keep in mind that just because a person is strongly oriented toward one type of motive doesn't necessarily mean that he or she will be "low" in another motive. For example, a person might be "high" in both affiliation and power needs—and possibly in achievement needs too. You'll need to consider the mix and the situation when making personnel decisions. In addition, people vary in their energy levels and in the degree of positive, constructive outlook. For example, it is quite possible that an energetic person with an approach to life that is usually very positive and constructive would be more highly motivated by needs for affiliation, power, *and* achievement than would a passive, lethargic person with a rather sour, pessimistic viewpoint.

Structuring the Work Environment

We've been focusing on building a highly motivated work team by achieving the best fit of worker to job and situation. You can also plan and organize the work itself to enhance motivation. You can provide workers with relevant information, and you can encourage them to participate in planning and decision-making.

Structuring Jobs Five key characteristics of job tasks that significantly affect motivation have been researched by J. Richard Hackman and others, as shown in Exhibit 8-2. These five task characteristics determine the type and level of certain psychological states that are critical to high motivation and performance. The extent to which three of these task characteristics are present (skill variety, task or team/task identity, and task significance) directly affects how meaningful the work is to the worker. A fourth key task characteristic, the level of autonomy the worker has in performing job tasks, directly affects the extent to which he or she takes personal responsibility for work results. And the fifth characteristic, the kind of feedback the worker gets, directly affects his or her knowledge of the actual work results.

Three critical psychological states—(1) perceived meaningfulness of the work, (2) responsibility for work outcomes, and (3) knowledge of the end results of the work activities—in turn directly affect the workers' attitudes and behaviors. In other words, the level of your workers' internal motivation, work performance, job satisfaction, and attendance rate are all directly related to these psychological states. Your challenge, therefore, is to structure the tasks and the atmosphere in which they're done so as to provide the needed levels of skill variety, task identity, task significance, autonomy, and feedback.

Ideally, workers should be the first ones to get feedback on their performance so they can practice as much self-evaluation and self-control as is feasible, as discussed in the section on planning in Chapter 10. When the feedback is given by you, take a problem-solving approach, as discussed in

EXHIBIT 8-1: Matching Workers' Needs to Job Requirements

When the job allows or requires workers to:	Look for people who:

Affiliation Orientation

Interact with numerous people on a daily basis	Relate well to other workers and go out of their way to make friends with new workers
Have access to interaction with numerous people in his or her working area	Get involved in group projects
Have significant free time to interact with people on nontask matters	Are sensitive to other people's feelings
Gain the cooperation of co-workers to successfully accomplish the task	Make special efforts to get personally involved with bosses
Be able to maintain long-term worker relationships	Don't like to work alone

Power Orientation

Personally direct coworkers	Especially like to be their own boss, even in situations where they need help or where cooperative effort is needed
Spend a significant amount of time dealing directly with the boss(es)	Enjoy a good argument
Spend a significant amount of time in personal interactions	Seek positions of authority where they can give orders rather than take them
Have significant control over his or her work pace and methods	Like to take charge of situations
Be reasonably free to come and go as she or he pleases, as long as the work gets done	View status symbols as especially important and use them to gain influence
Have significant opportunities for advancement	

Achievement Orientation

Have a great deal of freedom in setting his or her work pace and designing own work methods	Are eager to accept responsibility
Usually choose when and where to get help or direction	Like to set and meet measurable standards of high performance
Perform effectively and efficiently because company sales or profits are directly affected	Stick with tasks until they are satisfactorily completed
Always know how well she or he is doing	Enjoy difficult, challenging tasks
Be continually challenged to develop abilities and skills	Work better when the job is challenging or a deadline must be met
	Try to find out how they are doing, like to get as much information as possible to help meet goals and standards
	Enjoy a fairly high degree of freedom, responsibility, and competition

Adapted from George H. Litwin and Robert A Stringer, Jr., *Motivation and Organizational Climate* (Cambridge, Mass.: Harvard University, Graduate School of Business, 1978), pp. 105–110.

EXHIBIT 8-2: How Task Characteristics Affect Work Motivation

Task Characteristics	Critical Psychological States	Effects on Attitude and Behavior
Skill Variety—The number of different tasks, their level of challenge, and the variety of skills and talents needed to accomplish them *Task Identity*—How well a worker can identify with a distinct or tangible piece of work he or she can claim as the result of his or her effort or *Team/Task Identity*—How well workers can identify with a small team which in turn can claim a distinct piece of work as the result of its own joint effort- *Task Significance*—How important the task is; how much it affects the work or the lives of others	*Meaningfulness of the Work*— as perceived by the worker	High internal motivation to work High quality of work performance High satisfaction with work Low absenteeism, turnover rates
Autonomy—The level of freedom the worker has to plan tasks and to decide on procedures for carrying them out	*Responsibility for Outcomes of the Work*—as perceived by the worker	
Feedback—The extent, type, and immediacy of information about how well the worker is performing assigned tasks	*Knowledge of Actual Results of the work activities*	

Adapted from Richard Hackman and G. R. Oldham, *Work Redesign* (Reading, Mass.: Addison-Wesley, 1980).

the section on delegating in Chapter 12. In addition to information on their performance, workers frequently need other kinds of information in order to take full responsibility for their jobs.

Providing Information If workers are to accomplish their job goals and make contributions to company goals, managers must see that they get all possible information that can be helpful. Workers should receive relevant information on a regular basis and as a matter of course. Therefore, managers must arrange for information to flow routinely to workers who need it. The information should be specific, readily identifiable, and readily digested by the worker. In other words, workers should not have to wade through pages of reports or stacks of computer print-outs in order to sift out and interpret the information they need.

Providing for Planning and Decision-Making by Workers When the people who will actively undertake work assignments participate in making some decisions and have latitude to make others on their own, they gain stature within the company and in their own eyes. Their expertise and their capacity for rational action in making creative contributions is more fully utilized and developed. Their interest in their jobs and their sense of responsibility are enhanced.

If workers are not allowed to participate in planning and other decisions concerning their jobs, the company is in effect telling them that they have no prospect of becoming really involved in the company's affairs. If they are not involved, how can we expect them to be motivated? (See Chapter 10.)

Putting It All Together

In the final analysis, you cannot motivate anyone but yourself. You certainly cannot successfully manipulate motivation in others for very long. Neither will occasional "rewards," such as company picnics, gold watches, or even a pat on the back have any real effect if the job itself and the work environment do not enhance the worker's self-motivation.

The key, then, is to determine: (1) What needs create a readiness in the worker to act and (2) what rewards the worker values and is willing to put forth extra efforts to obtain.

You then can structure job content and work environment to enhance the workers' self-motivation. You can help your people see how meeting the job goals and standards you have jointly set can help them satisfy personal needs and get the rewards they want. Finally, through the way you interact with your people and your communication with them—such as giving immediate feedback on the desired behavior—you can further enhance the workers' self-motivation.

Now, try your hand at applying your knowledge of motivational theories and approaches by analyzing the motivational problems involved in the Leslie case, Exercise 8-5.

SUMMARY

A major reason that most employees aren't committed to their work is that managers rely more on position power than on personal leadership. The key to exercising leadership is to understand the psychological needs of individual workers and to help them satisfy their needs through their own actions—actions that also contribute to organizational objectives.

Perhaps the most widely used motivational theory is Maslow's hierarchy of needs, which is based on various levels of innate needs. Only when a person has adequately satisfied a lower-level need, will he or she be motivated to satisfy needs at the next level of the hierarchy. Most American workers are motivated to higher performance through expectation of rewards connected with the higher-level needs.

David McClelland suggests that many human needs are learned rather than innate. He discusses three basic categories of socially acquired needs: affiliation, achievement, and power. These motivators have special significance for women. As children we acquire needs (and motives) in the process of solving problems and reducing anxiety. Most women have received the greatest rewards and reduced anxiety most effectively through affiliative behavior. Many women have also received significant rewards for achievement-oriented behavior, but usually only until they reach adolescence. On the other hand, most have experienced censure and anxiety as a result of power-oriented behavior. Since problem-solving behavior is learned, women can make new decisions about the values implied by the behavior and its rewards. They can adopt new behaviors that will enhance their career goals.

Maslow's and McClelland's theories focus on what people want. Expectancy theory focuses on how desire can become action. Before people will act, they must generally expect that they will actually be able to perform the act and that they will get the reward they want as a result.

You can increase your workers' motivation to perform, their job satisfaction, and their acceptance of you as manager by combining expectancy theory with a path-goal approach. Recognize and arouse workers' needs for results over which they have some control. Increase personal payoffs to workers for attaining job goals. Make the path to such payoffs easier to travel by giving effective coaching and direction. Help workers clarify their expectations. Minimize frustrating barriers. Increase opportunities for personal satisfaction dependent on job performance. Use directive leadership when the demands of tasks are ambiguous or when organizational procedures, rules, or policies are unclear. Use supportive leadership when tasks are stressful, frustrating, or dissatisfying. Use achievement-oriented leadership when ambiguous, nonrepetitive tasks are required.

Above all, focus on selecting the right people for the right jobs. In general, look for these matches: affiliation motive—coordinators, integrators, trainers, service people who help others; power motive—upwardly mobile managers; achievement motive—certain staff specialists, commission salespersons, professionals, entrepreneurial types.

Finally, structure the work environment to provide a motivational climate. Provide information needed to perform well. Design the flow of information so that people routinely get information they need in the form they need it. Structure jobs so that dead-end jobs are eliminated, workers' creativity and intelligence are used, and workers can set meaningful, attainable job goals. Provide for decision-making by workers.

ADDITIONAL EXERCISES

EXERCISE 8-4: MATCHING NEEDS TO JOBS

Assuming you have a fair understanding of the predominant needs of the people you're placing in various jobs, what type of person would you place in each of the jobs listed below. (Use the categories Aff for affiliation, Ach for achievement, or Power.)

_____ 1. *EDP program librarian:* Responsible for maintaining the on-line and off-line libraries of production programs; keeps track of program revisions.

_____ 2. *EDP systems analyst:* Works with users to define data-processing projects or project segments, or to iron out details in specifications.

_____ 3. *Personnel interviewer:* Involved in all phases of screening prospective employees. Processes changes in employee status and conducts exit interviews.

_____ 4. *Word-processing operator:* Uses automated equipment to format, produce, and revise letters and complicated documents from complex sources, including electronic files. Must be able to act independently and assume full responsibility for the accuracy and completeness of documents.

_____ 5. *Word-processing supervisor:* Has technical skills of word-processing operator. Responsible for the operation of a word-processing center. Schedules and coordinates the work flow, assists operators, helps set and maintain standards. Evaluates procedures and identifies potential improvements.

_____ 6. *Labor relations specialist:* Is responsible for good labor-management relations, formulates the company's labor relations policy for top management's approval. Represents management in labor relations, including collective-bargaining negotiations.

_____ 7. *Personnel benefits administrator:* Administers benefit programs. Advises employees on eligibility for programs. Maintains benefit records and implements benefit coverage.

_____ 8. *Purchasing analyst:* Compiles and analyzes data to determine the feasibility of purchasing products, determines price objectives, keeps up-to-date on price trends and manufacturing processes.

_____ 9. *Buyer:* Obtains materials, products, equipment, and/or services. Checks requisitions, obtains quotations from vendors, examines bids, and makes awards. Evaluates vendor reliability. Develops new supply sources. Coordinates purchasing activities with production department, maintaining inventories at planned levels.

_____ 10. *Account executive:* Serves as connecting link with advertising agency and its clients. Meets client needs while maintaining agency's creative concepts and budget limitations. Brings in new accounts; maintains good relations with existing accounts. High visibility; high turnover based on success or failure with clients.

EXERCISE 8-5: THE LESLIE CASE

Lin Leslie was enthusiastic when she first took over as Customer Accounts Supervisor for the SuAnne product line. She enjoyed her contacts with the customers and felt a sense of achievement in seeing that all the accounts were handled properly. Lately, however, her enthusiasm is waning because of a continuing problem with three of her clerical people.

The three clerks—Barbara, Vickie, and Alice—are fresh out of high school and seem to be interested mainly in boys, parties, girlfriends, and clothes. They are rarely absent or late for work, but they don't accomplish much once they are on the job. The three have become good friends in recent months. (They were hired at about the same time last June. Leslie became supervisor about six weeks ago, in August.) Therefore, they usually take coffee and lunch breaks together and frequently stretch their breaks by anywhere from five to fifteen minutes. In addition, their legitimate discussions concerning accounts often get sidetracked onto personal matters, and prolonged personal conversations regularly take place in the hallway and restroom. All this results in a significant decrease of hours actually devoted to their work.

To compound the problem, all three frequently make errors in their work and fail to follow prescribed procedures. They just don't seem to care enough to thoroughly check their work and concentrate on doing it correctly.

1. If you were Lin, how would you handle this situation?

2. What motivational factors do you see in operation?

3. Can Lin do anything to enhance the motivation of the three clerks?

If your instructor has asked you to discuss this case with a group, jot down your own ideas first. If you're working on your own, write down your responses and then compare them with the main points mentioned in the answer key.

REFERENCES

1. Hackman, J. Richard, and G. R. Oldham. *Work Redesign.* Reading, Mass.: Addison-Wesley, 1980.

2. House, Robert J. "Path-Goal Theory of Leader Effectiveness." *Administrative Science Quarterly* (September 1971), pp. 321–28.

3. Lawrence, P. R., and J. W. Lorsch. *Developing Organizations: Diagnosis and Action.* Boston: Addison-Wesley, 1980. An excellent analysis of the origin of various needs and motives. Helpful for understanding the physiological aspects of motivation.

4. Litwin, George H., and Robert A. Stringer, Jr. *Motivation and Organizational Climate.* Cambridge, Mass.: Harvard University Graduate School of Business, 1978. A thorough discussion of the practical applications of the theory of socially acquired motives.

5. McClelland, David C., and David G. Winter. *Motivating Economic Achievement.* New York: Free Press, 1969. A thorough examination of the theory of socially acquired motives by the originator of the concept.

6. Maslow, Abraham H. "A Theory of Human Motivation." *Psychological Review,* Vol. 50, No. 4 (July 1943), pp. 370–96.

7. Sherwin, Douglas S. "Strategy for Winning Employee Commitment." *Harvard Business Review on Management.* New York: Harper & Row, 1975.

8. Svenson, Arthur L. "Moratorium on Motivation." *S.A.M. Advanced Management Journal* (April 1971), pp. 26–31.

Chapter Nine

Problem-Solving and Decision-Making

> *"Don't agonize. Organize."*
> *Florynce Kennedy*

The major barrier to effective problem-solving and decision-making for most women is the myth that women are innately weak in these areas. The truth is that you are likely to have special strengths that will become ever more valuable as you move to higher levels of management that call for broader types of decisions. In this chapter we'll explore the value of such special strengths as practicality, intuition, and preventive or constructive attitudes toward problems.

Specifically, in this chapter you will have the opportunity to learn more about

1. Recognizing the special strengths and weaknesses of women as problem-solvers and decision-makers

2. Developing a decision-making style that enhances your management style

3. Developing ways of preventing problems through the use of Murphy's Law

4. Focusing on prevention and rewarding preventive strategies

5. Stressing solutions instead of problems

6. Viewing problems as challenges to be met or as needs to be filled

7. Defining and analyzing problem situations and developing and evaluating alternate solutions to problems

8. Deciding on an action plan, committing to it, and then communicating, selling, implementing, evaluating, and modifying it

9. Deciding when and how to include groups in the problem-solving/decision-making process

---

 Breaking Murphy's Law

"Well, Carrie, how is your strategy for taming the savage sales staff working?" asks John Brockfield as he sinks into the chair by her desk.

"Just great, John. I guess there's nothing like a little honesty. Without coming right out and saying it, I got across the message that I realized I had made a false start and wanted to get back on the right foot. They responded like troopers. Now not only are they producing well, but I sense a high level of enthusiasm and team spirit."

"That's the impression I'm getting, too. They respect your savvy and willingness to level with them. They know you want the department to excel, and they feel a lot of support from you in helping them do their part. Congratulations, Carrie, I had a feeling you could carry it off."

A few minutes later Carrie's Assistant Sales Manager, Brian O'Hara, drops in. "Hi, Carrie. I got your note about a new assignment. What's up?"

"Brian, you know Jan Arguello in headquarters has asked us to do something brand new for the Resort/Holiday Fashion Preview this fall."

"Yes, I read a copy of the memo. It's going to be quite a job to play host to all the major buyers in the country."

"But it really gives us a chance to show what we can do, here in San Diego. All the top headquarters executives will be here along with some of the top buyers in the country. Brian, how would you feel about handling most of the details for this show?"

"Well, I don't know. I would hate for things to go wrong when so much attention is being focused on us."

"You know, Brian, I had the same kind of fears about my first big assignment. Here was my chance to shine—or to blow it. Luckily I had a boss who showed me how to use Murphy's Law."

"Murphy's Law?"

"Yes. You know: 'If something *can* go wrong, it will.' "

"That's just what I'm afraid of, Carrie!"

"Ah, but you can use it to *avoid* unpleasant surprises."

"How's that?"

"Well, for example, what are some of the things that *can* go wrong at the Resort/Holiday showing? Things that you fear happening?"

"You mean like some of the samples won't be ready on time? *(Carrie nods.)* All the invitations have the wrong date on them? Or they get lost in the mail? *(Brian warms to the subject.)* Or the hotel doesn't honor room reservations for some of the bigwigs . . . and they have to stay in some inferior, inconvenient place . . . and there's a howling rainstorm the day of the show . . . and taxis are practically impossible to find . . . "

"Enough, enough. You've got the idea. But that's just the first step in using Murphy's Law. The next step is figuring out ways to prevent those problems or to handle them most effectively if they can't be prevented."

"Like giving early deadline dates for completion of samples? *(Carrie nods.)* And having alternate back-up samples? Like having two or three people check the master copy of the invitation list to be sure all details are correct . . . and having extra invitations run in case some get lost in the mail . . . "

"That's right. Now start organizing those points into a list. As your plans progress, stop periodically to visualize the entire process of putting on the show, all the necessary steps, and everything that could go wrong at each step. Keep adding to your list. Of course, some possibilities are so remote or the consequences so trivial that you won't need to bother with preventive action. The main idea is to have no unpleasant surprises."

"Say, I'm already learning things from this project."

Later that day, Lin Leslie, Customer Accounts Supervisor, bursts into Carrie's office near tears.

"Why, Lin," says Carrie, "What's the matter?"

"I'm at my wits' end. This job is just too much for me. People keep pestering me for decisions before I'm ready to make them. Besides that, there's just one crisis after another."

"Sit down, Lin. Now, first, who's pestering you for decisions?"

"Today it seems like everyone! But I guess it's mainly the clerks in my unit. I do my best to motivate them, but they just don't seem to be able to handle problems that come up. I'm not sure whether they're incapable or just don't care."

"So you end up solving most of the problems?"

"That's right, Carrie."

"And making all the decisions?"

"Well, I know it's my job to make the decisions for my unit. But people are always wanting to know what to do about something when lots of times I haven't had a chance to look into it thoroughly."

"Lin, are you and your people getting the information you need to make decisions about the work?"

"Well, yes, I guess so. But, well, let's face it. I'm still not really comfortable with making so many decisions. I know the guys who are supervisors around here are used to making decisions—and they are good at it, for the most part—but I guess I'm more of a typical female when it comes to problems and decisions."

---

1. As you read this story, what actions and attitudes did you think were especially effective? Why? _____

2. What impact are those effective actions and attitudes likely to have on others?
_____

3. What actions and attitudes did you think were especially ineffective? Why? _____
_____

4. What impact are those ineffective actions and attitudes likely to have on others?
_____

VIEWING WOMEN AS LOGICAL PROBLEM-SOLVERS AND CONFIDENT DECISION-MAKERS

Many women have grown up with the assumption that girls are not as good as boys in math, science, sports, and finance—areas that call for logic, strategy, and good problem-solving and decision-making abilities. Therefore, many women feel inferior to men when it comes to logical problem-solving and confident decision-making. When we think of a competent executive who rationally, coolly, and calmly reviews the facts and reaches a decision, most of us picture a man. Lately, however, that picture has been expanded to include the female executive. As a matter of fact, some women have always been excellent problem-solvers and decision-makers. Others can acquire these skills with a little help and encouragement.

You may have to deal with others' stereotyped notions (and perhaps your own?) of the female decision-maker: She is perhaps charming but somewhat scatterbrained, vague, and emotional. She dithers and worries a great deal about problems and alternative solutions. "She just can't make up her mind." When she finally does reach a decision, she relies on intuition and emotions more than on the facts. She communicates her decisions in rather vague, emotional terms. She seems tentative about the entire matter.

Needless to say, this approach does *not* inspire confidence in those who must carry out the decisions. Finally, she confirms that age-old saying "It's a woman's prerogative to change her mind" by immediately reversing her decision when minor barriers to carrying out the plan arise.

Because of these stereotypes, you must communicate with people about your problem-solving and decision-making activities in as logical, rational, and businesslike a manner as possible. In this chapter we will discuss each step of the process. Some steps call for curiosity, creativity, intuition, the ability to tune in to people and their feelings—all traits that women have been blessed with and have developed to fairly high levels. Take advantage of your strengths in these areas, but watch how you refer to them in communicating with others. Stress the rational, logical, factual aspects of problem-solving and decision-making—as well as your know-how in preventing problems.

Just as important as being able to effectively solve problems and make decisions is knowing how to prevent problems (and the resulting need to make decisions). Therefore, we'll look at some methods of prevention before going on to cures.

PREVENTING PROBLEMS

The best way to avoid problems is to plan and prepare thoroughly. The best way to teach your people to prevent problems is to reward them for doing it. Next best is to give them training and information that will let them solve their own problems. Train them to have at least a tentative solution in mind if they must bring a problem to you, so that they won't get in the habit of dumping problems on you. Now for the details of these strategies.

Using Murphy's Law

According to **Murphy's Law:** "If anything *can* go wrong, it *will*." At first glance, this seems to reflect an extremely negative viewpoint. As Carrie discovered, however, it can be useful in a very positive way. If you start by anticipating all the things that can go wrong instead of blithely expecting things to occur as planned, you can then make back-up plans to (1) prevent as many problems as possible and (2) handle problems that do occur with minimal disruption.

Let's look at some elaborations on Murphy's Law contributed by Arthur Bloch [4, p. 11]:

Murphy's Second Law: Nothing is as easy as it looks.

Murphy's Third Law: Everything takes longer than you think.

Murphy's Fourth Law: Left to themselves, things tend to go from bad to worse.

Murphy's Fifth Law: If there is a possibility of several things going wrong, the one that will cause the most damage will be the one.

We've all experienced these truths, and the only reason for recalling them is to see what lessons we can learn. Ask yourself, "How can my experience of past disasters help me to prevent future problems?" The more important the project, the more thoroughly you'll need to apply Murphy's Law. An awareness of it can help you prevent problems, for example, when (1) you're tackling a certain type of project for the first time, (2) the results of the project will be highly visible and will affect your reputation, or (3) the assignment is a pet project of one of your bosses.

After you've planned the project, ask yourself some probing questions: Suppose

Jones doesn't show up that day? What if Smith is late? What will we do if the equipment isn't available? Or breaks down? What if a key person didn't get my memo? Or forgets to look at her calendar? What if twice as many people show up as I expect? Half as many? Suppose the printer doesn't get the handouts done in time?

Your list of questions will depend on your particular project. Develop your own questions by mentally living through the implementation of your project step by step. Each step of the way visualize all the problems that could possibly arise. Develop a plan for either preventing or handling each one. Make this your motto: "No Surprises!"

Developing a Preventive Attitude

Constructively applying Murphy's Law is only one facet of avoiding problems. Another is making sure the right people are aware of the thought, expertise, and effort you put into managing your project so smoothly. To be really successful, one must overcome Zimmerman's Law of Complaints [4, p. 12]: "Nobody notices when things go right."

Who gets the most favorable attention in your company? The person who runs her operation quietly and smoothly? Or the person who is always having to cope with crises and somehow "pulls her people through them to go on to bigger and better things?" The manager who trains her people to prevent problems and make correct decisions? Or the manager who is "indispensable" and is always rushing in to rescue her people from messes? The person who works at a steady, unhurried pace? Or the person who is aways getting "snowed under" (but who also has frequent slack periods)? Ask yourself, "What are the payoffs for managers and for workers in my company for preventing problems and crises?" It may be that managers and workers who *cope* with problems and crises are given more favorable attention than those who *prevent* them. People tend to behave in ways that get them favorable attention. You can help break such a cycle in your company.

To get the payoffs you deserve for preventing problems, you must be sure your bosses know about and understand what you are doing. By the same token, you need to be especially alert in order to give your subordinates more favorable attention when they prevent problems than when they merely cope with them. Let your people know what's important to you by training them to prevent problems and by giving them the information and guidelines they need for making decisions that are appropriate to their job responsibilities and their career potential.

Training Solutions-Oriented Workers

When problems *do* arise, you can minimize their burden to you or your boss by thinking in terms of solutions. Whenever possible, insist that your people bring you solutions along with the problems. If they keep dumping problems in your lap, don't automatically accept each problem and start trying to solve it.

If the decision can be postponed, ask the person to come back later with a list of all the possible solutions she or he can think of, along with the advantages and disadvantages of each. Ask for a ranking of the solutions according to their chances of success. If possible give the worker time to sleep on it and the next day or so go over the list and help her or him analyze the advantages and disadvantages of each solution.

If action is needed immediately, sit down

with the worker and try to get her or him to come up with at least one possible solution. Ask the worker to identify the advantages and disadvantages of any proposed solutions and to recommend one over the others. Then give your opinion and jointly come to a decision. By taking people step by step through the same process you use to make effective decisions, you help train them to make decisions on their own.

On the other hand, at times you will need further information, expertise, or authority from *your* boss in order to solve a problem. Even when you lack vital information, try to show your boss that you are thinking in terms of a solution rather than merely dumping a problem in her or his lap. Try to come up with some ideas or solutions, even if you feel they are not the greatest. Present your ideas or solutions along with your thoughts and feelings about them.

Preventing Problems Through Participative Decision-Making

There are many advantages to training your people to solve problems and to make appropriate decisions. Not only can you establish a preventive attitude, but you can also provide a more motivating work environment for most people. In Chapter 8 we discussed briefly some of the benefits of providing subordinates with the information and guidelines they need to make the decisions necessary to carry out their job responsibilities. In Chapter 7 we discussed participative versus authoritarian management. The more that managers tend toward Theory Y, concern for people, and therefore a participative approach, the greater is the area of freedom for their people to solve problems and make decisions, as indicated in Figure 9-1. The most extreme example of managerial

FIGURE 9-1: Extent of Participation in Decision-Making

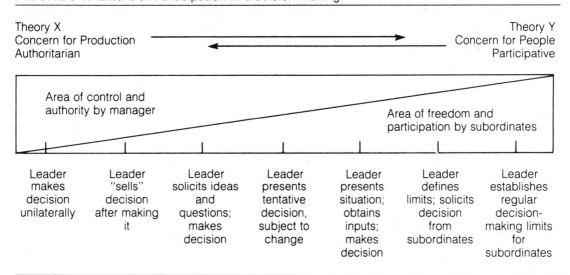

Adapted from Robert Tannenbaum and Warren H. Schmidt, "How to Choose a Leadership Pattern," *Harvard Business Review* (March–April 1958), p. 96. Copyright © 1958. Reprinted by permission of the President and Fellows of Harvard College.

control and authority is the leader who makes decisions unilaterally. At the opposite extreme is the leader who establishes regular decision-making limits for subordinates so that they have maximum freedom to make their own decisions and to participate in higher-level decisions.

You must use your own judgment about the degree of freedom each worker should have in making decisions in various situations. Sometimes crises do arise even with the best of planning, and it may be necessary for you to take charge and make timely, unilateral decisions. Moreover, some people need more training, experience, support, and encouragement than others before they are ready for increased decision-making freedom. If you keep these kinds of exceptions in mind, *as a general rule the more decision-making responsbilities you can train your people to handle, the more successful your group is likely to be.*

AN OVERVIEW OF THE PROBLEM-SOLVING/DECISION-MAKING PROCESS

So far our discussion has focused more on attitudes toward problems and their prevention than on the actual process of solving problems and making decisions. Perhaps the clearest way to view the problem-solving/decision-making process is to divide it arbitrarily into three major phases: (1) problem-solving, (2) decision-making, and (3) implementing (see Exhibit 9-1).

Let's look at each phase in detail, along with suggestions for effectively completing each step of the process.

THE PROBLEM-SOLVING PHASE

We've discussed the desirability of welcoming constructive criticism about work performance in your area of responsibility and of evaluating that criticism objectively and acting on it accordingly. One advantage of such openness is that it allows you to become aware of problems at an early stage of their development. Then you can analyze the problem to determine if it's merely a symptom of a deeper problem. Once you have defined the root problem, the best approach is to consult people who have valuable information about the problem and its possible solution and people who will be affected by the final solution you decide upon. After you gather the information you need to formulate possible solutions, analyze it carefully. See how many workable solutions you can put together. This problem-solving approach is outlined in Exhibit 9-1 as the first four steps of the problem-solving/decision-making process. Let's examine each step in detail.

Becoming Aware of the Problem

Managers typically deal with two distinct types of problems: (1) problems in implementing currently accepted policies, procedures, and approaches to achieving company, unit, or individual job objectives, and (2) problems in developing new, improved approaches to achieving objectives—approaches that might result in the ability to set completely new and different kinds of objectives.

Managers deal most often with problems of the first type. This category includes small, everyday problems such as maintaining workers' productivity, as well as occasional major problems such as dealing with a sudden, unexplained decrease in company sales. You need to be alert to problems of both types, however. If you're aware of how well objectives are being accomplished and of new and better ways of doing things, you're likely to recognize quickly the problems that need attention.

EXHIBIT 9-1: The Problem-Solving/Decision-Making Process

1. Becoming aware of the problem
2. Defining the root of the problem rather than its symptoms or results
3. Gathering information and consulting people who will be affected by the decision or have valuable information
4. Analyzing the information and formulating possible solutions

} Problem-Solving

5. Weighing possible solutions (alternative courses of action)
6. Selecting what appears to be the best course of action
7. Making a commitment to the success of the action plan

} Decision-Making

8. Communicating and selling the decision to those who will be involved in it
9. Directing the implementation of the plan
10. Evaluating the results of the action plan
11. Modifying the action plan in response to new situations and information

} Implementing

Each step should be taken separately and in proper sequence. The extent of participation by subordinates in each step will vary. Maximum participation that is feasible will give greatest payoffs in motivation and productivity.

Managers who do not dread dealing with problems are likely to be more open to recognizing and facing them. Therefore, it helps to view each problem as a need to be filled or as a challenge to be met. You can learn, grow, and profit from filling needs and meeting challenges. If you want to earn a reputation as a truly productive problem-solver—not just someone who puts out fires that should have been prevented in the first place—keep an open mind, be curious and inquisitive, and keep asking key, probing questions, both of yourself and of others.

Defining the Root of the Problem Rather Than Its Symptoms

Once you become aware of a problem, don't waste your time gathering information about it until you've satisfied yourself that it is not merely a symptom of a deeper problem. First ask, "Who is responsible and who has authority in this situation?" Is it really

your baby? If so, be sure to include in the problem-solving process the people who have some responsibility and authority for solving the problem and reaching the decision. Then try to get at the root of the problem by asking certain questions in the sequence shown in Exhibit 9-2.

This process of problem definition is similar to the one described in Chapter 3 for setting objectives and separately listing activities that can help you achieve those objectives. By keeping activities or approaches separate from objectives or purposes, you may delve deeper into the reasons behind your objective and realize that there are many more ways to achieve what you want than you originally thought. You may even redefine your objective. (You may want to look at the personal objectives you set in Chapter 2. Use the process shown here to see whether any of them should be redefined. You can also apply it to planning objectives, which are discussed in Chapter 10.)

EXHIBIT 9-2: Finding the Root of the Problem

Problem: What is the problem?

Purpose: What do you want to achieve in this situation? What is the purpose of solving this problem?

Why? Why do you want to accomplish this purpose?

Possible approaches: What approaches could accomplish this purpose?

Best approach: All things being equal, which approach will let you accomplish your purpose in the most effective way?

Redefine purpose: Having worked through the preceding steps, do you think the purpose needs to be modified?

Redefine problem: Do you think the problem needs to be redefined?

   Here is an example of the use of this method to define a problem.

Problem: Vince Dietz, head of the Accounting Department, has been by-passing Carrie and taking requests for information and other matters to her subordinate, Jack Ames.

Purpose: To prevent Jack Ames from taking over in areas where Carrie should be supervising.

Why: To maintain Carrie's authority and control over the work of her department.

Possible approaches: (1) Talk with Dietz about procedures to follow in making requests, etc. (2) Arrange a joint meeting with Ames, Dietz, and the General Manager in order to reach an understanding about procedures. (3) Instruct Ames to refer Dietz to Carrie in the future. (4) Ask the General Manager to instruct Ames and Dietz to handle requests through Carrie.

Best approach: Carrie decides her best initial approach is number 2, arranging a joint meeting.

Redefine purpose: To establish procedures for work assignments that all concerned understand and follow.

Redefine problem: Maintaining Carrie's authority and control over the work of her department.

Gathering Information and Consulting People

Once you have clearly defined the problem, the next step is to gather information in order to identify, explore, and develop as many workable alternatives as possible.

Pinpointing Information Sources   You need as many facts and knowledgeable opinions as you can afford to gather. *Decisions can be no better than the information they are based on. However, you must weigh the cost and time required to gather that information against its value in contributing toward a better decision.* How much potential profit and cost is involved in a decision? Obviously, you will want to spend more time and money gathering information in

order to select a new computer system, for example, than in selecting a new typewriter. Set appropriate time limits, then make a list of the most likely sources of the information you'll need, using Exhibit 9-3 for ideas.

Being Objective   Be sure you get the whole picture—not just the part you *want* to see. If you are in doubt about any important facts, double-check or cross-check. Look for another source, a person who has no personal involvement in the situation. For example, people in the Sales Department may exaggerate sales figures; people in the Production Department may inflate production figures and minimize errors and rejects. Double-check their reports by asking people outside their departments for the same information.

EXHIBIT 9-3: Checklist of Information Sources

Publications of all types	Personnel records:
Company files, newsletters, magazines, brochures	Staff selection, retention, and promotion records
Knowledgeable people in your company and other companies	Job descriptions, standards, and performance records
Other experts in the field	Absentee and employee turnover figures
Interviews and conversations	Union agreements
Library reference files	Annual reports to stockholders
Computer files	Press clippings
Company policy or procedures manuals	Universities and other institutions—the appropriate department

Keep asking questions until you're satisfied you have a fairly accurate picture of the situation. List appropriate questions, using those shown in Exhibit 9-4 for ideas.

Taking a Survey This is often one of the best ways to get information. Your survey may include people who have handled similar problems, experts in a particular field, or the people who will be affected by the decision you make in this situation. Get out and talk with these people; watch the people who will be affected as they go about their jobs. Experience for yourself the problems involved and people's responses to them. Give these firsthand impressions time to knock around in the conscious and subconscious areas of your mind. They can lead to flashes of insight and later help you put the pieces of the puzzle together.

Try brainstorming (which we'll discuss later in this chapter). This technique can be effective in the fact-gathering phase. Ask a person or a group to brainstorm facts that might be relevant to solving the problem. You can also use brainstorming to get advice and opinions. Sometimes the seemingly least likely fact or bit of advice turns out to be a key to solving a problem.

It's sometimes a good idea to give people time to think about the questions you are asking and then follow up later. People will often come up with more and better ideas and comments after they have mulled a question over for a while. Treat these inputs with respect and give immediate positive reinforcement for all sincere suggestions, advice, and information. Be careful not to commit yourself to following a suggestion or idea too soon, however. Give yourself time to collect all the facts you must have and to analyze and weigh them.

It's also wise to test people's reactions to your ideas about the situation by asking them what they think. But avoid giving the impression that you've already made the decision and just want support for it.

Consulting People This is perhaps the most important factor in the problem-solving/decision-making process. It gives you the best chance to get essential information and to get people involved. This suggestion is worth framing: *Before you make a decision, check out the facts you have gathered and ask for the viewpoints, advice, and information of the people who will be affected by the decision.*

You'll nearly always find there is something important you haven't grasped. Often you've missed important facts or gotten them wrong. By involving people, of course, you also make your job easier when you get to

EXHIBIT 9-4: Fact-Finding Questions

1. How is the problem situation similar to other situations? Different from others?
2. How long has this situation been in existence?
3. How did it get started?
4. What is its history?
5. What are the outstanding developments?
6. What are the major advantages of the current situation? The major disadvantages?
7. What are the major functions to be performed in this situation?
8. What functions are being neglected?
9. What is the situation related to, both in the past and currently?
10. What are the latest developments in the field that are relevant?
11. Are there opposing opinions?
12. What does the future appear to hold?
13. What further avenues should be investigated?

the later step of selling or communicating the plan. At the same time, you lay the groundwork for effectively implementing the plan. When people have been involved in making a decision, they're more likely to be cooperative, and even enthusiastic, about carrying it out than if it's handed down to them from "on high."

Analyzing Information for Possible Solutions

Once you have the necessary facts, your next step is to study them, analyze them, and use them to formulate creative alternate solutions. Don't evaluate at this stage. Save that for the next step.

Get into a Creative Mood Creativity is not some mystical quality enjoyed by only a few special people. All of us are capable of creative thinking and problem-solving. The key is to keep an open mind and a flexible attitude. You can allow your natural creativity to come forth by encouraging certain tendencies that, to some degree, we all have:

An open mind: Willingness to change viewpoints and approaches and to try new things and experiences

Curiosity: A spirit of inquiry, a realization that there is much to learn, a keen enjoyment of learning

Ability to concentrate: An interest in delving below the surface of situations, willingness to apply energy and effort to solve problems, an enjoyment of working on complex problems, willingness to spend considerable time alone thinking

Persistence: Willingness to keep working on a problem until a satisfactory solution is found, patience in working out solutions

Confidence: Willingness to risk being ridiculed by others for unconventional ideas and approaches, optimism and enthusiasm about finding and implementing solutions to problems

Cooperation: An ability to work productively with others to define problems, formulate solutions, and implement action plans; flexibility in adapting to the realities of situations.

Review Your Purpose and All the Facts Why do you want to solve this problem? What is the major goal you want to achieve? What facts are relevant? Organize them in a way that is meaningful to you so that you have them clearly in mind.

Analyze the Information Ask yourself what ideas, facts, or things can be put together or combined; changed, modified, or rearranged; substituted for something else. What items can be magnified, increased, made larger (advantages or assets); minimized, reduced, made smaller (disadvantages or faults); reversed, handled in exactly the opposite way; broken down into smaller parts and then each segment dealt with? Can any ideas or items be applied to similar problems or products? Can any be simplified, removed, or added?

Questions like these can spur your creative thinking. Another technique is to list advantages and disadvantages of the present situation or system. This may help you form a better picture in your mind of what the ideal solution should include.

Consider role-playing at this stage, either in your head or with another person. This can be especially effective when the cooperation of two or more factions is required. Pretend you are a key member of one faction. Discuss the current situation and each alternate solution from that viewpoint. Then take the role of a key member of the other faction and do the same thing. Get a debate going. Play the Devil's advocate. This technique can help you identify needs and concerns that pertain to the problem. As you answer the needs with suggestions to fulfill them, you will stimulate new ideas for a solution.

Investigate other special analytical techniques that might throw light on alternate solutions. You'll have a chance to review three of them (Program Evaluation Review Technique, Critical Path Method, and Force Field Analysis) later in this chapter. Exhibit 9-5 lists these and some other types you might want to investigate on your own.

Formulate as Many Alternate Solutions as Possible Don't stop when you have only one or two plausible solutions. Keep asking, "What else might work?" One of the most common barriers to effective problem-solving is putting unnecessary limitations on the number and variety of alternate action plans. Remember, at this stage *don't evaluate* the solutions that pop into your mind.

Write Down Alternate Solutions Each time a solution occurs to you, no matter how wild or far-out, write it down. Schedule definite times to work on the problem, but be ready to record ideas any time they occur—even in the middle of the night. Try to have note pads on hand in strategic spots.

EXHIBIT 9-5: Special Analytical Techniques

Experiments and pilot projects	Program Evaluation and Review Technique (PERT)
Test runs	Critical Path Method (CPM)
Decision matrix	Force Field Analysis
Model making	Other types of flow charts and structured analytical procedures
Algorithms and decision trees	
Problem analysis and synthesis	Other quantitative and statistical techniques
	Other computer-based techniques

Verbalize Possible Solutions After you've had time to analyze the facts and think about alternate solutions, discuss them with people. Strangely enough, you may find yourself describing an action plan you weren't even aware you had formulated until you started talking! Or you may find that you've selected one without being aware of it. The act of discussing the problem and its possible solutions in a relaxed atmosphere at this point may help all the pieces fall into place for you.

Following these steps should result in a top-notch list of alternate solutions. Next you're ready to make a decision.

THE DECISION-MAKING PHASE

Making decisions involves letting the alternate solutions "simmer" for a while, then weighing them, and finally selecting one. In this section we will examine specific techniques you can use for doing this, and pitfalls you'll want to avoid.

Weighing Possible Solutions

Some of the techniques for analyzing the information may be appropriate for evaluating the effectivenss of alternate solutions before you decide to adopt one of them.

Relax and Forget the Problem for a While Once you have formulated as many alternate solutions or action plans as possible, shelve the whole project for a few hours, days, or weeks, depending on the magnitude of the problem and your time targets. If you choose a course of action too soon, you'll be overlooking one of your major assets—your wonderful brain and its ability to process information at a subconscious level. Some people call this waiting time the

"incubation period." Others say it is a "simmering" process that leads to illumination, insight, regeneration, and the crystallization of ideas.

Turn your mind to other activities and forget the problem as completely as possible. If it's a major creative project, plan some activities or pastimes that are especially relaxing and pleasant to you. At least try to get a good night's sleep before you make your selection. If you have a tight time schedule, get it clearly in mind, tell yourself that you will come up with the best solution on time, then forget it. Most people find that the best solution will indeed pop into their minds unexpectedly and within the time target they specified.

The optimal simmering time needed for different types of projects varies for each person. Pay attention to your timing needs by noting the time-lag between when you shelve a problem and when you get a flash of insight or inspiration about how to handle it. The time-lag is *not* wasted time, especially if you are productively working on other matters. Once you get back to the problem after the proper simmering period, you'll come up with a far better action plan in a fraction of the time it would have taken if you had hurried into that phase too soon.

Weigh the Alternatives There are several evaluative techniques that will let you weigh alternatives.

1. *List the goals and* **criteria** *for making the decision.* Criteria are specifications of the quality a good solution would have. They help distinguish between good and bad alternatives. They are the standards a solution must meet in order to be acceptable. How well does each alternative measure up? Exhibit 9-6 shows a **criteria matrix** for accomplishing this.

   The matrix is a table in which the alternative actions, solutions, or selections are

EXHIBIT 9-6: Criteria Matrix for Weighing Alternatives

Step 1: Determine the criteria for making the decision. List them across the top of the matrix, one criterion per column.

Step 2: Determine what alternatives are available. List them vertically below the "alternative" heading.

Step 3: Rate each alternative on how well it meets each criterion. Use either "yes" and "no" or a scale of 1 through 5 for rating.

Step 4: Find the total number of "yes" responses or the sum total for each alternative by adding across.

Step 5: Rank each alternative from highest to lowest.

Numerical System for Rating Each Alternative

5 = Highest Rating

4 = Good

3 = Fair to Middling

2 = Poor

1 = Lowest Rating

| | Criteria | | | | |
Alternative	1. Less Than $10,000	2. Will Work Well for at Least 5 Years	3. Good Editing and Storage Functions	Total for Each Alternative	Rank of Each Alternative
CBX Magtape	1	5	4	10	1
Vymax Display	2	2	3	9	2
Ramses Memory	2	2	1	5	4
Xerxes Model Z	4	1	1	6	3

listed vertically as line headings. The major criteria that have been decided upon for measuring each alternative are listed horizontally as column headings. The criteria matrix allows you to organize and display all the alternatives and criteria related to a decision. Within the matrix, you record your evaluation of how well each alternative meets each of the criteria by assigning each evaluation a number. You then total the numerical ratings for each alternative and rank them accordingly. You should not decide automatically that the top-ranking alternative is the one to select because you'll need to weigh other factors too. But you can clarify complex situations and weigh alternatives with greater objectivity when you use the criteria matrix as a selection tool.

The criteria matrix shown in Exhibit 9-6 was developed by a group of workers who met with their manager to solve a written communications problem. They decided that the goal was to improve efficiency and timeliness of written communications through purchasing electronic typing equipment. They established three criteria for selection of the equipment: The unit must (1) cost less than $10,000, (2) stay relatively free of repairs for at least five years, and (3) have storage and editing functions to meet their needs.

Four types of electronic typewriters appeared likely to meet the criteria—CBX Magtape, Vymax Display, Ramses Memory, and Xerxes Model Z. The workers rated each one according to how well it measured up to their criteria and ranked each accordingly. They found CBX and Vymax to be the superior choices. Now they can concentrate on comparing these two alternatives.

In some cases, of course, one alternative emerges as the best choice and the decision can be made immediately. To simplify our example, we assumed that all criteria were of equal importance. In actual practice, however, the criteria can be weighted. In the example shown in Exhibit 9-6, if criterion 3, editing and storage functions, were considered twice as important as the other two criteria, you would place "× 2" above that column and multiply each number in the column by 2. The ratings for how well the four alternatives met criteria 3 would then be 8, 6, 2, and 2 respectively instead of 4, 3, 1, and 1. The total for each alternative would be 14, 12, 6, and 7 instead of 10, 9, 5, 6. Although the rank of each alternative wouldn't change in this instance, the degree of difference between the top two and bottom two alternatives is increased.

2. *List all events that are likely to occur in the future.* Include all events that might affect the action plan. Try to categorize events that have a cause and effect relationship or are related in some other meaningful way (see Exhibit 9-7). Which action plan would be best for each set of events?

This process can help you clarify how well each action plan fits with various types of future developments and circumstances. It can help you weigh the risks involved in adopting each action plan.

3. *List all possible consequences of each plan.* Project yourself into the future and visualize the plan in action. Try to foresee consequences and list them.

4. *Compare* **opportunity values** *of alternate action plans.* Keep in mind that when you select one plan you commit resources that would otherwise be available to take advantage of alternate or unforeseen opportunities. Try to estimate the potential value of the opportunities you'll be forced to pass up. Are the payoffs from your selected action plan worth it? Ask yourself and others some key questions: What would happen if we didn't do anything about this problem? What risks are involved in each plan? What payoffs are probable from each? What resources will we need for each? What limitations will be necessary for each? What tradeoffs are practical between the time and money invested and the possible payoffs for each

---

EXHIBIT 9-7: Factors to Consider When Weighing Alternatives and Risks

Costs, expenses, potential profits	Attitudes and reactions of the people involved
Available resources	Long-range consequences
Budgets	New problems that the action plan may create
Trained staff or workers	Union contracts and relationships
Tools and equipment	Morality and legality
Facilities	
Efforts involved	
Impact on company objectives and policies	

plan? What specific conditions require specific actions?

Keep the timing factor in mind. Although you don't want to jump to the commitment phase too soon, you must be aware of the consequences of postponing the decision. Sometimes putting it off is disastrous. At other times postponing can be a blessing because it allows you to take advantage of new developments, new information, and—perhaps most important —new insights and ideas that occur to you or your people.

5. *List the advantages and disadvantages of each action plan.* Include the people who will be involved, if possible. Make your list as complete as you can.

6. *Clarify how each action plan will be carried out.* Answer these questions: Who will be responsible for each phase? How will they carry it out? What will they do? When will they do it? Where will they do it?

Considering these questions can help you select an action plan that can be carried out. The people who will be responsible for carrying out the action plan must be capable of doing so. Assess the strengths and weaknesses of your people.

The action plan must also be acceptable to the people who will carry it out. You must be sure you will have adequate resources to implement your plan. In addition, ask yourself how flexible each action plan is and how much it will cost in money, time, and effort to change the plan if new developments and conditions call for change.

7. *Review your purpose in solving this problem.* Remember what you wanted to achieve in this situation. Which action plan is most likely to lead to the achievement of those objectives?

Selecting the Best Course of Action

The next step is to choose the option that best meets the objectives and priorities of the situation. If you have followed the step-by-step process and suggestions given here, the best solution will probably become fairly obvious. Occasionally, one action plan stands out as far superior to any others. In most situations, however, you will have to think in terms of *degrees* of effectiveness rather than right versus wrong solutions. Since you will rarely find a perfect solution, you will have to be willing to take calculated risks.

Holding out for the perfect solution is only one of the decision-making traps to beware of. We'll review typical traps poor decision-makers get caught in, as well as suggestions for making especially difficult decisions.

Poor Decision-Makers Many of the common decision-making traps managers fall into occur at the selection stage. In *Developing Decisions for Action*, Phillip Marvin describes typical types of poor decision-makers [8, pp. 30–42]. Here is Marvin's analysis, adapted for the woman manager.

The *decisionless decider* is the manager who keeps putting off decisions without proper regard to the optimal timing for making decisions. She overlooks the fact that making *no* decision is actually deciding to go along with the status quo, at least for the time being.

The *priority fumbler* is the manager who is not clear about objectives and priorities, fails to put first things first, and overlooks the fact that a short-range decision may have a long-range impact.

The *detail person* is the manager who, as she moves up, keeps making detailed decisions for her subordinates instead of focusing on higher-level decisions.

The *wheel-oiler* is the manager who avoids making decisions whenever possible. She makes decisions only when people complain loudly and long enough. She "oils the squeaky wheel" by attempting to solve the problem they are complaining about. This means that the problems that most need solving may be neglected. Only problems considered important by the loudest, most aggressive people in the company may be addressed.

The *perfectionist* is the manager who keeps waiting for the perfect solution. She thinks in terms of right and wrong solutions rather than degrees of effectiveness. She may become a facts junkie, going overboard in gathering more and more facts before making a decision. She overlooks the high cost, the time factor, and the possible loss of opportunity while she is looking for a riskless decision. She tries to substitute facts for her own good judgment.

The *know-it-all* is the manager who mistakenly thinks she knows enough about the situation to make a decision without investigating or consulting people. She is "sensitive to the situation" or "has a feel for the problem" and doesn't want to be bothered with the facts.

The *mare with blinders* is the manager who is so concerned with her bailiwick that she doesn't see the big picture. She therefore neglects to consider all the dimensions of the problem and its impact on others outside her department. She overlooks both positive and negative factors that should affect her decision.

The *yesteryear expert* is the manager who doesn't take into consideration the constantly changing conditions that affect business decisions. She made some effective decisions in the past, and she keeps looking back to those successes rather than looking forward to current and future conditions.

The *face-saver* is the manager who becomes ego-involved in her decisions and thinks in terms of right versus wrong decisions. If she makes a poor decision, she clings to it like a survivor clinging to a sinking ship. She may surround herself with "yes people" who keep telling her that she is right.

The *ball-dropper* is the manager who makes a good decision and then drops the ball by not following through by effectively communicating and selling the decision to those who will be affected by it. She therefore fails to properly implement her plan.

Do you recognize any of these characters? We've all seen people who have fallen into one or more of these traps. Of course, *you* can avoid these decision traps by following the suggestions given in this chapter.

Now evaluate your own decision-making approach by completing Exercise 9-1. Then compare it with those of typical Chief Executive Officers and successful entrepreneurs by checking the decision-making profile shown in the answer key.

Difficult Decisions In some situations the best solution is so difficult to determine that you will have to rely heavily on your own judgment in reaching a decision. You probably have an edge over your male peers here since judgment involves intuition.

When you use your intuition effectively, you're in good company. Recent research indicates that the higher a manager goes in an organization, the more she or he relies on soft data and intuition in making decisions [10, p. 96]. Most top-level decisions involve broad policy matters rather than operational details and have such general implications that managers cannot depend on hard facts and figures alone in reaching them. Although effective executives certainly won't ignore relevant facts and figures, they must also take into consideration the feelings and opinions of other people, information gleaned from the company grapevine, and their own feelings and intuition.

EXERCISE 9-1: DISCOVERING YOUR APPROACH TO DECISION-MAKING

Each numbered pair presents two opposing attitudes or actions. Decide which attitude in each pair best reflects the way you respond to decision-making situations and the extent or frequency of that response. Then place an "X" in the appropriate space.

	Usually	Frequently		Frequently	Usually	
1. Solve problems.	___	___		___	___	1. Capitalize on opportunities.
2. Generally dissatisfied with things as they are.	___	___		___	___	2. Satisfied with things as they are.
3. Don't care what others think.	___	___		___	___	3. Want to know what others think.
4. Get things going.	___	___		___	___	4. Avoid making waves.
5. Want to continue doing what I'm doing.	___	___		___	___	5. Want to shift to more rewarding activities.
6. Keep learning within my area of expertise.	___	___		___	___	6. Still in the process of searching for my best area of expertise; quickly bored.
7. Tend to do things in well-tested ways.	___	___		___	___	7. Tend to develop new ways of doing things.
8. Get ready for tomorrow's job while doing today's job.	___	___		___	___	8. Concentrate on today's job.
9. Do it myself.	___	___		___	___	9. Seek available counsel and advice.
10. Do what I'm told to do.	___	___		___	___	10. Make continuing reappraisals of the value of what I'm doing.
11. Adhere to rules.	___	___		___	___	11. Will break rules; rules are only guidelines.
12. Avoid risk as a matter of principle.	___	___		___	___	12. Accept "calculated" risk when it may optimize achievement.

Some people are startled to discover that top executives depend on intuition so much. It's not surprising to others who believe that intuition is actually the result of a process of analyzing and synthesizing information and experiences that are stored in the brain's memory—and doing so at lightning-fast speeds—at a subconscious level. In other words, intuition may be a short cut to problem-solving and decision-making, not a completely different process. If this is true, top-level executives who rely on intuition are actually relying on the vast knowledge, information, and experience stored in their brains, as well as on a high level of intelligence and an ability to relax and tune in to what their subconscious is trying to tell them.

The time to use your judgment and intuition is when no one solution stands out as unquestionably better than the others. For example, the decision that is needed may not be the obvious one or the easiest one to choose. In some cases there may be no "good" decision; you may have to select the "least worst" option, which may even be sticking with the status quo. If many people have been geared up to anticipate a change, you may find this difficult to do. When you firmly believe that no change is best, however, it's a good idea to have the courage of your convictions and convince the people involved that you have made the best decision.

When it's impossible to tell which solution will turn out to be the best one, decide arbitrarily. If necessary, flip a coin. The essence of a good decision is timing. Once it is time to make a decision, don't falter, waiver, or dither. Decide! Then commit yourself wholeheartedly to making the decision work.

Making a Commitment to the Success of the Action Plan

Once you have sidestepped the pitfalls and have selected a solution, you must be committed to making it succeed—even if you flipped a coin to decide. This doesn't mean you should stubbornly refuse to see that the action plan is not working or that you cling to a sinking plan as the "face-saver" does. You must remain flexible to changing conditions and open to new information. At appropriate intervals you must reevaluate the plan and modify it when necessary.

Making a commitment to the success of the plan means giving it the best you've got, so it has the best chance to succeed. If *you* are not committed to making the plan work, you can't expect others to become committed. Your attitude comes through to the people who must implement your plans: Commitment and enthusiasm can be contagious. Your leadership may make the decision work out even if it was not the best one available.

THE IMPLEMENTING PHASE

If you'll always include the implementing phase when you think about the problem-solving/decision-making process, you'll avoid dropping the ball the way so many managers do. Often managers tend to think that, once they've solved a problem and made a decision, what remains is merely detail work for subordinates to carry out. However, even the most brilliant problem-solving and decision-making achievements can be worthless if the manager fails to direct the effective implementation of the action plan.

Communicating and Selling the Decision

Once you're firmly committed to your decision, you are in a good position to convince others that your plan is a good one. If you do so effectively, you help ensure that your plan will be carried out successfully. Plan to announce the plan to your people as a group, then follow up as necessary with individual meetings and written instructions.

Briefing People in Groups If you brief and instruct people together rather than separately, you'll save yourself innumerable communication problems. When everyone knows what everyone else is responsible for, it's easier for them to coordinate their work and to cooperate with each other to carry out the plan. Also, many heads are better than one; the questions of the various members of the group will help clear up vague or uncovered aspects of the plan. Overlooked points tend to surface and can be dealt with.

Another advantage of briefing people in groups is that you avoid the false rumors, the needless chitchat on the office grapevine, and the resulting possibility of misunderstandings and ruffled feelings that frequently occur when decisions are communicated piecemeal. For this reason it's a good idea to call your meeting as soon as possible after the decision has been made—before people hear about it from some other source.

In your briefing, you may want to cover these seven points: (1) the specific objectives to be achieved in this situation, (2) the action plan you've decided on, (3) time targets for the plan, (4) changes that will take place— where and when, (5) how the plan will be carried out, (6) who will be affected, and (7) why this course of action was selected to solve the problem.

The "why" of the decision is often overlooked by managers. This is unfortunate because people rarely become committed to implementing a decision unless they understand how it was reached and why a particular action plan was selected. At this point it's up to you to sell the "why" of your decision. Point out all the benefits and advantages of the action plan.

As you prepare for the briefing meeting, put yourself in the place of those who will be attending. Be sure your briefing adequately informs each of them about (1) what is going to happen to them and the reason why, (2) what they are responsible for and when, (3) any worries and misunderstandings they may have. You might want to try your briefing out on your secretary or another trusted confidant to see whether there are any noticeable gaps in the information you intend to convey. Since you have been immersed in the problem, it's easy for you to overlook points that may be vague or unclear to others.

Be sure to cover the major effects of the action plan as well as the side effects. If you are unclear about all the side effects that may occur, at least deal with this point in the meeting and give a tentative date as to when resulting side effects will be known and handled. If you fail to address these issues, people may go away feeling very insecure about what's going to happen to them as a result of the decision.

Following Up If the plan is complex, you'll need to meet with individual subordinates on a one-to-one basis to develop specific objectives for each individual. Everyone responsible for implementing the plan must be clear about the results they're aiming for and how these results contribute to the achievement of the specific objectives for the action plan as a whole.

Follow up this briefing with a written confirmation of the action plan. Include key points, who is responsible for what, and time targets. However, do not rely on a memo initially to communicate the action plan without first holding a briefing. It's important to communicate face to face when you first present your plan so you can sell the decision, answer questions, and clear up any misunderstandings.

Directing, Evaluating, and Modifying the Plan

Once you have communicated and sold your action plan, you must follow through by directing the people who will carry out the plan. Be sure that action commitments are clear to everyone involved. Spell out (1) who is responsible for what specific results, (2) exactly what each person will do, (3) when they will do it (give target dates), and (4) where they will do it.

If your action plan involves many changes, they may have to be phased in one step at a time. If the plan will be implemented over a period of time, you must fix target dates for the completion of each stage. Mark your calendar or follow-up file and check to see what progress has been made at each stage. Where appropriate, make the rounds and observe what is happening and how people are carrying out the plan. Be prepared to work out problems that arise. Use the appropriate management and supervision techniques covered in other chapters of this book.

Even then your job is not finished, because there's only one sure thing about the business world: It is constantly changing. Therefore, your action plan should be subject to continuing review and update as required by changing conditions. Once you decide on a plan, don't close the door to revising it later. A good plan is flexible enough to be changed as times and conditions demand. Here are some suggestions for evaluating the results of your decision.

1. Keep your purpose firmly in mind.

2. Look at the specific objectives you developed for your action plan. How well are they being achieved?

3. Are target dates being met?

4. How well are the people responsible for carrying out the plan doing? Is each person achieving his or her individual objectives on target? If not, why?

5. What new or unforeseen factors are affecting the plan?

6. Do the objectives need to be modified or changed?

7. Does the plan need to be modified or changed? In what way?

8. How will any proposed changes affect other aspects of the plan?

Treat any major modifications just as you would a new problem and resulting decision. In other words, go through the entire process again, remembering to consult people as well as to communicate and sell the modification to the people who will be affected by it.

FACILITATING GROUP PROBLEM-SOLVING

So far we have discussed problem situations in which the manager takes the major responsibility for solving the problem. In many situations there's a high payoff for involving your people in the problem-solving process. Although management specialists agree that managers should make the *final* decisions in matters involving two or more subordinates, it's usually best to include them in some phases of the process.

Assessing the Desirability of Group Input

You as manager must decide the optimal level of group input in each problem-solving/ decision-making situation. In each situation ask yourself, "Which phases of the process might benefit from group effort—defining the problem, gathering information, analyzing the information, weighing possible solutions?" In the process of setting unit or department objectives, you might include your subordinates in all these steps.

At times you will undoubtedly be involved in group problem-solving and decision-making with your peers and colleagues. You can take a leadership role in these sessions if you are aware of effective approaches and techniques for group work. Whether you are leading subordinates or working with peers in one or more steps of the process, however, it is critically important to keep the steps separate and in sequence. Separate information from opinion or evaluation. If the group is evaluating a solution, be sure they know about *all* solutions and discuss them before evaluating *any* of them. Display all alternate solutions on a flip chart, chalkboard, or overhead projector so everyone can be clear about them.

Identifying the Type of Decision Needed

As a manager you must also be alert and aware of the best approach to each problem-solving/decision-making situation. You must define that approach to the subordinates involved in the process leading to a decision. Here are five distinct types of situations, each calling for an approach that is quite different from the others.

Debatable Decisions (Finding a Better Way) These are decisions to be reached when there is general agreement about the goal and methods for dealing with a problem. For example, everyone agrees that the goal is to increase sales by 10 percent and that the major method is through developing new accounts. The group needs to decide on a better way to build these new accounts.

Encourage the group to specify productivity objectives. In joint meetings with the leader of the group, each member makes quality and quantity commitments with time targets. After that there may be occasional joint meetings, but people generally coordinate their efforts by communicating and cooperating directly with each other. It's up to the manager in charge to encourage professionalism, commitment to shared group objectives, concern for the quantity and quality of actions, as well as efficiency and effectiveness.

Exploratory Decisions These are decisions to be reached when no agreed-upon method of dealing with the problem exists. For example, everyone agrees on the goal of finding a new product to develop and market, but people are unclear and undecided about the best way to go about it. Use brainstorming techniques in order to explore as many alternatives as possible.

Negotiated Decisions These are decisions to be reached when people are strongly divided and in conflict about methods or goals. Each side is committed to a different course of action even though the values or logic of both are generally acceptable to all.

For example, one group wants to adopt a new group insurance plan that provides increased benefits but will require larger monthly contributions from both the company and the employees. The members of the other group agree that increased coverage is valuable and understand that it will cost more. However, they strongly believe that their monthly insurance costs should not be increased and that the current insurance coverage is adequate for most employees.

Negotiated decision-making calls for an impartial leader or chair who follows parliamentary procedures. If the number of people in the two factions is unequal, each group should have the right to veto any vote that they don't agree with. The goal is to reach a compromise acceptable to both sides. The leader should encourage participants to express their viewpoints frankly and to be open to opposing viewpoints and compromise solutions.

Also, participants should be encouraged to see conflict as a healthy and natural process for free-thinking individuals rather than as a disaster. You can point out that conflict can lead to better decisions because the ramifications of various alternatives are more thoroughly explored.

Routine Decisions These are everyday decisions for which there are adequate guidelines, rules, procedures, or policies to provide a framework for making a choice. For example, hiring new workers, preparing production schedules, or making ordinary purchases. When there are no new significant factors to consider or any major changes involved, the decision falls into the routine category. These decisions rarely require a great deal of time or energy, although they may require going through each of the steps.

Emergency Decisions These are decisions to be reached in problem situations that call for clear, quick, and precise action to prevent or handle a crisis such as an injury, accident, or breakdown. Your goal is to have *no surprises*. Apply Murphy's Law and try to anticipate every type of crisis that could occur. With each plan of action, visualize you and your people carrying it out and all the problems that could arise. Decide in advance how you'll handle crises that could occur even though every precaution has been taken. For example: What will you do if the computer is down when the payroll is due? What if there's a fire? What will you try to save if there's time? How will your people get out? What procedures will they follow? By thinking ahead in this way, you avoid making poor snap decisions.

Selecting Appropriate Tools for Group Action

Once you've identified the best approach to reach the type of decision needed, you're in a position to review specific techniques that can facilitate group problem-solving and decision-making. Your job as a manager or team leader is to select or suggest techniques that are most appropriate to each type of decision situation, the people who are participating, and the problems involved. Here is a summary of some group techniques that may be valuable to you (Consult the business or educational section of your library for more details about these techniques.)

Procedure-Setting The group should decide on procedures at the time it is formed and before beginning the problem-solving or decision-making process. A major question the group should consider when setting procedures is: Who will make the decision? *One person* who has the authority and responsibility for seeing that it is carried out? If so, who is this person? Is the authority and responsibility clear? *The majority?* If so, will a vote be taken? *The entire group?* Is consensus essential or possible? *The minority?* Can the objections of a minority cause one of the alternate solutions to be dropped? If an alternate solution is mentioned and there is no response or comments, does that mean it will be dropped?

Problem Determination The chair gives everyone an opportunity to state what problems or matters pertaining to a problem should be discussed. Group members can state what aspects of the problem should be included and what alternative problems, solutions, or issues should be considered. The chair has a recorder list and post each suggestion so everyone can see all suggestions. These items may be used to guide discussion at the current meeting or to set a future agenda. This technique gets people involved and participating.

Force Field Analysis The group is asked to think of any driving forces in the problem situation that tend to push toward improvement. These items are listed on a flip chart. Then the group identifies restraining forces in the situation—forces that resist improvement and change and keep the problem a problem (see Figure 9-2). These items are listed. Then the lists of driving and restraining forces are posted in a conspicuous place and kept in mind during the brainstorming phase.

Brainstorming This technique is especially helpful when creative ideas are needed. If Force Field Analysis is being used, the group will be looking for actions likely to strengthen the driving forces for improvement and to reduce the restraining forces that are resisting improvement. The goal is to come up with as many ideas as possible within a specified time period. A recorder is designated to list *all* ideas on a flip chart. The ideas are then posted where everyone can see them. The group suspends all judgment and criticism of ideas and encourages the flow of ideas.

After the brainstorming phase, members may participate in an evaluation phase. Then they give each idea a critical look and evaluate it for feasibility, practicality, and probable effectiveness. Sometimes ideas are combined, modified, or ranked in order of preference.

Buzz Groups If you are working with a large group, there might be times when it would be effective to divide into small subgroups to discuss a specific aspect of a problem or solution. This technique tends to increase involvement and participation and to reduce the inhibiting and cumbersome factors present in working with large groups. The purpose of the discussion may be to brainstorm new ideas or to evaluate and discuss each item in more detail than the larger group might be able to spend time on. Such buzz groups may discuss the same item, or each may be assigned a different item to discuss.

After the discussion, one member of each buzz group reports back to the group as a whole. These reports may mention which issues members agreed upon and which issues need further discussion.

Listening Teams This is another technique that involves forming small groups. When you begin the meeting with a guest lecturer, panel discussion, or other informational presentation, the participants may have difficulty grasping and remembering all the information presented to them. To eliminate this problem, listening teams can be assigned to pay special attention to particular

FIGURE 9-2: Force Field Analysis

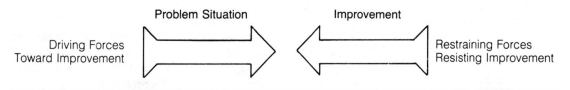

aspects of the presentation. Members can later serve as resource persons when the discussion moves to the aspects they were assigned to pay attention to.

Before the presentation, form teams and assign each team a different listening task. One group may listen for causes of the problem, for example, another for possible solutions, and a third for the possible results of each solution. After the presentation, each group takes a few minutes to prepare a master list of their recollections. When discussion begins, all members of the team serve as resource persons on the team's assigned topic.

Individual Polling This technique can be effective in conflict situations and situations where a negotiated decision may be necessary. It is used to get the viewpoints of *all* members, regardless of their shyness or their intimidation by the more powerful group members.

The chair asks each person to list the advantages and disadvantages of each solution being considered. After twenty minutes, the lists are turned in. A reporter posts a master list of all advantages and disadvantages.

Next, members have ten minutes to rank all advantages and disadvantages from highest priority to lowest priority. These lists are turned in, and an "average" master list is made while members take their break or address other issues. The rank-ordered lists are posted and used as the basis for discussing alternative solutions. The discussion now reflects the viewpoints of all members, regardless of their status or degree of assertiveness.

The Two-Column Method This method may also be used in conflict situations where two distinct viewpoints have developed. It can help all members see that each position has merits as well as weaknesses. The chair asks each person to express favorable and unfavorable points about each position. A re-

corder places two columns on the chalkboard or flip chart, one column for each position. Each point mentioned is placed in the appropriate column. The goal is to list as many points as possible in the shortest time. The list forms the basis for discussion of the merits of each viewpoint, how to resolve differences, and comparison of the advantages and disadvantages of each position.

This procedure gets all the items on the table before members get bogged down in arguing over one point or another. It tends to reduce the tendency to become firmly attached to one viewpoint, and it facilitates compromise and negotiation.

Action Plan Risk To facilitate the implementation of the decision, you may wish to learn what each member sees as the major "risk" involved with adopting and carrying out the action plan decided upon. These concerns can then be discussed by the group one by one. This technique can help you nip in the bud any unfounded fears and perhaps uncover serious reservations of members that can't be easily overcome. If these kinds of barriers to implementing the plan exist, you need to know about them and deal with them *before* you adopt the plan.

PERT and CPM PERT (Program Evaluation and Review Technique) is a good technique for reviewing all the steps necessary to carrying out a complex plan. It deals with the sequence in which steps should be performed, how long each step will take, and what resources and materials are needed. The steps are outlined in a flow chart.

CPM (Critical Path Method) is used to set time targets. Sometimes two or more of the steps or tasks necessary to implement the plan can be performed at the same time. The "critical path" is the cumulative time path for the most time-consuming task in each group of tasks that will be performed simultaneously. By following the critical path on the flow chart, the manager can determine the total number of work days the project will require.

PERT and CPM involve setting a target date and working backward from that date to see when each task must be initiated. Here are the major steps [9, p.15].

1. Determine the final step—in other words, how the solution should appear when it is fully operational.

2. List any events that must occur before the final goal is realized.

3. Arrange these events in chronological order.

4. Develop a flow chart of the process and all the steps in it.

5. List all the activities, resources, and materials needed to accomplish each step.

6. Estimate the time needed to complete each step.

7. Determine which steps can be accomplished at the same time. Add all the estimates to get a total time for the implementation of the plan.

8. Compare the total time estimate with deadlines or expectations and correct as necessary (for example, by assigning more workers to a task or by allowing less time for a given step).

9. Determine which members of the group will be responsible for each step.

Using Work Performance Teams

A special tool—for both solving problems and increasing productivity—that deserves special mention here is work performance teams (similar to "Quality Control Circles" used in some companies). The groups may consist of from three to seven workers (and their supervisor), who volunteer to meet approximately one hour a week on company time. Here are some key points for successfully using teams.

Ask the group to tackle a fundamental question, such as "Why are we getting so many customer complaints?" or "Why are we making so many errors on the customers' accounts?" Be prepared to deal with hostile replies, but listen for helpful ones. Focus on constructive problem-solving so the meeting doesn't become merely a gripe session.

Start with one experimental team. Once it is working well, you can add others to tackle other problems. Comprehensive programs at some large companies are structured in this way: (1) A consulting firm oversees the initiation of the program. (2) A coordinator has overall administrative responsibility for the program. (3) A training coordinator develops and implements the training materials and techniques to be used. (4) Facilitators receive two 40-hour training courses, one in the classroom and the other in actual practice. Facilitators help the supervisors or managers to set up teams and to operate them until they're ready to function on their own. (5) Team leaders receive a 24-hour leader-training course. They also meet once a month for additional training and to share their experiences and techniques with other leaders.

If your company will not or cannot establish a full-blown productivity improvement program, what aspects of the program can you establish and implement within your own unit or department?

Include a union representative if your people are union workers. Unions can sabotage the implementation of the teams' suggestions and probably will if they view them as a threat to their members or an attempt to weaken the union. For example, uninitiated union representatives may feel that some solutions could lead to an increase in members' work quotas or that the increased productivity resulting from the team suggestions could lead to layoffs. They may also fear that the teams will lead to direct negotiations between workers and management, by-passing union involvement.

Integrate the program into your departmental planning and control system. Don't just tack it onto the present system as an added gimmick. One way is to adapt all successful ideas to suit the department's special needs. Another is to have workers set objectives and standards that integrate the solutions developed by the teams. Reexamine the program periodically. Are teams dealing with the most crucial problems? What other problems might be dealt with? Finally, integrate the system into your performance appraisal system so that bonuses, raises, and promotions are based on the increased productivity coming out of team solutions.

SUMMARY

Many women believe the myth that they are not good at rational, logical, cool-headed problem-solving and decision-making. This misconception, however, can easily be overcome. The techniques and procedures for reaching effective decisions are easily learned. Not only that, the higher an executive goes, the more the decisions to be made are based on soft rather than hard facts. Since women have usually received a great deal of reinforcement for sensitivity to people's feelings and the use of their intuition, they have a special advantage in making these kinds of decisions. The main thing for the woman manager to keep in mind is the importance of communicating with people about her problem-solving and decision-making activities in a logical, rational, and businesslike manner.

According to Murphy's Law: "If anything *can* go wrong, it *will*." If you use Murphy's Law to anticipate everything that can go wrong, it can help you to (1) prevent many problems and (2) handle problems that do occur with minimal disruption. When you're tackling new projects, highly visible projects, or pet projects of a boss, it's especially important to take time to apply Murphy's Law.

Your attitude toward preventing problems, rather than allowing crises to occur and then galloping to the rescue, affects all your subordinates. Be sure to give more favorable attention and rewards to individuals who prevent problems than to those who merely cope with them. Your boss may be delinquent in this area. Nevertheless, be sure to let him or her know when *you* are preventing instead of coping.

Train your people to think in terms of solutions rather than in terms of problems. Require them to formulate at least one solution for each problem they bring to you. Do the same when discussing problems with *your* boss.

The sequence in which you tackle a problem and arrive at a decision is one key to success. For best results, use this sequence: (1) Be alert to problems. (2) Define the problem, not its symptoms or results. (3) Gather information and consult people who will be affected by the decision or have valuable information. (4) Analyze the information for possible solutions. (5) Weigh possible solutions or alternative courses of action. (6) Select what appears to be the best course of action. (7) Make a commitment to the success of the action plan. (8) Sell or communicate the plan to those who will be involved. Brief in groups first; if necessary follow up individually and in writing. (9) Direct the implementation of the plan by making assignments, setting target dates, and checking to make sure proper progress is being made. (10) Periodically evaluate the results of the action plan. (11) If necessary, modify the plan to respond to new situations and information.

It's impossible to have a really participative style of management without involving your people in the problem-solving/decision-making process. Doing so will increase the motivation of your people—and their productivity. In each situation ask yourself, "Which phases of the process might benefit from group effort?" Identify the type of decision needed so that you can determine the best approach to take. Ask whether the decision is debatable, exploratory, negotiable, routine, or emergency. Then review the techniques or tools commonly used in group problem-solving and select those that will be most helpful. Consider establishing work performance teams as an ongoing means of preventing and solving problems.

ADDITIONAL EXERCISES

EXERCISE 9-2: THE MANNING CASE

Mary Manning has her work cut out for her. Her proposal for a campaign to publicize the Laura Lee line of resort wear was accepted by the Executive Committee, thanks to the support of Jan Arguello. This is Mary's first chance to gain some real visibility at Lighthouse Designs. Some members of the Executive Committee were skeptical about her ideas, but they went along at Arguello's insistence.

Manning works days, nights, and weekends for the next two weeks mapping out complete plans, procedures, and strategies for the campaign. When her plans are complete, she calls the people who will be working with her, one by one, and tells them about their duties and responsibilities in carrying out the campaign. She sends memos to the Regional Sales Managers explaining the campaign and giving instructions for cooperating.

The Laura Lee campaign is scheduled to begin on November 1 with simultaneous fashion shows, news releases, and department store advertisements. Suddenly Manning starts experiencing problems. For example, some of the Regional Sales Managers haven't coordinated the department store ads in their localities with the New York fashion shows and press releases. Some of the styles pictured in the ads and planned for the fashion shows are not ready in time, so customers become confused about what styles are available. Worst of all, Mary doesn't learn about any of these problems until it's too late to remedy them.

1. What do you see as some of the sources of Manning's problems?

2. How could she have handled the situation more effectively?

3. What effect do you think this project will have on her status at Lighthouse?

4. Can she recoup her losses or redeem herself? If so, how?

Compare your responses with the answer key in the back of the book.

EXERCISE 9-3: MAKING DECISIONS UNDER PRESSURE

You left Monday morning for a one-week company-sponsored training program in supervisory leadership. Your department was turned over to Rose, but she became ill and went home. It was then turned over to Ken, but his mother became critically ill, and he flew home. You were called two hours ago to return on an emergency basis. You arrived five minutes ago. The time is 1:00 p.m. The day is Friday. As you walk into your office, you face ten immediate problems.

These problems are listed below. First read, evaluate, and decide on the relative importance of each problem. Then decide on the sequence in which you would handle the problems. Take only five minutes to read the problems, rank them in order of importance, and set up a sequence for handling them. Put your responses in the appropriate spaces to the left of each problem.

Compare your responses with the answer key in the back of the book.

Order of Importance	Sequence of Handling	Problem
_____	_____	A. You have received a report from Peggy in Personnel that Scott is looking for another job outside the company. She wants you to talk to him. You figure this would take you about fifteen minutes.
_____	_____	B. Your boss left word that he wants to see you in his office immediately upon your return. Anticipated time: sixty minutes.
_____	_____	C. You have some very important-looking un-opened mail (both company and personal) on your desk. Time: ten minutes.
_____	_____	D. Your telephone is ringing.
_____	_____	E. A piece of equipment has broken down, halting all production in your department. You are the only one present who can fix it. Anticipated time: thirty minutes.
_____	_____	F. A most attractive young man is seated outside your office waiting to see you. Time: ten minutes.
_____	_____	G. You have an urgent written notice in front of you to call a Los Angeles operator. Both your mother and the company headquarters are located in Los Angeles. Time: ten minutes.
_____	_____	H. Jim, head of Production, has sent word he wants to see you, and has asked that you return his call as soon as possible. Time: ten minutes.
_____	_____	I. Ann, one of your workers, is in the women's lounge and claims to be sick. She wants your permission to go home. It would take at least fifteen minutes to get down there and get the facts.
_____	_____	J. In order to get to your office by 1:00 p.m., you had to miss lunch. You're very hungry, but figure it will take at least thirty minutes to get some substantial food.

REFERENCES

1. Adams, James L. *Conceptual Blockbusting.* New York: Norton, 1979. Adams, a Stanford professor, discusses various types of blocks to creative problem-solving. He then provides individual and group "blockbusters" that provide breakthroughs to better ideas.

2. Albert, Kenneth J., ed. *Handbook of Business Problem Solving.* New York: McGraw-Hill, 1980. In this book, ninety top managers describe how to solve complex business problems in every major business function.

3. Arnold, John D. *Make Up Your Mind!* New York: AMACOM, 1978. An excellent, practical process for reaching decisions, using seven basic building blocks.

4. Bloch, Arthur. *Murphy's Law.* Los Angeles: Price/Stern/Sloan, 1979. A humorous look at the trials and tribulations of managers. Reading this book can help you feel that you are not alone; it can give you a few laughs; and it might even give you some insights.

5. Cornell, Alexander H. *The Decision-Maker's Handbook.* Englewood Cliffs, N.J.: Prentice-Hall, 1980. This text focuses on quantitative tools such as cost/benefit analysis, present value, and systems analysis.

6. Dean, Douglas, et al. *Executive ESP.* Englewood Cliffs, N.J.: Prentice-Hall, 1974. Dean and his associates at the Newark College of Engineering used scientific approaches to obtain reliable information about the effects of extrasensory perception on executive decision-making.

7. Huber, George P. *Managerial Decision Making.* Glenview, Ill.: Scott, Foresman, 1980. A well-rounded discussion of decision-making. The chapters on decisions involving multiple goals and especially risky or uncertain situations are particularly helpful.

8. Marvin, Phillip. *Developing Decisions for Action.* New York: Dow Jones–Irwin, 1971. An excellent source of ideas and techniques for making managerial decisions.

9. Seibold, David R. "Making Meetings More Successful: Plans, Formats, and Procedures for Group Problem Solving." *Journal of Business Communication,* Vol. 16, No. 4 (Summer 1979), pp. 15–17.

10. Tannenbaum, Robert, and Warren H. Schmidt. "How to Choose a Leadership Pattern." *Harvard Business Review* (March–April 1958), p. 96.

Chapter Ten

Planning and Organizing for Results: Productivity Through Performance Planning

> *"A woman is known for the company she organizes."*
>
> *Pamela M. Suber*

The two keys to effective managerial planning are (1) focusing more on end results than on activities and (2) including your subordinates in the planning process, rather than doing it yourself and then telling them. To use the first key, you should understand the difference between efficiency and effectiveness. Peter Drucker has defined it this way:

Efficiency = Doing things right

Effectiveness = Doing the right things

Think about it. How many people have you known who focused on increasing their speed and accuracy in completing detail work, yet failed to move ahead in their careers? The promotable woman looks at the total picture and sets her objectives and priorities to assure she is doing the right things—those things that will move her toward her top objectives.

In this chapter you will have the opportunity to

1. Learn the basic components of planning systems

2. Develop clearly stated job objectives and performance plans

3. Design appropriate standards and controls for achieving objectives

4. Understand how participative performance plan systems operate

5. Learn the bases for organizing work— organizational structure, departmental structure, and individual job design

6. Understand tactics for using your planning and organizing skills to best advantage

The Best-Laid Plans

Carrie smiles as Brian, her assistant, walks through the door. "Say, Brian, you did a great job of handling that Resort/Holiday Fashion Preview. There was no sign of Murphy's Law in action."

"Thanks to your coaching," Brian responds. "But I guess there's no rest for the weary—what's this I hear about a new line of sportswear?"

"Oh, the new Viva line. I think it will be a real winner, and headquarters is planning to spend plenty to promote it. Now we've got to decide how we're going to promote it at the regional level. We need to develop some departmental goals for this line, set quotas for each of the sales people, come up with job assignments for the other personnel in the department, and work out the details for advertising, merchandising, and generally promoting the line."

"Wow. And when do we need all this—yesterday?"

Carrie laughs. "Almost. I'm calling a staff meeting two weeks from today; so you and I should meet every morning till we get our plans in good shape."

Two weeks later, Carrie and Brian are rehashing the staff meeting held earlier in the day.

"Do you think they really understood our goals for the Viva line, Brian?"

"Well, they must have. Only two or three people had questions—and those were on minor items."

"We did cover everything didn't we?" Carrie looks over her notes. "Explanation of the new line and its target market, departmental goals, quotas, job assignments. Somehow I thought there would be more discussion. I just feel the others aren't as enthusiastic as we are."

A month later, Carrie and Brian are going over sales reports for the Viva line.

"Brian, I'm a little disappointed in these figures. I thought we'd be getting bigger orders than this by now—and more of them."

"Maybe the sales reps need a little motivating."

"Well, I've been praising those people who seem to be paying special attention to the Viva line. And I've called in several who aren't and stressed its importance. I don't know. Part of it may be that we didn't get as much budget money for the promotion as we requested. And I have to fight for any support from Advertising and from Administrative Services. How can I support my sales people properly if I can't get the support I need myself?"

At the end of the quarter, a couple of the top sales people are discussing the salary/commission situation:

"You know, Dickeson *talks* a lot about rewarding performance, but when it comes to recommending people for raises, she pays a lot more attention to who gets their paperwork in on time," says Frank Andreini.

"Yeah," responds Ken Cypert, "and a lot depends on who she likes to have lunch with. Like Joe—I just found out he was recommended for a bigger raise than I was. I think I did a better job pushing the new line than he did!"

Frank shook his head. "These women are hard to figure out. I'm never sure exactly what she's looking for or how well I'm doing."

"Yeah," agreed Ken. "I'm getting pretty fed up. I think I'll start looking around."

Word of dissatisfaction filters back to Carrie. She's not surprised; she's been sensing it for some time. She picks up the phone.

"Jan, I'm in trouble. I need help, and you're the best person at managing sales that I know. When can we get together?"

---

1. What planning strategies do you think Carrie has overlooked? _____

2. How has her method of planning affected the motivation of her people? _____

3. Is she using good decision-making strategies in formulating her plans? _____
   Explain your response. _____

4. If you were Jan, what suggestions would you make to Carrie now? _____

THE PLANNING PROCESS— AN OVERVIEW

All the planning skills in the world will do you no good unless you have a positive attitude toward planning so that you actually use your skills at the right time. Therefore, we'll first analyze attitudes toward planning, including why managers don't plan when they should and the payoffs for planning before taking action. Next, we'll look at the planning process as a system that involves the whole organization. You'll see how an ideal system of organizational planning might work. Then we'll discuss in more detail some key aspects of planning, and you'll have a chance to improve your planning skills by applying planning techniques to actual situations. First, to stimulate your thinking further about payoffs for planning, complete Exercise 10–1.

Why Plan?

In one sense, effective planning is the essence of good management. It is impossible to manage without planning. If you don't plan properly, then you are managed by the circumstances that surround you, instead of managing your environment to achieve your objectives and make the full contribution you're capable of making. Since it's so vital to good management, why do you suppose planning is so often neglected by managers?

To Make Things Happen Some managers are frightened by "thinking big." Setting up a year's objectives and action plans overwhelms them. Some managers don't like the risks involved in committing themselves to challenging objectives. They're more comfortable with day-to-day or week-to-week activities. What they call "objectives" may be merely intentions or hopes to complete certain activities. Such managers will never be leaders who make things happen.

An anonymous wit has been quoted as saying, "There are three kinds of people: (1) people who make things happen, (2) people who watch what is happening, and (3) people who ask, 'What happened?'" Of course, you want to be a manager who makes things happen, not a passive observer. When you plan effectively, you make those things happen that you want to happen. You get the results you intend to get.

Planning is more important than ever in these times of rapid change. New technology, products, and services are increasingly available. Other products, services, and ways of providing them are becoming obsolete. Companies are reorganizing, eliminating some old jobs and creating new ones. All aspects of modern business are touched by rapid change.

You can make plans to anticipate these changes and take advantage of the opportu-

EXERCISE 10-1: ANALYZING ATTITUDES TOWARD PLANNING

Why don't managers take time to plan when they should?

1 _____

2 _____

3 _____

Why should managers take time to plan? When should planning be done?

1 _____

2 _____

3 _____

nities they offer. Such plans can give direction to your own activities and to your subordinates' activities. By planning to anticipate and create change, you avoid becoming a passive victim of its effects. Instead, you *make things happen*.

To Become Promotable Managers who don't take adequate time to plan don't fully understand that it can put them in control of their destiny. When managers focus on activities—the "doing" of their jobs—they have little chance of creating constructive changes that will make them visible to top management. Such changes require effective planning, which in turn is based on well-conceived, clearly stated objectives. Other managers say they rarely have time to sit down and plan. They haven't learned that adequate time spent planning complex projects or tasks saves time in actually doing the job. Planning efforts pay off, also, in better results. In a nutshell, the ability and tendency to plan well are key factors in being pegged for promotion.

To Provide an Effective Framework for Decision-Making You won't always have as much time as you'd like to work out a decision. If you have clearly stated job objectives, however, you can make good decisions even under pressure. You brainstorm possible courses of action. Then you select the alternative that seems most likely to move you toward your objectives.

To Eliminate Unpleasant Surprises Don't wait until crises occur to think about how you will handle them. As soon as you acquire new responsibilities, start analyzing the types of problems that could crop up, ways of preventing them, and your objectives for handling each of them. Then formulate plans you can put into action readily should the need arise. That way you won't be caught by surprise and perhaps make a poor crisis decision. The larger the organization, the less its top management likes surprises.

Managers who are caught by surprise can cause significant financial loss or embarrassment for the company and can find themselves quickly relieved of their responsibilities. Regardless of the size of your organization, you'll get more predictable results if you anticipate all eventualities. Then plan either to make them happen, to prevent them, or to cope with them.

To Give Direction to Motivational Drive
To get something you want, you must have both motivational drive and direction. When you select goals that have value and meaning to you and to your company, goals that are worth the effort, then you tie your goals to your drive to achieve. You give the necessary direction to that drive by taking time now to decide on future actions. Some people think of planning as "coming up with a lot of stuff I've got to do, stuff that I'll feel guilty about if I don't get it done." High achievers think of it as essential to getting what they want. If you can sell your people on this idea, you'll gain a group of eager planners.

You can use the type of planning we'll discuss here to increase your own productivity and that of your subordinates, even though your organization has no integrated planning system. The truth is that most organizations still engage in formal planning only at the top and inform middle managers of what they want from them. Then middle managers direct others in ways they hope will produce the expected results. Workers seldom see the big picture and frequently are unclear about why they are performing certain tasks. Formal planning, like anything else, can be overdone, but the problem in most organizations tends to be inadequate planning.

Suppose you're fortunate enough to find an organization that uses planning on a systemwide basis. In other words, everyone in the firm is involved in planning, and all plans are integrated so that they work together and support each other in achieving the organization's objectives. We'll look first at how such a planning process might be set up (see Figure 10-1). Then we'll look at the role supervisors and middle managers play in the planning process, ways of improving your planning skills, and how to help your workers become skilled planners. Since virtually every step of the planning process involves decision-making, you should first develop problem-solving/decision-making skills, which were covered in Chapter 9.

How an Organizational Planning Process Works

A system of organizational planning, as shown in Figure 10-1, normally begins with top management's selecting a mission and setting organizational objectives based on forecasts of business opportunities and the company's capabilities. Top management then develops strategies and policies to guide middle managers in carrying out their plans to support the objectives. In participative companies middle managers help formulate these organizational plans. Middle managers in turn call in supervisors to set departmental objectives and to develop tactics, rules, and procedures to guide supervisors in carrying out their plans to support department objectives. Next, supervisors include their work teams in setting unit objectives that support the department objectives. Each supervisor then meets with each worker to set individual worker objectives that support the work unit's objectives. Supervisors and workers also jointly develop the action steps, standards, and controls that will guide workers in the day-to-day activities necessary to attain individual and work-unit objectives.

Defining the Mission Initial organizational planning begins even before a company starts operating, of course, and begins with

FIGURE 10-1: An Organizational Planning Process

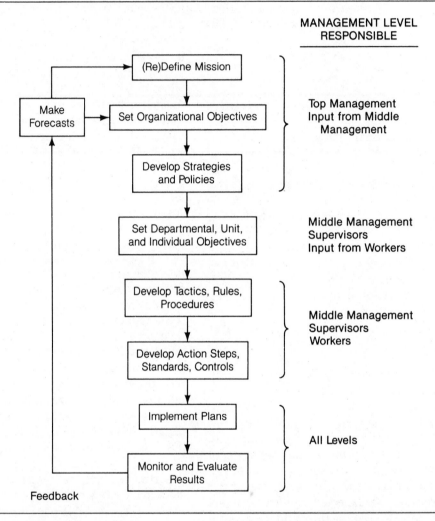

MANAGEMENT LEVEL
RESPONSIBLE

(Re)Define Mission

Make Forecasts → Set Organizational Objectives

Develop Strategies and Policies

Top Management
Input from Middle
Management

Set Departmental, Unit, and Individual Objectives

Middle Management
Supervisors
Input from Workers

Develop Tactics, Rules, Procedures

Develop Action Steps, Standards, Controls

Middle Management
Supervisors
Workers

Implement Plans

Monitor and Evaluate Results

All Levels

Feedback

top management's vision of the customer or client needs the company intends to meet—its reason for existence. This vision should include how the company differs from other, similar companies in type of customer, products or services the company provides, and/or the way it provides them. To be successful, a company should see itself as being at least slightly unique in some way. This

reason for being is often referred to as the company's mission—and defining it, along with making forecasts, is the first step in the planning process shown in Figure 10–1.

Successful companies not only manage to select an appropriate mission, they regularly reassess it as client needs, technology, and markets change—and they reformulate it when it begins to become obsolete. Lighthouse Design's mission was "providing women's clothing for the mass market in the top-of-the-moderate price range in misses sizes." This mission was effective for over twenty years, but recently they forecast changing demands and responded to them. Now they've expanded their mission to: " . . . in misses, petite, and large sizes."

Making Forecasts Top management is also responsible for developing effective forecasts about how much the company can expect to sell during the coming year(s); how much it can produce; what its needs for financing, supplies, and workers will be; and other factors necessary for effective planning. The middle managers whose departments deal directly with these aspects of company operations are of course called upon to help develop forecasts. The more accurate the forecasts, the more effective the company's objectives are likely to be. Challenging yet attainable objectives must be based on realistic forecasts.

Formulating Objectives, Strategies, and Policies Next, top management sets long-range (about five years) and short-range (usually one year) objectives for the entire organization, again with the input of the middle managers whose departments will carry out the resulting plans. Do you remember what you learned about stating effective personal goals in Chapter 2? We used the term "goal" there because it has a clear personal meaning for most people. In this chapter we'll use the term "objective" to discuss all types of organizational goals, from systemwide to individual worker goals. "Objectives" and "goals," as used in this book, have exactly the same meaning— that is, an end result we intend to achieve at some point in the future. Since most business organizations use the term "objectives" to refer to targeted business results, we'll use that term in this chapter.

After top management has developed forecasts, defined or redefined the organization's mission, and set long-range and short-range objectives, it develops strategies for attaining the objectives and policies to guide managers in carrying out plans. Strategies are broad decisions about the company's style or approach, including how to budget money, staff, facilities, and other resources. One Lighthouse Design strategy, for example, is "to work closely with retail store buyers in developing new fashion lines."

The activities required to achieve organizational objectives will be carried out at lower levels and are often expressed as objectives at those levels. An organizational objective of "to increase sales by 15 percent" will be supported by a number of Sales Department objectives. "To increase market share to 30 percent in the Western Region" might be one. What the Sales Department might view as activities for increasing the market share ("obtain $10,000 in orders from the Village Life clothing chain") would become an objective for a particular salesperson. That salesperson's activities in turn would be viewed as "call on every Village Life buyer at least once a month."

The planning process shown in Exhibit 10–1 can apply to nonprofit organizations as well as profit-making firms. Profit-making firms are primarily concerned with providing particular goods or services within specific cost and profit constraints. Their objectives reflect this by focusing to some extent on profitability and productivity. On the other hand, nonprofits are concerned mainly with cost constraints; the budget and funding are of prime importance. Their objectives revolve around providing a specific service within specific budget limits and reflect a higher relative stress on social responsibility.

Deciding on Tactics, Rules, Procedures Middle management is usually responsible for developing tactics, rules, and procedures for carrying out the activities that will lead to the attainment of the objectives. Supervisors and workers participate in this ongoing process to the extent that their work is affected (in companies that practice participative management). Middle managers are usually in the best position to identify effective tactics. For example, a tactic Carrie Dickeson used to carry out the organizational strategy of "working closely with retail buyers in developing new fashion lines" was "to invite key buyers to preview the colors and base fabrics to be used in new lines."

Setting Up Action Steps, Standards, Controls On the other hand, supervisors are often in the best position to develop or evaluate rules and procedures that affect their workers. And workers can often develop or improve upon action steps, standards, and controls for carrying out their jobs. However, supervisors are responsible for approving and monitoring these aspects of the planning process.

Monitoring, Evaluating Once plans are made, everyone in the company has individual objectives as well as guidelines for ways of achieving them. When objectives and standards are clear, specific, and measurable, and when the information necessary to monitor actual performance is readily available, everyone in the company has the tools to practice self-control and self-evaluation of their own performance. With effective worker self-monitoring, the supervisor's role can truly become one of resource person and coach. Performance problems might signal the need for joint problem-solving rather than reprimands. Actual performance provides feedback on how well plans were carried out and input for making new forecasts and setting new objectives.

DEVELOPING PLANNING SKILLS

Now that you have an understanding of how an organizational planning process works, let's focus on your role as supervisor or manager and the planning skills you need to work with your boss and your people on departmental, work-unit, and individual worker objectives. The key aspects of your role in the planning process, as shown in Figure 10-2, are helping people identify the contributions they can make; setting clearly stated, effective objectives; developing challenging, attainable standards for measuring performance; and establishing controls for monitoring performance.

Identifying Contributions People Can Make

The contributions a work unit or a department is able to make toward organizational objectives depends of course on what the individuals in that group can and will do. Chapter 8 gives suggestions for identifying the types of tasks that tie in to different kinds of needs that motivate people to perform, such as achievement, affiliation, and power. Chapter 12 gives further suggestions for assigning tasks.

The most powerful position you can take, however, in matching people to tasks, is to let them take the lead while you serve as resource person. So instead of initially suggesting contributions your people can make, ask them to do their own thinking about contributions. Not only will you get a more accurate picture of what they're able and willing to do, they're likely to see themselves as capable of making greater contributions than you could require of them. In turn, they're likely to set up more challenging objectives and standards for themselves than you could impose—and to attain them.

FIGURE 10-2: Departmental Planning Process

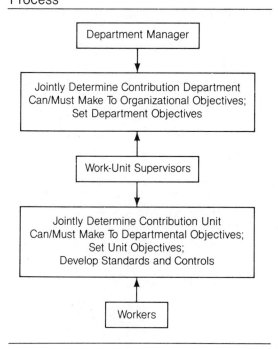

If you ask your people to identify any obstacles they see to making each contribution, you're likely to gain much valuable information about what your people are thinking, department problems that need solving, and ways of training and developing your people. Exercise 10–2 provides a structure for identifying possible contributions and obstacles to making them and for analyzing obstacles and attitudes. This exercise works well for managers too; so try it now for yourself.

Setting Clearly Stated, Specific Objectives

Clearly stated, specific objectives are the basis of all good plans, yet an amazing number of workers, and even managers, don't know what their boss expects of them, much less what her or his objectives are or how to formulate them effectively. How much do you know about the objectives of

EXERCISE 10-2: IDENTIFYING YOUR CONTRIBUTIONS TO THE COMPANY

Step A. Think about what you see as the greatest contributions that you, in your present position, can make to the company. List them in the left-hand column. Then ask yourself what obstacles are keeping you—or will keep you—from making those contributions. List them in the righthand column.

Contributions to the Organization	Obstacles to Making Those Contributions
1 _____	1 _____
_____	_____
2 _____	2 _____
_____	_____
3 _____	3 _____

Step B. Look at the obstacles you listed and answer a few questions about them. How many of them are *really* obstacles?

1. Do any of the obstacles originate within *you* rather than with external circumstances? How?

_____

2. Would changing your viewpoint or behavior remove any of the obstacles? How?

_____

3. Are any of the obstacles caused by a lack of clearly stated objectives?

_____

4. Think about your attitude toward your job when you believe you're making a contribution. Describe your thoughts and feelings.

_____

5. Think about your attitude toward your job when you believe you're "just working." Describe your thoughts and feelings.

_____

6. Think about your productivity and effectiveness when you believe you're making a contribution rather than just working. Describe the differences.

_____

the firms you've worked for? Complete Exercise 10–3 before we talk about techniques for writing objectives. Later you may want to rewrite the objectives in Exercise 10–3, stating them more clearly.

A format for stating objectives clearly and specifically is shown in Exhibit 10-1. The most effective objectives always include an action verb and a single key result that expresses just what you intend to accomplish, as well as a deadline date. Where possible your single key result (for example, "in-

crease sales") should include a standard that is measurable (for example, "by 10 percent," or "to $500,000"). Where possible, your objective should also include a measurable cost (for example, "at no increase in salary expense," or "using no more than 300 additional work hours"). After all, it's fairly easy to attain some objectives if you spend enough money on extra help, equipment, or advertising. If your boss expected you to do it with no increase in those budget items, you may be in trouble.

EXERCISE 10-3: OBJECTIVES THAT AFFECT YOU

Note: If you are not working now, use the last job you had for this exercise.

1. What is one organizational objective that your company as a whole now has? _____

   _____

2. What is one objective for your department or unit? _____

   _____

3. What is one personal, job-related objective that you have? _____

   _____

4. If you were unable to answer any of the above questions, is it because no objectives exist? _____ If they exist, how can you find out about them? _____

   _____

The best way to determine if an objective is specific enough is to ask yourself, "On the deadline date will it be clear to me and my boss whether or not I have achieved this objective? Is there room for argument? Will we agree on how close I've come or how far I've exceeded it?" A clearly stated, specific objective leaves no room for argument as to whether or not it has been achieved.

Using the model for stating objectives shown in Exhibit 10-1 and the examples of clearly stated, specific objectives shown in Exhibit 10-2, rewrite any poorly stated objectives shown in Exercise 10-4.

Planning with Your Boss   In the planning process described in this chapter, you as a work-unit supervisor or department manager (and your peers in your department) will be expected to meet with your boss in formulating the objectives for his or her department or division (see Figures 10-1 and 10-2). You'll need to help forecast opportunities, problems, and capabilities that involve your work area. Once the objectives have been set for your department or division, then it's your turn to meet with your people (as shown in Figure 10-2) to get their input on what the contributions and resulting objectives for your own department or work unit should be.

Planning with Your Work Team   Of course, it's quicker—and perhaps easier in the short run—to merely set the objectives for your unit on your own. After all, it's your re-

EXHIBIT 10-1: Format for Stating Objectives in Clear, Specific Terms

To: . . . (Action or Accomplishment Verb)
(Single Key Result)
By: . . . (Target Date)
At: . . . (Cost)

EXHIBIT 10-2: Examples of Objectives at Various Organizational Levels

Organizational Level	Departmental Level	Work-Unit Level	Individual Level
1. To increase total sales by 10% by June 1, 19xx, at no more than 2% increased overhead cost	To increase sales of SuAnne Sportswear by 10% by June 1, 19xx, with 2% increase in promotional costs.	To increase sales of SuAnne Sportswear in Nevada by 10% by June 1, 19xx, with a 2% increase in promotional costs	To increase my total sales to all outlets by 10% by June 1, 19xx
2. To reduce customer complaints by 25% during 19xx at no increased cost	To increase quality standards for SuAnne Sportswear during 19xx at no increased cost	To increase quality control inspections from 25% of pieces produced to 100% during 19xx by changing procedures for self-monitoring	To decrease defective merchandise that leaves my work station to zero during 19xx
3. To reduce operating costs by 8% during 19xx	To save the company $120,000 in computer costs during 19xx by installing a new input system	Install computer input system and have it operating by June 1	Write programs for accounting input to new computer system and have them debugged by May 1

sponsibility, and in many companies your peers will be doing just that. On the other hand, there's a great deal of long-range power to be gained from getting your people involved in setting the objectives for the work unit or department you manage. When people have a real, meaningful share in creating a plan, they are almost certain to become committed to making that plan work. So in the long run, you'll save time and get better results by taking time in the beginning to include your people in the planning.

In fact, the objective-setting session should include some development of action steps, standards, and controls that will make the plan work. A problem-solving team ap-

EXERCISE 10-4: MAKING OBJECTIVES CLEAR AND SPECIFIC

Do you think the following statements are clearly stated objectives? If so, write "o.k." beside the statement. If not, rewrite it, adding any assumed information you need. Remember to include measurable standards where possible.

1. Capture as much of the petite-size clothing market as we can. _____

   _____

2. Achieve maximum profit. _____

   _____

3. Increase the level of training for supervisors. _____

   _____

4. Improve the quality of our sweater imports. _____

   _____

5. Develop additional sources of supply. _____

   _____

6. Reduce the number of employee grievances. _____

   _____

7. Establish a research and development department. _____

   _____

8. Carry out assigned responsibilities within approved budget. _____

   _____

9. Conduct a market research survey. _____

   _____

10. Install a new computer system. _____

    _____

proach usually leads to good results. In fact, if your work group is large—over twenty or thirty people—you may want to ask work teams of five to seven each to work out proposals for plans that the entire group can then discuss and decide upon.

Planning with Each Team Member Once you've settled on the specific objectives for your work unit or department, it's time to meet with each of your people and to determine jointly what their contributions toward these objectives will be. Of course you should discuss individual contributions at the very beginning of your work relationship with each person. It's also a good idea to review and update understandings about these contributions and obstacles to making them. This review can provide the basis for setting the individual's objectives for the coming year.

After you've settled on three to five major objectives, let the worker take the lead in formulating the action steps needed to attain each objective. Although each objective will include some measurable standards, they may not be sufficient to cover all the action steps leading to the objective. So you'll need to reach an agreement about any standards needed for the action steps. For example, an objective of the shipping clerk at Lighthouse is "To ship all orders for SuAnne products so that customers receive them within the time specified on the order at no increase in shipping budget." One action step is "Package merchandise for shipping." What performance standards might be included here? "So that no merchandise is damaged because of inadequate packaging"? "Within an average of fifteen minutes per order"? The key is to look for the level of performance—how much and how well—the worker will be aiming for.

Next, the two of you must decide how the worker, and you, will know if these stan-

dards are being maintained. What sort of recordkeeping or feedback from others must be set up? But that comes under the heading of controls, which we'll discuss in the next section.

A word to the wise on setting individual objectives: *Keep them simple and few in number.* People can remember three to five simple objectives easily, and you want those objectives to be up front in their awareness every day. Then anytime they need to make a quick decision, such as what to do next, they can choose the alternative that will best move them toward one of their objectives. It's a good idea to rank the objectives in order of priority, for the same reason.

Later in this chapter we'll discuss individual performance plans, which are simply a comprehensive set of objectives and action steps developed or updated by each employee and approved by his or her manager each year. They include standards for quantity and quality of performance.

Developing Effective Controls

Controls are simply ways of determining how well plans are being carried out and when corrective or preventive action needs to be taken. Exhibit 10–3 shows some types of controls management uses for various purposes.

Standards provide the basis for controlling or monitoring progress toward objectives. Measurable standards can be expensive to measure and control objectively, especially quality standards. It makes sense therefore to weigh the costs of setting up control measures for standards against the payoffs the firm can expect from their use. In the tactic for conveying a company image mentioned earlier, for example, management must decide whether the cost of a client survey can be justified in terms of a probable

EXHIBIT 10-3: Types of Controls and Their Purpose

Purpose of Control	Form of Control
To standardize quality of product or service	Employee training, inspections, statistical quality control, employee incentive systems
To standardize performance	Production schedules, written procedures, inspections
To protect assets (from theft, waste)	Division of responsibility, dual authorization, auditing procedures, recordkeeping requirements
To limit individual power	Job descriptions, accounting requirements, policy directives, rules

short- or long-range sales increase. Or would it make more sense for the management team to use their subjective judgment in evaluating the effectiveness of the tactic?

Preventive Controls These are measures taken to minimize deviations from plans before they have a chance to occur. They in turn minimize the need for corrective action. Some examples include training and coaching individuals in performing their job responsibilities; providing job-related information; and setting up procedures and rules, such as those governing the handling of cash.

Corrective Controls These are measures taken to correct a significant deviation after it occurs. Since errors or deviations will occur occasionally, even with the best of preventive controls, checkpoints must be established to identify these deviations. In the manufacture of equipment, for example, the manager along with the workers must decide which parts can and should be tested before assembly of the equipment proceeds. In the textbook publishing business, the editor and author must decide at what stages of book development the materials will be sent to reviewers for evaluation.

The corrective control process often includes the following elements:

Define the subsystem. Is the control process established to monitor an individual's performance? A department's? The entire organization's? Or is it designed to monitor specific inputs (such as raw materials), production processes (such as assembly of certain parts or the actual performance of certain services), or outputs (such as inventory of finished goods on hand or service jobs completed)? The category you select is referred to here as the subsystem.

Identify characteristics to be measured. What are the most vital elements of the subsystem that account for most of the major variations in performance? How can they be measured most effectively and economically? Carrie determined that an up-to-date, accurate record of items sold by salespersons would help her know where efforts needed to be increased as early as possible. She arranged for salespersons to carry portable microcomputers with them when they call on buyers. Not only can they immediately enter items ordered, they can access the headquarters computer via a telephone modem and tell buyers what items are on hand for immediate delivery. At the end of each day, they report total items sold.

Set standards. What measures will you use for determining if the activities undertaken by the subsystem are acceptable— that is, if the quantity and quality of the subsystem's output is adequate to support organizational objectives? With input from all salespersons, Carrie and her sales people set quantity standards as part of departmental sales objectives. The one they set for this year, "To increase sales by 10 percent over last year," reflects a quantity standard of "10 percent increase." The quality standard is expressed in another objective, "To reduce customer service complaints by 15 percent." This approach assumes that customer complaints are a valid measure of the quality of service provided by salespersons.

Collect information. How will you get information on how well each of the selected characteristics of the action plan is being handled? From oral or written reports? Mechanical or computerized readouts? From the people who perform the activities? Inspectors? Auditors? Customers? Will feedback on performance be automatic—that is, built into the process? If not, how will it be activated or initiated? At what points in the process (checkpoints)?

Compare. Determine what differences exist between what is being done (performance) and what should be done (standards). If there are no significant deviations, then no further action needs to be taken except to continue collecting information.

Diagnose deviations and implement corrections. Determine the types, amounts, and causes of any deviations from standards. Decide on the best course of action for eliminating these deviations and determining how the new action plan will be monitored.

When establishing controls, try for the following: Establish as many preventive (versus corrective) controls as feasible. Set up checkpoints as early in the process as feasible. (Generally speaking, the sooner errors or deviations are caught, the easier it is to correct them.) Look for controls that can be built into the system, that give feedback automatically, that let the individual performer know almost immediately when a deviation occurs. Where appropriate, adopt controls suggested by the individuals or groups they're designed to monitor. You're more likely to get their cooperation in making the control work.

Built-in controls and worker participation in establishing controls foster self-control. And assuming that people are committed to achieving their job objectives, the more they can exercise self-control, the more productive they tend to be.

ORGANIZING FOR PRODUCTIVITY

An integral part of planning for results is determining how to divide the total work of the organization into divisions, departments, and work units. Top management wants to design the best structure for helping people work together to fulfill the firm's mission, carry out its strategies, and achieve its objectives. An organization's structure is the arrangement and interrelationships of its various parts and job positions. The structure defines the formal division of work activities and shows how all functions or activities are linked together. It also indicates the organization's formal hierarchy and authority structure and shows reporting relationships.

First we'll discuss some elements common to all organizations that affect their structure. Then we'll look at some key factors top management must consider when they organize and some types of organizational structure (ways of dividing into departments) you should be familiar with. Finally, we'll talk about ways of organizing the work within a department and a work unit, right down to designing individual job positions.

Structuring Organizational Activities

The structuring of activities begins at the top when management initially decides on an organizational plan and periodically re-evaluates and modifies it. To help you understand how this process works, let's look at some common elements that affect structure, some key factors in determining structure, and some ways of structuring activities into departments or divisions.

Elements of Organizational Structure Management normally must take into consideration at least five common elements of organizational structure when deciding how to organize its activities: (1) degree of job specialization, (2) degree of standardization of job procedures, (3) size of work unit, (4) type and extent of coordination of activities, and (5) degree of centralization of decision-making.

The first three elements, specialization, standardization, and size of work unit, pertain mainly to individual job positions or to work teams, so we'll discuss them in the next section. The fourth, coordination of activities, refers to ways management ensures that all departments and units work together to achieve organizational objectives. The fifth, centralization and decentralization of decision-making, refers to ways of delegating decision-making power. The more decentralized decision-making is, the more autonomy managers and workers at all levels are likely to have in planning, implementing, and controlling their own performance.

Key Factors in Determining Organizational Structure The five elements just discussed are experimented with and finally established in the process of designing an organizational structure. Four key factors that determine *how* they are decided upon and set up are the following:

The strategy for achieving the organization's mission and long-range objectives is important, especially in determining the lines of authority and channels of communication between various managers and subunits. It also affects how information flows along those lines and what mechanisms are used for planning and decision-making. For example, some companies have adopted a strategy of staying in close touch with customers in order to anticipate their wants and satisfy their needs. To implement this strategy, they may decide to divide activities according to type of customer to be served.

The technology used to create the products or services the organization offers especially affects the degree of standardization and specialization of work activities. It also affects the size of work units, the level at which decisions are made, and how units are coordinated. The rapidly changing technology of the computer-manufacturing industry, for example, creates a need for flexible structures that provide for experimentation and team problem-solving. Industries based on a more established technology may have evolved to a fairly high degree of specialization and standardization that is very efficient.

The people involved in the organization's activities affect every aspect of organizational structure. The attitudes, beliefs, and abilities of managers, workers, customers, suppliers, and others—and their need to work with each other in specific ways—must be taken into account. When the work of the organization involves large, long-term projects that require the expertise of people from various functional areas, for example, a matrix or project type of organization may work best. Any structural form that is highly decentralized and depends on worker participation in planning and decision-making must be staffed with people who believe such a system can work and who are willing to accept responsibility.

In the past most companies have viewed such factors as capital assets, products, competitive position, or unique technology as the foundation for success. Today organizations that focus on their human resources as the foundation for success are emerging as the leaders in their respective fields [9, pp. 263–264].

The size of the overall organization and its major divisions, if any, affects the need for specialization and standardization. Generally, the larger the organization, the higher the degree of specialization and standardization needed in order to maintain adequate control and coordination of activities. For this and other reasons, facilities with fewer than 100 employees are often perceived by workers as "better places to work," and levels of motivation and productivity appear to be higher [3].

Types of Organizational Departmentation
Organizations are usually divided into departments according to (1) the functions workers are to perform, (2) the products or services produced, (3) the location of the markets that are serviced, (4) the type of customer buying the products or services, or, most frequently, (5) some combination of these categories (see Figure 10-3). We'll pay special attention to the combination

known as a matrix structure, shown in Figure 10-4.

Functional departmentation is by far the most common and basic type of division of organizational activities. All persons engaged in one type of activity, such as sales, manufacturing, finance, personnel, and so on, are grouped into a department. Functional departmentation fosters a higher degree of specialization. For example, when everyone involved in sales belongs to one department, specialized sales skills may become increasingly sophisticated. If the firm becomes quite large, however, it may become difficult to coordinate sales of many products to large and diverse markets.

Product or market departmentation is usually used, therefore, when an organization becomes so large that basic functional departmentation is unwieldy. In small- to medium-sized companies the top managers are usually functional managers in charge of all sales or some other function for the entire company. In larger companies top managers may be in charge of a product line, all operations in a geographic location, or all operations for a particular customer category rather than heading up one functional area. Each of these divisions may have its own sales, manufacturing, accounting, and other functional departments. Each division may also be accountable for its own profits, operating almost as a separate business but with some direction from home office top management. Let's take a look at product or market divisions and some combinations.

Product departmentation is often used by large manufacturers, such as General Motors (Chevrolet Division, Cadillac Division, and so forth). It may also be used

FIGURE 10-3: Organizational Structure; Product Division Combined with Other Forms

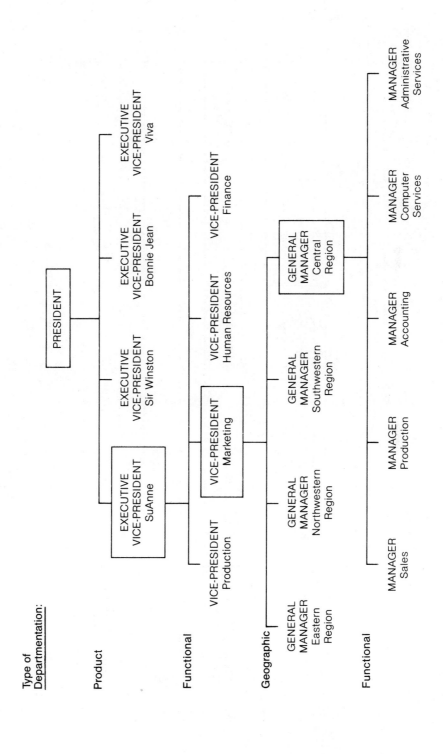

FIGURE 10-4: Matrix Organization

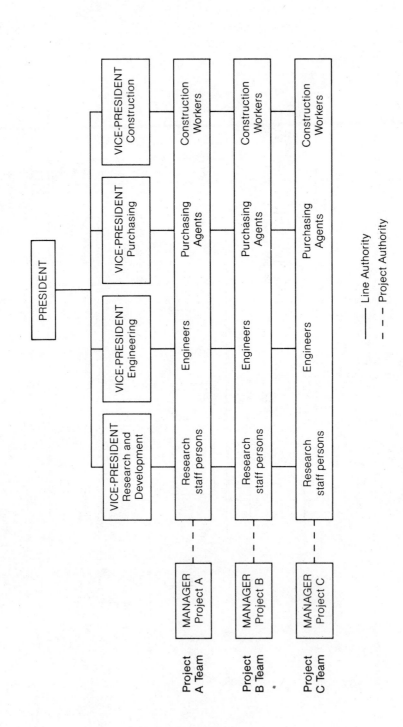

by large construction companies and other firms that engage in large, long-term projects; a department may be formed for each project. Lighthouse Designs has a SuAnne Division responsible for women's fashion wear in missy sizes, a Sir Winston Division responsible for men's sportswear, a Bonnie Jean Division responsible for women's fashion wear in large sizes, and a Viva Division for petite-size clothing. The partial organization chart shown in Figure 10-3 shows this division by product with further division of work activities by function and location.

Geographical divisions are formed when activities must be performed close to (1) major markets, such as bank customers or product buyers in foreign countries, (2) major sources of raw materials, such as oil to be refined or coal to be mined, or (3) specialized labor markets, such as computer specialists in the "Silicon Valley" area near San Francisco. When location is of prime importance, then each region may be headed by an executive vice-president with functional vice-presidents serving under her or him. In the example shown in Figure 10-3, the type of product is most important to the company, so regional division occurs further down the hierarchy.

Customer divisions may be formed when the operations involving various categories of customers are distinctly different. For example, a meat-packing plant may have different divisions for handling products going to grocery stores, to restaurants, and to institutions.

Combinations of these types of work division are used more often than a pure form. Normally there is a functional division at the top, with a vice-president overseeing sales of all kinds, for example.

Under that vice-president there may be a further division by product, customer, and/or geography. A combination that has received much attention because it violates a strict chain of command is the matrix structure.

Matrix structure is a composite of a basic functional structure with an overlay of project or product teams, each with its own project managers. This structure is frequently used by companies that contract for large projects (such as power plant or airport construction) that may last for months or years. Teams made up of various types of designers, engineers, skilled workers, and staff people are needed to complete the project. Each team member has a home base within a functional department (such as plant design or electrical engineering) but spends most of his or her time working with a project team. As soon as work on one project is completed, team members are normally assigned to a newly organized project team.

This dual structure, shown in Figure 10-4, complicates the chain of command because project team members report to two managers, the head of their functional (home-base) department and the project team manager. When an employee reports to two bosses, the authority and control of each boss can be weakened. The potential problems this situation might create must be weighed against the major advantage of bringing together specialized skills from various departments to focus on the problems of a particular project. Since these persons become a team, working together as a group, coordination problems are minimized. Also, each project is assigned only the number of people it needs, which minimizes duplication of effort and therefore costs.

Structuring Work-Unit and Individual Job Activities

Now let's talk about the design of your work unit (if you're in a small facility, it may be referred to as a department). Your structure of course will be based on your unit objectives and the tactics you'll use in attaining them. How much freedom you have to set these objectives and tactics and to organize your unit accordingly will depend on the philosophy of the firm's top management. The more you can involve your workers in dividing up the activities necessary to attaining objectives, the better.

During the organizing process, keep in mind the elements, key factors, and ways of departmenting we just discussed. Which concepts can help you determine the best way of organizing your unit's activities? Two elements of special significance at this level are degree of specialization and standardization. The degree of specialization addresses the question, How routine or complex shall various jobs be? The degree of standardization looks at the question, How much autonomy shall workers have in doing their jobs?

Degree of Specialization   Both during and after the objective-setting process, you and your people should jointly determine just what work must be done within the work unit in order to achieve its objectives. Next you must determine just how that work will be divided into tasks that individual or work teams will perform. Will each person get a large chunk of a task or project—a chunk that includes a variety of activities? Or will each person specialize in a small part of each project—doing that part over and over in project after project?

The answers to these kinds of questions can greatly affect the level of motivation and productivity in your unit. The more routine, or repetitive and specialized, the

job is, the easier it is to master and the more likely workers are to become quickly bored once they become expert at it. On the other hand, the more complex the job and the more varied the functions included in it, the more difficult the job is to learn and the longer it takes the workers to become productive. However, the challenge and variety are likely to be motivating to workers if they are able eventually to master the job.

Degree of Standardization   How much guidance and control will you exercise over the tasks you delegate? Will you design jobs that are highly standardized and controlled, thus providing the worker with guidance in tried and proven procedures? At the other extreme, job design can provide the worker with maximum autonomy in deciding how to achieve job objectives. Such a design may result in false starts and dead-end approaches but will enhance the motivation of most capable workers. The degree of standardization in most jobs falls somewhere between these two examples. Your decision will depend on the type of work to be done, the technology involved, the demands of the situation, the needs and abilities of your workers, and the attitude of top management toward worker participation and autonomy.

Job Designs That Motivate   Of course, you'll want to design jobs for the greatest employee motivation and productivity. You know from our discussion on motivation in Chapter 8 that workers are most likely to be productive on a long-term basis when (1) the work is meaningful to them, (2) they feel responsible for the outcome of their work, and (3) they get timely feedback on the actual results of their work activities. You also know that when job design calls for (1) a variety of skills and activities, (2) chunks of projects that are large enough for the worker to identify as his or hers, and (3) results that are viewed as significant, the worker tends to view the job as meaningful.

Work teams can be one solution to the problem of degree of specialization and standardization. Team members can gradually train each other in their respective specialties, for example, and then decide on how to rotate jobs to enhance skill variety. The work team can be responsible for a larger chunk of the work and therefore experience the feelings of pride, or disappointment and renewed determination, that go along with task identity and significance.

Once teams experience a sense of responsibility for what they produce, members usually begin to monitor each other, and peer pressure effectively replaces some of the external control that was previously necessary. Your role may become that of facilitator of group-planning, problem-solving and decision-making, and the teams may become relatively self-managed and therefore relatively autonomous. Such a design works best when teams operate democratically.

On the other hand, if your organization and its workers are committed to a traditional type of work structure, you will need to determine which jobs carry more authority and responsibility than others. Then establish a hierarchy for coordinating the activities of your unit. Delegation and building work teams is discussed in more detail in Chapter 12.

A PARTICIPATIVE PERFORMANCE PLANNING SYSTEM

A Participative Performance Planning System is one approach to planning that uses the type of planning process and the kinds of planning and organizing skills we've discussed so far. The performance plans developed by every person, managers and workers alike, are designed to support organizational objectives and strategies, as well as departmental, unit, and work-team objectives and tactics, as indicated in Figure 10-5. One major purpose of this system is to encourage people to think in terms of objectives and priorities instead of duties and tasks. Another major purpose is to provide the basis for self-appraisal and self-control of performance.

The development of individual performance plans includes the following steps, as shown in Figure 10-6: (1) Each employee meets with his or her manager for a one-on-one initial Planning Conference at which the employee presents an initial draft of a performance plan. The draft is jointly refined, and a Performance Plan is agreed upon that includes ongoing and periodic objectives and the action steps needed to attain them. (2) Regular, spontaneous conferences and coaching augment self-evaluation of the individual's achievement of objectives throughout the year. (3) One year later the employee and manager hold a one-on-one Yearly Planning Conference to discuss formally achievement of the past year's objectives and to plan the coming year's objectives. (4) At this conference they verbally describe the past year's performance and document it, along with the coming year's plan, in a Yearly Performance Planning Report.

The Performance Plan

It is all too common to encounter employees who focus on activities, duties, and tasks, some of which may be spelled out in a job description. Other employees are not even sure what their job description entails. It is relatively rare to encounter employees who are clear about their job objectives and priorities—who can reel them off on a moment's notice. Performance Plans are more comprehensive and results oriented than traditional job descriptions. A job description

FIGURE 10-5: A Participative Performance Planning System

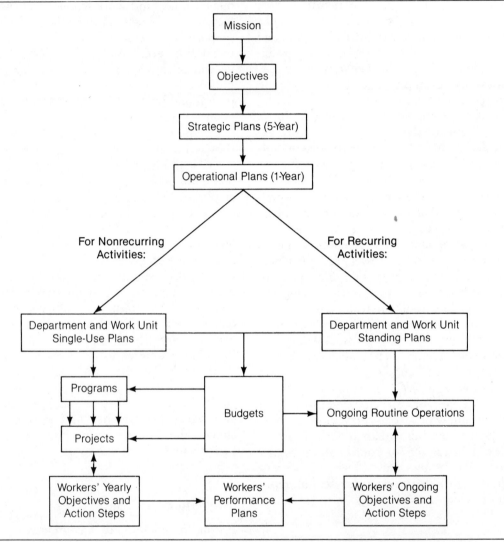

usually consists of a list of functional responsibilities and tasks with perhaps a statement of the level of education and experience required, as shown in Exhibit 10-4.

On the other hand, Performance Plans reflect the planning aspects of the job. They are operating plans that go beyond the job description by describing not only functional responsibilities (performance areas) but the key results that should be achieved in each area (performance objective). Performance Plans not only describe the tasks (action steps) entailed in the job, they relate the tasks to the achievement of objectives. In addition to these ongoing objectives, new organizational objectives are agreed upon

FIGURE 10-6: A Participative Performance Planning Process

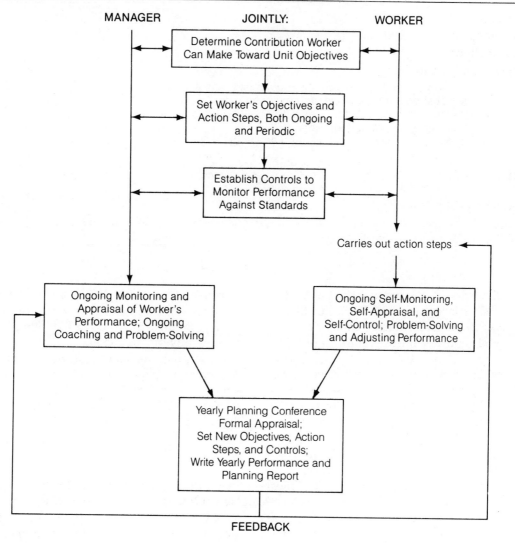

MANAGER   JOINTLY: WORKER

Determine Contribution Worker
Can Make Toward Unit Objectives

Set Worker's Objectives and
Action Steps, Both Ongoing
and Periodic

Establish Controls to
Monitor Performance
Against Standards

Carries out action steps

Ongoing Monitoring and
Appraisal of Worker's
Performance; Ongoing
Coaching and Problem-Solving

Ongoing Self-Monitoring,
Self-Appraisal, and
Self-Control; Problem-Solving
and Adjusting Performance

Yearly Planning Conference
Formal Appraisal;
Set New Objectives, Action
Steps, and Controls;
Write Yearly Performance and
Planning Report

FEEDBACK

each year, and the employee integrates these periodic objectives into his or her Performance Plan, as shown in Exhibit 10-5.

Ongoing (Standing) Plans When individuals sit down to prepare their Performance Plans, they start with their existing job de-scriptions, if available. If not, they must start from scratch in identifying performance areas (or functional areas) they are responsible for on an ongoing basis. These responsibilities support the organization's standing plans. The next step is to formulate a key objective for each performance area.

EXHIBIT 10-4: Job Description

Job Title: Buyer 1
Functional Area: Manufacturing
Subfunctional: Purchasing
Primary Responsibility:
Assist in obtaining materials, components, equipment, and services.
Check requisitions, obtain quotations, and examine bids.
Learn to coordinate purchasing activities with Manufacturing and Engineering Departments, maintaining inventory at planned levels.
As required, monitor the cost, schedule, and scope aspects of assigned subcontracts.
Job Level:
Entry level: Learn to use professional concepts and company's internal policies and procedures to solve routine problems.
Education/Experience:
Two years of college or equivalent. No prior experience necessary. Good writing and verbal communication ability preferred.

Individuals at the managerial or professional staff level may find it helpful first to list two major performance categories: professional and technical. The professional category includes the ongoing managerial functions present in every manager's job, such as planning, organizing, leading, and controlling. The individual should formulate a key ongoing objective in each major functional area for which he or she is responsible. Technical subcategories will vary according to the particular position. For example, an advertising manager's technical functions might include "identify target markets for xyz product; create advertising materials that will appeal to target markets; identify optimal media sources for advertising materials."

The next step is to develop a miniplan for each major objective. That miniplan must include what the individual will do to achieve the objective, deadline dates for key actions, and standards that state the level of achievement desired—the quantity and quality of output from these activities. It might also include tactics for achieving the

objective. One tactic might be to delegate certain action steps to subordinates or an ad agency; another might be to use only certain types of advertising media.

These plans make up the basic, ongoing performance plan for achieving recurring job objectives. The individual and his or her manager formally update it each year. It should tie in with the manager's performance plan and support the work-unit objectives.

Single-Use Plans (Special Projects, One-Time Objectives)   Individuals are also assigned periodic, nonrecurring responsibilities that contribute to the programs and resulting projects that are developed to meet nonrecurring organizational or departmental objectives. The other part of your performance plan will consist of specific objectives for meeting these responsibilities, along with key action steps for achieving each objective. For example, the objective "to develop an advertising campaign for ABC product" might call for the following action steps: (1) Select an ad agency using screening steps

EXHIBIT 10-5: Partial Performance Plan

Name: Jean Casey
Position: Buyer
Department: Purchasing
Performance Areas:

1. Production buyer
2. Responsible for past-due purchase orders
3. Maintain purchase price variance
4. Responsible for returning defective merchandise or overshipments of merchandise to vendor
5. Interface with Accounts Payable
6. Responsible for revision changes with vendor
7. Responsible for all change orders received from Production Planning Department

Performance Area 1:   Production Buyer

Ongoing Objective:

To purchase product materials in a cost-effective and timely manner in order to meet production work schedule determined by corporate requirements.

Action Steps:

1. After receipt of Traveling Requisition (TR) from Production Planning Department, contact vendor(s) (at least three) for pricing and delivery, after checking Approved Source List (APSL). Quotes may be verbal or written as required.
2. Select vendor, based on best price/delivery quotes and/or level of service offered.
3. Issue Purchase Order (PO) to vendor with TR data.
4. Complete TR card with vendor data.
5. Deliver TR card to Purchasing Clerk for computer entry and typing.
6. TR is returned with confirmation PO for signature and quotation summary if dollar amount exceeds $1,000.
7. Review weekly PO status report for accuracy.
8. Attend SuAnne production meetings when necessary.
9. Interface with designers and manufacturing engineers for verification of APSL or to establish an alternative material.
10. Consult with Production Planner as required.

Yearly Objective:

To decrease cost of materials purchased by 3 percent, without decreasing quality, during fiscal year 19xx.

Action Steps:

1. Contact other Lighthouse Designs buyers for vendor information.
2. Contact buyers at other manufacturing companies for vendor information.
3. When time permits, contact more than three vendors for quotes.

Note: Although detailed objectives and action steps for only the first performance area of this plan are shown here, detailed plans are developed for all performance areas.

listed below; (2) develop standards for acceptance of advertising materials from the agency, based on policy guidelines; (3) interpret marketing information from company sources and communicate it to the agency so they can develop appropriate advertising materials as evaluated by Executive Committee.

The formal written Performance Plan that is confirmed by an individual's boss may contain only major objectives and action steps, along with any standards that can be built in. But informal planning doesn't stop there; the written plan is merely the broad base for more detailed advance planning, for daily planning (see Chapter 13 for daily planning suggestions), and for monitoring of performance and results. Each broad action step may need a detailed plan of its own, with appropriate standards. These detailed action plans may be formalized into procedures for recurring objectives. Control plans should also be included in the Performance Plan, where appropriate. They should state when, where, and how performance will be checked against standards.

Ongoing Self-Evaluation and Monitoring

When the Performance Plan system is used effectively, it eliminates the individual's dependence on formal performance appraisals, which are generally ineffective and are usually dreaded by both employees and their managers. Instead of waiting for a formal performance appraisal to find out how the boss thinks they are doing, individuals are guided by the Performance Plan in practicing self-evaluation on a continuous basis. This continual self-evaluation is essential to the success of the Performance Plan system. The plan must become a guide for making

decisions, managing time, and allocating resources.

Also essential to the success of the system is the use the individuals' managers make of the Performance Plan. The managers must use it consistently to monitor the individuals' performance and to provide a fair and understandable basis for giving needed feedback, coaching, information, and other resources. Obviously, there need be no surprises when it's time for the Yearly Planning Conference, since both the individual and the manager know specifically how performance has measured up to plans throughout the year.

Yearly Planning Conference

At the end of the year individuals meet with their managers for a Yearly Planning Conference, which replaces the traditional performance evaluation with a more positive process. Here the focus is on the broad view of the employee's role and contributions in interacting with all elements of company operations. It is a joint endeavor in which employee and manager look at past experience, present status, and future needs and plans. Actual performance for the past year is surveyed in light of the Performance Plan. Achievements, areas of needed development, and career direction are discussed and identified.

Individuals and their managers agree on the level of the individual's achievement for the past year as specified and agreed upon during their planning conference the previous year. They must describe the achievement level, both quantitatively and qualitatively, where appropriate, for each performance objective. Such verbal descriptions tend to be individual and appropriate to each employee's unique job situation, and therefore they are more effective than filling in checklist appraisal forms.

Managers tend to inspire a higher level of employee motivation and accountability when they encourage employees to take the lead in evaluating their own performance, in pinpointing accountability for results, and in generating objectives for the coming year. When handled effectively, the conference eliminates the negative connotations for the employee of being evaluated. However, it still requires that the employee be responsible for his or her own performance.

The Yearly Planning Conference is much more future oriented than the traditional performance appraisal session. The conference provides a chance to step back and get an overview of the past year's performance. Employee and manager discuss important experiences in trying to meet last year's objectives and attempt to learn from those experiences. They identify what functional areas, action steps, and skill areas need to be expanded. For example, employees might attempt to identify what performance areas or portions of performance areas they enjoy the most and what future job position would allow them to use the skills involved in that performance area.

The Yearly Performance and Planning Report

The documentation process begins with the individual and his or her manager's determining whether or not each objective was achieved. Then they verbally describe the level of achievement—that is, how close, over or under, the employee came to meeting the target. If the objective was not achieved, they note any action steps that were taken or were overlooked. If similar objectives will be set in the future, they note any action steps that will be changed, added, or omitted. They also evaluate the performance of the action steps leading to each objective in order to gain a more detailed, specific picture of employee performance. This evaluation can help to pinpoint strong areas and problem areas.

The form provided for documenting the Yearly Performance Planning Report does not provide performance categories with boxes for easy checkoff. When such appraisal forms are used, managers tend to stereotype employees as generally excellent, average, or poor. The forms are so quick and easy that managers often don't carefully analyze the employee's performance in each category listed. On the other hand, when people must verbally describe an achievement level for each objective and its action steps, they tend to become more engaged in the process, and a higher level of involvement and communication results.

This yearly conference and report process results in the employee's and manager's agreeing upon Performance Plan Development Areas. These are the areas for training, coaching, growth, and development. They represent not only areas that need strengthening in order to achieve objectives in present performance areas, but areas that need to be developed for future career expansion and movement. These areas are included in the report.

Finally, the employee offers his or her ideas on what objectives and action steps should be included in the Performance Plan for the coming year. These ideas are discussed, the manager offers his or her ideas, and the two reach an agreement on a plan the employee is willing to make a commitment to achieving. The new objectives become a part of the Yearly Performance and Planning Report as well as a part of the Performance Plan for the coming year. Thus the cycle is completed and the stage is set for goal-directed action and ongoing self-evaluation for the future.

Why the System Works

The Participative Performance Planning System works because the individuals themselves formulate the contributions they intend to make toward organizational objectives. They develop a clear picture of the expectations they, and their boss, have for their performance. They therefore know exactly how they are going to be measured. And when they are actually measured according to the stated objectives and agreed-upon action steps, they are better able to perform at a level of productivity that gives them the satisfaction of achievement and also meets management's expectations.

THE POLITICAL SIDE OF PLANNING AND ORGANIZING

All management functions have their political aspects. We've talked about the more formal aspects of planning and organizing. Now let's discuss some of the political aspects—namely, how actual priorities and power lines may differ from formal plans and organization charts, how to use a planning system to get what you want, and what to do when your boss resists formal planning.

Reading Between the Lines: What Formal Plans and Organizational Charts Don't Tell You

The larger the organization, the more deviation you may discover between formal, published objectives, policies, and so forth, and what your boss considers most important. The more complex the company, the greater the power gap may be between lines of authority shown on the formal organiza-

tion chart and the actual informal power people can muster.

A major company objective and supporting policies may be to improve product or service quality. However, your boss' top priority may be to increase profits. He or she may prefer to sacrifice a little on quality if the resulting increase in profit is large enough. Don't assume therefore that formal organizational plans tell the whole story. Discuss them with your boss and other key decision-makers to determine where they really stand.

In a similar vein, the formal organizational chart may indicate that a certain person has only a staff relationship to your department and therefore has no line authority over you. Find out what authority such people actually wield. It's not rare for a strong person who has the support of someone in top management to turn a staff job into a powerful position that carries the equivalent of line authority. Also, a certain group, either formal or informal, may have the ear of key decision-makers and therefore exercise informal power and influence that far exceed their formal authority as shown on the organization chart.

The point is, don't be naïve enough to assume that the formal planning system tells the whole story or that the organization chart gives the full picture of power and authority relationships. Try to determine where your boss and other key people really stand. Chapters 1 and 3 discuss some of these political aspects of power and authority. As pointed out in Chapter 3, you'll need to become aware of alliances, support networks, and cliques, as well as enmities, skirmishes, and vendettas in order to deal knowledgeably and effectively with people. Such savvy can help you tie into the right support networks and gain the cooperation of others. It can help you to recognize and overcome barriers created by conflict between two managers. And it can help you steer clear of battles that don't directly concern you.

Using Your Plans—Beyond Formal Objectives

By now you're probably convinced that developing objectives for your work unit, yourself, and your people can lead to higher levels of achievement. You can also use your plans politically to increase your personal and managerial effectiveness.

With Your Boss If your boss is also involved in formal planning, you're in a good position to deal with him or her in terms of priorities and objectives. For example, what if your boss keeps piling too much work on you or your department without giving you additional resources for getting the work done? Instead of playing the passive martyr, you can suggest that you'll handle work necessary to attain top-priority objectives and put other work on the back burner. Or you can suggest that if you try to complete all the work, top-priority work will probably be neglected. Or you can ask your boss to specify priorities for completing various items.

When you want additional resources, such as more workers, equipment, or supplies, show how they will help meet work-unit and department objectives. Do the same when you're defending budget requests.

When asking for a raise or promotion, refer to your record of achieving objectives. Chapter 14 discusses this in more detail.

With Your Peers What if one of your peers makes unreasonable demands or requests for service from your department? An acceptable way of refusing may be to explain that if you comply with such a request, you will have to neglect high-priority work that is necessary to meet departmental objectives.

Sometimes peers simply don't understand what your people are trying to do. When you have a performance plan on file for everyone, you can easily communicate the objectives and activities involved in every position.

With Your Work Team You'll probably get the most mileage out of a planning sytem within your own work unit. After all, workers can make unreasonable requests and demands too. And it helps when you evaluate requests, make decisions, and explain them in terms of how they tie in with department objectives.

The planning process helps you nail down each worker's willingness and ability to perform. It can help you pinpoint areas that need changing or reorganizing, such as dividing work loads, shifting responsibilities or activities, or reorganizing work flow. It can help separate important from unimportant activities so they can be managed on a priority basis. This in turn helps eliminate energy drains and time-wasters.

From the time a worker comes on board until he or she moves out of the department, the planning process can pay off in greater effectiveness. Performance plans can be tools for orientation, career development, coaching and counseling, evaluation, and salary and promotion decisions.

A new worker can use the performance plan of the worker who previously held the position to gain a comprehensive, detailed, goal-oriented picture of job responsibilities and tasks.

By studying others' performance plans, you and your workers can pinpoint jobs in a career path leading to achievement of their career goals.

A well-developed performance plan helps you evaluate performance objectively because it provides specific, agreed-upon areas of responsibility, objectives, tasks, and standards.

It enables you to identify areas of needed development as well as areas of strength that can be expanded and enhanced. Therefore, you can do a better job of coaching workers to higher performance and counseling them in self-development.

Perhaps the major use you can make of the planning process is to motivate workers. A good planning process provides a higher level of autonomy, attainable challenges, guidelines for success, and the satisfaction of experiencing and being recognized for achieving specific results.

Performance plans also provide a fair basis for granting merit increases based on specific performance and results. In fact, they must be tied in with the reward the company gives if they continue to have meaning for workers. It's also crucial to base personnel decisions on how well workers meet performance objectives. Reward those who perform well with the promotions, transfer those who need development in other areas, and terminate those who repeatedly fail to perform adequately.

Every manager dreads firing a worker. A good planning process provides the basis for making such a decision and explaining it to the worker. When you explain it in terms of the necessity for meeting specific objectives and standards, you separate the decision from the personalities involved. You can take a counseling approach in guiding the worker toward needed development or other occupations better suited to the individual's abilities and interests.

When There's No Formal Planning in Your Firm

While adopting a formal planning system will not automatically eliminate organizational problems, numerous research studies indicate that it will result in a higher level of organizational achievement. In spite of these facts, you may find yourself in a firm where little or no formal planning exists, especially below the top-management level. Management consultant Paul Warner confirms the observations of many planning consultants when he discusses how the bright, well-educated young woman with planning skills and ideas can threaten an older male manager: "Most men at middle management level in small to medium-sized organizations, where most of the jobs are, don't engage in formal planning and have no training in it. Most of the training that does take place occurs in university business schools."

Such managers may feel threatened by a woman with a business degree who comes to him with planning ideas and suggestions. The subordinate he previously viewed as average he now sees as someone able to "work smarter" than he works. The fact that the subordinate is a woman may intensify his discomfort. Of course, female bosses may also feel threatened in such circumstances. If you have such a boss, and you push the planning issue, she or he may develop an antiplanning bias. On the other hand, you needn't abandon your planning expertise. Just adopt an informal, nonthreatening planning approach that is sensitive to your boss' preferences.

Start with Your Own Job Needs Instead of pushing for a large-scale planning system, settle for getting some commitment from your boss on what your own job objectives should be and the basis she or he will use for evaluating your performance. First, carefully work out the plan *you* would like to establish—do this privately, even at home. And leave any formal written versions of it there. Then find a quiet time at the office to have a relaxed discussion with your boss.

Avoid the Vocabulary of Formal Planning Carefully select the words you use to discuss matters pertaining to your privately developed performance plan. Instead of talking about strategic planning, objectives, tactics, action steps, and standards, ask your boss' opinion about what you should be accomplishing. You can say you have given some thought to this and you want to touch bases to be sure you're on the right track. You might ask what you need to work on in order to receive a good evaluation, a promotion, a raise, or whatever payoff seems appropriate for your situation.

Keep It Informal Chances are your boss will not be able to come up with many specific objectives you should be working toward, much less standards, tactics, or key action steps. This can be to your advantage if you play your cards right because it means you can probably get agreement on the plan you've developed. But remember, you've left your written plan at home. You now discuss just the meat of the plan with your boss. "I thought one area I could work toward would be decreasing shipping errors, even reducing them to no more than 1 percent of all orders by the end of the year. What do you think?" Go through your key objectives in this manner, getting your boss' ideas and reaching a mutual understanding on each.

Document by Informal Memo Only Written planning documents tend to be viewed as much more formal, and therefore threatening, than oral discussion. However, it's to your advantage to follow up this meeting with an informal memo, using such terminology as "confirming our discussion about job direction." You might mention that you want to be sure you're clear about his or her thoughts on the subject. If appropriate, you might flesh out the discussion by saying, "In the meantime, I've had some additional thoughts . . ." Add more items to your plan, and conclude, "I'll assume this follows the thrust of our talk and meets with your approval unless I hear otherwise."

Carefully file away your copy of this memo. Of course, you'll be using your more complete, formal performance plan between now and evaluation time. Just before your formal evaluation, review the memo to refresh your memory as to just what your boss agreed to. If his evaluation is not based on those items and seems unfair to you, you now have a leg to stand on. Remind him tactfully of your agreements; if necessary, you can later produce a copy of them to refresh his memory.

Use Similar Tactics for Your Subordinates You can use these same nonthreatening tactics in working with your people to improve their productivity. You can establish the entire planning process, merely changing the vocabulary to terms your boss and other key managers are comfortable with and documenting with informal memos. If your firm has a formal performance appraisal program, adapt the process to it.

SUMMARY

The two keys to effective managerial planning are (1) focusing more on end results than on activities and (2) including your subordinates in the planning process rather than doing it yourself and then telling them. When you focus on end results, you are more likely to be effective—to do the right things, the things that will bring about those results. This is much more important than being efficient—focusing on activities and doing them right—which can cause you to do relatively unimportant things at the expense of crucial items.

You must learn to plan effectively if you want to make things happen rather than be a passive bystander. Good planning (1) makes you more promotable, (2) provides you with a basis for making effective decisions, (3) can eliminate unpleasant surprises caused by lack of forecasting, and (4) gives direction to motivational drive—yours and your workers'.

The organizational planning process begins at the top-management level and includes defining the organization's mission, making forecasts, and setting organizational objectives. The next phase involves formulating strategies and policies that help achieve objectives. Middle management then develops departmental objectives, along with tactics, rules, and procedures for implementing them. Supervisors and workers set up work-unit and individual objectives, along with action steps for reaching them. They also devise standards and controls to help monitor and evaluate performance.

Important steps in the planning process include identifying the contributions each person can make and developing clearly stated individual objectives that support company objectives. Performance standards provide the basis for controls. These controls should serve to alert the right people to deviations from standards and allow corrections to be made before problems develop.

An integral part of planning for results is determining how to divide the total work of the organization into divisions, departments, and work units. Top management wants to design the best structure for helping people work together to fulfill the firm's mission, carry out its strategies, and achieve its objectives. An organization's structure is the arrangement and interrelationships of its various parts and job positions. The structure defines the formal division of work activities and shows how all functions or activities are linked together. It also indicates the organization's formal hierarchy and authority structure and shows reporting relationships.

The structuring of activities begins at the top when management initially decides on an organizational plan and periodically reevaluates and modifies it. Some key factors to consider when determining organizational structure are (1) the strategy for achieving the organization's mission and long-range objectives, (2) the technology used to create the products or services the organization offers, (3) the people involved in the organization's activities, and (4) the size of the overall organization and its major divisions.

Organizations are usually divided into departments according to (1) the functions workers are to perform, (2) the products or services produced, (3) the location of the markets that are serviced, (4) the type of customer buying the products or services, or, most frequently, (5) some combination of these categories.

When organizing the work in your unit and the individual job activities of your workers, pay special attention to the degree of specialization and standardization that will produce the best results. Look for job designs that motivate, such as self-managed work teams that provide a variety of activities and needed skills along with a measure of autonomy.

A Participative Performance Planning System encourages people to think in terms of objectives and priorities instead of duties and tasks. It provides the basis for self-control and self-appraisal of performance. The Performance Plan includes: (1) an initial planning conference at which worker and manager agree to ongoing and periodic objectives and action steps for the coming year; (2) regular, spontaneous conferences and coaching throughout the year; (3) a Yearly Planning Conference at the end of the year to discuss formally the achievement of the past year's objectives and to develop the coming year's objectives; and (4) the documentation of the Yearly Planning Conference, called the Yearly Performance Planning Report.

In addition to gaining knowledge and skills in planning and organizing, you will be wise to gain an understanding of the political aspects. Your boss' actual priorities and objectives may differ from his or her formal ones. Formal organization charts never show all the lines of informal influence and power.

You can use your plans politically to increase your effectiveness with your boss, your peers, and your work team. For example, you can base either agreement to or refusal of requests on how they affect objectives. You can use Performance Plans to help orient, develop, evaluate, motivate, coach, and counsel your workers. Performance Plans must be tied in with the rewards of salary increase and promotion if they are to be meaningful.

Your planning and organizing skills may threaten bosses who don't have such skills. You can still use them, beginning with setting objectives for your own performance. Be sensitive, however, to your boss' resistance to formal planning by using informal language and documentation. Use the same nonthreatening approach when you establish a planning process with your work team—keep it informal.

ADDITIONAL EXERCISES

EXERCISE 10-5: DEVELOPING OBJECTIVES AND CONTROLS WITH YOUR SECRETARY OR ASSISTANT

You have accepted the position of National Convention Chairperson for your professional association. This of course means you are responsible for the entire national convention that will be held in your city six months from now. You want your assistant to assume responsibility for all routine correspondence in connection with the convention. You ask him to develop a set of attainable yet challenging objectives, standards, and controls for this area of responsibility. In the meantime, develop your own set so that you will be ready to discuss these items with your secretary and make needed suggestions.

1. Objective(s) _____

_____

2. Additional standard(s) _____

_____

3. Controls _____

_____

EXERCISE 10-6: DEVELOPING YOUR PERFORMANCE PLAN

If you are now working, develop a Performance Plan for your current job. If you are not working, develop a Performance Plan for any job you previously held, either part-time or full-time.

Performance Areas: _____

_____

_____

Performance Area 1—Key Ongoing Objective: _____

_____

Action Steps: _____

_____

_____

Performance Area 1—Periodic Objective: _____

_____

Action Steps: _____

_____

_____

Note: Using additional sheets of paper, repeat this process for each performance area.

EXERCISE 10-7: DEL ORO—DESIGNING AN ORGANIZATIONAL STRUCTURE

You are the manager of a Del Oro Boutique that sells apparel and gifts imported from Mexico. The boutique is part of Del Oro Enterprises, owned by Vickie Drew and her cousin Maria Sanchez. Seven years ago they started with a small Mexican restaurant in the Dallas-Fort Worth Metroplex. The business has grown to include eight restaurants with adjoining boutiques and Mexican delicatessens, scattered across a sixty-mile radius.

Almost from the beginning the restaurants displayed a few gift items Maria bought on her frequent trips to Mexico to visit her father's relatives. They sold so well that separate boutiques were set up at each restaurant location. Because of the many requests Del Oro received to cater parties in private homes and to provide take-out food, the cousins eventually opened a separate but adjacent Mexican Deli. This operation was so successful that delicatessens are now included at each of the eight restaurant locations.

Recently sales of Mexican beer and Margarita ingredients have been so great that the cousins are considering adding bottle shops at some of the locations. If they are successful, they would add bottle shops at all locations.

So far Vickie has been overseeing all aspects of the restaurant operations, Maria is mainly responsible for the boutique operations, and they have been sharing responsibility for the deli/catering operations. At each of the eight locations they have three managers who are responsible for the restaurant, boutique, and deli operations, respectively. Today they are holding a special meeting with these twenty-four local managers to begin plans for reorganizing the company.

Vickie: We've experienced fantastic growth in the last few years, so we must have been doing something right. But Maria and I feel it's time for a reevaluation of our organizational structure.

Maria: Yes. For one thing, Vickie and I feel things have gotten a little beyond our control. It's difficult for us to keep up with our diverse operations.

Vickie: And we may be missing real growth opportunities. We think this bottle shop idea may be very profitable, but frankly Maria and I don't feel like taking on more complexity when we can hardly manage what we have now.

Maria: That's right. Vickie and I have been working sixty to seventy hours a week with very few breaks for the past seven years. Basically, our headquarters staff consists of several highly paid assistants and secretaries who have learned various aspects of the business. Their titles don't begin to reflect their duties and responsibilities. It's time we promoted some people and perhaps hired some specialists for certain areas. We need some help in managing this operation, but we haven't decided just how to go about it. We're open to suggestions.

Your assignment:

Step 1. Draw a rough sketch of the Del Oro Enterprises organizational structure as it now exists. Indicate type of departmentation.

Step 2. Determine at least two ways the company could be reorganized. Draw rough sketches of the resulting organizational structure for each.

Step 3. Discuss the advantages and disadvantages of each type of organizational structure you devised in Step 2. Which would you recommend?

REFERENCES

1. Bickel, Joyce. Director of Imports and Sweater Division, Koret of North America, San Francisco.

2. Drucker, Peter. *Management.* New York: Harper & Row, 1974. A classic— required reading in nearly all business schools. If you can read only one basic management book, read this one.

3. Hackman, J. Richard. *Improving Life at Work.* Santa Monica, Calif.: Goodyear, 1977.

4. Hellriegel, Don, and John W. Slocum, Jr. *Management.* 3d ed. Reading, Mass.: Addison-Wesley, 1982.

5. Mescon, Michael H.; Michael Albert; and Frank Khedouri. *Management: Individual and Organizational Effectiveness*. New York: Harper & Row, 1985. Excellent discussions of MBO, planning, and control with models and diagrams to clarify.

6. Newman, William H. *Constructive Control: Design and Use of Control Systems*. Englewood Cliffs, N.J.: Prentice-Hall, 1975. An extensive examination of control systems with models, diagrams, examples, and explanations.

7. Peters, Thomas J., and Robert H. Waterman. *In Search of Excellence*. New York: Harper & Row, 1982.

8. Schneider-Jenkins, Carol. Human Resources Manager, Oximetrix, Inc., Mountain View, Calif.

9. Stoner, James A. F. *Management*. 2d ed. Englewood Cliffs, N.J.: Prentice-Hall, 1982.

10. Warner, Paul H. Executive Director, Management Resource Group, Consultants in Strategic Planning, Product Development, and Marketing, 11 Embarcadero West, Oakland, Calif. 94607

Chapter Eleven

Understanding the Financial Aspects of Planning

"Humans must breathe, but corporations must make money."
Alice Embree

In the discussion of planning in Chapter 10, we talked about the desirability of including costs in the objectives you set. We also noted that you are more likely to get the resources you need when you can show how they will help you achieve your objectives. A very important part of planning, then, is financial planning. If you work for a business organization, the major focus of the financial system is planning for a profit. If you work for a nonprofit organization, the major focus will be planning to justify, obtain, and allocate (spend) funds.

The management responsibility that typically tends to intimidate women more than any other is financial responsibility. Yet interpreting financial statements and preparing budgets are skills that are relatively easy to learn. The information in this chapter is not designed to make you an expert in financial systems, but it should help you to become more comfortable with the financial aspects of your managerial role. We'll discuss details of a typical financial system that Carrie Dickeson learned about and some of the details of Lighthouse Designs' system.

Although a manufacturing company is used as an example, many of the basic aspects discussed here apply to any organization.

In this chapter you will have the opportunity to

1. Become aware of how much you already know about company finances

2. Gain confidence in your ability to handle the financial aspects of your job

3. Become comfortable with discussing company finances

4. Understand the basic aspects of a financial management system

5. Interpret some company financial statements

6. Compute simple profit margins, investment turnover, and return on investment

7. Understand the process of financial planning, including the preparation of operating budgets, capital budgets, and cash budgets

8. Understand the basic aspects of a cost control system

9. Apply techniques for controlling and reducing costs

 ## Finance Without Fear

Carrie is speaking to her people at a special staff meeting called to iron out the problems in promoting the Viva line.

" . . . so I need your help in formulating some new department goals. What do you think we as a department should aim for? What contributions do you feel you can make? Then I'd like you each to formulate what you think your quota or job assignment should be. I'm setting aside all day one week from today for us to work on this. We'll have a staff meeting in the morning, and I'll meet with each of you individually during the afternoon."

A couple of weeks later, at the weekly staff meeting, Carrie says, "I think all of you can be proud of this plan. You have all been willing to contribute to it, and the results reflect your good work. We make a pretty darned good team—and I think we can beat every region in the country in selling this line next quarter. What do you say?"

"Go for it!" "We're ready!" "Let's go!" the group responds.

After the meeting most of the people mill around for a while. Many of them discuss the new plan among themselves, and several come up to discuss it with Carrie and to express their approval.

Later, on the phone to Jan, Carrie beams, " . . . and it's just like a whole different group, Jan. They're really with me."

"You've just had the best lesson in planning that you could have—there's no lesson like experience, and you really felt this one, right down to your toes. I'll bet you *never* forget to include your people in the planning process again, huh, Carrie?"

"That's for sure. And I'll never forget how you helped me bail myself out of this one."

Later that day John Brockfield drops by Carrie's office. "Say, Carrie, you know I've been fairly happy that I took your recommendation and promoted Kate Blakeley to Administrative Services Manager, but lately I'm beginning to wonder if we had her pegged right."

"What's the problem, John?"

"Well, I called her in the other day to talk about preparing the annual budget, and . . . "

J: Kate, I'm going to need your preliminary operating budget by the fifteenth.

K: Preliminary operating budget?! But John, I don't know anything about budgets! Can't someone else handle that?

J: Kate, preparing the preliminary operating budget is your responsibility. Since you're going to have to defend it in order to get what you need for your department—and since you'll have to live with what you get for the coming year—I would think you'd be eager to oversee that responsibility personally.

K: John, you know I'm great at working with sales people, planning sales campaigns, and that sort of thing. But I'm not really a financial type.

J: I think you're letting this upset you needlessly. I'm sure you can learn what you need to do. I'm going to be tied up the next couple of weeks, but maybe we can get someone in Accounting to help you. (*To himself*): She's acting like a scatterbrain. I thought she was management material, but I'm beginning to wonder . . .

Carrie smiles, "Come on, John. Don't overreact. When George first turned the budget over to me, I had some of the same misgivings Kate has. As we're growing up, many of us women pick up messages that we're not supposed to be good with figures or know much about money. If we can get over that barrier, most of us are pretty good with budgets. Why don't I have a talk with Kate?"

"Thanks, Carrie. Do what you can."

A few days later, Carrie and Kate settle down in Carrie's office for a long chat about budgets.

"Kate, have you and your husband ever sat down together to figure out some sort of household budget?"

"Sure, we do that about once a year—or whenever we get a raise or make a big purchase."

"That's a start. How do you two go about deciding on a budget?"

"Well, we add up all our sources of income, which is mainly our two salaries. Then we add up all the costs we can't easily change, such as house payment, utilities, and any other regular monthly payments. Then, let's see . . . "

"You figure your total income or revenue. Then you figure your *fixed costs*. Do you make any provision for what you want to save?"

"Right now we're trying to save about 10 percent of our take-home pay."

"You're making sure that there is some money left over just for you, then. And if you're like me—and most people I know—you find that if you wait until *all* the bills are paid to see what's left over, you usually wind up with nothing."

"Too true! We learned we had to decide ahead of time exactly how much we want to save. Then we have to figure out how we can keep our spending down in order to be sure we meet our *savings goal*."

"In a business setting, that's called setting a *profit target*—deciding what the company wants to have left over for itself. Then what?"

"Then we consider all the types of expenses we have that we can modify fairly easily, such as food, clothing, entertainment, travel, and personal expenses. We divide up the money that's left over into these categories."

"You make a plan for your *current expenses*. Do you stick to that plan?"

"To some extent. However, Bud and I agree occasionally that we want to splurge a little in one area and cut back in another. But we try to stay within our total plan and just shift occasionally among the categories—unless of course we get a raise or get hit with some unexpected expense."

"So your budget is flexible? (*Kate nods.*) And you use it as a day-to-day plan to help you conduct your personal business so you'll end up having the things that are most important to you and Bud. Kate, you have a great deal of experience with preparing and implementing an *operating budget*. You've done it on a small scale, true. But your department operating budget is not that different. And the overall company budget is handled in the same way, but it's apportioned among the departments as well as among categories of expense."

"When you put it like that, I feel a lot less ignorant."

"Now let's take a look at what you know about *capital budgets*. Do you and Bud make special plans for major purchases?"

"Sure. We planned and saved for three years in order to buy our house. We also plan to trade in our car every five years. Oh, and we keep a special savings account for buying furniture and appliances. We like to have ready cash available for special sales and auctions."

"Well, those plans constitute your capital budget."

"Really?"

"Sure. The procedures your company uses to develop its capital budget are more formal and complex, of course, but the general idea is the same. The company requires its managers to submit proposals for projects that require major purchases of land, buildings, or equipment. Once these proposals are approved, they become part of the capital budget, which is the company's plan for those major items it will purchase over the next five years.

Now let's talk about the third type of budget you probably use: the *cash budget*. How do you and Bud make sure you will have enough cash in your checking account to pay your bills as they come due?"

"Well, we keep fairly close track of our bank balance, so we know the balance we have to work with. Then we look at our monthly budget of income, savings, and expenditures. We also take into consideration any large bills that will come due, such as yearly insurance premiums and vacation travel, to make sure we'll have enough to pay them."

"The finance officer in your company does the same type of thing. It's especially important for a business organization to watch its cash. It's easy to tie up huge sums of money in raw materials and inventory. It may take several months to make, sell, and ship the completed product, and then to bill customers, and finally to get paid. In the meantime the company can spend all its remaining cash and be forced

to borrow. It's even possible for the company to borrow all the banks will loan it and still run short of money. This type of cash-flow mismanagement can force a company into bankruptcy—even though it may be making good profits on highly successful products. You probably know people who are successful, have large incomes, invest in items that will appreciate and eventually pay off, but still have creditors after them all the time."

"Yes—and I can see that I already have a great deal of experience with budgets. Now could we discuss some of the detailed procedures companies use to develop their budgets and my role in the company's financial system?"

Carrie and Kate spend an hour or so discussing the financial aspects of Kate's job. After this session, Kate feels confident about her ability to catch on quickly to Lighthouse Designs' financial system and budgeting process. The next day she gets a copy of the company manual on budgeting procedures from the Accounting Department and studies it.

---

1. Do you think Kate Blakeley's attitude toward business finance was typical? _____ How? _____

2. What messages did you receive when you were growing up about women's role in handling money and understanding finance? _____

3. What experiences do you have in handling money and making financial plans? _____

4. How can you use that experience as a strength to base further financial skills upon? _____

Kate's initial response to the financial aspects of her job reflects the all-too-prevalent fears many women have about dealing with money and finance. When *Ms.* magazine questioned twenty thousand women about their attitudes toward money, the responses frequently reflected a puritanical taboo [5; 6]. Women report that both money and sex are very difficult for them to discuss, especially with men. Many of the women had picked up the belief from their parents and others that women shouldn't know about money. It was expected that their fathers would worry about the family finances and provide these women with what they needed until they married. Then their husbands would take over this responsibility. Later, when their husbands died, their sons or some other male family member would take over.

On the other hand, most of the women said that they controlled their own money in actual practice. Most prepared their own income tax returns and made their own financial decisions or, if married, shared them with their husbands. Most women, then, *do* have experience in handling personal finances and taking responsibility for them.

It's obvious that this knowledge and experience can be applied to handling the financial aspects of a manager's job.

MEASURING MANAGEMENT'S EFFECTIVENESS

New business ventures have a high rate of failure. In fact, the large majority of them fail in less than three years. Even a large, well-established business must perform all the management functions effectively in order to stay in business. Since poor financial management is perhaps the most common direct cause of failure, it's important that all the managers in a company understand the basic aspects of financial management, so they can contribute to the company's financial success.

Management might be described as coordinating all the resources of an organization through the processes of planning, organizing, staffing, directing, and controlling in order to achieve the organization's objectives. Managers do this through *people*, usually considered the organization's major resource. The whole process is illustrated in Figure 11-1.

Since all the resources cost money, an inherent part of the management process is managing the costs of resources and making the money to pay for them. Managers must

FIGURE 11-1: The Management Process

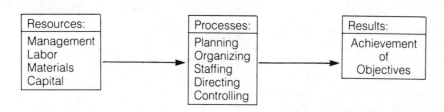

estimate the amount of goods or services the company will sell (dollars in) and the amount of money needed to provide the resources necessary to provide those goods and services (dollars out). In that way, managers contribute to the preparation of budgets, which are specific plans for allocating resources in dollar amounts and are based on the estimates. Managers must also control costs and expenses so that they stay within the budgeted amounts.

Instead of handling the making of money and the controlling of costs in a hit-or-miss fashion or viewing them as somewhat isolated functions, most large firms have a financial management system. A system is an arrangement of parts or subsystems that interact to form a complete, harmonious, and workable design or effect as a whole.

A stereo set is an example of a system. Its subsystems may consist of a tuner, amplifier, speakers, radio, tape-player, and record-player. By integrating these parts into one system, the manufacturer can provide you with higher-quality performance than would be possible if you purchased a radio, record-player, and tape-player separately. If one of the subsystems, such as the record-player, quits functioning properly, the stereo system may partially function. It will not be fulfilling your expectations, however, or providing the range of services you paid for.

The more effectively the parts of an organization work together, the better the entire organization will function and the more productive it will be. In dealing with finances, as well as with other aspects of the business, the organization should be viewed as an entity with each unit and department contributing to the organization's objectives, as we saw in Chapter 6. A good financial management system has three elements: (1) an objective, (2) a measuring device, and (3) a control device. The objective of the **financial management system** of a business is to make

a specific dollar profit. The measuring device is the company budget. The control device is the **management control system,** which ensures that managers stay within their budgets. We'll discuss these three elements in detail later. First, let's look at the end result of the entire system, which is reported in the company's annual financial statements.

Interpreting Financial Statements

Most companies prepare **annual reports** that show their financial performance for the year. In fact, you can appraise top management's performance by analyzing the annual report. It contains two separate financial statements that provide the information that stockholders and others need to evaluate management's effectiveness: (1) the profit and loss statement and (2) the balance sheet. The **profit and loss statement** (also called the income statement) shows how much money the company has made (or lost) during the previous year. The **balance sheet** shows the net worth of the company at the end of the year based on what it owns and what it owes.

Profit and Loss Statement The profit and loss statement summarizes the financial result of the company's activities each year. It has three main categories: (1) total sales or revenue, (2) costs and expenses, and (3) profit (or loss), as shown in Exhibit 11-1.

1. *Total sales or revenue.* This is the money the business takes in from all sources. For manufacturing companies such as Lighthouse Designs, the main source of revenue is product sales. For banks, it's interest on loans and income from investments; for law firms, it's fees for services performed.

EXHIBIT 11-1: Lighthouse Designs, Inc., Profit and Loss Statement for Year Ending 19xx ($ in Millions)

Total Sales	$200	
Costs and Expenses	180	
Profit (before taxes)		$20
Less Income Taxes		10
Net Profit (after taxes)		$10

2. *Costs and expenses.* This is the money spent to produce revenue. Costs include such things as the cost of materials and the wages of the workers who make the product. Expenses include such things as the salaries of managers and clerical workers, maintenance and replacement of worn-out or obsolete equipment, and office supplies. Income taxes are paid on the excess of sales over costs and expenses, which is $20 million in Exhibit 11-1 ($200 minus $180). In this example, the company paid half of this excess, or $10 million, as taxes. The remaining profit is referred to as **net profit**.

3. *Profit (or loss).* Net profit is the money that is left after all costs and expenses, including income taxes, have been deducted from revenue. If costs are *higher* than revenues, then the bottom line shows a loss.

The profit and loss equation is simple:

Revenue − Cost = Profit (or Loss)

Balance Sheet   The three main elements of the balance sheet are (1) assets, (2) liabilities, and (3) net worth.

1. *Assets.* These are everything owned by the company—for example, cash, buildings, equipment, money owed by customers.

2. *Liabilities.* These are everything the company owes and claims against the assets by nonowners—for example, money due suppliers, bank loans, unpaid taxes.

3. *Net worth.* This figure reveals the extent of the owners' claims against assets. In an individual proprietorship, net worth represents the current value of the owner's investment. For example, Anita Loos started a small automobile rental agency on June 15 by purchasing three autos at $5,000 each for a total of $15,000. She invested $10,000 of her own money and borrowed $5,000 from the bank. On the day she started the business, her assets were $15,000 worth of automobiles, her liabilities were the $5,000 she owed the bank, and her net worth was $10,000, the amount she invested.

The balance sheet gets its name from the fact that it has two sides that must be in balance (see Figure 11-2). *Total assets always equals net worth plus total liabilities.* The equation used to arrive at net worth (sometimes called capital or capital investment) is:

Assets − Liabilities = Net Worth

To see how the balance sheet changes as business activities are carried out, let's look at Anita's business six months after opening. Her three automobiles are now worth only $12,000, but she's kept them rented most of the time and therefore has a $6,000 balance in her business checking account, for a total of $18,000 in assets. Since she owes only

FIGURE 11·2: How the Balance Sheet Balances ($ in Thousands)

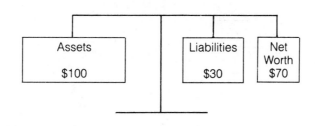

$4,000 to the bank now, her net worth is $14,000 ($18,000 in assets minus $4,000 in liabilities).

A balance sheet is normally prepared to show the firm's financial status on December 31 or the end of the fiscal year that the firm designates for accounting purposes. One may also be prepared any time management needs to establish the current net worth of the firm. In a corporation, net worth is the value shown on the company's books (book value) of all stock owned by the stockholders. In a partnership, net worth is the book value of the partnership shares owned by the partners. In these cases, net worth represents the money invested by all persons who own a share of the company, and the balance sheet shows the current status and value of that investment.

If net worth is a minus figure, the business is insolvent. For example, if the company owes $15 million and owns $5 million, its net worth is − $10 million ($5 − $15 = − $10), and its creditors are likely to file bankruptcy proceedings. Exhibit 11-2 shows the format of a balance sheet.

Measures of Effectiveness

From the profit and loss statement and the balance sheet we can figure three indicators of top management's effectiveness: (1) profit margin, which shows what percentage of sales was kept as profit; (2) investment turnover, which shows how well management used its "bankroll" of assets to drum up sales; and (3) return on investment, which combines the first two indicators to show how well management used its assets to capture sales and to earn a profit.

The financial statements and the performance ratios derived from them are important management tools for planning. They provide essential information about how well the company is doing in specific areas and therefore what needs to be done during the coming months or years.

Profit Margin   The **profit margin** measures how effective management has been in generating dollars of pretax profit out of dollars of sales revenue. It is figured in this way:

$$\text{Profit Margin} = \frac{\text{Profit}}{\text{Sales}}$$

Lighthouse Designs' profit margin (from Exhibit 11-1) is

$$\text{Profit Margin} = \frac{20}{200}$$
$$= 10\% \text{ or } 10¢$$
$$\text{per dollar of sales}$$

The profit margin can be computed for total sales and for individual product lines or items. It helps management make decisions about increasing or decreasing production of an item. After all, *it doesn't make sense to in-*

EXHIBIT 11-2: Anita Loos Car Rental Agency, Balance Sheet as of June 1, 19xx ($ in Thousands)

Assets		Liabilities	
Xxxxxx	$_____	Xxxxxx	$_____
Xxxxxx	_____	Xxxxxx	_____
Xxxxxx	_____	Total Liabilities	$ 5
Xxxxxx	_____	Net Worth	10
Xxxxxx	_____	Total Liabilities and Net Worth	$15
Total Assets	$15		

crease the volume of production of an item when *you're losing money on every item you sell!* Investors can compare Lighthouse's profit figure with the profit margins of other clothing manufacturers to see how Lighthouse management is doing.

Investment Turnover The profit margin is figured from the profit and loss statement alone. The second measure of management effectiveness, **investment turnover,** is figured from both the profit and loss statement and the balance sheet. Investment turnover, sometimes called capital asset turnover, measures management's effectiveness in using money invested in company assets and/or management's effectiveness in generating sales volume from the capital assets the owners have invested in. Here's how it's figured:

$$\frac{\text{Investment}}{\text{Turnover}} = \frac{\text{Sales}}{\text{Total Investment (Assets)}}$$

Dividing Lighthouse Designs' sales of $200 million (see Exhibit 11-1) by its total assets of $100 million, we get

$$\text{Investment Turnover} = \frac{200}{100} = 2$$

(To simplify, we assumed total assets were the same at the beginning and end of the year.) This computation shows that Lighthouse "turned over" its assets twice during the year: Management generated $2.00 in sales for every dollar invested in capital as-

sets. The more times a company can turn over its investment each year, the better is the grade we can give management. To make the most of this indicator, however, we must also look at the turnover rates of Lighthouse's competitors, its past performance, and management's objectives. In that way we get a more complete picture of what management is doing and how its performance compares with its own past performance and its competitors' performance.

Return on Investment The return on an owner's or stockholder's investment, **ROI**, is the most revealing measurement of management performance in generating sales and turning over investment in assets. It combines the effects of the profit margin (before taxes) and the investment turnover rate:

ROI = Profit Margin
   × Investment Turnover

Using the Lighthouse data in Exhibit 11-1 and the profit margin and investment turnover rates just calculated, we see that

ROI = 10% × 2
ROI = 20%

So last year, Lighthouse Designs' return on investment was 20%.

We can also figure ROI without first figuring net profit margin and investment turnover:

$$ROI = \frac{Profit\ (20)}{Sales\ (200)} \times \frac{Sales\ (200)}{Investment\ (100)}$$

$$= \frac{4,000}{20,000}$$

$$= 20\%$$

We can simplify our figuring, as follows:

$$ROI = \frac{Profit}{Sales} \times \frac{Sales}{Investment}$$

$$ROI = \frac{Profit\ (20)}{Investment\ (100)} = 20\%$$

The formula normally used for figuring return on investment, therefore, is

$$ROI = \frac{Profit}{Investment}$$

and you simply divide Profit by Investment to arrive at your answer.

ROI is a direct measure of top management's performance, and it is also an indirect measure of effectiveness at every level of the company. Every manager has an impact on the profit of the company. How effectively you run your department, the level of productivity you get from your people, how closely you estimate the funds you'll need to run your department, and how well you keep your expenditures within the budgeted amounts—all affect your company's profit at the end of the year and therefore its ROI. If Lighthouse wants to improve its return on investment, management must either generate more profit from each dollar of sales (increase profit margin) or use assets more efficiently (increase investment turnover rate).

Let's put the idea of return on investment on a more personal level. Suppose a friend told you, "I made two hundred dollars playing blackjack in Las Vegas last weekend." That information alone does not give an accurate picture of your friend's proficiency and luck as a blackjack player. If he was

working with a bankroll of $50, his winnings are very impressive. A $200 return on an investment of $50 would be remarkable indeed. On the other hand, if he had $500 to play with, his winnings of $200 above his initial bankroll would be less remarkable.

Now try your hand at figuring profit margin (before taxes) and investment turnover rate and evaluating overall financial performance by completing Exercises 11-1, 11-2, and 11-3.

PLANNING FOR SPECIFIC FINANCIAL RESULTS

The profit and loss statement summarizes the financial activities of the company over the past year. The balance sheet tells something about financial solvency at the end of the year. Managers must also look ahead. Forecasting, or estimating what will happen in future months and years, is essential to effective management.

The first step in financial planning and budget preparation is forecasting sales and estimating revenue for the coming year. Then management sets a profit goal and makes plans for budgeting costs and expenses. Once these plans are made, it is the job of the operating managers to achieve the stated profit goals of the company.

The budget is the formal documentation of management's plans for making a profit and controlling costs. It is the basic plan for operating the business for a particular time period in such a way that the stated objectives of the company are achieved within the targeted level of income. A diagram of the relationship of the budget-planning process before the year begins and the resulting profit and loss statement at the end of the year is shown in Figure 11-3.

EXERCISE 11-1: COMPUTING PROFIT MARGIN

Figure the profit margin of Nob Hill Designs (Lighthouse's competitor) from its profit and loss statement. Check your response with the answer key.

Nob Hill Designs, Inc.
Profit and Loss Statement for Year Ending December 31, 19xx
($ in Millions)

Total Sales	$100	
Costs and Expenses	92	
Profit		$8
Less Income Taxes		4
Net Profit		$4

EXERCISE 11-2: COMPUTING INVESTMENT TURNOVER

Using the balance sheet below and the profit and loss statement shown in Exercise 11-1, figure Nob Hill's investment turnover rate. Check your response with the answer key.

Nob Hill Designs, Inc.
Balance Sheet as of December 31, 19xx
($ in Millions)

Assets		Liabilities	
Xxxxxx	$_____	Xxxxxx	$_____
Xxxxxx	_____	Xxxxxx	_____
Xxxxxx	_____	Total Liabilities	$40
Xxxxxx	_____	Net Worth	20
		Total Liabilities	
Total Assets	$60	and Net Worth	$60

Management must include profit goals in company budget plans for the same reasons individuals must include savings goals in their personal budgets. The human tendency is to let costs and expenses creep upward. When we plan to set aside a specific amount for profit or savings, however, we're more likely to operate within the remaining amount of income available to us. We tend to devote extra effort and energy to controlling costs in order to meet our profit or savings goals. Therefore, management must plan in advance to keep part of the estimated revenue for profit and to operate the business with

EXERCISE 11-3: EVALUATING OVERALL FINANCIAL PERFORMANCE

Here is a comparison of Lighthouse Designs' performance ratios with those of similar clothing manufacturers.

	Lighthouse	Laurette's	Alexis	Nob Hill
Profit Margin	10%	9%	14%	8%
Investment Turnover	2	3.1	1.2	1.7
Return on Investment	20%	28%	17%	13%

Which company had the best overall financial performance? Why?

_____ Lighthouse   _____ Laurette's   _____ Alexis   _____ Nob Hill

Check your response with the answer key.

FIGURE 11-3: Relationship of Budget-Planning and the Profit and Loss Statement

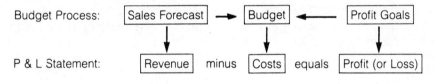

the balance. Furthermore, when the budget is based on return on investment rather than merely on a planned profit margin, management is recognizing the need to maximize the investment turnover rate *as well as* the need to make the planned profit.

Having looked briefly at the overall process of financial planning, we'll now discuss budget preparation in a company.

Preparing the Company Budget

Just as individual and departmental objectives are based on organizational objectives and contribute to achieving them, unit and de-partmental budgets are parts of the organizational budget. An effective manager cannot prepare her budget in isolation. She must bring it into line with the company budget. Likewise, when top management sets company objectives, limitations, and constraints, it must consider the effect of these decisions on each department and unit. The step-by-step process of budget preparation for Lighthouse Designs, Inc., is shown in Figure 11-4. The figures represent a composite of the operating, capital, and cash budgets, which we'll examine in detail later in the chapter. First we'll discuss each step of the budget-making process.

FIGURE 11-4: Budget Preparation by Lighthouse Designs, Inc., 19xx ($ in Millions)

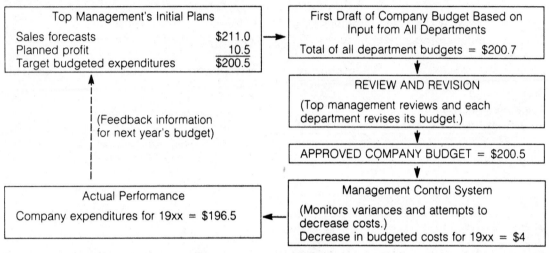

Sales Forecasts The Sales Department develops sales forecasts. These forecasts predict the total amount of money Lighthouse can expect to take in to cover its costs and planned profit.

Planned Profit and Target Expenditures Top management reviews company objectives for amount of dividends to pay to stockholders, company expansion, new product development, research, new equipment, and so forth. Management then determines what profit is necessary to achieve these objectives. When planned profit is deducted from expected sales, the remaining funds are what is available to cover the costs necessary (target budgeted expenditures) to meet the projected sales demand. Top management communicates these figures to the appropriate department and unit managers.

First Draft of Company Budget Each manager is responsible for preparing a prelimi-

nary budget for her or his department. The total of the department budget figures goes into the first draft of the company budget. As Figure 11-4 shows, the first draft of the Lighthouse budget pegs expenditures at $200.7 million, which is $200,000 over the target. This situation is typical, since each manager tends to think his or her department needs a little more money than is actually necessary.

Review and Revision When departmental budgets reach top management, conflicts over how the money will be spent must be ironed out. During the review and revision stage, managers are asked to tighten and trim their original budgets. This step is repeated until the total of the department budgets does not exceed the target company budget. Each manager will virtually always get his or her original budget back for cutting at least once. In some cases a department budget must be revised downward three or four times before it is accepted by top management.

Approved Company Budget When all the department budgets have been accepted, we have an approved company budget. We also have an objective in the form of planned profit and a measuring device in the form of a budget.

Management Control System Most companies devise comprehensive procedures by which managers ensure that resources are obtained and used effectively and efficiently in meeting company objectives. Part of this management control system involves cost control. Managers are responsible for operating within the planned budget. Through monitoring costs and continually devising ways to decrease them, managers work toward budget goals and sometimes even surpass them. Their *actual performance* is recorded through the accounting system, and top management compares it with the budget. Any difference is noted. A manager who spends less than the amount budgeted shows a positive difference. One who overspends shows a negative difference. By comparing budgeted performance with the actual performance of his or her department, a manager can plan action to eliminate negative differences. We'll discuss specific ways of doing this later. A manager with budget surpluses should check to see whether the quality of performance is up to standards and all critical activities are being carried out.

The Profit Center Approach

Lighthouse Designs designates each of its divisions as a profit center. This means that each division is expected to budget and achieve a net profit margin as if it were a separate company. For budgeting and ac-

counting purposes each division is treated almost as if it were a separate entity. This approach works well for Lighthouse because each division operates in a relatively independent manner and has its own market. Some companies even attempt to treat separate departments or product lines as profit centers. However, this sometimes leads to a degree of provincialism and competitiveness *within* the company that eventually harms the overall performance of the company.

The budgeting principle we've discussed for the company as a whole applies to profit centers as well. The company budget is a compilation of the budgets of its profit centers. The major advantage of the profit center approach is the manager's increased motivation to produce more and spend less in order to get credit for increased profits. The major disadvantage is that managers tend to neglect the overall welfare of the company.

Testing Your Understanding

To check your grasp of the principles of budgeting, consider the following problem. You are the general manager of a division of Lighthouse Designs. You have just finished reviewing the first draft of your budget for next year. It is a compilation of the budget figures prepared by each of your department heads:

Sales − Budgeted Costs = Profit
$70,000,000 − $66,700,00 = $3,300,000

The company expects you to make a profit of $3,000,000 next year. What should you do and why should you do it?

1. Increase costs by $300,000 before submitting the budget for corporate approval?

2. Tell your department heads to review and revise their budgets downward?

3. Submit the budget as is for company approval, stressing that you expect to exceed the profit goal?

You're on the right track if you chose the second response. Although it is very rare that a preliminary budget is less than the targeted amount, the manager should still insist on the review and revision step. It's quite likely that some departments or units have asked for too much money, either because they naturally feel their department needs and deserves more or because they expect their requests to be cut and are therefore trying to add enough to offset any reduction. Even though the review process sometimes uncovers items that should have been included in the budget but were overlooked, you will almost certainly be able to reduce the budgeted cost figure by going through this step.

Now evaluate this financial system: The financial system devised by Alexis Fashions includes (1) an accurate sales forecast, (2) realistic budgeted costs, and (3) a satisfactory profit goal before the company starts its operations each year. Would you say that the company's financial system is (a) adequate for a small company, (b) not adequate, or (c) very good? Explain your answer.

You're developing a good understanding of the basic requirements for a financial management system if you chose the second response. Alexis' system is incomplete and inadequate. The company has a realistic goal (profit) and a measuring device (the budget), but there is no control device to identify deviations between budgeted and actual performance during the year. Overspending, for example, could reach disastrous proportions before it's discovered and corrected.

Now that you know something about the overall process of financial planning and budget preparation, we'll look at three specific types of budgets—operating, capital, and cash—what they include, and how they're used.

LIVING WITHIN AN OPERATING BUDGET

The operating budget is the financial plan for conducting the normal business activities of the company. It is the budget that supervisors and middle managers deal with the most. The sales forecast on which it is based should take into consideration the capacity of the Production Department to deliver the goods and the capacity of other departments to provide adequate customer services. Making as many sales as possible, therefore, is not always a valid goal in the long run because unfilled orders and poor service can result in alienation of both established and potential customers.

Once the sales forecast has been developed, each department predicts what level of spending will be necessary to produce the products and services needed to provide for this expected level of sales. Figure 11-5 shows that an operating budget may be broken down into three major categories: (1) production budget, (2) design and tooling expense budget, and (3) sales and administration expense budget.

The **production budget** is the plan for all the costs necessary to make a product. The three main kinds of manufacturing costs are (1) direct material, (2) direct labor, and (3) manufacturing expense (see Figure 11-6).

Direct material cost refers to all material that enters into and becomes a part of the finished product. It also refers to material that can be directly identified with the production of a specific item or unit. Three types of direct material are (1) raw materials used to make a product or a part of the product,

FIGURE 11-5: Operating Budget for Lighthouse Designs, Inc., 19xx

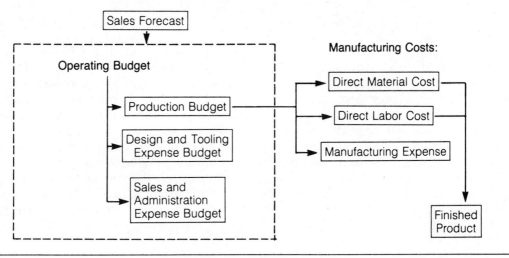

such as bolts of fabric for making clothing or yarn for weaving sweaters; (2) purchased parts already fabricated, such as belt buckles and buttons that become part of a garment; (3) bulk material that is used in the final product but has no definite dimensions, such as a spray-on fabric coating to give a garment body or water-repellence.

All labor that changes the nature, shape, or form of the material that enters into a product is known as *direct labor cost*. It includes such costs as the wages of cutters, who cut fabric into the pieces of a garment, and seamstresses, who sew the garment together; overtime payments; shift bonuses; and cost-of-living allowances paid to workers who make the product.

The indirect costs of making a product— the cost of items that don't become part of the product or change the nature, shape, or form of the material that enters into the product—are called *manufacturing expense*. They include (1) indirect labor, such as the salaries of janitors, plant superintendents, and supervisors, foremen, plant clerks and checkers, and plant physicians and nurses;

FIGURE 11-6: Total Costs and Expenses Lighthouse Designs, Inc.

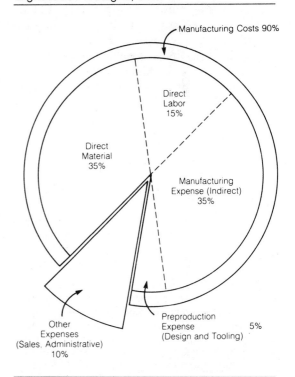

(2) indirect material, such as office supplies, maintenance equipment and supplies, bagging and shipping supplies, testing supplies, fuel and lubricants; (3) indirect expenses for data processing, losses, errors, manufacturing defects, **fixed costs*** such as depreciation and obsolescence of buildings and equipment, property insurance, and taxes.

The *design and tooling expense budget* deals with the costs of getting ready to make a product. Design and tooling expenses are preproduction costs for product design and styling or engineering, original tooling (making or modifying tools and equipment to be used to manufacture the product), and plant rearrangement.

The *sales and administrative expense budget* covers the cost of departments that are not directly involved in the manufacturing process but are essential to the operation of the company. These departments are usually *not* located in the manufacturing plant. They're part of what's known as "the office." They include top management and staff (President, Vice-Presidents, legal and financial officers) as well as the Accounting, Sales, Administrative Services, and Personnel Departments.

Operating Budgets Based on Standard Volume of Sales

A major problem in predicting the level of spending necessary to produce the right

amount of product is determining plant and major equipment needs. If management invests *too much* in plant and equipment—that is, if sales volume or equipment capacity is miscalculated—the plant will not be used as fully as it could be, and a large fixed cost will have to be charged against each unit produced. As a result, the unit or product may not be competitive, or the company profit on each unit will have to be reduced.

On the other hand, if management invests *too little* in plant and equipment, it may lose sales because it could not turn out enough units to meet demand. Customer demand may vary significantly from one year to the next, further complicating plant capacity decisions.

If managers use annual sales volume predictions to determine the amount of fixed costs to charge against each unit of product, their unit costs will change a lot from year to year. In order to have a more reasonable base point from which to figure fixed costs, many companies base their budgets on a long-range sales forecast called **standard volume**. Standard volume is the *average* yearly volume expected over a specified period of years (a **business cycle**).* **Index volume** is the forecast of next year's sales volume.

By using standard volume for a period of several years, companies can write off fixed plant and equipment costs at an even rate per unit each year. This rate will be a little above the actual cost one year and a little below it another year, but it will even out over the period of the business cycle. It's easier for management to make plans and prepare budgets when the sales volume figure is sta-

---

*In most manufacturing firms, a large part of the company's assets is in the form of plant and equipment. These assets are "fixed" in the sense that they are not available for day-to-day use in purchasing raw materials, paying salaries, and meeting other current financial needs. The investment in fixed assets must be recovered by figuring a portion of their cost into the cost of each item that is produced. When these fixed costs are depreciated (spread over the number of years of useful life of the building or piece of equipment), they are referred to as a fixed charge (or expense).

---

*A business cycle is a period during which there is a pattern of fluctuation in consumer demand for a product or service. In a typical cycle, consumer demand increases until it reaches a high point and remains there for a time. Then it begins to decrease until a low point is reached and remains there for a time until the next cycle begins.

ble and can be counted on from year to year rather than changing and therefore unknown. For example, management can more readily predict the price to be charged for the product and make marketing and advertising plans based on the price.

Standard volume doesn't affect decisions to decrease production when demand is off or to increase production when sales are increasing. It's merely a base point for figuring *fixed costs* and unit costs. Index volume—how many units the company expects to sell next year—is the basis for making **production schedules**. These detailed plans of the number and types of items to be produced are adjusted from week to week as demand changes. Index volume therefore affects decisions that are based on the production schedule, such as how many employees will be used and how much material will be purchased. These are **variable costs**.

Now try your hand at figuring profit margins for budget purposes, using standard volume, by completing Exercise 11-4. Figuring profit margins is essential in setting and translating profit goals. We know budgets are based on these sales forecasts and profits. The next step is figuring budgeted costs, as shown in Exercise 11-5, on page 412.

Do you see that if 10 percent of all money made from sales of the product is kept as profit by the company, that leaves 90 percent of sales for all the costs involved in making the product and running the company?

EXERCISE 11-4: FIGURING PROFIT MARGINS

Lighthouse Designs manufactures three completely different lines of clothing. In preparing its budget for next year, the company wants to establish a 20 percent return (before income taxes) on the assets (ROI) employed in producing each product.

The products, standard volumes, assets employed in producing them and the income forecasts are as follows:

Product line	Standard Volume (Units)	Assets Employed	Sales Forecast
Bonnie Jean	2,600,000	$ 35,000,000	$ 70,000,000
Sir Winston	2,800,000	50,000,000	100,000,000
SuAnne	2,100,000	25,000,000	50,000,000
Total	7,500,000	$110,000,000	$220,000,000

In past years, Lighthouse has been able to turn over its investment (assets) employed in producing each product twice a year and is expecting to accomplish this again next year. For this reason, the profit target of a 20 percent return on investment translates into a 10 percent profit margin on sales.

Profit Margin × Investment Turnover = Return on Investment
10% × 2 = 20%

Looking at the sales forecast for each product line, figure the planned 10 percent profits and write them below. Check your answers with the answer key.

Bonnie Jean $_____

Sir Winston $_____

SuAnne $_____

Now return to the discussion on page 411.

EXERCISE 11-5: FIGURING BUDGETED COSTS

The preliminary drafts of Lighthouse Designs' product budgets for next year appear in the following table. Figure the budgeted total costs for each product (90 percent of the sales forecast shown in Exercise 11-4; remember that 10 percent went for profits). Write them in on the bottom line of the table. Check your answer with the answer key, and return to the discussion on page 411.

Account	Bonnie Jean	Sir Winston	SuAnne
Direct Material	xxx	xxx	xxx
Direct Labor	xxx	xxx	xxx
Indirect Labor	xxx	xxx	xxx
Operating Supplies	xxx	xxx	xxx
Expense Tools	xxx	xxx	xxx
Utilities	xxx	xxx	xxx
Maintenance	xxx	xxx	xxx
Losses, Errors, and Defects	xxx	xxx	xxx
Fixed Charges—Depreciation and Obsolescence, Property Taxes and Property Insurance	xxx	xxx	xxx
Miscellaneous Manufacturing Expense	xxx	xxx	xxx
Purchasing	xxx	xxx	xxx
Production Control	xxx	xxx	xxx
Accounting	xxx	xxx	xxx
Product Design	xxx	xxx	xxx
Personnel	xxx	xxx	xxx
Proposed Costs	$63,300,000	$89,500,000	$46,500,000
Budgeted Costs	$_____	$_____	$_____

Therefore, you simply multiply the sales forecast by 90 percent (.90) to get the maximum amount that can be budgeted for costs. Now compare these figures by completing Exercise 11-6.

When the product-line manager is proposing total costs that are less than the maximum amount that can be budgeted, the variance is favorable. Any time proposed costs for a product line are more than the maximum amount that can be budgeted, the variance (difference between the two) is unfavorable and something must be done to eliminate the unfavorable difference.

Unfavorable variances might be dealt with in several different ways. At this stage of the budgeting process, which alternative is best: to (1) increase the sales price, (2) reduce the profit objective, or (3) reduce the proposed costs? Think about what you would do and why you would do it.

The best alternative is to reduce the budgeted costs by returning all three proposed budgets for further cutting. The Bonnie Jean and SuAnne proposals are definitely unacceptable because the variances are unfavorable. The Sir Winston budget shows a favorable variance but should be reviewed for further savings. It is not unusual for preliminary budgets to go over the targeted cost limits. That's why the review step is an essential part of the budgeting process.

Increasing the sales price, the first alternative, would be unwise at this stage. This alternative might be considered if all possible costs have been reduced and the profit margin is still unacceptable. But even then a price increase may not be a workable solution, for customers may turn to competitors who sell at a lower price.

Reducing the profit objective, the second alternative, should not be considered until all possible cost savings have been made and product pricing has been reexamined. If Lighthouse moves in this direction, they should also consider how far they can afford to go, whether they could recover the profit by redesigning the product line or improving the method of production, whether they should stop making this line or switch to a completely different line.

You have learned a great deal about financial management systems, especially about preparing operating budgets based on standard volume. Next, we'll discuss flexible operating budgets.

Flexible Operating Budgets

By stabilizing fixed costs and unit costs, standard volume helps managers deal with some of the problems caused by the business cycle. Fluctuating customer demand also cre-

EXERCISE 11-6: EVALUATING PRELIMINARY BUDGETS

Determine whether each product line has a favorable or unfavorable preliminary variance. Compare proposed costs with budgeted costs in Exercise 11-5. Compare your responses with the answer key.

Product	Favorable	Unfavorable
Bonnie Jean	_____	_____
Sir Winston	_____	_____
SuAnne	_____	_____

ates problems of changing variable costs, such as raw materials and employee salaries. (To provide a larger quantity of the product, the company must buy more raw materials and hire more workers.) **Flexible operating budgets** help solve these problems.

Flexible budgets change as the level of business changes. Figure 11-7 shows roughly how periodic forecasts of sales volume are sometimes higher and sometimes lower than standard volume, which represents the yearly average of a long-range forecast. If actual sales volume for several years were added together and averaged, the resulting annual figure would be very close to the standard volume established earlier from a long-range sales forecast.

Notice that the flexible budget doesn't fluctuate as sharply as the periodic sales forecasts. Its fluctuations represent variable costs that are easily increased or decreased as the volume of production changes. When actual sales turn out to be much higher than the forecast, operating departments are usu-

ally instructed to meet the demand and are given extra funds (increased budgets) to do so. When sales fall below the forecast, departmental budgets are reduced accordingly.

Of course fixed costs are not flexible. The cost of a building, for example, is spread equally over many years and remains the same for years. Fixed costs generally remain the same through short-term fluctuations in the volume of production (see Figure 11-8). Variable costs are directly tied to the volume of production, and they rise (or fall) with production (see Figure 11-9).

For budgeting purposes, all costs are considered to be either fixed or variable. (Costs that don't fall readily into either category are arbitrarily assigned to one or the other.) Each unit of product incurs both fixed and variable costs. Figure 11-10 shows how the two determine total costs. The variable cost has been added to the total cost at each level of volume. Fixed costs go on even when production stops. Therefore even if there were no variable costs involved, the unit

FIGURE 11-7: Flexible Operating Budget Based on Standard Volume

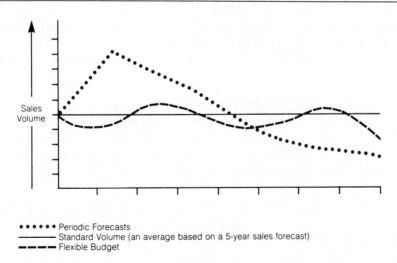

•••••• Periodic Forecasts
——————— Standard Volume (an average based on a 5-year sales forecast)
━ ━ ━ ━ Flexible Budget

FIGURE 11-8: Production Volume Does Not Affect Fixed Costs

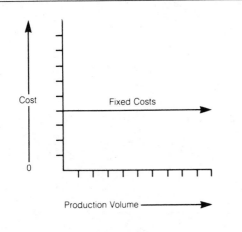

FIGURE 11-9: As Production Volume Increases, Variable Costs Increase Proportionately

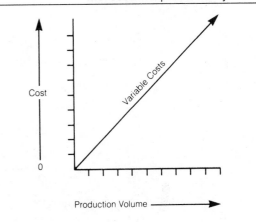

cost of the product would at least equal the fixed cost.

Flexible budgeting therefore is based on these conditions:

1. Fixed costs remain the same during the year.

2. Variable costs are based on the volume of production as it changes during the year. More money is allocated for the necessary variable costs when sales demand exceeds the forecast and less when it falls below the forecast.

3. Each unit supervisor or department manager is responsible for controlling variable costs, especially when volume decreases.

Relationship Between Fixed Costs and Plant Capacity

To understand the relationship between fixed costs and plant capacity (the maximum number of units that can be manufac-

tured in a plant per year), compare the graphs shown in Figures 11-11, 11-12, and 11-13. An understanding of this relationship can also help you realize the importance of capital budgets, which are discussed later in this chapter. Figure 11-11 shows the lowest possible fixed cost, the lowest plant capacity, and the lowest **break-even point**—the volume at which total revenue equals total costs. If you drop a vertical line from the point at which the revenue and total costs lines intersect, you'll find that the break-even point is about 275,000 units. This means that the company must sell at least 275,000 units to break even. All sales above 275,000 units represent a profit; failure to sell 275,000 units means a loss.

The advantage of being able to turn a profit after producing "only" 275,000 units is more than offset by the fact that in this case plant capacity and standard volume are the same. The plant can produce no more than 400,000 units, which is the long-range forecast of average annual demand (standard volume) that fixed costs are based upon.

FIGURE 11-10: Variable and Fixed Costs = Total Costs

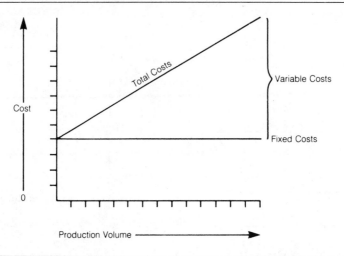

FIGURE 11-11: Minimal Plant Capacity

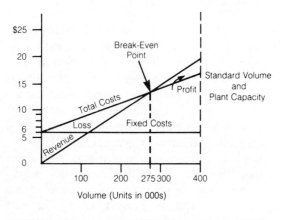

Volume (Units in 000s)

What would happen if customer demand increases to substantially more than 400,000 units? Since the company doesn't have the plant capacity to meet such a greater-than-average demand, potential customers will have to buy a similar product from one of the company's competitors, and the com-

pany will lose an opportunity to make additional profits.

Figure 11-12 reflects a company that has invested too heavily in **fixed assets** (buildings and equipment). The fixed costs are so high that the break-even point is about 375,000 units—so close to the standard volume of 400,000 that there is very little profit to be made when between 375,000 and 400,000 units are produced. Profitability between 400,000 and 500,000 units of volume is not as high as it is in Figure 11-13, and the opportunity to make money above 500,000 units may never arise since this demand is so far above average.

Figure 11-13 reflects the best mix. The break-even point is approximately 325,000 units, well below the average annual long-range forecast of 400,000 units (standard volume). Operations will be increasingly profitable up to 125 percent of standard volume (500,000 units). The company will make *some* profit even though it falls short of making standard volume by up to about 75,000 units (that is, the company will start making a profit once it makes and sells 325,000 units).

FIGURE 11-12: Excessive Fixed Costs and Plant Capacity

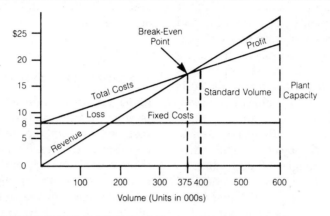

FIGURE 11-13: Optimal Plant Capacity

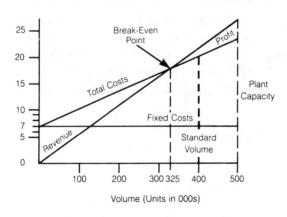

Zero-Base Budgets

We've discussed two budgeting procedures that help overcome different types of budgeting problems: (1) basing fixed costs on standard volume and (2) using flexible budgets. A third procedure, **zero-base budgeting**, is designed to help prevent cost control problems.

In most organizations managers begin working on their initial budget proposals for the coming year by looking at the current year's budget figures. They then estimate increases or decreases in each category for the coming year. One item might be 8 percent less than this year's amount, or 92 percent of it. Another item might be 20 percent more than this year's amount, or 120 percent of it. This is the traditional approach to estimating expenses for budget purposes.

Zero-base budgeting, developed in the late 1960s, is a new approach that is steadily gaining acceptance. It has been especially useful for government budgets, for large business organizations, and for other operations where management must exercise a fairly high degree of control over expenditures.

As its name implies, zero-base budgeting is a system in which managers analyze each item in the budget from a starting point of zero. They must justify estimated expenses anew each year. In traditional budgeting procedures, managers frequently assume that certain expenditures will be necessary in the future simply because they were considered necessary in the past.

In zero-base budgeting, managers analyze each item—both old and new—to determine how necessary it is to helping them achieve the company's stated objectives. They calculate costs and determine benefits for various *levels* of service, quality, performance, and activities rather than assuming that one particular level is optimal. As a result, managers can map out several alternative approaches to achieving objectives and compare the costs versus the benefits of each alternative plan. For example, they can determine the minimum level of service or activity required to fulfill each particular objective. Then they can study the advantages of upgrading to higher levels. The process includes enforced ranking of priorities to help in the analysis of the various levels of service or activities.

Leaming and Motley in *Administrative Office Management* [3] mention four ways that zero-base budgeting differs from traditional budgeting:

1. It does not build from a base of the previous year's budget.

2. It examines the costs and benefits of all activities.

3. It emphasizes the purpose of each activity prior to the allocation of dollars.

4. It encourages the examination of alternative approaches.

The prior year's budget is used for comparative purposes only, after the final zero-base budget is prepared; it does not serve as the basis for the budget. The entire system includes a method of follow-up and documentation of actual income and costs. Some organizations have also developed programs for recycling data and information to help managers evaluate decisions they made about providing various levels of service or activities. Such information also helps managers prepare subsequent budgets. Each of these further steps to expand the concept of *zero-base budgeting* into a *system of zero-base planning*

helps to integrate the planning, managing, budgeting, and controlling of the organization.

The Cost Control System

Managers are responsible not only for preparing operating budgets, but for seeing that costs stay within the budgeted amounts. If they are to do this effectively, top management must establish and implement a **cost control system.** An effective cost control system provides top management with an accurate picture of how well each department is staying within its budget from day to day, week to week, and month to month. The system includes

1. A reasonable budget, which is the company's plan for making a profit by making effective use of all its resources (capital assets, materials, supplies, and people)

2. A reporting system that determines the differences between budgeted dollars and actual dollars spent in each significant budget category

An effective reporting system provides these figures at the appropriate time to the right first-line, middle, and top managers so they can make intelligent decisions for keeping costs within the budgeted amount. To make these decisions, managers need to be able to differentiate various types of costs and to implement workable procedures for controlling and reducing operating costs in their areas of responsibility.

Differentiating Costs If managers are to make the right decisions about spending money and cutting costs, they must differentiate costs that are directly related to the manufacture of a product or to the providing of a service from those costs that are indirect, preproduction, or sales and administrative. The more directly related the cost is to producing the firm's major products or services, the more its reduction is likely to affect the firm's capacity to deliver and the quality of its products or services.

In retail operations the distinction is between administrative costs and costs directly related to securing and selling merchandise. In service operations it's between sales and administrative costs and the costs directly related to providing the service, such as salaries of the service workers and the supplies they need to perform the service.

In most manufacturing operations, costs directly and indirectly involved in making the product account for about 90 percent of the total company cost and expense. The other 10 percent may be categorized as "other expense" (see Figure 11-6), which includes sales (to wholesalers or retailers) and administrative expense.

Taking Responsibility for Budgeting and Cost Control Generally, all managers are expected to take some responsibility for budgeting and cost control. This is usually a top priority for managers who directly supervise a group of workers. Here are some specific actions that you, as a manager, may be expected to take responsibility for

1. Deciding the number of positions required to operate your department

2. Establishing a performance planning system for setting objectives and standards, giving feedback, and making formal performance evaluations (see Chapter 10)

3. Preparing a preliminary budget for your department and cooperating in arriving at a final budget

4. Staying within your budget by controlling and reducing your department's operat-

ing costs and by working with subordinates to establish objectives for improving departmental performance

Your ability to stay within your approved budget is an important indicator of your effectiveness as a manager. In order to determine how well your department is staying within its budget, you must take these actions:

1. Get regular, timely information (reports, computer printouts, and so forth) on the areas you are responsible for.

2. From this information, identify negative differences in your department's performance and budget figures as soon as possible after they occur.

3. Determine the causes of any negative differences and decide what actions should be taken to correct the deficiency. (Be sure to include subordinates in this step.)

4. Follow through to see that action is taken, and evaluate its effectiveness.

Sometimes it's difficult to *get* the exact data you need to determine how well your department is doing. Figures need to be broken down by department or unit. Item-by-item differences are often necessary to pinpoint where the problem lies. Sometimes it's difficult to *identify* the data you need on computer printouts. Take the initiative to find out where and how you can get the feedback you need in order to make informed decisions. If that information is not currently available, make every effort to find a way to start getting it. Explain to your boss the advantages of obtaining early, timely, usable information in meeting your objectives and staying within your budget.

One of your key functions is to control and reduce your department's operating costs. This is the way you help the company reach its profit target. Much of what you do as a manager involves seeing that your people have the resources they need to meet their objectives even while you're minimizing costs.

Cost control involves procedures for assuring that your people stay within your budget. You must plan in advance how you will keep your expenditures within the budget and how you will correct deficiencies when costs are too high. If you have no negative differences between budget and actual costs, you are probably doing an effective job of cost control.

Cost reduction refers to procedures for eliminating part or all of a particular cost or expense. The idea is to find new and better ways of doing things and to discover what things can be eliminated entirely. If managers are not constantly alert to areas of possible cost reduction, the company's competitors will soon become more efficient. The competitors' lower costs will make it difficult for the company to meet its profit objectives and may eventually run the company out of business.

Here are some suggestions for reducing costs.

1. Approach cost reduction positively. Taking the attitude that "There must be a better way" will help you and your people think creatively.

2. Get all your people involved in the cost reduction process. Not only will they be likely to come up with valuable ideas, but they will be more highly motivated to perform. Also, people are more likely to accept the changes resulting from cost reduction decisions if they have participated in the decision-making process.

3. Ask pointed questions about current procedures. Ask them in this order:

   What are we doing in this task? Is this the best way to do it? Is there a better or faster way? Has everyone involved been asked for suggestions?

   Why are we doing this? Do we really need it? What would happen if we stopped doing it? Before you can establish *why* you are doing something, you need to be clear about exactly *what* you are doing. Once you've determined that a task must be done, ask the following questions to determine how it can be done more efficiently and effectively.

   How much of this do we really need? Could we get by with less? Could we substitute something that costs less?

   Who is doing the job? Could anyone else do it better? How many other people are able to do it?

   When is the job being done? Is that the best time? Could it be combined with other jobs to save time and money? Can we improve it by different sequencing, grouping, or accumulating?

   Where is the job being done? Is this the best place? Do other activities in this area interfere with getting the job done? Could another department or unit do it at less cost?

Here are some steps for controlling and reducing operating costs.

1. Identify those costs that you cannot influence. Fixed costs, such as property insurance, property taxes, and depreciation, may be based on standard volume and budgeted over a period of years. They cannot be changed during the year. The only way you can influence them is on a long-term basis in planning purchases of capital equipment. You may also be unable to influence some variable costs that are controlled by someone else but are charged to your department.

2. Identify the costs you can influence—variable costs that change as business activity fluctuates and are related to the amount of work your department does.

3. Analyze the costs by category and by item to see which ones need to be reduced.

4. Determine ways to reduce costs. (Be sure to include subordinates in this step.)

Here are some suggestions for controlling operating costs by controlling expenditures for direct labor and manufacturing.

Cost standards for *direct labor* are usually fairly accurate and complete because productivity is measured fairly easily by observing the number of items produced in a specific time period. First-line supervisors and managers are responsible for controlling excessive absenteeism and tardiness, the quality of workmanship, efficiency, and work procedures—all of which affect direct labor cost. Supervisors and managers can also help control direct labor costs by making sure that poor work conditions—inefficient equipment layouts, inappropriate work standards, unbalanced work flows, poor scheduling, defective material—are improved.

Manufacturing expense presents a more difficult control problem than direct labor and direct material costs because standards of quality and work performance are not directly tied to the product. These expenses can be controlled, however, by actions such as these:

1. Select clerical, staff, and supervisory people who are well qualified.

2. Train and follow up properly.

3. Encourage suggestions for improvement.

4. Serve as a resource person for improved procedures and methods; coach your people in improved methods.

5. Provide proper tools, equipment, and supplies.

6. Don't overstaff. Have enough work to keep everyone busy.

7. Maintain good housekeeping and efficient use of space to eliminate unnecessary handling of material.

8. Handle operating supplies properly by being sure to personally inspect and sign requisitions, question the need for and use of each item requested, instruct people in the proper use of equipment and supplies, let people know the cost of each item they use, know the normal life and usage of each item, and check used supplies for possible salvage or use in another department.

9. Keep utility costs in check by having someone eliminate leaks, repair broken windows, and put signs by light switches and equipment switches as reminders to turn them off when not in use.

10. Prevent undue fixed charges by using good layouts that make the best use of available floor space (consider vertical storage of materials), removing any equipment that is unnecessary, eliminating hazards and practicing fire prevention techniques in order to reduce insurance rates, and getting maximum production from equipment by using the best methods and making mechanical improvements.

11. Keep losses, errors, and defects to a minimum by taking steps to be sure proper material and parts are used to train people well, stress quality standards, tell people how much scrap costs, keep a constant check on machine setup and work flow, report substandard material, practice preventive maintenance on

equipment, have malfunctioning equipment repaired promptly, and see that persons responsible for the recordkeeping and accounting of assets are *not* also responsible for negotiations involving those assets or physical custody of those assets (to protect the company from employee dishonesty).

Now that you have an overview of how operating budgets are prepared and used, we'll discuss capital budgets.

PLANNING FOR SPECIAL PURCHASES THROUGH A CAPITAL BUDGET

The overall company budget normally contains a capital budget as well as an operating budget. The **capital budget** is the plan for acquiring fixed assets such as new plants, office space, and machine tools. These expenditures are planned over a period of from two to ten years. Although supervisors and middle managers are usually involved in capital budgeting in only a limited way, it's important that they understand capital budgeting and the role it plays in the company's financial management system.

Distinguishing Between Fixed and Current Assets

The key to distinguishing between the operating budget and the capital budget is an understanding of the difference between fixed assets and current assets.

Fixed Assets   Capital budgets reflect management's plans for investing in land, buildings, machine tools, and other assets that are "fixed" in the sense that the company doesn't normally sell them as long as they adequately meet the needs of the business. The

costs resulting from the purchase of fixed assets are said to be "fixed" because they do not go up and down with the volume of production, if the company uses standard volume. They are charged to indirect manufacturing expense and are recovered over a period of several years.

Current Assets   These assets are items that are converted into cash at regular intervals in the normal process of doing business. They include raw materials on hand, work in process, finished goods, and accounts receivable (money owed the company by its customers). As a general rule, more than half of a manufacturing company's assets are current assets. They are sometimes referred to as "working capital" because they are actively "working" on a day-to-day basis as the company goes through the continuous process of converting them from cash to finished goods to cash. This process, shown in Figure 11-14, is called the **production cycle** by most managers. Accountants call it the working capital cycle.

The faster management can convert current assets from cash into goods (or service in a service-oriented company, merchandise

FIGURE 11-14: Production (Working Capital) Cycle

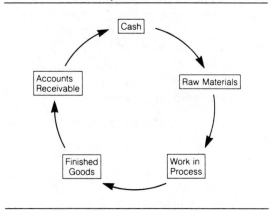

in a retail operation) and back into cash again, the higher the profit margin is likely to be. Operating budgets provide measures of management's efficiency in using current assets.

Striking a Balance One of the main goals of financial planning is to arrive at the best mix of current and fixed assets. In order to survive in a competitive environment, management must make the most of each dollar it spends and earn a profit adequate to compensate the owners or stockholders for the risk they take when they invest their money. The company must also keep up with new technology, meet new customer needs and desires, and anticipate new requirements. Management must invest in the fixed assets necessary to meet all these needs. But it must also be sure there is always enough cash on hand to pay current bills. Although the Treasurer or Controller of the company is ultimately responsible for maintaining an adequate cash flow, all managers are expected to cooperate.

Distinguishing the Capital Budget from the Operating Budget

An understanding of the difference between capital and operating budgets is closely related to an understanding of fixed and current assets. When part of the cash is put aside in a capital budget to buy new fixed assets, the contribution to profits from these assets will occur over a much longer period of time than is the case when current assets are purchased. Management must determine which fixed assets will give the best return on investment. For example, certain assets will increase the firm's ability to offer new and better products. Others will enable the firm to operate more efficiently and therefore reduce costs. The result will be increased sales and wider profit margins.

Capital budgeting procedures differ from operating budgeting procedures in several respects.

Capital budgeting is long-range planning based on standard volume over a period of years.

Capital decisions made today have a long-term effect on the business.

Because mistakes cannot be easily corrected and frequently must be lived with for years, special precautions must be taken to ensure that capital expenditures will achieve the desired purpose.

In addition, the benefits of alternate plans must be compared and the limited cash available must be spent where benefits will be greatest—that is, where the efficiency of operations will be affected most positively.

Preparing the Capital Budget

Taking some responsibility for capital budgeting is wise even though you may not be in a position to prepare capital budget requests. For example, every manager is responsible for developing more effective work procedures and for recommending any capital equipment needed to implement new work procedures. You will be expected to take the initiative in making these needs known to the people who can get them included in the capital budget. You will also be expected to report wornout or obsolete equipment and to request appropriate replacements. Find out the capital budgeting procedure for your company.

The capital budgeting procedure used at Lighthouse Designs is shown in Figure 11-15. We'll discuss each step in detail.

Forecasting Proposed Projects Any manager who is planning a major project within

FIGURE 11-15: Capital Budgeting Procedures Used by Lighthouse Designs, Inc.

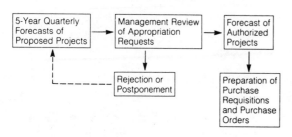

forecast of proposed projects to the forecast of authorized projects. If it is not approved, the manager submitting it may revise it and submit it again later or kill it.

Forecasting Authorized Projects The forecast of authorized projects provides the company with the following information to use in planning capital, operating, and cash budgets: (1) the company's likely requirements for capital tools and project expenses for the next five years; (2) information to be considered in the preparation of budget items, such as added depreciation to be charged against profits, project expenses (noncapital expenditures) to be charged against profits, cash requirements and timing, and staffing requirements to accomplish the work. Once the project is approved, the manager goes through normal procedures for purchasing any tools and equipment and securing any other resources needed to complete the project.

the next five years must submit a proposal together with all the costs of accomplishing the project. The forecast of proposed projects is a compilation of all proposals that require capital expenditures throughout the company. It is revised at the end of each quarter.

Partial plans are not acceptable because the rejection of plans to complete a project might mean that the money used to get a project underway was wasted. For complex projects, a sketchy preliminary proposal may be submitted to alert management to the type of project being planned. Later, a complete proposal indicating what will be achieved, how much the project will cost, when it will be completed, and what benefits it will provide must be submitted. A proposal must be resubmitted each quarter, with revised expenditures and timing (if necessary), until it is authorized, rejected, or withdrawn by the manager who submitted it.

Management's Review of Appropriation Requests The appropriation request is the formal request for the capital funds necessary for the project. This request includes a breakdown of costs for capital, special tooling, and other expense items. Appropriate line and staff managers review and evaluate the proposal. If the appropriation request is approved, the project is transferred from the

Making Purchase Requisitions If you need equipment for a major project, you will justify the need when you make the appropriation request for the entire project. If your equipment requests are approved when management reviews the project, then preparing purchase requisitions and purchase orders requires merely following routine procedures.

When you need new equipment that's *not* part of a major project, you'll need to justify your purchase requisition. You must show how the equipment will save the company money, how much it will save and by when. What will be the measurable gains in the productivity of your people through the use of this equipment? How much time will it save? Figure the salary cost of that time saved when you compute the total savings to the company. In estimating your equipment needs, consider what equipment you have now, what items you need to replace, what additional equipment you will need for use by employees you now have, and what additional equipment you will need for people you plan to add to your staff.

You need to know how equipment is classified in order to determine which budget to include it in. Let's look at three major categories: capital equipment, nominal value assets, and expense items.

Capital equipment consists of items that cost more than $500 and have a useful life of more than one year—for example, a $5,000 automated typewriter. Capital equipment needs are included in your department's forecast of proposed projects. After they are approved, they are included in the capital budget.

Nominal value assets are items that cost between $100 and $500 and have a useful life of more than one year—such as a $200 electronic desk calculator. These items are normally not provided for in the operating budget. An appropriation request is made for them.

Expense items are things that cost less than $100 and have a useful life of less than one year—for example, a ream of bond paper. These items are included in the operating budget.

See whether you can categorize some typical office items by completing Exercise 11-7.

Now that you've learned something about preparing and using operating and capital budgets, we'll discuss the cash budget.

TIMING COLLECTIONS AND PAYMENTS THROUGH A CASH BUDGET

The managers of a company can do a great job of carrying out plans for operating the business and for acquiring new equipment,

building space, and other resources, yet they may still be faced with bankruptcy. The operating budget and the capital budget don't include plans for assuring that the business always has enough money to meet its obligations. A cash budget is needed for that.

The **cash budget** is the plan for balancing expenditures with expected revenues so that there will be enough cash on hand to pay bills as they come due. Through cash budgeting, the company is assured of an adequate **cash flow** to pay the bills resulting from operating and capital budget expenditures. The department directly responsible for company finances is the one most concerned with this budget. However, managers of other departments may be asked to cooperate by either deferring expenditures and payments or accelerating sales and collections at certain times.

The Finance Department (sometimes given other titles in various companies) usually prepares and administers the cash budget. In times of high inflation and high interest rates, investing surplus cash at optimal rates until it is needed to pay bills becomes almost as important as ensuring an adequate cash flow to pay bills when they come due. In some companies the investment of surplus cash becomes a major source of income.

Perhaps the most difficult part of preparing a cash budget is actually done in the process of preparing the operating budget—that is, estimating income and expenses for the coming year. Normally a financial manager breaks down these annual estimates into quarterly estimates. Then it is a simple matter to figure whether income will be sufficient to cover expenses for each quarter. For example, suppose ABC Company's expected income for the year is $100 million and its anticipated expenses are $80 million. Does that imply ABC will take in $20 million more than they spend, so why worry about a cash budget? Exhibit 11-3 shows what can happen.

EXERCISE 11-7: CATEGORIZING OFFICE INVENTORY

Classify each item by placing a checkmark in the appropriate column.
Check your responses with the answer key.

Item	Capital Equipment	Nominal Value Asset	Expense Item
Office space (12' × 14')			
Dictation machine			
Tapes for dictation			
Walnut desk			
Desk chair			
Three reams of company letterhead			
Electric typewriter			
Typewriter table			
Pens (2 dozen)			
Company directory			
Framed picture			
Business cards—box of 100			
Ruler			
Office keys			
Wastebasket			
Bookcases (3)			
Four-drawer file cabinets (2)			
Desk calendar			
Stapler and staple remover			
Box of staples			
Two file baskets			
Armchairs			

In this case, ABC Company would have had to borrow money for the first nine months of the year in order to pay its bills on time. If creditors became impatient or banks were unwilling to keep lending, the company could be forced into bankruptcy. This is true even though the company made its targeted income of $100 million and kept its expenses within the targeted amount. Exhibit 11-4 shows that ABC Company actually made a profit of $20 million for the year but was in financial trouble all year because management didn't plan adequately for balancing income and expenditures.

Now try your hand at figuring a cash budget by completing Exercise 11-8, on page 428.

EXHIBIT 11-3: ABC Company, Cash Flow for 19xx ($ in Millions)

First quarter
Cash on hand at beginning of year ... $10
Income taken in during the 1st quarter ... +10
$20
Less: Expenses incurred in the 1st quarter ... −30
Cash balance—deficit ... ($10)

Second quarter
Income taken in during the 2nd quarter ... $20
Less: Expenses incurred during the 2nd quarter ... −25
Difference for the quarter—deficit ... ($ 5)
Cash balance—deficit ... ($15)

Third quarter
Income taken in during the 3rd quarter ... $30
Less: Expenses incurred during the 3rd quarter ... −15
Difference for the quarter ... $15
Cash balance ... -0-

Fourth quarter
Income taken in during the 4th quarter ... $40
Less: Expenses incurred during the 4th quarter ... −10
Difference for the quarter ... $30
Cash balance at the end of year ... $30

EXHIBIT 11-4: ABC Company, Summary of Income and Expenses ($ in Millions)

Income		Expenses	
1st quarter	$10	1st quarter	$30
2nd quarter	$20	2nd quarter	$25
3rd quarter	$30	3rd quarter	$15
4th quarter	$40	4th quarter	$10
	$100		$80

SUMMARY

In order to achieve desired results, managers must estimate the amount of goods or services the company will sell and how much will be needed to provide the resources necessary to provide those goods and services. That means managers must contribute to the preparation of budgets, which are based on these estimates. Managers must also control costs and expenses to see that they stay within the budgeted amounts. Every organization should have a workable financial management system that includes (1) an objective, (2) a measuring device, and (3) a control device.

EXERCISE 11-8: FIGURING A CASH BUDGET

Blakely Clothing Store's expected income and expenses for next year are shown below. Does management have a workable cash budget? Explain your answer. Then check the answer key.

	Forecast	
Quarter	Income	Expenses
Balance forward	$ 30,000	
1st quarter	115,000	$120,000
2nd quarter	115,000	125,000
3rd quarter	105,000	125,000
4th quarter	120,000	120,000

The annual report of a company might be considered the performance appraisal of its management. It contains two separate financial statements that provide the information needed to evaluate management's effectiveness: (1) The profit and loss statement summarizes the financial result of the company's activities each year. (2) The balance sheet shows the assets, liabilities, and net worth of the firm at the end of the company year.

From the profit and loss statement and the balance sheet we can figure three indicators of top management's effectiveness: (1) Profit margin measures how effective management has been in generating dollars of profit out of dollars of sales revenue. (2) Investment turnover measures management's effectiveness in using the money invested in company assets to generate sales. (3) Return on investment (ROI), which is based on the profit margin and the investment turnover rate, gives a more revealing, comprehensive measurement of a company's profitability.

Estimating or forecasting what will happen in future months and years is essential to the effective management of business organizations and to the process of financial planning. The first step in financial planning is the estimate of future revenue based on the sales forecast. Management then plans its costs along with a profit figure based on the sales forecast. It's the job of operating managers to achieve the stated goals of the company once these budget plans are made. To be most effective, the budget is based on ROI, which recognizes the need to maximize the investment turnover rate as well as the need to make a planned profit margin.

The operating budget for a typical manufacturing firm is broken down into three major categories: (1) The production budget is the plan for all the costs necessary to produce the product. (2) The design and tooling expense budget deals with the costs of getting ready to make the product. (3) The sales and administrative expense budget is the total of the budgets of the departments that are not directly involved in the manufacturing process.

Operating budgets based on standard volume are used by many manufacturing firms to provide a reasonable base point from which to figure fixed costs and, in turn, unit costs of products. The use of standard volume helps to spread fluctuations in sales volume and in capital investment in plant, equipment, and other assets over a period of several years. Standard volume is the *average* yearly volume expected over a specified period of years (a business cycle). Index volume is the forecast of next year's actual sales volume. Flexible budgets, in turn, allow for unexpected increases or decreases in sales volume by providing for corresponding changes in variable costs.

An effective cost control system provides management with an accurate picture of how well each department is staying within its budget from day to day, week to week, and month to month. The system includes a reasonable budget, an effective reporting system, and a way to differentiate various types of costs.

The capital budget reflects management's plans for investing in fixed assets, such as land, buildings, and major equipment. These plans should consider the optimal balance of fixed and current assets. Every manager is expected to recommend capital equipment needed to implement new work procedures and to replace wornout or obsolete equipment.

A cash budget is essential for assuring that the company always has enough money to meet its obligations. Operating managers are expected to provide prompt information about the expected timing of sales receipts and expense payments so that the finance department can prepare and implement a cash budget.

REFERENCES

1. General Motors Education and Training. *Financially Speaking.* Flint, Mich., 1977.

2. *Industrial Engineering Handbook.* Edited by H. C. Maynard. New York: McGraw-Hill, 1980. See especially cost control and profit prediction.

3. Leaming, Marj P., and Robert J. Motley. *Administrative Office Management.* Dubuque, Iowa: Wm. C. Brown, 1984.

4. Stonich, Paul J., and Associates. *Zero-Base Planning and Budgeting.* Homewood, Ill: Dow-Jones-Irwin, 1982.

5. Tazris, Carol. "Money: The Subject Harder to Talk About Than Sex." *MS.,* Vol. 6 (November 1977), pp. 63–67.

6. Tazris, Carol. "20,000 Women Reveal Their Fears, Splurges, and New Confidence—About Money." *MS.,* Vol. 6 (May 1978), pp. 47–51.

7. Turecamo, Dorrine. "Education: Visiting Scientists" and "New Office: You Can Take It With You." *Working Woman* (September 1983), pp. 100–118.

Chapter Twelve

Building Your Team: Supervising, Selecting, and Training Workers

"Management is getting work done through people."

Mary Parker Follett (1925)

You will incorporate all your personal and managerial skills in the supervision of your unit or department. "Supervision," as the term is used here, refers to your day-to-day responsibilities for selecting and training workers, delegating tasks, assessing and evaluating the performance of workers, and coaching them to improve their performance.

In this chapter you will have an opportunity to learn more about

1. Delegating tasks in ways that provide for the most effective and appropriate training and development of all types of subordinates

2. Analyzing performance problems and coaching workers to top performance

3. Evaluating workers' performance coherently and fairly to enhance motivation

4. Interviewing and selecting the most suitable subordinates for building a productive work team

5. Orienting new workers in ways that enhance both their motivation to achieve and their future productivity on the job

 The Magic of Involvement

"You must have had a good day," Murray smiles at Carrie as she breezes through the front door.

"Oh, Murray, I think this job is really beginning to click! And it all seems so easy, now that I know what to do."

"Sure. I knew you would do it. And to what do you attribute your sudden success?"

"I've finally learned how to get people involved. Now I know how to include them in the planning, the problem-solving, and the decision-making and still maintain their respect—you know, still project the right image of power and authority. It's like I use that sense of power to challenge them to learn and grow and achieve, but they also know I respect them and support them. Oh, I'm high on this feeling of success!" Carrie twirls around the room.

"Say, it sure makes things nice around here, too," Murray grins, catching her in his arms. "What do you say we celebrate with a night on the town?"

Carrie is tuned in to the feelings of her staff. Just that day Frank Andreini, one of her salespersons, ran into Hal Roach, a former Lighthouse salesman under George Rodriguez.

F: Hi, Hal. How are things at the Nob Hill shop?

H: Oh, so-so. How about the scene at Lighthouse? I hear you have a lady boss now.

F: That's right. Carrie Dickeson. Yeah, things are going real well. We have a whole new system of doing things. At first I didn't know how I was going to like all this, but it's working out okay. I never made so much money. The customers like what we're doing. And the best part is, the company lets me in on what's going on—in fact, they adopted a couple of my ideas.

H: That's a switch. I remember we were in the dark a lot of the time at Alexis, and I feel even more that way at Nob Hill.

F: It really makes a difference when you know what's going on. Why, I can see that I could move into a Sales Manager's slot and do a darned good job of it.

H: Hey, that's even more of a switch. Remember when you swore you'd never put up with management hassles?

F: Yeah, but Dickeson's been giving me some management responsibilities, and

I've been getting a lot done without much hassle. Matter of fact, it's a kick—something new, you know.

H: You? A management type?

F: Well, I'll have to give some of the credit to Dickeson. She's a good coach—doesn't throw everything at you at once or expect you to be an expert right away.

H: *Or* look over your shoulder, like she doesn't trust you?

F: No—she's given me some pretty tough assignments, too, but she takes plenty of time to go over everything and explain the end results she's looking for. I like her style.

H: Well, my boss, Jane Osgood, is really getting on my nerves.

F: How's that?

H: Well, it's mainly this heavy, oppressive maternal "presence." She hovers.

F: (*Grinning*) Well, at least you know she cares.

H: Not really! There's not even that saving grace. Oh sure, she cares how *she* looks to the top brass. But I don't get the message that she cares much about what happens to me. The other guys say you really have to be careful—she'll leave you high and dry if you blow an assignment. You're better off to keep checking with her and let her make all the real decisions. Of course, she takes most of the credit if things turn out well—but then she can't very well blame you if they don't work out.

F: Have any of the guys ever complained to her?

H: Yeah. One of the guys told me he tried to talk to her about it, but she ducked the issue. She makes a big thing about the "one big happy family" within our department. I get the impression she wants to think of it that way. She doesn't want to be bothered by any facts that show otherwise. So people generally either keep their problems and complaints to themselves or gripe to each other.

---

1. What effective management attitudes and actions did you see revealed in this story?

2. Why are they effective? _____

3. What ineffective attitudes and actions did you see? _____

4. Why are they ineffective? _____

DELEGATING EFFECTIVELY: THE KEY TO WORKERS' DEVELOPMENT AND TRAINING

When we think of day-to-day supervision, we usually think first of delegating tasks. In the broadest sense, delegation involves the training and development of your workers and your team, the direction and followup of assignments, the analysis of performance problems, coaching to overcome problems, as well as periodic formal evaluations of performance. Let's begin by discussing how effective delegation of tasks can help train and develop your people into a top-notch team.

Basing Delegation on the Worker's Readiness to Grow

Once you have had a chance to observe and interact with the workers in your department, you need to devise plans for training and developing each of them most effectively. A key aspect of training and development is selecting tasks you can delegate and matching them to the workers with the readiness to successfully complete the tasks and benefit from the assignments. An approach many effective executives use to accomplish this goal begins with ranking workers according to their readiness to learn and grow. Next, you divide the ranked list into top, middle, and bottom groups for training purposes. Then, you can work on upgrading the performance of the bottom group, the marginals; developing the top group, the promotables, into managers; and designing a program by which the middle group of average performers become assistants to the promotables.

Identifying Workers' Levels Although you will of course deal with each worker's strengths and weaknesses on an individual basis, ranking can help you to clarify in your own mind which people you consider the promotables, the weak links, and the average, reasonably competent workers. If your group is larger than fifteen or twenty people, first break up the group into logical smaller units that will be easier to rank and group. The smaller groups might be based on the type of job members do or other workable criteria.

It's important to keep an open mind about who belongs in each category. If a worker improves dramatically, you must be willing to handle her or his training and development differently. Likewise, if an apparently growing performer fizzles out, you may need to adjust your thinking.

One approach to ranking within a group is to ask yourself, "Which of these people seems likely to go the farthest?" That person is ranked first. Then ask, "Which one will probably have the hardest time advancing here?" That person is ranked last. Repeat the two questions until all the others are ranked. Then go back and divide the group into promotables, weak links, and average workers.

Another approach is to visualize a situation in which you are forced to lay off some of your people. Really get into it, and as realistically as possible decide whom you would let go first if you had to do it tomorrow morning. Which worker would you lay off next? Keep going until you're left with only one person—your most valuable worker, obviously. Now it should be easy to rank the group according to readiness for further growth.

Once you have ranked your workers by performance, you have a framework for concentrating your efforts to upgrade overall group performance. Most of your efforts should go into the top and bottom groups. This involves three main tactics: (1) Upgrade the weak links or move them out, eliminating marginals from your unit. (2) Groom the promotables to take your place (or another manager's place). Your special attention to these strong performers can pay off exceptionally well in increased motivation, productivity, and team spirit. As promotables get promoted, you can select the best qualified people available to replace them. You can attract better people because your unit becomes known as a steppingstone to higher-level jobs. (3) Make the middle group assistants to the star performers. The "middles" get a challenging change of pace while the promotables get a chance to develop managerial skills.

Handling Marginal Performers You should always be looking for the weakest persons in your group. You may want to concentrate on one or two at a time for development. Do what you can to train them, help them, give them some new skills, develop them. In the process, it is important to give them honest evaluations of their performance so they know exactly where they stand and how they are doing.

If they come around, they are no longer marginals. If they don't, you must either transfer them to more appropriate jobs within the company or let them go. Then you can start working with the next weakest links in order to upgrade them to the middle group. Theoretically, at least, you will end up with a weak link that is merely the least outstanding of a group of unusually fine performers.

The key to developing marginal performers is to determine the reason for their poor performance. See the discussion of performance analysis later in this chapter. Also see Chapters 8 and 10 for suggestions on setting objectives and enhancing motivation.

Some workers are marginal because they are simply not capable of mastering difficult tasks. Try to select tasks these people will be able to master. Such tasks might be assignments that would quickly bore more able performers but present continuing challenges to marginals.

Workers who are chronically and irremediably lacking should be removed as soon as you are sure that they won't work out. Over a reasonable period of time, your face-to-face evaluations and ratings should have made it clear that you are dissatisfied with the marginal worker's performance. In the later stages the worker should know without doubt that she or he will be leaving unless there is adequate improvement in performance. Specific objectives make it clear exactly what constitutes adequate performance. This doesn't mean that it is wise to use threats, but a candid discussion of the consequences of continued poor performance is only fair to the worker. Document these discussions to provide legal protection for you and the company. The Personnel Department can advise you on the steps you should take leading up to the discharge.

When you do give up on someone, it's important for you to take action as soon as possible. Don't wait until the worker does something that angers you so you can fire him or her in the heat of the moment. Doing it rationally and with consideration is more efficient in the long run. And it is certainly kinder. Perhaps most important, discharging the worker in the right way has a positive effect on other workers. Word gets around that you are fair and feel reasonable concern for them, their problems, and their welfare.

Do everything you honestly can within company policy to make it easy for people you fire—for example, allowing them to officially resign, to choose between working for a few more weeks or receiving severance pay instead, and to use their office while looking for another job. Find out what the worker wants others in the group told and honor this request if possible. In other words, treat the worker as well as you can.

Developing the Promotables   Once you have developed a plan for handling your marginal employees, your next step is to work on a plan for the promotables. The best way to train and develop people is to train them as if they are to be your replacement. Although the idea of grooming people to replace you may go against your natural impulses, it is a powerful concept that is essential to managers with the ambition to keep moving up.

It is fine to make a job *function* or your special expertise indispensable to your boss or the company. But if you don't want to get stuck in that job, you had better train some of your subordinates in the same job function or area of expertise. You know from reading previous chapters that this approach will attract better people to your team and keep them more highly motivated to learn and achieve.

Let's look at some common pitfalls in selecting candidates for your job.

Looking at performance alone and not giving enough weight to potential managerial ability. Everyone who is potential management material *is* a good performer, but every good performer does not necessarily make a good boss.

Being overly impressed with surface razzle-dazzle and making judgments too hastily. Consider all your people with an open mind and look long and hard at their strengths and weaknesses.

Grooming only one person to step into your job. Train *all* the people who appear to be managerial material so that any one of a fairly large group could step into your job. Train them all for *either* your job *or* some undefined managerial position at some unspecified future date. This provides growth, recognition, and motivation for *all* your best people.

Naming a successor too soon. Wait until you're ready to move before announcing your replacement. This maintains a spirit of healthy competition (assuming other aspects of the work situation also promote healthy competition). It also prevents unhealthy alliances by rivals against the named successor before she or he even has a chance to assume authority.

How do you tell if a person will make a good manager? First, see how she or he performs the functions. Then, determine whether she or he really *wants* to manage.

Review the kinds of things a manager must do well (see Chapter 7). Then ask yourself how well Jane or Joe performs as an organizer, administrator, communicator, trainer, evaluator, and so forth. If you don't know, give the person some assignments that require these skills. Give some suggestions and guidelines; be available as a resource person; give some coaching where needed; and see how the person performs.

Next you must determine whether Jane or Joe really *wants* to manage. To be successful, a manager must have a keen interest in the process of management—an interest that overrides the professional or technical area of expertise. There are several signs to look for in determining whether people have the desire to manage.

One is the need for power (see Chapter 9). Subordinates who take all the authority they can and are willing to be judged by the results—rather than asking the boss for his or her blessings on every decision they make—probably have an adequate need for power.

The ability to look at all questions in an original way and the practice of coming up with unexpected rather than pat answers is the sign of a good manager. Promotables can recognize the important issues and analyze the impact these issues are likely to make on their own area of authority. They do their own thinking and arrive at their own conclusions.

Quickness in spotting key issues without having everything spelled out is essential. A general manner of assured confidence that comes from being prepared and reflects a probing, sensitive intelligence.

A manager must be articulate and fluent in communicating, which includes the ability to organize thoughts, solve problems, and express thoughts convincingly.

Finally, the potential manager should have a sense of team membership—being able to work on a situation until the other person feels comfortable with it. And an effective manager must be willing to work for solutions the team can live with, even though he or she could impose the solutions on the group.

Once you've identified those workers most ready to grow, you must decide the best way to develop their talents. Your goal is to train them so they could replace you. Keep in mind these two key factors in successfully training potential replacements:

(1) Leave them alone once you have given them an assignment. The tendency is to look over their shoulders, to oversupervise. You must not only let go of them, you must train them to let go of their subordinates. (2) Plan an individualized training program tailored to each subordinate's needs. This takes a great deal of insight and thoughtfulness; it's the opposite of a stereotyped or "canned" program. Remember these factors as you move through the three training phases described in Exhibit 12-1.

Designing an Assistant Program for Average Performers A training and development program that is effective with the average, reasonably competent worker is one in which everyone in the group becomes a sort of part-time assistant manager or assistant to an assistant manager. We might refer to it as an "assistant program." The people in this middle group may currently lack the motivation, ambition, or the ability of the promotables. Their jobs may seem rather dull and boring to them. They turn in an adequate performance, but they get most of their kicks from other activities. Appropriate delegation to these people by either you or your promotables can greatly improve their level of productivity and motivation. It can even bring some of these people along to the point that they become top performers. Here's how the program works.

Many of the tasks you or your top performers consider routine would be an interesting challenge to someone in the middle group. These are tasks that were interesting to you before you mastered them and repeated them time and again. They are not mere drudgery. This is an important distinction because selecting tasks that will be interesting and challenging is the key to success in this kind of program.

Another type of task that is ideal for delegation to the middle group is any project that has been shelved for a while—one you

EXHIBIT 12-1: Steps to Develop the Managerial Potential of Top Performers

Phase 1: Initial Broadening: Even top performers have areas of weakness that may become a problem. Giving them responsibilities in those areas helps them overcome the human tendency to move toward their strengths and dismiss functions they know nothing about as being unimportant. When such areas suddenly become part of promotables' jobs and they must learn more about the functions, they begin to respect the area's values.

Phase 2: Assumption of Your Authority: This step-by-step process involves your letting go of central parts of your job. Doing this is quite difficult for most managers, so you must mentally prepare and remind yourself that it's necessary for your own continued advancement. If you plan carefully, you can schedule the delegation of tasks so that the promotables take them over and you let them go with minimal disruption.

1. Turn over the technical aspects of one of your job functions. Break the job down into logical segments. Give the subordinate responsibility for one segment at a time, keeping a close watch only until you are sure things are going smoothly.

2. Turn over the judgment aspects of that same job function. Review every decision at first, then review only occasional decisions until the candidate is finally taking full responsibility.

3. Let go gradually. This is an essential part of the process. The subordinate is still working under your direction, but you avoid interfering or oversupervising. Once you let go of a particular area, it may be helpful to arrange a business trip for a few days or at least to get very involved in other projects for a while in order to signal that the candidate is now on his or her own.

Phase 3: Delegation to Workers in Other Groups: Once candidates are performing well in a new area of responsibility, it's time to start turning them into good bosses. In all probability it will be next to impossible for them to deliberately delegate some of those central duties to less capable people, knowing they are still accountable for the results.

1. Push and coach them to delegate to others. You will probably have to arrange matters so that they are forced to delegate. Keep piling on the work so that they *must* delegate and depend on others in order to get everything done on time. Coach them in delegation techniques discussed in this chapter. If they still won't delegate, they have failed a vital test.

2. Later, require formal training plans that you both review periodically. The training plan should at least indicate the next logical step for every subordinate your candidate is working with.

3. Set a good example in the way *you* train, direct, control, reward, and discipline. Your example is the most powerful influence in teaching them to deal with *their* work team. When you report on an assignment to your boss, take along the promotable who worked on it. Showing how you relate to your boss teaches them how you want them to relate to you. As a further example, send them copies of reports you write to your boss. This also helps them understand your approaches and thought processes.

4. Maintain control of results because you're still held accountable. Once your promotables start delegating to the middle group, you're even further removed from the activities that lead to results. Set up checkpoints and follow up regularly.

or one of your top performers have been meaning to get around to one of these days but somehow it never gets done. Or delegate *part* of a project—a fact-finding assignment, analysis of a problem and possible solutions, collection of data for a report or a presentation, preparation of rough drafts or written materials, for example.

A somewhat different approach is similar to job rotation but involves only certain assignments rather than entire jobs. It might be called "assignment rotation" or "task rotation." Let workers swap assignments or projects so they can learn more about the various functions and operations of the unit or department. An assignment that used to "turn on" one person but has become "old hat" will be interesting and exciting to someone else because of its newness and challenge. Talk this over with your people and get their ideas about advantageous swaps.

Your top performers should eventually pass on to someone in the middle group any duty that calls for less than their full talent. There will still be parts of their jobs, of course, that are less than thrilling, but now the routine will be enlivened for all groups. Everyone can experience being interested in at least part of his or her job.

Some of the middle group will take such interest and pride in successfully completing more demanding assignments that they will begin to see possibilities for advancement. Your policy of promoting top performers can keep this new-found ambition alive and will result in middle-group people moving into the top group. Not everyone will respond so well, of course, but most will at least experience a heightened interest in their jobs. If a worker doesn't respond at all well to the program, that's your signal to weed him or her out.

The essence of the assistant program is that each worker's job takes on a new importance since it now includes assignments once carried out at a higher level. The two most important elements in enhancing each worker's feelings about this increased job importance are (1) the delegator's attitude toward the assignment—your promotable (or you) shows by what she or he says and does that she or he considers the task important; (2) prompt recognition and appropriate rewards for accomplishments.

Perhaps the key way to signal that an assignment is important is the sense of urgency with which you treat all aspects of it. For example, if you can't respond to a request for approval or for information within two days, go to the worker personally and tell him or her why. If you are not around,

have your secretary or assistant relay the message.

Another example: Your people need information or material from another department, and their assignment is being held up because they have been unable to get it. If you as boss take on the head of the department in question in order to get things moving, you signal to everyone that you care how and whether your people perform. So be alert to bottlenecks, as well as self-defeating bottleneck policies and outmoded traditions.

Before we discuss additional techniques for effective delegation, examine your ideas on the subject by completing Exercise 12-1.

Deciding When to Delegate

Whether you are doing the delegating yourself or are training your promotables to delegate to others, you need to understand typical barriers to delegation and how to decide when to delegate. First, let's review some reasons why supervisors don't delegate as much as they should.

Why Supervisors Don't Delegate You've given your ideas on this question in Exercise 12-1. Compare your responses with the summary of barriers to delegation—in the delegator, the delegatee, and the situation—listed in Exhibit 12-2.

Now we'll discuss some of these barriers in detail, along with attitudes and actions that can help you to overcome them.

It's easier to do it myself, and I know it will be done right if I do it. This is a short-range view, of course. Sure, it may take extra time and effort to train subordinates to take over certain tasks. However, once they are properly trained, your time is freed up for more productive tasks. Also, with proper training and controls some

EXERCISE 12-1: EXAMINING YOUR APPROACH TO DELEGATION

Why don't managers delegate when they should?

1 _____   4 _____

2 _____   5 _____

3 _____   6 _____

When should managers delegate?

1 _____   4 _____

2 _____   5 _____

3 _____   6 _____

---

subordinates may eventually do an even better job than you are doing.

I don't have enough confidence in my subordinates. You may doubt that a subordinate can handle the task properly. This may be a valid reason for not delegating at times. Take a look to see whether you have properly evaluated your subordinate's potential. Perhaps you need to weed out some of your marginal people and replace them with people you can have more confidence in.

I'm afraid of what my boss will think. This fear can come from being unclear about what your boss expects of you. If you are going to advance in your job, you must train and develop your own people. You must use some of your time to grow and develop by taking on new challenges. Discuss this with your boss. If your boss is unwilling or unable to see the value of

your delegating to subordinates, consider looking for a different position under a more enlightened boss.

I like to get personal credit for these tasks. Sometimes we don't realize that the higher we go in management, the less we actually *do* on a project and the more we *get done* through our subordinates. That means our value, and therefore the source of our personal credit, lies in our subordinates' achievements. By delegating to subordinates and giving them personal credit for accomplishing the tasks, we demonstrate our managerial ability.

I thought I had plenty of time to do it myself. Sometimes we simply bite off more than we can chew. One way to avoid this trap is to always ask first, "How much of this can I delegate?" instead of, "How much of this can I do myself?" Delegate as much as possible.

EXHIBIT 12-2: Barriers to Effective Delegation

Barriers in the Delegator

Preference for operating rather than planning when both need doing (delegating requires planning)	Lack of confidence in subordinates
	Perfectionism, leading to overcontrol
Demand that everyone "know all the details"	Lack of organizational skill in balancing the workload
The "I can do it better myself" fallacy	Failure to delegate authority commensurate with responsibility
Lack of experience in the job or in delegating	
Insecurity	Uncertainty over tasks and inability to explain them
Fear of being disliked by subordinates	Disinclination to develop subordinates
Refusal to allow mistakes	Failure to establish effective controls and to follow up

Barriers in the Delegatee

Lack of experience	Disorganization
Lack of competence	Overload of work
Avoidance of responsibility	Immersion in trivia
Overdependence on the boss	

Barriers in the Situation

One-man-show policy	Urgency, leaving no time to explain (crisis management)
No toleration of mistakes	
Involvement of critical decisions	Confusion in responsibilities and authority
	Understaffing

Adapted from R. Alec MacKenzie, *The Time Trap* (New York: McGraw-Hill, 1982), p. 133.

I'm afraid the worker will feel I'm imposing on him or her. This reason tends to come from women managers, almost never from men. Remember, your *job* is to assign tasks; you must become comfortable in that role.

Think of assignments as opportunities for the worker to contribute, not as impositions.

When Supervisors Should Delegate   You're on your way to recognizing barriers that prevent you from delegating. Next, look at some typical situations in which you'd be wise to delegate.

Delegate when doing so will help develop and motivate the subordinate. We discussed this in detail in the previous section. In the long run, this is the key to deciding when and what to delegate.

Delegate when you can do more productive work. This includes any time a higher-level task can be worked on (for example, one that requires longer-range planning, greater risks, a larger impact on departmental objectives, and so forth). It also includes any time there are assignments or projects to be done that will help you learn and grow.

Delegate when doing so won't show undue favoritism. It's easy to give all the most challenging tasks to your star performers. It's also tempting to always send a star to represent you in meetings with higher-level bosses because you know they'll make you look good. It makes sense to have different patterns of development for top performers, marginal performers, and the middle group of workers. It's also a good idea to pass around some of the plum assignments, where appropriate, so that you gain a reputation for being fair and for giving everyone a chance to shine.

Delegate when you are continually under too much time pressure. When you regularly find yourself struggling to meet even your top-priority objectives and the others get no attention at all, it's definitely time to look for areas where you can delegate. Work out a plan for easing your burden by training your subordinates to take over appropriate tasks.

Delegate when you are willing to take the time and effort to turn over the job skillfully. It's better to do a job yourself and do it right than to dump it on subordinates, expecting them to sink or swim. This approach usually leads to anxiety and resentment on the subordinate's part and to your having to salvage poor-to-disastrous results before the job is completed.

When Supervisors Should Do It Themselves Some management experts believe that a line supervisor should not be doing the actual work of the unit or department more than 20 percent of the time. When *is* it appropriate for a line supervisor to be doing the actual work? Here are some suggestions.

1. To instruct new people

2. To test or check out equipment

3. To try out a new method

4. When available people are overloaded due to a temporary, abnormal situation and it is impractical to recruit additional workers (If this is a frequent occurrence, you may not be foreseeing and avoiding problems adequately.)

5. When operating difficulties occur and corrective measures are beyond the ability of the workers (If this occurs frequently, you may not be training workers properly.)

Turning Over Tasks to Subordinates

Once you have decided that a task should be delegated, the next step is to turn over the job as skillfully as possible. Here are some suggestions.

Practice Delegation To become skilled at delegating and comfortable with it, you must practice. Delegating becomes easier as you go along. Don't get directly involved with the work you delegate. Instead, spend your time and effort trying to see that it gets done effectively by others. Set a goal that delegated work will be done entirely by others and will be done well.

Match the Job to the Worker As thoughtfully and carefully as possible, select both the job and the worker who will do it. Consider short-range, long-range, practical, and psychological factors in deciding on the best match.

Prepare Yourself and the Worker Think through the key aspects of the task. Visualize yourself doing it and make notes of key tasks. Take time to do it right. Meet with the worker in private; try to avoid having interruptions during the session. Put the worker at ease. Where possible, recall past successes she or he has experienced in similar situations. Review the task thoroughly and, where necessary, give appropriate training. Prepare the worker by first giving a general overview of the task. Find out what the worker knows about it already.

Explain the Assignment Start with why the task must be done. The more routine or repetitive the job is, the more essential it is for the worker to understand its importance. You must convey that you believe the task is important. Explain how completion of the task will help meet objectives—the worker's, the unit's, the department's, the organization's. In other words, help the worker understand how completion of the task fits into the big picture, the overall scheme of things. If you think of the task as mere drudgery or dirty work, your attitude will come across to the worker and will have a powerful demotivating effect.

Focus on the Goal for the Task Give the worker as clear a picture as possible of the end result you expect. Set target dates or times for completion of each phase of the project. Give the worker as much leeway as possible to reach the end result. In other words, if there are several ways or methods of achieving the goal, let the worker determine the best way, where possible.

Review the Assignment Thoroughly If appropriate, go over the task step by step, explaining it by telling, showing, illustrating. Keep explanations as simple and logical as possible. Use visual illustrations or examples where appropriate. Stress each key point. Don't give workers more than they can master at one time. When complex tasks are involved, consider holding several training sessions.

Check for Understanding Where appropriate, have workers perform a sample of the task. Have them explain key points to you as they understand them so you can identify and correct misinterpretations. Ask for questions, but don't depend on "Do you have any questions?" to verify that subordinates understand how to do the job. Ask the subordinate to repeat back what you have said, to walk through the job, or to perform part or all of it. Ask "smoke-out" questions: "Suppose you don't get all the statements by the fifteenth, what will you do?" "What's the next step?" "What do you have to do before sending the invoices to the Accounting Department?" Determine what training, if any, the worker needs in order to succeed in this assignment.

Discuss Standards of Performance Let workers know what you expect. Where appropriate, reassure subordinates that standards will be relaxed until they have had time to learn the job and gain skill at it. Transmit confidence that with experience they will perform well. Then discuss the quantity and quality of work you will eventually expect. Remember that standards should be challenging but realistic in light of the individual's ability.

Provide Necessary Support Be sure you delegate both the authority the worker will need to accomplish a task and the responsibility for getting the job done and maintaining minimum standards. Define the limits of responsibility and authority. Give as much decision-making authority as is feasible.

For example, suppose you make your secretary responsible for getting a report done on time, and she needs information from one or more persons in the company in order to complete it. Let those people know that she is responsible for the report and that you have given her the authority to set deadlines for getting the necessary information. If these persons are your subordinates, give them a directive to comply with her requests. If they are someone else's subordinates, get their boss' cooperation so that they are directed to comply.

Remember to see that the worker gets all the information she or he will need to do the job. Provide for the proper flow of information.

Encourage Independence   Give workers time to try out new tasks without peering over their shoulders. But let them know you are available to help. Check at appropriate times to see how they are doing.

Follow Up, Give Feedback, and Maintain Control   Remember that you are responsible for the results of the task even though you have delegated it to a subordinate. Set up a system of periodic reports or checkpoints so you can review progress.

Consider keeping a delegation file. Include in it all information about the tasks and projects you have delegated to someone else, including objectives, standards, and deadline dates. Also put deadline dates for completion of key parts of each delegated assignment on your calendar, or in your tickler file. This procedure will help to ensure that you follow up on subordinates' progress at appropriate times in order to maintain adequate control.

There are many ways to keep in touch with what's going on. One that's often overlooked is "management by walking around." This involves moving around among your people as often as necessary. Wander around and directly observe what's going on. Casually ask questions. If this is done in a friendly, offhand way, it won't be interpreted as peering over the shoulder—and in fact is not. Occasionally ask, "What are you working on today?" as you pass by someone's desk, especially if the work looks interesting or different. When you pass someone in the hall, occasionally ask about a project or assignment to see how well informed a worker is about what's going on. You don't have to play detective all the time, but remember it's your business to know what's going on. Also, your presence and your interest alone tend to keep people on the ball.

Evaluate and Give Feedback   Let subordinates know how they are doing at appropriate checkpoints. Then immediately after the assignment has been completed, give them a clear picture of your evaluation of the performance. Objectives and standards set earlier will be the basis for the evaluation. Give ample praise and recognition for good performance. If the performance was poor, ask the worker first for a self-evaluation. If there is a weak area the worker isn't aware of, you can say something like, "I think you could have done better on that. What did you learn from it?" We'll discuss other aspects of evaluating workers later in this chapter.

Keeping Delegated Tasks in the Subordinate's Court

Sometimes subordinates will try to throw a large portion of a delegated task back on you by tactics such as (1) asking you to solve problems that arise, (2) asking you to make tough decisions, or (3) expecting you to put the finishing touches on the project or to check for their errors. If you allow subordinates to get away with this, you're teaching them by your actions that it's okay to stay dependent on the boss and dump problems back in his or her lap. You are also partially defeating the purpose of freeing up your own time.

The first step to solving this problem is identifying *why* the worker is dumping problems back on you. Is it to avoid taking risks? Is the worker afraid of being criticized for making a mistake? Does the worker lack confidence? Does the worker lack necessary information or resources? Or are *you* the main source of the problem?

Pay special attention to the last possibility. Do you need to be needed? Do you want to feel indispensable? Your attitude comes across to your people. Examine it. Do you find it impossible to say "no" when the worker runs to you for help? Use your judgment, say "no" assertively when appropriate; otherwise, you'll be inviting the ball back into your court.

To keep the ball in their court, insist that workers come up with at least one possible solution to a problem before discussing it with you. If a problem is really thorny, give the worker just enough help so that she or he begins to see possibilities for a solution.

If possible, tell workers to make the decisions involved. Unless the decision turns out to be a poor one that would be really costly, support it. Discuss how to improve the decision next time around.

At the very least, insist that workers make a firm recommendation when they bring you a problem: "Come back when you can tell me which course of action *you* think would be best."

Remember that people must have the freedom to make *some* mistakes in order to become confident and independent. If they are constantly running to you for solutions to problems and for decisions, you're not doing the job of training and developing properly. On the other hand, when they successfully work through problems (with minimal coaching), they experience more satisfaction and enjoyment.

Another approach to delegation that's designed to keep the ball in the subordinate's court is called "managing by exception."

Managing by Exception

Once a team member knows the job you've delegated, you may want to try management by exception (or reporting by exception). Meet with the worker and agree on the limits of his or her authority. Everything outside those limits is considered an exception—significantly different or of greater magnitude or importance than usual: "If you have never had anything like it before, check with me." "If it involves more than X dollars, let me see it."

The same applies for reporting progress toward meeting objectives. Agree upon minimum progress that must be achieved at certain points and instruct your people to report to you immediately when they begin to fall behind in quantity, quality, or timing. In some cases you may need to set upper limits to be sure that necessary adjustments are made to handle any extra load on the system: "Let me know if sales go above X units."

One of the advantages of management by exception is that everything is handled at as low a level as possible, with a minimum drain on the time and attention of higher authority at every level. Another is that the manager spends time on the things that need special attention rather than on the routine or on what went right. (You can spend 75 percent of your time reading and listening to subordinates' reports on what went right, which leaves you inadequate time for dealing with problems—what can and does go wrong.)

A potential disadvantage of managing by exception is succumbing to the temptation of requiring subordinates to report routine transactions on your pet project or in an area that was formerly your specialty. Although you may find it difficult to let go of the details in those situations, doing so is essential to your progress.

The major disadvantage of managing by exception is the tendency to focus on the negative. You can offset this by giving credit and recognition when people meet objectives.

When no exceptions are reported, you know your people are on top of things—or are they? After all, exceptions are, at least to some extent, admissions of failure. Therefore people may shade exceptions in their favor. You can overcome this tendency by actively monitoring their progress. First, figure out which elements of a person's job may vary and which elements are most likely to have a decisive effect on whether a worker meets the objectives. Then determine beforehand what could become reportable exceptions and stay on top of them. Use your tickler file or calendar notations to remind yourself when to make inquiries or to schedule periodic reviews so that projects don't get lost in the shuffle.

Evaluating and Coaching for Top Performance

Once you've effectively handed over an assignment, the next step is to follow up and evaluate how well the worker is performing. If evaluation is to result in improved performance, you and the worker must identify areas of strength and weakness. Then the two of you must analyze any problems to determine their cause. Only then can you take specific action to improve performance.

One approach to analyzing performance problems is to first determine which of three basic categories they fall in:

1. *Environmental circumstances.* The worker has the skills and the desire to perform the tasks satisfactorily, but some barrier affecting the work situation prevents him or her from doing so.

2. *Skill deficiency.* The worker is unable to meet acceptable standards for performing the task because he or she lacks the necessary skills.

3. *Attitude deficiency.* The worker *could* perform the task satisfactorily but doesn't.

Exercise 12-2 lists a number of typical performance problems. How would you categorize them?

EXERCISE 12-2: ANALYZING PERFORMANCE PROBLEMS

Categorize each problem by determining whether its source is most likely a skill, attitude, or environmental deficiency. Place the number 1 under the category that represents the most likely source. If you think that more than one category may be the source, rank the deficiency by placing 1, 2, and possibly 3 in the appropriate spaces.

Performance Problem	Skill Deficiency	Attitude Deficiency	Environmental Deficiency
1. Arrives at work late	_____	_____	_____
2. Has a sloppy appearance	_____	_____	_____
3. Works slowly and creates bottlenecks	_____	_____	_____
4. Makes too many mistakes in paperwork	_____	_____	_____
5. Doesn't follow necessary procedures	_____	_____	_____
6. Gives fellow workers incorrect information	_____	_____	_____
7. Leaves work early	_____	_____	_____
8. Takes sick leave too frequently	_____	_____	_____
9. Leaves out important steps of task	_____	_____	_____
10. Is rude to customers	_____	_____	_____
11. Misses deadline dates	_____	_____	_____
12. Sends letters to wrong addresses	_____	_____	_____

Actually there are no right or wrong answers. The aim of the exercise is to help you experience the difficulty of dealing effectively with performance problems without first analyzing them thoroughly. Such analyses usually involve asking yourself a series of questions about the situation as well as asking the worker some probing questions. Only then can you determine the probable source of the problem. Robert Mager, in *Analyzing Performance Problems*, has suggested a sequence of steps [7, pp. 50–60].

Describe and Evaluate the Discrepancy First, describe as specifically as possible the performance discrepancy. For example, item 1 in Exercise 12-2 is "arrives at work late." A specific description would be "Has arrived at work late as follows: October 1, 15 minutes late; October 6, 20 minutes late; October 9, 30 minutes late."

Then determine whether the discrepancy is important. In the example just given, the lateness would be very important if the worker is responsible for serving customers or handling callers. There might be situations, however, where the behavior would be unimportant, such as when a technical or professional person is working in relative isolation and is meeting objectives satisfactorily.

Categorize the Source of the Discrepancy If there is a problem, determine its probable source. First, ask if it might be the result of environmental circumstances. If not, look next at the possibility that the worker is lacking in some skill. If neither of these categories appears to be the source of the problem, it may be the worker's attitude.

The simplest deficiencies to correct are often environmental ones, so look for them first. If the problem appears to result from an *environmental deficiency*, meet with the worker to attempt to discover the obstacles to performance. Your first step is to determine whether the worker understands the objectives and standards. Find out if the worker knows what is expected; is clear about timing, deadlines, and workflow; has conflicting demands on his or her time.

The second step is to determine whether the worker has the resources necessary to perform adequately. Does the worker have the authority necessary to complete the task? Has he or she been given a reasonable length of time to complete the task and the tools, staff support, and other resources needed to perform adequately?

The third step is to determine whether there are bottlenecks or other barriers to performance. Are there bottlenecks that can be eliminated? Can the flow of work or paper to the worker be improved? Does company policy or the attitudes of the worker's peers or supervisors need to be changed? ("That can't be done." "We have always done it this way.")

Physical factors may be creating barriers to performance. You may need to change lighting or colors, modify the work position, reduce noise, provide more privacy, or take other steps to increase the worker's comfort. Are interruptions creating problems? If so, focus on reducing phone calls, visitors, "crises," and other demands that are more immediate but less important than the tasks in question.

If the problem is not an environmental one, chances are it's caused by a *skill deficiency*. There are three steps you can take. The first is to meet with the worker to try to determine these things:

1. Could the worker do the task satisfactorily if he or she really had to (if it were a matter of survival)? Under normal circumstances, are the worker's present skills adequate for the desired performance?

2. Was the worker able to perform the task satisfactorily in the past? If not, consider

providing formal training. If so, has the worker forgotten how to perform the task satisfactorily?

3. How often is the skill used? If the worker rarely performs the task, consider providing opportunities for practice.

4. Does the worker find out how well he or she is doing? Does the worker routinely get feedback about performance? If not, consider devising standards and control systems so that the worker gets feedback as frequently and automatically as is feasible.

The second step is to determine whether you can solve the problem by changing the job, providing written instructions or checklists, showing the worker how to perform, or providing informal on-the-job training.

The third step is to determine whether the worker has the aptitude to gain the necessary skills. Could the worker learn the job with a reasonable amount of formal training? Does he or she have the physical and mental potential to perform adequately, or is the worker overqualified for the job?

After you've eliminated the possibility of environmental or skill deficiency, you're left with the probability that the source of the performance problem lies in the worker's attitude. Inspiring others to change their attitudes is a challenging task! All you can do is give it your best shot—and, remember, it's up to the worker to make the grade or not.

If the problem appears to reflect an *attitude deficiency*, meet with the worker to attempt to discover the source of the unproductive attitude. First, determine whether the results of performing well are perceived as rewarding or as punishing by the worker. Find out what the worker sees as the consequences of performing well. Does he or she think there are certain penalties for performing well—for example, that standards will probably be in-

creased and more work will be required? Does the worker feel his or her world would become a little less pleasant or interesting if he or she performed better, or does the worker anticipate rewards for performing well?

Next, determine what payoffs the worker gets for *not* performing well. Find out specifically what the worker gets out of doing it his or her way instead of your way. Look for payoffs the worker gets from his or her present performance—for example, group belonging, prestige, status, revenge, attention, help, sympathy, pity, more time and energy for personal or favored activities.

Does the worker need more attention? Perhaps he or she gets more attention for poor performance than for satisfactory performance. Perhaps you are inadvertently rewarding poor performance with attention and ignoring good performance.

Finally, determine whether the worker perceives good performance as important. Find out how important satisfactory performance is to the worker. Does he or she anticipate a favorable outcome for performing well and an undesirable outcome for performing poorly? Does the worker receive any personal satisfaction from good performance, and is he or she able to take pride in good performance as an individual and as a member of a group? Are any of the worker's needs satisfied through good performance?

Determine the Optimal Solution   After you've analyzed the deficiency, select the best solution to the performance problem and see that it is carried out. Determine which solutions are most appropriate and feasible and which solutions are obviously too costly.

First, figure out the cost (including time and energy) of carrying out each solution and the resources needed. Next, figure the added value to the company of successfully carrying out each solution. Then you can decide whether each solution is worth carrying out. You can compare to see which will probably give the best results with the least effort and which you are best equipped to try. Keep in mind the intangible factors, too, such as which solution will be the most interesting to those involved and the most visible to superiors.

Making Coherent Formal Evaluations

One of the most powerful signals about what you think is really important is the way you handle formal evaluations, raises, and promotions. The first thing to remember is that evaluations must not be limited to a formal procedure. They should be ongoing and as immediate as possible.

Another key point to remember is that trivia should never be included in your evaluation. When you evaluate, focus on important matters. Be sure to evaluate the subordinate's performance, not the person. Be as specific as possible about what achievements were satisfactory or unsatisfactory.

It may help clarify the situation to tell subordinates how they rank within the department. For example, a statement such as "You rank third out of the fifteen people in the unit with comparable jobs" tells a worker that he or she is doing well and is valued. It also lets the worker know that there is some room for improvement. On the other hand, "You rank eleventh out of the fifteen people with comparable jobs" may serve as a spur to those who never before realized how much room they have for improvement. And it can do so without creating a problem of personal jealousies through comparison by names.

If you're responsible for giving or recommending merit raises, use the ranking technique for categorizing your people into top, average, and marginal performers. If you encounter a borderline case, discuss it with your boss. In fact, you should routinely review all evaluations with your boss before formal sessions with your subordinates.

Of course you will try to get as much in your budget for merit raises as possible. If you are responsible for dividing the money up, consider using a ratio of 2:1:0. The top performers get twice as much as those who made some progress, and the marginals get nothing.

Next you must decide whether the amount to be divided up among each group will be based on a percentage of each person's salary or whether the same lump-sum increase will be given to everyone in a particular group. The main thing to remember is to be consistent in your actions and to explain your line of reasoning to all concerned.

Your goal is to reward the accomplishment of specific objectives you and your workers have agreed upon and to do it in as fair and reasonable a way as possible. Giving merit increases to those who don't deserve them waters down the impact of what the top performers get and encourages marginal workers to disbelieve what you *say* about the need for improved performance.

SELECTING WORKERS FOR YOUR TEAM

Periodically you will be selecting and training new workers. Be sure to take full advantage of this opportunity to add persons of your own choosing. Your goal is to build an effective work group. You may inherit someone else's mistakes—people who are difficult to work with and perhaps even more difficult to move into different departments. It is worth taking special precautions to avoid creating your *own* mistakes and to assure that each person you hire is the best one available for the job and for your team.

The process of selecting workers differs from company to company, depending on company size, policy, and job requirements. You may have complete responsibility for selecting new workers—from announcing job openings to making the final decision about who is hired. On the other hand, if your company is one of those rare ones in which the Personnel Department handles the entire selection process, you may have virtually no say about who is hired. In most cases, however, you will at least interview applicants for jobs in your unit or department and have some input into the hiring decision.

Your main goal in interviewing is to determine which applicants are likely to be successful or unsuccessful in the job position. Once you have differentiated between probable successful and unsuccessful candidates, your goal is to determine which of the successful ones is best suited to the position. In order to achieve these goals, you must (1) distinguish between your own personal biases, prejudices, or stereotypes and your valid intuitive judgment of each person's suitability for the job, (2) devise a form and procedures for recording your evaluations of the candidates' qualifications, (3) determine relevant questions to ask, and (4) establish an atmosphere that brings out essential information about each candidate's skills, knowledge, experience, and social/ motivational aptitude for the particular position. (See Exercise 12-5 for practice at interviewing.)

Identifying Personal Biases

Only you can determine whether your positive or negative feelings about a job applicant reflect an inappropriate bias or a valid intuitive judgment. An inappropriate bias can cause you to select a person who is unsuited for the job or to reject a person who is well suited.

For example, you may take an immediate liking to an applicant who reminds you of a good friend or relative. You may subsequently assume that the applicant has the same admirable personal characteristics of your friend. However, the applicant may in fact have quite different characteristics that you failed to discover because of your false conclusion.

On the other hand, you may immediately take a negative attitude toward a candidate who reminds you of, say, your brother-in-law, whom you believe is lazy, inconsiderate, and generally obnoxious. Unless you are aware of your bias and make a special effort to dig deeper and try to determine just what this applicant is really like, you may pass over the best candidate for the job.

Exercise 12-3 is designed to help you become aware of some of your biases and to pinpoint some areas where you will want to be especially cautious about jumping to false conclusions. In this exercise you have a chance to identify general categories in which you are biased, such as "same sex." Under that category, you will list specific types of people of the same sex that you have a positive bias toward—for example, "liberated women." Then you will list factors you have especially noticed and admired about this type of person—for example, "assertive, independent, direct in their dealings." You will also list specific types of people you have a negative bias toward— for example, "catty women." And you will mention negative factors about these people, such as "concerned with trivialities; tend to be sneaky."

Providing Necessary Structure

In addition to being aware of your personal biases, you must establish an atmosphere conducive to open communication. Then you must ask questions that will help you uncover the factors that are essential to making the best decision about whom to hire.

EXERCISE 12-3: IDENTIFYING PERSONAL BIASES

In the first column, list specific types of people toward whom you have positive or negative biases. In the middle column, list *positive* factors (traits, actions, attitudes) that you especially notice and *like*. In the last column, list *negative* factors that you especially notice and *dislike*.

Object or Cause of Bias	Positive Factors	Negative Factors
	Same Sex	
_____	_____	_____
	Opposite Sex	
_____	_____	_____
	Minorities	
_____	_____	_____
	Age	
_____	_____	_____
	Appearance	
_____	_____	_____
	Education	
_____	_____	_____
	Socioeconomic or Ethnic Background	
_____	_____	_____
	Lifestyle	
_____	_____	_____
	Religion	
_____	_____	_____
	Other	
_____	_____	_____

Most of the experts who have researched the field of interviewing agree that the structured interview usually gives the best results. As a matter of fact, most interviews could be improved by more advance planning and structure. This includes formulating a set of questions to ask to be sure you cover all bases with every applicant. Good questions will help you predict a good fit in the social/motivational aspects of the job as well as in the skill/knowledge aspects.

Prepare for the interview thoroughly so you can make it as effective and relaxed as possible. Here are some suggestions.

1. Examine the job requirements and the application form.

2. Map out the areas that need to be covered by the interview.

3. Review, select, or develop a rating form that you will use for the candidates for this job. (A discussion of rating forms follows.)

4. Plan and organize questions that will help you get the essential information in each of these areas without violating EEO guidelines on discrimination. (A discussion of effective questions follows.)

5. Try to interview each applicant in the same setting so that the only element that's altered is the applicant being interviewed. In this way your comparisons will have more validity.

6. Pick a setting that's pleasant and quiet. Take steps to prevent interruptions during the interview.

7. Before each candidate arrives, review his or her completed application form. Look for gaps in education and employment. Decide which items on the form need to be discussed so you can better understand the applicant's qualifications. From the application form determine what things

about the candidate need to be confirmed or explained in the interview. Add these individualized questions to your list of questions designed for all candidates for this job position.

8. Keep the questions and the rating form handy for reference as you conduct the interview.

Select or Develop a Rating Form A rating form will help you record and evaluate whether each candidate has the characteristics of a person likely to be successful in the particular position. Figure 12-1 depicts the process of selecting the best job candidate. Your first step as interviewer is to determine the characteristics necessary for success in the job. The next step is to discover each applicant's relevant characteristics. Then you compare the two sets of characteristics in order to determine how well they fit and to decide whether the applicant merits further consideration. After this initial screening of applicants, you compare the relative suitability of the top candidates and make a final decision about who will receive the job offer.

Only you can formulate what you think are the essential characteristics for success in the position you have available. It is a good idea to consider more than the skill, experience, and education required for success. Look also at how well the person will fit in with the people already on your team. Ask yourself, "Will the applicant probably be happy and motivated to perform well in this work situation?" In other words, consider the social and motivational factors in job success as well as the technical factors.

Exhibit 12-3, which begins on page 453, is an example of a rating form that covers technical, social, and motivational predictors of job success. It can give you some ideas about devising your own form. Exhibit 12-4 provides a format for summarizing the content of the rating form.

FIGURE 12-1: Finding a Good Applicant/Job Position Fit

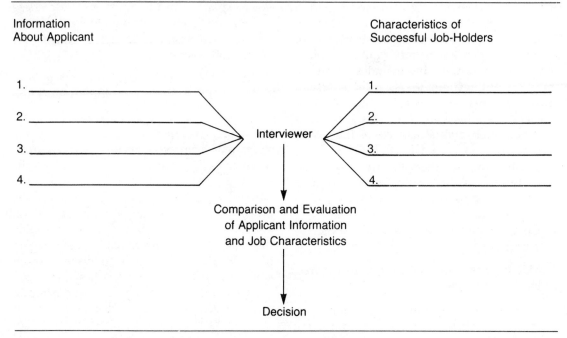

Information
About Applicant

Characteristics of
Successful Job-Holders

1. _____

2. _____

3. _____

4. _____

1. _____

2. _____

3. _____

4. _____

Interviewer

Comparison and Evaluation
of Applicant Information
and Job Characteristics

Decision

Plan and Organize Questions The questions you pose to a candidate should ferret out the necessary facts without violating **Equal Employment Opportunity (EEO) laws** concerning discrimination against women and minorities. Avoiding illegal questions while giving applicants an opportunity to express their ideas and feelings candidly requires special thought.

Any question that focuses on an applicant's sex, race, ethnic origin, religion, physical condition, or age is off limits *unless* it's a **Bona Fide Occupational Question (BFOQ).** BFOQ, a term used in connection with EEO laws, refers to interview questions that are necessary to determine an applicant's *bona fide*, or relevant and essential, qualifications for the job. All qualifications set up for the job must be (1) objective, stated in terms of basic and observable facts; (2) uniform in application to all candidates; (3) consistent in

their effect on all candidates; and (4) essential to the successful performance of the job. An effective interview question is helpful in gathering job-related information, is tactful, and is in compliance with Equal Employment Opportunity guidelines. Here are some examples.

1. *Work Experience*

"One of the things I am particularly interested in is your work experience. Will you please describe your current position?"

"What do you feel have been some of your particularly strong points in accomplishing your work? Why?"

"What are some of the things about your present job that you have found difficult to do? Why?"

EXHIBIT 12-3: Applicant-Rating Form

Applicant's Name _____   Date _____

Position Available _____   Interviewer _____

Detailed Evaluation in Each Area

Place a plus sign (+) or minus sign (-) to the left of relevant items to show positive or negative factors. After completing the items in a numbered section, make a general evaluation of the applicant's suitability in that area by checking the appropriate box on the right of the numbered heading.

Note: Only relevant items should be marked plus or minus.

General Evaluation in Each Area

1	2	3	4	5	6	7
Lowest	Low	Below Avg.	Average	Above Avg.	High	Highest

1. Knowledge, Skills and Abilities. . . . . . ☐ ☐ ☐ ☐ ☐ ☐ ☐

    (Write your own as required by the job, listing specific areas.)

    _____   _____

    _____   _____

    _____   _____

2. Work Experience. . . . . ☐ ☐ ☐ ☐ ☐ ☐ ☐

    (Extent to which applicant's work history indicates an ability to learn and understand the job requirements)

    _____ Experience in performing tasks   _____ Past job assignments

    _____ Past failures due to lack of   _____ Assignment to task forces
           ability   or special projects

    _____ Knowledge of equipment, tools,   _____ Achievement in special
           and work procedures   projects, task forces

	Lowest	Low	Below Avg.	Average	Above Avg.	High	Highest
3. Training.	☐	☐	☐	☐	☐	☐	☐

_____ Adequate education for job position

_____ Relevant on-the-job training

_____ Relevant vocational or trade school training

_____ Participation in seminars, workshops, continuing education classes, etc.

_____ Self-study (programmed instruction, correspondence courses, etc.)

4. Ability to Understand and Respond to Questions	☐	☐	☐	☐	☐	☐	☐

_____ Listening skills

_____ Clear, concise answers

_____ On-target, relevant responses

5. Ability to Communicate Ideas.	☐	☐	☐	☐	☐	☐	☐

_____ Ability to organize and present ideas coherently

_____ Ability to communicate feelings, as well as logical thoughts and ideas, appropriately

6. Manner and Appearance	☐	☐	☐	☐	☐	☐	

(Prediction of how others will react to applicant)

_____ Overall appearance

_____ Tactfulness

_____ Self-confidence

_____ Sensitivity to others' needs

_____ Appropriateness of dress

_____ Health and physical condition adequate for job duties

7. Congeniality.	☐	☐	☐	☐	☐	☐	☐

(Prediction of ability to get along with others and work as a member of a team)

_____ Previous problems with supervisors, peers, or subordinates

_____ Preference for working with others

_____ Tendency to be a "loner" in social activities

_____ Involvement in community, social, religious, or athletic activities

_____ Excessive reaction to criticism

_____ Openness and candidness in communication

	Lowest	Low	Below Avg.	Average	Above Avg.	High	Highest

8. Goal Congruence. . . . . □ □ □ □ □ □ □

(Prediction of extent to which applicant's goals and aspirations are
consistent with available opportunities)

_____ Level of ability and qualifica-   _____ Level of ambition is con-
tions are consistent with   sistent with available
available opportunity here   opportunity in the company

9. Job Satisfaction . . . . □ □ □ □ □ □ □

(Prediction of the extent to which
applicant will be involved in the job
and will gain personal satisfaction
from it)

_____ Past participation in job-   _____ Degree of success and sat-
related activities (societies,   isfaction in school and
associations, etc.)   work situations

_____ Participation in company-   _____ Personal interest in
sponsored opportunities to   goals, hobbies, avocations
develop job-related skills   that fit in with job activities

10. Reward Structure . . . . □ □ □ □ □ □ □

(Prediction of the extent to which
rewards available in this position
will be perceived as motivational
rewards by the applicant)

_____ Will soon expect higher pay   _____ Needs more recognition
than will be available   and praise than job offers

_____ The job itself will be rewarding

	Lowest	Low	Below Avg.	Average	Above Avg.	High	Highest
11. Initiative and Productivity.	☐	☐	☐	☐	☐	☐	☐

(Prediction of applicant's ability to use good judgment in doing the job, taking initiative when appropriate, and getting help when needed)

_____ Ability to think and act independently to meet work standards

_____ Ability to exercise leadership when appropriate

_____ Willingness to take responsibility for work delays and interruptions as well as for producing results

_____ Capacity for persistence, thoroughness, "professionalism"

_____ Past record for meeting deadlines and achieving objectives and standards

	Lowest	Low	Below Avg.	Average	Above Avg.	High	Highest
12. Poise and Stability.	☐	☐	☐	☐	☐	☐	☐

(Prediction of applicant's ability to perform well under pressure and to respond effectively to emergencies)

_____ History of reactions in emergencies (impulsive or composed)

_____ Indications of the quality of applicant's work in emergencies or under pressure (suffers or remains high)

_____ Ability to adjust to changes in work procedures

_____ Ability to adjust to changes in work environment, such as work interruptions or schedule changes

	Lowest	Low	Below Avg.	Average	Above Avg.	High	Highest
13. Dependability.	☐	☐	☐	☐	☐	☐	☐

(Prediction of applicant's work habits and attendance record)

_____ Past attendance record (absenteeism, lateness, regularity, promptness)

_____ Previous reprimands or commendations for work performance

_____ Safety record (instance of involvement in accidents, work interruptions, accident prevention, etc.)

_____ Other indications of work habits

EXHIBIT 12-4: Summary of Applicant-Rating Form

Transfer ratings from each category of the applicant-rating form to make overall evaluations and comparisons with other candidates.

Hired ☐   Applicant's Name _____ Date _____

Rejected ☐ Job Title _____

	1 Lowest	2 Low	3 Below Avg.	4 Average	5 Above Avg.	6 High	7 Highest
1. Knowledge, skills, and abilities	☐	☐	☐	☐	☐	☐	☐
2. Work experience	☐	☐	☐	☐	☐	☐	☐
3. Training	☐	☐	☐	☐	☐	☐	☐
4. Ability to Understand and Respond to Questions	☐	☐	☐	☐	☐	☐	☐
5. Ability to Communicate Ideas	☐	☐	☐	☐	☐	☐	☐
6. Manner and Appearance	☐	☐	☐	☐	☐	☐	☐
7. Congeniality	☐	☐	☐	☐	☐	☐	☐
8. Goal Congruence	☐	☐	☐	☐	☐	☐	☐
9. Job Satisfaction	☐	☐	☐	☐	☐	☐	☐
10. Reward Structure	☐	☐	☐	☐	☐	☐	☐
11. Initiative and Productivity	☐	☐	☐	☐	☐	☐	☐
12. Poise and Stability	☐	☐	☐	☐	☐	☐	☐
13. Dependability	☐	☐	☐	☐	☐	☐	☐

Factual Reasons for Hiring: _____

_____

_____

Factual Reasons for Rejecting: _____

_____

_____

_____

"How much supervision do you have? Do you feel that's the most appropriate amount for you?"

"What do you feel are the major problems that you have encountered and how have you solved them?"

2. *Feelings and Attitudes About Past Jobs*

"Do you consider your progress in your present position representative of your ability? Why or why not?"

"How do you feel about the progress that you have made with your present employer?"

"In what ways do you feel that your present job has developed you to assume greater responsibilities?"

"How do you feel about the responsibilities that you have assumed in former positions?"

"What part of your job do you enjoy the most? the least? why?"

"Do you feel that your salary is adequate for the work you now perform? If not, why?"

"What are your reasons for wanting to leave your present job?"

3. *Attitude Toward the Job Being Offered*

"What are some of the things in a job that are most important to you?"

"How do you feel this company can provide what's important for you?"

"What do you feel should be the qualifications for this job?"

"What do you feel you'd like best about this job?"

"What do you expect would be the typical problems in this job?"

"What reservations do you have about this job?"

"What do you think is likely to make the difference between success and failure in this position?"

4. *Relationships with Others*

"Describe the perfect boss for you. How does your boss differ?"

"What kinds of people upset you the most?"

"What are some of the problems you've encountered while working with other people?"

"What would you like to do to strengthen your dealings with superiors, peers and subordinates? How?"

"How do you feel your supervisor has increased your capabilities, or not developed them?"

"How do you feel your previous or current supervisor would describe you?"

5. *Self-Esteem*

"What are some of the things in a job that motivate you?"

"What has been your biggest disappointment? Why? How did you handle it?"

"What kind of situations make you feel tense or nervous?"

"What obstacles have you had to overcome?"

"What's the hardest thing you've ever done?"

"What do you feel is your greatest strength?"

"What do you feel you could most improve upon?"

"What are you doing to improve those things which you feel need improvement?"

6. *Career Goals*

"What is your long-range career goal?"

"How do you plan to reach this goal?"

"How do you feel this company can help you reach your career goals?"

"What do you want from your next job that you are not getting from your current job?"

"What kind of position do you want to have in five years?"

Conducting the Interview

You'll want to do a thorough job of both preparing for and conducting the job interview because it's your best chance to get and give essential information and to make a personal impact on potential team members. Keep in mind that top applicants will be interviewing you and the company too. Therefore it is important to put your best foot forward in order to attract the best people to your team. Here are some pointers.

Opening the Interview Begin the interview with a few minutes of light conversation, putting the applicant at ease as much as possible. Start establishing an atmosphere of trust and open communication. Next, ask the applicant how she or he learned of the job. This can help you establish a relationship between the applicant and the company. Mention early in the interview how much time you can spend. Mention again when you have only five or ten minutes left to talk so that important questions and information can be exchanged.

Exchanging Relevant Information Move into important topics as soon as some rapport is established. Describe the essential responsibilities and requirements of the job. Clarify any job requirements the applicant is not clear about.

Use appropriate questions and techniques to get the information you need. Try to use the same sequence of questions with all applicants to help in making valid comparisons. Begin with broad general questions to give the applicant an opportunity to show what she or he thinks is most important for you to know. Probe incomplete answers and problem areas while maintaining an atmosphere of trust. Make followup comments and summaries of the discussion where appropriate.

Avoid questions that can be answered "yes" or "no" when you want complete information. Use open phrasing that encourages the applicant to give a complete idea or thought: "What did you like best (or least) about school?" rather than "Did you like school?" However, if you are having trouble getting an answer from an applicant who rambles and digresses, you may want to ask some closed questions, such as "Can you operate the XYZ machine without further training?" Other types of questions to be avoided are those that

Prompt a specific kind of reply (leading questions): "Working as part of a team is very satisfying, isn't it?"

May be argumentative: "Wouldn't you have more flexibility if you were willing to transfer?"

Have no bearing on the applicant's qualifications for the job

Tend to be viewed as discriminatory (such as some questions regarding children, arrests, religion, military discharge, credit rating, and age)

Have been answered adequately on the application form

Avoid interjecting your own opinion or attitude in your questions or comments without good reason. For example, do not make remarks such as these: "It's difficult to work with that type of person." "I wouldn't put up with that either." When an applicant makes a statement that is too general to be meaningful, ask for specifics to clarify what is meant. For example, the applicant says, "I'm good at planning and organizing." You respond, "Could you give me some examples of how you have used those abilities?"

Take notes during the interview so you will be able to recall important factual items clearly, as well as your feelings and general impressions about each candidate. If the applicant seems tense about note-taking, explain its purpose in a reassuring way. Note *how* a person answers questions as well as *what* is said. Does the applicant get to the point or wander and ramble? Answer concisely and clearly? Listen to questions closely? Second-guess what the question will be?

Throughout the interview, show concern for the applicant's feelings but maintain control of the interview. React appropriately to applicant's comments and questions as well as to nonverbal messages. Set a tone of warmth and trust by showing a positive interest in the applicant and by using encouragement and praise where appropriate.

Let the applicant do most of the talking while you focus on getting the information you need to make a decision. Give the applicant adequate time to formulate thoughts into logical replies. Don't feel you have to keep the air filled with words. In fact one technique for getting more information is simply to pause for a few seconds. The applicant will usually volunteer an additional response.

For a further discussion of open and closed questioning, listening responses (both verbal and nonverbal), and identification and clarification of applicants' key thoughts, see Chapter 6.

Closing and Documenting the Interview
Your main goal when closing is to leave the applicant feeling that she or he has been treated fairly, courteously, and with consideration. Whether the applicant is eventually hired or rejected, it's important that she or he leave with positive feelings about the company. A major factor in treating applicants fairly is to be as candid as possible about the status of their applications.

When the applicant *will not be hired,* use this procedure: If you have already decided that the applicant is not adequately qualified for the job, give him or her the decision and the reasons for it. Use only job-related reasons for not hiring applicants. This helps avoid feelings of discrimination. Where appropriate, offer suggestions for gaining the knowledge or experience needed to become qualified for such a job.

Be as tactful as possible in informing applicants that they will not be hired. Take special care to be encouraging and supportive so that the applicant will retain a positive image of the company.

When the applicant *may be hired,* use this procedure: Tell the applicant that he or she is qualified. Reveal the approximate number of other applicants you are considering and express this in terms of any one applicant's probability of being hired: "I'm interviewing ten or so people. Therefore, there is roughly one chance in ten that any one of you will be hired." By giving this kind of information, you help the applicant formulate reasonable expectations. A subsequent refusal is less likely to be incorrectly interpreted as a case of discrimination.

Tell qualified applicants how you will notify them of the final decision and approximately when they may expect to hear from you.

Studies show that vital information given toward the end of an interview is often not heard or remembered accurately. Therefore, be sure you present a clear plan of action to the applicant when closing the interview. A clear, concise summary of this plan should be repeated to be sure there is no misunderstanding.

Proper documentation of the interview process can save you and your company from the ordeal of a discrimination suit. By taking notes and by using a rating form correctly, you can explain to anyone why a particular applicant was hired or rejected.

Don't allow any interruptions until you have completed the rating form. Research indicates that even one phone call between the end of an interview and the documentation of it reduces your ability to remember all the essential information you gained during the interview.

The summary rating form shown in Exhibit 12-4 calls for *factual reasons* for hiring or rejecting an applicant. The term "factual" as used here refers to specific actions or statements made by the applicant rather than vague, general statements or your personal feelings and opinions about the person. For example, "sloppy appearance" is an opinion, not a fact. "Applicant was wearing soiled, wrinkled, patched jeans and a tee shirt. He was wearing sandals with no socks." These are facts that are specific. They can readily be verified by others who met the applicant.

"Applicant is not highly motivated" is an opinion, not a fact. "Applicant stated that she had difficulty sitting at a desk for long periods of time. She stated that her family thought that she should work in a bank." These are specific, factual statements.

"Applicant lacks the necessary skills" is a vague statement. "Applicant's shorthand dictation speed tested at 60 W.P.M., which is 20 W.P.M. below minimum job standards. She has no experience with automated typewriters, which is required." These are specific reasons for rejection.

Selecting the Best Candidate Once you have completed interviewing all the applicants, you're ready to carefully analyze the information you obtained about them. If you have taken adequate notes and have completed your rating form properly, you'll have a good picture of each applicant and his or her qualifications and characteristics. The job of matching the best applicant to the characteristics essential to job success will be simplified by completing the summary rating forms and spreading them before you. In this way you can best evaluate them in terms of job requirements and reach a final decision that you're confident is a good one.

A word to the wise: Don't hire men or women who are openly hostile or reticent about working for a woman manager. There's no need to burden yourself unnecessarily with the tough and thankless job of trying to win them over.

ORIENTING WORKERS: GETTING TEAM MEMBERS OFF TO A GOOD START

Once you have hired the best person for the job, you'll want to retain his or her positive image of the company, and you'll also want to help the new worker get off to a good start. Perhaps the most common mistake supervisors make in orienting new workers is throwing too much information at them at one time. Another common mistake is devoting too little time to preparing for and orienting the worker. Too often the new worker gets a half-day orientation—much of it conducted on the spur of the moment or almost as an afterthought. On the other hand, supervisors sometimes depend on canned, superficial presentations by the Personnel Department for nearly all of the orientation process.

An effective orientation not only gives new workers basic information about the company and the job, it also enhances their motivation to achieve and their future productivity on the job. First, decide which workers you will ask to help with the orientation; select people you think will relate well to the new employee, people with positive, enthusiastic attitudes toward the work and the company. Next, decide what information and training should be included in the orientation and how long the orientation period needs to be. Then prepare a brief written outline showing information that will be presented on each day of the orientation period. Plan short daily sessions designed to give the new employee a little information or instruction each day for about two weeks. The worker can spend the remainder of each day applying any instruction to job tasks. The exact pattern and length of time for orientation will of course depend on each specific situation.

Now we've come full circle. After the new worker has had time to master the job and establish a fairly stable level of performance, your next step is to delegate appropriate new assignments. As you develop your skills in selecting and orienting workers, then delegating, coaching, and evaluating effectively, you'll find yourself also developing a top-performing team—one your bosses will notice and your colleagues will envy.

SUMMARY

"Supervision," as used here, refers to your day-to-day responsibilities for delegating tasks, assessing and evaluating work performance, coaching workers in improving their performance, and selecting and training new workers. The key to effective supervision is knowing when and how to delegate. To build a top-performing team, you must match tasks to be delegated to workers with the potential to successfully complete the tasks and benefit from the assignments. One way of accomplishing this is to rank your people into three groups: top, average, and marginal performers. Then you can upgrade the weak links or move them out; groom the promotables to take your place; and make the middle group assistants to the top performers, giving both groups a challenging change of pace.

By delegating as many tasks as possible, you free up your own time for doing more productive tasks and acquiring new skills. You also provide training and development opportunities for your people, increasing their level of interest, challenge, and motivation. You can adopt various strategies for overcoming barriers to effective delegation within you, the workers, or the environment. Once you delegate a task, don't let the worker dump it back on you. Insist that she or he come up with at least tentative solutions, recommendations, or decisions before you step in to help.

Since you can spend as much as 75 percent of your time dealing with reports about what went right on assignments you delegate, consider using the management by exception technique. You become involved only in the exceptions to the routine—decisions outside the limits of subordinates' authority, or their failure to make minimum progress in terms of quantity, quality, or timing of performance. Avoid potential problems with this technique by establishing an effective followup system.

When you evaluate a worker's performance of delegated tasks, carefully analyze any performance problems before attempting to deal with them. First describe as specifically as possible the performance discrepancy and determine whether it's important. If it is, try to categorize it as a skill, attitude, or environmental deficiency. Then meet with the worker to further investigate and determine the source of the problem. Finally, select the best solution to the performance problem and see that it is carried out.

When you make formal evaluations, stick with the really important matters. You may help the worker to understand the situation if you explain how his or her performance ranks within the department. Be consistent in your actions and explain your line of reasoning to all concerned. Reward the accomplishment of specific objectives.

The job interview is your key tool to selecting the best workers for your team. First you must determine which applicants are likely to be successful or unsuccessful in the job. Then you determine which of the successful ones is best suited to the job.

To prepare properly for the interview, formulate a predetermined set of questions to ask so you'll cover all bases with every applicant. Good questions will help you predict a good fit in the social/motivational aspects of the job as well as the skill/knowledge aspects. They'll also help you comply with EEO guidelines.

Close the interview so the applicant leaves feeling that she or he has been treated fairly, courteously, and with consideration. Immediately document what happened so you can refer back to key points. Proper documentation helps you explain to anyone why a particular applicant was hired or rejected; it can save your company from the ordeal of a discrimination suit. When documenting factual reasons for hiring or rejecting an applicant, refer to specific actions or statements made, not vague, general comments or your personal feelings and opinions about the applicant.

Once you have selected a new worker, plan an effective orientation that provides basic information about the company and the job and also enhances motivation to achieve. Any plan should spread the orientation over a period of several days to give the new team member adequate time to comprehend and absorb all the information.

ADDITIONAL EXERCISES

EXERCISE 12-4: DELEGATION

Jill has taken a deep look at herself and her department and has decided she must delegate more to her employees for the following reasons: (1) She has been working fifty hours a week instead of forty. (2) The pressure of getting everything done has put her on edge with some of the staff. (3) She has not been sleeping well because of worry. Last night she spent three hours formulating a list of responsibilities she might delegate to her five employees. The list is below. What goals should Jill keep in mind when she ranks these tasks in order of priority for delegating? Rank the tasks in order of priority for delegating.

Priority
Ranking:

_____   A. A weekly report that takes fifty minutes to prepare. This report could easily be delegated to Rose, but it would reveal certain departmental figures that have always been kept away from the employees in the past. There is nothing secret about the data, but Jill feels she might lose some control if everybody knows what goes on.

_____   B. A weekly fun job that Jill has always enjoyed doing. Frances would love to do the job (she would probably do it better than Jill), but Jill wants to keep it because it keeps her closer to her employees and facilitates communication. The job usually takes about one hour.

_____   C. A very routine weekly stock or supply room count that takes one hour and a half. Jill has delegated this job before, but she always winds up taking it back because the grumbling from the employee disturbs her more than doing the job herself. Besides, sometimes the count is wrong and she winds up doing the job herself anyway.

_____   D. A short (fifteen-minute) telephone call every day at 4:00 P.M. to get some data to the computer center. Jill has refused to delegate this because if it is not done accurately, she will be reprimanded by her boss. Calvin would be able to do the job and not be overloaded.

_____   E. A daily (ten-minute) delivery job of a special report to top management. Jill has kept this to do herself because it gives her a chance to have a cup of coffee and she can play a little politics with middle- (and sometimes top-) management executives.

_____   F. A special routine meeting each month, which many supervisors already delegate to a subordinate. George could learn a lot from this assignment. Jill has
kept it to herself because she is afraid that something will happen at the meeting
that she won't know about. The meetings last from one to two hours.

EXERCISE 12-5: INTERVIEWING: QUESTIONING TECHNIQUES

This activity will help you become more skillful in conducting interviews
through using open-ended questions, responding to free information, and
paraphrasing. (See Exhibit 12-5 and the accompanying discussion on
phrasing questions.)

Interview your partner for a job in your office. Concentrate first on using open-ended questions, then on responding to free information, and
finally on integrating paraphrasing into the interview. Switch roles.

Exhibit 12-5 presents some examples of closed and open-ended questioning and some possible responses. Note that closed questions can be
answered by a simple yes or no, but open-ended questions call for a
more detailed reply. Although some individuals *may* respond more fully
to closed questions than shown here, nonassertive people frequently won't.
Open-ended questions offer more encouragement to talk extensively.

EXHIBIT 12-5: Closed and Open-ended Questions

Closed Questioning	Open-ended Questioning
Q: Were you a salesman at Apex?	Q: *What* did you do at Apex?
A: Yes.	A: I was a salesman for the first two years and a sales supervisor for the last six months.
Q: Did you like being a sales supervisor?	Q: *How* did you feel about being a sales supervisor?
A: No.	A: It was frustrating because I really liked to sell and I'm not comfortable supervising others.
Q: And you supervised the Central City Territory?	Q: *Tell me* about the Central City Territory.
A: Yes.	A: Well, it includes twenty-one major accounts and

Another way to encourage conversation is to occasionally respond to
the *free information* the other person gives to your open-ended questioning
and give your own opinions, disclosures, or information:

Q: How were your commissions paid at Apex?

A: We received two percent of gross sales each quarter.

Q: Our commissions are comparable, and they are paid each month. Most salespersons really appreciate getting that check every month.

If you don't have anything to say in response to your partner's free information, yet you'd like for her to continue talking on the topic, try *paraphrasing:*

Q: How is the sales department structured at Apex?

A: There are four hundred or so salespersons reporting to thirty or so sales supervisors. Supervisors are expected to make a few calls with each sales person every month.

Q: It sounds as if the supervisors have their hands full.

REFERENCES

1. Deal, Terrence E., and Allan A. Kennedy. *Corporate Cultures*. Reading, Mass.: Addison-Wesley, 1982. The rites and rituals of corporate life are based on common values and reveal a great deal about how your management style fits in.

2. Drucker, Peter F. *Management*. New York: Harper & Row, 1974. This text is somewhat difficult to apply to everyday management situations. However, it is considered a classic.

3. Grove, Andrew S. *High Output Management*. New York: Random House, 1983. The president of Intel discusses how managers can dramatically increase productivity in their departments.

4. *Harvard Business Review on Management*. New York: Harper & Row, 1975. This book has been published annually for a number of years. It contains some of the outstanding articles published in the *Harvard Business Review*, a journal for the continuing education of business executives. Thirty-nine articles by leaders in their fields provide a wealth of information for the new manager.

5. Kanter, Rosabeth Moss. *The Change Masters*. New York: Simon and Schuster, 1983. Kanter discusses the importance of innovation in the American corporation as the key to raising productivity levels.

6. MacKenzie, R. Alec. *The Time Trap*. New York: McGraw-Hill, 1982. MacKenzie discusses delegation techniques as a major approach to executive time management.

7. Mager, Robert. *Analyzing Performance Problems*. Belmont, Calif.: Fearon Pitman, 1980. A thorough discussion of setting behavioral objectives and standards and analyzing performance problems in meeting those objectives and standards.

8. Maier, Norman R. F. *The Appraisal Interview: Three Basic Approaches*. La Jolla, Calif.: University Associates, 1976. The author discusses the problem-

solving approach to working with subordinates. Although he applies the approach mainly to the appraisal interview in which the subordinate's performance is reviewed, the approach can easily be adapted to all kinds of management situations.

9. Peters, Thomas J., and Robert H. Waterman, Jr. *In Search of Excellence*. New York: Harper & Row, 1982. The authors discuss nine basic lessons they gleaned from their research on America's best-run companies. They discuss the importance of developing and communicating simple, clear corporate values and visions.

10. Schoenberg, Robert J. *The Art of Being Boss*. New York: Lippincott, 1978. Perhaps the one best all-around reference for the new manager. Schoenberg has interviewed top corporate executives to learn the secrets of their success. The resulting text gives practical, down-to-earth, workable ideas that all managers can use.

11. Wachs, William. *Managerial Situations and How to Handle Them*. West Nyack, N.Y.: Parker, 1976. This book gives numerous everyday management situations with examples of how to handle them constructively.

Chapter Thirteen

Managing Your Time Productively

"Lost time is like a run in a stocking. It always gets worse."

Anne Morrow Lindbergh

We have discussed some underlying theories and philosophies of management, motivation, problem-solving, and decision-making. We have also discussed applying these theories in day-to-day management situations so that your management style in general and your supervision skills in particular are effective and help you achieve your specific objectives.

By now you have probably become aware that the functions of management and the various types of management skills cannot really be divided into neat categories. They overlap greatly. One category can rarely be discussed without bringing in aspects of other categories. We use these categories merely for the sake of looking at a few aspects of management at one time.

All the management skills we have discussed so far are affected by your attitude toward time, the way you use your time, and the way you expect your subordinates to use theirs. Your time management approach certainly affects your management style and supervision techniques—how you delegate, for example. It has a profound impact on

your own motivation and the motivational climate you create in your department. It can create or alleviate problems for you and your subordinates, and it affects the timeliness and effectiveness of your decisions. Conversely, the way you manage your time will depend to a great extent on your management style, your approach to problem-solving and decision-making, and so forth.

In this chapter you will have the opportunity to learn more about

1. Developing a constructive attitude toward time, its value, and its use

2. Making the best use of time for your individual working style and energy-level patterns

3. Creating a personal environment for effective time management

4. Focusing on results instead of activities

5. Scheduling your day to accomplish *your* goals rather than other people's goals

6. Making and using "To Do" lists

7. Cooperating with your boss, subordinates, secretary, and peers to weed out time-wasters

8. Streamlining paperwork so that you normally handle each piece of paper only once

9. Minimizing interruptions so you can complete your top-priority tasks

10. Analyzing activities in order to improve the workflow in your department

11. Using your travel time productively

12. Planning, directing, and completing large, complex projects with minimal procrastination and a greater sense of satisfaction

---

 ## Freewheeling or Frantic?

8:00 A.M.: Carrie smiles as she sails by her secretary's desk. "Another gorgeous San Diego day, Amy. And I'm ready to tackle that summer sportswear project." Carrie enters her office. "Ah, nothing like a nice, clean desk to start a nice, clean day."

"Oh, come on," laughs Amy, poking her head in the door. "Sometimes your efficiency becomes absolutely Pollyannish. I assume you want me to keep the pack at bay for the next hour."

"You bet," responds Carrie, picking up the file folder lying on her otherwise empty desk and patting it. "The good old sales campaign for summer sportswear gets my undivided till 9 A.M. or a dire emergency—whichever comes first."

9:00 A.M.: Carrie checks with Amy to see who has called or asked to see her. Randy Perkins, one of the new salesmen, wants to see Carrie before he leaves the office to call on customers this morning. Carrie asks Amy to call Randy's extension and to ask him to drop by now. Meanwhile, she starts going through the high-priority mail that Amy has sorted and placed on her desk. She makes instructional notes to Amy on a few of them. (Amy writes many of the letters in response to requests for information and other routine transactions. She also delegates routine items to others in Carrie's department.)

9:15 A.M.: Randy enters Carrie's office. "Hi, Carrie. Thanks for taking the time to see me this morning. I know you're busy with the new sales campaign."

"Glad to see you, Randy. The sales campaign is coming right along. It's exciting to work with such a well-executed line of sportswear. I think you'll enjoy selling it, too. It should make a lot of money for us and for our customers. Here, take a look at these preliminary sketches."

"Say, these *are* good looking! They'll practically sell themselves."

"I agree. Now, what can I do for you this morning, Randy?"

"Well, I'd like your opinion on the Wingate account . . . (Randy discusses a potential problem concerning one of Lighthouse Designs' oldest and largest customers. Carrie listens, making appropriate, helpful comments from time to time.) I see now exactly what I've got to do. I think I mainly just needed to talk to someone who understands the situation. Just talking about it and getting a few pointers from you has clarified the whole situation for me."

"Good, I'm sure you can handle it well, Randy. If you want to discuss it further, though, be sure to drop by."

"Thanks, Carrie. See you at the next staff meeting, if not before. By the way, when will our next meeting be?"

"I'm not sure yet, but I'll give you plenty of notice. Things are going pretty smoothly right now, and there are not enough discussion items to warrant a meeting at this time. As soon as we need a meeting, I'll let you know."

"Okay. See you later."

9:30 A.M.: Randy stops at Amy's desk on the way out. "You know, Amy, we're both lucky to have a boss like Carrie. I don't know how she manages to get so much done and still have plenty of time to listen to everyone's problems and requests. Are you the one who keeps her organized?"

"Well, let's just say we work together to keep the office running smoothly. Carrie *lets* me help her—more so than any boss I've ever had. And she helps me, too."

Kate Blakeley's secretary, Phil, is sitting by Amy's desk, going over some items Amy is sending to the Administrative Services Department.

"You really are lucky, Amy. Kate drives me buggy sometimes. I wish she'd get her act together the way your boss does."

"Oh, Phil. Surely it's not all that bad."

"Okay. yesterday was a typical day. Let me give you a rundown. Pretend we're hiding behind a candid camera."

8:00 A.M.: Kate Blakeley comes bustling in. She rushes toward her office, barely nodding to people as she dashes by. She has several meetings to attend today, including the weekly staff meeting of her sales people. She simply must spend an hour or so with Phil, her secretary, dictating important correspondence and giving him instructions on handling some matters while she's in her meetings.

K: Good morning, Phil, would you come in right away and let's get on these letters.

P: Sure thing. Ah . . . Frank LeFavor just came by. He needs to see you to find out what you want him to do about the materials for Schroeder's Department Store.

K: Well, get him on the phone and tell him I'm here. I'll try to get this over with as soon as possible and then we'll work on the correspondence. Meantime, I'll start on these telephone calls. (She picks up several telephone message slips left over from yesterday afternoon.)

8:20 A.M.: When Frank gets to Kate's office, she's on the telephone and waves for him to come in and sit down. Frank waits patiently as Kate tries to finish the call. She occasionally glances at Frank, raises her eyebrows, and shrugs her shoulder as the long-winded person on the other end of the line keeps talking.

8:30 A.M.: Finally Kate is able to complete the call and turns to Frank.

K: Now, Frank, let's discuss the Schroeder problem . . .
Frank tries to explain to Kate what he has learned about the Schroeder problem. During the discussion, Kate excuses herself two different times to take important phone calls. She's aware that the morning is slipping by and she still hasn't finished preparations for her staff meeting. She glances at her watch several times. Finally at 9 A.M. she interrupts Frank.

K: Why don't you put this all in a memo to me and let me study it.

F: But I'm supposed to call on Schroeder tomorrow . . . Well, all right. I hope you can give me an answer within the next few days.
Kate manages to complete most of the dictation and instructions to her secretary. Then she takes a few minutes to prepare for her weekly staff meeting, which is scheduled for 10 A.M.

10:10 A.M.: Kate rushes into the meeting.

K: Good morning, people. Now we've a number of items to cover this morning, so I'll get right down to business . . .

11:05 A.M.: The meeting adjourns. Frank LeFavor and Bill Waldheim walk together toward their offices.

B: You know, I'm wondering what we really accomplished in that meeting.

F: I thought the same thing after several of the meetings lately. It seems to me that at least half of these meetings could be eliminated and everyone would be a lot better off.

B: Yeah. I need to finish the Viva job today. Now the day's nearly half gone.

F: Why does she think we have to meet every single week?

B: Oh, she thinks we need the regular contact so that we feel like one big happy family.

F: Some family! I went in this morning to try to get an answer from her on the Schroeder job, and I felt like I was talking to a brick wall.

Amy sighs. "Yeah, I see what you mean, Phil. Kate needs help. Well, maybe I can drop a hint to Carrie. She's great at working with people on these problems—and she does it in a way that makes people feel good about themselves."

———————————

1. As you read this story, what effective time management attitudes and actions did you notice? ———————

———————————

2. What impact or effect did these practices have on people? (For example, on moti-

vation and productivity?) ——————

———————————

3. What ineffective time management attitudes and actions did you observe? ————

———————————

4. What impact or effect did these practices have on people? ———————————

DEFINING ATTITUDES TOWARD TIME

> Yesterday is a cancelled check.
> Tomorrow is a promissory note.
> Today is ready cash. Use it!

This statement by an anonymous philosopher vividly conveys the importance of making the most of the present moment. Think about it. The present moment is all you *really* have.

How can we make the most of time? First of all, even though we speak of managing *time*, what we can actually do about time is manage our *activities* so that they produce the most effective results. We conduct our activities within a frame of reference called "time." Time marches on, and there is nothing we can do to change that. What we *can* do is change our activities so that they give the best results.

It has been said that "Time is money." Most effective managers share that viewpoint. When employees' time is wasted, the dollars the company pays them in salary are being wasted. Not only that, but wasted time can mean lost opportunities to make money, costly delays that not only tie up other workers' time but perhaps increase storage costs, transportation costs, insurance costs, and other costs.

Thinking of your time and your subordinates' time in terms of hourly pay will help you to put wasted time in proper perspective. To figure approximate hourly pay, divide annual salary by 2,000 hours. For example, if you make $20,000 a year, your hourly rate is about $10 per hour ($20,000 ÷ 2,000). The hourly rate for $8,000 a year is $4, and the hourly rate for $50,000 a year is $25. Remember, though, that this doesn't include "perks" or fringe benefits, which frequently amount to one-third of the salary. The estimated cost of some typical executive time-wasters is shown in Exhibit 13-1.

When you adopt the attitude that indulging in time-wasters is similar to taking a match to company money and burning it, you are likely to guard your precious time and make the most of it. This attitude can influence your subordinates too. You can go over the monetary value of their time by calculating with them the cost of a coffee break or bull session, interruptions, and other time-consumers.

Using your time productively is intertwined with other good management practices, such as setting objectives so that you focus on effectiveness rather than on efficiency; setting priorities and time targets so that the most important objectives are given top priority; planning activities ahead by identifying and ranking them on a "To Do" list so that you schedule your day for the activities most likely to achieve the objectives; concentrating on a single item at a time; delegating effectively and establishing a good followup system; and making timely, appropriate decisions. All these practices also tend to prevent harmful tension that leads to stress. Instead, they promote beneficial tension—that is, challenge and enthusiasm. Stress management and time management are both enhanced by an awareness of personal energy-level patterns (**body time**) and a soothing external environment. To take advantage of the time management techniques suggested here, however, you must analyze your attitude toward time and focus on payoffs for practicing time-saving techniques.

Delegating: The Key to Time Management

We have discussed how important your attitude toward delegation is for keeping your subordinates motivated and enthusiastic and how important it is to your upward mobility.

EXHIBIT 13-1: Estimating the Cost of Wasted Time

Someone comes into your office uninvited = $5

That's the average value of the time you lose from the interruption of your work and the unproductive time you spend.

You accept a phone call outside your preset phone hours = $6.50

If you're not a salesman or a customer relations specialist, you can restrict unwanted calls and save this expenditure.

You pick up a piece of paper = 50¢

If you put the paper down without working on it, you've thrown that money away.

You stop what you're doing to do something else = $1.75

That's the approximate cost of switching from one task to another, especially when the first task isn't finished.

You dictate a letter = $5 to $15

The exact cost depends on your salary and your secretary's salary. Is this letter really necessary?

Adapted from EXECU*TIME, Vol. 2, No. 8 (August 1979), p. 2.

Another important benefit of delegating effectively is the time it frees up for you to devote to higher-priority items such as planning and organizing or mastering higher-level skills.

Focusing on One Task at a Time

Your attitude toward balancing projects is important too. Regardless of your individual working style, you must focus on one task at a time for maximum effectiveness.

Some people work best with several irons in the fire at once. They like to have several projects going—each at a different stage in its development. In that way they can be thinking about one when they have a breather in another. They can assign the solution of certain problems on one project to their subconscious while the conscious part of their mind focuses on another project. When they feel blocked, tired, or bored with one project, they can frequently make progress on a quite different one.

If this is your style, you can still focus on one task at a time, even while "keeping all your irons hot." Try these suggestions.

1. As soon as one project is underway, look for another that is ready for action.

2. Make a step-by-step plan for each project.

3. Delegate as much of the work as you can.

4. Set a schedule for following up on each one.

Other people prefer to focus on one project at a time. They become intensely involved with it, living with it almost day and night until it is completed.

If this is your style, try these techniques.

1. Choose the one project that promises to be most fruitful and is best suited for you.

2. Make a plan for completing it.

3. Delegate other projects that will need attention before your number one project is completed.

4. Stick with your project until it is finished.

Regardless of which style best suits you, it's important to focus on one *task* at any one point in time. Other tasks and other projects may be simmering in your subconscious, or subordinates may be working on them. But at any one moment you are totally focused on the task at hand—whether it is planning a step, discussing a task with a subordinate, carrying out a task yourself, or handling some other aspect of the multiple projects you may have going.

Using Awareness of Body Time

Your attitude toward your activities and the pace at which you accomplish them is strongly affected by your energy level at various times of the day [4, p. 3]. As a rule, workers between 18 and 30 years of age start the slowest, begin to peak after lunch, and are still going strong even when the office is closing up. Workers between 31 and 40 start to peak very early in the morning and slow down by 2 P.M. Workers between 41 and 55 peak at midmorning and taper off gently throughout the day. On average, the energy of all workers is highest at 10:30 A.M. By the end of the day, 20 percent are "exhausted."

Try to schedule projects and tasks that require the most concentration, creativity, analysis, synthesis, and decision-making for your higher-energy hours. If you find that your peak hours simply don't coincide with the needs of your job, it may be possible to change your peaks by changing your sleeping habits. People who are convinced they are "night people" are often surprised to find that they become more of a "morning type" after a few months of changed sleeping habits. When they are required to arise early every morning for a few months and in turn to retire early, they soon find themselves waking earlier on their own and peaking at an earlier hour.

Locating Time-Wasters and Energy Drains

The first step in locating the major time-wasters and energy drains in your life is to keep a log of your activities for a week or two. Exercise 13-1 offers suggestions for setting up such a log and analyzing it to determine how well your activities support your top priority goals.

Developing a Constructive Attitude Toward Time Management

Your viewpoints about the value of time, the role of delegation, your individual working style, and the use of your body time patterns all work together to form a constructive (or not so constructive) attitude toward time management. Another vital factor is how you use rewards to motivate yourself to reach your time management goals.

First, give yourself permission to have regularly scheduled rewards. You may find yourself torn between what you *should* do and what you *want* to do. It's natural to want immediate payoffs—to have fun and feel good *now*. Therefore, if you don't arrange some regular short-term payoffs, you may end up sabotaging your own efforts, usually without knowing why.

Find rewards that are satisfying but create minimal delay and expense in meeting your objectives. Only you can decide how simple or sophisticated, how large or small, how often and in what pattern they must be to keep you happy. Experiment with rewards such as these to find out what works for you:

A snack break, coffee break, special lunch or dinner, cocktail, weekend trip, or vacation days off—once you complete a certain task or project

A shopping trip, the purchase of a little luxury item, or simply a stroll through an interesting shop or mall—upon completion of a task or project

An interesting new "toy" such as a new dictating machine, a calculator, a personal computer, or other equipment that turns you on and helps get the work done

A favorite beverage or goodie to sip or munch as you concentrate on an especially tedious project (watch out for calories, sugar, alcohol, too much caffeine, and other problems)

A thick piece of carpet under your desk to work your toes into after you've quietly slipped off your shoes

A red marker for drawing nice big lines through items on your "To Do" list as you complete them

A trip down the hall or to another floor to enjoy a nice view for a few minutes

You may be carrying around old parent messages that interfere with your enjoyment of these rewards, such as: "You're just coddling yourself and wasting time." "Buckle down and get your work done." "Quit acting like a child." If so, simply remind yourself that you'll be more productive in the long run if you enjoy yourself along the way.

If you still have trouble motivating yourself to use constructive time management techniques, find out what payoffs you're getting for *not* managing your time well. Use the same process you followed in Chapter 5 for analyzing payoffs for nonassertiveness.

EXERCISE 13-1: LOGGING AND ANALYZING YOUR ACTIVITIES

Step 1. *Identify goals.* If you are working, first analyze your job description or determine what is expected of you; then identify your major areas of responsibility. In any case, identify your top-priority goals in all areas of your life.

Step 2. *Set up a time log.* A fairly large daily appointment calendar with space to record items for each hour of the day can be purchased at an office supply store, or you can easily set up your own log sheets.

Step 3. *Log activities and body time.* Pick two weeks that are fairly typical and log all your activities. Include weekends. Note times when your energy level is especially high or low, when you especially enjoy being with people or prefer to be alone (sociability level), or when you feel especially influential or ineffective (charisma level). Also note any variations in the work pace you prefer at various times.

Step 4. *Set up summary sheets.* Prepare a summary form for each week that will help you analyze the percentage of time you spent on various types of tasks. You can use the form shown in Exhibit 13-2 or design your own.

Step 5. *Fill in summary sheets.* Identify the main activities that occupy your time and make up your work load, as shown on your log sheets. Each major activity becomes a column heading on your summary form opposite "Task." The sample summary sheet shown is abbreviated. Your own summary sheet will probably have a dozen or so major types of activity. Referring to your log sheet for each day, record the hours you spent on each type of task under the task column heading and in the appropriate horizontal row indicating the day the task was worked on.

Step 6. *Analyze summary sheets.* You should be able to see how much time you spent on each task and the daily and weekly pattern of effort toward each task by looking down each column. You can also see the daily and weekly pattern of time allocated to all major types of tasks by looking horizontally across the row for each day.

Step 7. *Identify time-wasters and energy drains.* Does the amount of time you're spending on each type of task adequately support your top-priority goals? If not, how can you reprioritize your activities? Are you making best use of peak body times? If not, how can you change the timing of your activities?

EXHIBIT 13-2: Example of Summary Sheet for Analyzing Logged Activities

Task: No. of Hours:	Research for Marketing Report		Reading for Management Seminars		Team Meeting		Food Shopping Preparation, Cleaning		Total	BODY TIME SUMMARY:*			
										Energy	Sociability	Charisma	Work Pace
Mon.	2	½	2	—	3	½	3	—	11	9-11 H 5-6 L			9-11 = F 2-3 = S
Tue.													
Wed.													
Th.													
Fri.													
Sat.													
Sun.													
Week's Total													
SUMMARY TOTAL (all weeks)													
PERCENTAGE OF TOTAL TIME													

*H = High
L = Low
F = Fast
S = Slow
M = Moderate

Setting the Stage for Effective Time Management

Not only is your internal environment important for effective time management, your external environment has a strong impact also. Eliminate or improve as many situations that regularly irritate you as possible. For example, if your daily route to work is unpleasant, the trip to the office may have a depressing effect on you. It may be worth a few extra minutes of commuting time to take a more pleasant route. If you find yourself in regular contact with people who are insulting, confront them assertively or find a way to avoid them. If you find yourself regularly waiting in line and hating it, use problem-solving techniques to figure out ways to avoid lines. In other words, clean up your life as much as possible by eliminating any negative junk that is surrounding you. These irritants and depressants are energy drains.

Remember, your physical working environment has a strong psychological effect on your attitude and your work habits. Determine what you need to make you feel comfortable with your office and enjoy being in it and modify your work space. Set the stage for effective time management by organizing your desk, setting limits on your weekly work hours, and learning to say "no" to some requests.

Keeping an Uncluttered Desk Nearly everyone finds that a well-ordered desk improves mood and efficiency; it also signals an executive attitude. In most companies the higher up in the corporate hierarchy one goes, the cleaner are the managers' desks. So get papers off your desk and onto someone else's (or into the wastebasket) when possible. Avoid in- and out-baskets; keep them on your secretary's desk or use your desk drawers for this purpose.

Limiting Your Work Except for short periods when you're learning the ropes of a new job or completing a special project, avoid working more than forty-five hours a week. If you must work overtime, consider doing it early in the morning rather than staying late; this signals that you're on top of things instead of floundering.

You will profit from directing most of your energy toward career-related objectives, especially while you're trying to make your mark. Everyone who succeeds pays those kinds of dues. However, don't confuse long hours and hard work with achieving objectives. Don't bury yourself in piles of work and neglect opportunities to make important contacts, become professionally involved, and learn important new skills.

Try to get all your work done at the office so you won't need to carry it home. If this is your intention and your goal, you'll rarely need to take work home and you'll probably be a better manager. When you get in the habit of thinking, "If I don't finish it today, I can always do it at home tonight," your *intention* changes and your incentive for managing your time effectively takes a nosedive.

Learning to Say "No" If you don't learn to say "no" to tasks, nominations, meetings, and other time-consuming activities people request you to participate in, you will end up managing your time according to other people's objectives and priorities rather than your own (see Chapter 5 on assertiveness). Of course your priorities should be congruent with your boss'. If they are not, perhaps you should think seriously about changing jobs. At times, it may even be wise to say "no" tactfully to your boss. At least discuss how completion of the activities the boss is requesting fits in with the objectives the two of you agreed upon for your job.

USING OBJECTIVES AND PRIORITIES FOR DIRECTING ENERGY

Before you can direct your energies into channels that are most productive for you, you must know what you are trying to achieve. Time management rests on management by objectives, which implies effective action rather than merely efficient action, getting results rather than merely making an effort. To lay the necessary foundation for using your time effectively, therefore, look at the list of activities you made for achieving your career objectives (Exercise 2-8). Are you actively engaged in these activities now? Are they moving you toward your most important objectives? Do you need to add new activities and weed out unproductive ones? How about the time targets for completing them? Do you need to rethink the deadlines you've set?

Setting Deadlines

It's important to set deadlines for completing your activities and achieving your objectives—and to have your workers set deadlines. It's also important to observe them. According to **Parkinson's Law:** "Work expands to fill the time available for its completion."

People who don't have a deadline tend to put off getting started on a task and to dawdle once they do start. Some keep working toward perfection rather than being satisfied with reasonable effectiveness or excellence. Perfectionism is extremely costly. In fact, it's prohibitive over the long term. Successful business people adopt the principle of "sensible approximation." Ask yourself, "If my life depended upon doing this task in half the time I have allocated, what shortcuts would I take? Is there really any reason *not* to take them?" Set intermediate deadlines for long-term projects so that you keep working at a steady pace rather than finding yourself swamped near the deadline date.

Scheduling Your Day

If you don't plan your day, you'll end up doing whatever comes up. This means that other people's actions may determine your priorities instead of the goals you have set for yourself. It also means, as Edwin Bliss points out in *Getting Things Done,* that you will make "the fatal mistake of dealing primarily with problems rather than opportunities" [1, p. 81]. You're likely to be solving other people's problems instead of working on that new idea, system, or proposal. Remember, one of the most productive uses of your time is planning ahead. The better you plan a project in advance, the less time it takes to complete it successfully. Don't let busy-work crowd out your planning time.

Using a "To Do" List   The key to successful use of "To Do" lists is actually *using* them. That means referring to your list the first thing every morning and checking it regularly during the day to be sure you are making the best use of your time all through the day. Especially good times for checking your list are just after an interruption, when you're torn between two activities, when you're running out of energy or interest in your current activity. Use whatever format and ma-

terials work best for you but avoid using small pieces of paper. They tend to get scattered all over the place, making you feel scattered rather than organized and integrated. Put everything on one sheet of paper or in one notebook.

Perhaps you need to get a clear picture of your major responsibilities and deadlines for each week, each month, or perhaps even for a year. Experiment by either trying out various "To Do" sheets and pads from office supply stores or by designing your own format. After a tryout period, stock up or have your own format typed and reproduced. Be sure to always have an adequate supply of sheets at your desk. If you date your "To Do" sheets, they can do double duty as an appointment calendar and tickler file. Figure 13-1 shows a format that is helpful for many managers. Use the "follow-up" section for jotting down reminders by turning ahead to the appropriately dated "To Do" sheet. Later, on that day, your reminder will be waiting for you.

Preparing for Tomorrow   Not only is it important to check your "To Do" list first thing every morning and at intervals throughout the day, it's also important to take a few minutes in the afternoon before going home to work on your list for the following day. Why should you make it in the afternoon? For one thing, doing so gives you a feeling of closure and completion of the workday. Also, in the morning, you are pressured by other duties and are likely to prepare the "To Do" list haphazardly. The main reason, however, is to give your subconscious mind time to work on your list during the intervening time, even while you sleep.

After you have made your list for the next day, clear your desk before leaving the office. Try setting just one important project out on your desk and putting everything else in a file drawer or cabinet that's easy to

FIGURE 13-1: Format for "To Do" Lists

TO DO TODAY

DATE _____

TO DO		
Task		Priority

TO SEE		
Time	Person or Group	Place

FOLLOWUP

TO PHONE		
Person	Objective of Call	Priority

reach. When you come in the next morning, work on that one project as long as you can.

Eliminating Activities Remember that sometimes the activities that are most important for reaching your objectives are not urgent—for example, writing an article, working up a proposal, or working out the details of a new idea. If you find yourself transferring an item from your "To Do" list day after day, ask yourself: "Is this item really important?" "Am I procrastinating?" "Should this go in the tickler file?" There is no need to list routine items that you do regularly. List only the items that have high priority today and might not get done unless you give them special attention.

For each item, ask yourself, "What can I delegate?" Then, for each activity, beginning with the one ranked lowest, ask, "What would happen if I didn't do this?" If the answer is "maybe nothing" or "not much," give the activity an aging period. If there is no followup from anyone and no repercussions, you have saved that time to spend on high-priority items.

Custom Tailoring Your List As you schedule your time, keep in mind three major considerations.

Practical considerations: Match items that require concentration with times when you are reasonably certain of having an uninterrupted period of peace and quiet. If special equipment or facilities are necessary, are they available only at certain hours? Might there be a waiting time to consider? Do you need to see other people in order to complete the task? When will they be available?

Body time considerations: Wherever possible, schedule activities to take advantage of your prime times. Reserve routine tasks for times when you are fairly alert but not at your peak. Try to use peak hours for top-priority projects, tasks that require intense concen-

tration or original thinking, or tasks that are stressful or unpleasant but important. Use your low-energy times for catching up on professional reading, proofreading and signing letters, planning the next day, and so forth.

If you must schedule a task that calls for high energy during a low-energy time, boost your energy by taking a brief rest period followed by a nutritious snack (and see the relaxation exercises at the end of Chapter 4).

Preferred pace considerations: Some people require pressure to work at top capacity. If that is your style, use it. However, be sure you plan ahead enough to get the information, approvals, documentation, and other items you need to complete the job so that pressure doesn't turn into panic or disaster. If you like to schedule your day very closely, from hour to hour, be sure you still build in at least an hour a day for unexpected events and for breathing space.

For most people, crash programs are far inferior to well-planned and well-timed programs. Knowing when to stop work on a project is as important as knowing when to start because overwork leads to diminishing returns, such as increased errors and sloweddown responses. When your muscles are aching or you find yourself reading the same sentence two or three times, it's usually time to quit.

Whenever you possibly can, schedule your time in large blocks so you won't have to constantly switch back and forth from one type of activity to another. Leave some unscheduled time for visitors, phone calls, unforeseen emergencies, and other unexpected tasks. If it turns out you don't need all that unscheduled time, count your blessings and return to the next item on your "To Do" list.

Remember to schedule some quiet time for relaxation and meditation. At least find some time to back off from the rat race; stand back and gain some perspective on what is going on. This can help you be more objective about minutiae and pettiness when you go back to your tasks.

Setting Special Emphasis Goals Allan Lakein, in *How to Get Control of Your Time and Life,* suggests that in order to increase your level of motivation and enthusiasm, you should set a "special emphasis goal" that lasts from a week to a couple of months [7]. The goal might be to come up with one new idea for some special project each day, to go after one big customer each day, or to figure out a way to streamline one activity (yours or a subordinate's) each day. Then do something every day to squeeze in at least one top-priority activity for each special emphasis goal.

This technique is a great morale-booster because every day you see yourself come closer to your top-priority objectives by remembering what you want to do and doing it. Obviously, then, working with your subordinates to set special emphasis goals can also pay off handsomely.

Using "Dead" Time We all have a certain amount of "dead" time when we are not doing anything that directly leads to the accomplishment of top-priority objectives—the time we spend waiting for someone or something, sleeping, engaging in early morning activities or inertia, commuting, taking lunch and coffee breaks, and so forth. It is up to you to decide how much of that time should remain "dead" and how much of it you want to liven up by making it do double duty.

There is no need to become an overworked time management "nut" by frantically packing every moment full of activity. But you will no doubt experience times when dead-time activities are boring. You may feel a sense of frustration at such a low-level use of your time when you are itching to work on a top-priority activity. It can be fun to figure out your own preferred pace and see how creative you can be in making the best use of your dead time.

Try keeping a file folder of "quick tasks." During the day, drop into it items that can be done during dead time. Drop the folder in your briefcase when you leave the office. Then when you are faced with dead time and want to work on some high-priority activity, you will have some quick tasks with you. Also, be sure to take your file folder along to meetings and appointments when you may need to wait for someone.

Use your commute time to think about activities for the coming day. This time can be extremely valuable in mentally rehearsing the best ways to handle problems, situations, and tasks. Consider carrying a small tape recorder so you can dictate "To Do" list reminders for the future, items for your expense report, and dates you want to remember. If you are not doing the driving, you can even dictate detailed memos and letters. Your secretary can sort out the items and transcribe them later.

Evaluating Objectives, Activities, and the Daily "To Do" List Frequent evaluation helps you to stay flexible and ready to change plans and priorities as circumstances change. Once every month or so keep a detailed log of how you spend one day. Choose a fairly typical day; then ask yourself as you get ready to begin an activity, "If I weren't already doing this, would I start it now?" If the answer is "no," why not cut your losses and drop it? If the answer is "yes," calculate how much time that item deserves and limit your involvement to that much time and no more. This practice will keep you aware of good time management. It will help you focus on objectives that enhance your effectiveness and activities that get results rather than on merely keeping busy and working hard.

Documenting Your Achievements Keeping track of what you've accomplished is easy if you keep your used-up "To Do" lists in special file folders. Be sure they include a notation indicating whether you completed each item. For special activities or projects, note (1) everything you did well, what made it successful, and how you went about it; (2) everything that went wrong, why, and how to prevent problems from happening again. File these sheets where you can easily find them when you begin planning a similar activity or project.

Some people make an "I Love Me" (ILM) folder for their achievement records. They add to it letters of appreciation, congratulation, and praise written to them by others. They also include special reports, articles, or letters they have written that reflect high-quality work or special achievement. Keep this file at home to maintain privacy and prevent loss.

Review your special files when it's time for a performance appraisal, a raise or promotion request, or an update of your résumé or biography, and on any other occasion involving your performance. In this way you can base your comments on specific achievements that you can back up with accurate facts and figures.

FINDING TIME-SAVERS AND WEEDING OUT TIME-WASTERS

In Chapter 2 you developed a list of clearly stated objectives, ranked in order of importance, and a list of activities that will lead to achieving those objectives, ranked in order of priority. In this chapter you have reviewed techniques for using a daily "To Do" list that includes those activities and other tasks, ranked in order of importance. You're well on your way to managing your time as effectively as possible. All that remains is for you to weed out time-wasters that may creep into your well-planned day and replace them with time-savers—whether the

source of the waste is your boss, your subordinates, your peers, or the system.

We'll look at cooperating with others on time-savers first and then at effective ways to handle workflow, interruptions, the telephone, paperwork, and travel time. Finally, we'll cover procrastination, which is especially common, and deadly, to large, complex projects that tend to be rather overwhelming.

Cooperating with Others on Time Management

Your best efforts at managing your time effectively can be sabotaged by your boss, your subordinates and your peers. It is up to you to use Murphy's Law in order to foresee and circumvent as many obstacles as possible.

Your Boss   If your boss pushes you to complete an item that is low on your priority list, tactfully discuss your conflict rather than meekly complying. Talk in terms of achieving objectives and doing what's best for the boss, the department, and the company. Make sure the boss knows what other items are pending on your "To Do" list and is aware of their impact on your objectives.

If your boss is difficult to find when you need an approval, decision, or information, plan ahead to avoid delays. If that doesn't work, discuss the problem with the boss.

Some bosses don't delegate effectively; others postpone decisions too long. No matter what time management problem your boss is creating for you, a tactful, open discussion about the impact of the boss' actions on your productivity is usually the key to improving the situation. Of course you never want to appear critical of your boss' behavior. To avoid the impression of evaluating your boss in a negative fashion, take a problem-solving approach. Stress the possibilities for improvement of your performance with the boss' help.

Your Subordinates Encourage your subordinates to think about time management and to speak up when you ask them to do things they think are ineffective or time-wasters. Work with them on making the best use of your time and theirs.

You can waste your subordinates' time by communicating instructions poorly or in other ways delegating ineffectively—for example, when you don't select the right job for the right person or don't train the person properly. When you keep your subordinates waiting, you are wasting their time and the company's money. Be prompt for appointments and meetings with them. If you see that you're going to be late, let them know so they can be using their time constructively until you *are* ready to see them.

Be sure that you don't interrupt your subordinates' work unnecessarily. Ask yourself: "Is this interruption really necessary, or could it wait?" "Could I ask this subordinate to drop by when he reaches a stopping point?" "Could she call me?" "Could a secretary or receptionist give this subordinate the message during a break?"

That Special Subordinate: Your Secretary The most important subordinate, so far as helping you manage your time is concerned, is your secretary or assistant. The first step in using this asset is to select an intelligent, well-trained secretary who approaches the job as a professional. Pay him or her as much as you can. The next step is to *treat* your secretary as a professional who will be working with you as a teammate. Delegate as much of the paperwork and as many of the communications tasks as you can to your secretary. Keep your secretary fully informed so that he or she knows what you would do in almost any situation.

Upgrade your secretary's duties. Work with him or her to eliminate useless typing chores and to streamline paperwork. In this way

you will free up some valuable administrative talent. Work together to make the best use of it. Set decision-making guidelines and define areas of authority for your secretary. Inform others of these developments and instruct them to cooperate with your secretary.

Keep your secretary's workflow in mind as you plan and execute yours. Some bosses sit on their paperwork all day and then dump it on the secretary late in the afternoon. That practice can be harmless *unless* you expect to have it all handled before quitting time.

Remember that work variety is important, and that secretaries can suffer from mental fatigue and boredom. Help your secretary to have variety in the course of a day, week, and month. Be sure your assignments provide adequate challenge and opportunity for growth. Your secretary will probably respond by working more efficiently and effectively. It pays, therefore, to work out a pattern of assignments that meets both your needs and your secretary's needs.

Keep your secretary informed about your priorities. Assign priority numbers to tasks you give your secretary, or have him or her rank the items after checking your "To Do" list. Prioritizing avoids the overwhelming effect of dumping work in a heap on your secretary's desk. It lets your secretary know which tasks to tackle first even when you assign a large number of tasks at one time.

Work together. Work with your secretary to devise procedures for screening calls, visitors, and mail. For example, some managers enlist their secretary's help in bringing appointments to a close: When someone is scheduled to see you in your office, decide how much time you want to allot to the meeting, and tell your secretary to call you when the time is up. Respond in a way that clearly indicates to your visitor that the meeting will have to end.

Keeping your desk organized can also be a joint project. One way to work together on this is to have a couple of "Do Not Disturb" paperweights. Your secretary can then be authorized to straighten or clear anything that doesn't have one of the signs on it. He or she can keep you organized in other ways, too. For example, your secretary can suggest items for your "To Do" list, help you monitor the progress of projects, take minutes at staff meetings, and handle the followup on actions delegated to subordinates at staff meetings. Here are some additional time-saving practices that require working cooperatively.

Be prepared for dictation to avoid delays, searches, and changes.

Every time you leave your office, let your secretary know where you're going and when you'll return.

Ask for suggestions on how you can help your secretary be more effective.

Give your secretary the same kind of feedback, professional development, support, decision-making autonomy, and recognition that you give your other subordinates.

Work together to arrange, keep, and cancel appointments; keep your secretary informed. The same goes for following up with information and decisions others have requested of you.

Your Peers The heads of other units or departments in your company can create all sorts of bottlenecks and delays in your plans. It's up to you to foresee and prevent as many of these problems as possible. When you are discussing the need for action with a peer, stress how the completion of the task in question helps achieve a specific objective. Tie the objective in with an organizational objective that your peer is committed to. In other words, find a common goal in order to motivate your colleague to cooperate more fully.

Here are additional techniques for eliminating time-wasters in your dealings with peers (as well as with subordinates and others) in meetings and discussions.

Set a closing time for all meetings and keep them as short as possible.

Consider scheduling meetings just before noon so that everyone will leave for lunch at the appointed time.

When you want to end an informal discussion, simply push back your chair, stand up, and start walking slowly toward the door as you end the discussion.

When someone drops by your office unannounced and you don't have time for a visit, stand up and remain standing as you talk. This signals that the conversation will have to be brief and prevents a "settling in" for a long session.

If you don't have time for a discussion in your office, but you want to at least acknowledge someone, walk out of your office and talk with the person on his or her way down the hall.

Improving Workflow

Sometimes the source of time-wasters—and a fertile area for finding time-savers—lies in the workflow system rather than in the people you deal with. To improve the workflow to, within, and from your unit, the first step is to work out regular times for doing *your* routine or recurring tasks so others can adjust *their* workflow, timing of calls, and other contacts with you accordingly.

Next, analyze routine tasks to see which ones (yours and your subordinates) can be performed more effectively so that workflow is improved. Do this by breaking down the tasks into steps and then concentrating on all aspects of each step, searching for alternative ways of handling each one.

Obviously the tasks that occupy the most time offer the most opportunity for real breakthroughs in time savings. So look first for problem areas where you can get the highest possible return on the time you invest in analysis and improvement. Focus more on what can be improved than on what is being done wrong. See whether you can make even small changes that will have big results. If you can, your motivation—and your workers'—to continue working toward improvement will be boosted.

Here are suggestions for finding *break-through problem areas*.

1. Develop a specific objective for the improvement; state it in measurable terms.

2. Start with the bottom line and work backward. For example, start with profits, items produced, costs, savings, or some other measure of effectiveness. Then work backward until you find an activity that controls or significantly affects this measure of effectiveness in some way.

3. If you come up with several ideas for change, look for the one that requires the least change, effort, cost, or lead time. The easiest, smallest changes are often the best, especially to begin with, unless there is a basic flaw in the entire system or procedure.

4. Before focusing on special tasks, look at repeated routine tasks, which offer greater opportunity for savings. The most typical types of problems to look for are [5, pp. 72–84]:

Bottlenecks: A person, task, or spot that creates delays in other people's work by backing up everything that precedes it, holding up everything that follows it, or both. Do a separate study of each delay to find out why it's happening and how it can be corrected.

Time-consumers: Tasks that take a long time to finish.

Run-abouts: Tasks that involve a great deal of dashing around or flurries of phone calls and paperwork.

Hidden time-wasters: These are the most difficult problems to identify because everybody is so busy. Remember, however, that well-organized tasks create a minimum of fuss and bother. Therefore, be suspicious of too much hustle and bustle. Ask, "Are the *right* things being done?"

Exercise 13-2 gives you an opportunity to analyze a workflow problem in your organization. As you make your analysis, be sure to include the people involved in each step. Ask them for their ideas and suggestions for improvement. It is a good idea to ask for input even on your own workflow problems—the ones that you personally create. Sometimes we are blind to solutions that an outsider can readily see; we are just too close to the problem. You may benefit by stepping aside and letting someone else take a look.

Were you able to eliminate or change any steps in the job you selected for Exercise 13-2? Now look at the performance steps that are left. Ask some "where, when, who, and how" questions for each one. Follow each question with a "why" question and a question that searches for alternatives.

The sequence in which you ask the questions is important. How the task is done should *not* be the first question. Changing the location, time, or person doing a task can be a great deal easier and simpler than coming up with an improved method for doing it. Therefore, the answer to the where, when,

EXERCISE 13-2: ANALYZING WORKFLOW PROBLEMS

Identify a job or task in your organization (or any personal task); then analyze it step by step, listing each step in sequence. Ask yourself why each step is necessary. Begin with the performance steps because if you can eliminate any of them, you'll probably automatically eliminate some planning and followup steps. Next ask yourself what else could be done that might give you the same or even better results. To further analyze each step, see the suggestions that follow.

Job: _____

Job Step	*Why Is It Done?*	*What Else Could Be Done Instead?*
	Performance Steps	
1 _____	_____	_____
2 _____	_____	_____
3 _____	_____	_____
4 _____	_____	_____
5 _____	_____	_____
6 _____	_____	_____
7 _____	_____	_____
8 _____	_____	_____
9 _____	_____	_____
10 _____	_____	_____
11 _____	_____	_____
12 _____	_____	_____
	Planning Steps	
1 _____	_____	_____
2 _____	_____	_____

Job: _____

Job Step	Why Is It Done?	What Else Could Be Done Instead?
3 _____	_____	_____
4 _____	_____	_____
5 _____	_____	_____
6 _____	_____	_____

Followup Steps

1 _____	_____	_____
2 _____	_____	_____
3 _____	_____	_____
4 _____	_____	_____
5 _____	_____	_____
6 _____	_____	_____

and who questions may eliminate the need for the how question.

Here are specific questions about each step.

1. Where is this task being done? Why there? Where else can it be done as well?

2. When is it done? What is the timing and sequence of the actions taken? Why then? What other time could it be done as well?

3. Who does it? What individual, group, or classification of persons has responsibility? Why is it done by them? Who else could do it as well?

4. How is it done? Why that way? How else could it be done as well?

As you search for ways to overcome workflow problems, it's important to deal with facts; look for causes; look for reasons, not excuses; and make the activity a team effort. As you look for improved methods of completing jobs (the "how"), you might decide to

Eliminate steps. Ask, "What would happen if we didn't do this?"

Combine steps to consolidate time, space, or people.

Rearrange the sequence of steps. Identify steps that can be done at other times or at any time. This will show where your flexibility lies.

Simplify steps. Can an existing step be simplified? If you come up with a *new* method, ask yourself, "Is each step in the new procedure done as simply and easily as possible?"

When you are ready to try out your improved procedures, approach, or system, continue to involve those who will carry out the plan.

Minimizing Interruptions

A common complaint of new managers is that they can't find time to work on high-priority projects because of constant interruptions. Finding large blocks of uninterrupted concentration time can be a real time-saver. It takes ten minutes for most of us to get deeply focused on a task that requires our full attention and intense concentration, and we can sustain this concentration for twenty minutes or so [3, p. 2]. After that, most of us take a break of some kind. Therefore, when your top-priority activity requires concentration, you may find yourself actually spending about half of your time on getting into the task, resting, switching to lower-priority items, and so forth. If you can build up your concentration span from twenty minutes to forty minutes, you get a real bonus in prime productive time. So time yourself and see whether you can stick it out for a few more minutes each time.

As you learn to concentrate for longer periods of time, you may find that you can focus in much faster and feel less tired when you are done. As a matter of fact, for most people one hour of continuous concentration on a project usually yields better results than two hours spent in ten- to twenty-minute work sessions. Eventually you may be able to concentrate for as long as three hours, if necessary, with only a ten-minute break each hour.

In order to make the best use of your concentration time, then, you must have at least one-hour blocks when you are free from interruptions. Nothing is more tiring and frustrating than handling continual interruptions when you are attempting to concentrate on a task. It's especially important to have a quiet time when you are faced with a high-priority project that is rather large or complex. You can accomplish this by establishing a daily **quiet hour** and by using other techniques for minimizing interruptions, such as scheduling "open-door" times and screening telephone calls.

The Quiet Hour The key to minimizing interruptions during times when you need to concentrate is to establish a quiet hour in your schedule. During this time, have your secretary hold all your calls and tell visitors you are unavailable. If you don't have a secretary and you can't stand ringing telephones, devise some way to keep your phones from ringing and people from knocking on your door. Put a sign on your door saying "Quiet Time" and perhaps the time when you will be available again. Alternatively, you might install a schedule board outside your door showing times when you will meet with people and times when you will be unavailable.

If you are convinced that the quiet hour is valuable and indeed necessary, you will probably be able to convince your boss and subordinates to respect it. In fact, you may be able to institute a quiet hour throughout the unit, department, or company that might follow these procedures: During this hour no phone calls are put through, no visitors are admitted, and there is no unnecessary talking or moving about. Management teams can meet and concentrate on tasks and people can focus on individual tasks. Encourage your people to plan, get organized, dream up new projects or new solutions to problems, or concentrate on their single most important task of the day. During the quiet hour the clerical and secretarial people can put their work in order, catch up on paperwork, and intercept stray phone calls and visits to their bosses.

If the quiet hour is the first hour of the day, the effect on customers is no more drastic than if office hours were 9 to 5 instead of 8 to 5. If you *do* institute a quiet hour for everyone, remember to renew commitment to it periodically. Otherwise "exceptions to the quiet hour rule" tend to increase until the quiet hour eventually becomes like any other hour.

Other Techniques In addition to the quiet hour, you can try a number of other techniques for keeping interruptions to a minimum. An **open-door policy,** for example, reflects a willingness to listen to subordinates' ideas and problems and an openness to accepting and trying out their suggestions. If you take it too literally, however, you're likely to sabotage your own efforts to improve your productivity by inviting constant interruptions. To forestall that problem you can (1) require your people to schedule the times they will meet with you, (2) have them hold less-urgent matters until you can visit them, or (3) have them hold most matters for regularly scheduled meetings.

Let people know what times you prefer to be available. This approach doesn't necessarily violate the concept of an open-door policy, and it allows you to set aside large blocks of time in the morning and afternoon to concentrate without interruption. An added bonus is that during the waiting period workers often figure out solutions to problems on their own.

Placing a barrier in front of your office door can help prevent constant interruptions. Some possible "protectors" are your secretary's desk, a screen, or a table. Closing your office door at least part of the way also helps discourage people's tendency to interrupt.

Avoid needless communication by analyzing your company's communication system. Are appropriate people informed in advance of changes, events, and other matters so they don't need to call you for the information? Is the company's telephone directory clear, accurate, and current so you needn't spend time redirecting calls? To further minimize telephone interruptions, either have your secretary screen your calls, or simply say, "I'm busy (or tied up) now. May I call you back at eleven?"

If all else fails, when you must concentrate on a project without interruption, trade offices with someone else, find a quiet spot in the company or public library, or even consider working at home.

Taming the Telephone

Your telephone can either be a time-saver or a time-waster, depending on how you use it. Analyze the purpose and pattern of your calls. When you need to communicate with someone, take a moment to reflect on the advantages and disadvantages of doing so by telephone, face-to-face meeting, or written message. Is your purpose to discuss (1) detailed items that you need to confirm in writing anyway, (2) complex items that the receiver will have to think about before giving you a firm reply, (3) important items that require approval at several levels? Will a phone call now really do any good? If it will, then have your points and all materials at hand *before* you dial.

Bunch your telephone calls by making several calls during one time period. This leaves blocks of time when you can be uninterrupted.

Decide on a policy about being put on hold. Either avoid it and call back, or keep your file of quick tasks handy so you can keep busy while you're waiting.

Consider using special telephone equipment and arrangements, such as a speaker phone or a shoulder rest that leaves your hands free to handle files and perform other tasks. A telephone headset with a long cord frees your hands and still maintains your privacy. An automatic dial system for frequently called numbers also saves time. A telephone charge card for calls made away from the office can be handy. You don't have to worry about finding change for calls, and you'll get a record of all calls made with your card.

When your business is over with, get off the phone. Practice the quick ending: "I'll let you get back to your business." "Well, thanks so much. I must dash to a meeting now." "Fine. If we've covered everything, I'll let you go and get back to you later."

Analyze the pattern of both incoming and outgoing calls for a while to see which types can be eliminated through delegation, re-routing of written notices, screening, or other methods. Streamline incoming calls by finding out what a caller wants as soon as possible. Ask probing questions tactfully or say, "What can I do for you?"

Streamlining Paperwork

Now you know how to sidestep the worst hazards of the telephone. It's time to face a similar danger—becoming swamped in paperwork. Many articles and books have been written about handling the "paper explosion" and avoiding paper-pushing all day. W. J. Reddin states in *Effective Management by Objectives* that the less paperwork an organization produces, the more effective its planning system is likely to be [10, p. 16]. When people are preoccupied with documenting actions, they spend less thought and

energy on actually doing the things that contribute most to achieving specific objectives. Here's where working closely with your secretary or assistant can really pay off. Ask for suggestions.

The first step in streamlining paperwork is to work out a plan for minimizing and organizing the flow of paper. Establish procedures for sorting and handling your mail effectively. Experiment until you find the best procedures for your situation. Then stick with your plan until and unless you come up with something better. Minimize both the time you spend writing letters, reports, and other documents, and the number of papers you file. Organize your files so that you can make the best use of them.

The second step is a part of your plan. As a daily practice, make this your goal: Once your incoming mail is sorted, *handle each piece of paper only once.* This is a goal, of course, not a rigid rule. But if you haven't tried it, you may be surprised at how seldom you really need to violate it.

Handling Your Mail Effectively A workable system for sorting and handling mail is a prerequisite to handling each piece of paper only once. Have your secretary divide your mail into the categories that work best for you. Here are some categories to consider.

Immediate action—high priority

Pending action—high priority (needs research, consultation, or approval)

Can be done later—low priority

To read later, file, or distribute

Throw away

Of course you judge the priority of each piece of mail according to how it fits in with your objectives and the activities designed to achieve them. Remember to give low-priority items an aging period because the need for many of them may disappear.

One of the most common sources of poor time management is the practice of working on low-priority items just because they seem to be immediate, demanding, easy, or short. At times the only high-priority tasks you have are either difficult or time consuming. Nevertheless, it's generally more productive to keep chipping away at large, high-priority tasks than to sail through low-priority ones. (Later in this chapter we'll discuss ways of breaking down large projects into quick tasks or manageable tasks.)

Train your secretary to handle as much of the mail as possible without your needing to see it. For the things you do read yourself, try using a four-color pen so you can signal by color the type of action your secretary should take on an item. One executive uses this system: When she uses red ink to jot a note on a piece of mail or related item, her secretary knows he must complete the instructed action himself. A note in green signals the secretary to type an item, blue to file it, and black to route it to the person noted. Such color coding lets you avoid the time-waster of writing the same instructions over and over.

Streamlining Your Correspondence Procedures Writing letters and reports in minimal time is also an integral part of handling each piece of paper only once. Use dictation equipment for most letters and reports. Dictate from a *brief* outline of points you want to cover. To make retyping unnecessary, include information about format, stationery, and number of copies needed at the *beginning* of each dictated item, and learn to make corrections on the tape properly.

Consider using form letters, preprinted cards, and form paragraphs. You and your secretary can keep a file of well-worded, numbered paragraphs. Then simply dictate

the paragraph numbers and any other necessary information. If you have access to a word-processor, you can have the paragraphs stored and reprinted electronically. For many messages, of course, you can simply dictate key ideas and let your secretary compose the letter or memo.

Look for other ways to simplify your correspondence. On the bottom portions of the letters you receive, write short replies or have longer ones typed. If you need a copy of the transaction, have one made on the copy machine. Try speed forms for the correspondence you initiate; they provide a place at the bottom for quick replies. Use simplified formats for letters, memos, reports, and forms. Post bulletins for general-interest messages rather than making copies and routing them. Make changes and corrections on the carbon copies of your letters so your secretary need retype only the original. Make creative use of the new pre-inked rubber stamps for reducing writing and typing time.

Streamline reports by developing standard procedures for authorizing and auditing new forms and periodic reports. The procedures should provide a double-check for duplication of effort, real need, and distribution lists. Can some reports be combined? Can routine reports be computerized?

Keeping Lean Files The third aspect of handling each piece of paper once is minimizing and organizing the papers you file. Always ask, "What are the probabilities of our ever needing this piece of paper again? If we eventually need some information it contains, could we get it elsewhere? What would happen if we didn't have a written record of it?"

Many people ask, "Could we possibly need this ever again?" In other words, they retain records on the basis of *possibilities*— remote possibilities—rather than on the basis of *probabilities*. Even if it might be handy to have an item in the file at some future time, the item may be relatively unimportant and the consequences of producing or not producing it may be trivial. Meanwhile, the item is adding to the clutter in your files, and you must contend with this growing profusion of paper every day. So think in terms of high priorities and probabilities and dump papers that don't measure up.

Avoid dealing with needless paper by asking to have your name removed from mailing lists and routing slips for materials that have little or no value to you. Don't file (1) memos that are routine and are on file somewhere else in the company, (2) announcements of meetings, (3) directives that have since been revised, or (4) company newsletters, minutes, announcements, and other material that's on file elsewhere. It's been estimated that about 75 percent of the items in most files should have been thrown away. Be ruthless in throwing out papers, and you will avoid crowded files, a messy desk, an overworked secretary, and a confused mind.

Finally, experiment to find the filing system that works best for you. Your system might include such categories as "tickler," "current projects," "to read," "creativity," and "travel," as well as a general file.

A *tickler file* is kept handy to remind you to initiate or follow up on transactions. It consists of day folders numbered 1 through 31, for each day of the month. In the appropriate day's folder for the current month, you place letters, memos, reminders, notes, reports, and other items that you want to handle on that day and that do not need to be placed in some other file. You might also need folders labeled for each month of the year, which you'll review on the first day of each month, and folders labeled for each of the next several years, which you'll review at the beginning of each year. On the first

day of each month, file all the items from that month's folder into the day folders. Then each January the items in that year's file are placed in the appropriate monthly folders.

Your tickler file can supplement the "To Do" sheets you dated ahead and jotted reminders on. Each afternoon when you work on your "To Do" list for the next day, pull the tickler file folder for the following day. You can think of it now as your "Do Today" folder that keeps all those notes and papers organized and off your desk.

A *current projects file* should also be within easy reach. It consists of file folders that contain the working papers, correspondence, reports, ideas, and plans for all projects you and your subordinates are currently working on. If you set up your folders well, you can easily and quickly clear your desk of all paper and still have everything at your fingertips. In fact, you will find it easier to lay your hands on an item at any one time than if you have stacks and piles of papers all over the place.

Create as many new folders for each project as you need, but categorize and title them in ways that are meaningful to you and work for you. You can put notes about priorities, starting dates, and deadlines for the projects in your tickler file or on your "To Do" list, depending upon their length and detail.

A *"to read" file* is a handy place to group and store all the journal articles, reports, book summaries, newspaper items, and other information you need currently or will need in the future. Categorize the file according to subjects that interest you. For example, an accountant who works for a computer company and is involved in professional accounting associations might be interested in such subjects as tax law, accounting associations, computer technology, and standard accounting practices.

To make the best use of your "to read" file, have your secretary scan the tables of contents of books and journals, checking articles or chapters you might be interested in. She or he might even read certain items, marking important passages so that you can scan them quickly later. Have your secretary prepare a "reading record," a sheet for recording all items as they are placed in the "to read" file. Figure 13-2 is an example of how a reading record can be set up.

The subject columns of your reading record become the subjects of your "to read" file folders. Each article placed in a folder and each journal and book placed in a box or on a bookshelf is recorded on the reading record sheet and is numbered sequentially. This identifying number is also written on the book, journal, or article so that it's easy to spot. The subject(s) the item refers to are checked in the appropriate subject column(s) of the reading record. This record is a handy reference of sources for projects, speeches, reports, or other assignments. Refer to it also when you want to quickly pull items for your briefcase—to have on hand for dead-time reading or a business trip.

A *creativity file* is a handy place to store new ideas for projects and improvements, future plans and goals, and other ideas, hopes, and dreams. We've stressed the importance of keeping pad and pen handy for jotting down ideas wherever they occur. Record all ideas and drop them into your creativity file. You may want to categorize them by subject matter, by project, or by more

FIGURE 13-2: Example of a Reading Record

Item No.	Source	Tax Law	Acctg. Assn.	Standard Acctg. Practice	Computer Tech.	Reports	Other
1	The Accountant, June 10, p. 22	✓		✓			
2	Computing Newsletter, June 17, p. 43				✓		
3	CPA Journal, July 5, p. 67		✓	✓			
4	Jones Audit Report					✓	
5	Fortune, July 12, p. 105						Motivation

general categories such as "ideas," "plans," and "projects." You may also want folders that indicate a stage of development, such as "rough ideas," "developing ideas," and "refined ideas."

A *travel file* can be a great help if you travel often in your job. You might have a file folder for each location you regularly visit or anticipate visiting. Put into these folders items concerning people to see; information to gather or to check on; information about plane, train, rental car, limousine, and other transportation services; tips on good hotels, restaurants, and entertainment; and any other information that might be helpful. Also, for each business trip prepare a file folder, such as "Boston trip—June 10." Keep it handy and as you receive your plane tickets, hotel confirmations, phone numbers, contracts, and other working papers, put them in it. By the time you leave, everything you need will be accumulated in your trip folder. This habit helps prevent leaving important items behind.

The *general file* is where you store everything else. You may categorize by subject, alphabet, geographical locations, number, or any combination of these. You and your secretary can devise the system that works best for you.

Finally, just as important as a system for categorizing and arranging items in files is developing a workable system for periodically removing from the files items with a low probability of being needed again. If space is limited, you may need to have an active general file and an inactive general file. Items should be periodically removed from the active file and placed in a less accessible inactive file. These items are usually kept for legal or tax reasons and shouldn't clutter prime filing space.

Organizing Travel Time

Telephoning and paperwork are time-consuming activities that all managers must control. For those managers who frequently travel, conserving their time and energy on the road is also a major time management consideration. We've already discussed some ways to save travel time—by using conference calls and by keeping trip files, for example. Look for additional ways you can handle business in other cities without spending your precious time and energy in airports and taxis. At times, of course, there's no substitute for an in-person appearance. The more frequently you must travel, the more important it is to make the most of your travel time.

Packing   Let's begin with packing. Stay partially packed all the time. Keep extra toiletries, medication, first-aid items, business cards, and other trip items in a bag at home. Some people include a travel hair dryer, special high-steam iron, and heating rod for boiling water.

Travel Agent   Next, get a good travel agent if your company doesn't already have one. Air fares are so complicated these days that even professional travel agents have difficulty keeping track of them. Because of their daily contact with the airlines, agents can usually get you a better deal and can do it quickly and efficiently. It costs you nothing and saves your time as well as your secretary's time.

Airline Clubs   If you travel often, consider joining one or more airline clubs. Some of the benefits may be

Access to a members-only lounge at most airports, which includes telephones and free local calls, free coffee, peace and quiet, and sometimes meeting rooms, free drinks, free continental breakfast, color TV, and other amenities

The airline's special telephone numbers for preferred customers (You can get through on these unlisted numbers even when the airline's other lines are busy.)

Special check-in privileges with no waiting in line

Hotel and car rental discounts

Check-cashing privileges

Car Rental Agencies Consider opening business accounts with a couple of car rental agencies. You can negotiate a significant business discount, so shop around. Rental agencies with offices some distance from airports are frequently less expensive. If you reserve a car before arriving at your destination, it will be delivered to you at the airport. It's a good idea to reserve your car ahead regardless, especially if you are arriving on a weekend in a popular resort area. Also, during the fall months there are usually fewer cars available as agencies reduce their inventories and get ready to buy new models.

Itinerary Be sure to leave a detailed itinerary with appropriate people so important messages can reach you. If you subscribe to an itinerary service, you can call in for messages at any time of the day or night. You give a special toll-free number to people who might need to call you. Also, some hotels will rent you a beeper so that you can immediately get messages left at the hotel desk. You don't have to keep calling the hotel to check for messages or wait in your room for calls to come through.

Notebook A pocket-sized loose-leaf notebook for your appointments, brief "To Do" lists, and other notes is a great organizer. You can choose from handy printed pages to set up your own system—for example, week-at-a-glance pages with space for notes on appointments and reminders, expense record pages, address and phone pages that can be arranged alphabetically by company

or person's name, and plain, lined pages for notes.

When it's time to go, you'll need to spend minimal preparation time if you have kept a trip file, your other files are in order, your bag is partially packed, and your pocket notebook is current. Of course, you can use part of your flight time to work on tasks. Rank them in order of priority just as you do in the office.

Pace Yourself Last but not least is making plans to pace yourself and to manage the stress that travel creates. Plan for extra rest on the first evening you arrive, especially if you take a two-hour or longer flight. Many people become ill immediately after they return from business trips. The reason is frequently fatigue, even though the traveler may not feel tired. Take steps to prevent illness by getting extra rest, even though you're full of nervous energy.

Don't try to pack too much into one trip. Decide what's most important and allow enough time to accomplish it, including time to rest and relax. Usually three major meetings a day are the most you can expect to handle well. After that, you will probably lose your ability to concentrate and perform well. Also, allow plenty of time to get from one place to another. Ask local people about distances and traffic patterns, and then estimate travel time within an area.

AVOIDING PROCRASTINATION IN TACKLING LARGE PROJECTS

Now you have the tools for managing your time on a day-to-day basis. Before you assume that your time problems are licked, however, you must face the question of how effectively you complete the large projects that are essential to achieving some of your major objectives. One of the problems with working on big projects—and one of the reasons people procrastinate on them—is the feeling of leaving loose ends after a work session on the project. Yet the project is much too big to finish in one time block. Here are some ways to overcome that problem.

Organizing Projects into Manageable Segments

First, be clear about specific objectives to be achieved through completion of the project, and write them down. Next, break the project up into major segments. Do this as soon as you receive the assignment (or conceive of it), and do it in writing. Block the project into tasks you can complete in one work session. Making a written plan helps you tackle each segment with minimal time-loss from building up momentum again, retracing steps, reviewing what you've done, and getting your thoughts and materials in order.

When you start a task, finish it. Savor the moment by congratulating yourself and taking time to enjoy the satisfaction of having completed that part of the project. This helps reinforce a sense of closure each time you work on it. Also consider rewarding yourself in other appropriate ways.

If you must leave a task uncompleted, note the next step so you won't waste time when you come back to it. Once you start a major project, be sure to keep working on the segments until you finish the project. Avoid having too many large projects going at once. If you accumulate a backlog of partially finished projects, it becomes more and more difficult to finish any of them and to have a sense of satisfaction and closure.

Figure 13-3 presents a format for planning large, complex projects. After you break the project down into major segments and the manageable tasks involved in each segment from start to finish, you determine which tasks can be delegated. Then you estimate how long each task will take. (Consider doubling that estimate to give yourself plenty of lead time and to build in flexibility.) Which tasks can be overlapped or done simultaneously? List starting dates and target completion dates. Put these dates on your "To Do" list daily calendar sheets as reminders of when to begin, assign, follow up, or complete each task. Finally, note the date each task is actually completed on your planning sheet.

Identifying Quick Tasks

If you have trouble getting started on a major segment of the project, look for "quick tasks" that can be done in five minutes or so. Quick tasks are great for getting overwhelming projects underway. To set the wheels in motion, try tactics such as these:

Contact someone to get information that you need.

Spend a few minutes planning some procedures for the project.

Set up a simple filing system for the project.

Do some reading that will be helpful.

Locate some sources of information or material.

After you have completed a few quick tasks, you may find yourself being pulled into the project. Completing the tasks tends to generate interest and involvement and to build momentum.

Using Other Techniques

If you find yourself still procrastinating, try some other techniques.

FIGURE 13-3: Planning Sheet for Large, Complex Projects

Project _____ Objectives _____

Major Segments	Tasks	Do Myself or Delegate	Estimated Time for Completion	Starting Date	Target Completion Date	Actual Completion Date

Do the most unpleasant task first, if possible. Get it out of the way so you don't waste energy "doing it in your head over and over." Congratulate yourself for getting it done. Notice the light, satisfied feeling you get from completing the task and take time to enjoy that feeling. If you give yourself this positive reinforcement, you'll soon get in the habit of getting necessary unpleasant tasks done fast.

Take advantage of your current mood. Keep returning to the project in your mind. Keep asking yourself, "What am I especially in the mood to do today that could move the project along?"

List the advantages and disadvantages of start- ing now. You'll usually see that the disadvantages are trivial and the advantages significant. This can quickly boost you into action.

Analyze your motives. If these direct techniques aren't working, maybe you need to delve deeper. Perhaps fear of failure or fear of success is blocking you. Are you afraid of succeeding at the project? Women frequently *do* fear the changes in their lives that accompany success in a career. Look deep within. If that's your problem, ask yourself, "What's the worst that can happen?" You will probably realize either that your fears of the worst are absurd or that you *can* face the worst and handle it comfortably.

Are you afraid of failing at the project if

you start it? If so, remind yourself that if you give it a good try, you may succeed; but if you don't, you guarantee failure. If you do your best and it's not good enough, you can at least learn from your mistakes. Studies show that people who work toward success are happier and accomplish more than those who fear (and therefore expect) failure. Everyone who makes it to the top experiences some failure along the way. It's what they do with that failure—the lessons they learn from it—that makes them winners.

SUMMARY

Your attitude toward time is the most important aspect of time management. Time is money. When your time and subordinates' time is being wasted, the dollars the company pays in salary are also being wasted. Not only that, wasted time can mean costly delays or lost opportunities to make money. Major attitudinal keys to time management include constructive attitudes toward delegating, balancing tasks and projects (the ability to focus on one task at a time even though you may have many irons in the fire), and using body time productively (scheduling your day to make best use of your energy, sociability, and charisma levels as well as your preferred work pace).

Another key is the ability to overcome nonproductive parent messages about what you *should* do and to provide yourself with small rewards for completing tasks, meeting deadlines, weeding out time-wasters, and discovering time-savers. Your attitude toward time management is also affected by your internal and external environment—your ability to eliminate or rise above minor depressants and irritants in your life, to say "no," and to arrange a pleasant, practical physical work space.

Using your objectives and priorities to direct your energy is the key to actually making the most of your time. Your goal is to focus on doing the right things at the right time, rather than merely working hard and doing things correctly and efficiently. This means making a daily "To Do" list of tasks that lead to achievement of your top-priority objectives.

Cooperating with others on time management can help you eliminate time-wasters and discover time-savers that others create in your workday. It also includes helping your boss, subordinates, and peers make the best use of their time. Getting your boss to practice more effective time management calls for tact; however, if you stress the good of the company in your discussions, your suggestions will probably be accepted.

Your greatest opportunity to influence others' time management practices, of course, is in dealing with subordinates. The way you handle *your* time makes the greatest impact because it sets a noticeable example; it's also important to respect their time. The person who can help you the most in your time management efforts is your secretary. Treat your secretary as a professional, keep him or her informed about your priorities, listen to his or her suggestions, and work with your secretary as a teammate in keeping your desk, your calls, your correspondence, your calendar, and *you* organized.

Your peers can create all sorts of bottlenecks and delays in your plans. Therefore, when you are discussing the need for action with a peer, stress how the completion of the task in question helps to achieve a specific objective. Tie the objective in with an organizational objective that the peer is committed to helping achieve. Be businesslike in your dealings with peers to avoid wasting time in needless chatter.

Improving workflow, both yours and your subordinates', can pay off in big time-saving benefits. Working out regular times for handling recurring tasks is a first step in improving workflow. Analyzing routine tasks to see which ones can be performed more effectively so that workflow is improved is next. Look for typical barriers—bottlenecks, time-consumers, run-abouts, and hidden time-wasters.

Minimizing interruptions is essential if you are to make the best use of your concentration time. You need at least a one-hour block of uninterrupted time when working on complex projects. The solution is to establish a "quiet hour" in your schedule. Other techniques include scheduling meetings with subordinates and others for certain times of the day, informing others of your work patterns so that they'll know when to contact you without needless interruption, working with your secretary to screen calls and visitors, and maintaining a businesslike manner.

Telephoning can help you save time, or it can be one of your worst time-wasters. Analyze the best way to handle a communication. Prepare adequately for placing calls. Bunch calls to eliminate unnecessary interruptions. Have your calls screened when you need uninterrupted time. And be businesslike and to the point when making telephone calls.

Streamlining paperwork is essential to avoid becoming swamped in the "paper explosion." Start by sorting your mail by priority (or having your secretary sort it). Keep in mind that your goal is to handle each piece of paper only once. Learn to use dictation equipment for most of your letters and reports, and use it correctly in order to save your secretary's time. Do everything you can to cut down on paperwork and files and to keep them out of sight. One way to organize current paperwork is to keep special files, such as a tickler file, a current projects file, a "to read" file, a creativity file, and a travel file. Everything else goes into the general file, which should be categorized in the way that works best for you and your secretary. Finally, develop a workable system for periodically cleaning out the files.

You can plan your travel time to make the most of it. First, look for ways you can handle your business in another city *without* having to be there in person. Then keep a bag partially packed with essentials you use over and over on your trips. Use a good travel agent and appropriate credit and membership cards. Leave a detailed itinerary so your office can get in touch with you. Take a pocket-sized looseleaf notebook for your appointments, "To Do" lists, and other essential notes. Protect your health by getting plenty of rest and pacing yourself properly. Use the time en route to accomplish some of your tasks, but don't overdo.

You can overcome procrastination and complete large, complex projects by first breaking them down into manageable segments. Give yourself an appropriate reward each time you complete a segment, and build in as much pleasure and satisfaction as you can. Remember to identify quick tasks that can be done in five minutes or so to help you get started and to build momentum.

REFERENCES

1. Bliss, Edwin C. *Getting Things Done.* New York: Scribner, 1980. An excellent resource for managing your time and producing results.

2. *EXECU*TIME,* Vol. 2, No. 8 (August 1979). *EXECU*TIME* is a monthly newsletter that is a valuable source of ideas for making the most of your time. It is published by MRH Associates, P.O. Box 11318, Newington, CT 06111.

3. *EXECU*TIME,* Vol. 2, No. 3 (March 1979).

4. *EXECU*TIME.* Special Bulletin (1979).

5. Fuller, Don. *Manage or Be Managed.* Boston: Cahners Books, 1970. Fuller was an engineer who became a top executive. He gives his secrets of success and offers especially valuable suggestions for increasing effectiveness and efficiency.

6. Grossman, Lee. *Fat Paper.* New York: McGraw-Hill, 1980. This book is full of excellent suggestions for streamlining paperwork, including files, correspondence, reports, copies, and forms.

7. Lakein, Allan. *How to Get Control of Your Time and Life.* New York: McKay, 1983. Perhaps the most widely used source for time management techniques. Lakein, a former Harvard professor, has done extensive business consulting.

8. Lefsky, William. "Are Your Phone Calls Being Screened Tactfully?" *Supervisory Management* (December 1969).

9. MacKenzie, R. Alec. *The Time Trap.* New York: McGraw-Hill, 1982. One of the best all-around books on managing your time. The chapter on working with your secretary is especially helpful.

10. Reddin, W. J. *Effective Management by Objectives.* New York: McGraw-Hill, 1971. This text integrates management by objectives and time management.

Chapter Fourteen

Getting a Promotion (and a Raise)

"Being good at something is only half the battle. The other half is mastering the art of self-presentation, positioning, and connecting."

Adele Scheele

The culmination of developing and managing yourself and of developing and practicing effective management skills is getting the promotions that move you on up the ladder to your ultimate career goal. Whether that ultimate goal is head of the Personnel Department of a relatively small company or Chief Executive Officer of a large multinational corporation, you must know how to negotiate promotions and raises in order to get there. Although you will base your requests on specific achievements and results, you must develop negotiating skills and techniques in order to make the most of your accomplishments.

In this chapter you will have an opportunity to learn how to

1. Base your requests on standards and accomplishments

2. Set job standards you can meet

3. Learn how your work affects the company's profits

4. Get around promotion blocks

5. Size up your competition

6. Study your boss' position in the promotion game

7. Get rid of your false fears

8. Overcome barriers in your boss' mind

9. Stand up for your ideas without antagonizing the boss

10. Time your request

11. Adapt your visibility during the raise-getting period

12. Turn negatives into positives for promotion purposes

13. Handle special problems during promotion negotiations

14. Create demand for your services

15. Close the promotion negotiation proceedings

16. Position yourself for your next promotion

17. Deal with unfair discrimination

501

Sweet Success

"For she's a jolly good fellow, for she's a jolly good fellow..." Carrie's eyes are misty as she looks around at the staff of the San Diego branch, their glasses raised in a toast to her, their voices raised in song at this, her farewell party.

John Brockfield holds up his hand. "I just want to say that I've never seen a better Sales Manager than our Carrie. You've touched all our lives, Carrie, and we'll always remember you—even when you're ensconced in that big new Sales Executive office in San Francisco, hobnobbing with all the bigwigs."

Carrie laughs. "And I'll never forget a one of you—I'll always remember all I've learned from you and all we've done together."

Next day, as Carrie is packing the items she plans to take to San Francisco with her, Kate Blakeley enters her office.

"Carrie, before you get away, you've got to give me one more lesson—on getting promotions. I heard you had some stiff competition for this new Sales Executive position they created at headquarters—like Fred Rosen, who's already a Sales Account Executive at headquarters, and Margo Malquist, who's made a name for herself at the New Orleans branch. Tell me, how did you pull it off?"

Carrie searches Kate's face. "All right, Kate, but this is just between the two of us. Well, first I sized up my competition and figured that Margo was my closest competitor. The advantage she had over me was her computer knowledge. So my next step was to do some 'horse trading' with Vince Dietz."

"Oh, the head of our Computer Department," responds Kate. "But—horse trading?"

"Sure. Vince wanted to know more about the sales end of the business, so I swapped my knowledge about that for his knowledge of our computer setup and how to use it. In the meantime, I worked on my ILM file."

"What, pray tell, is an ILM file?"

Carrie grins. "I love me. Jan coined the term, I guess, and told me about it. It's just a way to remind yourself vividly that you should be your own best friend. One way of doing that is to document your achievements—goals you've reached, deadlines you've met, increases in sales volume you've effected, decreases in expenses. You see, the President is a financial type; he understands people who talk in terms of the dollar value of their contributions and how resources should be allocated. I felt that Jan probably favored me for the promotion, but she had to sell her recommendation to the Executive Committee—mainly the President. So I needed to provide her with a strong case on my behalf."

"So, did she recommend you to the Committee?" prompts Kate.

"Yes, and they approved the promotion, but I had to go before them to discuss the terms and conditions of the appointment—meaning mainly the salary I would get. I was nervous, but I did my homework. You know, like my contribution to company profits, how I'd maintained an adequate profit margin, how my department's efforts affect cash flow. The Committee did raise some questions and objections, but I kept returning to my main points. I figured I might as well go for the best raise possible. So I laid the groundwork for computing my value to the company in dollars and cents, tracing my work in the Sales

Department down to that magic 'bottom line.' "

Carrie continues, "My main point was that I had achieved every one of the goals John Brockfield and I agreed on for my department earlier in the year. We increased the number of customer accounts by 15 percent, which gave the company the opportunity to expand its market in the San Diego region. In addition, my people increased our sales volume by 20 percent. And in spite of the extra expenses such increases always incur, I held the expense increase down to 9 percent. Finally, I provided the Committee with a table showing item by item how these and other achievements of my department had contributed to the net worth and the profit of the company."

"But how did you know how much to ask for?" Kate asks.

"To begin with, I let them make an offer first, just to be sure I didn't ask for too little. When they asked what amount I thought was fair, I said I'd like to hear what the Committee thought about that. They mentioned a 15 percent increase over my present salary. I had laid the groundwork for showing how I had made contributions beyond those of any previous Sales Manager—contributions worth well over 50 percent of my present salary. I said I felt it was only fair for them to split the difference and give me a 25 percent raise."

"And they bought it?" asks Kate.

"Yes. They all got a kick out of my line of reasoning. They said I was just the person to sell the Board on the new projects we'll be lining up. Believe me, I assured them that I'd make them look good and that they were making a good investment."

Kate sighs. "What a lovely success story. I hope I can tell one like it myself some day. But wait—I almost forgot the most important question: How did you convince a confirmed San Diegan like Murray that he should move to San Francisco?"

Carrie smiles. "Pure luck. He was looking around for a new job opportunity anyway, and he always wanted to try living in the Bay Area."

Kate hugs her friend. "You're just an inspiration, Carrie, because you're managing to have it all—a good career, a good marriage, and real personal growth. And you deserve it all."

Where Did They Go Astray?

You have just seen how a successful campaign for a promotion can work. For every success story, however, there are probably a dozen stories of frustration, rejection, or disappointment. Let's look at a couple of them.

Too Little Margo Malquist knows that she deserves a promotion. She has improved productivity and lowered expenses significantly during the past year. She discusses her performance and her hopes with her colleague Lee Chin.

"Lee, I know Ms. Arguello's pleased with the job I've been doing. Nearly every time I see her, she comments about the great results I'm getting and how much improvement she sees in my department. I sure hope she recommends me for this promotion. I need a good raise too."

"Have you asked her about it, Margo?"

"No, I don't want to appear too greedy or pushy. Ms. Arguello tells me how much she appreciates my devotion and loyalty to the company. We have such a good relationship; I don't want to take a chance on upsetting it. I think she'll take care of me at promotion time and she'll probably recommend an even bigger raise if I let her decide on the amount."

"But what if she doesn't?"

"Well, at least our rapport will not be damaged. If I don't put her in a position of having to turn me down, then we won't have any negative feelings to have to work through."

As we know, Malquist doesn't get the promotion. She feels disappointed and finds it a little difficult to maintain her previous level of enthusiasm. She holds on to her hopes, however, that someday she will get the promotion she deserves.

Actually, Arguello decides that the new job assignment would be too tough and demanding for Margo. Handling some of the characters she would have to deal with in the new position requires more savvy and drive than she seems to have.

Too Much Back at headquarters, Fred Rosen, Sales Account Executive, decides to go all out for the promotion. He makes it a point to fully support Arguello's every idea, suggestion, and action. She can always depend on Rosen to agree with her.

Fred also wants Jan to see that he is a person who knows how to dress and how to live. He wears his best Italian-made shoes to the office. When he takes Jan to lunch he drives his new foreign sports car. And he invites her and several colleagues to dinner at his swank apartment with an impressive view of the city.

He makes sure Jan knows that he's aware of the pressing problems of the organization and that he needs Jan's advice and guidance. He looks for problems he can bring to her to solve.

To impress Jan with his diligence and dedication, Fred begins to show up much earlier and to stay much later at the office than usual. The amount of paperwork coming out of his office nearly doubles, with copies of almost everything going to Jan to be sure that she's aware of his activities.

Fred discusses the details of his campaign with his colleagues in order to get their reaction and to encourage them to share techniques with him. He begins to feel sure he'll get the promotion. In fact, he's so sure that he's already planning how he'll spend the raise that goes with it. He mentions a few of his plans to colleagues.

When it's announced that Carrie Dickeson is getting the new position, Fred is upset and resentful. He can't understand why he failed after putting so much time and energy into his campaign.

---

1. As you read this story, what actions and attitudes did you think were most effective in preparing for and getting a promotion? Why? _____
_____

2. What actions and attitudes were most ineffective? Why? _____
_____

ONGOING STRATEGIES FOR PROMOTABILITY

In most companies, upward mobility and power go hand in hand. In Chapter 1 we discussed Rosabeth Kanter's finding about the difficulty of managers in dead-end, low-power positions. Most managers consider it crucial to keep moving up. More than three years in a job is probably a danger sign of being "stuck." After completing Chapters 1 and 3, you should have some tools for developing an effective career path within your company. When you feel it is time for you to be promoted or to receive a raise, you'll need to apply your assertiveness skills and plan a promotion campaign.

Overcoming Archaic Attitudes

Winning the right promotion and the raises and privileges that go with it is the proof of the pudding. These are the rewards that really count, the outward proof of your success as a manager and as an astute organization person. The further up you attempt to go, the more likely you are to encounter barriers based on stereotyped ideas about the roles women are suited for, what women *really* want, what women need (such as less money than men), and so forth. To overcome these barriers, you will need to use all the experience and knowledge you have gained about the hierarchy, influence and power, organizational politics, the mentor relationship, and management skills.

Perhaps the barriers you face are more internal than external. Take a good look at your own attitude toward taking the initiative to wage an assertive promotion campaign. Since women have traditionally been spectators rather than participants in the money game of business, they can be handicapped in successfully negotiating higher positions and salaries.

Have you, like most women, been taught that if you work hard and wait, you will be rewarded, that it's bad taste to make monetary demands? This defensive attitude places more value on approval than on money. It also overlooks the viewpoint of business executives who understand that they work for a proportionate share of the company's money—a share that reflects the value of their contributions.

Furthermore, anyone who is "worth his [or her] salt" is expected to ask for substantial raises. Waiting for a promotion or raise is low-echelon thinking. If you never ask, you're not likely to ever get what you're worth. Moreover, if you don't place a high value on your worth, no one else will. Regular merit increases are almost always mere tokens of

appreciation, as small as the company can get away with and still keep satisfactory employees quiet.

As discussed in Chapter 1, women frequently view risk in a negative way. Examine your attitude toward the risks involved in pushing for a promotion or a significant raise. What are the possible payoffs? What are the possible negative results? Are you hanging back because the status quo is comfortable and that higher-level job is a little scary? What do you really have to lose? Will it be the end of the world if you don't succeed?

Once you've decided to go for the next promotion, give it all you've got. Be persistent and assertive.

Clarifying Your Career Goals

Before you start selecting specific strategies for waging your promotion campaign, first be sure the promotion you have in mind will lead into jobs that will further your career. Carefully consider any promotion offer that is not a part of your plan. It may be best to turn down a promotion that will not help you acquire the experience you need for your long-term goal. To determine whether a promotion is right for you, ask yourself questions such as these:

"Will the new position lead directly to a higher position?"

"Will I gain experience in the job that will make me more valuable to the company?"

"Will this job give me an opportunity to make more or bigger decisions?"

"Is this job a good temporary step—even if it's not in the direct line of my career goal? (For example, you could learn about many phases of company activities by working for a short time as an assistant to a senior executive. Be careful, however, that the new position isn't a dead end—and that you stay in it no longer than a couple of years.)

Once you're sure what your next position should be, you can focus your energy on ways of lining it up.

Expanding Your Present Job

Suppose you find yourself with a company you like and want to stay with. However, your upward mobility is temporarily blocked by older people above you, people waiting to retire, and lack of company growth. What can you do? Two likely approaches are to (1) enlarge your job or (2) get some small jobs attached to your position—jobs that show on the organization chart and that you can take on while you're holding down your main job. Here are some specific tactics.

Volunteer for jobs no one is doing anything about. Look for things you can tackle. If the boss asks you to look into a project or problem, even very informally, accept the assignment happily and begin to formalize the request through the reports you write and by your attitude.

Make yourself visible as someone who is interested in company progress and problems and studies company records.

Send your boss some progress reports with copies to others who might be interested.

Talk to appropriate department heads and other executives.

See whether you can get some colleagues to work with you on the project. Their reasons for working on it may be similar to yours. Now you have a task force.

Try to get your new responsibilities or positions formalized on the organization chart. Whether you are able to do so or not, you can provide your boss with justification for giving you a raise outside the salary range for your position.

Executives who get what they want expend about half their time performing their work and the other half calling attention to it in an assertive, nonbragging manner. The decision-makers in your company must value your presence before they'll promote you, and they can't value what is not visible.

Creating Demand for Your Services

Without neglecting or jeopardizing your job, never miss an opportunity to make contacts with other companies, departments, or executives who might be interested in hiring you. There are several advantages to doing this.

Your confidence and self-esteem are enhanced when you get job offers without soliciting them.

Word may get around to your boss without your saying anything. As a result, you will appear more valuable to him or her while incurring no risk to yourself.

During the promotion or raise negotiation period, you may be able to use other offers to reinforce your case. Be careful not to threaten or bluff, however, unless you're ready to carry it out.

If you're turned down, you can always come back with the news that you have a firm offer that's better than your present salary.

Basing Your Requests on Standards and Accomplishments

Your boss will certainly be unwilling to lose you if he or she is clear about what you have contributed in the past and can contribute in the future. Rather than thinking in terms of how much additional money you need, therefore, focus on how much you're worth in the current job market and in terms of what you can produce.

Setting Job Objectives and Standards You Can Meet When the boss criticizes your performance and performance standards have previously been set, get your boss' comments on how the job could be done better, no matter how vague they may be. Get his or her agreement on what good performance would consist of. Get yourself in a position to suggest objectives and standards yourself. When you do, don't make them too easy but be sure that they are attainable (see Chapter 6).

To prevent unfair or unexpected criticism of your performance, develop a plan, including times when you will report your results to the boss. Set deadlines for accomplishment of each goal. Then make an appointment for a discussion with the boss in a relaxed atmosphere (preferably in your office so you'll have a "home court" advantage). During the meeting, get the boss to talk about what she or he thinks is important in your job. Get clarification on how your role fits into the overall scheme of the business. This information will help you to pinpoint attributes you possess that are important to the company and to know what points to stress later when you ask for a promotion.

When the boss gives you a lead in an area you handle well, follow it. Agree with the idea that this is truly a vital function and you'll do your best to achieve more than has ever been accomplished before. Reach an agreement on objectives and standards you know you can meet. Try to phrase them in words that will either give a great deal of credit to your boss or will help him or her report your achievements in glowing terms when justifying your promotion at some future time.

If you have some weak areas that the boss mentions or that you're sure will inevitably surface in carrying out your responsibilities, invite the boss' recommendations. If he or she has no good ones, take the opportunity to discuss the awesome difficulty of achieving in this area. Then work toward the establishment of a standard that involves motions without necessarily involving accomplishment—for example, paperwork and meetings. Turn the negative into a positive by at least appearing to be working on it and improving.

Once you have a set of goals and standards that you like, document them. Send your boss a followup memo confirming the conversation. Such records will serve you well when you prepare your case for getting a promotion or raise.

Learning How Your Work Affects the Bottom Line Compute the value of your achievements, your productivity. To do this, learn the arithmetic of your business and how it affects you. Find out how to understand financial statements and talk about them (see Chapter 11). You'll become identifiable as a profit-minded person and will probably learn more than your associates—and perhaps more than your boss—about the financial end of the business. Team up with someone who works with the finances of the company and exchange information. You can learn about the profits, losses, expenses, and costs of the business and teach your friend about your end of the business.

If you work in a staff position rather than as a line manager, your department will probably be viewed as an expense rather than as a profit source. Don't let that intimidate you. The services of your department must be contributing to the overall profit of the company or they would soon be eliminated. Your services at least indirectly affect profits. What would happen if these services were not provided by your department? Would the company pay free-lance people to provide them or farm them out to another firm that specializes in such services? How much would that cost? What advantages does your company enjoy by securing these services through your department instead? The answers to these questions can help you figure the dollar value of your contributions.

Perhaps your services have resulted in a decrease in company expenses as well as an increase in profits. Have you reorganized the workflow, restructured job descriptions, developed new procedures, or formulated better controls that resulted in a saving of time, money, or both? Time saved represents money saved. Convert the time you've saved the company into the hourly wages of the workers, who can now use that time to accomplish other tasks and therefore to achieve a higher level of productivity.

If you're a manager in a government or nonprofit organization, your department is contributing a valuable service to the public; otherwise it wouldn't be in existence for long. With a little thought and ingenuity, you can place a value on your services. What would they cost if they were provided by a profit-making organization? How much do they add to the lives of the people who receive them? What would happen if these services weren't provided at all? What resulting costs would society have to pay? Analyze also the increases in productivity and reductions in expenses you've been responsible for and translate them into dollars.

If you're a secretary or an assistant to a manager, your value is tied in with your boss' contributions. What does your boss do to increase profits and decrease expenses? What value can you place on his or her overall contribution to the organization each year? How do you help the boss in making that contribution? What percentage do you contribute to the boss' value to the company? Twenty-five percent? Fifty percent? Are there any projects or procedures you have pursued on your own for increasing departmental productivity or decreasing expenses? Figure dollar values and add them all together to arrive at a figure representing your achievements.

Whether you are a manager or a worker; in a profit-making, government, or nonprofit organization; in a line or staff position, you can make some effort to determine your value to the firm. You *must* do it if you want to prepare the most effective case possible for getting a promotion or raise. Follow the suggestions we've just discussed to complete Exercise 14-1.

Setting Your Asking Price   Now you should have some basis for determining the size of your next raise. In figuring an exact asking price, keep in mind that you should always ask for more than you expect to get and you should phrase the increase in thousands of dollars per year. Here are some other factors to consider in setting your asking price:

What you have contributed or can contribute to the firm

How the rate of inflation has affected the buying power of your salary dollars since your last raise

What the *men* who perform similar functions in the company are making

The top figure your boss is probably willing to give you

EXERCISE 14-1: ESTIMATING YOUR VALUE TO THE ORGANIZATION

Analyze your activities and your achievements in terms of how much they contribute to company profits and how much they've helped the company save on costs and expenses. Evaluate time saved in terms of salary expense for each hour saved. If you can't determine exact amounts, make the closest estimate you can.

Activities That Increased Profits $ Value

Activities that *directly* increased profits

1 _____ $ _____

2 _____   _____

3 _____   _____

Activities that *indirectly* increased profits

1 Services you provided and cost to firm if firm had to buy your services from free-lancers or other firms

_____   _____

2 Increased productivity of other persons resulting from services you provide

_____   _____

Total $ _____

Activities That Helped Decrease Expenses $ Value

Activities that *directly* decreased expenses

1 _____ $ _____

2 _____   _____

Activities that *indirectly* decreased expenses

1 _____   _____

2 _____   _____

Total $ _____

Your Market Value to Other Similar Organizations	Probable Starting Salary
Firm A _____	$ _____
Firm B _____	_____
Firm C _____	_____

Other Factors

1 How inflation has affected your spending power since your last raise _____% $_____

2 New skills and knowledge gained since your last raise _____

_____

_____

3 Average salary increase for managers in your field (or managers in general) during the past year, according to the *Wall Street Journal* or other sources _____% $_____

The bottom figure you are willing to take

What competing firms are willing to pay you

The difference between the bottom figure you are willing to take (a $5,000 raise, for example) and the top figure your boss is willing to give ($3,000, for example) is the area of negotiation. Your goal is to negotiate for as close to your figure as possible. If you asked for $1,000 more than you expected to receive and are able to convince your boss that you deserve $4,000, you will each have made a $1,000 concession and you'll still end up with the raise you expected. Identify perks, benefits, and other rewards you would be willing to accept in lieu of cash. Be sure to consider all tax implications.

Building on Your Reputation for Assertiveness

You establish a reputation as a promotable woman beginning with the job interview and continuing through every phase of establishing yourself in the company. Keep in mind that you want your boss to respect you without feeling threatened by you. Therefore you don't want to be a "yes person," but you won't want to antagonize either. In other words, assertiveness with your boss throughout the year pays off at promotion time.

Occasionally disagree or express strong reservations about some idea or position of your boss. Don't make your disagreement too visible or too personal, however. Express it in a way that doesn't cast doubts on the boss' intelligence or reasoning power. If the boss strongly backs his or her position, come around to agreeing. You want to be known as a person who is not afraid to speak up but one who is also willing to listen to reason. If it later turns out that you were partially or completely right on the point, don't bring it up. Don't let any "I told you so" messages come through, however subtle. You also want to be known as a person who may disagree but then forgets her disagreement and pitches in to get the job done.

PREPARING TO ASK FOR A PROMOTION AND RAISE

In addition to ongoing strategies for moving into your next job position, you can adopt some specific strategies as you approach the time to discuss your promotion request. These include sizing up your competition, studying the boss' position, anticipating and overcoming barriers in your boss' mind, and getting rid of your false fears.

Sizing Up Your Competition

You need to understand the circumstances that will affect your chances of getting a promotion. Therefore it is important to size up the people who will be competing with you for the position you want. Exercise 14-2 provides some questions to consider. Of course you will *not* use this information to attack your competitors; in fact, you won't even mention rivals in most cases. When you're having your interview with your boss about your promotion, your competition is a strong *unmentioned* presence. Therefore stress at least one area in which you are unique or unquestionably stronger even though you don't make comparisons or even mention your competition. This gives your boss some

ideas for justifying his or her selection of you. If you must discuss areas where your competition is stronger than you, associate yourself with your competitor. Talk about how you work together in these areas and the similarities you share.

In getting raises, strangely enough, your biggest problem may be the competitor that is an "old reliable" who never asks for a big raise. This person may have been around longer than you and on the whole may even do a better job than you. The boss is aware of "old reliable's" quiet worth and may mentally compare you with him or her. Since the boss may hesitate to give you a larger increase than "old reliable," your own chances of getting a good raise may be greatly increased if you can convince your complacent colleague to ask for more.

How you go about this will depend on the situation. Use the same rationale you use to determine your own worth to the company and the amount of increase you should get to convince your colleague of his or her worth and why he or she should receive a larger increase.

Studying Your Boss' Position

Perhaps the most important suggestion for successfully getting a raise or promotion you want is to put yourself in your boss' shoes. To do this, try to study his or her position—upward, downward, and laterally—in the raise-getting process within the company.

Your boss has many concerns besides your promotion. Before planning your approach to getting a promotion or raise, study the situation from your boss' viewpoint. Your boss is your adversary, even if you're the best of friends, if he or she is the one who has the most influence over the size of your raise. If you can determine the answers to the questions posed in Exercise 14-3, you'll go a long

EXERCISE 14-2: EVALUATING YOUR COMPETITION

Focusing on the person in your classification who seems to be your strongest rival, answer the following questions.

1. How long has Rival A been here? _____

2. How good is Rival A? _____

3. What is management's perception of how good Rival A is? (The answer to this one is often quite different from how well your competitor actually produces.) _____

4. What are Rival A's strong points? _____

5. What are Rival A's weak points? _____

6. How do I compare to Rival A, point by point? _____

7. What is management's perception of my strengths? _____

8. What is management's perception of my weaknesses? _____

9. How much is Rival A probably making? _____

10. What kind of raise is Rival A likely to ask for? _____

11. Does Rival A seem to be successful in getting promotions and raises? _____

Adapted from John J. Tarrant, *How to Negotiate a Raise* (New York: Simon and Schuster, 1984), pp. 81–82.

way toward understanding your boss' viewpoint.

How do you get good answers to all these questions? Sometimes the best way is through informal channels: getting to know as many people as possible who have access to the information you want, chatting with them occasionally about what's going on in the company, chatting with your boss about his or her plans. Listen, observe, ask questions. By all means, get all the *official* information you can through the Personnel Department, company manuals, annual reports to stockholders, minutes of meetings, accessible files and records, and so forth. But don't depend on easily available data to give you the whole picture.

Overcoming Barriers in Your Boss' Mind

Remember that bosses *do* think about how the employee will use the raise. Plant the seed of need in the boss' mind, but be sure the picture he or she gets about how you'll spend the raise will not trigger resentful, envious, or disapproving feelings. Male bosses frequently believe women don't *need* as much money as men because they don't have the financial obligations men do. Watch for that

EXERCISE 14-3: STUDYING YOUR BOSS' POSITION

Study the official position of your boss and of the company. Ask yourself
these questions.

1. What is the pattern of raises given to me and to others in similar jobs? _____

2. To what extent is compensation a part of a fixed budget process? _____

3. What degree of freedom does the boss have in deciding on raises? _____

4. What's the current condition of business within the company and industry? _____

5. What are the company's plans for the immediate future? _____

6. What's the boss' overall pattern of conduct toward me? _____

7. To what degree does she or he praise or criticize parts of my performance? _____

8. What is the boss' position in the firm and ambitions for growth? _____

9. To what extent does she or he take me for granted? _____

10. How much knowledge does she or he have of exactly what I do
    and how valuable that work is? _____

Adapted from John J. Tarrant, *How to Negotiate a Raise* (New York: Simon and Schuster,
1984), p. 13.

barrier so you can change his picture. Get
across the idea that money represents the
company's recognition of your achievements, not just buying power to you, and
that therefore raises and promotions keep
you motivated to perform better.

Getting Rid of False Fears

Get rid of any fear or apprehension you have
about asking for an increase. Let's look at
two major reasons we don't like to ask for a
raise or promotion: (1) fear of being turned
down and (2) fear of losing rapport with the
boss.

These are false fears. Actually, the employee who doesn't take initiative on raises
and promotions may give the impression of
being too satisfied and too "nice" to handle
a more difficult job assignment. If necessary,
review the techniques for asserting yourself
in Chapter 5 and select and complete appropriate exercises at the end of that chapter.
Also, use the relaxation and visualization
techniques described at the end of Chapter 4.

MAKING YOUR REQUEST

In addition to adequately preparing, you
must consider strategies for actually making
your promotion request. You must decide
exactly when to make it and be aware of
your image in the boss' mind as part of your
timing. Once you go into the meeting, you
should be prepared for any response the

boss makes and be ready to turn negatives into positives. Know what you plan to do if the boss balks or says "no."

Timing Your Request

If you've estimated your boss' position adequately, you'll know when budget requests are made and adjust your timing accordingly. Regardless of this, don't overlook the importance of asking for a promotion or raise shortly after you've done an outstanding job, made your boss look especially good, greatly outshined all your competitors, or otherwise pulled off a coup. Strike while the iron is hot. Even if the boss can't come through immediately, you may be able to extract a promise for a promotion or raise later.

Don't let your request for a raise or promotion be handled in a casual, spur-of-the-moment, or offhand manner. If your boss attempts to handle it that way, tell him or her you think this is not a good time to discuss the subject and ask for an appointment. If all else fails, ask for an appointment to discuss another work-related topic and bring it up then.

When should you reveal how much you're asking for? Should you announce the amount in advance of the interview or toward the end of the interview? Exercise 14-4 can provide guidelines for making that decision.

Fine-Tuning Your Image

Once your boss knows you're asking for a raise or promotion, he or she will be looking at you in a different light for a while. Give some thought to how you look during this period. Here are some dos and don'ts.

Don't make waves, although it's all right to talk to your boss about making waves

that will support him or her if you think a show of assertiveness will be helpful. However, don't get involved with your own in-fighting now.

Don't bring major problems or sticky questions to your boss if you can avoid it. If you have a good solution to the problem, fine. Otherwise, try to postpone it until after you get your raise.

Don't try to make a good impression by drastically changing your work habits or behavior. You probably won't fool anyone, and it may well go against you.

Don't talk about the progress of your raise or promotion with anyone. The only time you should talk about that is after you've received a tentative turndown or when you're being stalled. Then you might want to rally support.

Don't be away from the work scene if you can help it. Even if you're doing important work elsewhere, long absences sometimes unjustly trigger the suspicion that you're goofing off.

Do be a problem-solver. In fact, you can even emphasize your image as a problem-solver if you postpone solving small, nagging problems until the campaign period. Make sure you get credit—not by boasting but by making modest references to all the help other people gave you, including the boss.

When it comes to big problems, you may not have a solution. However, there may be something you can do toward solving them, such as reporting ways in which similar problems have been handled in other companies, by describing the difficulty in a way that gives clues to what must be done, or at least by showing you're determined to overcome barriers to getting the problem solved.

EXERCISE 14-4: DECIDING WHEN TO REVEAL THE AMOUNT YOU'RE RE-QUESTING

Rate each factor as it applies to your job situation by placing the appropriate number in the space provided.

0 = Not a factor
1 = Somewhat a factor
2 = Definitely a factor
3 = Weighs heavily as a factor

Conditions Conducive to Telling How Much You Want in Advance

_____ 1. You have a strong case, one that is likely to be strengthened by developments between the time you tip your hand and the actual negotiation.

_____ 2. Your boss needs time to get used to the idea and he or she is not likely to use the time to figure out ways to combat you.

_____ 3. Your boss must make preliminary judgments about how much of a gross figure he or she must set aside for raises.

_____ 4. Other conditions:

Factors Indicating You Should Wait to Reveal the Amount You Want

_____ 1. Little or nothing is going to happen in the interim to make you more deserving.

_____ 2. The boss is known as a haggler or bargainer who will begin to carve away at your request as soon as he or she knows what it is.

_____ 3. The boss has the leeway to make the decision and is apt to make it fast. (You want him or her to make it *after* you've presented a strong case.)

_____ 4. You are thinking of taking a strong stand, boldly striking for a very large amount, and you plan to win agreement through persuasion.

_____ 5. Your boss has to sell your raise to others and needs full knowledge and coaching in the supporting arguments you can provide. (You don't want him or her to start selling until you've provided that support.)

_____ 6. News of your request is likely to get around and stimulate others to jack up their own demands.

_____ 7. Other factors:

Adapted from John J. Tarrant, *How to Negotiate a Raise* (New York: Simon and Schuster, 1984), p. 100.

Do maintain a confident—but not complacent—attitude. Be positive in your communications.

Do make the boss look good while you are making yourself look good. You can avoid being a "yes person" and at the same time make your boss look good. For example, ask searching questions about his or her plans or proposals at meetings only when you are fairly sure he or she will be able to back them up with facts and figures and therefore win points with the others.

Do make life easier for your boss and give reassurance that he or she can depend on you to take care of responsibilities in a way that makes the boss look good with minimal hassle. Try to contribute to your boss' peace of mind. At the same time, you should appear to be working effortlessly.

In summary, fine-tune your image so the boss pictures you as a calm, efficient, supportive, positive manager with a forward-looking focus on solving problems and achieving goals that contribute to company profits.

Turning Negatives into Positives

Some of the most valuable strategies you can learn involve ways of turning negatives into positives, especially in the promotion raise interview.

What should you do if you think your boss will fight your request for a promotion or raise by criticizing an area where you've been weak? What can you do to offset this attack? First, prepare yourself by finding some evidence—no matter how small—of progress in your weak area. At least try to come up with something that can be considered hopeful. Don't reveal it to the boss until you're in the interview; you don't want to give him or her extra time to pick it apart.

If the boss brings up the weak area, don't deny that it is a problem. Instead, encourage the boss to focus on this problem. Try to get him or her to verbalize it as the main or only obstacle to granting your request. Don't give your boss any solutions or progress reports until he or she has done this. The boss who thinks he or she is making a strong case you can't refute is more likely to concentrate on the weak area to the exclusion of any others.

Next, get the boss to express support for your work in other areas. Your boss will be more comfortable supporting you if he or she thinks your request can reasonably be denied because of your poor showing in the weak areas you've been discussing. If possible, get the boss to state that he or she would take a supportive position toward your request when and if you show improvement in the weak area.

Now produce evidence of improvement or reason for hope. This can be some minor result, some form of solution, a plan of action, or anything that shows promise. State clearly how you intend to take advantage of this improvement and what your plan of action is. Remind the boss that you can do your best work once your request has been granted and your mind is free to concentrate fully on the job.

Mention the job objectives and standards the two of you agreed on at the last interview of this type. Stress how well you have met most of them. Go over your strengths and your weakness, stressing that your evidence indicates that this weakness is in the process of becoming a strength. Keep stressing your strong points and achievements during the interview.

If the boss argues that your evidence is weak, counter with the fact that his or her objections were based on *complete* lack of results in the weak area. Appeal to his or her sense of fairness in giving you credit. Ask the boss whether he or she *really* demands perfect performance in every area before giving promotions or raises. Mention how monetary recognition of your achievements provides a strong stimulus to your becoming more effective and productive. Ask for advice and support in making improvements. Stress the boss' value to you as a leader and guide in achieving these improvements.

Be patient and firm in maintaining your position that the boss was prepared to accept a slight show of progress and that you have given him or her that as well as a strong showing in other areas.

What if you've botched an assignment? How can you redeem yourself? As soon as you know how extensive the problem is, have a frank discussion about it with your boss. Get it over with right away—as far in advance of promotion or raise discussions as possible. Give him or her all the facts; get across the feeling that you are really leveling.

Don't give excuses or alibis, even though justified. Take responsibility for the problem. Express your concern and dismay and don't try to minimize the problem. If anything, let the boss reassure you and put things in perspective. Let him or her make you feel better, but stress that you have learned a lesson.

In the weeks that follow, don't go overboard in compensating for your error. However, when you're able to call the boss' attention to a real achievement, even though minor, indicate that you were able to learn from your previous error. When the promotion or raise negotiation period arises and you present your supporting evidence, be frank about the fact that you botched an assignment. Indirectly remind the boss that he or she said it wasn't so bad and that you have learned from your mistake.

Coping with the Boss Who Balks

It is possible to overcome all the barriers mentioned so far and still be faced with a boss who won't say "yes." Here are some strategies for handling the balky boss.

The Boss Who Says Money Is in Short Supply Prepare yourself for a disagreement. Collect facts that support your claim that the operation has been functioning properly and at a profit. Collect company statements and comments of executives that refute a "no money" argument. Find out the percentage of increase the top executives received last year, including stock options and other "perks."

The Hostile Boss If your boss gets angry when you ask for a promotion or raise, remain cool. Try to get as much information as you can about whether his or her upset is directed at you or is a general one. If the boss is displeased with your work, try to find out whether the displeasure is aimed at one particular area of your performance or several. Once you've discovered the major problem, you can then select the tactics you want to use.

The Boss Who Says "Trust Me" or Delays Making a Decision If your boss won't make a commitment, use one of these responses: (1) Appeal to his or her self-image as a decision-maker, someone who quickly and easily makes on-the-spot decisions. (2) Tactfully hint at the possible unfortunate results of delaying or giving a negative answer. (3) Reassure the boss that he or she will not regret a decision in your favor. Indicate that you will be appreciative and do everything in your power to merit an affirmative answer. When you've done everything you can do, stop talking. Use one more powerful tool—silence, no matter how long it gets.

Closing the Raise or Promotion Negotiation Proceedings

When you feel it's time to bring negotiations to a close, take the initiative and move on. Base your statements on the assumption that all questions are answered and that the promotion or raise will be granted. Summarize the main arguments for the promotion and ask for it.

If your boss balks, smoke out the main objection. Focus on *it* as the main obstacle to granting your request, answer the objection, and then restate your request. Imply the negative results that may result from delay or from a "no," and reassure the boss that he or she will be making the right move by saying "yes." If necessary, make one concession and then wait for the boss' answer.

If you get the promotion or raise, thank the boss, and reassure him or her that the decision is a sound one. Write a brief memo summing up any agreements and repeating your thanks.

POSITIONING FOR THE NEXT RAISE

As soon as the promotion or raise interview is over, regardless of its outcome, it's time for you to start positioning yourself for your next promotion.

If You Get the Promotion or Raise

First, do anything you can to help the boss resolve any ambiguous feelings about granting your request. Don't give the least reason to suspect you're gloating about getting a "yes" answer. Show how seriously you take your job, how much you appreciate the granting of the request, and stay busy.

Don't go all out to show an artificially high level of performance immediately after the increase. When you can't keep it up, the boss will later become disappointed. Don't hang around the boss asking numerous questions about your job. This may merely create more problems for the boss. Just do your job and be reasonably natural.

Reassure your boss of your good intentions by outlining the big plans you've made, the big problems you're going to solve, and the big goals you will begin to accomplish (long-term items are even better than short-term ones). Above all, give your boss reassurance that he or she made the right decision. Start positioning yourself for your next raise.

If You Don't Get the Promotion or Raise

If the boss says "no" and sticks with it, handle the turndown gracefully but show your concern. Ask for specific reasons why your request was denied. Pin down exactly what you must do in order to ensure getting it the next time around. Focus on your career goals rather than on blaming or complaining. If you do in fact achieve the objectives stated by your boss as criteria for promotion, you'll be in a stronger position next time. You can use the fact that you were previously turned down as a "playing chip," subtly implying "You owe me one."

If you've created a demand for your services from other firms, now may be the time to pin them down on the terms of an offer. Then you can tell your boss that you're seriously thinking of taking the offer, even though you'd prefer to stay with the company if they can match the offer.

You can say you realize that your job, as it's presently described, isn't worth the salary you expect. Then ask for promotion to one that is, or ask if there's any way of broadening your present duties or changing the title so both you and the company will be getting fair value. This strategy can open the door for renegotiation, and your boss can change the original decision without losing face.

If You Are Being Discriminated Against

If you think you haven't been promoted as fast as you should have been, or you think you haven't been given as much responsibility as a male counterpart would have been given, ask yourself whether your employer is unfairly discriminating against you because you are a woman. If you think the answer is "yes," here are some steps to consider.

1. Talk the problem over with your immediate boss, even if you are sure it won't do any good. Remember, your boss may resent your stand and seek revenge. On the other hand, he or she may respect your assertiveness and bend over backward to prevent accusations of discrimination. Either way, it's best to decide whether you are prepared to take the matter further before you talk it over with your boss. If you do confront your boss, keep in mind these suggestions:

   Talk about unfairness rather than discrimination so the boss won't overreact to what appears to be a threat of legal action.

   Give specific examples of unfairness.

   Talk about the facts of the situation without blaming or accusing.

   Take an effective, problem-solving approach, not an emotional one or one that reflects "just a gripe."

   Be clear about your exact purpose—what you want from this meeting. Prepare before you go in. Make a list of your specific complaints and of specific results that show what you've been producing. Practice what you're going to say.

2. If you are not satisfied with what your boss says or does, then go to his or her boss or to the Personnel Department.

3. If you have done everything you know to do within the company without getting satisfactory results, and if you want to stay with the company, contact the nearest Department of Labor, Wage and Hour Division; Equal Employment Opportunity Commission office; and/or a lawyer experienced in handling discrimination cases. It's usually best to select a female lawyer who will have a special interest in the case and a rapport with your situation. Be aware that taking legal action should be a last resort since these cases usually take several years to resolve.

HANDLING YOUR SUBORDINATES' REQUESTS FOR PROMOTIONS

You now have some strategies for getting your boss to grant your request for a promotion or a raise. Now switch to the other side of the desk and ask yourself what you need to keep in mind when your subordinates come in with their own requests for promotions or raises. Perhaps the first point to remember is that since you are familiar with most of the strategies, you can more easily prepare yourself to respond appropriately to them.

Base your decision on how well the subordinate has achieved the objectives the two of you agreed upon earlier. If the objective-setting process is to have any meaning and impact, it must be the basis for these kinds of personnel decisions. Be sure the subordinates understand this basis for your decision. Whether your answer is "yes," "no," or somewhere in between, communicate specific reasons that are clearly tied in with the subordinate's performance.

Remember that Rosabeth Kanter found that subordinates will do almost anything for a boss who has power and is willing to fight for them. So where appropriate let subordinates know you are willing to go to bat for them in getting their requests approved. However, guard against making promises you're not sure you can fulfill.

If you must deny all or part of the request, be firm but encouraging. Where appropriate, offer helpful suggestions for bringing performance up to par, gaining needed knowledge and experience, and so forth. Ask yourself about the basic needs of this particular subordinate (see Chapter 8). Social? Belonging? Status? Recognition? Self-Development? Other? Will the promotion or raise really fulfill these needs best? What else can you offer this person? Consider other rewards, such as more authority, status, or time off. Benefits or perks that are not taxable for the employee might be as satisfactory as twice the amount of straight salary increase.

How does your decision fit in with company and departmental needs and plans? See Chapter 12 for suggestions on evaluating, categorizing, and ranking workers' achievements and giving merit raises.

Effectively handling requests for promotions and raises is an important skill to develop. The major goals involved are making the best use of available job positions and salary funds while keeping workers' morale and productivity high, effectively training and developing workers, and providing for company needs and goals.

SUMMARY

You will need to use all the knowledge you've gained from this book and all your experience to get the promotions you want and the salary you're worth. First, you may need to overcome some archaic attitudes about women and salaries—both others' and your own. Before you go for a particular job move, clarify your career goals and be sure the new job will contribute to your plan.

Get around promotion blocks by enlarging your job or by getting small jobs attached to it—jobs that show on the organizational chart and that you can take on while holding down your main job. Gain all the visibility you can.

To strengthen your hand, create a demand for your services from other departments and other companies. Of course, you don't want to jeopardize your job in the process.

Base your requests on your standards and accomplishments. Think and talk in those terms, beginning with the job interview and carrying through with every discussion of performance or rewards. Set realistic job standards and objectives that you're reasonably sure you can meet. Learn how your contribution affects company profits. The more you can quantify your achievements, the more likely you are to be compensated for them.

Size up your competition so you can stress areas in which you're unique or unquestionably stronger when you meet with your boss. Don't knock your competitors. Instead, if one of their strengths must be discussed, talk about similiarities you share and how you work well together in those areas.

Prepare well for the promotion interview by studying your boss' position so you'll understand his or her viewpoint and be able to anticipate arguments, responses, and ploys. Get rid of false fears of being turned down or losing rapport with the boss. Your assertiveness will be respected. Overcome barriers in your boss' mind about your need for the raise.

Time your request for best results. Don't allow the request to be handled in a casual or offhand manner. Study the conditions surrounding your situation and determine whether it's best to tell your boss in advance how much salary increase you want or to wait until the meeting. Adapt your visibility during the performance evaluation period. The boss is most likely to base the evaluation on your most recent behavior. Make it good, but don't overdo it.

Turn negatives in your performance into positives by focusing on progress, strong areas, plans for improvement, and evidence that objectives and standards have been met.

Close the promotion interview by summarizing your main arguments and requesting the promotion. If the boss has objections, determine the major one and focus on it by answering it and repeating the promotion request. If necessary, make one concession and wait for the boss' response.

Position yourself for the next promotion or raise by going about your business in a natural way and following through with the plans and agreements you made in the promotion interview. If you got the promotion or raise, make the boss glad he or she recommended it. If you didn't, find out exactly what you need to do to get it next time. If you deliver, you're in a stronger position for having requested and been turned down before.

If you're being discriminated against, talk the problem over first with your boss. Remain objective and factual by discussing unfairness rather than discrimination and by giving specific examples. If you're not satisfied with your boss' response, go to his or her boss or to the Personnel Department. If you still get poor results, contact the nearest EEOC office and/or a lawyer.

Handle your subordinates' requests for promotions and raises constructively by basing your decision on how well he or she has achieved the objectives and met the standards you agreed upon earlier. Guard against making promises you can't fulfill; then fight for rewards your people deserve. If you must deny part or all of a request, be firm and specific but encouraging.

REFERENCES

1. Administrative Management Society. *AMS Guide to Management Compensation*. Maryland Road, Willow Grove, PA 19090.

2. Chastain, Sherry. *Winning the Salary Game*. New York: John Wiley & Sons, Inc., 1980. A detailed guide to negotiating salaries, raises, and promotions, this book offers creative as well as practical suggestions.

3. Fisher, Roger, and William Ury. *Getting to Yes: Negotiating Agreement Without Giving In*. New York: Penguin Books, 1983. The authors provide practical suggestions based on their experiences directing the Harvard Negotiation Project.

4. Greenburger, Francis. *How to Ask for More and Get It*. Chicago: Contemporary Books, 1981.

5. Tarrant, John J. *How to Negotiate a Raise*. New York: Simon and Schuster, 1976. A detailed, thorough, and extremely helpful guide to getting raises and promotions.

6. Wright, John W. *The American Almanac of Jobs and Salaries*. New York: Avon Books, 1984. See the listing in Chapter 2 References.

Networks: Women's Organizations

Every large city in the United States has numerous organizations devoted to promoting equal opportunity, career education, and upward mobility for women. To find the organizations that suit you, check your telephone directory and watch for newspaper stories that mention them. Magazines such as *Executive Female* and *Savvy* also provide networking information. At least two books provide lists of local, state, and national organizations as well as information on using networks and starting your own network. They are *Networking* by Mary-Scott Welch (New York: Warner Books, 1980) and *Women's Networks* by Carol Kleiman (New York: Ballantine Books, 1981).

The list of national offices shown here may give you some idea of the types of organizations in existence. You can call or write to get addresses and phone numbers for the local chapters nearest you.

American Alliance of Women
 Entrepreneurs
1710 Connecticut Ave. NW
Washington, D.C. 20009
Phone: (202) 387-6060

American Assn. of University
 Women
2401 Virginia Ave. NW
Washington, D.C. 20006
Phone: (202) 785-7750

American Business Women's
 Assn.
National Headquarters
9100 Ward Parkway
P.O. Box 8728
Kansas City, MO 64114
Phone: (816) 361-6621

American Economic Assn.
Committee on the Status of
 Women in the Economics
 Profession
c/o Elizabeth Bailey
Federal Aviation Agency
Washington, D.C.

American Newspaper Women's
 Club
1607 22nd Street NW
Washington, D.C. 20008

American Society of Women
 Accountants
35 E. Wacker Drive
Chicago, IL 60601
Phone: (312) 341-9078

American Women's Economic
 Development Corp.
1270 Ave. of the Americas
New York, NY 10020
Phone: (212) 397-0880

American Women's Society of
 Certified Public Accountants
500 N. Michigan Avenue
Chicago, IL 60611
Phone: (312) 661-1700

American Women in Radio and
 Television, Inc.
1321 Connecticut Ave. NW
Washington, D.C. 20016
Phone: (202) 296-0009

Assn. of Business &
Professional Women in
Construction
331 Madison Ave.
New York, NY 10017

Association for Women in
Computing
41 Strawberry Circle
Mill Valley, CA 94941

Business and Professional
Women's Foundation
2012 Massachusetts Ave. NW
Washington, D.C. 20036
Phone: (202) 293-1200

Career Alternatives for Teachers
Support Network
738 North LaSalle
Suite 200
Chicago, IL 60610
Phone: (312) 664-6650

Catalyst
14 East 60th Street
New York, NY 10022
Phone: (212) 759-9700

Clearinghouse on Women's
Issues
1346 Connecticut Ave. NW,
Suite 924
Washington, D.C. 20036
Phone: (202)466-3429

Coalition for Women in
International Development
c/o Overseas Education Fund
2101 L Street NW, Suite 916
Washington, D.C. 20037

Coalition of Women in National
and International Business
1900 L Street NW
Washington, D.C. 20036
Phone: (202) 833-5580

ERAmerica
1525 M Street NW
Washington, D.C. 20005
Phone: (202) 833-4354

Executive Women's Division
National Savings & Loan
League
1101 15th Street NW
Washington, D.C. 20005

Federally Employed Women,
Inc.
1010 Vermont, Suite 821
Washington, D.C. 20006
Phone: (202) 638-4404

Federation of Organizations for
Professional Women
2000 P Street NW
Washington, D.C. 20036
Phone: (202) 466-3547

International Association of
Personnel Women
P.O. Box 3057
Grand Central Station
New York, NY 10017

International Association for
Personnel Women
5820 Wilshire Boulevard
Suite 500
Los Angeles, CA 90036
Phone: (213) 937-9000

International Network of
Business & Professional
Women
6424 NE Mallory
Portland, OR 97211
Phone: (503) 289-0400

International Organization of
Women in Telecom-
munications
342 Madison Avenue
New York, NY 10017
Phone: (212) 370-1867

The International Women's
Writing Guild
Box 810, Grace Station
New York, NY 10028
Phone: (212) 737-7536

Leads Club
Box 24
Carlsbad, CA 92008
Phone: (619) 434-3761

The National Alliance of
Professional & Executive
Women's Networks
1 Faneuil Marketplace
Boston, MA 02109
Phone: (617) 720-2874

National Assn. of Bank Women
500 N. Michigan Ave.
Chicago, IL 60611
Phone: (312) 661-1700

National Assn. of Business &
Industrial Saleswomen
90 Corona, Suite 1407
Denver, CO 80218
Phone: (303) 777-7527

National Assn. of Commissions
for Women
Mary Burke Nicholas, President
1350 Avenue of the Americas
New York, NY 10019

National Assn. for Female
Executives (NAFE)
(Publishers of *Executive Female*)
160 E. 65th Street
New York, NY 10022
Phone: (212) 371-8086

National Assn. of Insurance
Women
Furlong Insurance Company
280 NW 42nd Avenue
Miami, FL 33126
Phone: (305) 446-0832

National Assn. of Insurance
Women
1847 E. 15th Street
P.O. Box 4694
Tulsa, OK 74104

National Assn. of Media
Women
157 W. 126th Street
New York, NY 10027
Phone: (212) 666-1320

National Assn. of Office
Workers
Working Women
1224 Huron Road
Cleveland, OH 44115

National Assn. of Minority
Women in Business
City Square Center
P.O. Box 26412
Kansas City, MO 64169
Phone: (816) 421-3335

National Assn. of Women
Business Owners
2000 P Street NW, Suite 410
Washington, D.C. 20036
Phone: (202) 388-8966

National Assn. of Women in
Construction
2800 W. Lancaster
Fort Worth, TX 76107
Phone: (817) 335-9711

National Assn. for Professional
Saleswomen
Box 255708
Sacramento, CA 95865
Phone: (916) 484-1234

National Assn. for Women
Deans, Administrators, and
Counselors
1028 Connecticut Ave. NW
Washington, D.C. 20036
Phone: (202) 659-9330

National Coalition for Women
and Girls in Education
One Dupont Circle NW
Washington, D.C. 20036
Phone: (202) 296-1770

National Commission on
Working Women
1211 Connecticut Ave. NW,
Suite 310
Washington, D.C. 20036

National Council of Career
Women
608 H Street SW
Washington, D.C. 20024

National Federation of Business
& Professional Women's Clubs
2012 Massachusetts Ave. NW
Washington, D.C. 20036
Phone: (202) 293-1100

National Federation of Press
Women
721 Massachusetts Ave. NE
Washington, D.C. 20002

National Network of Graduate
Business School Women
MBA Program Office
Carroll Hall
University of North Carolina
Chapel Hill, NC 27514

National Savings & Loan
League
1101 15th Street NW
Washington, D.C. 20005

National Identification Program
for Advancement of Women
in Higher Education
Administration
c/o American Council on
Education
Office of Women in Higher
Education
One Dupont Circle NW, Room
829
Washington, D.C. 20036
Phone: (202) 833-4692

NOW (National Organization
for Women)
425 13th Street NW, Suite 1001
Washington, D.C. 20004
Phone: (202) 347-2279

National Women's Education
Fund
1410 Q Street NW
Washington, D.C. 20009
Phone: (202) 462-8606

National Woman's Employment
Project
1609 Connecticut Avenue NW
Washington, D.C. 20036
Phone: (202) 797-1384

National Women's Political
Caucus
1411 K Street NW, Suite 1110
Washington, D.C. 20005
Phone: (202) 347-4456

National Women's Studies
Assn.
Elaine Reuben, Coordinator
University of Maryland
College Park, MD 20742

Planning & Women
A Division of American
Planning Assn.
1776 Massachusetts Ave. NW
Washington, D.C. 20036

Professional Connections
Savvy
111 Eighth Avenue, Suite 1517
New York, NY 10011

Women in Communications,
Inc.
National Headquarters
Box 9561
Austin, TX 78766
Phone: (512) 345-8922

Women in the Economy:
Project Conference on State and
Local Policies
1901 Q Street NW
Washington, D.C. 20009
Phone: (202) 234-7014

Women in Government
Relations
1801 K Street NW, Suite 230
Washington, D.C. 20006
Phone: (202) 833-9500

Women in Information
  Processing Inc. (WIP)
P.O. Box 39173
Washington, D.C. 20016
Phone: (202) 298-8000

Women Leaders Round Table
1299 F Street NW
Washington, D.C. 20006
Phone: (202) 331-6049

Women in Municipal
  Government
c/o National League of Cities
1620 I Street NW
Washington, D.C. 20006
Phone: (202) 293-7310

Women Officials in NACO
c/o National Assn. of Counties
1735 New York Ave. NW
Washington, D.C. 20006
Phone: (202) 785-9577

Women in Sales Assn.
8 Madison Avenue
Valhalla, NY 10595
Phone: (914) 946-3802

Women's Educational Service
  Assn.
363 West Drake Road
Fort Collins, CO 80526
Phone: (303) 223-9372

Women's Equity Action League
  (WEAL)
805 15th Street NW, Suite 822
Washington, D.C. 20005
Phone: (202) 638-4560

Women's Lobby
201 Massachusetts Ave. NE
Washington, D.C. 20002

Women's Institute for Freedom
  of the Press
3306 Ross Place NW
Washington, D.C. 20008
Phone: (202) 966-7783

Women's National Book Assn.
60 West 60th Street, 16-A
New York, NY 10023

Women-Owned Business
  Directory
P.O. Box 1166
Pittsburgh, PA 15230

Women's Workforce
c/o Wider Opportunities for
  Women
1649 K Street NW
Washington, D.C. 20006
Phone: (202) 638-4868

Magazines for Career Women

Business Woman   THA, Inc., P.O. Box 23276, San Jose, CA 95153.
A bimonthly magazine distributed nationally which includes networking information for California women.

Executive Female   421 Fourth Street, Annapolis, MD 21403
A bimonthly publication of the National Association for Female Executives (NAFE). This magazine offers a fairly sophisticated level of helpful articles for women managers. Each issue usually centers around a particular theme, such as functional skills, working relationships, or financial savvy. You must join NAFE in order to receive the magazine. Some advantages of membership include (1) access to a list of NAFE network directors as well as the opportunity to become a network director yourself, (2) a career placement service called MATCHPOINT, (3) career aids such as aptitude testing, résumé guidance, and a credit handbook, (4) personal benefits such as a group hospitalization option and hotel and car rental discounts.

Ms   370 Lexington Ave., New York, NY 10017
A monthly publication that includes articles on the sources and impact of sex-role stereotyping, discrimination, networking, sources of supportiveness for women, and other items of interest to women. It's an excellent source of current information on women's rights and the women's movement.

New Woman   314 Royal Poinciana Way, Palm Beach, FL 33480
A bimonthly publication that bridges the gap between *Good Housekeeping* and *Ms*. This magazine is for women who are just beginning to look seriously at alternate lifestyles and career choices. Some articles on self-development of interest to the aspiring woman manager are included.

Savvy   111 Eighth Ave., Suite 1517, New York NY 10001
A sophisticated monthly publication that combines some aspects of *Ms*. and *Executive Female*. This is an excellent, well-rounded magazine for the woman manager.

Women's Health Rodale Press, Emmaus, PA 18049.
This monthly newsletter takes a preventive, assertive approach to health care. It features news you won't find in newspapers or most women's magazines.

Working Mother McCall Publishing Company, 230 Park Avenue, New York, NY 10169
A bimonthly magazine that includes articles of interest to all working women as well as information and advice specifically geared to the working mother.

Working Woman P.O. Box 10132, Des Moines, IA 50340
An excellent monthly magazine for women who are thinking about upward mobility and for new women supervisors and managers. Basic articles of interest to working women at all levels are included.

Answers to Selected Exercises

Exercise 1-1: Assessing Viewpoints That Affect Promotability (pp. 5–7)

Scoring Instructions: Place a check mark in the space to the left of the answer that corresponds to your responses for each of the ten items. For example, if your response to Item 1 was "a," place a check beside "1a" below. When you have checked off all the items, add the number of check marks you have in each column and write the total for each category on the bottom line.

Category A (Viewpoints typical of the promotable woman)	Category B (Viewpoints typical of the marginally promotable woman)	Category C (Viewpoints typical of the nonpromotable woman)
_____ 1c	_____ 1a	_____ 1b
_____ 2b	_____ 2a	_____ 2c
_____ 3b	_____ 3c	_____ 3a
_____ 4a or c	_____ 4b	_____ 4d
_____ 5b	_____ 5a	_____ 5c
_____ 6b	_____ 6a or c	_____
_____ 7a	_____ 7c	_____ 7b
_____ 8a	_____ 8b	_____ 8c
_____ 9b	_____ 9a	_____ 9c
_____ 10b*	_____ 10a	_____ 10c
_____ Total	_____ Total	_____ Total

Scoring Interpretation: You can make a general evaluation of your current level of promotability by merely noting the category in which you have the highest score. The more detailed explanation that follows in the book can help you further diagnose your areas of strength and weakness.

---

*You should include in your plans how many people you'll need in order to handle the increased workload.

Exercise 1-3: Pinpointing Your Attitude (pp. 37–38)

This exercise is designed to pinpoint any conflict you may harbor about career success. Do any of the statements in your story reflect negative consequences? Negative consequences might include any form of social or family difficulty or rejection; some decrease in eligibility or desirability as a date or marriage partner; becoming isolated, lonely, or unhappy in some way as a result of succeeding. Expecting negative consequences leads to the arousal of some degree of fear of success, which in turn leads to self-sabotage unconsciously designed to avoid the negative consequences.

Exercise 3-1: Self-Assessment: Making the Transition from Worker to Manager (pp. 99–101)

Scoring Instructions: Transfer the numbers you placed in the blanks in Exercise 2-1 to the corresponding blanks shown here. Add the numbers in each column to get your total score in each category.

Category 1 (Savvy manager)	Category 2 (Aggressive/loner)	Category 3 (Submissive detail person)
_____ 1b	_____ 1c	_____ 1a
_____ 2a	_____ 2b	_____ 2c
_____ 3c	_____ 3a	_____ 3b
_____ 4b	_____ 4c	_____ 4a
_____ 5c	_____ 5b	_____ 5a
_____ 6a	_____ 6c	_____ 6b
_____ 7b	_____ 7c	_____ 7a
_____ 8c	_____ 8b	_____ 8a
_____ 9b	_____ 9a	_____ 9c
_____ 10a	_____ 10b	_____ 10c

Scoring Interpretation: You can make a general evaluation of your readiness to make a successful transition by simply noting the categories in which you scored the highest and the lowest. The categories may be interpreted as follows:

Category 1, Savvy manager—Your identification with these responses indicate that you're already tuned into ways of projecting a competent, professional image. You can probably avoid the typical problems that face the new woman manager.

Category 2, Aggressive/loner—Your identification with these responses may indicate a tendency to "go it alone" and to sometimes overreact to others' stereotypes of women in the business world. Actions perceived as over-aggressive may leave you wide open to being labeled a "women's-lib type" or a grouch. Loner actions may create barriers to developing a support network. See Chapter 5 for suggestions on changing your aggressiveness to assertiveness.

Category 3, Submissive detail person—Your identification with these responses may indicate that you strongly identify with typical female behavior patterns. While these patterns can contribute to success in secretarial/clerical roles, they are nonproductive in a managerial role. Focus on seeing the "big picture," on taking a power stance, and on upward mobility for you and your subordinates. See Chapter 5 for developing your assertiveness.

Exercise 3-2: The Dawson Case (pp. 134–135)

1. Major problems Vickie must deal with in her new job:
   a. A patronizing boss, Phil Crain. While he may mean well, Crain is reinforcing Vickie's image as a secretary rather than as a manager. He's also reinforcing cultural stereotypes about women's roles and managerial abilities.
   b. Subordinates (Bob and Olivia) who want to continue being buddies and to take advantage of their former relationship with Vickie.

c. Male subordinates who are testing Vickie to see how far she will bend (Ben and others).

2 and 3. Some attitudes, approaches, and actions Vickie can take, in order of priority:

a. Establish her image as a competent, fair manager.

—Focus on identifying and communicating current department and individual job objectives and on the results people achieve.

—Let former buddies know that while she has not changed as a person, her role and responsibilities have changed. Therefore, some of her relationships must change. As man-

ager, she must avoid playing favorites and she must exhibit fairness to all the workers.

b. Delegate as much of the paperwork as possible. If necessary, catch up at home, but avoid neglecting other managerial functions in order to complete paperwork at the office.

c. Put together a support network that includes subordinates, peers, and top management.

d. Start working privately on plans for major departmental improvements. Later discuss them with supporters. Finally present them to the entire department.

Exercise 5-2: Identifying Assertive, Aggressive, and Nonassertive Behavior (pp. 172–174)

1. As 2. N 3. Ag 4. As 5. Ag 6. As 7. N 8. As 9. Ag 10. N 11. As 12. As
13. N 14. As 15. N 16. As 17. As 18. As 19. Ag 20. Ag

Exercise 5-11: Giving Feedback Messages (p. 210–211)

If possible, get someone to read your response and to define or summarize it by selecting one verb that best represents its tone. Some possibilities: assume, evaluate, praise, blame, solve, lecture, psych, sympathize, accuse, warn, scold, order, imply, question, hint, kid. If you can't get someone to read your response, evaluate it yourself *after* you read the following discussion.

Underline any judgmental or evaluative words you can find in your response. Do any of your statements imply that Lois' behavior is bad or wrong in and of itself? Consider the fact that her behavior might seem good to some apartment mates, who would be happy that Lois likes to really relax and let her hair down once in a while. Such behavior could conceivably put such a partner at ease so that she would feel free to behave in a similar manner herself.

Here is an example of a feedback message that objectively describes Lois' behavior: "Lois, I want to talk with you. I notice that your coat, shoes, and briefcase are lying in the entry hall, that some of your clothes and the newspaper are lying around the living room, that there are peanuts and an empty beer can on the floor, and that the TV is playing

loudly. This is the third or fourth time this has occurred. When it happens, I feel . . . (angry/frustrated/unhappy/glad to see you relaxed but worried about the furniture/that guests might drop in/etc.)"

Do you see that objectively describing behavior is merely repeating the specific actions as you observe them? Words such as "mess, lazy, sloppy, inconsiderate" are judgmental and should be avoided. A matter-of-fact tone should be used with no hint of hostility or resentment.

The feedback message should also include the effects Lois' behavior has on her roommate. For example, "I am beginning to hesitate to invite people over." At some point in the conversation the message should also include the specific behavior the sender would prefer. In most cases, including this one, the most effective approach is to get the receiver's ideas about behavior change first. However, if the receiver does not propose a change that is satisfactory to the sender, the sender should assert herself clearly by making tactful queries or suggestions. For example, "When you relax in this way, could you confine your activities and possessions to your bedroom?"

This feedback message may not "work" in the sense that you and Lois are able to reach a mutual agreement on lifestyles and housekeeping habits. In fact, you may decide now or later that you should not share an apartment because of these differences. However, if you have given effective feedback messages, both you and Lois will be clear about exactly why the living arrangement didn't work out. This way, Lois will not worry and wonder about what went wrong. She's not likely to think you dislike her as a person or even that you have negative emotions in connection with other aspects of her behavior. Therefore, unfounded resentments and hurt feelings are likely to be avoided. While Lois may not like your honesty at the time, she's likely to respect it and to respect you. Your chances of an amicable living arrangement—or an amicable parting—and good will in the future are enhanced through effective feedback.

Exercise 6-2: Preparing Action Agenda Items (p. 237)

Here are some possible ways of phrasing the agenda items as action questions: 1. What will be our sales target for 19xx? OR How can we increase sales by 10%? 2. Shall we develop the new XYZ product? OR How can we best market the new XYZ product? 3. How can we improve our layoff policy? OR What shall our layoff policy be? 4. When should we meet again?

Exercise 6-4: Choosing the Best Graph (p. 257)

1. Broken-line.   2. Bar.   3. Pie.   4. Broken-line with projection in dots or similar differentiation. Text or footnote should give basis for projection and statistical technique used.   5. Bar, each bar with three differentiated segments.   6. Bar, if for comparison.   7. Broken-line.   8. Pie.

Exercise 6-5: Constructing and Interpreting a Graph (p. 258)

1. True.
2. You can't tell. You can only make projections, using statistical treatment.
3. You can't tell—*something* does.
4. You can't say, since you have no costs or expenses shown.
5. True.
6. June and July, but not October.

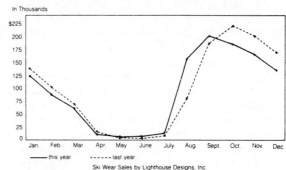

Ski Wear Sales by Lighthouse Designs, Inc.

Exercise 7-2: How Do You View Subordinates? (p. 273)

Answers to odd numbered questions (1, 3, 5, 7, 9):

Total of + scores	_____
Total of − scores	_____
Difference	_____ (Y) score

Answers to even numbered questions (2, 4, 6, 8, 10):

Total of + scores	_____
Total of − scores	_____
Difference	_____ (X) score

Interpretation:
A Y-Score or an X-Score of 7 to 10 indicates you are strongly oriented toward that theory. A Y-Score or an X-Score of 4 to 7 indicates you are moderately oriented toward that theory. A Y-Score or an X-Score of 3 to 0 or any minus amount indicates little or no orientation toward that theory.

Exercise 7-4: Identifying Behavior Characteristics of Defensive and Supportive Climates (p. 287)

	"a" Response	*"b" Response*
1.	Control	Cooperation
2.	Superiority	Equality
3.	Description	Evaluation
4.	Indifferent	Concerned
5.	Know-it-all	Open to ideas
6.	Manipulative	Spontaneous

The purpose of this exercise is to reinforce concepts and to stimulate thinking, not to determine "right answers." The answers shown here are merely intended to suggest the categories of behavior involved in each of the situations.

Exercise 8-1: Identifying Motivational Priorities (p. 303)

Your self-assessment will depend on how you interpret each factor, of course. Most of the managers who have worked through Exercise 8-1 have interpreted these factors as follows:

Factor	*Suggested Level—Maslow's Hierarchy*
Salary	Physiological or security
Responsibilities assigned	Self-actualization
Relationship with fellow employees	Social
The work itself	Self-actualization
Opportunity for advancement	Ego or self-actualization
Working conditions	Safety
On-the-job achievement	Self-actualization
Kind of supervision received	Social
Recognition	Ego
Company policy	Security
Personal growth opportunities	Self-actualization

Exercise 8-4: Matching Needs to Jobs (pp. 320–321)

The responses can vary depending on the particular job situation and the unique combination of needs perceived by each person. The responses shown are to stimulate your thinking.

1. *EDP program librarian:* Ach. The job is highly task oriented with little interaction with other people.
2. *EDP systems analyst:* Ach/Aff. The job calls for task-oriented technical skills as well as good human relations skills. Need to listen, question, identify others' needs, and communicate effectively.
3. *Personnel interviewer:* Aff. Extensive interaction with people. High level of human relations skills required.
4. *Word-processing operator:* Ach. Highly task-oriented job with almost immediate feedback and measurable results.
5. *Word-processing supervisor:* Aff/Ach. Although a task-oriented background is required, at this level human relations skills are more important. Much interaction with people; ability to keep workers and users satisfied is important.
6. *Labor relations specialist:* Power/Aff. To the extent the union is demanding and hostile, ability to project and exercise power is crucial, es-

pecially in negotiations. High level of human relations skills is also required to anticipate others' behavior, to communicate effectively, and to smooth over ruffled feelings.

7. *Personnel benefits administrator:* Ach. Highly task-oriented job. Little interaction with people.
8. *Purchasing analyst:* Ach. Highly task oriented; little interaction.
9. *Buyer:* Aff/Power. Much interaction with vendors; some interaction with production people. Good human relations skills, ability to communicate well are important. To extent management allows autonomy in bargaining with vendors and deciding on bids, power needs may be met.
10. *Account Executive:* Ach. Since results are so important and visible, and since they depend so greatly on the individual's effort and abilities, this job is first and foremost an achievement-oriented one. Since it requires a high level of interaction and human relations skills, it may also satisfy affiliation needs. However, the successful account executive is comfortable with risk-taking and uncertainty. Because success can lead to rapid advancement, the job can also meet power needs.

Exercise 8-5: The Leslie Case (pp. 321–322)

The clerks are exhibiting strong affiliation needs at the expense of achievement or power needs. Here are various steps Lin can take to handle the situation and to enhance the motivation of the clerks.

1. Discuss goals and standards; implement the concepts of performance planning.
2. Attempt to find a way to achieve goal congruence and to channel the affiliation needs of the clerks so that the goals of the unit are also met.
3. Consider organizing the clerks formally into a project team with specific goals.
4. Consider separating the clerks on the job, putting them into jobs that will allow maximum

contact with others and giving them adequate responsibility to keep them challenged. Consider transferring them to other departments in carrying out this action.

5. Determine if achievement needs lie hidden behind the obvious affiliation needs. If so, try to find out what rewards are most motivating: recognition? training for more responsible tasks or positions?
6. If affiliation is actually the predominant motive, what types of rewards will be more satisfying than socializing on the job? Praise? Giving challenging tasks that require interaction with interesting people?

7. Determine if the clerks are viewing their jobs as mere drudgery. If so, how can she make the jobs appear more important and essential to them.

8. Determine if she can delegate some of her tasks to the clerks, tasks that will be rewarding to them.

9. Watch for opportunities to reward the clerks when they are obviously concentrating on work and performing tasks effectively.

Exercise 9-1: Discovering Your Approach to Decision-Making (p. 341)

Phillip Marvin found that the typical successful entrepreneur and top-level executive exhibits the decision-making profile shown here:

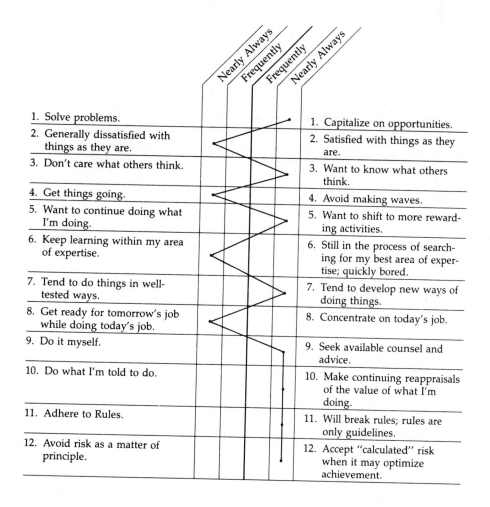

Exercise 9-2: The Manning Case (pp. 351–352)

1. Some of the sources of Manning's problems are: (a) Lack of a preventive attitude toward problems. (b) Failure to use Murphy's Law to prevent unpleasant surprises. (c) Failure to consult the people who are involved in carrying out the decisions. (d) Failure to brief people in groups, face-to-face, where possible. (e) Lack of participation of others in the decision-making process; for example, in deciding how details of the campaign will be carried out. (f) Lack of adequate controls to assure that any deviations from the plan will be discovered in time to prevent failure.

2. By using the techniques mentioned above, Mary could have handled the situation more effectively.

3. Mary is in real trouble because she has blown her first real chance to show her managerial effectiveness. What's worse, the results will be visible to the top decision makers in the company.

4. The best approach Mary can take now is to admit her problems and seek help. The first step would be to think through her problems and figure out how some can be remedied and how to prevent any of them from occurring again. Then go to Jan Arguello and discuss the whole matter, sharing her insights and asking Jan for her own advice. If Mary shows that she has learned a great deal from this experience and is determined to perform better in the future, she may be able to redeem herself eventually.

Exercise 9-3: Making Decisions Under Pressure (pp. 352–353)

The key to handling this situation effectively is the decision you make regarding Item E. Any time all production is halted in your department, your company is losing money rapidly. If the average salary of your workers is $20 an hour including benefits and you have ten workers, the company loses $200 worth of productivity for each hour your work unit is idle or unproductive. Since you're the only one who can fix the equipment (a situation that should be remedied in the future, by the way), you must handle this item at once if you are to get everyone else back to work as soon as possible.

Meanwhile, how are you going to salvage some productivity from your idle workers? Are you going to run around frantically trying to handle all the listed items by yourself while they sit around watching you? If you didn't decide to delegate as many of the other items as possible, you need to work on your attitude toward delegation! Pay special attention to this section in Chapter 12.

Here are suggested priorities and sequence of handling the items:

Importance	Sequence	Item
8	11	A
2	2	B
6	9	C
4	1	D
1	8	E
6	4	F
5	5	G
6	7	H
7	6	I
3	3	J

Suggestions for handling items in sequence shown below.

Item D. If a worker is nearby, have her or him answer the phone and take the message. If not, answer it, ask them to hold, then get someone to take the message.

Item B. Send someone to your boss to explain the situation and to set up a later appointment.

Item J. Send someone to get a sandwich or other fast food that you can eat when you finish repairing the equipment.

Item F. Send someone to find out what the young man wants and to get his name and number so you can call him next week.

Item G. Have someone call the Los Angeles operator and talk with the party to determine whether or not it is an emergency.

Item I. Send someone to the lounge to relay your permission to Ann; let her go home.

Item H. Send someone to tell Jim of your situation and to get a message from him as to the nature of his call and/or how long it can wait.

Item E. After you have delegated the above

items, which should take no more than 5 minutes, repair the equipment.

After the equipment is repaired, review the messages returned to you by the workers you sent on errands. Decide which need handling first and whether any can be further delegated.

Item C. You could have delegated the opening of the company mail earlier. (If you have a secretary, she should routinely open all company mail anyway.) Since anyone with an urgent time target would not handle a request by mail, you can assume the mail can wait. However, you may want to check it by midafternoon in case you want a reply to go out in the Friday afternoon mail.

Item A. Your talk to Scott can wait till next week. Think about it over the weekend.

Exercise 10-4: Making Objectives Clear and Specific (p. 367)

1. This statement needs to be more specific and measurable. A possible rewrite: Increase our share of the petite-size clothing market from 10 percent to 25 percent by January 19xx with no more than a 2 percent increase in our department budget.
2. A possible rewrite: Increase our net profit to 12 percent of sales for fiscal year 19xx.
3. A possible rewrite: Provide at least 100 contact hours of appropriate classroom training for each supervisor during fiscal year 19xx within a budget of $25,000.
4. A possible rewrite: Set quality control standards for sweater imports to meet or exceed those of Competitors X and Y, while maintaining a profit margin of 13 percent.
5. A possible rewrite: Develop twelve additional sources of supply by January 1, 19xx, at a cost of no more than 100 working hours.
6. A possible rewrite: Reduce the number of employee grievances to no more than ten per quarter by quarter ending April 1, 19xx, at a cost not to exceed $2,000.
7. A possible rewrite: Establish a research and de-

velopment department with a staff of twelve and a first-year operating budget of $100,000 by September 1, 19xx, at a developmental cost of $65,000.
8. Ideally, an objective does not represent an "assigned responsibility." It is a measurable goal to be achieved by a certain date. "Carrying out assigned responsibilities" carries the connotation of "just working" to most people. The estimated resources to be used in achieving the objectives are agreed upon by worker and boss during the objective-setting process. Securing the necessary resources is part of the action or implementation process. Therefore, "within approved budget" is inappropriate language for stating clear objectives.
9. A possible rewrite: Conduct a market research survey to determine the major emerging styles desired by business women; results to be reported by March 1, 19xx; budget allowance, $2,000.
10. A possible rewrite: Install XYZ system by October 15, 19xx, at a cost not to exceed $150,000.

Exercise 10-5: Developing Objectives and Controls with Your Secretary (pp. 389–390)

There are many possible responses to this exercise. Here is one:

1. Key objective: To initiate and respond to all routine correspondence in connection with the XYZ convention to be held on April 8, 19xx.
2. Additional standards: (1) All letters and memos will be effective; that is, they will get the desired results. (2) All letters and memos will be grammatically correct. (3) All correspondence will be typographically correct (no uncorrected errors). (4) The normal length of time for completing an average letter (one-half to one page long) will be fifteen minutes.

3. Controls: During the first few weeks of this project, you will sign all correspondence before it is sent. You should check each letter thoroughly before signing it, using standards (1) through (3) as the basis for approval. Later, you will only spot-check routine correspondence. During the entire project, your secretary will practice self-evaluation, using all agreed-upon standards. Standard (4) is difficult to control when the secretary has a variety of duties and may be frequently interrupted. However, it can serve as a guideline.

Exercise 10-7: Del Oro Enterprises—Defining an Organizational Structure (pp. 391–392)

Current Organizational Chart:

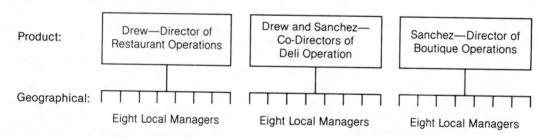

Possible New Chart A—Using Product Deparmentation:

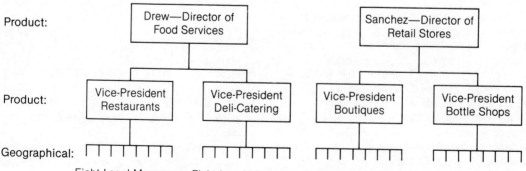

(continued on next page)

Possible New Chart B—Using Functional Departmentation:

Functional:

		Executive Committee Drew and Sanchez		

Vice-President Marketing

Vice-President Retail Operations

Vice-President Human Resources

Vice-President Food Services

Vice-President Finance

Geographical:

Eight Local Boutique Managers

Eight Local Bottle Shop Managers

Eight Local Restaurant Managers

Eight Local Deli Managers

The Current Organizational Chart and the Possible New Chart A show departmentation by product or service: (1) in-house food service, (2) take-out or off-premises food service, (3) boutique products, and (4) alcoholic beverage products.

In Chart A Drew and Sanchez capitalize on their individual strengths—Drew's in food services and Sanchez' in the buying/selling game of retail operations. Each has two vice-presidents reporting directly to her, which will help take some pressure off their jobs and yet provide top-management coverage of all areas. A disadvantage of this structure is that all four top managers must oversee all functional areas within their product areas. They may lack needed expertise in some functional areas, and there will probably be some overlap and duplication of functions.

Chart B shows departmentation by functional area. The operations area (equivalent to production in a manufacturing operation) is divided into two functional areas: Food Service Operations, covering restaurant and deli operations, and Retail Operations, covering boutique and bottle shop operations. These two types of operations are significantly different and call for different types of experience and expertise. Functional expertise can be brought to other areas too, such as marketing. The Vice-President of Marketing can handle promotion and advertising for all operations, possibly resulting in significant savings and better results. The major disadvantage is that the vice-presidents will be reporting to two bosses, and the lines of authority for Drew and Sanchez are not as clear-cut as in Chart A.

Exercise 11-1: Computing Profit Margin (p. 404)

$$\frac{\text{Profit}}{\text{Sales}} = \frac{\$8M}{\$100M} = 100\overline{)8.00}^{.08} = 8\%$$ Profit margin is 8%.

Exercise 11-2: Computing Investment Turnover (p. 404)

$$\frac{\text{Sales}}{\text{Total investment (Assets)}} = \frac{\$100M}{\$60M} = 60\overline{)100.00}^{1.66}$$

$$
\begin{array}{r}
60 \\ \hline
400 \\
360 \\ \hline
400 \\
360 \\ \hline
40
\end{array}
$$

Investment turnover is 1.6. Management "turned over" the assets more than 1½ times during the year. It generated sales of more than 1½ times the dollar value of the assets.

Exercise 11-3: Evaluating Overall Financial Performance (p. 405)

Laurette's has the best overall financial performance because it has the highest return on investment (28%). ROI is the best overall measure of financial performance because it combines the profit margin and the investment turnover.

Exercise 11-4: Figuring Profit Margins (pp. 411–412)

Figure 10% of the sales forecast for each product line.

Bonnie Jean	$7,000,000
Sir Winston	$10,000,000
Su Anne	$5,000,000
Total	$22,000,000

Projected profit margins can be figured by multiplying the dollar amounts the company expects to take in from sales by the profit margin (expressed as a percentage) the company expects to achieve. To figure the Bonnie Jean product line, for example:

$$\begin{array}{r} \$70,000,000 \\ \times\ .10 \\ \hline \$\ 7,000,000.00 \end{array}$$

When a number is multiplied by 10% of course, the shortcut of merely moving the decimal point one place to the left is used to get the same answer.

Exercise 11-5: Figuring Budgeted Costs (p. 412)

Figure 90% of the sales forecast for each product line (shown in Exercise 11-4).

Bonnie Jean	$63,000,000
Sir Winston	90,000,000
Su Anne	45,000,000
Total	$198,000,000

Budgeted costs may be figured by taking the percent remaining after the profit margin is figured (in this case 100% less 10% for profit equals 90% for costs) and multiplying the sales forecast for each product line by it. Budgeted costs for Bonnie Jean are figured as follows:

$$\begin{array}{r} \$70,000,000 \\ \times\ .90 \\ \hline \$63,000,000.00 \end{array}$$

Exercise 11-6: Evaluating Preliminary Budgets (p. 413)

Bonnie Jean has an *unfavorable* preliminary variance (proposed costs of $63,300,000 with budgeted costs of $63,000,000). Sir Winston has a *favorable* preliminary variance (proposed costs of $89,500,000 with budgeted costs of $90,000,000). Su Anne has an *unfavorable* preliminary variance (proposed costs of $46,500,000 with budgeted costs of $45,000,000).

Exercise 11-7: Categorizing Office Inventory (p. 426)

Item	Capital equipment	Nominal value asset	Expense item
Office space (12' x 14')	✔		
Dictation Machine		✔	
Tapes for dictation			✔
Walnut desk	✔		
Desk chair		✔	

(continued on next page)

Three reams company letterhead			✔
Electric typewriter	✔		
Typewriter table		✔	
Pens (2 dozen)			✔
Company directory			✔
Framed picture		✔	
Business cards—box of 100			✔
Ruler			✔
Office keys			✔
Waste basket			✔
Bookcases (3)		✔	
Four-drawer file cabinets (2)		✔	
Desk Calendar			✔
Stapler and staple remover			✔
Box of staples			✔
Two file baskets			✔
Arm chairs		✔	

Exercise 11-8: Figuring a Cash Budget (p. 428)

No, management does not have a workable cash budget. During the third quarter the company will run out of cash. It will have to operate for the remainder of the year on borrowed funds and begin the following year with no cash of its own.

Balance forward	$ 30,000	
Income first quarter	115,000	
	145,000	
Expenses first quarter	– 120,000	
Cash balance		$ 25,000
Income second quarter	115,000	
Expenses second quarter	– 125,000	
Difference for the quarter—deficit		(10,000)
Cash balance		15,000
Income third quarter	105,000	
Expenses third quarter	– 125,000	
Difference for the quarter—deficit		(20,000)
Cash balance (deficit)		(5,000)
Income fourth quarter	120,000	
Expenses fourth quarter	120,000	
Difference for the quarter		-0-
Cash balance at end of year (deficit)		($5,000)

Exercise 12-4: Delegation (pp. 464–465)

Rationale for Priority Ranking: (1) The amount of time that Jill will free up for herself. (2) The extent to which workers' jobs will be enriched, their skills expanded, and their motivation increased without overburdening them. (3) The extent to which Jill will be focusing on higher-level functions rather than routine details.

If Jill delegates all the tasks listed except E, she can reduce her workweek by an average of five hours, to forty-five hours per week. Perhaps she can shave off another five hours by streamlining some of her procedures for her remaining tasks. She can also help her workers streamline their tasks. As workers gain skill in performing current and new tasks more efficiently, Jill can delegate even more of her activities to them.

Priority Ranking	Job No.	Delegatee	No. Hours Involved (Per Week)	Comments
1	D	Calvin	1¼	Enrich Calvin's job. Train properly and maintain close control until confident Calvin will maintain accuracy.
2	C	Rotate	1½	Rotate the job each week to a different worker. Develop detailed written procedures for doing the task and include it in each worker's job description and performance plan. Maintain close control; require worker to redo task if count is wrong.
3	A	Rose	¾	If there is nothing secret about the data, Jill should let go and delegate the task. Job enrichment for Rose and free time for Jill should receive higher priority. Jill could stress the importance of the job and its confidentiality to Rose.
4	F	George	½ (Two per month)	If the other supervisors don't attend, it's unlikely Jill will miss much of importance. She can instruct George about the types of information he should note and report back to her.
5	B	Frances	1	Enrich Frances' job and develop her skills. Jill should find other, less time-consuming ways to interact with workers. If this proves difficult, she may decide to keep this job for herself. If not, delegating it should rank third in priority because of the relatively large amount of time that can be saved.
6	E	None	1¼	It has been estimated by many experts that about 75 percent of managerial failures are due to office politics rather than to incompetence. Maintaining constructive political contacts is a crucial part of Jan's job. She should delegate this task only on extremely busy days; then rotate it.

Key Terms

Achievement need A socially acquired need to continually set and achieve personal goals. It implies a willingness to solve problems, take calculated risks, and seek feedback on performance.

Active listening An approach to interacting constructively with another person through listening with a specific purpose in mind, such as identifying the speaker's key thoughts, habit patterns, or desire for change; reflecting back main ideas; checking out the speaker's feelings.

Affiliation need A socially acquired need to be with others, to be liked and approved by them, and to relate to them in a mutually supportive, positive way.

Affirmative action guidelines Specific policies and procedures for achieving the goals of an affirmative action program within a prescribed time period. Guidelines may cover practices in employment, upgrading, demotion, transfer, recruitment, layoff, termination, salary, benefits, and training of employees.

Affirmative action program A set of specific results-oriented actions, commitments, and procedures designed to systematically achieve an equitable redistribution of both sexes in all racial groups within a work force.

Affirmative action target dates Deadline dates built into a company's affirmative action program for achieving various goals.

Aggressiveness Standing up for personal rights and expressing thoughts, feelings, and beliefs in ways that violate the rights of another person. Such expressions are usually inappropriate, domineering, manipulative, humiliating, degrading, belittling, or dishonest in some way.

Analytical messages Messages that can be broken down into parts so that each part can be examined to see how it relates to a particular situation or problem.

Annual report A report of a firm's financial performance for the preceding year. It includes a profit and loss statement and a balance sheet.

Assertiveness Standing up for personal rights and acting in ways that express thoughts, feelings, and beliefs in direct, honest, and appropriate ways that don't violate another person's rights.

Balance sheet A statement of the net worth of a firm at a particular point in time, based on what it owns and owes.

Bar graph A graph consisting of bars that represent events that occurred at the same time or during the same period of time. Effective for making comparisons.

Body time Personal patterns of body functions that include preferred hours of waking, sleeping, and working; fluctuations in energy level; degree of sociability; and amount of charisma.

Bona Fide Occupational Question (BFOQ) A term used in connection with EEO laws. BFOQs are interview questions that are necessary to determine an applicant's bona fide, or relevant and essential, qualifications for a job.

Break-even point The level of production at which total revenue equals total costs. At this point the firm shows neither a profit nor a loss; it breaks even.

Broken-line graph A graph consisting of one or more lines that show progress such as trends and fluctuations over a period of time.

Business cycle A period during which there is a pattern of fluctuation in consumer demand for a product or service. Typically, demand increases until it reaches a high point, remains there for a time, begins to decrease until a low point is reached, and remains there for a time until the next cycle begins.

Cafeteria approach   Allowing employees to choose from an array of possible benefits to tailor a "benefit package" (within a set budget) that fits their particular needs.

Capital budget   An organization's plan for acquiring fixed assets, usually covering a two- to ten-year period.

Cash budget   An organization's plan for balancing expenditures with expected revenues so that there will be enough cash on hand to pay bills as they come due.

Cash flow   The timing and pattern of the collection of revenues and payment of costs and expenses.

Chain of command   An organizational structure in which each person is responsible to one immediate boss, who in turn is responsible to his or her immediate boss. If a worker goes to a Vice-president for an assignment instead of to his or her supervisor, he or she would be violating the chain of command.

Communication process   The steps involved in getting an idea from the mind of a sender to the mind of a receiver.

Company operations   The day-to-day business activities and transactions necessary to achieve company goals.

Comparable pay for comparable worth   Pay scales based on analyses of all types of jobs, male- and female-dominated, in which levels of education, experience, responsibility, difficulty, and hardship are the determining factors, rather than tradition or supply-and-demand.

Conformity pressures   The attempts of members of a group to influence the behavior of others to conform to the group's ideas. Tactics such as a show of approval, disapproval, acceptance, or nonacceptance may be used.

Confrontive assertion   Confronting a broken agreement by describing what the other person agreed to, what he or she actually did, and what the speaker wants done.

Content level (of messages)   The verbal content of the message that focuses on the topic being discussed.

Contract option   Giving a person who has violated your rights the chance to change his or her behavior before you take action to enforce your rights. A statement of the action you will take if the behavior is not changed.

Control checkpoint   A step in a work process at which the work is checked to see how well standards are being met.

Control system   The entire set of procedures established to provide feedback on the performance of a particular work process.

Controls   Methods or procedures established to keep both management and workers informed about how well objectives and standards are being met.

Cost control system   Procedures for ensuring that managers at all levels in an organization keep costs within the budgeted amounts. The system includes a reasonable budget and a reporting system that determines the differences between budgeted dollars and actual dollars spent in each budget category.

Cost reduction   Procedures for eliminating part or all of a particular cost or expense by finding new and better ways of doing things and by discovering what things can be eliminated entirely.

Criteria   Specifications of the quality a good solution should have. Criteria help distinguish between good and bad alternatives. They are the standards a solution must meet.

Criteria matrix   The matrix is a table in which the alternative actions, solutions, or selections are listed vertically as line headings. Major criteria that have been decided upon for measuring each alternative are listed horizontally as column headings. The criteria matrix allows you to organize and display the alternatives and criteria and to record your evaluation of how well each alternative meets each of the criteria.

Crunching numbers   Using mathematical, statistical, or financial skills to solve business problems.

Dead-end jobs   Positions that are not considered by top management to be on a career path leading to middle and upper management. People holding dead-end jobs are rarely if ever considered for promotion to "growth" positions. They are usually overlooked entirely by management in its planning for managerial training and development.

Dead-time A period of time when one is doing nothing that directly leads to the accomplishment of a high-level objective. Examples are time spent sleeping, eating, commuting, and waiting in line.

Decode To translate or interpret a message; to fit it into one's background of experience.

Dovetailing The coordinating of objectives at various hierarchical levels of an organization.

Encode To put a thought or feeling into some form for possible communication to another person.

Entrepreneurial Concerned with the process of searching for and finding promising business opportunities and taking calculated risks by investing money, time, and effort in business ventures with the expectation of making a profit.

Equal Employment Opportunity (EEO) laws Federal legislation designed to provide equal opportunity to be hired, retained, trained, and promoted for all persons regardless of sex, race, ethnic origin, religion, physical condition, or age.

Expectancy theory A motivational approach based on the assumption that people will not act to satisfy a need unless they believe they have the capability to perform satisfactorily so that their performance will actually lead to a reward that will satisfy the need.

Fast track A series of jobs leading to middle and top management in less time than usual. A career path chosen for "fair-haired boys" (and girls) by top-level decision-makers.

Fear of success Usually an unconscious fear of achieving career success based on an underlying belief that such success conflicts with other desirable female roles.

Feedback Information concerning a specific activity or performance.

Feedback assertion Information the speaker gives about how another person's specific behavior is violating the speaker's rights and affecting his or her life, the feelings the speaker has about the behavior, and what behavior the speaker would prefer.

Fiedlar's contingency theory A situational management philosophy that focuses on (1) leader/follower relations, (2) the leader's position power, and (3) the degree of structure in the workers' tasks as the three keys to determining the level of the manager's influence. A Theory Y approach works best in situations where a manager has moderate influence, a Theory X approach in situations of low or high influence.

Financial management system A coordinated arrangement of unit and departmental goals and budgets that results in a company-wide profit goal, budget, and management control system.

First-line supervisor A person who directly supervises the workers in an organization and who is usually skilled at doing the work itself. Her or his area of decision-making is usually limited to minor day-to-day operations within the work unit.

Fixed assets Assets such as buildings and equipment that are retained over a period of years.

Fixed costs Costs that remain the same regardless of the level of business activity, such as buildings, equipment, property insurance, and certain taxes.

Flexible operating budget An operating budget that is changed as the level of business activity changes. Variable costs are increased or decreased accordingly.

Flexitime A system of scheduling work hours so that all workers are on hand at core times during the middle of the day but have a choice of beginning and ending work hours.

Goal congruence A work situation in which the worker achieves some of his or her highly valued goals in the process of achieving specific organizational goals.

Groupthink A state that occurs when members of a group appear to think as one and any deviation by one member results in severe negative sanctions by the others.

Hidden agenda The personal goals for a meeting that an individual does not reveal to the group spontaneously for fear of rejection.

Housekeeping Activities involved in keeping a work station in a neat, safe, and well-functioning condition.

Human Resources Department This department is often called "Personnel." Its responsibilities include screening applicants for employment, maintaining current employee records, and conducting employee orientation and training meetings.

Index volume The forecast of next year's sales volume.

Input Incoming information.

Investment turnover A measure of management's effectiveness in using money invested in capital assets and management's effectiveness in generating sales volume.

I-message A statement that expresses the speaker's honest feelings and experiences without evaluating, judging, or interpreting the motives of others.

Job description A list of the typical functions, duties, skills, and tasks included in a particular position on an ongoing and continuous basis.

Job-sharing A setup where one job position is shared by two people—each working half of each day, week, or month (or other agreed-upon division).

Likert's approach A management approach based on types of leadership style: exploitative/authoritative, benevolent/authoritative, consultative, and participative.

Line jobs Positions in the organizational hierarchy that are directly in the flow of authority and responsibility from top manager to worker. Career paths to top management are usually through line jobs.

Management By Objectives (MBO) A results-oriented approach to managing that emphasizes forecasting and planning for future events. The focus is on participation by workers at all levels and on improvement of both individual and organizational effectiveness. The process includes formulating clear objectives, developing action plans to achieve them, systematic measuring of performance, and taking corrective actions necessary to achieve the planned results.

Management control system Comprehensive procedures for ensuring that managers obtain the resources they need and use them effectively and efficiently in meeting company objectives. The system includes a cost control subsystem.

Management functions Kinds of actions and areas of responsibility within a manager's job position, such as planning, organizing, and directing. Functional areas within a firm include sales, production, and personnel.

Managerial supervisor A person with a broader area of responsibility than the first-line supervisor. He or she may be responsible for two or more units, coordinating and directing their work, with the unit supervisors reporting to him or her. The managerial supervisor usually has some influence on departmental decisions.

Maslow's hierarchy of needs A motivational theory developed by psychologist Abraham Maslow that identifies five ascending categories of innate needs. The average person is motivated to act in ways that satisfy his or her most pressing unfulfilled need. Only when that need is adequately satisfied is a person motivated by a higher-level need.

Matrix organization A temporary organization of project teams that operates concurrently with the ongoing permanent organizational structure. Team members are pulled from various departments to work on projects and return to their departments upon the completion of each project.

Medium (of communication) The form a message takes, such as face-to-face meeting, letter, report, telegram, telephone call, or radio or television broadcast.

Mentor A person with experience and power within an organization who adopts a younger, less experienced protégé and helps him or her up the organizational ladder.

Middle manager A person who is responsible for a department, branch, or sometimes a division and who has a broader area of decision-making, coordinating and cooperating with other middle managers and top management in achieving organization goals. Middle managers usually have some influence on top-level policy-making and company direction.

Mind chatter The internal dialogue people carry on in their minds most of the time.

Murphy's law "If anything can go wrong, it will."

Net profit Money that is left after all costs and expenses of doing business have been deducted from total revenue.

New hires Recently hired employees of an organization.

Nonassertiveness Letting oneself be victimized by failing to act in ways that express honest feelings, thoughts, and beliefs, or expressing them in such an apologetic or unsure way that others can easily disregard them. Allowing one's rights to be violated without adequate challenge.

Nonprofit organization Any organization—governmental, charitable, or other publicly or privately funded group—that exists to provide a service rather than to earn a profit for owners.

Objectives Targets or goals to be achieved within a specific time frame.

Open-door policy A manager's stated practice of being regularly available to listen to subordinates' ideas and problems. The policy implies an openness to accepting and trying out worker's suggestions.

Operating budget The financial plan for conducting the normal business activities of an organization.

Operational decisions Those decisions that directly concern the day-to-day business activities of the company.

Operational employees The line employees who actually make the products or perform the services that bring in company revenue.

Opportunity value The value of opportunities that are given up when a particular course of action is decided upon. Because limited resources must be committed to carry out the chosen plan, they are not available to take advantage of other opportunities that may arise. The value of the chosen plan should therefore be greater than the anticipated value of the other opportunities that may be sacrificed.

Organizational hierarchy The various levels of authority and responsibility within a company beginning with the worker level and going up through the supervisory, middle, and top management levels to the board of directors, which represents the stockholders, who own the company.

Output Outgoing information.

Parent messages Instructions about how to behave that small children pick up from parent figures and internalize so that the messages become a subconscious part of the child's, and later the adult's, value system.

Parkinson's law "Work expands to fill the time available for its completion."

Path-goal approach A motivational approach to management that focuses on showing workers how meeting their job objectives will satisfy their personal needs and help them get some of the rewards they want most.

Personnel assessment center A private or company-sponsored service for analyzing and evaluating a person's education, experience, performance, and aptitude in order to recommend the types of jobs the applicant is likely to handle well.

Pie graph A circular graph the shape of a pie with the "slices" representing parts of the whole. Effective for showing how the proportion of each of the items in a group relates to the whole amount.

Plant capacity The maximum number of units that can be manufactured in a plant in a year.

Position power The power that is inherent in a particular job position regardless of the job-holder's personal traits and abilities.

Power base The political power gained through a combination of such factors as (1) support network, (2) job position, (3) visibility, (4) ability to fill a pressing company need, and (5) personal expertise, credibility, savvy, and charisma.

Power need A socially acquired need to gain and use power and authority over others.

Production budget The plan for all the costs necessary to make a product.

Production cycle The process of converting cash into finished goods and back into cash again. It's often called the working capital cycle by accountants.

Production department The department responsible for manufacturing the products the company is set up to make.

Production schedules Detailed plans of the number and types of items a company will produce. These schedules are adjusted from week to week as customer demand changes.

Profit and loss statement A summary of the financial results of a firm's activities for the preceding year, showing revenues, costs and expenses, and net profit or loss.

Profit center A unit, department, branch, or division of a company that is directly responsible for generating a portion of company profits. Its revenues and expenses are figured or estimated separately so that a specific profit figure is arrived at.

Profit margin A measurement of how effective the management of a firm has been in generating dollars of profit out of dollars of sales revenue.

Quality control circle A group of workers who hold regular problem-solving meetings. The group may analyze quality control problems, determining why standards are not being met and suggesting methods for improvement.

Quiet hour An hour set aside each day for uninterrupted concentration on work projects. No phone calls or visitors are received, and there is no unnecessary talking or moving about.

Relationship level (of messages) Predominantly nonverbal aspects of a message that focus on the way one person values or accepts the other person.

Resource person Someone who is available to others to provide information, expertise, advice, and instruction.

Resources Anything of value that is used in achieving company goals, such as cash; employees' labor, skill, and expertise; plant facilities; and equipment.

Return On Investment (ROI) A measure of management's effectiveness in generating sales, in generating dollars of profit out of dollars of sales, and in using money invested in company assets.

Role conflict A state of being in which a person believes that if she succeeds in one role she desires, such as manager, her success in another desired role, such as housewife, will be undermined. The resulting conflict often occurs at an unconscious level and leads to self-sabotage in one or both of the roles.

Sales forecast A prediction made by the Sales Department of sales volume for the coming year or years.

Self-actualization An ideal state in which a person achieves his or her full potential. Self-actualizing needs, the highest in Maslow's hierarchy, are needs for continuous growth and development in the pursuit of becoming all that one is potentially capable of becoming.

Self-concept The picture a person has of herself or himself, including strengths, weaknesses, looks, personality.

Socialization messages Parent-like messages that focus on "socially acceptable" behavior a child should adopt.

Socially acquired needs Needs that are socially acquired from interaction with people in a particular cultural environment, as differentiated from innate or biological needs.

Staff jobs Positions in the organizational hierarchy that are essentially advisory in nature. Staff departments specialize in a particular area of service or expertise and usually report to a line manager in an advisory capacity.

Standards Measures of acceptable work performance. A standard defines the cutoff point between acceptable and unacceptable performance of an activity engaged in to achieve a job objective.

Standard volume The average yearly volume expected over a specific period of years (during a business cycle).

Stereotype A belief about a certain group of people and their predictable characteristics that causes the holder to prejudge individual members of that group and to interpret their actions and motives according to predetermined expectations.

Stress Significant disruptions in an individual's environment, originating from within the person in such forms as fears and hurts or from the external environment in such forms as family conflicts or job promotions.

"Stuck" position A job position that the company decision-makers do not view as preparatory for promotion to other positions that in turn lead to top management.

Supervisor A lower-level manager who is directly responsible for getting workers to carry out the action plans of the organization. See First-line supervisor and Managerial supervisor.

Support system (or **Support network**) An assortment of people at various levels and positions in various departments within the company as well as outside the company who are carefully selected and developed by a manager for their ability and willingness to stand behind her or him. Ideally, supporters are selected from various areas so that the network is structured to enhance the manager's political power.

Synthesizing (messages) Putting together the parts of a message to understand the relationships between the parts. Putting together many messages to build a mental model of a situation, an organization, or a particular environment.

Territory A sphere of dominance, control, or power. Examples are a specific geographical space, a group of people, or an area of decision-making authority.

Theory X A management philosophy based on the assumption that people are basically lazy and unambitious, work mainly for security purposes, and therefore must be controlled and coerced to work toward organizational objectives.

Theory Y A management philosophy based on the assumption that workers will exercise self-direction in achieving the organization's goals if they believe their efforts will result in rewards they value. It assumes the average worker has the ingenuity to contribute to management decisions.

Theory Z A situational management philosophy that relies on a Theory Y approach to the extent that it leads to goal congruence. It falls back on a Theory X approach to the extent necessary to achieve the organization's goals.

"To Do" list A manager's daily plan of activities, noted in order of priority according to importance in achieving specific goals.

Top manager A high-level manager who is concerned with the overall mission and objectives of the company, its future direction, and the formulation of broad policies for implementing the objectives.

Transactional analysis (TA) A comprehensive approach to awareness of the subtleties and meanings that underlie people's behavior, interactions, motivations, and games. TA offers a model or framework for understanding oneself and others and for changing nonproductive behavior.

Transmit (a message) To deliver or broadcast a message from a person sending the message to a person receiving the message.

Variable costs Costs that can be readily increased or decreased as the level of business activity changes.

Wholistic (Holistic) An overall systems approach, as opposed to an approach that deals with only isolated parts or subsystems of something.

Wholistic health (or **Holistic health**) An approach to health care that recognizes the importance of every aspect of psychological and physical well-being and the effects of their interactions. This approach focuses mainly on the responsibility of each person for becoming aware of body signals and for preventing illness through optimal nutrition, exercise, mental attitude, and environmental control. Treatment of illness focuses on a patient/doctor partnership in which all relevant aspects of the patient's life situation are considered.

You-message Statements that focus on another person's actions or motives and are frequently judgmental.

Zero-base budget A system in which managers analyze each item in the budget from a starting point of zero rather than from a percentage increase or decrease of the prior year's budget for the item. Frequently, two or more alternate budgets are compared. Managers analyze the costs and benefits of providing alternate levels of quality in the products or services the firm offers.

Index